THE 1995 INFORMATION PLEASE®
WOMEN'S SOURCEBOOK

The 1995 Information Please® Women's Sourcebook

Lisa DiMona and Constance Herndon, Editors

Seth Godin Productions
and
Cader Books

Houghton Mifflin Company
Boston New York
1994

The editors of the *Sourcebook* would like to hear from you. Let us know what information is most interesting and most helpful and what you would like to see included in future editions. While we can't answer every letter, we promise that each suggestion will be carefully reviewed and included if possible.

Contact:

Internet: women@sgp.com
Fax: (914) 693-8132
Mail: P.O. Box 321, Dobbs Ferry, NY 10522

EDITORS' NOTE:

While the information in this book has been carefully vetted for accuracy and reliability, it does not provide a comprehensive guide to any single issue; women with detailed interests should use the book as a resource for obtaining further information directly from the sources we've listed. This suggestion obtains especially in the areas of health and law—the guidelines included here should not replace the professional advice a doctor can give a woman who is worried about breast cancer or a lawyer can give a woman facing a custody battle.

Sources for all information are given in the main text, but in most cases we have not provided sources for the marginalia. Curious readers should know that, unless otherwise noted, the marginalia comes from the same sources credited for the major features within each chapter.

ISBN: 0-395-70067-1

ISSN: 1077-5994

Printed in the United States of America

VB 10 9 8 7 6 5 4 3 2 1

CONTENTS

CONTENTS

EDITORS' PREFACE

When this book was conceived, we hoped to create a volume that would provide as much information as possible about the state of women in America today. To our delight, that turned out to be impossible: over the last decades, the number of organizations studying the lives of women, providing information about our options, and offering support in our endeavors has grown tremendously. Complementing the rich body of statistical data available, we found a dazzling number of groups that exist to provide information and support for women in every area of life, from health and work to childcare and education. Presenting even a small fraction of the substantive information now available, we realized, would require a multi-volume work. What we could provide, however, was an overview of the major issues facing women and a guide to finding the sources that we need to make informed decisions about our lives—a handbook for being a woman, as Governor Ann Richards has said.

The result is a comprehensive survey drawing on over 1,000 resources, organizations, and statistics that describe and influence the lives of American women today. With such a wide range of sources, we have necessarily been forced to limit the number of groups we can include. Our task, then, has been to cite reputable organizations recognized as leaders in their fields. And each section is carefully credited to its source—readers should recognize that the viewpoints expressed throughout the book are those of our sources, not the editors.

While our work with the groups mentioned in this book gave us insight into the condition of women in America today, our research did not directly involve individual women—at work, or at school, or at home. Their voices, we realized, were missing. To add a more personal perspective, we conducted two informal focus-group surveys, the first with a group of elementary-school girls, the second with a nationwide group of women from all backgrounds and of all ages. These sample surveys are not statistically significant, but the findings paint a fascinating portrait of what's on the minds of American women.

In the first focus group, we asked an ethnically diverse group of fourth-grade girls their opinions about role models, school, and career choices. The responses revealed a wide range of interests and ambitions.

When queried about their favorite school subjects, the girls ranked math in second place, just behind reading. Other favorites included social studies, gym, and the widely admired lunch period.

Asked "What do you want to be when you grow up?" the girls replied (in order of frequency): president, mom, lawyer, doctor, realtor, veterinarian, teacher, pilot, businesswoman, farmer, scientist, politician, television star, actress, dancer, and computer operator. When given a list of fifty careers to choose from, the girls most often selected U.S. senator, followed by artist, inventor, doctor, and lawyer.

On the subject of specific role models, the girls were asked to select which famous person they'd like to be, and their answers ran the gamut. In order of popularity:

1. Hillary Rodham Clinton
2. Mother Teresa
3. Barbra Streisand
4. Julia Roberts
5. "my mom"
6. Wynonna
7. Madonna

The answers these fourth graders gave were echoed somewhat in the second set of focus-group interviews we conducted. In this case, however, our respondents were adult women from across the country, women of all ages, professions, races, and economic backgrounds. The following three questions were asked:

1. Who are the three most influential women living today?
In further testimony to the impression she has made on women, Hillary Rodham Clinton was named in 78 percent of our interviews, receiving almost five times more votes than her closest runner-up, Janet Reno. "As a key advisor to the president of the United States," observed one woman, "she has tremendous influence on the executive branch."

The twenty women named most often were:

1. Hillary Rodham Clinton
2. Attorney General Janet Reno
3. Oprah Winfrey
4. Surgeon General Joycelyn Elders
5. Supreme Court Justice Ruth Bader Ginsburg (tie)
   Former Prime Minister Margaret Thatcher (tie)
   Mother Teresa (tie)
6. Madonna (tie)
   Gloria Steinem (tie)
7. Supreme Court Justice Sandra Day O'Connor (tie)
   Barbara Walters (tie)
8. Maya Angelou (tie)
   Princess Diana (tie)
   Martina Navratilova (tie)
   Elizabeth Taylor (tie)
9. Prime Minister Benazir Bhutto (tie)
   Elizabeth Dole (tie)
   Katharine Hepburn (tie)
   Diane Sawyer (tie)
   Barbra Streisand (tie)

2. What are the two greatest challenges women face today?
Two issues struck women as by far the greatest challenges facing them. The first, the balance between work and family, was mentioned by 54 percent of respondents, including retired women as well as those who have no children. The second most commonly mentioned challenge was gaining equality in the workplace, which came up in 19 percent of interviews.

The most important challenges mentioned by the women in our focus groups included:

1. The balance between work and family
2. Equality in the workplace
3. Equal opportunity

4. Reduction of violence against women
5. Health care
6. Abortion (tie)
   Being taken seriously (tie)
7. Child care (tie)
   Self-esteem (tie)
   Media images of women (tie)
   Sexism (tie)

3. If you could influence one sixth-grade girl today, what message would you want to get through to her?

Because of the more personal character of this question, the answers we received here cannot be as easily quantifed as those to the first two questions. If it is possible to generalize about the detailed answers women gave, however, the most common message they hoped to send to sixth-grade girls was one of hope and ambition: "You can do it all," one woman said. And, reflecting the interests expressed by our group of fourth-grade girls, she added, "Just because you are a female doesn't mean you can't be a scientist, a fireman (or a fireperson?), a cop, or even president of the U.S." Another respondent seconded these words, but added, "It's possible to have a career and a home life." And another urged, "Believe that you can do anything and be yourself without having to meet anyone's expectations of what the perfect woman should be."

Women also focused almost equally on self-esteem and education in the messages they wanted to send girls. "The key word is respect, for yourself and for others," one commented. And other women counseled, "Know you are valuable," "Never let anyone tell you that you can't do something," and "Trust your intuition and believe in your own ability regardless of what other people say." On the subject of education, one woman directed, "Read and educate yourself. This will empower you." But another observed, "Study hard, because education is the key to independence, and don't ever expect that someone else will take care of you (or any children you might have) financially forever." In a similar vein, girls were urged to "complete your schooling goals before you make other commitments in life. The rest will follow."

These informal focus-group discussions provide a snapshot of women's concerns today, one that bears out the overarching themes of this first edition of the Information Please Women's Sourcebook: women looking to other women for inspiration, support, and opportunity.

And those opportunities are expanding. The sheer volume of available resources, networks, support systems, organizations, and experts laid out here is a testament to this extraordinary development. Our hope is that the information we've included will provide not only immediate help for women in need of specific facts, statistics, and resources, but also a wealth of new ideas and opportunities.

A number of extraordinary people have made this book possible. We would like to thank Seth Godin and Michael Cader in particular, for their creative insights and unstinting support for this project. For their outstanding research efforts and for their good humor, we would also like to thank Megan O'Connor, Carol Markowitz, and Chris Angelilli. On the editorial end of the book, we are especially grateful for the efforts of Tom Dyja, Nanette Maxim, Alison Mitchell, and Judy Sandman. Special thanks are also due to Julie Maner, Karen Watts, Jennifer Gniady, Meredith Cristiano, Kate Grossman, Mike Eldridge, and Jennifer Jupp. In addition, Bob Moses and his staff at Working Media have done an extraordinary job of producing the book. Finally, we would like to thank our editor, Liz Kubik, and Borgna Brunner and Amy Smith, for their enthusiasm and thoughtful guidance.

Lisa DiMona
Constance Herndon

ACKNOWLEDGMENTS

More than 500 people and organizations contributed valuable insights, information, and advice to the creation of the Information Please Women's Sourcebook. We would like to thank the following in particular for their help:

INDIVIDUALS

Mesie Alemseged, National Committee on Pay Equity
Akiko Arakawa, Japan Society
Laura Kopulos Ashplund, American Society of Plastic and Reconstructive Surgeons
Elizabeth Austin
Teresa Awalt, Campus Violence Prevention Center
Louise Bacon, Society of Women Engineers
Mary Lou Ballweg, Endometriosis Association
Lucy Baruch, Center for the American Woman and Politics
Joel Beard, AIDS Treatment Data Network
Shanti Blanton, National Council of Negro Women
Barbara Brabec, National Home Business Report
Deborah Brice, National Association of Child Care Resource and Referral Agencies
Madeline Bryer
Andrea Camp, Congresswoman Patricia Schroeder's Office
Roxanne Camron, 'Teen
Carolyn Carreno
Lynne Casper, Fertility and Statistics Branch, U.S. Bureau of the Census
Stacey Charney, American Cancer Society
Kathleen Christensen, Work Environment Research Group
Jean Cilik, Women Work! The National Network for Women's Employment
Sarah Ciriello, Challenging Media Images of Women
Eric R. Claeys
Marlene Colburn, Lesbian Avengers
Congresswoman Cardiss Collins
Don Davis, Cosmetic Insiders Report
Carol DeVita, Population Reference Bureau
Catherine Didion, Association for Women in Science
Larry Doherty, Advertising Age
Paula Donovan, UNICEF
Linda Dozoretz
Kate Dunn, Catholics for a Free Choice
Marian Wright Edelman
Carolyn B. Elman, American Business Women's Association
Carol Espel
Mary Faber and Nessa Chapelle, National Education Association Women's Caucus
Carol Felton and Susan Tew, Alan Guttmacher Institute
Mary Ferrari, Ferrari Publications
Cyd Cherise Fields, Association of American Colleges Project on the Status and Education of Women
Marilyn Fingerhut, National Institute of Occupational Safety and Health
Debra Fishbach, American Woman's Economic Development
Lesley Lee Francis, American Association of University Professors
Pat Frank, National Federation of Democratic Women
Karen Furia, Work and Family Clearinghouse, Department of Labor
Lucy Garcia and Lynnore Lawton, Women's Sports Foundation
Violet Garcia, Women in Crisis
Denise Gayle, Women's Resource Center of New York
Dr. Susan Geller, American Mathematical Society Joint Committee on Women in the Mathematics Sciences
Linda Getchis, Security on Campus
Susan Gibbs, Susan B. Anthony List

Dr. Charmaine Gilbreath, Naval Research Laboratory
Joline Godfrey
Vance Grant, Education Information Branch, Department of Education
Liz Grossman, Occupational Safety and Health Administration
Diane Gruver, Federation of Feminist Women's Health Centers
Karen Haliburton, Essence
Roland Hansen, GLTF Clearinghouse, American Library Association
Robin Hardman, The Families and Work Institute
Maggie Harter, Kinsey Institute for Research in Sex, Gender, and Reproduction
Shirley Haruka Bekins, Organization of Pan Asian American Women
Renai Harvey, Concerned Women for America
Kathleen Flier Hawley
Howard Hayghe, Division of Labor Force Statistics, Bureau of Labor Statistics
Glory Hernandez, Education Development Center, Women's Educational Equity Act Program
Sharon Hershey, Population Reference Bureau
Professor Anita Hill
Lea Hill, Congressional Caucus for Women's Issues
Erika Hogarth, National Association of Anorexia Nervosa and Related Eating Disorders
Kay Hollestelle, The Children's Foundation
Renée Howard, International Lactation Consultant Association
Dr. Vicki Hufnagel
Emily Hume
Jennifer Isham, Mothers without Custody
Tamara Jackson, National Association of Child Advocates
Laine Jastram, Resources for Personal Empowerment
Karen Johnson, National Federation of Republican Women
Janet Justus, National Collegiate Athletic Association
Harriet Karp, National Institute of Mental Health, Violence and Traumatic Stress Branch
Gail Kaufman, Equal Rights Advocates
Jeannie Kelleher, American Psychological Association
Sandy Kewley, Child Care Council of Westchester
Jean Kilbourne
Lidia Kliner, Small Business Administration
Bob Kominski, Education Information Branch, Bureau of the Census
Carol Lacampagne, Mathematical Association of America, Committee on the Participation of Women in the Mathematical Sciences
Yvonne Lacey, Glass Ceiling Commission, Department of Labor
Frances Lear
Ulana Lesiv, National Maternal and Child Health Clearinghouse
Jill Lippitt, National Women's Mailing List
Melinda Lockner, Division of STD/HIV Prevention, Centers for Diseases Control and Prevention
Sarah Logan, American College Testing
Kathy London, National Center for Health Statistics
Al Lowman
Sara L. Mandelbaum,Women's Rights Project, American Civil Liberties Union
Al Marrewa, Powerflex USA
Kim Anne Martin, Working Woman
Frederica Mathewes-Green, Feminists for Life of America
Christine Mayman, National Criminal Justice Reference Service
Marena McPherson, American Bar Association, Commission on Women in the Profession

Mona Miller, Planned Parenthood Federation of America
David Mittman, The Clinicians Publishing Group
Dr. Caryn McTighe Musil, Association of American Colleges
Mary Anne Napoli, Center for Medical Consumers
Barbara Nardone, Wellesley College Center for Research on Women
Martina Navratilova
Jeannie Hwang Ng, Girl Scouts of the U.S.A.
Tanya Nieri, Women's Action Alliance
Martin O'Connell, Bureau of the Census
Vicki O'Reilly, Older Women's League
Stella Olgata
April Osajima, American Association of University Women
John Oseid
Kenya Ostermeier, Girls Nation
Pat Patriarcha, Bureau of the Census
Kathy Patrick, Coalition on Women and Job Training
Olivia Pickett, National Center for Education and Maternal and Child Health
Isabelle Katz Pinzer, Women's Rights Project, American Civil Liberties Union
Marva Price, Women's Cancer Prevention Program, Duke University Medical Center
Tricia Primrose, EMILY's List
Shelly Reecher, Project Safe Run
Nancy Risdon
Dr. Robin Robertson, Emma Willard School
John Rogers, Division of Consumer Expenditure Surveys, Bureau of Labor Statistics
Mike Russell, Office of the Surgeon General
Mary Ruthsdotter, National Women's History Project
Gail Ryan, C. Henry Kempe National Center for the Prevention and Treatment of Child Abuse and Neglect
Arlene Saluter, Marriage and Family Statistics Branch, Bureau of the Census
Dr. Bernice R. Sandler, Center for Women Policy Studies
Ronnie Sandler, Northern New England Tradeswomen
Bob Schaeffer, FairTest
Congresswoman Patricia Schroeder
Jadwiga Sebrechts, Women's College Coalition
Elizabeth Senema
Lisa Shraeder, American Bar Association, Family Law Division
Janet Simons, Adolescent Pregnancy Prevention Clearinghouse
Audra Singer, The National Osteoporosis Foundation
Karen Sisko, Working Woman
Pam Smith, American Franchise Association
Tom Smith, National Opinion Research Center
Shirley Smith, Lydia Scoon-Rogers, and Susan Donohue, Income Statistics Branch, Bureau of the Census
John Solomon, Lifetime TV
Vivian Staples, National Commission on Working Women
Abby Steele, Women's Bureau, Department of Labor
Robyn Stein, Planned Parenthood Federation of America
Dr. Jeanne Stellman
Karen Stevens, Ms. Foundation for Women
Rosalie Streett, Parent Action
Elizabeth Swasey, Women's Issues and Information, National Rifle Association
Peggy Tartaro, Women and Guns
Nancy Taylor, Menninger Clinic: The Women's Program
Nancy Triska, The National Center for Women and Retirement Research
Magaret Tunstall, American Association for the Advancement of Science

Diane Wagener, National Center for Health Statistics
Carol Wallace, Everywoman's Center, University of Massachusetts at Amherst
Julie Weeks, National Foundation for Women Business Owners
Diane Wiesen-Todd, Oryx Press
Mike Williams, Division of Statistical and Economic Analysis, Women's Bureau
Marianne Williamson
Virginia Woodruff, Working Woman
Laura X, National Clearinghouse on Marital and Date Rape
Sarah Yoo

ORGANIZATIONS

Aask America
Abortion Rights Mobilization
Abusive Men Exploring New Directions
Academy of Family Mediators
ACT-UP Prison Issues Committee
Action on Smoking and Health
Adolescent Pregnancy Prevention Clearinghouse
Adoptive Families of America
African Ancestral Lesbians United for Societal Change
Aid to Imprisoned Mothers
AIDS Coalition to Unleash Power
AIDS Treatment Data Network
Al-Anon
Alan Guttmacher Institute
Alcoholics Anonymous
Alliance of Genetic Support
Alliance of Minority Women for Business and Political Development
Alyson Publications
American Academy of Adoption Attorneys
American Academy of Dermatology
American Agri-Women
American Alliance for Health, Physical Education, Recreation and Dance
American Anorexia/Bulimia Association
American Arbitration Association
American Assembly of Collegiate Schools of Business
American Association for Marriage and Family Therapy
American Association of Homes for the Aging
American Association of Retired Persons
American Association of Sex Educators, Counselors and Therapists
American Association of Tissue Banks
American Association of University Professors
American Association of University Women
American Bar Association, Commission on Women in the Profession
American Business Women's Association
American Cancer Society
American Civil Liberties Union, Reproductive Freedom Project
American Civil Liberties Union Women's Rights Project
American College Health Association
American College of Nurse-Midwives
American College of Obstetricians and Gynecologists, Resource Center
American College of Radiology
American College of Sports Medicine
American College of Surgeons, Commission on Cancer
American College Testing
American Council for Career Women
American Council of Nanny Schools
American Council of Railroad Women
American Council on Education
American Dietetic Association
American Fertility Society
American Foundation for AIDS Research
American Franchise Association
American Heart Association
American Humane Association, Children's Division
American Indian AIDS Institute of San Francisco

American Institute of Architects, Women in Architecture Committee
American Institute of Stress
American Library Association Office for Personnel Resources
American Lung Association
American Lupus Society
American Mathematical Society Joint Committee on Women in the Mathematics Sciences
American Medical Women's Association
American National Cattle Women
American Nurses Association
American Psychiatric Association
American Psychological Association
American Society of Addiction Medicine
American Society of Plastic and Reconstructive Surgeons
American Society of Women Accountants
American Woman's Economic Development Corp.
American Woman's Society of Certified Public Accountants
American Women in Radio and Television
Amnesty International
Anorexia Nervosa and Related Eating Disorders
Asian AIDS Project
Asian Lesbians of the East Coast/ Asian Pacific Lesbian Network
ASPO/ Lamaze
Assisted Living Facility Association of America
Association for Children for Enforcement of Support
Association for Professional Insurance Women
Association for Women in Computing
Association for Women in Mathematics
Association for Women in Psychology
Association for Women in Science
Association for Women in Social Work
Association for Women Psychiatrists
Association for Women Veterinarians
Association of American Colleges, Project on the Status and Education of Women
Association of American Medical Colleges
Association of Executive Search Consultants
Association of Image Consultants International
Association of Occupational Health and Environmental Clinics
Association of Women in Architecture
Association of Women Psychiatrists
ASTRAEA National Lesbian Action Foundation
Ayuda
Bay Area Bisexual Network
Best Start
Big Brothers/Big Sisters of America
Black Gay and Lesbian Leadership Forum
Black Women in Sisterhood
Black Women Organized for Educational Development
Black Women's Health Network at Maryview Medical Center
Black Women's Professional Network
Boston Alliance
Boston Bisexual Women's Network
Boston Club
Breast Cancer Action
Brigham and Women's Hospital
Bureau of the Census
Bureau of Labor Statistics
Business and Professional Women's Foundation
C. Henry Kempe National Center for the Prevention and Treatment of Child Abuse and Neglect
California Urban Indian Health Council
Cambridge Documentary Films
Campus Violence Prevention Center
Capital Area Network
Career Women's Forum (Switzerland)
CareerTrack

Caribbean Women's Health Association
Catalyst
Catholics for a Free Choice
Center for Children of Incarcerated Parents
Center for Population Options
Center for Reproductive Law and Policy
Center for Substance Abuse Treatment
Center for the American Woman and Politics
Center for the Education of Women, University of Michigan
Center for Women Policy Studies
Center for Women's Global Leadership
Centers for Disease Control
Cesareans/Support Education and Concern
Challenging Media Images of Women
Chicago Network
Chicago Women's AIDS Project
Chicago Women's Health Center
Chicanos Latinos Unidos En Servicio
Child Care Action Campaign
Child Care Council of Westchester
Child Custody Services of Philadelphia Resource Center
Childbirth Education Foundation
Childhelp USA
Children Awaiting Parents
Children of Aging Parents
Children of Divorce and Separation
Children's Defense Fund
Children's Foundation
Children's Rights Council
Chimera
Church Women United
Clinicians Publishing Group
Co-Dependents of Sex Addicts
Coalition for the Medical Rights of Women
Coalition for Women's Appointments
Coalition of Grandparents Parenting Children
Coalition of Labor Union Women
Coalition of Trade Union Women
Coalition on Women and Job Training
Coalition to Support Women Prisoners at Chowchilla
College Board, Educational Testing Service
College Entrance Examination Board
Commission on Legal Problems of the Elderly
Committee for Mother and Child Rights
Committee for Single Adoptive Parents
Committee of 200
Committee on Women in Science and Engineering, National Academy of Sciences
Community Health Awareness Group
Compassionate Friends
Concerned Women for America
Congressional Caucus for Women's Issues
Congressional Hispanic Caucus Institute
Cooper Institute
Cornell University Institute on Women and Work
Custody Action for Lesbian Mothers
D.C. Rape Crisis Center
Democratic National Committee, Women's Outreach Desk
Department of Education
Department of Labor
Depression after Delivery
DES Action
Dignity USA
Down's Syndrome Congress
Duke University Medical Center, Women's Cancer Prevention Program
Eagle Forum
Education Development Center, Women's Educational Equity Act Program
Elderhostel
Emerge
EMILY's List
Endometriosis Association
EnTRADE, Tradeswomen, Women Empowering Women
Equal Employment Opportunity Commission
Equal Relationships Institute
Equal Rights Advocates

Equity Institute
Equity Policy Center
Eve's Garden
Evelyn H. Lauder Breast Center/Iris Cantor Diagnostic Center
Everywoman's Center, University of Massachusetts at Amherst
Executive Women International
F.E.M.A.L.E: Fomerly Employed Mothers at the Leading Edge
Facial Plastic Surgery Information Service
Fairness and Accuracy in Reporting
FairTest, National Center for Fair and Open Testing
Families and Work Institute
Families USA
Family Resource Coalition
Federal Bureau of Investigation
Federal Reserve System, Board of Governors
Federation of Feminist Women's Health Centers
Federation of Organizations for Professional Women
Feminist Majority Foundation
The Feminist Press
Feminists for Life of America
Fenway Community Health Center
Financial Women's Association of New York
Financial Women's International
Find Dad
Florida Women's Alliance
Food and Drug Administration, Department of Health and Human Services
Food and Nutrition Information Center
Forum for Women Business Owners
Forum of Executive Women
Foundation for Alternative Cancer Therapies
GABRIELA Network
Gannett News Service
Gay and Lesbian Advocates and Defenders
Gay and Lesbian Victory Fund
General Federation of Women'sClubs
Georgia Executive Women's Network
Giarretto Institute
Girl Scouts of the U.S.A.
Girls, Inc.
Girls Nation
GLTF Clearinghouse, American Library Association
Good Vibrations
Government Printing Office
Hay/Huggins
Health Crisis Network
Health Insurance Association of America
The Health Resource
HerBody
Herpes Resource Center
Hetrick-Martin Institute
Hispanic Health Council
Hispanic Women's Council
HIV Law Project
HIV/AIDS Aging Task Force of New York
Hollywood Women's Political Committee
Hopedale Medical Complex
HUB CO-Ventures (National Coalition for Women's Enterprise)
Human Nutrition Information Service
Human Rights Campaign Fund
Human Rights Watch, Women's Rights Project
Hysterectomy Educational Resources and Services Foundation
Independent Adoption Center
Independent Federation of Flight Attendants
Institute for Feminist Studies
Institute for Women and Work
Institute on Black Chemical Abuse
Internal Revenue Service
The International Alliance
International Association of Corporate and Professional Recruiters
International Association of Parents and Professionals for Safe Alternatives in Childbirth
International Black Women's Congress
International Cesarean Awareness Network
International Child Resource Institute
International Childbirth Education Association

International Community of Women Living with HIV/AIDS
International Gay and Lesbian Human Rights Commission
International Institute for Women's Political Leadership
International Lactation Consultant Association
International Network for Women in Enterprise and Trade
International Organization of Women in Telecommunications
International Tennis Hall of Fame
International Wages for Housework Campaign
International Women's Forum
Interpersonal Communication Programs
Jacobs Institute of Women's Health,
Japan Society
Joint Committee on Women in the Mathematics Sciences
Joint Custody Association
Judicial Arbitration and Mediation Services
Kinsey Institute for Research in Sex, Gender, and Reproduction
La Leche League
Lambda Legal Defense and Education Fund
Latin American Professional Women's Association
Leadership America
League of Women Voters of the United States
Lesbian AIDS Project, Gay Men's Health Crisis
Lesbian Avengers
Lesbian Community Cancer Project
Lesbian Herstory Archives
Lesbian Mothers National Defense Fund
Lesbian Resource Center
Libertarians for Life
Lifetime TV
Links
Look Consulting International
Lordly and Dame
Los Angeles Commission on Assaults Against Women
Lupus Foundation of America
MammaCare
Management Training Specialists
March of Dimes Birth Defects Foundation
Massachusetts Women's Forum
Masters & Johnson Institute
Maternity Care Hotline
Maternity Center Assocaition
Mathematical Association of America, Committee on the Participation of Women in the Mathematical Sciences
Media Action Alliance
Media Watch
Medical College of Pennsylvania, Center for the Mature Woman
Melpomene Institute
Men's Anti-Rape Resource Center
Menninger Clinic: The Women's Program
Metropolitan Life Insurance Company
Mexican-American Women's National Association
Midwives' Alliance of North America
Minnesota American Indian AIDS Task Force
Minority Health Resource Center
MOM: Alliance of Entrepreneurial Mothers
Momazons
Mothers Against Drunk Driving
Mothers and Others for a Livable Planet
Mothers at Home
Mothers of AIDS Patients
Mothers Without Custody
Ms. Foundation for Women
Multi-Focus
Names Project
National Abortion Federation
National Abortion and Reproductive Rights Action League
National Action Forum for Midlife and Older Women
National Adoption Information Clearinghouse
National Aging Resource Center on Elder Abuse
National AIDS Clearinghouse
National AIDS Hotline
National Alliance of Breast Cancer Organizations

National Alliance of Homebased Businesswomen
National Anorexic Aid Society
National Arthritis and Musculoskeletal and Skin Diseases Information Clearinghouse
National Asian Women's Health Organization
National Association for Female Executives
National Association for Home Care
National Association for Professional Saleswomen
National Association for Retarded Citizens
National Association for the Education of Young Children
National Association for Women in Careers
National Association for Women in Education
National Association of Anorexia Nervosa and Related Eating Disorders
National Association of Black Women Attorneys
National Association of Black Women Entrepreneurs
National Association of Child Advocates
National Association of Child Care Resource and Referral Agencies
National Association of Childbearing Centers
National Association of Childbirth Assistants
National Association of Insurance Women
National Association of Minority Women in Business
National Association of Perinatal Social Workers
National Association of Women Business Owners
National Association of Women in Construction
National Association of Women Judges
National Association of Women Lawyers
National Association of Working Women
National Black Women's Health Project
National Breast Cancer Coalition
National Businesswomen's Leadership Association
National Cancer Institute
National Caucus and Center on Black Aged
National Center for Education and Maternal and Child Health
National Center for Education Statistics
National Center for Health Statistics, Department of Health and Human Services
National Center for Lesbian Rights
National Center for Policy Alternatives, Women's Economic Justice Center
National Center for Women and Retirement Research
National Center on Women and Family Law
National Clearinghouse for Alcohol and Drug Information
National Clearinghouse for the Defense of Battered Women
National Clearinghouse on Child Abuse and Neglect Information
National Clearinghouse on Marital and Date Rape
National Coalition Against Censorship
National Coalition Against Domestic Violence
National Coalition Against Pornography
National Coalition Against Sexual Assault
National Coalition for Women and Girls in Education
National Coalition of 100 Black Women
National Coalition of Grandparents
National Coalition of Hispanic Health and Human Services Organizations
National Coalition to End Racism in America's Child Care System
National Collegiate Athletic Association
National Commission on Working Women

National Committee for Adoption
National Committee for Prevention of Child Abuse
National Committee on Pay Equity
National Congress of Neighborhood Women
National Consumers League
National Council for Research on Women
National Council of Career Women
National Council of La Raza
National Council of Negro Women
National Council of Senior Citizens
Nursing Home Information Service
National Council on Alcoholism and Drug Dependence
National Council on Child Abuse and Family Violence
National Council on Sexual Addiction and Compulsivity
National Council on the Aging
National Criminal Justice Reference Service
National Down Syndrome Society
National Education Association Women's Caucus
National Family Planning and Reproductive Health Association
National Federation of Business and Professional Women's Clubs
National Federation of Democratic Women
National Federation of Republican Women
National Forum for Executive Women
National Forum of Press Women
National Foundation for Depressive Illness
National Foundation for Women Business Owners
National Gay and Lesbian Task Force
National Heart, Lung and Blood Institute
National Institute of Aging
National Institute of Child Health and Human Development
National Institute of Mental Health, Violence and Traumatic Stress Branch
National Institute of Occupational Safety and Health
National Institute of Relationship Enhancement
National Institutes of Health, Computer Retrieval of Information on Scientific Projects
National Institutes of Health, Office of Research on Women's Health
National Latina Health Organization
National Legal Aid and Defender Association
National Lesbian and Gay Health Foundation
National Maternal and Child Health Clearinghouse
National Museum of Women in the Arts
National Network of Hispanic Women
National Network of Minority Women in Science
National Network of Women in Sales
National Network of Women in Science
National Network of Womens' Caucuses
National Opinion Research Center
National Organization for Men Against Sexism
National Organization for Victim Assistance
National Organization for Women
National Osteoporosis Foundation
National Perinatal Association
National Resource Center on Child Abuse and Neglect
National Resource Center on Child Sexual Abuse
National Resource Center on Women and AIDS
National Rifle Association
National Right to Life Committee
National Science Foundation
National Self-Help Clearinghouse
National Victim Center

National Women's Business Council
National Women's Coalition for Life
National Women's Educational (Economic) Alliance Foundation
National Women's Health Network
National Women's Health Resource Center
National Women's History Project
National Women's Law Center
National Women's Mailing List
National Women's Party
National Women's Political Caucus
National Women's Self-Defense Association
National Women's Studies Association
Native American Women's Health Education Resource Center
Network for Professional Women
Network of Executive Women
New Dawn
New Day Films
New York Asian Women's Center
Non Traditional Employment for Women
Northern New England Tradeswomen
Northwest Coalition for Alternatives to Pesticides
NOW Legal Defense and Education Fund
Nurturing Network
Occupational and Environmental Reproductive Hazards Clinic and Education Center
Occupational Safety and Health Administration
Office of the Surgeon General, Department of Health and Human Services
Older Women's League
Organization of Chinese American Women
Organization of Pan Asian American Women
Parent Action
Parents and Friends of Lesbians and Gays
Parents Anonymous
Parents Without Partners
Partnership for Training and Employment Careers
Pension Rights Center
People's Medical Society
Philadelphia Women's Network
Planetree Health Resource Center
Planned Parenthood Federation of America
PMS Access
Population Reference Bureau
Positive Pregnancy & Parenting Fitness
Powerflex USA
Practical Application of Intimate Relationship Skills
Pregnancy/Environmental Hotline
Premenstrual Syndrome Action
prePARE
President's Council on Physical Fitness and Sports
Pro-Life Alliance of Gays and Lesbians
Professional Women's Exchange
Professional Women's Network
Project Inform
Project Safe Run
Public Voice for Food and Health Policy
Real Men
Recovery
Referrals
Religious Coalition for Abortion Rights
Renfrew Center
Reproductive Health Technologies Project
Republican National Committee
Republican Network to Elect Women
Resolve
Resourceful Women
Resources for Personal Empowerment
Revlon/UCLA Women's Cancer Research Center
Rochester Women's Network
Roundtable for Women in Foodservice
St. Charles Medical Center
Seattle Bisexual Women's Network
Security on Campus
Self-Employed Women's Association Bank

Self-Help for Women With Breast or Ovarian Cancer
Senate Judiciary Committee
Serono Symposia, USA
Sex Addicts Anonymous
Sex and Love Addicts Anonymous
Sexaholics Anonymous
SHARE Pregnancy and Infant Loss Support
SIDS Alliance
Sex Information and Education Council of the United States
Simmons College School of Management
Single Mothers By Choice
Small Business Administration
Smith Management Program
Social Investment Forum
Society of Women Engineers
Soroptimist International of the Americas
Small Business Administration, Office of Women's Business Ownership
State of New York Governor's Office
Strang-Cornell Breast Center
Students Against Driving Drunk
Students Organizing Students
Stuntwomen's Association of Motion Pictures
Substance Abuse and Mental Health Services Administration
Susan B. Anthony List
Susan G. Komen Breast Cancer Foundation
T.H.E. (To Help Everyone) Clinic For Women
Teens and AIDS Hotline
Third Wave
UCSF AIDS Health Project
UNICEF
Unitarian Universalist Association, Office of Lesbian and Gay Concerns
United States Information Agency
University of Miami, Pediatrics Department
University of Michigan
University of Minnesota Talented Youth Mathematics Program
U.S. National Senior Sports Organization
Utah Department of Health, Pregnancy Riskline
VOICES in Action
Volunteers of America
Voters for Choice
Washington Alliance of Business Women
Wellesley College Center for Research on Women
Whitman-Walker Clinic
Widowed Persons Service
WISH List
Wishing Well
The Woman Activist Fund
Woman to Woman
Women Against Pornography
Women Against Rape
Women and AIDS Resource Network
Women Business Owners of New York
Women Coping
Women Employed
Women Employment Institute
Women Entrepreneurs
Women for Sobriety
Women in Advertising and Marketing
Women in Agribusiness
Women in Communications
Women in Crisis
Women in Film
Women in Fire Service
Women in Franchising
Women in Management
Women in the Motion Picture Industry
Women in the Nineties
Women Marines Association
Women of Color Resource Center
Women Organized Against Rape
Women Organized to Respond to Life Threatening Diseases
Women Organizing Women
Women Unlimited
Women Work! The National Network for Women's Employment
Women's Action Alliance
Women's Action Coalition
Women's Action for New Directions
Women's Bureau, Department of Labor

Women's Campaign Fund
Women's Cancer Resource Center
The Women's Center
Women's College Coalition
Women's Community Cancer Project
Women's Council of the Democratic Senatorial Campaign Committee
Women's Environment and Development Organization
Women's Health Action and Mobilization
Women's International League for Peace and Freedom
Women's International Network News
Women's Legal Defense Fund
Women's National Book Association
Women's National Democratic Club
Women's National Republican Club
Women's Ordination Conference
Women's Outreach Network of the National Hemophilia Foundation
Women's Political Committee
Women's Psychotherapy Institute
Women's Resource Center of New York
Women's Rights National Historical Park
Women's Sports Foundation
Women's Work
WOMONEY
Work Enviroment Research Group
World Health Organization
Y-ME, National Organization for Breast Cancer Information and Support

THE 1995 INFORMATION PLEASE®

WOMEN'S SOURCEBOOK

EDUCATION

EDUCATIONAL EQUITY

Progress Update on the Education Front

Women, compared to men, have shown tremendous gains in educational achievement over the last thirty years. Indeed, by 1989, women had 96% of the chance a man had to have completed four years of college—compared to less than 60% before 1965. This progress still appears to be continuing, so much so that experts predict we may soon see a woman's chance of earning an undergraduate degree surpass that of a man.

Despite the encouraging data, however, research suggests that women are still not receiving the same quality, or even quantity, of education as men. From gender bias in testing and the tendency of teachers to treat female students differently to the experiences girls have in math and science classes, educational equality remains a concern for women.

For a better understanding of the issues facing educators and policy makers, the following reports are highly recommended:

"The Classroom Climate: A Chilly One for Women?" Roberta M. Hall and Bernice Resnick Sandler (1982; available from the Center for Women Policy Studies, 2000 P Street, N.W., Suite 508, Washington, DC 20036).

Equity of Higher Education Opportunity for Women, Black, Hispanic and Low Income Students, American College Testing Program (available from the American College Testing Program, P.O. Box 168, Iowa City, IA, 52243, [319] 351-4913).

Failing at Fairness: How America's Schools Cheat Girls, Myra and David Sadker (New York: Charles Scribner's Sons, 1994).

"How Schools Shortchanged Girls: A Study of Major Findings on Girls and Education," American Association of University Women (Washington, DC, 1991; available from the AAUW, [800] 225-9998, or the Wellesley College Center for Research on Women, Wellesley College, Wellesley, MA 02181).

Meeting at the Crossroads: Women's Psychology and Girls' Development, Lyn Mikel Brown and Carol Gilligan (Cambridge: Harvard University Press, 1991).

"Women Faculty at Work in the Classroom, Or, Why It Still Hurts to Be a Woman in Labor," Bernice Resnick Sandler (1993; available from the Center for Women Policy Studies, 2000 P Street, N.W., Suite 508, Washington, DC 20036).

Sources: American College Testing; American Association of University Women: Center for Women Policy Studies

EDUCATIONAL EQUITY — RESOURCES

American Association of School Administrators
1801 N. Moore Street
Arlington, VA 22209
(703) 528-0700

American Association of University Women
Educational Foundation
1111 Sixteenth Street, N.W.
Washington, DC 20036
(202) 785-7722

American Civil Liberties Union
Women's Rights Project
123 W. 43rd Street
New York, NY 10036
(212) 944-9800

Association for Women in Science
1522 K Street, N.W., Suite 820
Washington, DC 20005
(202) 408-0742

Only 5.3% of all foundation dollars—$283.8 million out of $5.3 billion—is designated for programs that directly benefit women and girls.

"That is what learning is. You suddenly understand something you've understood all your life, but in a new way."—Doris Lessing, *The Four-Gated City*

More than $5 million is awarded annually in educational scholarships presented at the local, state, and national Miss America pageants.

Center for Women Policy Studies
2000 P Street, N.W., Suite 508
Washington, DC 20036
(202) 872-1770

The Equity Institute
P.O. Box 30245
Bethesda, MD 20824
(301) 654-2904

FairTest, the National Center for Fair and Open Testing
342 Broadway
Cambridge, MA 02139
(617) 864-4810

National Association for Women in Education
1325 Eighteenth Street, N.W., Suite 210
Washington, DC 20036
(202) 659-9330

National Coalition for Sex Equity in Education
Maryland State Department of Education
200 W. Baltimore Street
Baltimore, MD 21201
(410) 333-2239

National Education Association
Division of Human and Civil Rights
1202 16th Street, N.W.
Washington, DC 20036
(202) 822-7700

Wider Opportunities for Women
1325 G Street, N.W., Lower Level
Washington, DC 20005
(202) 638-3143

Women's Action Alliance
370 Lexington Avenue, Suite 603
New York, NY 10017
(212) 532-8330

EXTRACURRICULAR EDUCATION RESOURCES FOR GIRLS

Big Brothers/Big Sisters of America
230 N. Thirteenth Street
Philadelphia, PA 19107
(215) 567-7000

Girl Scouts of the U.S.A.
420 Fifth Avenue
New York, NY 10018
(212) 852-6548

Girls Incorporated
30 E. 33rd Street
New York, NY 10016
(212) 689-3700

Girls Incorporated National Resource Center
441 West Michigan Street
Indianapolis, IN 46202
(317) 634-7546

Girls' State/Girls' Nation
American Legion Auxiliary
777 North Meridian Street
Indianapolis, IN 46204
(317) 635-6291

New Moon: The Magazine for Girls and Their Dreams
New Moon Parenting: For Adults Who Care About Girls
New Moon Publishing
P.O. Box 3587
Duluth, MN 55803
(218) 728-5507

SCHOLARSHIPS AND FINANCIAL AID

Millions of dollars in scholarships and financial aid have been set aside for women. For more information the following resources are recommended:

Directory of Financial Aids for Women, 1993–1995, Gail A. Schlacter (San Carlos, Calif.: Reference Service Press, 1993).

Women's Information Directory, Shawn Brennan, ed. (Detroit: Gale Research, 1991).

Higher Education Opportunities for Minorities and Women: Annotated Selections (Washington, DC: U.S. Government Printing Office).

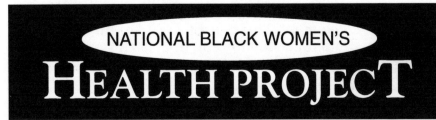

YES, I want to join NARAL's fight for reproductive freedom.
I would like to become a member of NARAL. Enclosed is my check for :

⬭ $10 ⬭ $25 ⬭ $50 ⬭ Other $ ________

Name ________________________________

Address ________________________________

City ________________ State ________ Zip ________

Telephone ________________________________

⬭ I would like information about the Friends of NARAL monthly gift program.

Contributions to NARAL are not tax-deductible as charitable contributions. NARAL cannot accept corporate contributions.

Please mail your contribution with this entire form to :

NARAL
Attention: Sandra Paul
1156 15th Street, NW, Ste. 700
Washington, DC 20005

ADULT EDUCATION—RESOURCES

For information on returning to school, literacy programs, or continuing education opportunities, the following organizations are recommended:

Education Development Center
Women's Educational Equity Act Program
55 Chapel Street
Newton, MA 02158
(800) 225-3088

Wider Opportunities for Women
1325 G Street, N.W., Lower Level
Washington, DC 20005
(202) 638-3143

Women Work! The National Network for Women's Employment
1625 K Street, N.W., Suite 300
Washington, DC 20006
(202) 467-6346

The fastest-growing group of college students is women over 35.

FEMALE-TO-MALE EARNINGS RATIOS BY EDUCATIONAL ATTAINMENT

This graph shows how much women earn for each dollar earned by men, ranked in 1992 for year-round full-time workers 25 and over.

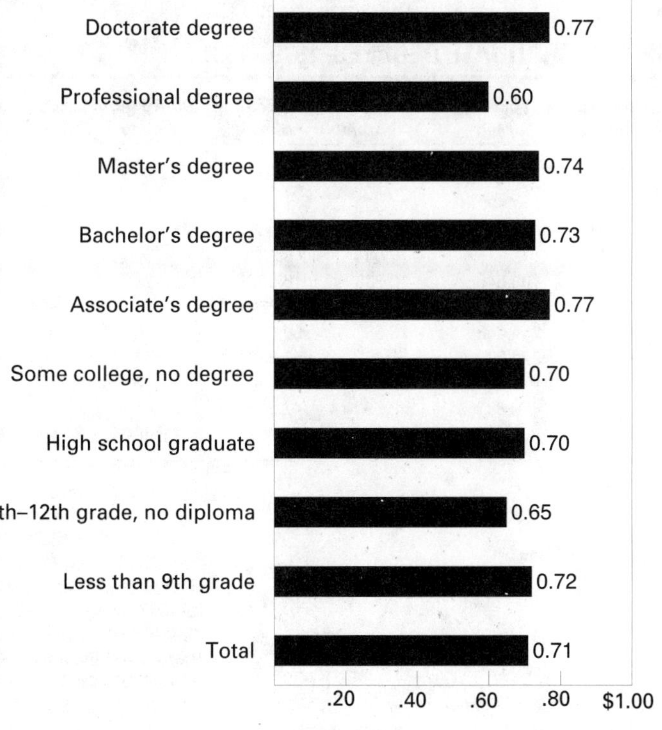

Source: Education Information Branch, Bureau of the Census, 1992

Two-thirds of the world's illiterate are women and girls.

Evelynn Hammonds and Robin Kilson, two professors at MIT, held the first Black Women in the Academy conference in January 1994.

WOMEN'S LITERACY—INTERNATIONAL HIGHS AND LOWS

Poor But Literate Countries
The following nations had per capita GNP below $1,000 in 1990, but female literacy rates of more than 60%.

	% of literate women
Philippines	90
Vietnam	84
Sri Lanka	84
Dominican Republic	82
Indonesia	75
Madagascar	73
Myanmar	72
Zimbabwe	72
Honduras	71
Bolivia	71
Zambia	65
China	62

Not So Poor, Not So Literate Countries
While these countries have per capita GNPs of more than $1,000, their female literacy rates are below 60%.

	% of literate women
Morocco	38
Iran	43
Congo	44
Algeria	46
Saudi Arabia	48
Gabon	49
Iraq	49
Libya	50
Syria	51
Tunisia	56

Source: UNESCO

COLLEGE AND GRADUATE DEGREES, 1879–1991

YEAR	BACHELOR'S DEGREES		MASTER'S DEGREES		DOCTORAL DEGREES	
	Women	*Men*	*Women*	*Men*	*Women*	*Men*
1879–80	2,485	10,411	11	868	3	51
1899–00	5,237	22,173	303	1,280	23	359
1919–20	16,642	31,980	1,294	2,985	93	522
1929–30	48,869	73,615	6,044	8,925	353	1,946
1939–40	76,954	109,546	10,233	16,508	429	2,861
1949–50	103,217	328,841	16,963	41,220	616	5,804
1959–60	138,377	254,063	23,537	50,898	1,028	8,801
1960–61	140,636	224,538	26,779	57,830	1,112	9,463
1970–71	364,136	475,594	92,363	138,146	4,577	27,530
1980–81	465,257	469,883	148,696	147,043	10,247	22,711
1990–91	590,493	504,045	180,686	156,482	14,538	24,756

Source: Department of Education, National Center for Education Statistics

HIGHEST DEGREES EARNED BY WOMEN AND MEN

Total Population Over 18

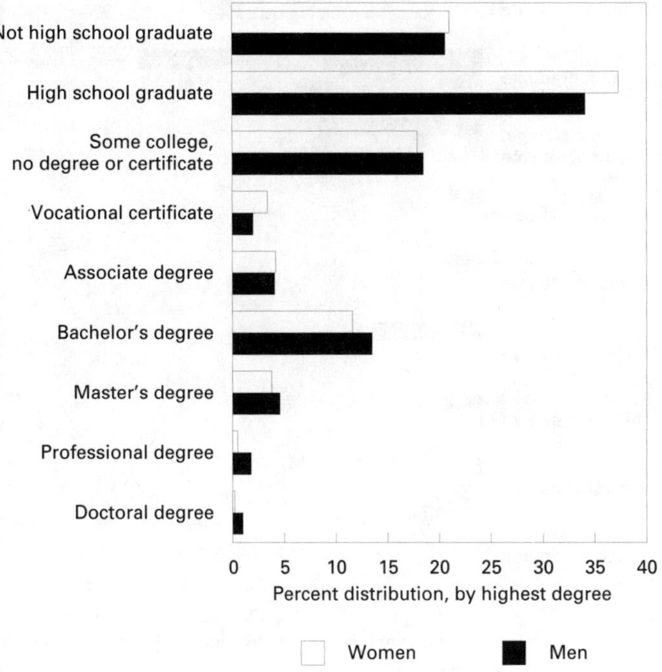

"Our goal is to raise strong, smart, and bold girls. And I don't mean a better version of a boy."—Isabel C. Stewart, National Executive Director, Girls, Inc.

Women earn 52% of all college degrees.

Women accounted for 55.9% of all college students in 1992. Twenty years ago, they constituted only 42.6%.

Women by Racial and Ethnic Group

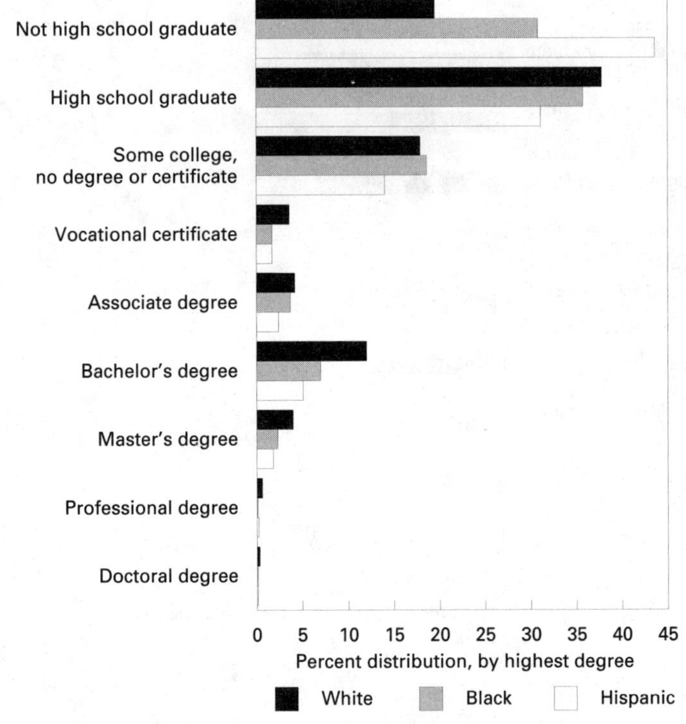

Source for above: Department of Education, National Center for Education Statistics

DROPOUT RATES

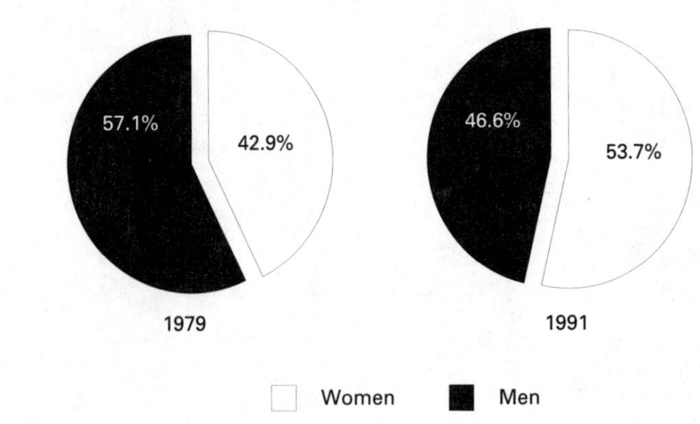

Source: Department of Labor, Bureau of Labor Statistics

FEMALE AND MALE EDUCATIONAL ATTAINMENT

By percentage, in the 25 largest states.

	% High School Graduate	% Bachelor's or More
Alabama		
Female	76.1	14.1
Male	76.0	15.2
Arizona		
Female	83.9	18.4
Male	83.8	27.1
Califonia		
Female	79.0	21.8
Male	80.4	28.3
Florida		
Female	80.1	16.8
Male	79.1	23.1
Georgia		
Female	73.6	20.0
Male	76.0	22.4
Illinois		
Female	78.4	18.8
Male	80.0	25.8
Indiana		
Female	79.8	10.6
Male	78.6	18.0
Kentucky		
Female	74.9	15.3
Male	72.6	19.3
Louisiana		
Female	72.4	14.6
Male	75.2	18.7
Maryland		
Female	83.2	23.8
Male	82.1	28.6
Massachusetts		
Female	84.1	26.8
Male	85.0	33.6
Michigan		
Female	81.4	17.0
Male	81.6	21.3
Minnesota		
Female	87.4	19.5
Male	84.6	27.4
Missouri		
Female	80.1	18.5
Male	80.4	22.4
New Jersey		
Female	81.0	23.2
Male	83.3	33.0
New York		
Female	79.8	21.7
Male	81.7	27.2
North Carolina		
Female	76.0	17.2
Male	73.5	19.9
Ohio		
Female	81.9	17.4
Male	83.7	21.9
Pennsylvania		
Female	78.6	15.8
Male	81.1	21.9
South Carolina		
Female	73.6	15.0
Male	72.8	18.5
Tennessee		
Female	74.1	15.1
Male	69.5	14.8
Texas		
Female	76.9	19.1
Male	77.8	25.2
Virginia		
Female	81.7	23.9
Male	79.7	27.8
Washington		
Female	88.8	25.9
Male	88.3	29.9
Wisconsin		
Female	85.2	17.6
Male	84.3	22.7

Source: Education Information Branch, Bureau of the Census

August Chapin is believed to be the first woman to receive an honorary doctorate. A minister, she was awarded an honorary divinity degree by Lombard University in 1893.

Women earn 29% of B.S. degrees in science and engineering, but only 18% of all employed scientists and engineers are women.

Rachel Carson earned an M.A. in zoology from Johns Hopkins University in 1932. Her best-selling book Silent Spring marked the birth of the environmental movement and is recognized as one of the most important books of our time.

FIELDS OF STUDY FOR GRADUATE DEGREES

	BACHELOR'S DEGREE		MASTER'S DEGREE		DOCTORAL DEGREE	
	Women	*Men*	*Women*	*Men*	*Women*	*Men*
Agriculture & natural resources	4,292	8,832	1,135	2,160	232	953
Architecture & environmental design	3,993	5,788	1,246	2,244	34	101
Area & ethnic studies	2,765	1,858	613	637	73	94
Business & management, business & office, marketing & distribution	117,902	132,058	27,489	51,192	320	923
Communications & communications technology	32,133	20,666	2,625	1,711	123	151
Computer & information sciences	7,357	17,726	2,761	6,563	92	584
Criminal justice	6,378	10,225	368	717	16	12
Education	87,565	23,445	68,118	20,786	3,892	2,805
Engineering & engineering technologies	10,957	67,907	3,529	21,430	485	4,787
Foreign languages	8,745	3,350	1,438	635	296	230
Health & health sciences	49,573	9,695	16,763	4,465	920	694
Home economics & vocational home economics	13,871	1,603	1,722	299	193	62
Law	1,185	573	614	1,443	25	65
Letters	35,345	17,535	5,215	2,595	784	632
Life sciences	20,118	19,412	2,463	2,302	1,516	2,577
Mathematics	6,917	7,744	1,478	2,137	188	790
Philosophy & religion	2,658	4,657	608	833	112	344
Physical sciences & science technologies	5,168	11,176	1,472	3,837	843	3,447
Psychology	42,412	16,039	6,756	2,975	2,094	3,128
Public affairs	11,558	5,418	12,375	6,159	240	190
Social sciences	56,293	68,600	5,140	6,929	1,056	1,956
Theology	1,164	3,649	1,586	2,922	138	937
Visual & performing arts	25,990	15,864	4,825	3,830	370	466
Women's studies	259	2	13	0	0	0

(Data from 1990–91)
Source: National Center for Education Statistics

AVERAGE TIME SPENT EARNING GRADUATE DEGREES

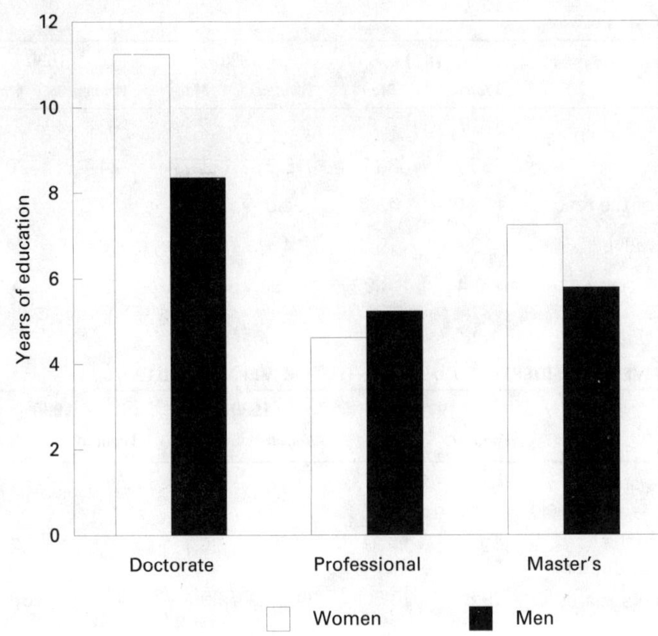

Source: National Center for Education Statistics, 1990

The U.S. Government Printing Office agreed to accept "Ms." as an optional title for women in government publications in 1972.

70% of students in female secondary vocational schools are enrolled in programs that lead to low-paying jobs traditionally held by women.

TRENDS AMONG COLLEGE FRESHMEN

Political Views

	1971		1980		1990	
	Women	***Men***	***Women***	***Men***	***Women***	***Men***
Far Left	1.9	3.5	1.9	2.2	1.4	2.3
Liberal	33.6	36.7	18.9	20.3	24.7	20.3
Middle of the road	50.6	43.6	64.0	55.8	57.3	51.7
Conservative	13.6	15.3	14.4	20.0	16.0	24.0
Far right	0.4	0.9	0.8	1.7	0.6	1.8

Objectives Considered to Be Essential or Very Important

	1971		1980		1990	
	Women	***Men***	***Women***	***Men***	***Women***	***Men***
Become an authority in my field	54.3	64.8	71.7	74.7	63.6	67.4
Influence the political structure	10.2	17.3	12.6	20.1	18.6	22.9
Influence social values	29.8	26.5	34.8	29.4	48.4	36.3
Be very well-off financially	28.2	50.2	57.8	69.4	70.3	77.7
Help others who are in difficulty	71.6	55.2	72.7	56.0	71.4	50.9
Develop a meaning ful philosophy of life	73.5	63.6	52.1	48.7	44.3	41.8
Keep up-to-date with political affairs	40.4	44.8	35.0	45.4	38.9	46.5

Self Ratings As Above Average or Top 10%

	1971		1980		1990	
	Women	***Men***	***Women***	***Men***	***Women***	***Men***
Academic ability	51.9	49.6	50.4	52.6	50.3	57.5
Drive to achieve	54.0	51.1	65.1	63.6	65.2	67.7
Leadership ability	30.4	38.6	43.9	50.2	46.1	56.5
Mathematical ability	25.5	37.6	29.2	42.4	30.4	45.5
Intellectual self-confidence	30.3	38.7	40.9	51.8	40.9	56.8
Writing ability	29.3	26.5	36.4	30.5	40.6	37.1

Source: The American Freshman: Twenty-Five-Year Trends, F. L. Dey, A.W. Astin, and W. S. Korn (Los Angeles: The Higher Education Research Institute, University of California, 1992)

ATTITUDES OF COLLEGE FRESHMEN

Those who agree strongly or somewhat with these issues.

	% Female	% Male
Too much concern for criminals	60.6	65.3
Abortion should be legal	73	68.1
Abolish death penalty	28.2	21.9
Sex okay if people like each other	32.9	58.8
Married women best at home	14.9	25.1
Prohibit homosexual relations	17.8	36.3
College increases earning power	53.2	66.9
Man not entitled to sex on date	96.1	87.2
Fed. government should do more to control handguns	91.7	75.8
Racial discrimination is no longer a problem	8.4	3.2
Regulate student publications	27.8	26.7
High school grading too easy	51.3	56.3
Prohibit racist/sexist speech	57.7	49.7

Source: The American Freshman: Twenty-Five-Year Trends, E. L. Dey, A.W. Astin, W. S. Korn, (Los Angeles: The Higher Education Research Institute, University of California, 1992).

Alice Gertrude Bryant and Florence West Duckering were the first two women admitted to the American College of Surgeons, in 1914.

TENTH GRADERS' ATTITUDES ABOUT SCHOOL

Class subject and opinion	% Male	% Female
Math		
Understood the material	60.4	61.3
Try very hard	75.9	84.6
Feel challenged	71.8	77.1
English		
Understood the material	50.2	51.5
Try very hard	75.5	83.2
Feel challenged	57.8	61.9
History		
Understood the material	34.0	31.0
Try very hard	53.4	53.7
Feel challenged	42.4	41.9
Science		
Understood the material	49.0	47.6
Try very hard	69.5	76.0
Feel challenged	65.0	68.1

(Data from 1990)
Source: Department of Education, National Center for Education Statistics

WHO DOES BETTER, GIRLS OR BOYS?

Juliette Gordon Low organized the first group of Girl Scouts on March 12, 1912, in Savannah, Georgia.

The Parent-Teacher Association (PTA), originally the National Congress of Mothers, was founded by Alice McLellan Birney in 1897.

These graphs cover a measurement of proficiency based on a scale from 0 to 500.

Reading Proficiency

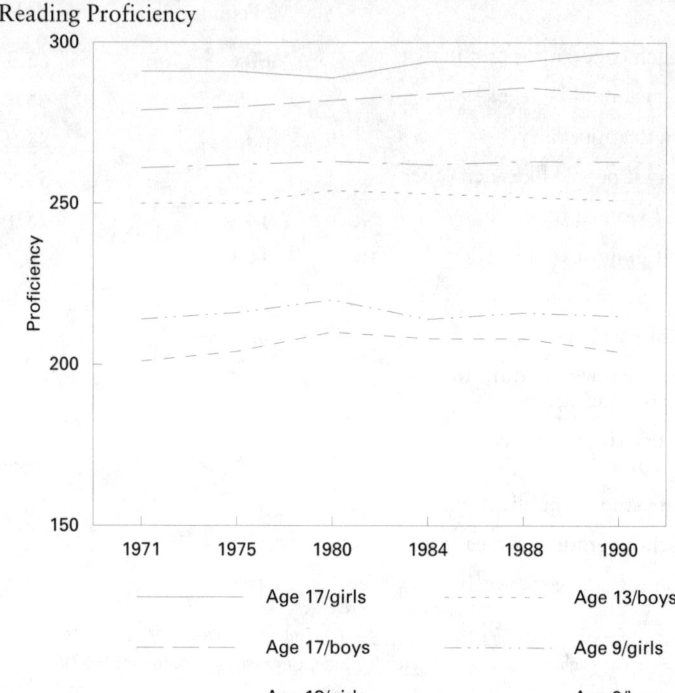

Writing Proficiency

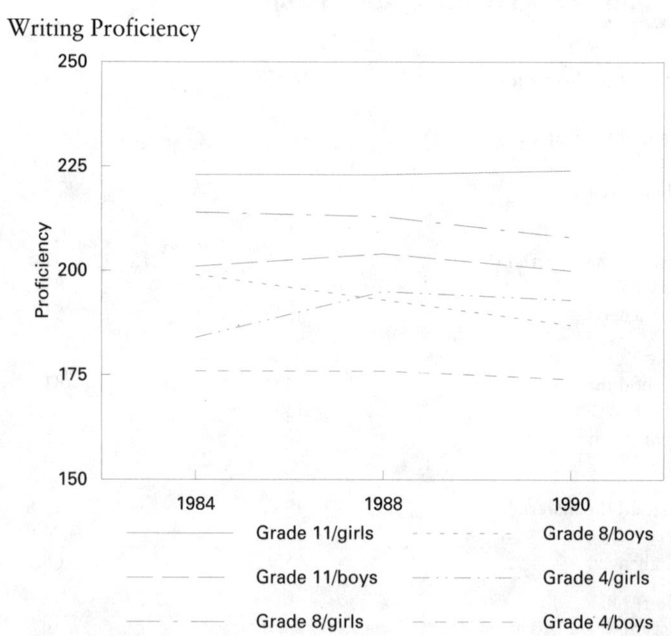

Science Proficiency

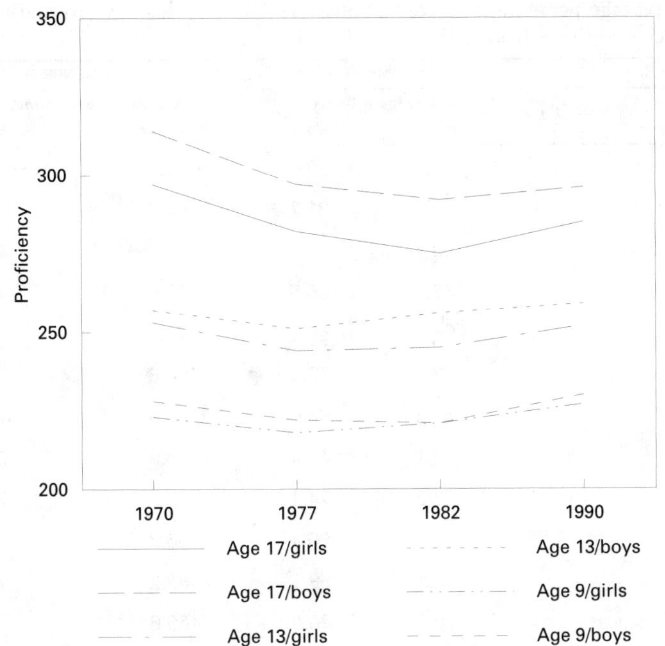

Source for above: "Trends in Academic Progress," Department of Education, National Center for Education Statistics

Julia B. Robinson was the first woman mathematician to be elected to the National Academy of Science, in 1976.

Marie Curie was the first woman to win the Nobel Prize for physics, in 1903.

INTERNATIONAL MATH AND SCIENCE SCORES

The average percentage of correct answers 13-year-olds gave to math and science questions, from 1991.

	MATH		SCIENCE	
	Average % Correct		Average % Correct	
Country	Female	Male	Female	Male
Canada	60.9	63.0	67.1	70.5
China*	78.5	81.7	64.8	69.4
England*	60.4	60.8	67.1	70.3
France	62.8	65.5	66.5	70.7
Hungary	68.3	68.5	71.4	75.6
Ireland	58.4	62.6	60.8	66.1
Israel	61.8	64.4	68.0	71.6
Jordan	39.1	41.4	55.9	57.1
Korea	72.2	74.4	75.0	79.6
Scotland	60.8	60.4	66.3	69.6
Slovenia	56.1	58.1	68.2	72.5
Former Soviet Union	70.3	70.0	69.6	72.9
Spain	53.8	57.1	66.0	69.2
Switzerland	68.7	72.8	70.9	76.4
Taiwan	72.4	73.1	74.9	76.3
United States	54.8	55.8	64.5	69.4

*Limited segments of these populations were tested; figures are not necessarily representative.

Source: Department of Education, National Center for Education Statistics

Rachel F. Brown was the first woman to win the Pioneer Chemist Award from the American Institute of Chemists, in 1975.

Three California schools, two public and one private, have begun offering all-girl math and science classes as a way of solving the problem of girls falling behind boys in these classes from middle school onward.

UNFAIR TESTING

Despite the widely noted fact that girls outperform boys academically by earning higher grades in the same classes, girls have consistently scored lower on the SAT and similar standardized tests. Since the only scientific purpose of the SAT is to predict first-year college grades, the test fails by its own standard by regularly underrating the abilities of girls. According to FairTest, the test's inherent discrimination can be traced to a great extent to the timed, speeded character of the tests, which works against women and members of minority groups. The nature of multiple-choice tests such as the SAT puts a premium on fast-paced strategic guessing while penalizing reflection, the inclination to look for shades of meaning in a question, and other cognitive characteristics more common among girls than boys. Gender and race-biased questions can also undercut the scores of girls and people of color, although some of the most egregiously biased questioning has been weeded out under pressure from women's and civil rights groups.

Source: FairTest, National Center for Fair & Open Testing

WOMEN RECEIVE FEWER SCHOLARSHIPS

• Each year many more men than women—about 60%—are awarded National Merit Scholarships, even though women earn higher grades in high school and college.
• Three-quarters of new federal scholarships designed to encourage students to study math, science, or engineering have gone to boys. Winners of these scholarships, worth $2.2 million in all, are chosen solely on the basis of their scores on the American College Testing Program Assessment, another test on which males score higher than females. The result is that women again receive fewer scholarships.
• A federal civil rights complaint was filed in Feburary 1994 against the Educational Testing Service and the College Entrance Examination Board, charging both with violating federal equal education law by administering and cosponsoring the exam used to determine which students will receive National Merit Scholarships. That exam, the Preliminary Scholastic Assessment Test (PSAT), is derived from the Scholastic Assessment Test (SAT), which test makers admit underpredicts the college performance of girls. Use of PSAT scores as the sole qualifying factor for scholarship eligibility denies girls an equal opportunity to receive the awards.
• In 1989 New York State's system of selecting Regents Scholarship winners was declared unconstitutional and in violation of Title IX. The previous system has been based exclusively on college admissions exam scores, which have been shown to discriminate against female students.

Sources: Feminist Majority Foundation/Fund for the Feminist Majority; FairTest, National Center for Fair & Open Testing

A study found that female characters in illustrations in Caldecott Medal–winning children's books were shown using household implements in 77% of cases, whereas 80% of the male characters used implements for work outside the home.

SCHOLASTIC APTITUDE TEST SCORE AVERAGES FOR COLLEGE-BOUND HIGH SCHOOL SENIORS

	Verbal score		Mathematical score	
	Female	Male	Female	Male
1966–67	468	463	467	514
1971–72	452	454	461	505
1976–77	427	431	445	497
1981–82	421	431	443	493
1986–87	425	435	453	500
1991–92	419	428	456	499

Note: Possible scores on each part of the SAT range from 200 to 800.
Source: College Board, Educational Testing Service

NATIONAL MERIT SCHOLARS

	1982	1992
Female	1,740	1,903
Male	2,830	3,192

Source: National Science Board, Science and Engineering Indicators, 1993

Women made up 9% of American math Ph.D.s in 1973–74; by 1992–93, that number had risen to 28%.

The first all-woman's secretarial school was Union School of Stenography, founded by Mary Foot Seymour in 1879 in New York City.

GIRLS' SCORES ON MATH SATS

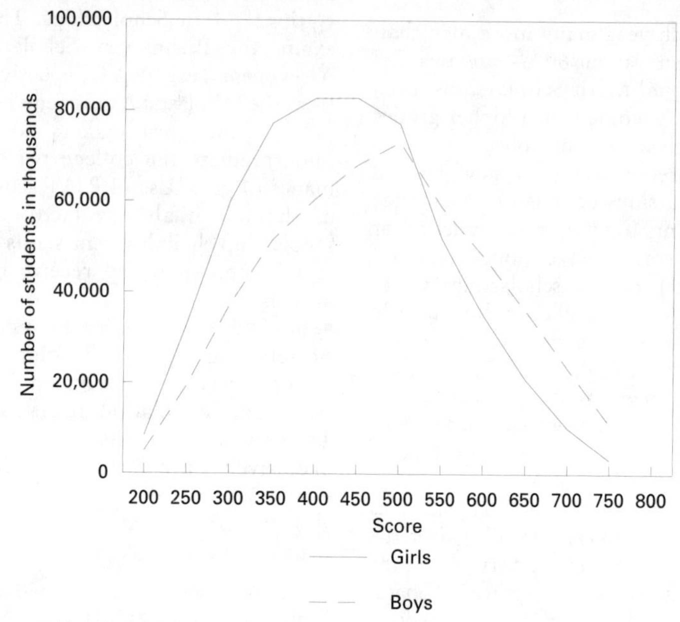

Source: College Board, Educational Testing Service

THE MATH MYTH

There Is No Math Gene

Despite the fact that the specter of a math gene favoring males is often in the news, there is strong evidence against biological/genetic causes of gender differences in math. These arguments include:

- The gender gap in mathematics is rapidly decreasing, while genetic differences tend to remain stable.
- The gap can be reduced or eliminated by changing teaching practices and providing opportunities for both girls and boys to build math skills; biological differences are not so easily influenced.
- Gender differences in math achievement are not consistent across racial/ethnic groups. If there were a sex-linked math gene, differences would be consistent across all groups.

Source: Patricia Campbell, Campbell-Kibler Associates, Groton, Mass.

Social Pressures Against Girls and Math

Very little evidence exists to support the claim that there are natural differences in math ability between boys and girls. But overwhelming evidence does suggest that differences in boys' and girls' performance and interest in science and math is strongly influenced by differences in their play and learning experiences and in their parents' expectations of them. Research has also shown that teachers, counselors, and fellow students typically expect girls *not* to like math and science and *not* to perform well in these classes, despite the fact that girls actually do as well or better than boys, especially in the earlier grades.

Source: American Association for the Advancement of Science

REASONS FOR NOT TAKING MATH AND SCIENCE CLASSES

The following survey was posed to high school seniors in 1993; the numbers represent the percentage of students who responded in the positive to each question.

Reasons	Math		Science	
	% Female	% Male	% Female	% Male
There were other courses I wanted to take.	40	34	42	38
I did not think I would do well in more advanced classes.	32	31	29	22
I was advised I did not need to take more.	32	28	34	28
I will not need the advanced course for what I plan to do in the future.	30	23	33	36

Source: National Science Board, Science and Engineering Indicators; 1993

More than 1.5 million adolescent girls live in poverty.

Annie Jump Cannon was the first person to systematically classify the heavens, in 1918.

GIRLS' AND BOYS' EXPERIENCE WITH SCIENCE EQUIPMENT

	Grade 7		Grade 11	
	% Female	% Male	% Female	% Male
Microscope	90	92	97	98
Telescope	64	80	71	85
Barometer	20	30	41	51
Electricity Meter	10	31	17	49

Source: The Science Report Card, National Assessment of Educational Progress, 1988

Harvard awarded a tenured position to a woman for the first time in 1956, when Cecelia Payne-Gaposhkin became professor of astronomy.

Nationally, 11% of all high school girls study mathematics past algebra II/trigonometry.

PROGRAMS TO ENCOURAGE GIRLS AND WOMEN TO PARTICIPATE IN MATH AND SCIENCE

Computer Equity Trainers
Women's Action Alliance
370 Lexington Avenue, Suite 603
New York, NY 10017
(212) 532-8330

Eureka!
Girls Incorporated National Resource Center
441 West Michigan Street
Indianapolis, IN 46202
(317) 634-7546

Girls and Science: Linkages for the Future American Association for the Advancement of Science
Directorate for Education and Human Resources Programs
1333 H Street, N.W.
Washington, DC 20005
(202) 326-6670

In Touch with Technology American Association for the Advancement of Science
Directorate for Education and Human Resources Programs
1333 H Street, N.W.
Washington, DC 20005
(202) 326-6670

National Science Foundation
Targeted Programs for Women/Girls
4201 Wilson Boulevard
Arlington, VA 22230
(703) 306-1234

National Science Partnership for Girl Scouts and Science Museums
Girl Scouts of the U.S.A.
420 Fifth Avenue
New York, NY 10018
(212) 852-6548

Operation SMART
Girls Incorporated National Resource Center
441 West Michigan Street
Indianapolis, IN 46202
(317) 634-7546

Science-By-Mail
Museum of Science
Science Park
Boston, MA 02114
(800) 729-3300

University of Minnesota Talented Youth Mathematics Program
115 Vincent Hall
Minneapolis, MN 55455
(612) 625-2861

Women and Mathematics
Mathematical Association of America
1529 Eighteenth Street, N.W.
Washington, DC 20036
(202) 279-2064

GENERAL RESOURCES FOR MATH AND SCIENCE

American Association of University Women Educational Foundation
P.O. Box 4030
Iowa City, IA 52243
(319) 337-1716

Association for Women in Science
1522 K Street, N.W., Suite 820
Washington, DC 20005
(202) 408-0742

The Equity Institute
P.O. Box 30245
Bethesda, MD 20824
(301) 654-2904

National Association of Women in Education
1325 Eighteenth St., N.W., Suite 210
Washington, DC 20036
(202) 659-9330

National Women's History Project
Science Department
7738 Bell Road
Windsor, CA 95492
(707) 838-6000

Fast Fact: The Importance of Math and Science Skills for Girls

Why are math and science skills so important for girls? Between 1984 and the year 2000, 25 million new jobs will be created in the United States. Four out of every ten of these will be technical or professional jobs in fields such as engineering, physics, chem-istry, health, and computer and engineering technology; it is estimated that 65% of these new jobs will be held by women.

Source: American Association for the Advancement of Science

G. CHARMAINE GILBREATH—A WOMAN IN SCIENCE

Dr. G. Charmaine Gilbreath has a Ph.D. in electrical engineering and is head of the electro-optics technology section at the Naval Research Laboratory. In this speech, she expresses her concern that more women are not pursuing careers in science and engineering

In college, I wanted to be a lawyer. My first undergraduate degree was in communications and the humanities, and then somewhere around my mid-20s, I had a midlife crisis. I realized that what I did to make myself happy were physics and geometry problems. It took me two years to get up the nerve to take a pre-calculus class. When I finally did, I was surprised to find that it was not that hard.

Later, when I returned to school to get my degrees in engineering science, I found my biggest obstacle was a fear of the subject itself. The litany I used then—and still use today, by the way—is "Humans invented this (mathematical or engineering) construct to understand this physical interaction. I am human. I can understand it, too." Essentially, like my female peers in engineering school, I learned to ignore society's traditional expectations of women and concentrated on learning the fundamentals of physical interactions, as we know them so far.

As a researcher at the Naval Research Laboratory, I do not have any official expertise in the area of education. My work actually involves projects like optical wavefront manipulation to improve data transfer, satellite laser ranging, and laser illumination of rocket plumes. I do, however, have perceptions that are shared by other women in the field [of engineering and science].

We are concerned that something is happening to our young women in the black boxes of high school and undergraduate school. There are those who survive the negative forces and, at best, ambivalence of high school and enter college with hopes to pursue engineering or science. However, these women are for the most part not emerging in the field after their undergraduate education. What is happening to them?

I feel there are two strong negative forces at work. I do not have any statistics but do base my feelings on a lot of anecdotal evidence as well as on the excellent recent survey on girls' self-esteem in high school conducted by the American Association of University Women. The first is that young women seem to have a "perfectionist" complex that sets in early. They feel that if they cannot get A's or B's in something, that they must not be good at the subject, and shy away from it. Young men do not seem to be so easily diverted. They will struggle through, persist in their studies, and get their engineering or science degrees. The world then opens to them, since training and credentials in engineering and science provide an excellent place from which to launch any kind of professional career.

Girls need to feel free to get C's from time to time in math and science. After all, math *is* hard; physics *is* hard; engineering *is* hard. I still overhear young girls say, "Algebra—eeeeew, I'm not taking that." We need to hear instead, "Algebra, yeah, it's hard, but I'm going to take it anyway."

How do we create the conditions in which our girls feel safe and free to learn these challenging subjects? Relaxation of academic standards is not the answer. After all, our scientists and engineers will be competing on a global scale. Freedom to struggle must be granted in the home. The burden must shift to the parents, who might say to their daughters, "Hey, a C is still okay.

Shall we get you a tutor? What didn't you understand? Did the course move too fast? What did you like about the subject?" etc. For families who cannot afford a tutor by themselves, it might be possible to hire a tutor with another family or two to teach more than one struggling girl, each of whom will be afforded the freedom to ask questions, be paced differently, and be able to fail from time to time without bearing the consequences of a bad report card.

For our young women who have made it to college with their aspirations intact, a tutor is still a good solution. So is slowing down. Why is it necessary to take a lot of killer courses in the same semester? To ease the financial burden of increased time in school caused by taking a more manageable load, our young women should be steered toward co-op programs. In a co-op program, an engineering or science student alternates between going to school for a term and working in the field for a term.

The second negative force, which is still surprisingly strong today, is the perception that excelling in math and science and pursuing related career disciplines is somehow de-feminizing. What can I say, I just gave birth to my second child. Many of us in the field are spouses and mothers. We can have it all—maybe not all at once—but we do not have to assume that we lose our fundamental femaleness just because we enjoy the satisfaction of understanding a physical process, or designing and building a good circuit, or solving a thorny equation.

This is a difficult problem since much of it is generated from peer pressure. To change our girls'—and boys'—perceptions requires exposure to role models. For this, I appeal to the other women in the profession. We need to participate in career fairs at high schools and colleges. We need to work with educators to expose our young women to women in the field.

Parents must play a strong role in exposing their girls to these options. For example, the parent must not let that Saturday trip to the mall take priority over a women-in-science career day. Television and the media can play a key role in featuring female protagonists who are not de-feminized by their careers in science and engineering. We in the field can play a part in educationg the media as well. And we must hire, train, and support our young women with real work as well as words whenever we possibly can.

This essay does not necessarily reflect the views of the Naval Research Laboratory.

WOMEN WHO RECEIVED PH.D.S IN MATHEMATICS

Racial/Ethnic Group	
Asian/Pacific Islander	11
Black	3
Native American, Eskimo, Aleut	0
Mexican-American, Puerto Rican, or other Hispanic	4
White (non-Hispanic)	126
Unknown	1

Source: American Mathematical Society, 1993

WOMEN ENGINEERING GRADUATES

Academic Year Ending in June	*% Bachelor's*	*% Master's*	*% Doctorate*
1955	0.3	0.3	0.0
1960	0.4	0.4	0.4
1965	0.4	0.4	0.5
1970	0.8	1.1	0.4
1975	2.3	2.4	1.8
1980	9.7	6.3	3.2
1985	14.8	11.3	5.7
1990	15.4	14.3	9.1
1992	15.7	15.5	9.9

Source: Society of Women Engineers

MEDICAL SCHOOL ACCEPTANCE RATES

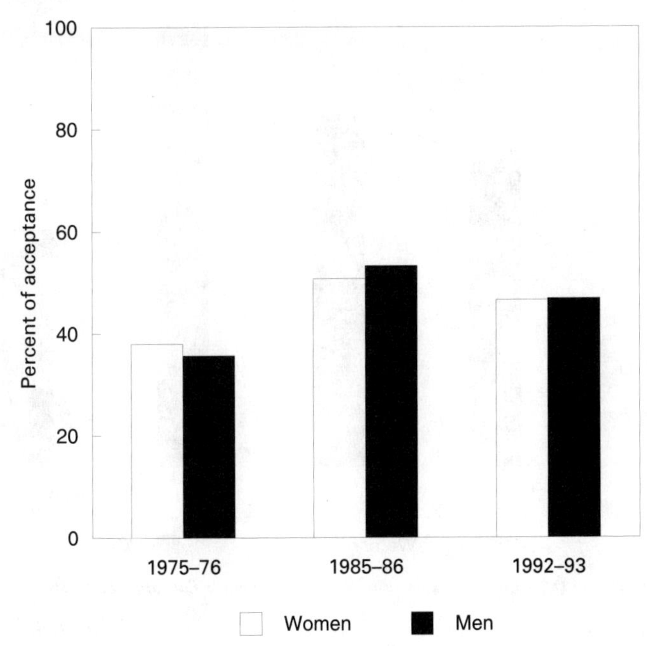

Source: Association of American Medical Colleges

Bette Nesmith Graham, a high school dropout and single mother who worked as a secretary, invented Liquid Paper. She sold the invention to Gillette in 1979 for $47.5 million, plus royalties.

Emma Sadler Moss was the first woman to be elected president of a major medical society (the American Society of Clinical Pathologists), in 1955.

MEDICAL AND DENTISTRY DEGREES

Maria Goeppert-Mayer was the first American woman to win the Nobel Prize for physics, in 1963.

Medical

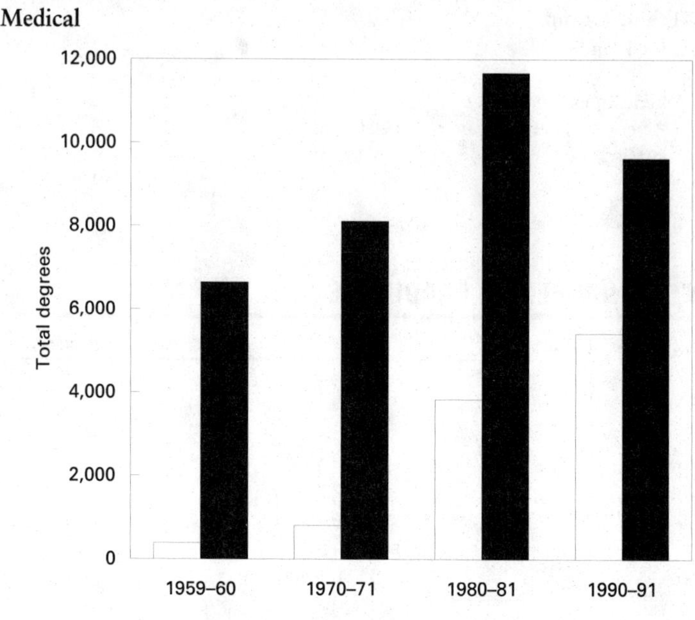

Dentistry

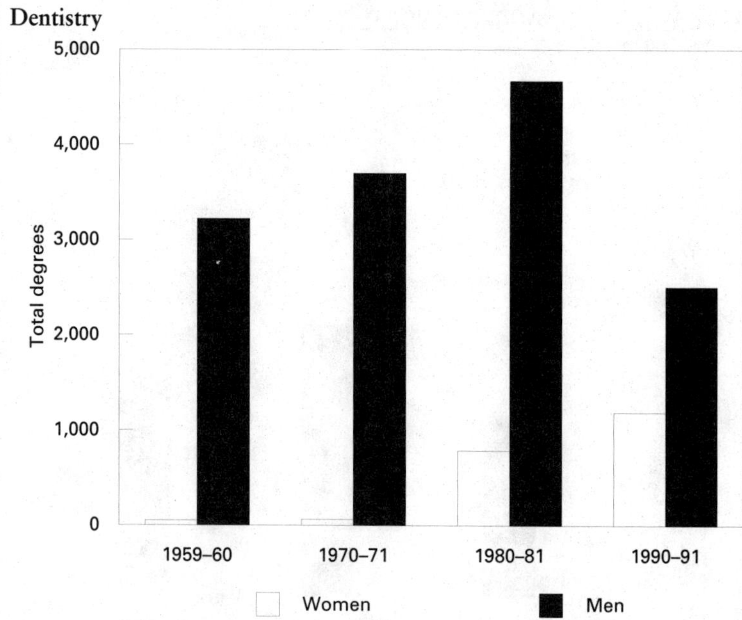

Source for above: Department of Education, National Center for Education Statistics

FEMALE BUSINESS AND MANAGEMENT GRADUATES

	% Bachelor's	% Master's
1962–63	7.8	3.7
1972–73	10.8	4.9
1982–83	41.9	28.8
1990–91*	47.1	34.9

*Preliminary, rounded-off figures

Source: American Assembly of Collegiate Schools of Business

LAW DEGREES CONFERRED UPON WOMEN AND MEN

	Women	Men
1959–60	230	9,010
1969–70	1,240	16,181
1979–80	11,768	24,563
1990–91	16,302	21, 643

Source: Department of Education, National Center for Education Statistics

The first American woman to win the Nobel prize in a scientific category by herself was Barbara McClintock, a geneticist, in 1951.

Fast Facts: Women in Legal Education

- 44% of law school students are women
- 27% of full-time faculty are women; of those 4% are women of color
- 7% of law school deans are women

Source: American Bar Association, Commission on Women in the Profession

"We don't accept the 'glass ceiling' notion here. The ceiling isn't glass; it's a very dense layer of men."—Anne Jardim, cofounder of Simmons Graduate School of Management

WOMEN NOBEL LAUREATES

Nobel Peace Prize

1992—Rigoberta Menchu Tum (Guatemala), activist on behalf of indigenous people in Guatemala.

1991—Aung San Suu Kyi (Myanmar), secretary general of National League of Democracy, a group advocating democracy in Myanmar (formerly Burma).

1979—Mother Teresa (India), leader of Missionaries of Charity, Calcutta.

1976 — Betty Williams (U.K., co-winner with Mairoad Corrigan), founders of the Northern Ireland Peace Movement (later named the Community of Peace People).

1946 — Emily G. Balch (U.S.), professor of history and sociology, honorary international president of Women's International League for Peace and Freedom, for contributions to the international women's movement for peace.

1931 — Jane Addams (U.S.), sociologist, suffragette, international president of Women's International League for Peace and Freedom.

1905 — Baroness Bertha von Suttner (Austria), writer, honorary president of Permanent International Peace Bureau, author of Lay Down Your Arms.

Nobel Prize for Chemistry

1964 — Prof. Dorothy Crowfoot Hodgkin (U.K.), "for her determinations by X-ray techniques of the structures of important biochemical substances."

1935 — Irène Joliot-Curie (France, co-winner with Frédéric Joliot), "in recognition of their synthesis of new radioactive elements."

1911 — Prof. Marie Curie (France), "in recognition of her services to the advancement of chemistry by the discovery of the elements radium and polonium, by the isolation of radium, and the study of the nature and compounds of this remarkable element."

Nobel Prize for Literature

1993 — Prof. Toni Morrison (U.S.),

14% of the women who head American colleges and universities are women of color, including 26 African-Americans, 17 Latinas, 5 Native Americans, and 2 Asian-Americans.

Martha Carey Thomas was the first female college faculty member to become a dean, in 1884.

"who in novels characterized by visionary force and poetic import, gives life to an essential aspect of American reality."

1991 — Nadine Gordimer (South Africa), "who through her magnificent epic writing has—in the words of Alfred Nobel—been of very great benefit to humanity."

1945—Gabriela Mistral (Chile), "for her lyric poetry which, inspired by powerful emotions, has made her name a symbol of the idealistic aspirations of the entire Latin American world."

1938 — Pearl S. Buck (U.S.),"for her rich and truly epic descriptions of peasant life in China and for biographical masterpieces."

1928 — Sigrid Undset (Norway), "principally for her powerful descriptions of Northern life during the Middle Ages."

1926 — Grazia Deledda (Italy), "for her idealistically inspired writings which with plastic clarity picture the life on her native island and with depth and sympathy deal with human problems in general."

1909 — Selma Lagerlörf (Sweden), "in appreciation of the lofty idealism, vivid imagination, and spiritual perception that characterize her writings."

Nobel Prize for Physics
1963 — Prof. Maria Goeppert-Mayer (U.S., co-winner with Prof. J.H.D. Jensen [West Germany]), "for their discoveries concerning nuclear shell structure."

1903 — Prof. Marie Curie (France, co-winner with Prof. Pierre Curie), "in recognition of the extraordinary services they have rendered by their joint researches on the radiation phenomena discovered by Prof. Henri Becquerel."

Nobel Prize for Physiology or Medicine
1988 — Gertrude B. Elion (U.S co-winner with Sir James W. Blac [U.K.] and George H. Hitching [U.S.]), "for their discoveries o important principles for drug treat ment."

1986 — Rita Levi-Montalcini (Italy co-winner with Stanley Cohe [U.S.]), "for their discoveries o growth factors."

WOMEN CHIEF EXECUTIVE OFFICERS AT U.S. COLLEGES AND UNIVERSITIES

	1975	1984	1992
Private	132	182	184
Public	16	104	164
Total	148	286	348

Source: American Council on Education, Office of Women in Higher Education, 1992

Fast Facts: Women Leading Major Academic Institutions

Judith Rosen, president of the Uni versity of Pennsylvania, is the firs woman to head an Ivy League insti tution. Other women to lead majo academic institutions include: W Ann Reynolds, chancellor of th City University of New York; Nan nerl H. Keohane, president of Duk University; Katherine Lyall, presi dent of the University of Wisconsin and Yolanda Moses, president o City College of the City University of New York.

SEX AND RACE OF ELEMENTARY AND HIGH SCHOOL TEACHERS

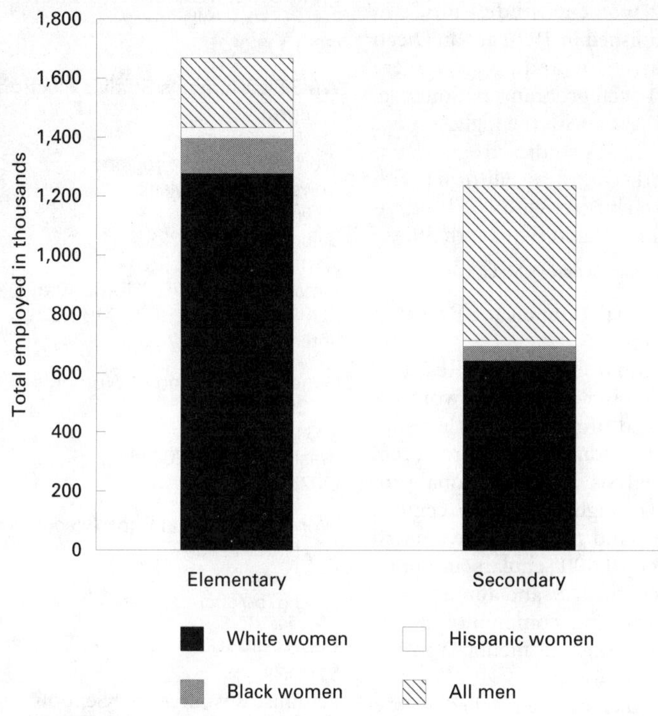

Source: Department of Labor, 1993

99% of women's studies programs are administered by women.

WOMEN VS. MEN IN PUBLIC EDUCATION

Position	% Women	% Men
Chief state school officials	18.0	82.0
School board members	33.7	66.3
Superintendents	4.8	95.2
Principals	27.7	72.3
Elementary and secondary teachers	72.0	28.0

Source: American Association of University Women and American Association of School Administrators

Boys Town began accepting girls in 1980, and in 1991 the village elected a girl, Sarah Williamson, 16, as its mayor.

WOMEN'S STUDIES

The first women's studies program was established in 1970 at San Diego State University, and by 1990 there were 621 such programs nationwide. The five states with the highest number of women's studies programs are New York with 69, California with 64, Massachusetts with 47, Pennsylvania with 41, and Ohio with 30.

Source: National Women's Studies Association

The National Council for Research on Women
The National Council for Research on Women is a coalition of women's centers and organizations that support and conduct feminist research, policy analysis, and educational programs. Through its member centers, affiliates, and projects, the council links over 10,000 scholars and practitioners in the U.S. and abroad, serving the academic community, public policy makers, the media, and the nonprofit sector.

The council can be reached at:
530 Broadway, 10th Floor
New York, NY 10012
(212) 274-0730

WOMEN'S STUDIES—RESOURCES

Institute for Feminist Studies
988 Market Street, Suite 609
San Francisco, CA 94102
(415) 922-3837

Lesbian Herstory Archives
P.O. Box 1258
New York, NY 10116
(212) 874-7232

National Council for Research on Women
530 Broadway
New York, NY 10012
(212) 274-0730

National Women's History Project
7738 Bell Road
Windsor, CA 95492
(707) 838-6000

National Women's Studies Association
University of Maryland
College Park, MD 20742
(301) 403-0525

WMST-L Women's Studies Electronic Forum
c/o Joan Korenman
Women's Studies Program
University of Maryland
Baltimore County
Baltimore, MD 21228
(410) 455-2040
E-mail: KORENMAN@UMBC (Bitnet)
KORENMAN@UMBC2.UMBC.EDU (Internet)

General Federation of Women's Clubs
1734 N Street, N.W.
Washington, DC 20036
(202) 347-3168

Women's National Book Association
160 Fifth Avenue
New York, NY 10010
(212) 675-7805

PUBLISHED RESOURCES FOR WOMEN'S STUDIES

Feminist Resources for Schools and Colleges, Anne Chapman (New York: Feminist Press, 1982).

All the Women Are White, All the Blacks Are Men, But Some of Us Are Brave: Black Women's Studies, Gloria T. Hull, Patricia Bell Scott, and Barbara Smith, eds. (New York: Feminist Press, 1982).

BOOKS BY WOMEN WHOSE WORDS HAVE CHANGED THE WORLD

The Women's National Book Association compiled this list of 75 books to commemorate its seventy-fifth anniversary in 1992.

Jane Addams	Twenty Years at Hull House
Louisa May Alcott	Little Women
Isabel Allende	The House of the Spirits
Maya Angelou	I Know Why the Caged Bird Sings
Hanna Arendt	The Human Condition
Jane Austen	Pride and Prejudice
Simone de Beauvoir	The Second Sex
Ruth Benedict	Patterns of Culture
Boston Women's Health Book Collective Staff	Our Bodies, Ourselves
Charlotte Brontë	Jane Eyre
Emily Brontë	Wuthering Heights
Susan Brownmiller	Against Our Will: Men, Women, and Rape
Pearl S. Buck	The Good Earth
Rachel Carson	Silent Spring
Willa Cather	My Antonia
Mary Boykin Chestnut	A Diary From Dixie
Kate Chopin	The Awakening
Agatha Christie	The Murder of Roger Ackroyd
Emily Dickinson	The Complete Poems of Emily Dickinson
Mary Baker Eddy	Science and Health
George Eliot	Middlemarch
Fannie Farmer	The Boston Cooking-School Cook Book
Frances FitzGerald	Fire in the Lake
Dian Fossey	Gorillas in the Mist
Anne Frank	Diary of a Young Girl
Betty Friedan	The Feminine Mystique
Emma Goldman	Living My Life
Germaine Greer	The Female Eunuch
Radclyffe Hall	The Well of Loneliness
Edith Hamilton	Mythology
Betty Lehan Harragan	Games Mother Never Taught You
Karen Horney	Our Inner Conflicts
Zora Neale Hurston	Their Eyes Were Watching God
Helen Keller	The Story of My Life
Maxine Hong Kingston	The Woman Warrior
Elisabeth Kubler-Ross	On Death and Dying
Frances Moore Lappe	Diet for a Small Planet
Harper Lee	To Kill a Mockingbird
Doris Lessing	The Golden Notebook
Anne Morrow Lindbergh	Gift From the Sea
Audre Lorde	The Cancer Journals
Carson McCullers	The Heart is a Lonely Hunter
Katherine Mansfield	The Garden Party
Beryl Markham	West With the Night
Margaret Mead	Coming of Age in Samoa
Golda Meir	My Life
Edna St. Vincent Millay	Collected Poems
Margaret Mitchell	Gone With the Wind
Marianne Moore	Complete Poems of Marianne Moore
Toni Morrison	Song of Solomon

Bill and Camille Cosby donated $1.8 million in March 1994 for a building in Washington, D.C., to be used for a national center for African-American women.

"If I read a book that impresses me, I have to take myself firmly in hand before I mix with other people; otherwise they would think my mind rather queer."—Anne Frank

Lady Shikibu Murasaki	The Tale of Genji
Anaïs Nin	The Early Diary of Anaïs Nin
Flannery O'Connor	The Complete Stories
Zoe Oldenbourg	The World Is Not Enough
Tillie Olsen	Silences
Elaine Pagels	The Gnostic Gospels
Emmeline Pankhurst	My Own Story
Sylvia Plath	The Bell Jar
Katherine Anne Porter	Ship of Fools
Adrienne Rich	Of Woman Born
Margaret Sanger	Margaret Sanger: An Autobiography
Sappho	Sappho: A New Translation
May Sarton	Journal of a Solitude
Mary Shelley	Frankenstein
Susan Sontag	Illness As Metaphor
Gertrude Stein	The Autobiography of Alice B. Toklas
Harriet Beecher Stowe	Uncle Tom's Cabin
Barbara Tuchman	A Distant Mirror
Sigrid Undset	Kristin Lavransdatter
Alice Walker	The Color Purple
Eudora Welty	Delta Wedding
Edith Wharton	Ethan Frome
Phillis Wheatley	The Collected Works of Phillis Wheatley
Mary Wollstonecraft	A Vindication of the Rights of Woman
Virginia Woolf	A Room of One's Own

Source: Women's National Book Association

WOMEN'S BOOKSTORES IN NORTH AMERICA

CANADA

Alberta

Calgary, A Woman's Place Bookstore

British Columbia

Nanaimo, Women's Work
Vancouver, Vancouver Women's Bookstore
Vancouver, Women in Print
Victoria, Everywoman's Books

Manitoba

Winnipeg, Bold Print

Ontario

Bloomfield, Food for Thought
Hamilton, Women's Bookstop
London, Womansline Books
Ottawa, Ottawa Women's Bookstore
Thunder Bay, The Northern Woman's Bookstore
Toronto, Toronto Women's Bookstore

UNITED STATES

Alaska

Anchorage, Alaska Women's Bookstore

Alabama

Birmingham, Lodestar Books

Arizona

Flagstaff, Aradia Bookstore
Tucson, Antigone Books

California

Auburn, Lotus Bookstore
Beverly Hills, Her Body Books
Claremont, Wild Iris Bookstore
Eureka, The Woman Reader's Bookshop
Fresno, Valley Women Books and Gifts
Kensington, Boadecia's Books
Laguna Beach, A Different Drummer Bookstore
Long Beach, Pearls
Los Angeles, Sisterhood Bookstore
Los Angeles, Her Body Books
Menlo Park, Two Sisters Bookshop
Oakland, Mama Bears
Pacific Grove, Raven in the Grove
Palm Desert, Her Body Books
Palo Alto, Stepping Stones
Pasadena, Page One—Books By and For Women
Sacramento, Lioness Books

San Francisco, Old Wives' Tales
San Jose, Sisterspirit
Santa Barbara, Choices
Santa Cruz, Herland Book-Cafe
Santa Rosa, Clairelight

Colorado
Colorado Springs, Abaton Books
Denver, The Book Garden

Connecticut
Bridgeport, Bloodroot
Hartford, The Readers' Feast
New Haven, Golden Thread Booksellers

Florida
Gainesville, Iris Books
Pensacola, Silver Chord
St. Petersburg, Brigit Books
Tallahassee, Rubyfruit Books

Georgia
Atlanta, Charis Books and More

Illinois
Arlington Heights, Prairie Moon
Bloomingdale, A Book for All Seasons
Champaign, Jane Addams Book Shop
Chicago, Women and Children First
Evanston, Platypus Book Shop
Rockford, Iris Gardens

Indiana
Bloomington, Aquarius Books
Indianapolis, Dreams and Swords

Kansas
Wichita, Visions and Dreams

Louisiana
Shreveport, PLU Books and Gifts

Massachusetts
Cambridge, New Words Bookstore
Haverhill, Radzukina's
Jamaica Plain, Crone's Harvest
Northampton, Lunaria
Provincetown, Now Voyager
Provincetown, Recovering Hearts Book and Gift Store
Provincetown, Womancrafts

Maryland
Baltimore, Thirtyfirst Street Bookstore

Maine
Freeport, Sister Creations
Gardiner, The Circle Shop

Michigan
Ann Arbor, Common Language
Ferndale, A Woman's Prerogative
Grand Rapids, Earth and Sky
Kalamazoo, Pandora Books for Open Minds
Marquette, Sweet Violets

Minnesota
Minneapolis, Amazon Bookstore
Minneapolis, Motherlode
St. Paul, Minnesota Women's Press

Missouri
Kansas City, Phoenix Books

North Carolina
Charlotte, Rising Moon Books and Beyond
Durham, Southern Sisters

North Dakota
Fargo, Food for Thought Alternative Bookstore

Nebraska
Lincoln, The Arbor Moon Bookstore

New Hampshire
Portsmouth, Lady Iris

New Jersey
North Haledon, Pandora Book Peddlers
Woodbury, Renaissance Bookstore and Coffeehaus

New Mexico
Albuquerque, Full Circle

Nevada
Reno, Grapevine Books

New York
Ithaca, Smedley's Bookshop
New York, Judith's Room
Rochester, Silkwood Books
Syracuse, My Sisters' Words

Ohio
Cincinnati, Crazy Ladies Bookstore
Cleveland Heights, Gifts of Athena
Columbus, Fan the Flames
Millfield, For Women Only
Toledo, People Called Women
Toledo, Tallulah's

Oklahoma
Oklahoma City, Herland Sister Resources

Oregon
Bend, NOW Underground Bookstore
Eugene, Baba Yaga's Dream
Eugene, Mother Kali's Books
Newport, Green Gables Bookstore
Portland, In Other Words
Portland, Widdershins

The number of feminist bookstores increased 27% in 1994, to 124 from 98.

The first woman to supervise a public school system was Amy Bradley, in Wilmington, North Carolina, in 1869.

The first coed class of Columbia University (the last Ivy League school to go coed) graduated on May 13, 1987.

The first higher education institution for women was Middlebury Female Seminary, founded by Emma Hart Willard in 1814.

The Trade School for Girls, the first girls' public vocational high school, opened in Boston in 1904.

Pennsylvania
Hallam, Her Story Bookstore
Lewisburg, The Dwelling Place
New Hope, Book Gallery
Pittsburgh, Gertrude Stein Memorial Bookshop

South Carolina
Columbia, Bluestocking Books
Greenville, Wittershins
Greenville, Avalon

Tennessee
Memphis, Meristem

Texas
Austin, Book Woman
Houston, Inklings
Lubbock, Ellie's Garden: Women's Books and More
San Antonio, Textures

Utah
Draper, A Woman's Place Bookstore
Park City, A Woman's Place Bookstore
Salt Lake City, A Woman's Place Bookstore

Virginia
Fredericksburg, Purple Moon Books
Newport News, Out of the Dark

Washington
Tacoma, Imprints Bookstore and Gallery

Washington, D.C.
Lammas Women's Books and More

Wisconsin
Beloit, A Different World Bookstore
Madison, A Room of One's Own

WOMEN'S COLLEGES

Numerical Breakdown
•Of the 84 women's colleges in th U.S., 53% are located in the North east, 25% in the South, 18% in th Central States, and 4% in California.
•Eighty-three percent are four-yea women's institutions and 17% ar two-year colleges. Fifty-one percen have religious affiliations; in addi tion, three are state-affiliated.

Enrollment Trends
•Since 1970, undergraduate enrol ments are up more than 18% at women' colleges, and full-time undergraduat enrollments are up more than 7%.

Graduates in the Workplace
•Nearly three-quarters of women' college graduates are in the workforce
•Almost half of the graduates wh work hold traditionally male-domi nated jobs at the higher end of th pay scale, such as lawyer, physician or manager.
•One-third of the women boar members of the 1992 Fortune 10 companies are women's colleg graduates.
•Of the 4,012 highest-paid officers an directors of 1990 Fortune 1000 com panies, 19, or less than half of 1% were women. But of these women 36% were women's college graduates
•Twenty percent of women identi fied by Black Enterprise magazine i August 1991 as the twenty mos powerful African-American wome in corporate America graduate from women's colleges.
•Of 54 women members of Congress 24% attended women's colleges.
•Graduates of women's colleges ar more than twice as likely as graduate of coeducational colleges to receiv doctoral degrees. And women's col lege graduates are also more likel than female graduates of coed institu tions to enter medical school.

Source: Women's College Coalition

HILLARY RODHAM CLINTON— MAKING WOMEN'S VOICES COUNT

First Lady Hillary Rodham Clinton delivered the commencement address at her alma mater, Wellesley College, on May 29, 1992.

This is my second chance to speak from this podium. The first was 23 years ago, when I was a graduating senior. My classmates selected me to address them as the first Wellesley student ever to speak at a commencement.

I can't claim that 1969 speech as my own; it reflected the hopes, values and aspirations of the women in my graduating class. It was full of the uncompromising language you only write when you're 21. But it's uncanny the degree to which those same hopes, values, and aspirations have shaped my adulthood.

We passionately rejected the notion of limitations on our abilities to make the world a better place for everyone. We saw a gap between our expectations and realities, and we were inspired to bridge that gap. On behalf of my class in 1969, I said, "The challenge is now to practice politics as the art of making what appears to be impossible, possible." That is the challenge of politics, especially in today's far more cynical climate.

The aspiration I referred to then was "the struggle for an integrated life . . . in an atmosphere of . . . trust and respect." What I meant by that was a life that combines personal fulfillment in love and work with fulfilling a responsibility to the larger community. A life that balances family, work, and service throughout life. It is not a static concept, but a constant journey.

[College] nurtured, challenged, and guided me; it instilled in me not just knowledge, but a reserve of sustaining values. I was here on campus when Martin Luther King was murdered. My friends and I put on black armbands and went into Boston to march in anger and pain—feeling much as many of you did after the acquittals in the Rodney King case.

Much changed—and much of it for the better—but much has also stayed the same, or at least not changed as fast or as irrevocably as we might have hoped.

Each generation takes us into new territory. But while change is certain, progress is not. Change is the law of nature; progress is the challenge of both a life and a society. Describing an integrated life is easier than achieving one.

What better a time to speak than in the spring of 1992, when the women's special concerns are so much in the news as real women seek to strike a balance in their lives that is right for them.

I've traveled all over America, talking and listening to women who are: struggling to raise their children and somehow make ends meet; battling against the persistent discrimination that still limits their opportunities for pay and promotion; bumping up against the glass ceiling; watching the insurance premiums increase; coping with inadequate or nonexistent child support payments; existing on shrinking welfare payments with no available jobs in sight; anguishing over the prospect that abortions will be criminalized again.

We also talk about our shared values as women and mothers, about our common desire to educate our children, to be sure they receive the health care they need, to protect them from the escalating violence in our streets. We sorrow about our children—something mothers do particularly well.

Women who pack lunch for their kids, or take the early bus to work, or stay out late at the PTA, or spend every spare minute taking care of aging parents don't need lectures from Washington about values. We don't need to hear about an idealized world that never was as righteous or carefree as some would like to think. We need understanding and a helping hand to solve our own problems. We're doing the best we can to fight for the right balance in our lives.

For some of you, your work may overlap with your contribution to the community. For some of you, the future might not include work outside the home (and I don't mean involuntary unemployment), but most of you will at some point in your life work for pay, maybe in jobs that used to be off-limits to women. You may choose to run for public office, you may choose to stay at home and raise your children—you can now make any and all of these choices for the work in your life.

It is a false choice to tell women—or men, for that matter—that we must choose between caring for ourselves and our own families, or caring for the larger family of humanity.

So you see, if you listen to all the people who make the rules, you might conclude that the safest course of action is to take your diploma and crawl under your bed. But let me propose another alternative.

Hold on to your dreams. Take up the challenge of forging an identity that transcends yourself. Transcend yourself and you will find yourself. Care about something you needn't bother with at all. Throw yourself into the world and make your voice count.

SINGLE-SEX EDUCATION READING LIST

Recent research indicates that a single-sex educational environment may be advantageous for girls. For more information on the subject, the following reports are recommended:

"Confident at 11, Confused at 16," Francine Prose, The New York Times Magazine (January 7, 1990).

"Girls Talk; Boys Talk More," The Harvard Education Letter (January/February 1991).

"How Schools Shortchange Girls: A Study of Major Findings on Girls and Education," American Association of University Women Report (February 1992).

Meeting at the Crossroads: Women's Psychology and Girl's Development, Lyn Mikel Brown and Carol Gilligan (Cambridge: Harvard University Press, 1992).

"Shortchanging Girls, Shortchanging America," American Association of University Women Report (January 1991).

SEXUAL HARASSMENT IN THE SCHOOLS

•In a survey of more than 1,600 public school students—African-American, white, and Hispanic; female and male—four out of five students in grades 8 through 11 report having experienced some form of sexual harassment in school.
•Seventy-eight percent of women students surveyed at Cornell University in 1986 said that they had experienced sexist comments, and 68% had received unwelcome attention from their male peers. At the Massachusetts Institute of Technology, 92% of women had experienced unwanted sexual atten-

NATIONAL WOMEN'S HISTORY MONTH

In 1987 Congress passed a joint resolution declaring March to be National Women's History Month. The annual celebration of women's history has become a regular part of the school curriculum in communities across the country. Inspired by the information that has come to light about women's history, many states and cities have instituted a "Women's Hall of Fame," or have published biographical materials about prominent women in the history of their particular locales. In many areas, state historical societies, women's organizations, and groups such as the Girl Scouts have worked together to develop joint programs recognizing the historical contribution of women.

For more information contact:

National Women's History Project
7738 Bell Road
Windsor, CA 95492
(707) 838-6000

Source: National Women's History Project

60% of elementary school girls say "I am happy with myself," but only 29% of tenth grade girls make the same statement.

The first woman to graduate from the Massachusetts Institute of Technology was Ellen Swallow Richards, in 1873. She was also the founder of the American Home Economics Associations, in 1908.

The University of Virginia officially banned sexual relationships between professors and undergraduate students in April 1993. The policy, the first of its kind, states that a professor "shall not engage in amorous or sexual relations with, or make amorous or sexual overtures to, any student over whom he or she holds a position of authority."

tion, and at the University of Rhode Island, 70% of women surveyed reported having been sexually assaulted by a man.

•While girls in grades 1–12 are most often harassed by fellow students, 4% reported being harassed by teachers, administrators, or other school staff.

•In over 2/3 of the incidents of sexual harassement reported in primary and secondary schools, other people were present. When students specifically told a teacher or school administrator that they had been harassed the schools took action in 55% o the cases.

•Almost 2/3 of girls being harasse told their harassers to stop, and ove 1/3 resisted with physical force.

•Three-quarters of the girls told at leas one person about being harassed.

Sources: "Hostile Hallways: The AAUW Survey on Sexual Harassment in America's Schools"; "Peer Harassment: Hassles for Women on Campus"; "Secrets in Public: Sexual Harassment in Our Schools"

TYPES OF SEXUAL HARASSMENT IN SCHOOL

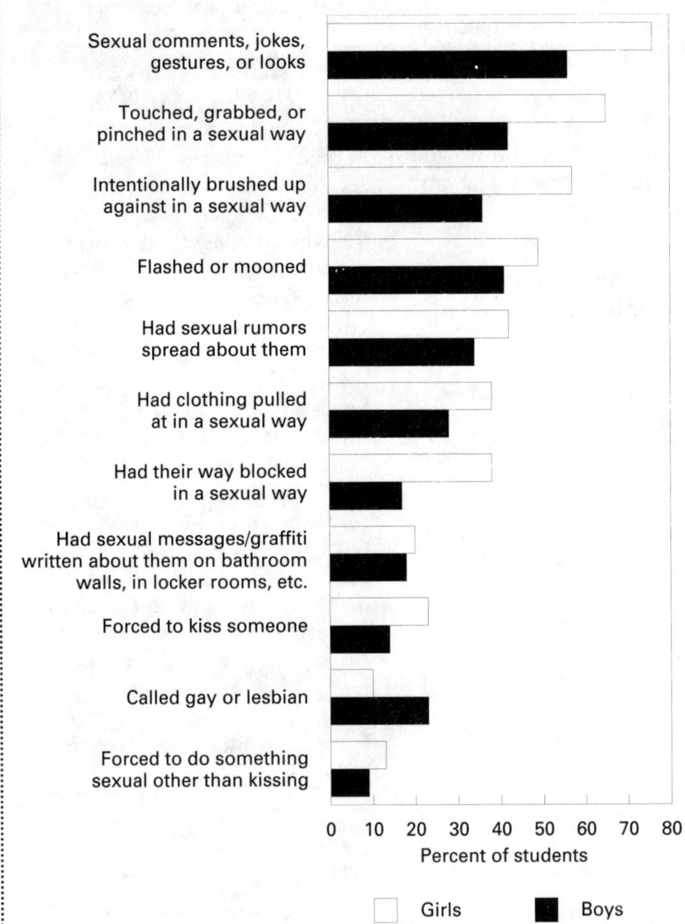

TYPES OF SEXUAL HARASSMENT AMONG GIRLS BY RACE

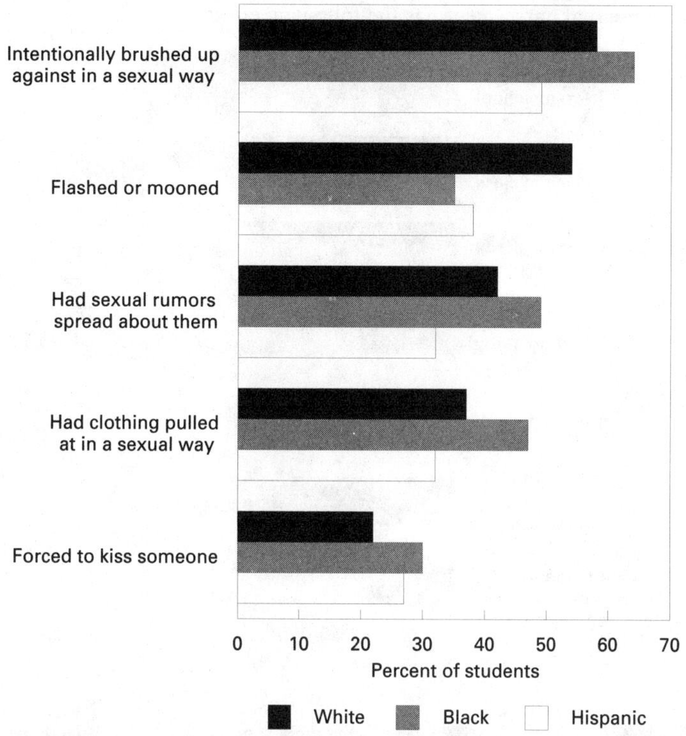

MAJOR REPORTS ON SEXUAL HARASSMENT IN THE SCHOOLS

"Hostile Hallways: The AAUW Survey on Sexual Harassment in America's Schools," Louis Harris and Assoc. (Annapolis Junction, Md.: American Association of University Women, 1993; available from AAUW, P.O. Box 251, Annapolis Junction, MD 20701 [800] 225-9998, x285).

"Peer Harassment: Hassles for Women on Campus," Jean O'Gorman Hughes and Bernice Sandler (Washington, D.C.: Center for Women Policy Studies, 1991; available from Center for Women Policy Studies, 2000 P Street, N.W., Suite 508, Washington, DC 20036 [202] 872-1770).

"Secrets in Public: Sexual Harassment in Our Schools," Nan Stein (Wellesley, Mass.: Center for Research on Women, 1993; available from Publications Department, Center for Research on Women, Wellesley College, Wellesley, MA 02181, [617] 283-2500).

EDUCATIONAL IMPACT OF SEXUAL HARASSMENT ON GIRLS

57% of female respondents to a recent poll said they believed there was a need for a strong women's movement, but 63% said they did not consider themselves feminists.

Girls say sexual harassment has the following effects on them.

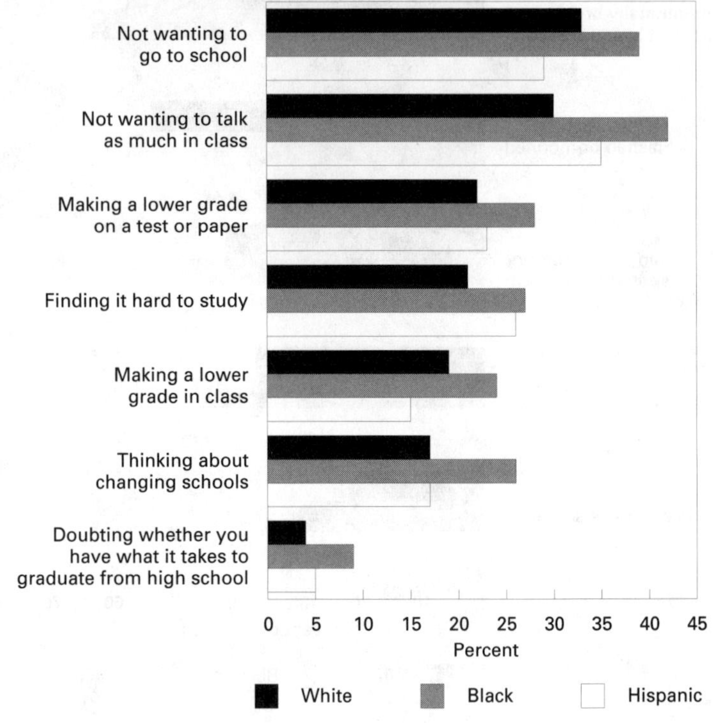

This chart is based on the 81% of students who report some experience of sexual harassment in school.

Source: Hostile Hallways, American Association of University Women Educational Foundation

WOMEN LOSE IN COLLEGE ATHLETICS SPENDING

The NCAA surveyed its members' expenditures for women's and men's athletics programs in 1991 and discovered that, while undergraduate enrollment was roughly evenly divided by sex, men constituted 69.5% of the participants in intercollegiate athletics, and their programs received around 70% of the athletic scholarship funds. In addition, men's programs were allotted 77% of funding for operating budgets and 83% of recruiting money.

Source: National Collegiate Athletic Association

EQUITY IN WOMEN'S ATHLETICS

Title IX of the Educational Amendments Act, passed in 1972, requires equity between men and women in three areas: equal opportunity to participate in sports in relation to the percentage of men and women in the student body; equal access to scholarship money; and equal facilities and support services. In an attempt to force colleges and high schools to comply with a federal law banning sex discrimination at educational institutions receiving federal funds, athletes across the country have begun filing, or threatening to file, sex-discrimination suits against those schools under the terms of Title IX.

- Howard University in Washing-ton, D.C., was ordered to pay $1.1 million to its women's basketball coach, Sanya Tyler. Tyler's salary was $44,000, while the men's coach received $78,500 plus a car. His office was air-conditioned and carpeted while Tyler shared a former closet, without air-conditioning, with the women's volleyball coach.
- In an out-of-court settlement, Karan Lafata, who coached a Mich-igan high school boys' junior varsity team, sued because a man with less experience was hired to coach the boys' varsity team, and she was passed over for the position. She was awarded $150,000, and now coaches a girls' varsity team.
- The women's golf coach at the University of Oklahoma, Anne Pitts, filed suit against the school in 1993 seeking equal pay to the men's golf coach.
- Nine women filed a sex discrimination complaint in 1993 against Cornell University because the women's gymnastics and fencing teams were cut. At the University of California at Los Angeles, the women's gymnastics team was reinstated after the athletes threatened a lawsuit.

Sources: National Association for Women in Education; Feminist Majority Foundation/Fund for the Feminist Majority

NOTABLE ATHLETIC PROGRAMS

The following schools are notable for their efforts to achieve parity in their sports programs:

Stanford University has implemented a multi-million-dollar women's sports enhancement program, which officials say will actually go beyond the requirements of Title IX. By the 1996–97 school year, Stanford will add three additional women's varsity sports for a total of 17, and will add 29 full athletic scholarships to the women's sports program. By that same academic year, the California school will have 730 athletes, of whom 325 (45%) will be female and 405 (55%) will be male; 102 scholarships will be set aside for women athletes and 144 for men.

The University of Iowa became the first major university to voluntarily commit itself to a new standard of gender equality. Announcing its plans in 1992, on the twentieth anniversary of Title IX, Iowa hopes to attain a 60:40 ratio of access to scholarships for female student athletes by 1997. That year, the opportunity to participate, as well as access to scholarships, will expand to a ratio reflecting the undergraduate enrollment of the university.

The University of Texas, after settling a Title IX class action suit, has implemented an enhancement program for women's athletics that will bring the institution into compliance with the regulations. With the addition of soccer in 1994, and with softball scheduled for 1997, UT will offer all those sports offered to high school girls at state-level competition. Each of the programs will be brought to NCAA Division I competition levels within three years. Eleven scholarhips will be available in each sport, bringing the total number of women's scholarships at UT to 93, the maximum allowed under NCAA guidelines.

The first women's college to be endowed by a woman was Smith College, in Northampton, Massachusetts. Heiress Sophia Smith established the college, chartered in 1871.

Clare Dalton, an attorney, sued Harvard University for sex discrimination over the decision not to grant her tenure as a law professor. She won $260,000 in an out-of-court settlement.

FEMALE PARTICIPATION IN ORGANIZED SPORTS, PRE- AND POST-TITLE IX

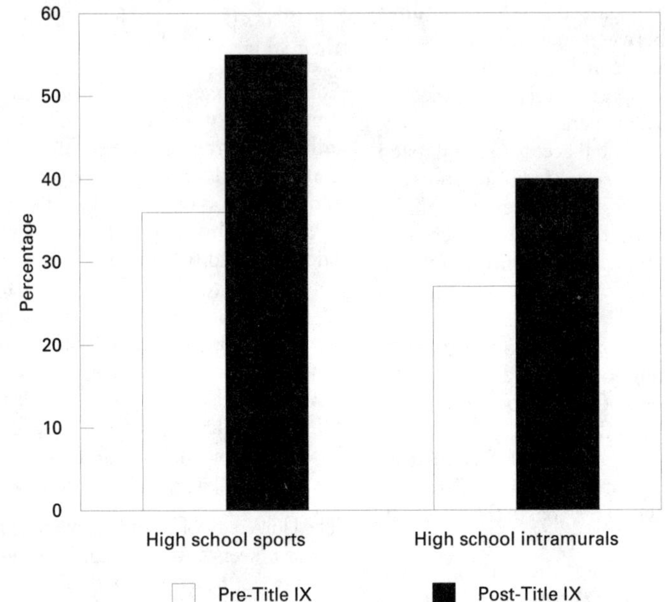

Source: Women's Sports Foundation

NCAA DIVISION I SCHOLARSHIPS

Sport	Average Scholarship Expenses	
	Women	Men
Baseball/Softball	$48,581	$78,556
Basketball	105,873	124,407
Cross Country	23,417	23,721
Football		629,880
Gymnastics	61,603	42,914
Ice Hockey		146,400
Lacrosse	28,379	53,730
Soccer	47,511	59,808
Swimming	65,141	57,861
Tennis	35,945	28,674
Indoor/Outdoor Track	63,332	70,006
Volleyball	63,870	34,019
Institutional Average	$372,800	$849,130

Source: National Collegiate Athletic Association

The first annual National Girls and Women in Sports Day was February 3, 1987. Female athletes met throughout the country to celebrate their achievements and lobby for equal opportunities.

The percentage of freshmen women who judged their mechanical abilities above average or better rose from 8.2% in 1971 to 40.7% in 1980.

COLLEGIATE ATHLETICS—RESOURCES AND READING

ORGANIZATION
National Collegiate Athletic Association
Education Services Group
6201 College Boulevard
Overland Park, KS 66211
(913) 339-1906

READING
The National Directory of College Athletics (Cleveland: Collegiate Directories; available from Collegiate Directories, P.O. Box 450640, Cleveland, OH 44145).

The Women's Collegiate Sports Scholarship Guide (New York: Women's Sports Foundation; available from the Women's Sports Foundation, 342 Madison Avenue, Suite 728, New York, NY 10173).

TITLE IX: WHAT IT IS, WHAT IT SAYS, HOW IT WORKS

Who is prohibited from discriminating?
Educational institutions that receive federal financial assistance, and educational programs of federally funded noneducational entities. Federal financial aid to an institution's students constitutes federal financial assistance to the institution.

What is prohibited?
Discrimination on the basis of sex against students *and* employees. Title IX forbids sex discrimination in all aspects of education (including recruitment, admissions, curricular and extracurricular opportunities, financial aid, rules of conduct, counseling, testing, fees, services and benefits, and other educational activities and opportunities); it also forbids sex discrimination in all aspects of employment (including hiring and promotion, tenure, salaries, benefits, training, demotion, layoff, firing, transfer, and other conditions of employment.

Is discrimination on the basis of pregnancy or marital/parental status covered?
Title IX regulations prohibit institutions from discriminating against students or employees on the grounds of their pregnancy, childbirth, or the decision to terminate a pregnancy. Institutions must treat disabilities related to pregnancy and childbirth as they treat other disabilities and must grant students and employees medical leave (without pay) for pregnancy if the institution has no other applicable leave policy.

*Is sexual harassment covered?**
Title IX protects students and employees from sexual harassment.

Are any institutions exempt from some or all of the law's requirements?
Public undergraduate schools that have traditionally been single sex, elementary and secondary schools (except for vocational schools), and private undergraduate schools may discriminate on the basis of sex *in admissions only*. Institutions con-

Rhodes scholarships were awarded to women for the first time in 1977.

*"Sexual harassment" is unwelcome sexual conduct that is a condition of employment or education. Harassing conduct can range from verbal sexual innuendo, jokes, and epithets through coerced intercourse and rape. To date the law has recognized two types of sexual harassment. "Quid pro quo" harassment occurs when the victim must submit to the unwelcome sexual conduct to obtain a job, promotion, admission to a school or educational program, or any other job-related or education-related benefit or opportunity. "Hostile environment" harassment occurs when the unwelcome sexual conduct is sufficiently pervasive or severe to create a hostile, offensive, or abusive workplace or educational environment interfering with the victim's performance or participation.

"The highest result of education is tolerance."—Helen Keller, Optimism

Approximately 200,000 collegiate women are currently active in social fraternities and sororities on campus.

trolled by a religious organization are exempt with respect to a particular policy required by Title IX if that policy is not consistent with the organization's religious tenets. Schools whose purpose is to train individuals for United States military service or the merchant marine are entirely exempt.

Which agency enforces the law?
The Department of Education has played the leading role in Title IX enforcement, handling both individual and class complaints. It accepts individual complaints of employment discrimination, but refers them to the Equal Employment Opportunities Commission (EEOC) for processing.

How is a complaint filed with the agency?
By a letter to or complaint form obtained from the regional or national office of the agency providing financial assistance to the institution. In most cases this will be the Department of Education or the Department of Health and Human Services. Complaints must be filed in 180 days.

Are institutions notified of complaints against them?
Yes. However, the Department of Education's policy is to avoid revealing complainants' names to the institutions charged with discrimination, doing so only with complainants' consent if necessary to conduct the investigation or enforcement action. If court action becomes necessary, the names of the parties involved are a matter of public record. Neither the institution nor the complainant are bound by any confidentiality requirements.

Is retaliation for filing a complaint prohibited?
Institutions may not discharge, threaten, harass, or otherwise discriminate against any person or organization for making a complaint. Such retaliation is itself a violation of Title IX, regardless of whether the institution is found to have committed the discrimination that was the basis of the original complaint.

What enforcement powers and sanctions does the agency have?
If the agency finds that the law has been violated, it tries to secure the institution's voluntary compliance. Should this fail, the agency may institute administrative proceedings to suspend or terminate federal assistance and/or bar future awards, or refer the complaint to the Department of Justice with a recommendation for court action. Courts may order the institution to stop violating Title IX and award victims of discrimination appropriate relief, including back pay where employment discrimination is involved. With the passage of the Civil Rights Act of 1991, both the EEOC and the Department of Justice may also seek monetary damages on behalf of victims of intentional discrimination. The amount of damages that may be awarded is capped according to a sliding scale based on the number of employees.

1–100 employees:	up to $50,000
101–200 employees:	up to $100,000
201–500 employees:	up to $200,000
over 500 employees:	up to $300,000

Can victims of discrimination file suits in court?
Yes. Victims need not file a grievance with the institution or a complaint with an agency before filing suit in court. Courts may award injunctive relief, back pay, and, in some cases of intentional discrimination, monetary damages according to the same scale described in the answer to the immediately preceding question.

For further information and relevant documents contact:

Regional office of the Department of Education, the Department of Health and Human Services, or other agency providing federal financial assistance to the institution, or

Office of Civil Rights
Department of Education
330 C Street, S.W.
Washington, DC 20202

Office of Civil Rights
Department of Health and Human Services
330 Independence Avenue, S.W., Room 5400
Washington, DC 20201

Source: Center for Women Policy Studies

FILING A TITLE IX COMPLAINT

If a violation of Title IX has occurred, an administrative complaint may be filed by an athlete, parent, or team, with the Office for Civil Rights. A letter should be sent to the Office of Civil Rights within 180 days of the discrimination. The letter must contain the name and address of the complainant and describe the person or group injured by the alleged discrimination. The institution that is alleged to have discriminated must be identified, and although the letter must be signed, the complainant may request confidentiality. An administrative complaint is not a lawsuit (see legal resources list also in this chapter).

For more information, or to file a complaint, contact one of the ten regional offices listed below:

Office of Civil Rights Regional Offices

Region I: Connecticut, Maine, Massachusetts, New Hampshire, Rhode Island, Vermont
Mr. Thomas J. Hibino
Regional Civil Rights Director
Office for Civil Rights, Region I
U.S. Department of Education
J. W. McCormack Post Office and Courthouse Bldg., Room 222, 01-0061
Boston, MA 02109
(617) 223-9662, or (617) 223-9695 (deaf access)

Region II: New Jersey, New York, Puerto Rico, Virgin Islands
Ms. Paula D. Kuebler
Regional Civil Rights Director
Office for Civil Rights, Region II
U.S. Department of Education
26 Federal Plaza, 33rd Floor
Room 33-130, 02-1010
New York, NY 10278
(212) 264-5180, or
(212) 264-9464 (deaf access)

Region III: Delaware, District of Columbia, Maryland, Pennsylvania, Virginia, West Virginia
Dr. Robert A. Smallwood
Regional Civil Rights Director
Office for Civil Rights, Region III
U.S. Department of Education
3535 Market Street
Room 6300, 03-2010
Philadelphia, PA 19104
(215) 596-6772, or
(215) 596-6794 (deaf access)

Region IV: Alabama, Florida, Georgia, Mississippi, North Carolina, South Carolina, Tennessee
Mr. Archie B. Meyer, Sr.
Acting Regional Civil Rights Director
Regional Civil Rights Director
Office for Civil Rights, Region IV
U.S. Department of Education
P.O. Box 2048, 04-3010
Atlanta, GA 30301
(404) 331-2954, or
(404) 331-7816 (deaf access)

Region V: Illinois, Indiana, Michigan, Minnesota, Ohio, Wisconsin
Mr. Kenneth A. Mines
Regional Civil Rights Director
Office for Civil Rights, Region V
U.S. Department of Education
401 South State Street
Room 700C, 05-4010
Chicago, IL 60605
(312) 886-3456, or
(312) 353-2541 (deaf access)

The first American nursery schools were set up by Joanne Bethune in New York City in 1827.

Region VI: Arkansas, Louisiana, Oklahoma, Texas
Mr. Taylor D. August
Regional Civil Rights Director
Office for Civil Rights, Region VI
U.S. Department of Education
1200 Main Tower Building
Suite 2260, 06-5010
Dallas, TX 75202
(214) 767-3959, or
(214) 767-3639 (deaf access)

Region VII: Iowa, Kansas, Kentucky, Missouri, Nebraska
Mr. Charles Nowell
Acting Regional Civil Rights Director
Office for Civil Rights, Region VII
U.S. Department of Education
10220 North Executive Hills Boulevard
8th Floor, 076010
Kansas City, MO 64153
(816) 891-8026, or
(816) 374-6461 (deaf access)

Region VIII: Arizona, Colorado, Montana, New Mexico, North Dakota, South Dakota, Utah, Wyoming
Ms. Lilian R. Gutierrez
Regional Civil Rights Director
Office for Civil Rights, Region VIII
U.S. Department of Education
Federal Office Building
1961 Stout Street, Room 342, 08-7010
Denver, CO 80294
(303) 844-5695, or
(303) 844-3417 (deaf access)

Region IX: California
Mr. John E. Palomino
Regional Civil Rights Director
Office for Civil Rights, Region IX
U.S. Department of Education
Old Federal Building, 09-8010
50 United Nations Plaza, Room 239
San Francisco, CA 94102
(415) 556-7000

Region X: Alaska, American Samoa, Guam, Hawaii, Idaho, Nevada, Oregon, Washington
Mr. Gary D. Jackson
Regional Civil Rights Director
Office for Civil Rights, Region X
U.S. Department of Education
915 Second Avenue
Room 3310, 10-9010
Seattle, WA 98174
(206) 442-6811, or
(206) 442-4542 (deaf access)

TITLE IX—RESOURCES

General Resources

American Council on Education
1 Dupont Circle
Washington, DC 10036
(202) 939-9300

National Coalition for Women and Girls in Education
c/o AAUW, Program and Policy Department
1111 Sixteenth Street, N.W.
Washington, DC 20036
(202) 785-7712

Women's Sports Foundation
342 Madison Avenue
New York, NY 10173
(800) 227-3988

Reading

Playing Fair: A Guide to Title IX in High School and College Sports (available from the Women's Sports Foundation, 342 Madison Avenue, New York, NY 10173).

TITLE IX—LEGAL RESOURCES

American Civil Liberties Union
122 Maryland Avenue, N.E.
Washington, DC 20002
(202) 544-1681

Equal Rights Advocates
Legal Advice and Counseling Hotline
(415) 621-0505

National Women's Law Center
1616 P Street, N.W.
Washington, DC 20036
(202) 328-5160

Northwest Women's Law Center
119 S. Main Street, Suite 330
Seattle, WA 98104
(206) 621-7691

NOW Legal Defense and Education Fund
99 Hudson Street
New York, NY 10013
(212) 925-6635

Women's Sports Foundation
Eisenhower Park
East Meadow, NY 11554
(800) 227-3988 (for a list of attorneys interested in Title IX cases)

WORK

RUTH BADER GINSBURG–A WOMAN AT THE TOP

After being nominated by President Bill Clinton in 1993, Ruth Bader Ginsburg became the second female justice of the Supreme Court. On June 15 of that year, she delivered this speech on the White House lawn.

Mr. President, I am grateful beyond measure for the confidence you have placed in me, and I will strive with all that I have to live up to your expectations in making this appointment.

The announcement the president just made is significant, I believe, because it contributes to the end of the days when women, at least half the talent pool of our society, appear in high places only as one-at-a-time performers. Recall that when President Carter took office in 1976, no woman had ever served on the Supreme Court, and only one woman, Shirley Hofstedler of California, then served at the next federal court level, the United States Court of Appeals.

Today Justice Sandra Day O'Connor graces the Supreme Court bench, and close to 25 women serve at the federal Court of Appeals level, two as chief judges. I am confident that more will soon join them. That seems to me inevitable, given the change in law school enrollment.

My law school class in the late 1950s numbered over 500. That class included less than ten women. As the president said, not a law firm in the entire city of New York bid for my employment as a lawyer when I earned my degree. Today few law schools have female enrollment under 40%, and several have reached or passed the 50% mark. And thanks to Title VII, no entry doors are barred.

My daughter, Jane, reminded me a few hours ago in a good-luck call from Australia of a sign of change we have had the good fortune to experience. In her high school yearbook on her graduation in 1973, the listing for Jane Ginsburg under "ambition" was "to see her mother appointed to the Supreme Court." The next line read, "If necessary, Jane will appoint her." Jane is so pleased, Mr. President, that you did it instead, and her brother, James, is, too.

I expect to be asked in some detail about my views of the work of a good judge on a high court bench. This afternoon is not the moment for extended remarks on that subject, but I might state a few prime guides.

Chief Justice Rehnquist offered one I keep in the front of my mind: a judge is bound to decide each case fairly in a court with the relevant facts and the applicable law, even when the decision is not, as he put it, what the home crowd wants.

Next, I know no better summary than the one Justice O'Connor recently provided, drawn from a paper by New York University Law School Professor Bert Nueborne. The remarks concern the enduring influence of Justice Oliver Wendell Holmes. They read: "When a modern constitutional judge is confronted with a hard case, Holmes is at her side with three gentle reminders: first, intellectual honesty about the available policy choices; second, disciplined self-restraint in respecting the majority's policy choices; and third, principled commitment to defense of individual autonomy even in the face of majority action." To that I can only say "Amen."

I am indebted to so many for this extraordinary chance and challenge: to a revived women's movement in the 1970s that opened doors for people like me, to the civil rights movement of the 1960s, from which the women's movement drew inspiration, to my teaching colleagues at Rutgers and Columbia, and for 13 years my D.C. circuit colleagues, who shaped and heightened my appreciation of the value of collegiality.

Most closely, I have been aided by my life partner, Martin D. Ginsburg, who has been, since our teenage years, my best friend and biggest booster, by my mother-in-law, Evelyn Ginsburg, the most supportive parent a person could have, and by a daughter and son with the tastes to appreciate that Daddy cooks ever so much better than Mommy and so phased me out of the kitchen at a relatively early age.

Finally, I know Hillary Rodham Clinton has encouraged and supported the president's decision to utilize the skills and talents of all the people of the United States.

And I have a last thank-you. It is to my mother, Celia Amster Bader, the bravest and strongest person I have known, who was taken from me much too soon. I pray that I may be all that she would have been had she lived in an age when women could aspire and achieve and daughters are cherished as much as sons. I look forward to stimulating weeks this summer and, if I am confirmed, to working at a neighboring court to the best of my ability and for the advancement of the law in the service of society. Thank you.

EMPLOYMENT OF WOMEN

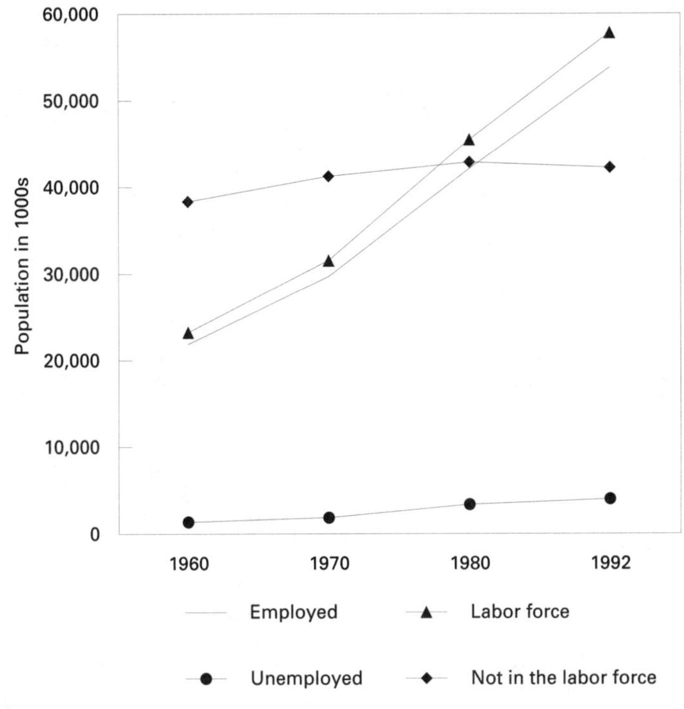

Source: Department of Labor

Women who love their work have the best marriages, according to a 1992 *Working Mother* survey; 60% of these women say that they make financial decisions with their husbands.

LABOR FORCE VS. HOUSEKEEPING

These charts show the labor-force status of women 25–54 years old in 1962 and 1990.

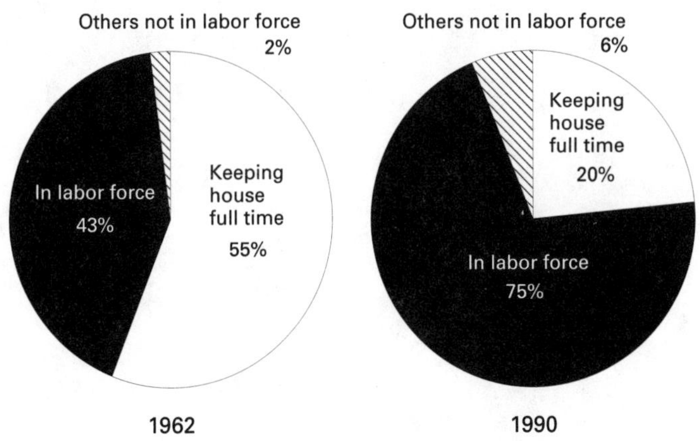

Source: Department of Labor, Women's Bureau

LABOR FORCE PARTICIPATION BY SEX AND AGE

More women than men work part-time because they cannot find full-time work. The rate of involuntary part-time work is 5.6% among women and 3.9% among men.

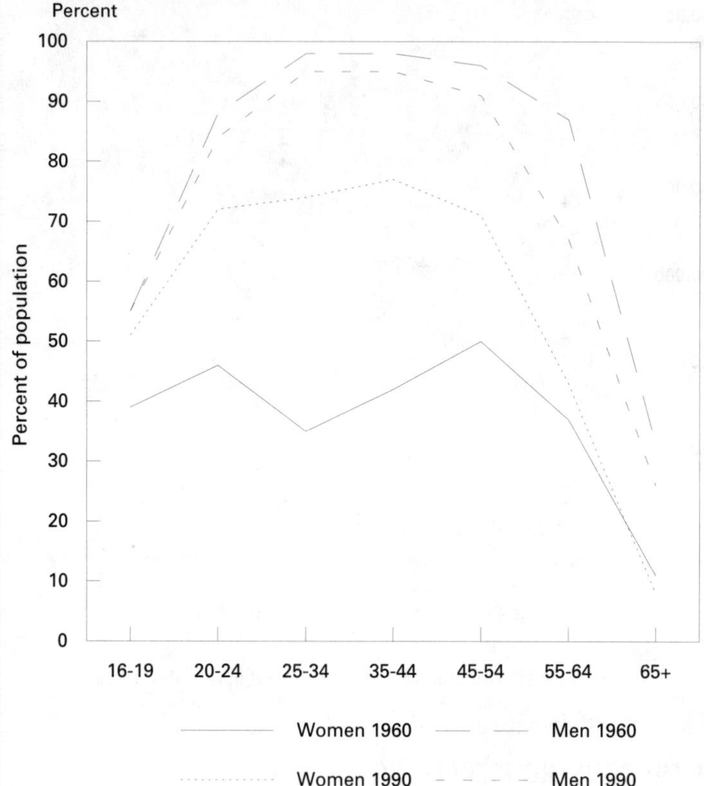

Source: Department of Labor, Women's Bureau

CURRENT EMPLOYMENT BY SEX AND RACE

In Labor Force

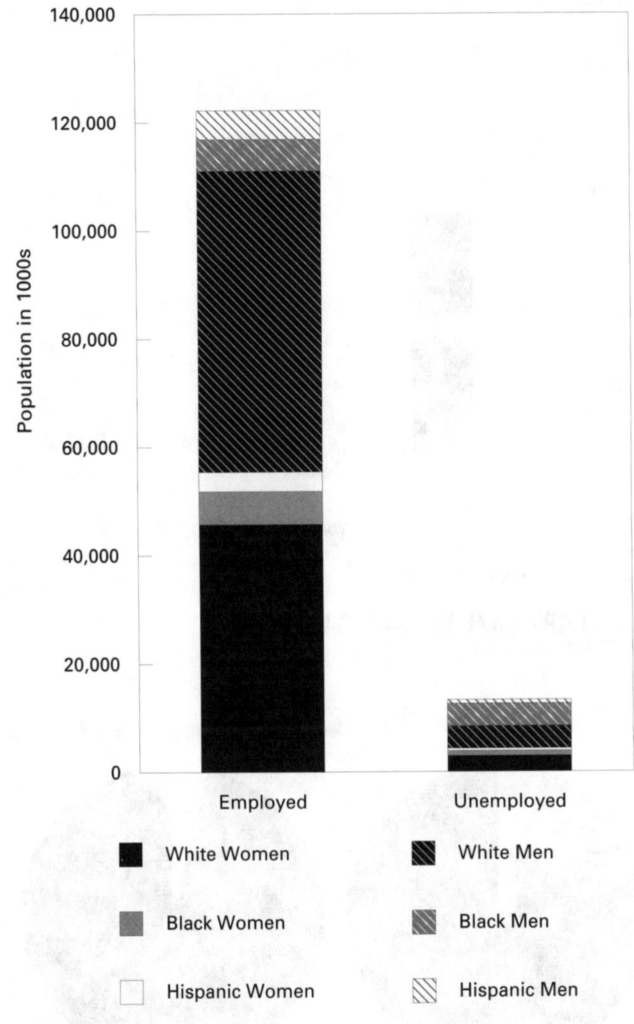

(Data from 1992)

Sally Ride was the first female American astronaut to blast off into space, on September 30, 1983.

The most likely cause of death on the job for women is murder (42% of work-related fatalities)—unlike men, who die on the job most often in highway vehicle accidents.

Not in Labor Force

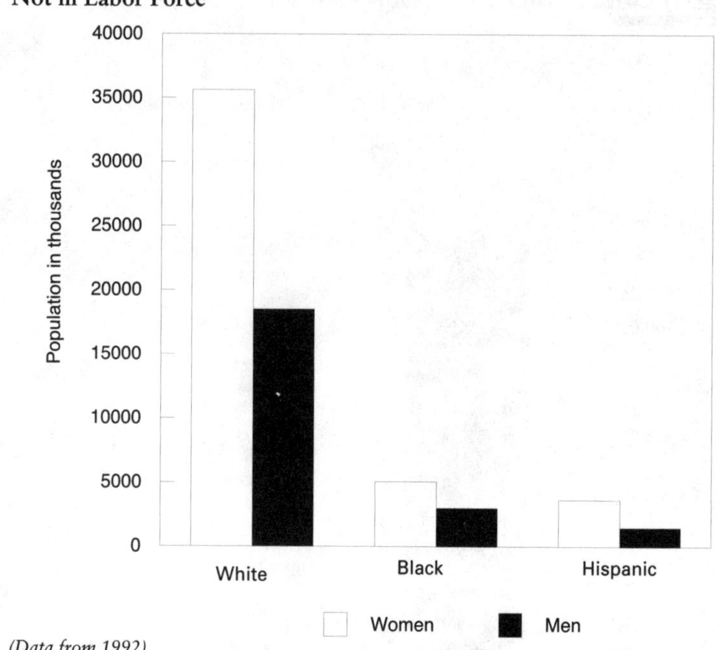

(Data from 1992)
Source for above: Department of Labor

FULL- AND PART-TIME WORKING WOMEN

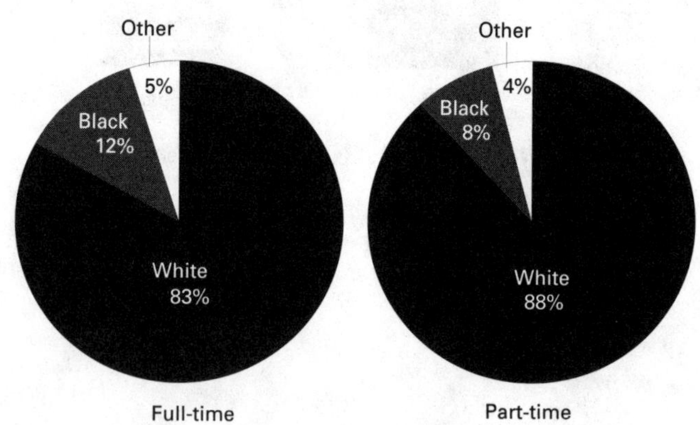

(Data from 1992)
Source: Department of Labor

MINORITY WOMEN IN THE LABOR FORCE

Employment Status of African-American Women

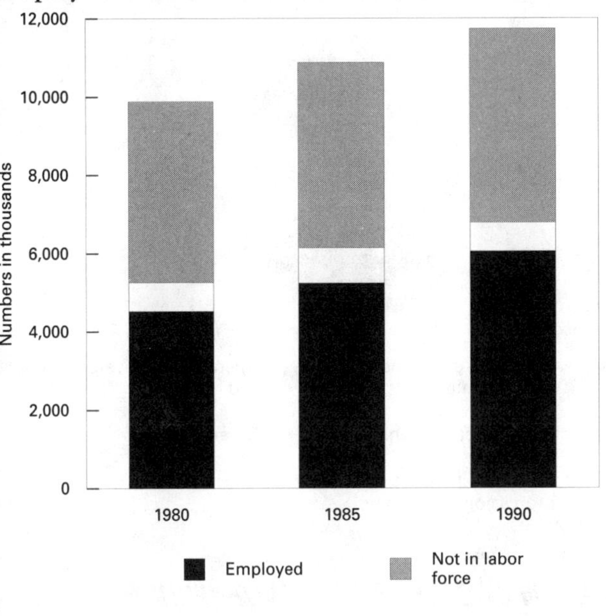

Source: Department of Labor, Women's Bureau

Employment Status of Hispanic Women

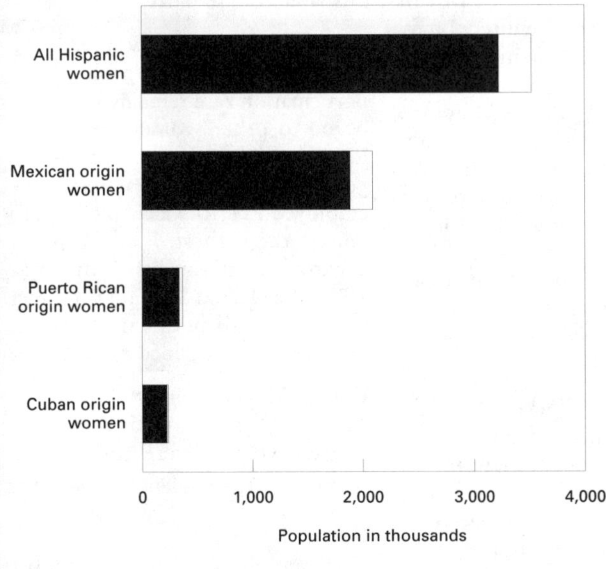

(Data from 1989)
Source: Department of Labor, Women's Bureau

While women earned 64 cents for every dollar earned by men in 1986, black women earned only 57 cents and Latinas 53 cents for every dollar earned by white men.

Mary Schmidt Campbell was named executive director of the Studio Museum in Harlem in 1977. It became the first African-American museum to be accredited.

Occupations of Employed Hispanic Women

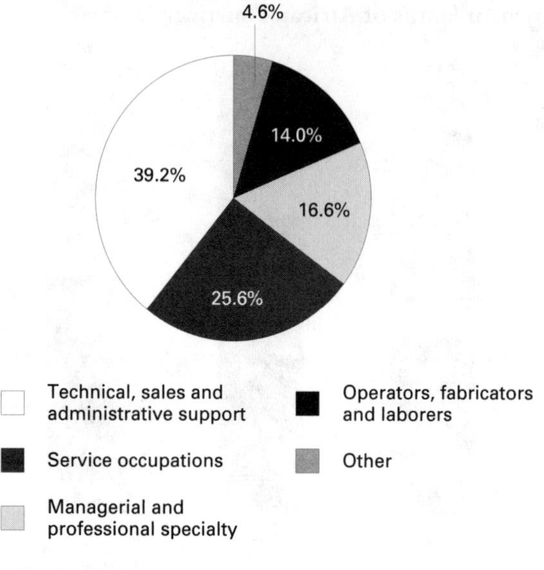

(Data from 1993)
Source: Department of Labor, Women's Bureau

WOMEN OF COLOR IN THE WORKFORCE

African-American Women Workers
Historically, African-American women in the United States have had higher participation rates in the labor force than white women or women of Hispanic origin. During the past decade, retail sales workers, nursing aides, secretaries, cashiers, cooks, elementary school teachers, janitors, and cleaners have been the most common jobs for black women—accounting for as much as 33% of the group's employment in 1990. African-American women make up only 1% (142,000) of the 4 million persons employed in the skilled trades.

Mexican Women Workers
Mexican women have lower incomes than almost any group in the U.S. Their median earnings in 1990 were $9,286, compared to $10,099 for all Hispanic women and $12,438 for non-Hispanic women. Almost half of all Mexican female-headed families were poor—45.7%. In addition, Mexican women experience higher unemployment rates than their non-Hispanic counterparts.

Puerto Rican Women Workers
The Puerto Rican female labor force participation rate remains low compared to other women and is the lowest of any Hispanic subgroup, yet the median earnings of employed Puerto Rican women are among the highest of all Hispanic subgroups, with median earnings in 1990 of $11,702. Still, almost three-quarters of all poor Puerto Rican families are maintained by women.

Cuban Women Workers
The 1990 median earnings of Cuban women were among the highest of any Hispanic subgroups at $13,124. Over 48% of employed Cuban women work in technical, sales, and administrative suppport positions.

Source: National Council of La Raza

UNEMPLOYMENT

Unemployment Rates of Women with Children

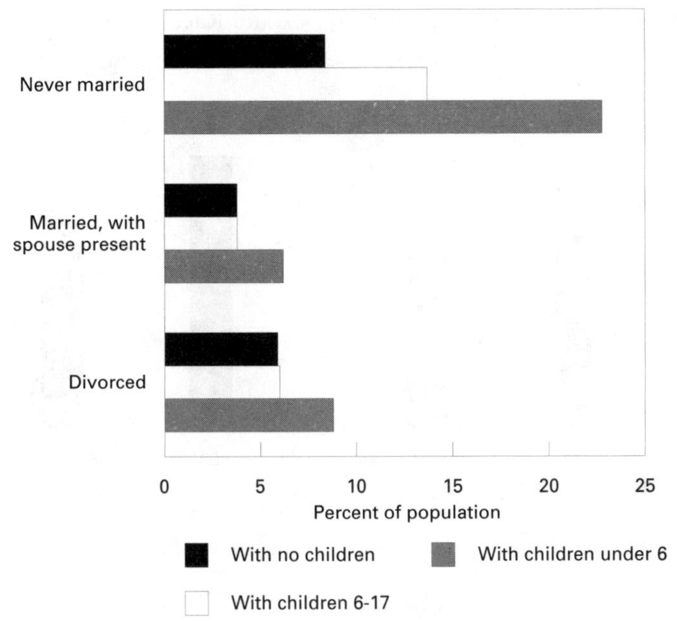

(Data from 1993)

Unemployment Rates, by Race

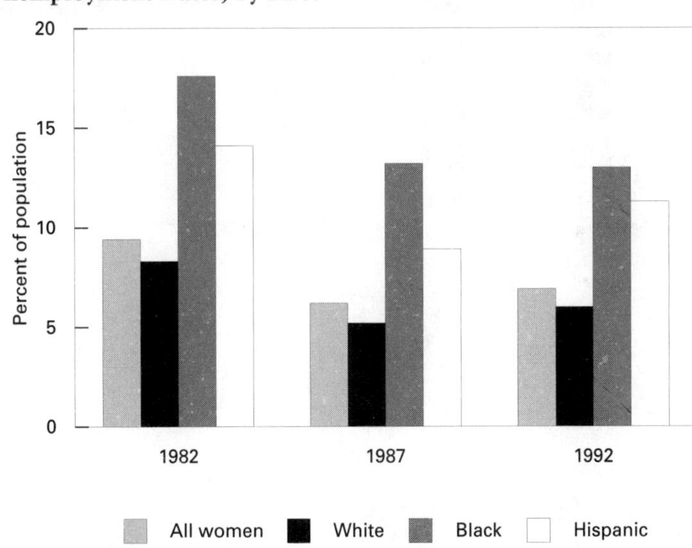

Source for above: Department of Labor, Bureau of Labor Statistics

The first all-woman baseball team, the Colorado Silver Bullets, was sanctioned by the National Association of Professional Baseball Leagues in 1994.

DISPLACED WORKERS

43% of men and 54% of women would prefer to work for a man, while 12% of men and 15% of women would prefer to work for a woman.

Displaced workers include those who have lost their jobs because of plant closings or employment cutbacks.

Percentage of Workers Displaced, by Sex and Race

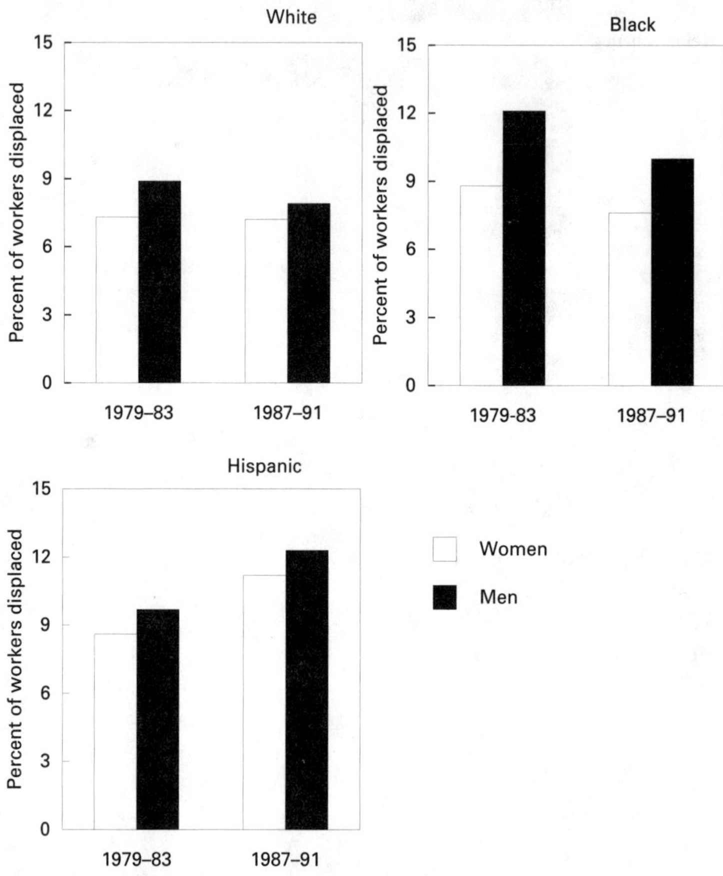

Source for above: Department of Labor, Bureau of Labor Statistics

Displaced Workers, by Reason for Job Loss

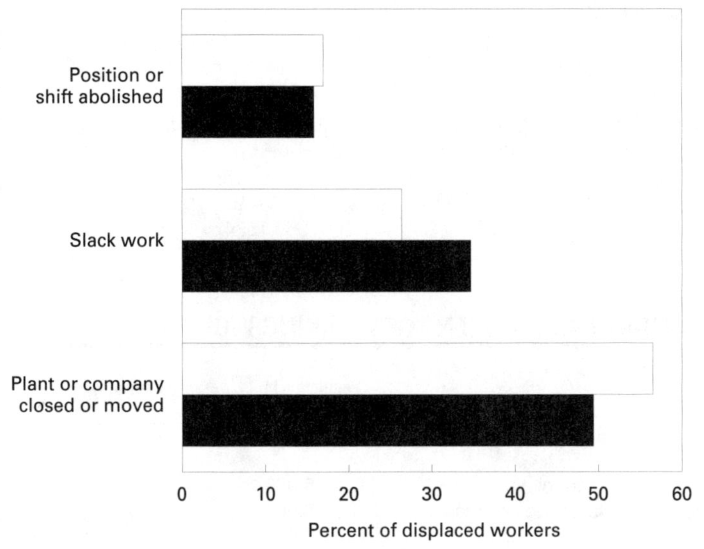

Source: Department of Labor, Bureau of Labor Statistics

At the nation's top 500 banks, more than 71% of employees were women in 1992, yet fewer than 1% of the CEOs were women.

THE WOMEN'S BUREAU

Created in 1920, the Women's Bureau of the U.S. Department of Labor serves as one of the best general resources for women in the working world. Through its regional offices, women can obtain information about job training, receive advice about discrimination, find referrals, and obtain educational and statistical data about women in the labor force.

Regional Offices of the Women's Bureau

Region I—Connecticut, Maine, Massachusetts, New Hampshire, Rhode Island, Vermont
One Congress Street
Boston, MA 02114
(617) 565-1988

Region II—New Jersey, New York, Puerto Rico, Virgin Islands
201 Varick Street, Room 601
New York, NY 10014
(212) 337-2389

Region III—Delaware, District of Columbia, Maryland, Pennsylvania, Virginia, West Virginia
3535 Market Street, Room 13280
Philadelphia, PA 19104
(215) 596-1183

Region IV—Alabama, Florida, Georgia, Kentucky, Mississippi, North Carolina, South Carolina, Tennessee
1371 Peachtree Street, N.E., Room 323
Atlanta, GA 30367
(404) 347-4461

Region V—Illinois, Indiana, Michigan, Minnesota, Ohio, Wisconsin
230 South Dearborn Street, 10th Floor
Chicago, IL 60604
(312) 353-6985

Region VI—Arkansas, Louisiana, New Mexico, Oklahoma, Texas
Federal Building
525 Griffin Street, Suite 731
Dallas, TX 75202
(214) 767-6985

Most women listed their jobs as their greatest worries in a recent poll.

Region VII—Iowa, Kansas, Missouri, Nebraska
911 Walnut Street, Room 2511
Kansas City, MO 64106
(816) 426-6108

Region VIII—Colorado, Montana, North Dakota, South Dakota, Utah, Wyoming
Federal Office Building
1961 Stout Street, Room 1452
Denver, CO 80294
(303) 844-4138

Region IX—Arizona, California, Hawaii, Nevada
71 Stevenson Street, Suite 927
San Francisco, CA 94105
(415) 744-6679

Region X—Alaska, Idaho, Oregon, Washington
1111 Third Avenue, Room 885
Seattle, WA 98101
(206) 553-1534

EDUCATIONAL ATTAINMENT OF WORKING WOMEN

	Population in labor force (in thousands)	Unemployment rate
All Women		
Less than a high school diploma	5,086	11.4
High school graduate, no college	18,080	6.2
Bachelor's degree	8,082	3.3
Master's degree	3,104	2.6
Doctoral degree	296	1.5
White Women		
Less than a high school diploma	3,886	10
High school graduate, no college	15,292	5
Bachelor's degree	6,958	3
Master's degree	2,724	2
Doctoral degree	254	1
Black Women		
Less than a high school diploma	952	15.5
High school graduate, no college	2,282	11.3
Bachelor's degree	672	3.3
Master's degree	251	2.1
Doctoral degree	22	*
Hispanic Women		
Less than a high school diploma	1,065	13.9
High school graduate, no college	1,018	8.2
Bachelor's degree	273	6.1
Master's degree	86	2.7
Doctoral degree	11	*

*Data is not shown when base is less than 35,000 (Numbers include those over age 25.)
(Data from 1992)
Source: Department of Labor, Bureau of Labor Statistics

WOMEN WHO MAINTAIN FAMILIES

A family maintained by a woman consists of two or more persons residing together who are related by birth, marriage, or adoption, where the householder (the person in whose name the home is owned or rented) is a woman without a spouse present.

After Bobby Riggs declared that even an over-the-hill man could beat any championship-class woman, Billie Jean King challenged him to a five-set tennis match and defeated him in straight sets in 1973.

Percentage of Families Maintained by Women in Poverty

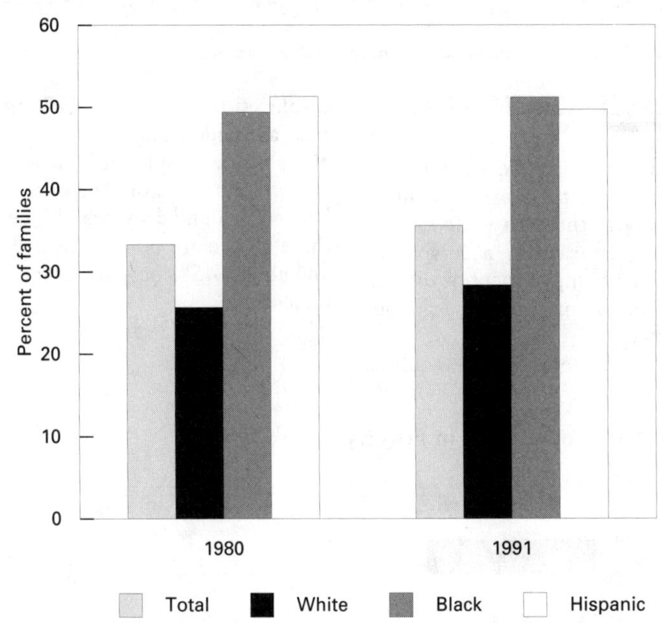

Unemployment Among Women Who Maintain Families

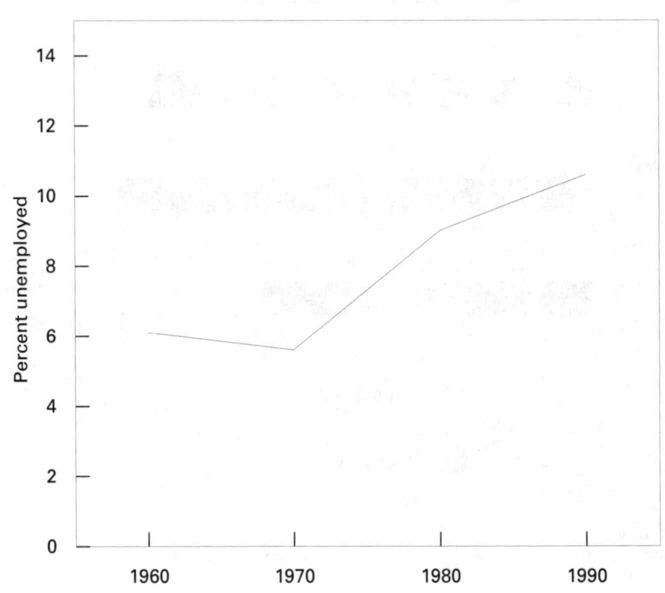

The median annual personal income for displaced homemakers is $6,766.

Family Incomes: Female Householders vs. Married-Couple Families

	1980	1985	1991
Female householder, no husband present	$10,408	$13,660	$16,692
Married-couple family	23,141	31,100	40,995
Wife in paid labor force	26,879	36,431	48,169
Wife not in paid labor force	18,972	24,556	30,075

Source for above: Department of Labor, Bureau of Labor Statistics

DISPLACED HOMEMAKERS

•Displaced homemakers are women who have lost their primary financial support through widowhood, divorce, separation, a husband's long-term unemployment or disability, or the discontinuation of public assistance.

•As of 1992, there were 15.6 million displaced homemakers, 12% more than a decade ago.

•One in four displaced homemakers is a woman of color, one in three is between 35 and 65 years old, nearly three in five are poor or near poor, and almost 45% have not completed high school.

Displaced Homemakers in Poverty

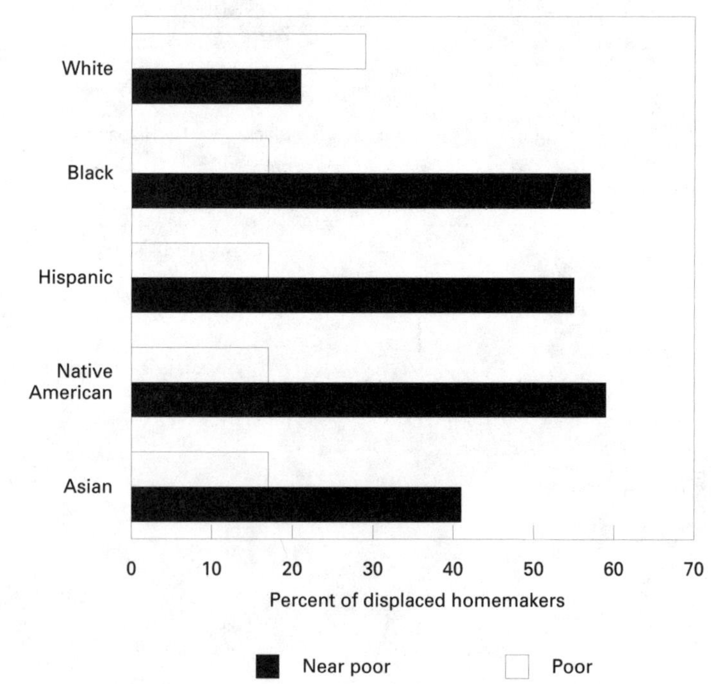

(Data from 1990)
Source: Women Work! The National Network for Women's Employment

Fast Fact: Women Work!

An organization devoted to advancing the cause of displaced homemakers, Women Work! provides women with job training, counseling, networking, and other forms of support. For more information, contact:

Women Work! The National Network for Women's Employment
1625 K Street, N.W., Suite 300
Washington, DC 20006
(202) 467-5366 or (800) 235-2732

The Coalition of Labor Union Women was formed on March 23, 1974.

WORKING WOMEN, BY INDUSTRY

These are averages for 1993, based on occupational totals for women 16 years and over.

	Total	*White*	*Black*	*Hispanic*
Accountants and auditors	683	569	59	29
Actors and directors	37	31	5	1
Airplane pilots and navigators	4	4	0	0
Architects	23	20	2	1
Athletes	19	18	1	0
Automobile mechanics	5	4	1	1
Bakers	55	49	5	2
Bank tellers	395	356	26	25
Bartenders	171	164	4	3
Bookkeepers, accounting and auditing clerks	1,642	1,516	69	69
Butchers and meat cutters	57	35	20	7
Carpenters	12	11	1	0
Cashiers	2,025	1,664	273	160
Child care workers	336	294	30	52
Clerks, traffic, shipping, and receiving	176	149	23	16
Computer operators	369	299	58	22
Computer programmers	182	152	17	7
Construction occupations, supervisors	14	13	2	0
Cooks	881	649	188	76
Dental hygienists	76	74	0	2
Dentists	16	13	1	1
Dressmakers	91	76	7	7
Drivers, bus	232	188	41	9
Drivers, taxicab and chauffeurs	21	16	4	1
Drivers, truck	126	114	8	4
Economists	56	51	3	3
Editors and reporters	129	118	8	4
Electricians	7	5	2	0
Engineers	148	124	11	7
Farmers	149	147	1	2
Firefighting occupations	6	6	0	2
Fishers, hunters, and trappers	3	3	0	0
Groundskeepers and gardeners, except farmers	48	41	5	3

Occupations with high concentrations of women of color are the lowest paid of all women's jobs, including household domestic work, agricultural labor, and garment production.

Hand packers and packagers	188	155	24	25
Hairdressers and cosmetologists	683	593	63	39
Household cleaners and servants, private	503	372	111	130
Insurance adjusters, examiners, and investigators	266	226	36	13
Insurance sales	194	179	13	10
Judges	7	6	1	0
Kitchen workers, food preparation	196	160	30	17
Lawyers	178	162	13	6
Librarians	172	156	10	5
Locksmiths and safe repairers	0	0	0	0
Machine operators, printing	104	97	5	10
Machine operators, textile, apparel, and furnishings	862	597	188	145
Machine operators, woodworking	17	14	3	0
Machinists	18	13	4	2
Mail carriers, postal service	95	85	9	1
Managers, marketing, advertising, and public relations	155	147	5	3
Musicians and composers	57	53	3	2
Nursing aides, orderlies, and attendants	1,510	999	467	109
Nurses, registered	1,754	1,516	147	50
Painters	28	27	1	1
Pharmacists	71	61	4	4
Photographers	35	33	2	1
Physicians	132	105	8	7
Police and detectives, public service	61	45	16	1
Psychologists	154	137	12	5
Real estate sales	365	346	9	11
Receptionists	874	778	72	66
Sales counter clerks	125	103	12	10
Sales workers, apparel	377	322	38	33
Secretaries	3,545	3,187	273	203
Social workers	403	307	85	20
Supervisors, general office	320	265	45	14
Teachers, college and university	328	288	22	14
Teachers, elementary	1,433	1,276	130	53
Teachers, secondary	711	642	54	23
Technicians, electrical and electronic	46	34	7	2
Telephone installers and repairers	24	21	2	1
Telephone operators	171	131	36	12
Typists	466	355	87	33
Veterinarians	19	19	0	0
Waitresses	1,131	1,032	46	64
Water and sewage treatment plant operators	4	3	1	0

(Numbers in thousands)

Source: Department of Labor, Bureau of Labor Statistics

LEADING WOMEN ON THE LECTURE CIRCUIT

1. Gail Sheehy, author of The Silent Passage; estimated fee: $15,000.
2. Anita Hill, law professor; estimated fee: $11,000.
3. Gloria Steinem, editor and feminist leader; estimated fee: $10,000.
4. Rosabeth Moss Kanter, former editor of the Harvard Business Review; estimated fee: $30,000.
5. Jane Bryant Quinn, financial columnist; estimated fee: $12,000.
6. Susan Faludi, author of Backlash; estimated fee: $7,500.
7. Linda Ellerbee, TV commentator; estimated fee: "upwards of $10,000."
8. Pat Schroeder, congresswoman from Colorado; fees and honorariums prohibited by law.
9. Faith Popcorn, futurist and trend prognosticator; estimated fee: $25,000.
10. Nancy K. Austin, co-author of A Passion for Excellence; estimated fee: $10,000.

Source: Working Woman, March 1993

TWENTY LEADING WOMEN'S OCCUPATIONS

Occupation	Number of women	Percentage	Median weekly earnings (both sexes)	Ratio of women's to men's
Total, 16 years and over	53,794	45.7	$445	75:4
Secretaries	3,663	99.0	373	*
Cashiers	1,997	79.3	219	94:8
Managers and administrators[1]	1,783	30.6	729	57:1
Registered nurses	1,702	94.3	662	104:7
Bookkeepers, accounting and auditing clerks	1,669	90.7	367	83:8
Nursing aides, orderlies, and attendants	1,407	89.4	266	96:0
Elementary schoolteachers	1,403	85.4	567	83:4
Sales workers, other commodities[2]	1,391	69.9	269	78:0
Sales supervisors and proprietors	1,353	34,8	479	67:2
Waiters and waitresses	1,089	79.5	222	83:9
Administrative support occupations[1]	1,006	76.3	428	74:0
Receptionists	868	97.3	309	*
Cooks	865	46.1	245	83.3
Machine operators, assorted materials	792	31.8	367	71:5
Accountants and auditors	699	51.2	600	73:4
Hairdressers and cosmetologists	688	90.8	263	*
Secondary schoolteachers	651	55.5	610	90:3
Janitors and cleaners	635	30.0	291	85:4
General office clerks	599	83.5	356	83:1
Textile sewing machine operators	591	87.4	217	91:9

* Median not available where base is smaller than 50,000 male workers.
1. Not elsewhere classified.
2. Includes food, drugs, health, and other commodities.
(Numbers in thousands for full-time workers)

Source: Department of Labor, Bureau of Labor Statistics

Alice Stebbins Wells became the first female police officer in the country on September 12, 1910.

Almost 14% of all working women had no health insurance in 1989; this included 26% of Latina, 19% of African-American, and 11.5% of white working women.

NONTRADITIONAL OCCUPATIONS FOR WOMEN

Nontraditional occupations are any in which women comprise 25% or less of the total employed.

Occupation	*Women employed*	*Percent women*
Operators, fabricators, and laborers	4,235	25.0
Optometrists	6	25.0
Precision production occupations	891	23.7
Sales representatives, commodities, except retail	343	21.8
Farm workers	187	21.6
Lawyers and judges	169	21.4
Barbers	18	20.9
Physicians	125	20.4
Handlers, equipment cleaners, helpers, and laborers	820	18.0
Engineering and related technologies, and technicians	161	17.5
Announcers	9	16.9
Supervisors, protective service	16	16.7
Police and detectives, public service	136	15.8
Farmers	174	15.7
Guards and police, except public service	113	15.4
Architects	21	15.3
Funeral directors	8	15.1
Farm managers	17	12.8
Motor vehicle operators	377	10.2
Engineers	149	8.5
Dentists	14	8.5
Clergy	27	8.4
Groundskeepers and gardeners, except farm	53	5.9
Forestry and logging occupations	6	5.4
Material moving equipment operators	45	4.5
Fishers, hunters, and trappers	2	3.9
Construction inspectors	3	3.8
Transportation occupations, except motor vehicles	6	3.6
Mechanics and repairers	148	3.3
Firefighting and fire prevention occupations	7	3.3
Airplane pilots and navigators	2	2.3
Construction trades	89	1.9

(Numbers in thousands; data from 1992)
Source: Department of Labor, Women's Bureau

WORKING WOMAN'S HOTTEST CAREERS FOR WOMEN

Information technology
Computer programmer
Database manager
LAN administrator
Systems analyst
Telecommunications manager
Education, training
Cross-cultural trainer
Employee trainer
Environmental consultant
50-plus marketer
School administrator
Health care
Family physician
Home-health-care nurse
Managed-care manager
Nurse practitioner
Physical therapist
Management
Diversity manager
Environmental manager
Ombudsman
Product manager
Small-business opportunities
Employee leasing
Financial planning
Private investigation
Professional-practice management
Professional-temp placement

Source: Working Woman, July 1993

WORKING WOMAN'S TEN WORST CAREERS FOR WOMEN

Cytotechnologist
Reasons: High-pressure, long and sometimes irregular hours, low pay.
Career military officer
Reasons: Advancement opportunities limited by restriction to noncombat duty, sexual harassment, discrimination, high susceptibility to job cuts.
Investment banker
Reasons: Long hours, decreasing salaries, little opportunity for advancement to highest management levels.
Farmer
Reasons: Dangerous work environment, exposure to insecticides and herbicides, fewer farms, more sophisticated educational requirements, low pay.
Flight attendant
Reasons: Lack of respect, tough work rules, low starting salaries and benefits, health risks from increased radiation at high altitudes.
Book editor
Reasons: Decreasing number of job opportunities, difficult work environment, lowpay.
Day-care worker
Reasons: Low pay, lack of benefits.
Retail buyer
Reasons: Fewer jobs, diminishing advancement opportunities, long hours, high pressure.
Large-firm attorney
Reasons: Sexual harassment, advancement opportunities limited by denial of litigation experience and other high-visibility assignments, old-boy network still in force.
Role model
Reasons: No pay, high stress, extreme scrutiny from others.

Source: Working Woman, July 1990

In a study of 400 frequent travelers, 68% of the men reported feeling lonely on business trips, compared to 46% of the women.

PAY EQUITY

The Earnings Gap

Even when men and women work in the same occupations, women earn between 60% and 80% of what men earn; though the gap appears to be closing in some areas, a portion of that improvement is the result of downward trends in men's earnings.

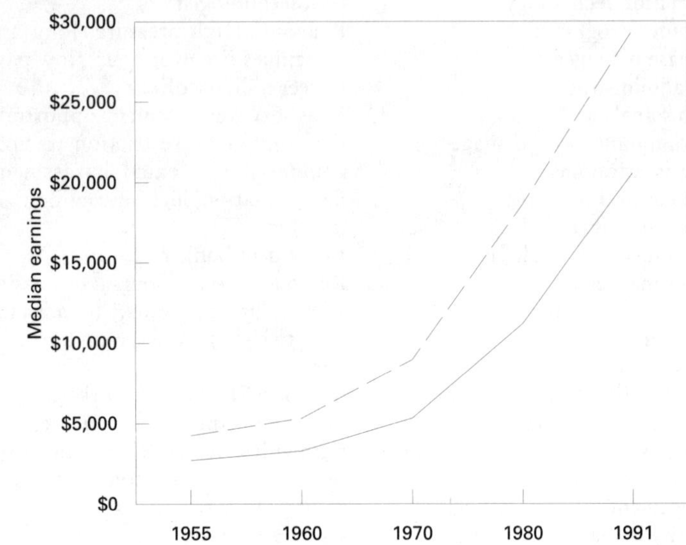

Source: Department of Labor, Women's Bureau

Women in their twenties have closed the pay gap; on average, they make as much or more than men their age.

Race and the Earnings Gap

Median earnings of year-round, full-time workers, 25 and over, 1992.

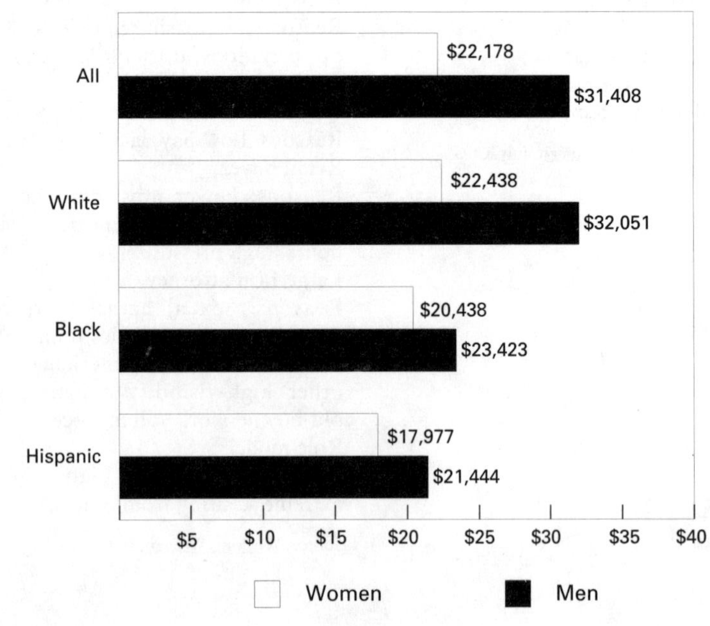

Source: Bureau of the Census

Age and the Earnings Gap
Percentage women earn vs. men, by age, 1960–1992.

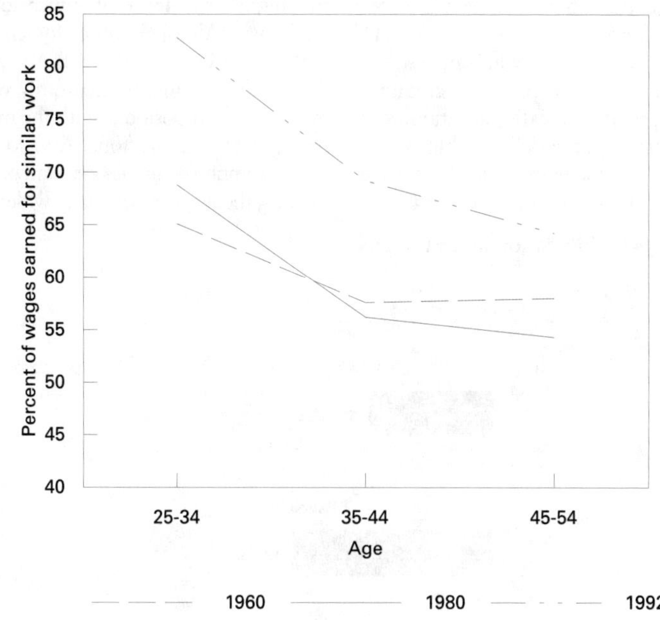

Source: Bureau of the Census

55% of the 3 million women employed by state and local governments work in the lowest-paying job categories, compared to 25% of the men.

EDUCATION AND THE EARNINGS GAP

90% of men and 92% of women feel that women are capable of being just as successful as men in the workplace.

Lower educational attainment is sometimes offered as a reason for the gap between women's pay and men's, but this can be only partially credited. While greater educational attainment helps broaden the fields within which women can find employment, the wage gap becomes even more pronounced the higher the level of educational attainment. Although more women are earning M.D.s, J.D.s, M.B.A.s and Ph.D.s, they're still not necessarily winning the prized positions with the most prestigious organizations. And so for women employed in the best-paid occupations, the wage gap actually widens.

Earnings by Education and Ethnicity

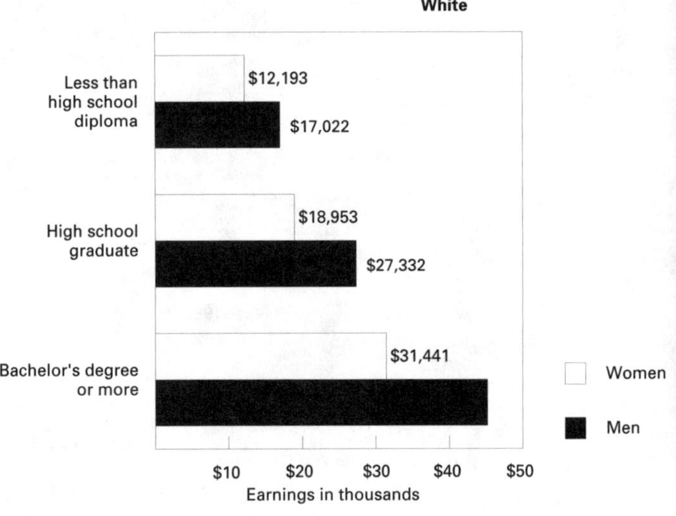

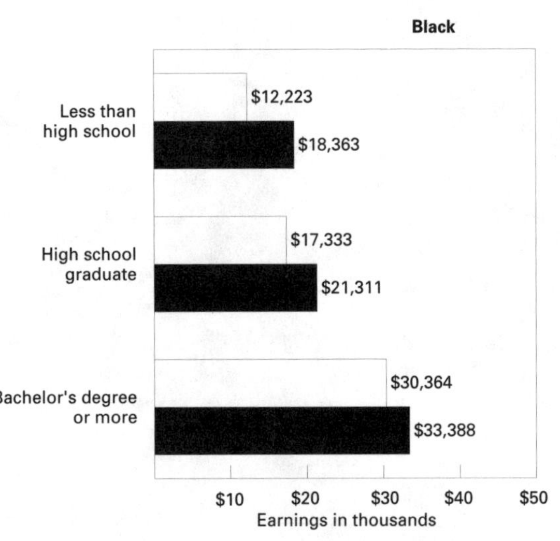

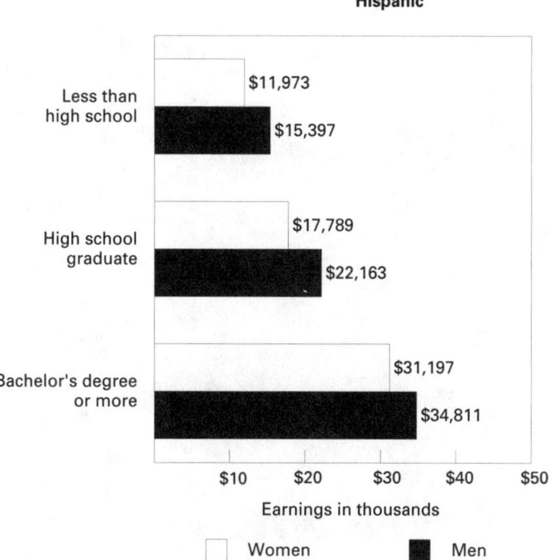

(Data from 1992)
Source for above: Bureau of the Census

EARNINGS GAP IN SELECTED PROFESSIONS

Annual median salaries as of 1993.

	Women	Men
Accountants	$26,936	$36,816
Computer programmers	31,616	37,596
Engineers	48,555	59,750
Financial managers	31,876	51,064
General surgeons	150,108	190,269
Insurance salespeople	23,504	35,308
Lawyers	47,684	61,100
Nurses	34,476	32,916
Obstetrician/gynecologists	180,800	202,956
Personnel, training, and labor specialists	29,120	39,572
Physical therapists (staff)	25,895	28,221
Pharmacists (independent)	44,000	45,600
Professors—public institutions	52,905	9,240
Psychiatrists	110,270	117,879
Public relations supervisor	41,707	59,627
Real estate salespeople	24,908	34,632
Teacher, elementary	28,548	34,216

Source: Working Woman, January 1994

The U.S. Air Force's first female pilot was First Lieutenant Jeannie Flynn.

REAL WAGES

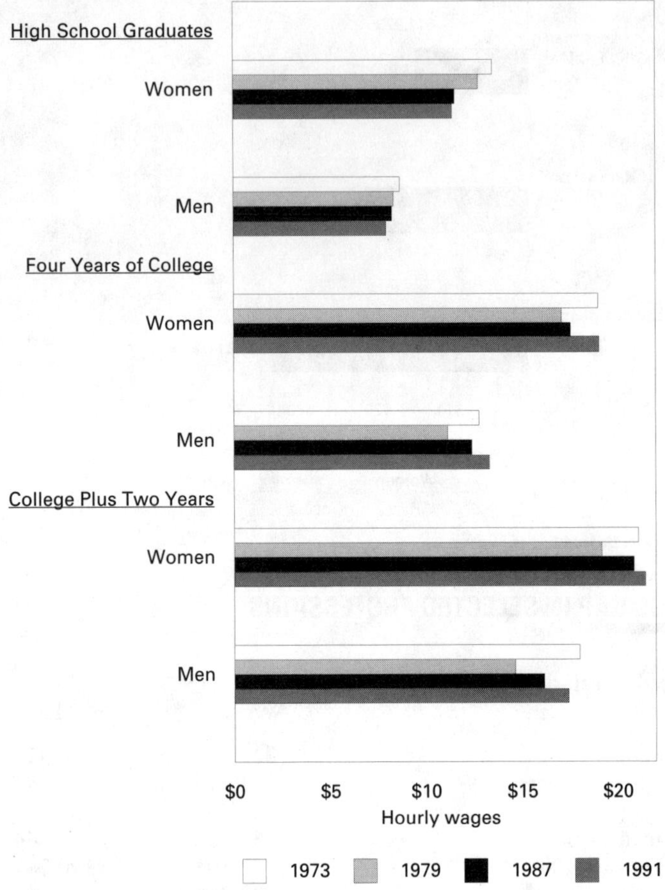

Source: Economic Policy Institute

PART-TIME EARNINGS

Median weekly earnings of part-time workers in 1993.

	Number of workers (in thousands)	Earnings
White women	11,527	$148
Black women	1,222	134
Hispanic women	878	129
White men	5,256	127
Black men	723	131
Hispanic men	596	139

Source: Bureau of the Census

9 to 5's GUIDELINES FOR GETTING THE RAISE YOU DESERVE

Be informed. Know your employer's raise policy and find out the going rate for work similar to yours in other companies.

Know your worth and be confident of it. Go in with a figure in mind and support it in a businesslike fashion with the reasons why you deserve more. Prepare a summary of your accomplishments and unique contributions, special projects, ways you've helped your company save money, newly acquired skills, and any written commendations of you or your work.

Ask! Remember that timing is all-important. Make sure to ask before your scheduled increase has been decided and don't choose a hectic day to make your request. If possible, ask after you've made a significant contribution.

Negotiate, barter, dicker, and insist! Be matter-of-fact and positive. Try for a commitment, but be prepared to set a date and follow up if needed. Have a compromise figure in mind. Ask for other improvements, such as more time off or tuition reimbursement.

Source: 9 to 5, National Association of Working Women

12.1% of officers and 11.7% of enlisted soldiers of the U.S. Army were women as of June 1992. Women also made up 11.8% of the officers and 10% of enlisted soldiers in the Navy and 3.3% of officers and 4.7% of enlisted soldiers in the Marines.

WHAT TO DO IF YOU'RE A VICTIM OF EMPLOYMENT DISCRIMINATION

Women who feel that they have been discriminated against in the workplace—on the grounds of unfair hiring practices, unequal pay, promotions, or benefits, sexual harassment, or pregnancy discrimination—should know that certain federal, state, and local laws have been created to protect them against employment discrimination. On the federal level, Title VII of the Civil Rights Act is the most commonly invoked, although in some cases state and local legislation may give women more rights, remedies, and favorable procedures. Women should check with their state and local departments of employment, human rights, or human relations for information on the scope and existence of these laws. (For further information about specific forms of sex discrimination in employment, see: Wage Discrimination, pp. 73–4; Sexual Harassment, pp. 75–80; and Pregnancy Discrimination, pp. 80–82.)

Title VII

Title VII of the Civil Rights Act covers many of the forms of sex discrimination you may encounter in decisions about hiring, firing, work assignments and conditions, promotions, benefits, training, retirement policy, and wages. Its broad language makes it applicable to many situations and groups, and as a result Title VII is one of the most commonly invoked laws in discrimination cases. Under its regulations, all intentional discrimination is prohibited, including sexual harassment and failure to pay according to the comparable worth of specific jobs, as well as more traditional forms of wage and employment discrimination.

If you think you have an employment discrimination case under Title VII, you can file a complaint with the Equal Employment Opportunity Commission (EEOC) or with the state or local human rights agency that enforces state and/or city equal employment laws. There is no fee for filing, and the agencies do not charge for investigating or attempt-

48% of Americans said that women did not have equal job opportunities with men in 1975. In 1993, this number rose to 60%.

ing to resolve your complaint.

When talking to federal and local agencies about discrimination or civil rights violations, find out the requirements for filing a claim. For further information, contact your regional office of the EEOC.

Source: NOW Legal Defense and Education Fund

EQUAL EMPLOYMENT OPPORTUNITY COMMISSION

General Information
(800) 669-4000 or (800) 800-3302 (deaf access)

District Offices:
Albuquerque, NM: (505) 766-2061
Atlanta, GA: (404) 331-6093
Baltimore, MD: (301) 962-3932
Birmingham, AL (205) 731-0082
Boston, MA: (617) 565-3200
Buffalo, NY: (716) 846-4441
Charlotte, NC: (704) 567-7100
Chicago, IL: (312) 353-2713
Cincinnati, OH: (513) 684-2851
Cleveland, OH: (216) 522-2001
Dallas, TX: (214) 767-7015
Denver, CO: (303) 866-1300
Detroit, MI: (313) 226-7636
El Paso, TX: (915) 534-6550
Fresno, CA: (209) 487-5793
Greensboro, NC: (919) 333-5174
Greenville, SC: (803) 241-4400
Honolulu, HI: (808) 541-3120
Houston, TX: (713) 653-3320
Indianapolis, IN: (317) 226-7212
Jackson, MS: (601) 965-4537
Kansas City, MO: (816) 426-5773
Little Rock, AR: (501) 324-5060
Los Angeles, CA: (213) 251-7278
Louisville, KY: (502) 582-6082
Memphis, TN: (901) 722-2617
Miami, FL: (305) 536-4491
Milwaukee, WI: (414) 297-1111
Minneapolis, MN: (612) 370-3330
Nashville, TN: (615) 736-5820
Newark, NJ: (201) 645-6383
New Orleans, LA: (504) 589-2329
New York, NY: (212) 264-7161
Norfolk, VA: (804) 441-3470
Oakland, CA: (510) 273-7588
Oklahoma City, OK: (405) 231-4911
Philadelphia, PA: (215) 656-7020
Phoenix, AZ: (602) 640-5000
Pittsburgh, PA: (412) 644-3444
Raleigh, NC: (919) 856-4064
Richmond, VA: (804) 771-2692
San Antonio, TX: (512) 229-4810
San Diego, CA: (619) 557-7235
San Francisco, CA: (415) 744-6500
San Jose, CA: (408) 291-7352
Savannah, GA: (912) 944-4234
Seattle, WA: (206) 553-0968
St. Louis, MO: (314) 425-6585
Tampa, FL: (813) 228-2310
Washington, DC: (202) 275-7377

DISCRIMINATION—GENERAL RESOURCES

For help in deciding whether or not you have a wage discrimination case or for guidance about to how to pursue a case, the following organizations can be of assistance:

ACLU Women's Rights Project
American Civil Liberties Union
132 W. 43rd Street
New York, NY 10036
(212) 944-9800

Business and Professional Women's Foundation
2012 Massachusetts Avenue, N.W.
Washington, DC 20036
(202) 293-1200

Center for Women Policy Studies
2000 P Street, N.W., Suite 508
Washington, DC 20036
(202) 872-1770

Equal Rights Advocates
1663 Mission Street, Suite 550
San Francisco, CA 94103
(415) 621-0672

National Committee on Pay Equity
1201 Sixteenth Street, N.W., Suite 420
Washington, DC, 20036
(202) 331-7343

National Employment Lawyers' Association
535 Pacific Avenue
San Francisco, CA 94133
(415) 227-4655

National Organization for Women
1000 16th Street, N.W., Suite 700
Washington, DC 20036
(202) 331-0066

NOW Legal Defense and Education Fund
99 Hudson Street, 12th Floor
New York, NY 10013
(212) 925-6635

9 to 5, National Association of Working Women
614 Superior Avenue, N.W.
Cleveland, OH 44113
(216) 566-9308 or (800) 245-9865

Women's Bureau
Department of Labor
Washington, DC 20210
(202) 219-6652

Women's Legal Defense Fund
1875 Connecticut Avenue, N.W., Suite 710
Washington, DC 20009
(202) 986-2600

LEGAL REMEDIES FOR WAGE DISCRIMINATION

Two federal laws prohibit wage discrimination: The Equal Pay Act (EPA) of 1963 and Title VII of the Civil Rights Act of 1964. The EPA is a narrowly tailored law addressing only the issue of sex-based wage discrimination and covering only situations of equal work, while Title VII is a broad civil rights statute designed to remedy a range of discriminatory practices.

The Equal Pay Act

To establish a violation of the Equal Pay Act (EPA), a plaintiff has the burden of proving two elements: that she performed "equal work" to male employees and that she was paid less than those male employees for the equal work. Once a plaintiff has established her case, the burden of proof shifts to the employer to explain wage disparities.

If you think you are not receiving equal pay for equal work, you may file a confidential complaint with the Equal Employment Opportunity Commission (EEOC), which enforces the EPA. If a violation is found, the EEOC will negotiate with the employer for a settlement, including back pay and appropriate raises in pay scales. They may also initiate court action to collect back wages.

Title VII

For further information on Title VII and employment discrimination in general, see Employment Discrimination, pp. 71–2. There you will also find contact information for the EEOC and its regional offices.

In 1970, about half of all adult women were earning a paycheck. Today, the figure exceeds two-thirds.

35 years ago, all the U.S. astronauts were men; today, almost one-fourth of the 103 astronauts are women.

WAGE DISCRIMINATION—RESOURCES

For help in deciding whether or not you have a wage discrimination case or for guidance about to how to pursue a case, the following organizations can be of assistance:

ACLU Women's Rights Project
American Civil Liberties Union
132 W. 43rd Street
New York, NY 10036
(212) 944-9800

Equal Rights Advocates
1663 Mission Street, Suite 550
San Francisco, CA 94103
(415) 621-0672

National Committee on Pay Equity
1201 Sixteenth Street, N.W., Suite 420
Washington, DC, 20036
(202) 331-7343

National Employment Lawyers' Association
535 Pacific Avenue
San Francisco, CA 94133
(415) 227-4655

9 to 5, National Association of Working Women
614 Superior Avenue, N.W.
Cleveland, OH 44113
(216) 566-9308 or (800) 245-9865

NOW Legal Defense and Education Fund
99 Hudson Street, 12th Floor
New York, NY 10013
(212) 925-6635

Women's Legal Defense Fund
1875 Connecticut Avenue, N.W.,
Suite 710
Washington, DC 20009
(202) 986-2600

WAGE DISCRIMINATION—RECOMMENDED READING

"Bargaining for Pay Equity: A Strategy Manual," (Washington, D.C.: National Committee on Pay Equity, 1990).

"Pay Equity Sourcebook," (Washington, D.C.: Equal Rights Advocates, National Committee on Pay Equity).

"25 Arguments Against Pay Equity and How to Answer Them," (Cleveland: 9 to 5, National Association of Working Women, 1987).

"A Working Woman's Guide to Her Job Rights," (Washington, D.C.: Department of Labor, Women's Bureau, 1992).

"The New 9 to 5 Office Worker Survival Guide" (Cleveland: 9 to 5, National Association of Working Women, 1990).

SEXUAL HARASSMENT

The Legal Definition

Sexual harassment in employment is defined as "unwelcome sexual advances, requests for sexual favors, and other verbal or physical conduct of a sexual nature." Courts have recognized two forms of sexual harassment claims: the "quid pro quo" claim and the "hostile environment" claim.

•A "quid pro quo" claim involves sexual harassment in which a supervisor demands sexual favors in exchange for job benefits.

•A hostile work environment claim involves unwelcome behavior of a sexual nature, which creates an intimidating, hostile, or offensive work environment or has the effect of unreasonably interfering with an individual's work performance. These claims may include unwelcome behavior of a sexual nature by anyone in the workplace, if the employer knows or reasonably should have known about the harassing conditions.

Sources: Business and Professional Women's Foundation; National Organization for Women

Statistics

•In a 1990 Department of Defense study of military employees, 64% of women said they'd been sexually harassed.

•Fifty-three percent of women in a 1991 poll by the National Association of Female Executives had either been sexually harassed or knew someone who had.

•Ninety percent of harassment cases involve men harassing women, 9% involve same-sex harassment, and 1% involve women harassing men.

•Only 1–7% of all women who report sexual harassment in surveys actually file formal complaints, largely because they fear retaliation or loss of privacy. The formal complaint rate in companies is 1.4 per thousand women employees.

•About 25% of sexually harassed women use leave time in order to avoid the situation. Of women who experience the harassment, about 5% quit, 10% leave their place of employment at least partially because of the harassment, and 50% try to ignore it.

•The annual cost of sexual harassment for each Fortune 500 company is estimated at $6.7 million; the federal government loses $267 million because of it.

Sources: Business and Professional Women's Foundation; 9 to 5, National Association of Working Women

FAST FACT: HARRIS V. FORKLIFT

The standard of what constitutes a hostile workplace has been clarified by the Supreme Court in Harris v. Forklift Systems, Inc., only the second sexual harassment case to be heard by the Supreme Court. In this case, the Court held that a sexual harassment victim does not have to show that she suffered "severe psychological injury" in order to state a claim, which is what some federal courts had been demanding.

The Supreme Court went on to establish a two-part test. The conduct complained of must be "severe or pervasive enough to create an objectively hostile or abusive work environment—an environment that a reasonable person would find hostile or abusive." And the victim must "subjectively perceive the environment to be abusive."

Source: National Organization for Women

Between 80-90% of Fortune 500 companies report having training programs to raise awareness of sexual harassment.

The U.S. Navy has dismissed 89 officers and sailors for sexual harassment since 1992.

ANITA HILL—SEXUAL HARASSMENT: THE NATURE OF THE BEAST

Oklahoma University law professor Anita Hill, and the idea of sexual harassment in general, first came into national focus during Senate Judiciary Committee hearings in which she charged Supreme Court nominee Clarence Thomas with sexual harassment. This article was based on remarks she delivered in 1992 as part of a panel on sexual harassment and policymaking.

The response to my Senate Judiciary Committee testimony has been at once heartwarming and heart-wrenching. In learning that I am not alone in experiencing harassment, I am also learning that there are far too many women who have experienced a range of inexcusable and illegal activities— from sexist jokes to sexual assault—on the job.

"The Nature of the Beast" describes the existence of sexual harassment, which is alive and well. A harmful, dangerous thing that can confront a woman at any time.

What we know about harassment, sizing up the beast:

Sexual harassment is pervasive . . .

1. It occurs today at an alarming rate. Statistics show that anywhere from 42% to 90% of women will experience some form of harassment during their employed lives.
2. It has been occurring for years.
3. Harassment crosses lines of race and class.

We know that harassment all too often goes unreported for a variety of reasons . . .

1. Unwillingness (for good reason) to deal with the expected consequences.
2. Self-blame.
3. Threats or blackmail by co-workers or employers.
4. What it boils down to in many cases is a sense of powerlessness that we experience in the workplace, and our acceptance of a certain level of inability to control our careers and professional destinies.

That harassment is treated like a woman's "dirty secret" is well known. We also know what happens when we "tell." We know that when harassment is reported the common reaction is disbelief or worse . . .

1. Women who "tell" lose their jobs.
2. Women who "tell" become emotionally wasted.
3. Women who "tell" are not always supported by other women.

What we are learning about harassment requires recognizing this beast when we encounter it, and more. It requires looking the beast in the eye.

We are learning painfully that simply having laws against harassment on the books is not enough. The law, as it was conceived, was to provide a shield of protection for us. Yet the shield is failing us: many fear reporting, others feel it would do no good. The result is that less than 5% of women victims file claims of harassment.

As we are learning, enforcing the law alone won't terminate the problem. What we are seeking is equality of treatment in the workplace. Equality requires an expansion of our attitudes toward workers. Sexual harassment denies our treatment as equals and replaces it with treatment of women as objects of ego or power gratification.

We are learning that women are angry. The reasons for the anger are various and perhaps all too obvious . . .

1. We are angry because this awful thing called harassment exists in terribly harsh, ugly, demeaning, and even debilitating ways.

2. We are angry because for a brief moment we believed that if the law allowed for women to be hired in the workplace, and if we worked hard for our educations and on the job, equality would be achieved. We believed we would be respected as equals. Now we are realizing this is not true. The reality is that this powerful beast is used to perpetuate a sense of inequality, to keep women in their place, notwithstanding our increasing presence in the workplace.

What we have yet to explore about harassment is vast. It is what will enable us to slay the beast.

How do we capture the rage and turn it into positive energy? Through the power of women working together, whether it be in the political arena, or in the context of a lawsuit, or in community service. This issue goes well beyond partisan politics. Making the workplace a safer, more productive place for ourselves and our daughters should be on the agenda for each of us. It is something we can do for ourselves. It is a tribute, as well, to our mothers—and indeed a contribution we can make to the entire population.

I wish that I could take each of you on the journey that I've been on during all these weeks since the hearing. I wish that every one of you could experience the heartache and triumphs of each of those who have shared with me their experiences. I leave you with but a brief glimpse of what I've seen. I hope it is enough to encourage you to begin—or continue and persist with—your own exploration.

Source: 65 S. Cal L Rev. 1445–1449 (1992), reprinted with permission of the Southern California Law Review.

Ruth Bader Ginsburg was the first woman faculty member at Columbia Law School, and became one of the first tenured women professors there.

WHAT TO DO IF YOU'RE SEXUALLY HARASSED

•An isolated incident of sexual harassment does not give you the right to file a claim, but at the same time you are not required to ignore such behavior. If an incident occurs, make it immediately clear to the harasser that you do not welcome the behavior and want it to stop.

•If the problems persists, inform your supervisor that you do not welcome the behavior; any future legal claims you may make can be hurt if you remain silent. Keep records of all conversations with your supervisor about the harassment.

•Informal actions by co-workers may also be sufficient to stop sexual harassment. Talk to people at your workplace and try to solve the problem. Co-workers may intimidate a harasser by organizing a series of lunchtime meetings to discuss sexual harassment or by gathering around your desk with notebooks to take down anything the harasser may say to you.

Source: National Organization for Women

WRITING TO YOUR HARASSER: NOW'S GUIDELINES

One of the most effective informal actions a harassed woman can take is to write a letter to her harasser. The National Organization for Women offers this sample letter:

Date

Dear Harasser:

I am writing this letter to inform you that I do not welcome and have been made to feel (uncomfortable) (intimidated) (angered) by your action(s). This (these) action(s) I am referring to is (include):

List specific incidents of harassing behavior, with dates and offending statements made by the harasser, if possible.

This behavior is offensive to me and constitutes sexual harassment. This (these) incident(s) has (have) created a (an) (unprofessional) (tense) (stressful) (detrimental) (harmful) working environment that interferes with my job performance, particularly in any matters that require contact with you. Therefore I am asking you to stop this illegal harassment now.

Optional Paragraph

If you continue with this behavior, or harass me further as a result of this letter, I will deliver a copy of this letter to (your supervisor, _________) (the Personnel Department) (my union representative) (the president of the company, _________). [NOTE: THIS CONTACT IS DEPENDENT ON THE EMPLOYER'S GRIEVANCE PROCEDURE, IF ANY EXISTS.] If necessary, I will file a formal complaint with the (Equal Employment Opportunity Commission) (state or local Fair Employment Practices agency), which investigates charges of employment discrimination.

Sincerely,

Harassee

(cc:________)
(encl. e.g. copies of notes)

Be sure to make copies of your letter. Also, be mindful of in-company grievance procedures that may give you an opportunity to rectify the situation before pursuing legal action.

Source: National Organization for Women

FILING A SEXUAL HARASSMENT COMPLAINT

If informal remedies do not stop the harassment, you may pursue a complaint. A victim of sexual harassment may file under Title VII with the Equal Employment Opportunity Commission (EEOC), unless she works for a firm with fewer than 15 employees, in which case she must file a claim with her state or local antidiscriminatory agency.

Under Title VII you cannot sue your co-workers for sexual harassment. However, you can sue your employer and high level supervisors for the harassing and discriminatory actions of your immediate supervisors or for knowingly allowing your co-workers to harass you and make the workplace a hostile environment.

Title VII remedies for sexual harassment include back pay, front pay under certain conditions, attorney's fees and costs, along with compensatory and punitive damages for intentional discrimination. The damages are capped at $50,000 for employers of 100 or fewer employees, $100,000 for 101–200 employees, $200,000 for 201–500 employees, and $300,000 for employers of more than 500 workers.

To file a complaint, contact the nearest EEOC office and/or the human rights agency that enforces your state and/or city equal employment laws. For a list of EEOC district offices, see the Employment Discrimination section, pp. 71–2.

Source: National Organization for Women

SEXUAL HARASSMENT—RESOURCES

ACLU Women's Rights Project
American Civil Liberties Union
132 W. 43rd Street
New York, NY 10036
(212) 944-9800

Equal Employment Opportunity Commission
(800) 669-4000 or (800) 800-3302 (deaf access)
For the phone numbers of EEOC district offices, see the Employment Discrimination section, pp. 71–2.

Equal Rights Advocates
1663 Mission Street, Suite 550
San Francisco, CA 94103
(415) 621-0672

National Organization for Women
1000 16th Street, N.W., Suite 700
Washington, DC 20036
(202) 331-0066

9 to 5, National Association of Working Women
614 Superior Avenue, N.W.
Cleveland, OH 44113
(216) 566-9308 or (800) 245-9865

NOW Legal Defense and Education Fund
99 Hudson Street, 12th Floor
New York, NY 10013
(212) 925-6635

Women's Legal Defense Fund
1875 Connecticut Avenue, N.W.,
Suite 710
Washington, DC 20009
(202) 986-2600

"If men can run the world, why can't they stop wearing neckties? How intelligent is it to start the day by tying a little noose around your neck?"—Linda Ellerbee

Ruth Nichols was the first woman to be a pilot for a commercial passenger airline (New York and New England Airways, 1932).

SEXUAL HARASSMENT—RECOMMENDED READING

Back Off!: How to Confront and Stop Sexual Harassment and Harassers, Martha Langelan (New York: Simon & Schuster, 1993).

"Crime of Power, Not Passion" (Washington, D.C.: Business and Professional Women's Foundation, 1992).

"Employment—Sex Discrimination and Sexual Harassment" (New York: NOW Legal Defense and Education Fund, 1992).

The 9 to 5 Guide to Combating Sexual Harassment, Ellen Bravo and Ellen Cassedy (New York: John Wiley & Sons, 1992).

"Sexual Harassment Policies Manual" (New York: NOW Legal Defense and Education Fund, 1992).

"Sexual Harassment: Research and Resources" (New York: National Council for Research on Women, 1991).

Sexual Harassment—Women Speak Out, Amber Coverdale Sumrall and Dena Taylor, eds. (Freedom, Calif.: Crossing Press, 1992).

Sexual Harassment—You Know Your Rights, Martin Eskenazi and David Gallen (New York: Carroll & Graf, 1992).

"Stopping Sexual Harassment" (Detroit: Labor Education and Research Project, 1992).

PREGNANCY DISCRIMINATION

Discrimination as a result of pregnancy was made illegal in 1978 when Congress amended Title VII of the Civil Rights Act with the Pregnancy Discrimination Act. The passage of the Family and Medical Leave Act in 1993, which guarantees pregnancy leave for working women, further undermined pregnancy discrimination. Still, between 1985 and 1990, studies showed that new mothers were ten times more likely to lose their jobs after taking disability leave than employees taking other kinds of medical leave. And so with 80% of women in the workforce of child-bearing age, and 93% of them likely to become pregnant at some point in their working lives, the issue remains an important one.

Recognizing Pregnancy Discrimination
The following are possible indicators of pregnancy discrimination:

- Forced leaves or firings due to pregnancy or health issues related to the pregnancy
- Lesser status upon returning to work, while other workers are allowed to take non-pregnancy-related disability leaves for periods longer than your pregnancy leave and return to their previous jobs
- Benefits do not cover pregnancy or pregnancy of a spouse
- Pay or promotions affected by your pregnancy
- Specific, necessary accommodations are not made for your pregnancy, although they are accorded to other workers.

What to Do
If you feel you have been discriminated against because of your pregnancy and you wish to challenge the discrimination, you should:

- Document your case
- Create a paper trail

•Consider using a grievance procedure
•Involve your union, if you have one
•File a formal discrimination complaint with the Equal Employment Opportunity Commission. (See the Employment Discrimination section pp. 71–2, for how to contact the EEOC.)

Source: Equal Rights Advocates

More than a third (37%) of all union members today are women. This includes 19.8% of African-American and 11.4% of Latina working women.

PREGNANCY DISCRIMINATION COMPLAINTS ON THE RISE

The number of complaints of pregnancy discrimination have risen since the passage of the Civil Rights Act of 1991 and the Family and Medical Leave Act of 1993. Both laws strengthened women's rights in this regard and heightened their awareness of these rights.

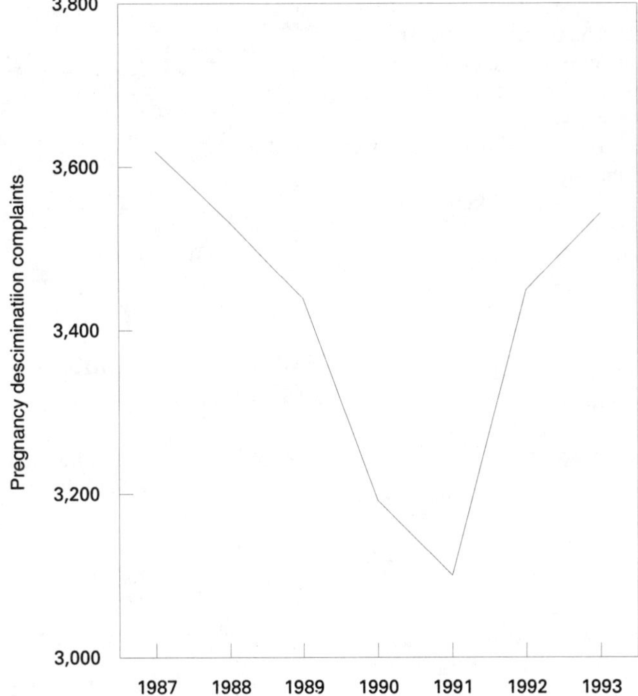

Source: Equal Employment Opportunity Commission

A statue of Eleanor Roosevelt, the first of a First Lady in the U.S., was unveiled in New York City in 1994.

PREGNANCY DISCRIMINATION—RECOMMENDED READING

Mothers on the Job: Maternity Policy in the U.S. Workplace, Lise Vogel (New Brunswick, N.J.: Rutgers University Press, 1993).

AGE DISCRIMINATION

One of the most common reasons for discriminating against older women is to avoid paying fringe benefits such as pensions. Although discrimination against older women may take many forms, employers most commonly discriminate against older women by:

- •Reinforcing unspoken youth requirements
- •Requiring unnecessary qualifications that operate to exclude older women from employment opportunities
- •Maintaining pay inequities between younger and older workers
- •Perpetuating negative stereotypes about older women

There are two federal laws which protect older women against discrimination: Title VII and the Age Discrimination in Employment Act of 1967. If you feel you have been discriminated against because of your age and sex, you may file a formal complaint with the Equal Employment Opportunity Commission. See the Employment Discrimination section, pp. 71–2.

Source: The Older Women's League

AGE DISCRIMINATION—RECOMMENDED READING

"Employment Discrimination Against Older Women," (Washington, D.C., The Older Women's League, 1992).

"Older Women and Job Discrimination: A Primer," (Washington, D.C.: The Older Women's League, 1984).

Fast Fact: The Older Women's League

The Older Women's League is an organization specifically designed to advance the needs of older women. It can be reached at:

666 11th Street, N.W., Suite 700
Washington, DC 20002
(202) 783-6686

WOMEN WITH WORK DISABILITIES

- •Of the 79.8 million working women in the U.S. in 1988, 6.7 million had a work disability.
- •Women with work disabilities are nearly three times as likely as nondisabled women to be unemployed, and tend to have poorer educational backgrounds.
- •Women who believe they have been discriminated against because of their disability can sue under the Americans with Disabilities Act. They should seek redress with the Equal Employment Opportunity Commission (EEOC); the remedies are reinstatement, back pay, and other forms of injunctive relief. For a list of EEOC district offices, see the Employment Discrimination section, pp. 71–2.

EARNINGS OF WOMEN WITH WORK DISABILITIES

This graph shows the mean annual earnings of disabled women in 1987, compared with all men.

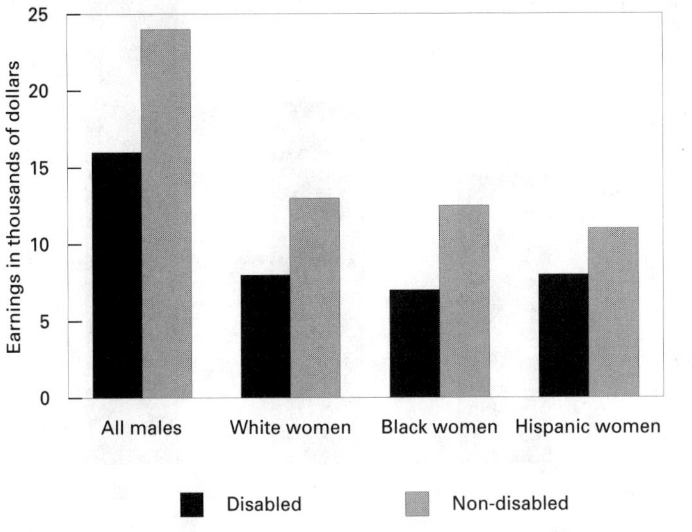

Source for above: Department of Labor, Women's Bureau

A group of Yves St. Laurent female staffers were thrown out of New York City's Plaza Hotel in the late Sixties for wearing pantsuits to lunch.

THE GLASS CEILING

"The Glass Ceiling" is a phrase that describes the artificial barriers, based on bias, that prevent qualified women from advancing within their organization and reaching their full potential. Despite the growing participation of women in the labor force, there has been only a slight increase in the representation of women and minorities in the top executive positions of the nation's companies, an increase that is even smaller among the largest 1,000 companies (women and minorities hold less than 5% of managerial positions in those companies).

Source: Glass Ceiling Commission

Fast Fact: Take Our Daughters to Work Day

Sponsored by the Ms. Foundation for Women, Take Our Daughters to Work Day is designed to give girls between 9 and 15 exposure to the working world. Parents, friends, neighbors, and relatives are encouraged to bring a girl they know to their workplace for the day to let her see where they work and to learn about the different jobs women have.

For organizers' kits, parents' guides, employers' guides, or girls' and boys' lesson plans, contact:

Ms. Foundation for Women
141 Fifth Avenue, Suite 65
New York, NY 10010
(800) 353-2525

Women in Management

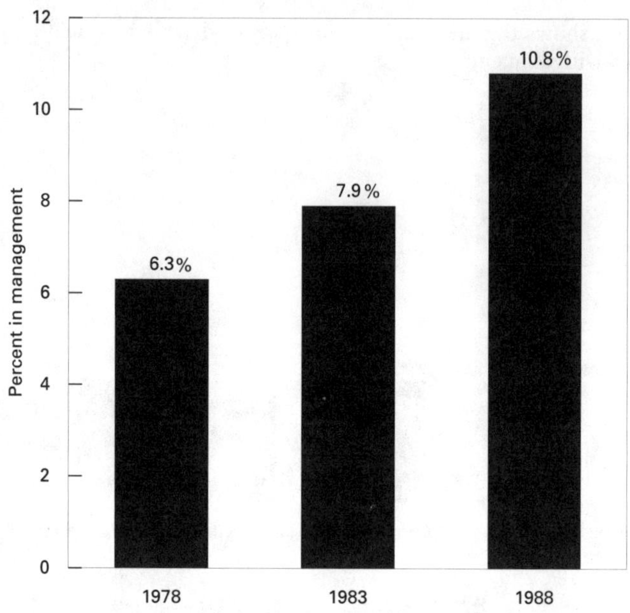

(Data from 1988)
Source: Department of Labor, Women's Bureau

Women in the Board Room

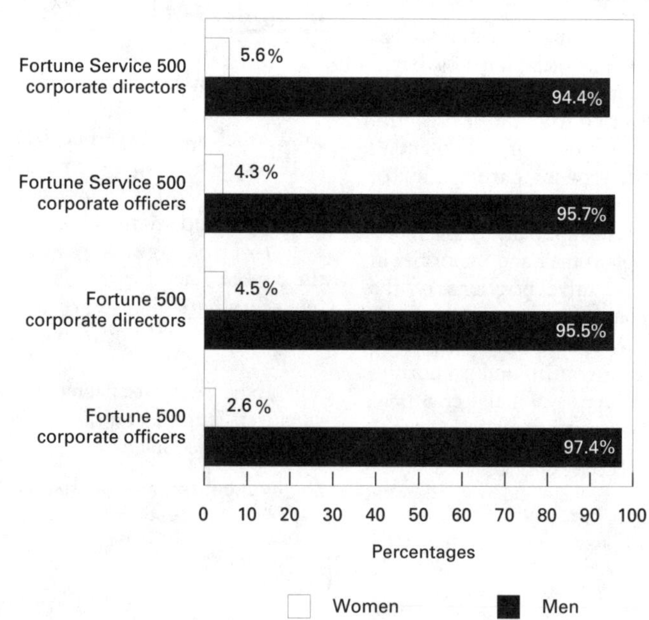

Source: Business and Professional Women's Foundation

GLASS CEILING BARRIERS

A number of barriers have been identified that contribute to the Glass Ceiling:

A lack of consistent recruitment practices to attract a diverse pool of talent
While entry-level corporate hiring is generally well-documented, systems of recruiting and tracking women generally do not exist above a certain level.

The Glass Wall
Women generally do not have the opportunity to move laterally in order to obtain the work experiences they need to advance vertically. Usually placed in staff positions such as personnel and human resources, women do not have the same exposure to sales, marketing, and other positions that contribute to the bottom line and that tend to serve as pools for management talent.

The old boys' network
Social contacts are a vital aspect of corporate development and women are very often barred from these informal, yet important, networking opportunities. Coffee chats, lunches, golf outings, clubs, and other traditional social settings remain in large part a male preserve within corporate America. Since management positions are generally filled through word-of-mouth in these social networks, denial of access represents a major obstacle for women.

Lack of effective role models and mentors
The corporate culture is not typically learned through formal orientation, but rather by casual discussion with more experienced members of the workforce.

Corporations not regarding equal employment opportunity as an organizational responsibility
While most CEOs in a Catalyst survey affirmed that their companies should change to meet the needs of women by addressing equal opportunity barriers, a large proportion of companies are not pursuing the strategies that they describe as critical to women's advancement, and rank development of high-potential women as a low priority.

Sources: Catalyst; Department of Labor

BREAKING THE GLASS CEILING

The Civil Rights Act of 1991 and the Equal Remedies Act represent essential steps toward breaking the Glass Ceiling. By providing compensatory and punitive damages for victims of sex discrimination, these acts create more effective economic incentives for companies to eliminate discriminatory practices. The establishment of the Glass Ceiling Initiative is also an important first step.

If you believe that you have been held back because of sex discrimination, you may also file a complaint with the Equal Employment Opportunity Commission (EEOC). (For regional offices of the EEOC, see the Employment Discrimination section, pp. 71–2.)

Source: Department of Labor

Genevieve Cline was the first woman to be appointed as a federal judge, in 1928.

Only 2% of women keep their maiden names after marriage. Those who do, keep them mainly because they have a professional reputation under that name.

Some companies with the best family-oriented benefits, such as day care, family leave, and flex-time, have some of the worst records for promoting women, according to the Wall Street Journal.

THE GLASS CEILING—RESOURCES AND READING

Resources

Business and Professional Women's Foundation
2012 Massachusetts Avenue, N.W.
Washington, DC 20036
(202) 293-1200

Catalyst
250 Park Avenue South
New York, NY 10003
(212) 777-8900

The Glass Ceiling Commission
Department of Labor
200 Constitution Avenue, N.W.,
Room S-2233
Washington, DC 20210
(202) 219-7342

Reading

Breaking the Glass Ceiling, Ann M. Morrison, Randall P. White, Ellen Van Velsor, and the Center for Creative Leadership (Reading, Mass.: Addison-Wesley, 1987).

"Pipelines of Progress: A Status Report on the Glass Ceiling" (Washington, D.C.: Department of Labor, 1992).

Fast Fact: The Glass Ceiling Commission

The Glass Ceiling Commission was created as part of the Civil Rights Act of 1991. The 21-member commission is chaired by the secretary of labor and is required to make a report on its findings and recommendations by November 1995. The report will focus attention on barriers to the advancement of minorities and women, and on promoting workforce diversity.

For more information on the Glass Ceiling Commission, contact:

Office of the Secretary
Glass Ceiling Commission
Department of Labor
200 Constitution Avenue, N.W.
Washington, DC 20210

WOMEN IN MANAGEMENT

The Growth of Women Professionals, 1980–1990

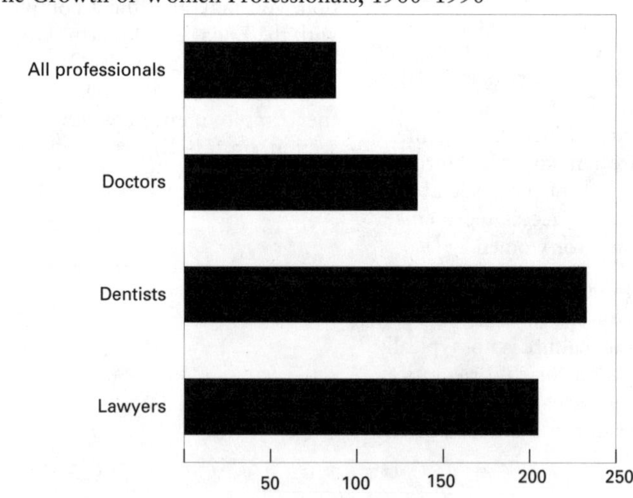

Source: Population Today, October 1993

Women Professionals, by Race
Race and ethnic composition as of 1990.

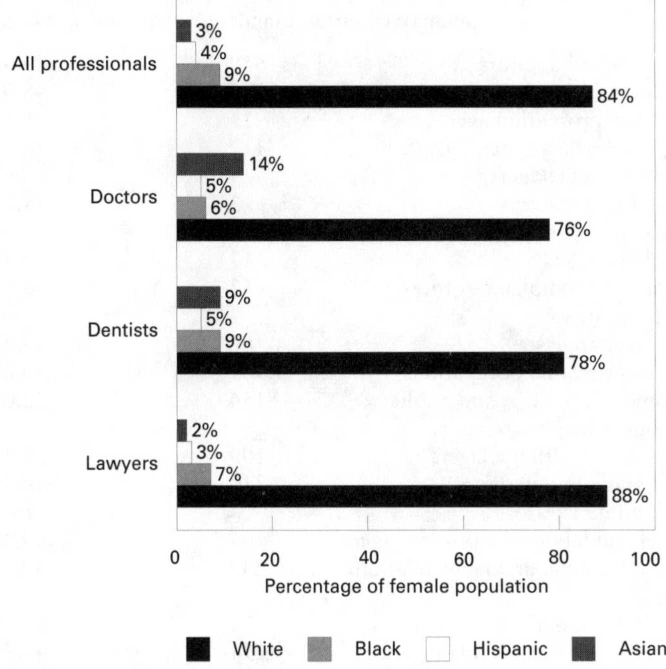

Source: Population Today, October 1993

The Women's National Bar Association was the first national women's group to promote the interest of women lawyers, in 1899.

Fast Fact: Minority Women in Management

As of 1988, 7% of employed African-American women and 6.7% of Hispanic women were in management occupations. Paralleling the trend among all women managers, the largest numbers of black women managers were concentrated in the services industries, followed by finance, insurance, and real estate. The largest numbers of Hispanic, Asian-American, and Native-American women managers were in finance, insurance, and real estate.

Source: Department of Labor: Women's Bureau

Half of women-owned businesses had sales of over $250,000 and 25% had sales of over $1 million between 1990 and 1992.

California had the largest number of women-owned firms and receipts as of 1987, accounting for 13.6% of all women-owned firms and 11.2% of their receipts.

Women Managers
By occupation of women over 16 years, as of 1988

	Total women employed, in thousands	Women as percent of total workers
Accountants and auditors	659	49.6
Administrators, education and related fields	275	48.9
Business and promotion agents	11	*
Buyers, wholesale and retail trade (except farm products)	117	50.2
Construction inspectors	3	5.0
Executive, administrative, and managerial	5,590	39.9
Financial managers	213	42.4
Inspectors and compliance officers (not construction)	52	26.8
Management analysts	66	33.2
Management-related occupations	1,909	50.6
Marketing, advertising, and public relations managers	154	32.0
Medicine and health managers	100	61.3
Officials and administrators, public administrators	210	44.5
Personnel and labor relations managers	64	49.2
Personnel, training, and labor relations specialists	230	59.0
Postmasters and mail superintendents	16	42.1
Properties and real estate managers	194	44.8
Purchasing agents and buyers	103	42.7
Purchasing managers	24	24.2
Underwriters and other financial officers	659	49.6

* Percentage not shown when base is less than 35,000
Source: Department of Labor, Women's Bureau

WORKING WOMAN'S TEN MOST ADMIRED WOMEN MANAGERS

Gwendolyn Calvert Baker—president and chief executive officer, U.S. Committee for UNICEF
Jill Barad—president and chief operational officer, Mattel
Jane Hirsch—chair and chief executive officer, Copley Pharmaceutical
Judy Lewent—chief financial officer, Merck
Ruth Owades—founder and president, Calyx & Corolla
Alicia Philipp—executive director, Metropolitan Atlanta Community Foundation
Clyda Rent—president and chief executive officer, First of America Bank, Northeast Illinois
Ella Williams—president and chief executive officer, Aegir Systems
Faith Wohl—director of human-resource initiatives, DuPont

Source: Working Woman, December 1993

WOMEN BUSINESS OWNERS

In 1992, an estimated 6.5 million women-owned businesses employed over 11 million people in the U.S., more than the Fortune 500 companies did worldwide. And the number of women-owned businesses and their importance to the economy continue to grow—by the year 2000, it is projected that 50% of all American businesses will be owned by women.

Black women own 3.8 % (102,600) of the 2.7 million women-owned sole proprietorships.

Number of Women-Owned Businesses, by Industry

	1986	1980	Percentage increase
Agriculture, forestry, and fishing	65	31	110.9
Mining, construction, and manufacturing	224	84	165.9
Transportation, communications, and electric utilities	52	28	86.1
Wholesale and retail trade	975	825	18.2
Finance, insurance, and real estate	451	355	27.2
Services	2,355	1,213	94.2

Source: Department of Labor, Women's Bureau

Women-Owned Firms and Receipts as a Percentage of U.S. Totals

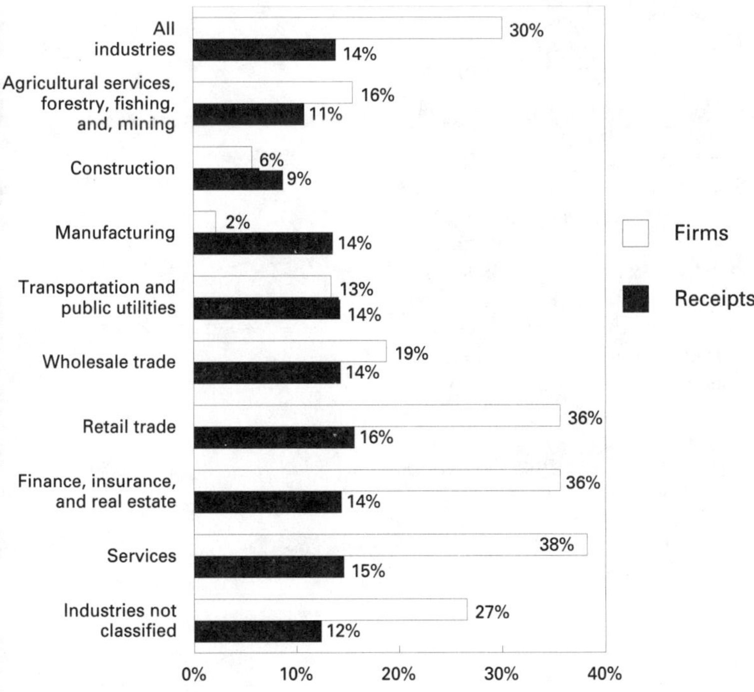

(Data from 1987)
Source: 1987 Economic Census of Women-Owned Businesses

Distribution of Women-Owned Firms, by State—1987

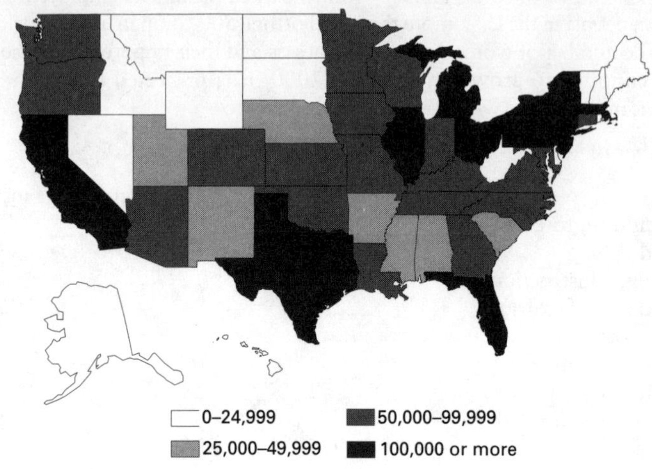

(Data from 1987)
Source: Bureau of the Census

Fast Fact: How Well Off Are Women-Owned Firms?

Receipts from women-owned businesses rose 183% from 1982 to 1987, increasing from $98.3 to $278.1 billion. Though impressive, this represented only 13.9% of the country's gross receipts, despite the fact that women-owned businesses accounted for 30% of all firms in the U.S. at that point. One factor that contributed to this disparity is that the majority of women-owned firms are concentrated in the service industries, which in 1987 accounted for 55.1% of all women-owned firms but only 22% of gross receipts.
Source: 1987 Economic Census of Women-Owned Businesses

THE TOP TWENTY WOMEN BUSINESS OWNERS

1. Marian Ilitch—secretary, treasurer, Little Caesar Enterprises. Trade: pizza, fast-food, chain restaurant. Sales: $2.3 billion. Employees: 25,200. Ownership: 50%.
2. Joyce Raley Teel—co-chair, Raley's. Trade: grocery store chain. Sales: $1.7 billion. Employees: 12,000. Ownership: 100%.
3. Lynda Resnick—co-chair, Roll Industries. Trade: teleflora, citrus growers, and Franklin Mint collectibles. Sales: $1.3 billion. Employees: 7,500. Ownership: 50%.
4. Antonia Axson Johnson—chair, Axel Johnson. Trade: telecommunications, multinational conglomerate, communications. U.S. sales: $800 million. U.S. employees: 2,000. Ownership: 100%.
5. Liz Minyard, Gretchen Minyard Williams—co-chairs, Minyard Food Stores. Trade: food. Sales: $760 million. Employees: 6,100. Ownership: The two sisters and a cousin each own 33.3%.
6. Linda Wachner—president, chair, CEO, Warnaco Group. Trade: intimate apparel, men's and women's underwear, clothing. Sales: $704 million. Employees: 12,700. Ownership: 10.3%.
7. Jenny Craig—vice chair, Jenny Craig. Trade: weight-loss diet plan. Sales: $465 million. U.S. employees: 6,500. Ownership: 61%, with husband.
8. Donna Wolf Steigerwaldt—chair, CEO, Jockey International. Trade: men's and women's underwear, clothing. Sales: $450 million. Employees: 5,000. Ownership: more than 50%.
9. Donna Karan—chief designer, CEO, Donna Karan. Trade: women's clothing. Sales: $408 million. Employees: 877. Ownership: 50%, with husband.
10. Helen Copley—chair, CEO, Copley Press. Trade: newspaper publishing. Sales: $63 million. Employees: 3,500. Ownership: 100%.
11. Barbara Levy Kipper—chair, Chas. Levy. Trade: wholesale distributor of magazines and books. Sales: $335 million. Employees: 2,330. Ownership: 100%.
12. Betty Martin Marsham—president, CEO, GEAR Holdings. Trade: home furnishings, linens. Sales: $335 million. Employees: 30. Ownership: more than 20%.
13. Susie Tompkins—co-founder, co-owner, Esprit de Corp. Trade: women's sportswear and shoes, clothing. Sales: $800 million. U.S. Employees: 1,230. Ownership: more than 20%.
14. Annabelle Lundy Fetterman—chair, Lundy Packaging. Trade: hog processing, food. Sales: $294 million. Employees: 900. Ownership: more than 20%.
15. Dian Graves Owen—chair, Owen Healthcare. Trade: health care services, pharmacy-management, hospital services. Sales: $291 million. Employees: 2,000. Ownership: 37.8%.
16. Carole Little—co-chair, Carole Little. Trade: ladies' ready-to-wear clothing. Sales: $283 million. Employees: 850. Ownership: 50%.
17. Ellen Gordon—president, Tootsie Roll Industries. Trade: candy, food. Sales: $260 million. Employees: 1,400. Ownership: more than 20%.
18. (tie) Josephine Chaus—chair, CEO, Bernard Chaus. Trade: ladies' ready-to-wear clothing. Sales: $230 million. Employees: 750. Ownership: 64%.
18. (tie) Christel DeHaan—president, CEO, Resort Condominium International. Trade: vacation, time-share, resort management, leisure. Sales: $230 million. Employees: 2,300. Ownership: 100%.
20. Linda Paresky—co-chair, Thomas Cook Travel. Trade: travel agency. Sales: $220 million. Employees: 3,500. Ownership: 50%.

Source: National Association of Women Business Owners

Women are forming small businesses at nearly twice the rate of men.

In 1959, Ruth Bader Ginsburg graduated first in her class from Columbia Law School, but found it difficult to get a job. Sandra Day O'Connor was also unable to find a job immediately after graduating third in her class at Stanford Law School in 1952.

FINANCING WOMEN-OWNED BUSINESSES

Three-quarters of all women-owned businesses sought short-term financing in 1993, and over half went to commercial banks, despite the problems often encountered in dealing with banks. As the size of the businesses increased, they were more likely to rely on commercial banks.

Short-Term Financing and Women-Owned Businesses
This graph shows the types of short-term financing used by women-owned businesses.

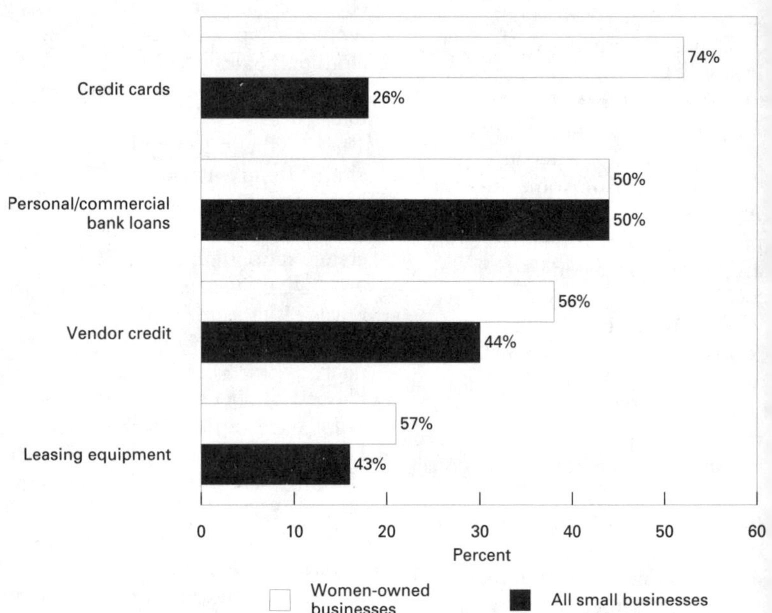

THE BEST COMPANIES FOR WOMEN

BE & K
Ben & Jerry's Homemade
Federal Express
1st Federal Bank of California
Mary Kay Cosmetics
Morrison and Foerster
Nordstrom
Patagonia
Pitney Bowes
Xerox

Source: The 100 Best Companies to Work for in America, Robert Levering and Milton Moskowitz (New York: Plume, 1994).

Long-Term Financing and Women-Owned Businesses
This graph shows the types of long-term financing used by women-owned businesses.

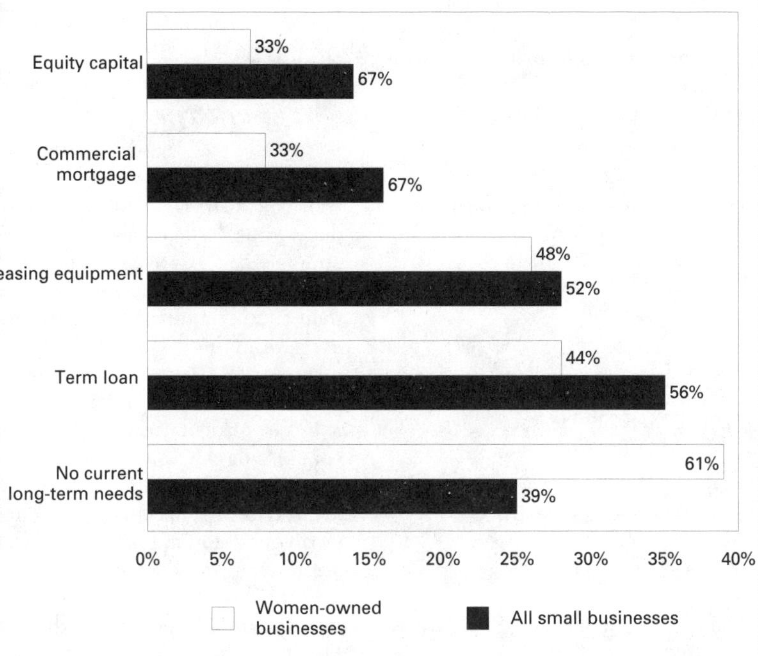

Source for above: National Foundation for Women Business Owners

Joan Wyatt was appointed a guard in the Iowa State Penitentiary, a maximum security prison, in 1973. One inmate filed a suit, claiming that her presence "inflames the passions of prisoners." A federal judge dismissed the suit.

COMPANIES WITH MENTORING PROGRAMS FOR WOMEN

AT&T
Champion International
Chubb & Son, Inc.
CIGNA
Colgate-Palmolive Company
Dow Jones & Company
Liz Claiborne, Inc.
NYNEX Corporation
Pitney Bowes
Procter & Gamble

Source: Catalyst

FINANCING SOURCES FOR WOMEN-OWNED BUSINESSES

PRIVATE

Capital Rose
(215) 687-1666

Inroads Capital Partners
(312) 902-5347

National Association of Female Executives/Venture Capital Fund
(212) 477-2200

New Era Capital Partners
(310) 284-8868

Sky Venture Capital Fund
(515) 248-1249

Women's Equity Fund (or American Women's Equity Fund)
(303) 443-2620

60% of women-owned businesses are either business services (where the failure rate is 21%, compared with a 13% overall average) or retail trade (where the profit margins are slim).

Government

The Office of Women's Business Ownership is perhaps the best place for women to start if they are interested in obtaining information or financial assistance with their businesses. Either national or regional offices can be of assistance.

Office of Women's Business Ownership
U.S. Small Business Administration
409 Third Street, S.W.
Washington, DC 20416
(202) 205-6673 or (202) 205-7333
(hearing impaired)

Regional Offices:

Region I
60 Batterymarch Street, 10th Floor
Boston, MA 02110
(617) 451-2023

Region II
26 Federal Plaza, Room 31-08
New York, NY 10278
(212) 264-7772

Region III
475 Allendale Road, Suite 201
King of Prussia, PA 19406
(215) 962-3750

Region IV
1375 Peachtree Street, N.E., 5th Floor
Atlanta, GA 30367
(404) 347-2797

Region V
230 S. Dearborn Street, Room 510
Chicago, IL 60604
(312) 353-0359

Region VI
8625 King George Drive, Building C
Dallas, TX 75235
(214) 767-7643

Region VII
911 Walnut Street, 13th Floor
Kansas City, MO 64106
(816) 426-2989

Region VIII
999 18th Street, Suite 701
Denver, CO 80202
(303) 294-7001

Region IX
450 Golden Gate Avenue
San Francisco, CA 94102
(415) 556-7489

Region X
2615 Fourth Avenue, Room 440
Seattle, WA 98121
(206) 442-5676

THE EQUAL CREDIT OPPORTUNITY ACT

The Equal Credit Opportunity Act makes it illegal for lenders to deny your loan application, discourage you from applying for a loan, or give you less favorable terms than another applicant because you are a woman or a minority group member.

In addition, the lender may not ask for information about your spouse unless he has some connection to the business, except if you are relying on his income to support your credit application, or you are relying on alimony, child support, or separate maintenance payments to establish creditworthiness. However the lender may ask you for information about your spouse if you are living in or are relying for security on property located in a community property state (Arizona, California, Idaho, Louisiana, Nevada, New Mexico, Texas, Washington, or Wisconsin).

If you are not granted credit by the lender and you believe the lender may have acted unlawfully, you can seek further assistance from the regulatory agency that supervises the institution.

Source: Small Business Administration

WORKING WOMAN'S FIVE BEST BUSINESS AREAS FOR WOMEN

Health Care—Women have tended to dominate the ranks of the lower-paying fields, such as home health care, physical and occupational therapy, laboratory analysis, nutrition, and, on the business side, medical-billing services. And that's exactly where some of the best moneymaking opportunities now lie.

Nondurable Manufacturing—This category encompasses a broad range of enterprises, such as soft-goods manufacturing, which includes plastic, rubber, and leather products, and the printing and publishing businesses. Estimated to be a $1.5 trillion industry, it is projected that this area will have an annual growth rate of more than 5% over the next five years in at least half the nondurable categories.

Environmental Products and Services—Removal and recycling are the two largest aspects of this rapidly expanding industry, but the redesign of products and services is the real future here.

Information Management and Technology—In terms of employment, the second- and fourth-largest-growing industries in the country are computer and data-processing services, and information management and public relations. Certain sectors, such as video and software production and CD-ROM publishing, grew at a rate of 20% or more in 1992.

Business Financial Services—These firms serve both large companies that are contracting out this work because of downsizing and small businesses that can't afford to have the work done in-house. Financial-services businesses are also attractive because they can be started on a shoestring.

Source: Working Woman, October 1993

WRITING A BUSINESS PLAN

In order to secure financing, it is necessary to write a business plan. Here are some basic Do's and Don'ts:

DO:

- Be brief. Identify your business early on.
- State the company's objectives and describe the strategy and tactics that will enable the company to reach its objectives.
- State clearly how much money the company will need, over what period of time, and how the funds will be used.
- State clearly when and how the money will be paid back.
- Be realistic in making estimates and in assessing your market and other potentials.
- Discuss your company's business risks.
- Be specific. Substantiate your statements with underlying data and market information.
- Use an attractive (but not overdone) cover on your plan.
- Provide extra copies of your plan.

DON'T:

- Include internal plans and budgets as part of your business plan. Summarize and structure them to facilitate review by outside parties.
- Use highly technical descriptions of your products, processes, and operations.
- Make vague or unsubstantiated statements.

Source: National Foundation for Women Business Owners, Coopers and Lybrand

Women-owned businesses receive only 1.5% of the $200 billion spent by the U.S. government to purchase goods and services.

Fast Fact: National Directory of Women-Owned Business Firms

When the government and major contractors look for women-owned businesses, they thumb through the National Directory of Woman-Owned Business Firms. Entrepreneurial women hoping to obtain government contracts can get a boost by arranging for a free listing for their companies.

To be listed, more than 50% of the business must be woman-owned and the principal owner must control the daily business operations. Listings are available by writing the publisher:

Business Research Services
4201 Connecticut Avenue, N.W., #610
Washington, DC 20008
(800) 325-8720

Women-owned companies are more likely to offer tuition reimbursement and flextime.

SELLING TO THE FEDERAL GOVERNMENT

Government procurement is big business, and federal agencies are actively seeking vendors among women-owned businesses. Because government contracting offices buy just about everything offered in the marketplace, every businesswoman has a potential share in govenment contracting. The Office of Women's Business Ownership of the Small Business Administration annually negotiates with federal agencies and departments to increase prime contracting goals for women-owned businesses.

For more information on how to sell to the federal government, see "Women Business Owners: Selling to the Federal Government," published by the Office of Women's Business Ownership. To contact the office, write to:

Office of Women's Business Ownership
Small Business Administration
409 Third Street, S.W.
Washington, DC 20416
(202) 205-6673

Source: Small Business Administration

FLEXIBLE WORK SCHEDULES

	Women	Men
Telecommuting	60%	40%
Regular part-time	77%	23%
Job sharing	94%	6%

Source: Flexible Staffing, Kathleen Christensen (New York: Conference Board, Research Bulletin no. 240, 1989)

TELECOMMUTING

Though American corporations are far from the futuristic idea of a scattered workforce at home, connected by computers, telecommuting is slowly becoming a viable way of arranging a flexible schedule. Corporations see benefits in the resulting lower capitol costs and the edge it gives them in recruitment. For workers, telecommuting can allow them to balance more successfully the responsibilities of home and office.

Most telecommuting situations involve splitting work weeks between home and the office, and 88% of those who telecommute are professionals or managers. Those who are considering telecommuting must also weigh the possible career drawbacks of lessened visibility within their company.

Source: Flexible Staffing, Kathleen Christensen (New York: Conference Board, Research Bulletin no. 240, 1989)

FRANCHISING

Franchising is a way for women who want to start companies to compensate for the difficulties they often face obtaining financing and because of their lack of managerial training. Over the last 10 years, the industry's size has more than doubled and sales are currently approaching $800 billion.

Burdena Pasenelli, assistant director of the FBI's finance division, is the first woman executive in the agency's history.

WORKING WOMAN'S 15 BEST FRANCHISES FOR WOMEN

Name	Type of Business	Investment	Royalty	Advertising fee	Financing	Phone
Callanetics Franchise Corporation	Fitness centers	$28,600 to $66,900	12%	4%	none	(800) 822-5526
A Choice Nanny	Child-care referral service	$40,000 to $50,000	10% of gross revenues per week or a minimum weekly fee of $75 to $150	3%	none	(800) 736-2669
Coffee Beanery	Gourmet-coffee stores	$150,000 to $250,000	6%	1%	yes	(800) 728-2326
Computertots	Computer classes for kids	$18,125 to $32,350	6%, $250 monthly minimum	1%	none	(703) 759-2556
Conroy's	Retail florists	$250,000 to $300,000	7.75%	3%	none	(800) 435-6937
Cost Cutters	Unisex hair salons	$59,000 to $110,800	6%, no royalties for the first 17 weeks	4%	none	(800) 858-2266
Gymboree Corporation	Parent-child play programs	$33,000 to $43,000	6%	between $100 and $300 quarterly (est.)	none	(415) 579-0600
I Can't Believe It's Yogurt	Frozen-yogurt stores	$150,000 to $200,000	5%	2%	none	(800) 722-5848
Jazzercise	Dance-fitness program	$2,010 to $4,500	20%	none	none	(619) 434-2101
Kinderdance International, Inc.	Dance fitness for preschoolers	$7,000	10% to 15% or $50 monthly,	3%	yes	(800) 666-1595
The Lemon Tree.	Unisex haircutters	$27,500 to $42,500	6%	$400 a week	yes	(516) 735-2828
Little Professor Book Centers Bookstores	$184,000 to $1 million	3%	1%	none	(800) 899-6232	
Shipping Connection	Packaging and shipping stores	$42,750	5%	2%	none	(800) 727-6720
Sox Appeal Franchising	Socks and hosiery stores	$90,000 to $140,000	5%	1%	none	(800) 966-7699
Travelplex International	Travel agencies	$70,000 to $100,000	$400 a month	$400 a month	yes	(614) 766-6315

Source: Working Woman, November 1992

Other Franchises of Interest to Women

Some franchisors actively try to build a diverse franchisee base or to attract women and minorities. Among them:

American Leak Detection
888 Research Drive, Suite 109
Palm Springs, CA 92262
(800) 755-6697

Chesapeake Bagel Bakery
1363 Beverly Road, Suite 104
McLean, VA 22101
(703) 893-0167

Decorating Den Systems
7910 Woodmont Avenue
Bethesda, MD 20814
(301) 652-6393

KFC Corp.
1441 Gardiner Lane
Louisville, KY 40213
(502) 456-8300

McDonald's
Kroc Drive
Oak Brook, IL 60521
(708) 575-6196

Manchu Wok
400 Fairway Drive, Suite 106
Deerfield Beach, FL 33441
(800) 423-4009

Source: Kiplinger's Personal Finance Magazine, March 1994

Fast Fact: Women in Franchising

Women in Franchising is a 100% women-owned firm that exists for the purpose of educating and training women and minorities about franchise business ownership. WIF, founded in 1987, provides franchise training seminars, development, and technical support for the U.S. Department of Commerce's Minority Business Development Agency. Both one-on-one consulting and classroom-style education and training are avilable.

Women in Franchising
53 W. Jackson Boulevard, Suite 756
Chicago, IL 60604
(312) 431-1467

HOME-BASED WORK—RESOURCES AND READING

Organizations

Mothers' Home Business Network
P.O. Box 423
East Meadow, NY 11554
(516) 997-7394

Mothers on the Move, An Alliance of Entrepreneurial Mothers
P.O. Box 64033
Tucson, AZ 85728
(602) 628-2598

National Home Business Network
P.O. Box 2137
Naperville, IL 60567

Recommended Reading

"Starting and Managing a Business from Your Home" (Small Business Administration, Office of Business Development, Starting and Managing Series, vol. 102).

Women and Home-Based Work, Kathleen Christensen (New York: Henry Holt, 1987).

Word Processing Plus: Profiles of Home-Based Success, Marcia Hodson (Galveston, Ind.: CountrySide Publications, 1991).

Working at Home Newsletter
P.O. Box 200504-HM
Cartersville, GA 30120

MARILYN QUAYLE—WOMEN, WORK, AND FAMILIES

Wife of the former vice president and a lawyer and mother, Marilyn Quayle addressed the Republican National Convention in 1992 and touched on the issues of work, values, and family life.

We are all shaped by the times in which we live. I came of age in a time of turbulent social change. Some of it was good, such as civil rights. Much of it was questionable; but, remember, not everyone joined the counter-culture. Not everyone demonstrated, dropped out, took drugs, joined in the sexual revolution, or dodged the draft.

The majority of my generation lived by the credo our parents taught us. We believed in God, in hard work and personal discipline, in our nation's essential goodness, and in the opportunity it promised those willing to work for it.

And so, most of us went to school, to church, and to work. We married and started families. We had a stake in the future, and though we knew some changes needed to be made, we did not believe in destroying America to save it.

For women, there were choices and challenges. Like many of you, I chose to have a career—I became a lawyer. Believe me, having a profession is not incompatible with being a good mother or a good wife. But it isn't easy. Women's lives are different from men's lives. We make different trade-offs. We make different sacrifices, and we get different rewards. Helping my children as they grow into good and loving teenagers is a daily source of joy for me. There aren't many women who would have it any other way.

Because my husband went from the publishing business into politics, I chose to leave my law practice and join his campaign. Our marriage is a partnership, and for me it was a reasonable decision. It wasn't caving in. When Dan married me, he married a budding lawyer. He wanted a partner, and he has one. Political liberals hold no monopoly on respecting women's abilities.

But there are differences. I sometimes think that the liberals are always so angry because they believe the grandiose promises of the liberation movement. They're disappointed because most women do not wish to be liberated from their essential natures as women. Most of us love being mothers and wives, which gives our lives a richness that few men or women get from professional accomplishments alone.

Nor has it made for a better society to liberate men from their obligations as husbands or fathers. Our generation's social revolution taught us that family life needs protection. Our laws, policies, and society as a whole must support our families. As we have matured and assumed the responsibilities of parenthood and community leadership, most of my generation has recognized that our parents were wise in ways we did not appreciate. We learned that commitment, marriage, and fidelity are not just arbitrary arrangements. Our generation has benefited, as no other, from the opportunities that America provides. So, now is not the time to turn away from the values that brought us here.

When it comes to rebuilding our families, our communities, the fabric of our society, our goals must be to go back to the future, a future full of promise for all Americans, because that future is built on a foundation of proven values of the past: responsibility, integrity, industry, morality, and respect for others.

About 6.5 million U.S. enterprises with fewer than 500 employees are owned or controlled by women.

THE TEN BEST CITIES FOR WOMEN ENTREPRENEURS

	Women business owners	% of all firms
Baltimore	7,827	34.1
San Francisco	19,894	33.3
San Diego	21,338	32.7
New York	109,903	32.4
Boston	8,318	32.3
Indianapolis	12,815	31.6
Chicago	29,812	31.0
Los Angeles	71,727	31.0
Columbus	8,318	30.9
Philadelphia	13,533	28.6

Source: Working Woman, March 1994

WOMEN-OWNED BUSINESSES—RECOMMENDED READING

"A Guide to Business Credit for Women, Minorities, and Small Business" (Board of Governors of the Federal Reserve System, Washington, D.C. 20551).

The Entrepreneurial Woman's Guide to Owning a Business (available from Entrepreneur magazine, P.O. Box 50369, Boulder, CO 80322, [800] 421-2300)

Our Wildest Dreams: Women Making Money, Doing Good, Having Fun, Joline Godfrey (New York: HarperBusiness, 1992).

Taking Control of Your Life: The Secrets of Successful Enterprising Women, Gail Blanke and Kathleen Walas (New York: MasterMedia, 1990).

"Women-Owned Businesses: The New Economic Force," 1992 Data Report, National Foundation for Women Business Owners (Washington, D.C., 1993).

WOMEN BUSINESS OWNERS—RESOURCES

American Business Women's Association
9100 Ward Parkway
P.O. Box 8728
Kansas City, MO 64114
(816) 361-6621

American Woman's Economic Development Corporation
71 Vanderbilt Avenue, Suite 320
New York, NY 10169
(800) 222-2933 or (212) 692-9100

National Association of Black Women Entrepreneurs
P.O. Box 1375
Detroit, MI 48231
(313) 559-9255

National Association of Negro Business and Professional Women
1806 New Hampshire Avenue, N.W.
Washington, DC 20009
(202) 483-4206

National Association of Women Business Owners
1377 K Street, N.W., Suite 637
Washington, DC 20005
(301) 608-2590

National Chamber of Commerce for Women
10 Waterside Plaza, Suite 6H
New York, NY 10010
(212) 685-3454

The National Foundation for Women Business Owners
1377 K Street, N.W., Suite 637
Washington, DC 20005
(301) 495-4975 or (301) 495-4979
(Research and education)

National Women's Business Council
409 Third Street, S.W., Suite 7425
Washington, DC 20024
(202) 205-3850

Office of Women's Business Ownership
Department of Small Business Administration
409 Third Street, S.W., 6th Floor
Washington, DC 20416
(202) 205-6673

NETWORKING

The following pages present information and resources about a wide range of jobs. The data has been organized by specific field in order to assist women interested in the network and support services available in their professional area. General organizations for women in business and the professions can be found immediately following the Networking listings, pp. 122–5; for women interested in the skilled trades (apprenticeship programs and general information), see the resources listed in Skilled Trades and Other Manual Occupations, pp. 126–9.

The Networking section includes information about the following fields:

Academia
Accounting
Advertising
Agriculture
Appraising
Architecture
Art
Automobiles
Aviation
Child care
Computers
Cosmetics
Culinary
Development
Economics
Education
Engineering
Fashion
Finance/Banking
Fire service
Government
Health/Medicine
Insurance
Law
Law enforcement
Library science
Media
- Communications
- Film/Television/Radio
- Journalism
- Publishing

Military
Mining
Music
Office work
Personnel
Planning
Politics
Public relations
Railroads
Real estate
Religion
Sales and marketing
Science
Social work
Sports
Travel agent

ACADEMIA

Women in Academia

Percentage of women by rank

	1975	1990
Professor	10.1	12.8
Associate	17.3	26.4
Assistant	27.9	39.5
Instructor	48.0	56.5
Lecturer	41.4	52.4
All ranks	22.5	27.4

Tenure

Percentage of full-time faculty that is tenured

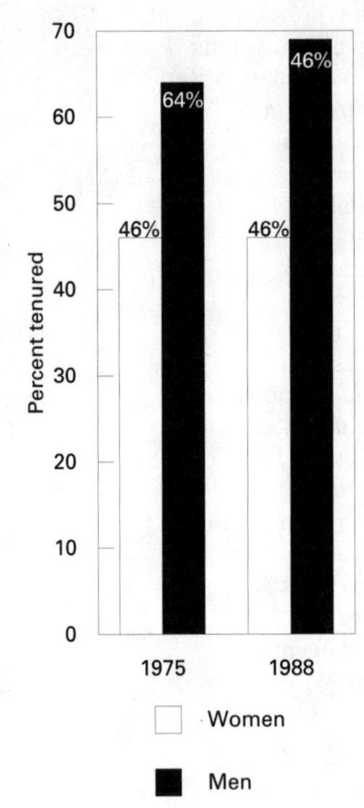

Source for above: American Association of University Professors

Resources

American Anthropological Association
Association for Feminist Anthropology
c/o Mary Moran
The Sociology/Anthropology Department
Colgate University
Hamilton, NY 13346
(315) 824-7548

American History Association
400 A Street, S.E.
Washington, DC 20003
(202) 544-2422

American Philological Association
Committee on the Status of Women and Minorities
Classics Department
Holy Cross College
Worcester, MA 01610
(508) 793-2203

American Philosophical Association
Committee on the Status of Women
Department of Philosophy
University of Delaware
Newark, DE 19716
(302) 831-1112

American Sociological Association
Committee on the Status of Women
1722 N Street, N.W.
Washington, DC 20036
(202) 833-3410

American Studies Association
Women's Committee
University of Maryland
Taliafero Hall
College Park, MD 20742
(301) 405-1355

Association of Black Women Historians
c/o Dr. Jacqueline A. Rouse
Association of African-American Life and History
National Director
1407 14th Street, N.W.
Washington, DC 20005
(202) 667-2822

Center for International Studies Women in International Security
University of Maryland
WIIS/CISSM, School of Public Affairs
Van Munching Park, Room 2101
College Park, MD 20742
(301) 405-6330

Committee on the Status of Women in Linguistics
1325 18th Street, N.W., Suite 211
Washington, DC 20036
(202) 835-1714

Committee on the Status of Women in Philosphy
c/o Alison Jaggar
University of Colorado
Women's Studies
Campus Box 246
Boulder, CO 80309
(303) 492-8997

Feministas Unidas
2101 E. Coliseum Boulevard
Fort Wayne, IN 46805
(219) 481-6636
Feminist scholars in Hispanic, Luso-Brazilian, Chicano, or Puerto Rican studies.

International Women's Anthropology Conference
Anthropology Department
New York University
25 Waverly Place
New York, NY 10003
(212) 998-8550

In the past 10 years, women in the accounting profession rose from 36% to 51%, in law from 13% to 21%, and in architecture from 7% to 18%.

37% of adults prefer a marriage where the husband provides for the family and the wife takes care of the house and children, while 57% prefer equal responsibilities for the husband and wife.

ACCOUNTING

Approximately 50% of all accountants and auditors are women. Since 1977, women in this field have shifted away from large national and international firms toward local and regional firms or they have started their own practices; 17.2% of female accountants were self-employed in 1992. Women who work in firms other than their own practices have also made significant gains in responsibility.

Status of Women in Accounting

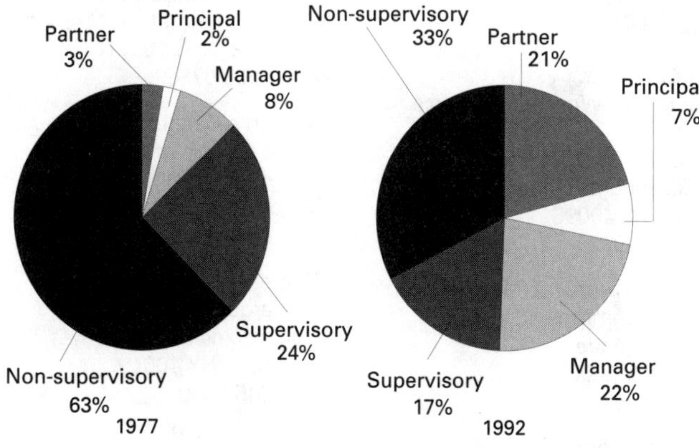

Source for above: The Educational Foundation of the American Woman's Society of Certified Public Accountants–American Society of Women Accountants

Resources

American Society of Women Accountants
1755 Lynnfield Road, Suite 222
Memphis, TN 38119
(901) 680-0470

American Woman's Society of Certified Public Accountants
401 N. Michigan Avenue
Chicago, IL 60611
(312) 644-6610

ADVERTISING

Women have historically had a large presence in advertising, though it was not until recently that they have begun to reach high visibility executive positions. In 1991, women took major positions at Ogilvy & Mather, DDB Needham, Young & Rubicam, and Ayer, and in 1992 Charlotte Beers became chair and CEO of Ogilvy & Mather Worldwide.

Resource

Women in Advertising and Marketing
4200 Wisconsin Ave. N.W.,
Suite 106-238
Washington, DC 20016
(301) 369-7400

AGRICULTURE

Resources

American Agri-Women Resource Center
c/o Marjorie Wendzel
785 N. Bainbridge Center
Watervliet, MI 49098
(616) 468-3649

American Farm Bureau Federation
Women's Committee
225 Touhy Avenue
Park Ridge, IL 60068
(312) 399-5795

American National Cattle Women
5420 S. Quebec
P.O. Box 3881
Englewood, CO 80155
(303) 694-0313

National Grange
Department of Women's Activities
1616 H Street, N.W.
Washington, DC 20006

Women in Agribusiness
P.O. Box 10241
Kansas City, MO 64171

ARCHITECTURE

Resource

American Institute of Architects Women in Architecture Committee
1735 New York Avenue, N.W.
Washington, DC 20006
(202) 626-7305

ART

Resources

Coalition of Women's Art Organizations
123 E. Beutel Road
Port Washington, WI 53074
(414) 284-4458

National Association of Women Artists
41 Union Square West, Room 906
New York, NY 10003
(212) 675-1616

Professional Women Photographers
c/o Photographics Unlimited
17 W. 17th Street, No. 14, 4th Floor
New York, N.Y. 10011
(212) 255-9678

Women's Caucus for Art
Moore College of Art
20th and The Parkway
Philadelphia, PA 19103
(215) 854-0922

Women's Interart Center
c/o Margot Lewitin
549 W. 52nd Street
New York, NY 10019
(212) 246-1050

AUTOMOBILES

Resources

United Auto Workers
Women's Committee
Region 9A
505 Eighth Avenue, 14th Floor
New York, NY 10018
(212) 736-6270

United Auto Workers
Women's Department
8000 E. Jefferson
Detroit, MI 48214
(313) 926-5237

AVIATION

Resources

Independent Federation of Flight Attendants
630 Third Avenue, 5th Floor
New York, NY 10017
(212) 818-1130

Ninety-Nines, International Women Pilots
Will Rogers Airport
P.O. Box 59965
Oklahoma City, OK 73159
(405) 685-7969

Whirly-Girls (International Women Helicopter Pilots)
P.O. Box 584840
Houson, TX 77058
(713) 474-3932

CHILD CARE

Resource

International Nanny Association
P.O. Box 26522
Austin, TX 78755
(512) 454-6462

COMPUTERS

Women in Computer-Related Occupations

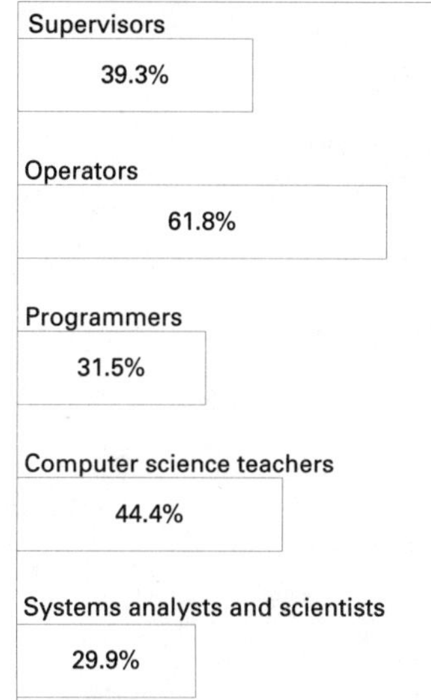

(Data from 1993)
Source: Department of Labor

Resource

Association for Women in Computing
41 Sutter Street, Suite 1006
San Francisco, CA 94104
(415) 905-4663

The first group of women to earn their wings as U.S. Air Force pilots did so in 1977.

The Association of Professional Flight Attendants went on strike in November 1993. After only five days President Clinton stepped in and brokered an agreement for arbitration, the proposal favored by the union. Denise Hedges, president of the association, led the successful strike.

COSMETICS

RESOURCE
Cosmetic Executive Women
217 E. 85th Street, Suite 214
New York, N.Y. 10028
(212) 759-3283

CULINARY

Women in Food Service

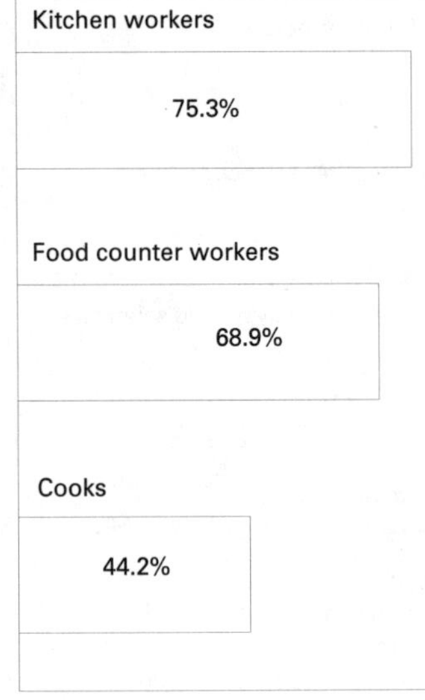

(Data from 1993)
Source: Department of Labor

RESOURCES
Association of Women in Natural Foods
10159 Brooke Avenue
Chatsworth, CA 91311
(818) 718-6230

Roundtable for Women in Foodservice
425 Central Park West, Suite 2A
New York, NY 10025

United Food and Commercial Workers International Union
Women's Affairs
1775 K Street, N.W.
Washington, DC 20006
(202) 223-3111

Women Grocers of America
1825 Samuel Morse Drive
Reston, VA 22090
(703) 437-5300

DEVELOPMENT

RESOURCE
Association for Women in Development
Virginia Tech
10 Sandy Hall, Room 1660, Litton Reaves
Blacksburg, VA 24061
(703) 231-3765

ECONOMICS

RESOURCE
Committee on the Status of Women in the Economics Profession
2040 Sheridan Road
Northwestern University
Evanston, IL 60208
(708) 491-4145

EDUCATION

RESOURCES
American Association of University Professors
Committee on the Status of Women in the Academic Profession
1012 14th Street, N.W., Suite 500
Washington, DC 20005
(202) 737-5900

American Educational Research Association
Research on Women and Education Group
1230 17th Street, N.W.
Washington, DC 20036
(202) 223-9485

American Federation of Teachers
Women's Rights Committee
Human Rights Department
555 New Jersey Avenue, N.W.
Washington, DC 20001
(202) 879-4400

Association of Black Women in Higher Education
Nassau Community College
1 Education Drive
Garden City, NY 11530
(516) 572-7160

National Association for Women Deans, Administrators and Counselors
1325 18th Street, N.W., Suite 210
Washington, DC 20036

National Association for Women in Education
1325 18th Street, N.W., Suite 210
Washington, DC 20036
(202) 659-9330

National Identification Program for the Advancement of Women in Higher Education Administration
American Council of Education
Office of Women in Higher Education
1 Dupont Circle
Washington, DC 20036
(202) 939-9390

United Federation of Teachers
Women's Rights Committee
260 Park Avenue South
New York, NY 10010
(212) 598-7738

ENGINEERING

Women Engineers

	%Women	%Men
Aerospace	7.2	92.8
Metallurgical	10.7	89.3
Petroleum	5.6	94.4
Chemical	10.3	89.7
Nuclear	10.0	90.0
Civil	9.5	90.5
Industrial	16.4	83.6
Mechanical	5.1	94.9

(Data from 1993)
Source: Department of Labor

Resource

Society of Women Engineers
120 Wall Street, 11th Floor
New York, NY 10005

FASHION

Resources

International Fashion Group
597 Fifth Avenue, 8th Floor
New York, NY 10017
(212) 593-1715

International Ladies' Garment Workers' Union
1710 Broadway
New York, NY 10019
(212) 265-7000

Ladies Apparel Contractors Association
450 Seventh Avenue
New York, NY 10123
(212) 564-6161

FINANCE/BANKING

Women in Financial Occupations

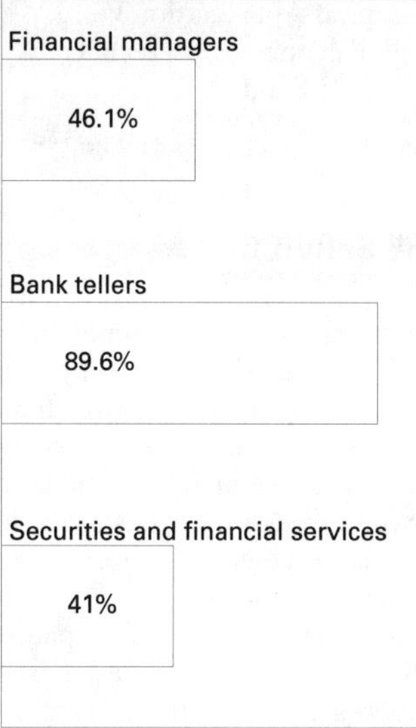

(Data from 1993)
Source: Department of Labor

Resource

Financial Women International
7910 Woodmont Avenue, Suite 1430
Bethesda, MD 20814
(301) 657-8288

The first woman to hold a seat on the New York Stock Exchange was Muriel Siebert, who took her place there in 1967.

Margaret Knight was a nineteenth-century inventor who patented more than 24 types of heavy machinery.

Women make up 37% of all new golf players, says the National Golf Foundation, as more and more businesswomen want to network through the sport.

WOMEN MANAGERS OF TOP MUTUAL FUNDS

Beth Terrana—Fidelity Equity Income Fund
Ellen Harris—Paine Webber Growth Fund
Dorothea M. Dutton—Delaware Group U.S. Government Fund
Carlene Murphy—Strong Common Stock Fund
Anne Hodsdon—John Hancock Sovereign U.S. Government Income Fund
Helen Young Hayes—Janus Worldwide Fund
Kathleen McClaskey—Pioneer Municipal Bond Fund
Fiona Biggs—Dreyfus Global Investing Fund and Dreyfus Strategic World Investing Fund
Catherine Dudley—Phoenix Capital Appreciation Fund
Nola Falcone—Evergreen Total Return Fund

Source: Working Woman, January 1993

FIRE SERVICE

•More than 3,500 women are at work in career-level fire-suppression positions in over 650 fire departments in the U.S.

•At least 20 women have made their way up through the ranks to the level of division chief, battalion chief, or district chief.

•Among the volunteer and paid-on-call fire and EMS forces, perhaps 30,000 are women firefighters, as are thousands more EMTs and paramedics.

•An estimated 11% of women career firefighters are African-American, another 4% are Hispanic, 1% Asian-American, Native American, or other women of color, and 84% Caucasian.

Source: Women in the Fire Service

Resources

Wildland Fire Fighter Apprenticeship Program
1780 Creekside Oaks Drive, Suite 500
Sacramento, CA 95833

Women in the Fire Service
P.O. Box 5446
Madison, WI 53706
(608) 233-4768

GOVERNMENT

Resources

American Federation of State, County and Municipal Employees
Women's Rights Department
1625 L Street, N.W.
Washington, DC 20036
(202) 429-5090

American Postal Workers Union, AFL-CIO
Post Office Women for Equal Rights
1300 L Street
Washington, DC 20005
(202) 842-4225

Center for Women in Government
University at Albany
Draper 302
135 Western Avenue
Albany, NY 12222
(518) 442-3900

Coalition for Women's Appointments
c/o National Women's Political Caucus
1275 K Street, N.W., Suite 750
Washington, DC 20005
(202) 898-1100

Federally Employed Women
1400 I Street, N.W., Suite 425
Washington, DC 20005
(202) 898-0994

National Conference of State Legislatures
The Women's Network
1560 Broadway, Suite 700
Denver, CO 80202
(303) 830-2200

National League of Cities
Women in Municipal Government
1301 Pennsylvania Avenue, N.W.
Washington, DC 20004
(202) 626-3017

Section for Women in Public Administration
1120 G Street, N.W., Suite 700
Washington, DC 20005
(202) 393-7878

Women in Government
c/o Joy N. Stone, Executive Director
1101 30th Street, N.W., Suite 200
Washington, DC 20006
(202) 333-0825

Women in Government Relations
1029 Vermont Avenue, N.W.,
Suite 510
Washington, DC. 20005
(202) 347-5432

WOMEN'S WIRE

Launched from South San Francisco by partners Nancy Rhine and Ellen Park, Women's Wire (Worldwide Information Resource & Exchange) claims to be the first computer network directed at women. As well as information on careers, health, and parenting, Women's Wire carries material such as the Department of Labor's Women's Bureau reports, White House position papers, and other materials relevant to women. The cost is $15 a month, which includes two hours of on-line time. To receive a free software start-up kit, call (800) 210-9999.

HEALTH/MEDICINE

Health care is an expanding sector of the American economy, and much of its growth is in areas that are traditionally strong in female participation, among them home health aides, X-ray technologists, medical secretaries, and physical therapists. There are acute shortages of nurses and pharmacists as well.

Women are less likely than men to have employer-provided health insurance. In the 1980s, 50% of women were covered by their employers, compared with 70% of men.

WOMEN IN HEALTH PROFESSIONS

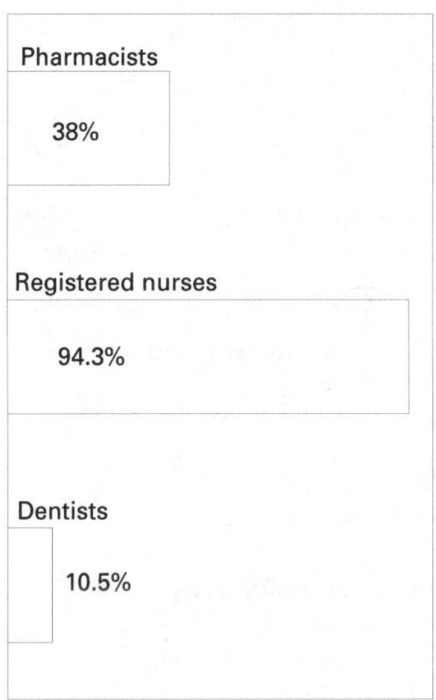

Source: Department of Labor

RESOURCES

American Association of Immunologists
Committee on the Status of Women
9650 Rockville Pike
Bethesda, MD 20814
(301) 530-7178

American Association of Women Dentists
401 N. Michigan Avenue
Chicago, IL 60611
(312) 644-6610

American Association of Women Radiologists
1891 Preston White Drive
Reston, VA 22091
(703) 648-8939

The number of women physicians has continued to rise in the last few decades, increasing nearly five-fold between 1970 and 1992.

Women Doctors

		1970	%	1992	%
All Physicians	Total	334,028		653,062	
	Women	25,401	7	118,519	18
Anesthesiologists	Total	10,860		28,148	
	Women	1,416	13	5,170	18
Cardiovascular	Total	6,476		16,478	
	Women	187	2	915	5
General/family practice	Total	57,948		71,688	
	Women	2,486	4	12,036	16
Internal medicine	Total	40,153		109,017	
	Women	2,383	5	23,043	21
Obstetrics/gynecology	Total	18,876		35,273	
	Women	1,337	7	8,721	24
Pediatrics	Total	18,332		44,881	
	Women	3,816	20	18,147	40
Plastic surgery	Total	1,600		4,688	
	Women	40	2	334	7
Psychiatry	Total	21,146		36,405	
	Women	2,459	11	9,028	25
Radiology	Total	10,524		7,848	
	Women	500	4	784	9

Source: American Medical Association

American College of Nurse-Midwives
818 Connecticut Avenue, N.W., Suite 900
Washington, DC 20005
(202) 289-0171

American College of Obstetricians and Gynecologists
409 12th Street, S.W.
Washington, DC 20024
(292) 638-5577

American Medical Women's Association
801 N. Fairfax Street, Suite 400
Alexandria, VA 22314
(703) 838-0500

American Nurses Association
600 Maryland Avenue, S.W.
Washington, DC 20024
(202) 554-4444

American Psychiatric Association
Association of Women Psychiatrists
9802 Farnham Road
Louisville, KY 40223
(502) 588-6185

American Psychological Association
Division of the Psychology of Women
Women's Program Office
750 First Street, N.E.
Washington, DC 20002
(202) 336-6044

American Public Health Association
Women's Caucus
1015 15th St., N.W.
Washington, DC 20005
(202) 789-5600

Association of American Medical Colleges
Women in Medicine Program
2450 N Street, N.W.
Washington, DC 20036
(202) 828-0575

Association for Women Psychiatrists
Erie County Medical Center
462 Grider Street
Buffalo, NY 14215
(716) 898-5275

Association of Women in Psychology
601 S. Vine Street
Chandler, AZ 85225

Black Women Physicians Project
3300 Henry Avenue
Philadelphia, PA 19129
(215) 842-7124

Council of Women Chiropractors
3415 Bell, Suite G
Amarillo, TX 79109
(806) 355-7217

International Association of Eating Disorders Professionals
123 N.W. 13th Street, #206
Boca Raton, FL 33432
(407) 338-6494

International Lactation Consultant Association
201 Brown Avenue
Evanston, IL 60202
(708) 260-8874

NAACOG: The Organization for Obstetric, Gynecologic, and Neonatal Nurses
700 14th Street, N.W., Suite 600
Washington, DC 20005
(202) 662-1600

National Association of Childbirth Assistants
205 Copco Lane
San Jose, CA 95126
(408) 225-9167

National Black Nurses Association
1011 North Capitol Street, N.E.
Washington, DC 20002
(202) 393-6870

National Council of Women's Health
Box 52
1300 York Avenue, Room D-115
New York, NY 10021
(212) 535-0031

National League for Nursing
350 Hudson Street
New York, NY 10014
(212) 989-9393

Ruth Jackson Orthopaedic Society
6300 N. River Road, Suite 727
Rosemont, IL 60018
(708) 698-1693

Society of General Internal Medicine
Women's Caucus
Montefiore Medical Center, Department of Medicine
111 E. 210th Street, Centennial 3
Bronx, NY 10467
(718) 920-4784

Woman's Organization of the National Association of Retail Druggists
205 Dangerfield Road
Alexandria, VA 22314
(703) 683-8200

INSURANCE

Resources

Association for Professional Insurance Women
1 Liberty Plaza
New York, NY 10006
(212) 225-7571

National Association of Insurance Women–International
1847 E. 15th
P.O. Box 4410
Tulsa, OK 74159
(918) 744-5195 or (800) 766-6249

LAW

Women in the Legal Profession

Federal judiciary
11% of circuit court judges
13% of district court judges
State judiciary*
10% of judges on courts of last resort
10% of intermediate appellate court judges
10% of trial court judges

Federal Government
35% of lawyers in executive branch agencies; of those, 5% are minority women

Corporate**
16% of corporate attorneys

Organized Bar
25% of American Bar Association membership
13% of state and local bar presidents

(All data from 1992, except *from 1991 and **from 1988)
Source: American Bar Association Commission on Women in the Profession

St. Louis Law School was the first law school to admit women, in 1869.

Belva Ann Bennett McNall Lockwood was the first woman lawyer admitted to practice before the U.S. Supreme Court, in 1879.

The presence of American women in the legal profession has risen from 3% in 1970 to 24% in 1990.

Women Partners at Large Firms

The following chart shows the percentage of women partners and those at partner level at the ten largest law firms in 1992.

	% partners	% at partner level
Baker & McKenzie (U.S. offices only)	7.9	(Not available)
Jones, Day, Reavis & Pogue	10.5	21.6
Skadden, Arps, Slate, Meagher & Flom	13.9	25.0
Gibson, Dunn & Crutcher	10.8	0.0
Sidley & Austin	11.7	12.0
Fulbright & Jaworski	9.3	50.0
Pillsbury, Madison & Sutro	13.2	20.0
Morgan, Lewis & Bockius	8.0	31.0
Morrison & Foerster	18.1	18.8
Shearman & Sterling	8.6	0.0

Source: The National Law Journal, January 27, 1992

Law Firms with the Highest Female Representation

Female Partners	Percent
Anderson, Kill, Olick & Oshinsky; New York	29
Kutak, Rock & Campbell; Omaha	23
Ross & Hardies; Chicago	23
Littler, Mendelson, Fastiff & Tichy; San Francisco	22
Thompson & Knight, Dallas	22
Female Associates	
Dow, Lohnes & Albertson; Washington, D.C.	62
Wyatt, Tarrant & Combs; Louisville	58
McDermott, Will & Emery; Chicago	54
Cooley, Godward, Castro, Huddleston & Tatum; San Francisco	53
Epstein, Becker & Green P.C.; New York	53
Heller, Ehrman, White & McAuliffe; San Francisco	53
Palmer & Dodge; Boston	53

Source: The National Law Journal

Resources

American Bar Association Commission on Women in the Profession
750 N. Lake Shore Drive
Chicago, IL 60611
(312) 988-5676

Association of American Law Schools
Section on Women in Legal Education
1202 Connecticut Avenue, N.W.
Washington, DC 20036
(202) 296-8851

International Federation of Women Lawyers
186 Fifth Avenue
New York, NY 10010
(212) 206-1666

National Association of Black Women Attorneys
3711 Macomb Street, N.W., 2nd Floor
Washington, DC 20016
(202) 966-9693

National Association of Women Judges
1020 19th Street, N.W., Suite LLO1
Washington, DC 20036
(202) 872-0963

National Association of Women Lawyers
750 N. Lake Shore Drive
Chicago, IL 60611
(312) 988-6186

National Bar Association
Association of Black Women Attorneys
134 W. 32nd Street, Suite 602
New York, NY 10001
(212) 244-4270

National Bar Association
Women Lawyers Division
c/o Brenda Girton
1211 Connecticut Avenue, N.W., Suite 702
Washington, DC 20036
(202) 291-1979

National Conference of Women's Bar Associations
P.O. Box 77
Edenton, NC 27932
(919) 482-8202

National Judicial Education Program to Promote Equality for Women and Men in the Courts
99 Hudson Street, 12th Floor
New York, NY 10013
(212) 925-6635

Women in Legal Education
1201 Connecticut Avenue, Suite 500
Washington, DC 20036
(202) 296-8851

THE MARGARET BRENT WOMEN LAWYERS OF ACHIEVEMENT AWARD

Named after Margaret Brent, the first woman lawyer in America, the ABA Commission on Women in the Profession established this award in 1991 to recognize and celebrate the accomplishments of women lawyers.

1991
Hon. Phyllis A. Kravitch
Andrea Sheridan Ordin
Justice Rosalie Wahl
Jeanette Rosner Wolman
Marilyn V. Yarbrough

1992
Prof. Anita F. Hill
Margaret L. Behm
Hon. Betty B. Fletcher
Dean and Prof. Herma Hill Kay
Justice Leah J. Sears-Collins

1993
Hon. Janet Reno
Hon. Betty Weinberg Ellerin
Hon. Ruth Bader Ginsburg
Elaine R. Jones
Justice Joyce L. Kennard
Esther R. Rothstein

Arabella Mansfield Babb was the first woman to be admitted to the bar, in 1869.

Women who worked for federal law-enforcement agencies were not allowed to carry guns until 1971.

The FBI opened its ranks to women for the first time on May 12, 1972.

LAW ENFORCEMENT

Women in Law Enforcement

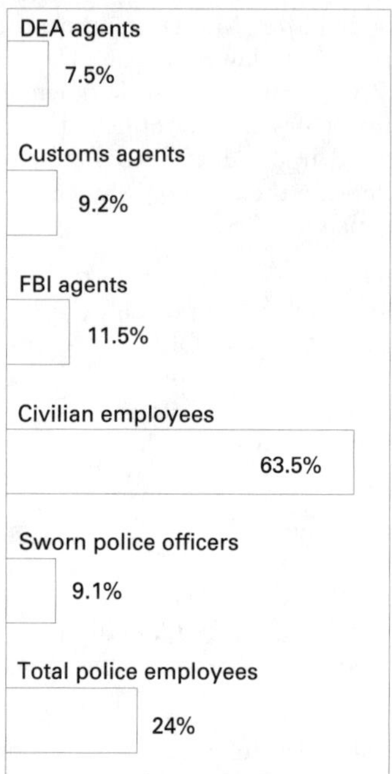

(Data for last three categories is from 1992)
Sources: Federal Bureau of Investigation Uniform Crime Report; Working Woman, March 1994

Resource

International Association of Women Police
P.O. Box 371008
Decatur, GA 30037
(404) 244-2856

LIBRARY SCIENCE

Resources

American Library Association
ACRL Women's Studies Section
50 E. Huron Street
Chicago, IL 60611
(312) 944-6780

Art Libraries Society/North America
Women and Art Round Table
3900 E. Timrod Street
Tucson, AZ 85711
(602) 881-8479

MEDIA

Communications—Resources

Communication Workers of America, AFL-CIO
National Women's Committee
501 3rd St., N.W.
Washington, DC 20001
(202) 434-1128

Women in Telecommunications
P.O. Box 96
Cupertino, CA 95015
(408) 451-9000 or (415) 677-7645

Film/Television/Radio—Resources

American Federation of Television and Radio Artists
National Women's Division
260 Madison Avenue
New York, NY 10016
(212) 532-0800

American Film Institute Directing Workshop for Women
2021 North Western Avenue
P.O. Box 27999
Los Angeles, CA 90027
(213) 856-7721

American Women in Radio and Television
1650 Tyson's Boulevard
McLean, VA 22102
(703) 506-3290

Stuntwomen's Association of Motion Pictures
13601 Ventura Boulevard, #94
Sherman Oaks, CA 91423
(213) 462-1605

Women in Broadcast Technology
P.O. Box 370772
Denver, CO 80237
(303) 745-7748

Women in Cable
c/o P. M. Haeger & Associates
500 N. Michigan Avenue, Suite 1400
Chicago, IL 60611
(312) 661-1700

Women in Film
6464 Sunset Boulevard, Suite 530
Hollywood, CA 90028
(213) 463-6040

Women Make Movies
462 Broadway, Suite 500
New York, NY 10013
(212) 925-0606

The Women's Film Company
9165 Sunset Boulevard, Suite 300
Los Angeles, CA 90069
(310) 271-0202

Journalism—Resources

American News Women's Club
1607 22nd Street, N.W.
Washington, DC 20008
(202) 332-6770

Association for Education in Journalism and Mass Communication
Committee on Status of Women
University of South Carolina
Columbia, SC 29208
(803) 777-2005

Association for Women in Sports Media
P.O. Box 4205
Mililani, HI 96789
(714) 733-0558

International Women's Media Foundation
2775 S. Quincy Street, #470
Arlington, VA 22206
(703) 820-0607

International Women's Writing Guild
Box 810, Gracie Station
New York, NY 10028
(212) 737-7536

National Federation of Press Women
Box 99
Blue Springs, MO 64013
(816) 229-1666

National League of American Pen Women
1300 17th Street, N.W.
Washington, DC 20036
(202) 785-1997

Women in Communications
3717 Columbia Pike, Suite 310
Arlington, VA 22204
(703) 920-5555

Publishing—Resource

Women's National Book Association
160 Fifth Avenue, Room 604
New York, NY 10010
(212) 675-7805

MILITARY

As of 1993, there were approximately 200,000 women on active duty in the U.S. armed forces.

Women and Men in the Military

	% Women (total)	% Men
Army	12.5 (70,797)	87.5
Navy	10.7 (54,190)	89.3
Air Force	15.0 (66,192)	85.0
Marines	4.4 (7,864)	95.6
Coast Guard	8.0 (3,036)	92.0

Source: Defense Advisory Committee on Women in the Service

Resources

Defense Advisory Committee on Women in the Services and Military Women
The Pentagon
Washington, DC 20301
(703) 697-2122

Women Military Aviators
P.O. Box 396
Randolph Air Force Base, TX 78148
(317) 688-2167

Black women make up 44% of women in the U.S. Army, with 8% from other minorities.

Women can now serve in all combat positions in the U.S. Navy except in Seal commando units and on nuclear submarines and minesweepers.

The top officer in the U.S. Navy said in May 1994 that he would speed up plans to assign women to all surface vessels, and possibly to submarines as well.

AWARD-WINNING ACTRESSES

Oscars

Katharine Hepburn, four Oscars
Morning Glory (1933)
Guess Who's Coming to Dinner (1967)
The Lion in Winter (1968)
On Golden Pond (1981)

Two Oscars each: Bette Davis, Jane Fonda, Jodie Foster, Olivia de Havilland, Vivien Leigh, Luise Rainer, Elizabeth Taylor, Shelly Winters

Emmys

Mary Tyler Moore, five Emmys
The Dick Van Dyke Show (1965/66)
The Mary Tyler Moore Show (1972/73)
The Mary Tyler Moore Show (1973/74)
The Mary Tyler Moore Show (1975/76)
Stolen Babies (1992/93)

Lucille Ball, four Emmys
Best comedienne (1952)
The Lucy Show (1966/67)
The Lucy Show (1967/68)
Governor's Award (1988/89)

Tyne Daly, four Emmys
Cagney & Lacey (1982/83)
Cagney & Lacey (1983/84)
Cagney & Lacey (1984/85)
Cagney & Lacey (1987/88)

Valerie Harper, four Emmys
The Mary Tyler Moore Show (1970/71)
The Mary Tyler Moore Show (1971/72)
The Mary Tyler Moore Show (1972/73)
Rhoda (1974/75)

Nancy Marchand, four Emmys
Lou Grant (1977/78)
Lou Grant (1979/80)
Lou Grant (1980/81)
Lou Grant (1981/82)

Rhea Perlman, four Emmys
Cheers (1983/84)
Cheers (1984/85)
Cheers (1985/86)
Cheers (1988/89)

Three Emmys each: Barbara Bain, Candice Bergen, Ellen Corby, Jean Stapleton, Patricia Wettig, Betty White

MUSIC

Resources

International League of Women Composers
ACU Station, Box 8274
Abilene, TX 79699
(915) 674-2044

Women Band Directors National Association
345 Overlook Drive
West Lafayette, IN 47906
(317) 463-1738

Women's Independent Label Distribution Network
1712 E. Michigan Avenue
Lansing, MI 48912
(517) 484-1712

GRAMMY-WINNING WOMEN SINGERS

Aretha Franklin, fifteen Grammys
"Respect" (1967), two awards
"Chain of Fools" (1968)
"Share Your Love with Me" (1969)
"Don't Play That Song" (1970)
"Bridge Over Troubled Water" (1971)
"Young, Gifted, and Black" (1972)
"Master of Eyes" (1973)
"Ain't Nothing Like the Real Thing" (1974)
"Hold On, I'm Comin'" (1981)
Aretha (1987)
"I Knew You Were Waiting [For Me]," with George Michael, (1987)
One Lord, One Faith, One Baptism (1988)
"Speech by Rev. Jesse Jackson, July 27" (1988)
Living Legend Award

Ella Fitzgerald, thirteen Grammys
Ella Fitzgerald Sings the Irving Berlin Song Book (1958)
Ella Fitzgerald Sings the Duke Ellington Song Book (1958)
"But Not For Me"(1959)
Ella Swings Lightly (1959)
"Mack the Knife"/Ella in Berlin (1960), two awards
Ella Swings Brightly with Nelson Riddle (1962)
Fitzgerald and Pass...Again (1976)
Fine and Mellow (1976)
A Perfect Match/ Ella and Basie (1980)
Digital III at Montreaux (1981)
The Best is Yet to Come (1983)
All That Jazz (1990)
Lifetime Achievement Award (1967)

Leontyne Price, thirteen Grammys
A Program of Song (1960)
Great Scenes from Gerswhin's Porgy & Bess (1963)
Berlioz: Nuits d'Eté; Falla: El Amor Brujo (1964)
Strauss: Salome ("Dance of the Seven Veils," Interlude, Final Scene); The Egyptian Helen (Awakening Scene) (1965)
Prima Donna (1966)
Prima Donna, Vol. 2 (1967)
Barber: Two Scenes from Antony and Cleopatra; Knoxville: Summer of 1915 (1969)
Leontyne Price Sings Robert Schumann (1971)
Puccini: Heroines (La Boheme, La Rondine, Tosca, Manon Lescaut) (1973)
Leontyne Price Sings Richard Strauss (1974)
Prima Donna, Vol. 5, Great Soprano Arias from Handel to Britten (1980)
Verdi: Arias (Leotyne Price Sings Verdi) (1982)
Leotyne Price and Marilyn Horne in Concert at the Met (1983)
Lifetime Achievement Award (1989)

Barbra Streisand, eight Grammys
The Barbra Streisand Album (1963), two awards
"People" (1964)
My Name is Barbra (1965)
Love Theme from A Star is Born (1977), two awards
The Broadway Album (1986)
Living Legend Award

Seven Grammys: Anita Baker, Bonnie Raitt, Tina Turner

The National Press Club voted to admit female members in 1970.

Only 6.4% of all car salespeople are women.

In 1932 an executive order decreed that only one spouse could work for the federal government, and thousands of women gave up their jobs. Married women who wanted to keep their jobs filed for divorce and continued to live with their ex-husbands.

OFFICE WORK

Twenty-seven percent of women work in administrative support jobs, more than in any other occupation.

Occupation	Percent
File Clerks	79.9%
Typists	88.8%
Bookkeepers	90.9%
Stenographers	93.6%
Receptionists	97.2%
Secretaries	98.2%

Source: Department of Labor

Resources

9 to 5, National Association of Working Women
614 Superior Avenue, NW
Cleveland, OH 44113
(216) 566-9308 or the 9 to 5 Hotline (800) 522-0925

Professional Secretaries International
10502 Ambassador Drive
Kansas City, MO 64153
(816) 891-6600

PLANNING

Resource

American Planning Association Planning and Women Division
1776 Massachusetts Avenue, N.W.
Washington, D.C. 20036
(202) 872-0611

POLITICS

Resources

G.O.P. Women's Political Action League
2000 L Street, N.W., Suite 200
Washington, DC 20036
(202) 785-8242

National Association of Minority Political Women
6120 Oregon Avenue, N.W.
Washington, DC 20015
(202) 686-1216

National Federation of Democratic Women
c/o C. Pat Frank
1 Plaza South, Suite 189
Tahlequah, OK 74464

National Federation of Republican Women
310 First Street, S.E.
Washington, DC 20003
(202) 547-9341

Women Executives in State Government
122 C Street, N.W., Suite 840
Washington, DC 20031
(202) 628-9374

PUBLIC RELATIONS

RESOURCE

Women Executives in Public Relations
P.O. Box 20766
New York, NY 10025
(212) 721-9661

RAILROADS

RESOURCE

American Council of Railroad Women
Norfolk Southern Corporation
185 Spring Street
Atlanta, GA 30303
(404) 529-2148

RELIGION

RESOURCES

African Methodist Episcopal Church
Women's Missionary Society
1134 11th Street, N.W.
Washington, D.C. 20001
(202) 371-8886

American Jewish Congress
Commission for Women's Equality
15 E. 84th Street
New York, NY 10028
(212) 360-1560

American Women's Clergy Association
P.O. Box 1493
Washington, DC 20013
(202) 797-7460

Black Women in Church and Society
c/o Interdenominational Theological Center
671 Beckwith Street, S.W.
Atlanta, GA 30314
(404) 527-7740

B'nai B'rith Women
1828 L Street, N.W., Suite 250
Washington, DC 20036
(202) 857-1300

Women's Ordination Conference
P.O. Box 2693
Fairfax, VA 22031
(703) 352-1006
An international group committed to the ordination of Roman Catholic women

SALES AND MARKETING

RESOURCES

National Association of Business and Industrial Saleswomen
90 Corona, Suite 1407
Denver, CO 80218
(303) 777-7257

Women in Sales Association
8 Madison Avenue
P.O. Box M
Valhalla, NY 10595
(914) 946-3802

The only two women to win all four grand slam tennis championships in one year are Margaret Court, in 1970, and Steffi Graf, in 1988.

SCIENCE

Resources

American Association for the Advancement of Science
National Network of Women in Science
Office of Opportunities in Science
1333 H Street, N.W.
Washington, DC 20005
(202) 326-6670

American Astronomical Society
Committee on the Status of Women in Astronomy
1630 Connecticut Avenue, N.W.
Washington, DC 20009
(202) 328-2010

American Chemical Society
Women Chemists Committee
1155 16th Street, N.W.
Washington, DC 20036
(202) 872-4000

American Meteorological Society
Board on Women and Minorities
45 Beacon Street
Boston, MA 02108
(617) 227-2425

American Physical Society
Committee on the Status of Women in Physics
1 Physics Ellipse
College Park, MD 20740
(301) 209-3200

American Physiological Association
Women in Physiology Committee
9650 Rockville Pike
Bethesda, MD 20814
(301) 530-7164

American Society of Bio-Chemistry and Molecular Biology
Committee on Equal Opportunities for Women
9650 Rockville Pike
Bethesda, MD 20814
(301) 530-7145

American Society for Microbiology
Committee on the Status of Women in Microbiology
1325 Massachusetts Avenue, N.W.
Washington, DC 20005
(202) 737-3600

American Statistical Association
Caucus for Women in Statistics
1429 Duke Street
Alexandria, VA 22314
(703) 684-1221

Association of American Geographers
Committee on the Status of Women in Geography
1710 16th Street, N.W.
Washington, DC 20009
(202) 234-1450

Association for Women Geoscientists
10200 W. 44th Avenue, Suite 304
Wheat Ridge, CO 80033
(303) 422-8527

Association for Women in Mathematics
4114 Computer/Space Sciences Building
University of Maryland
College Park, MD 20742
(301) 405-7892

Association for Women in Science
1522 K Street, N.W., Suite 820
Washington, DC 20005
(202) 408-0742

Association of Women Soil Scientists
c/o Margie Faber
P.O. Box 115, Ancram
New York, NY 12502
(914) 677-3194

Biophysical Society
Committee on Professional Opportunities for Women
9650 Rockville Pike
Bethesda, MD 20814
(301) 530-7114

National Academy of Sciences
Committee on Women in Science and Engineering
2102 Constitution Avenue, N.W.
Room GR412
Washington, DC 20418
(202) 334-2709

National Network of Minority Women in Science
c/o American Association for the Advancement of Science
Directorate for Education and Human Resources Programs
1333 H Street, N.W.
Washington, DC 20005
(202) 326-6670

New York Academy of Science Women in Science Section
2 E. 63rd Street
New York, NY 10021
(212) 838-0230

SOCIAL WORK

Resources

Association for Women in Social Work
University of Pennsylvania
Women's Center, 119 Houston Hall
3417 Spruce Street
Philadelphia, PA 19104
(215) 898-8611

Women in Community Service
1900 N. Beauregard Street, Suite 103
Alexandria, VA 22311
(703) 671-0500

SPORTS

Resources

International Curling Federation–Ladies Committee
c/o Luella M. Ansorage
4114 N. 53rd Street
Omaha, NE 68104
(402) 453-6574

International Women's Fishing Association
P.O. Drawer 3125
Palm Beach, FL 33480

Ladies Professional Bowlers Tour
7171 Cherryvale Boulevard
Rockford, IL 61112
(815) 332-5756

Ladies Professional Golf Association
2570 West International Speedway Boulevard, Suite B
Daytona, FL 32114
(904) 254-8800

National Association of Collegiate Women Athletic Administrators
c/o Marilyn McNeil
Cal Poly State University
Athletic Department
San Louis Obispo, CA 93407
(805) 756-2923

National Association for Girls and Women in Sport
1900 Association Drive
Reston, VA 22091
(703) 476-3450

National Intercollegiate Women's Fencing Association
3 Derby Lane
Dumont, NJ 07628
(201) 384-1722

North American Network of Women Runners
P.O. Box 719
Bala-Cynwyd, PA 19004
(215) 668-9886

United States Women's Lacrosse Association
45 Maple Avenue
Hamilton, NY 13346
(315) 824-2480

Women's Basketball Coaches Association
4646 B. Lawrenceville Highway
Lilburn, GA 30247
(404) 279-8027

Women's Professional Racquetball Association
153 S. Fifth Street
Souderton, PA 18964
(215) 723-7356

Women's Professional Rodeo Association
Rt. 5, Box 698
Blanchard, OK 73010
(405) 485-2277

Women's Sports Foundation
342 Madison Avenue, Suite 728
New York, NY 10173
(212) 972-9170

Women's Tennis Association
133 1st St. N.E.
St. Petersburg, FL 33701
(813) 895-5000

In the early years of the 1930s depression, women lost their jobs and stayed unemployed at almost twice the rate of men. However, by 1936, while the general unemployment rate still hovered around 20%, only about 10% of women workers reported themselves unemployed.

In 1970, about half of all adult women were earning a paycheck. Today, the figure exceeds two-thirds.

MISCELLANEOUS

Resources

International Association for Personnel Women
P.O. Box 969
Andover, MA 01810
(508) 474-0750

International Federation of Women's Travel Organizations
4545 N. 36th Street, Suite 126
Phoenix, AZ 85018
(602) 596-6640

National Association of Women Highway Safety Leaders
1321 Clara Avenue
Sheboygan, WI 53801
(414) 452-0905

Professional Women's Appraisal Association
8383 E. Evans Road
Scottsdale, AZ 85260
(602) 998-4422

Service Employees International Union
Women's Program
1313 L Street, N.W.
Washington, DC 20005
(202) 898-3410

Society for Women in Plastics
P.O. Box 775
Sterling Heights, MI 48078
(313) 949-0440

Women in Information Processing
Lock Box 39173
Washington, DC 20016
(202) 328-6161

Women in Mining National
1801 Broadway, Suite 400
Denver, CO 80202
(303) 298-1535

Women's Council of Realtors of the National Association of Realtors
430 N. Michigan Avenue
Chicago, IL 60611
(312) 329-8483

ORGANIZATIONS FOR WOMEN IN BUSINESS AND THE PROFESSIONS

National Groups of General Interest

American Business Women's Association
9100 Ward Parkway
P.O. Box 8728
Kansas City, MS 64114
(816) 361-6621

American Woman's Economic Development Corporation
641 Lexington Ave.
New York, NY 10022
(212) 688-1900

American Women in Enterprise
71 Vanderbilt Avenue, 3rd Floor
New York, NY 10169
(212) 692-9100 x18

The Committee of 200
625 N. Michigan Avenue, Suite 500
Chicago, IL 60611
(312) 751-3477

Executive Women International
515 S. 700 East, Suite 2E
Salt Lake City, UT 84102
(801) 355-2800

Federation of Organizations for Professional Women
2001 S Street, N.W., Suite 500
Washington, DC 20009
(202) 328-1415

The International Alliance
8600 LaSalle Road, Suite 617
Baltimore, MD 21286
(410) 472-4221

International Network for Women in Enterprise and Trade
P.O. Box 6178
McLean, VA 22106
(703) 893-8541

Management Training Specialists
550 Bailey, Suite 210
Fort Worth, TX 76107
(817) 332-3612

National Association for Female Executives
127 W. 24th Street, 4th Floor
New York, NY 10011
(212) 645-0770

National Chamber of Commerce for Women
10 Waterside Plaza, Suite 6H
New York, NY 10010
(212) 685-3454

The National Federation of Business and Professional Women's Clubs
2012 Massachusetts Ave., N.W.
Washington, DC 20036
(202) 293-1100
The organization also maintains a nonprofit education and research organization that provides scholarships to businesswomen who want to pursue further education. The foundation can be reached at (202) 293-1200.

National Women's Economic Alliance
1440 New York Avenue, N.W.
Suite 300
Washington, DC 20005
(202) 393-5257

Women in Management
30 North Michigan Avenue, Suite 508
Chicago, IL 60602
(312) 263-3636

National Groups for Women of Color

Latin Business and Professional Women
P.O. Box 45-0913
Miami, FL 33245
(305) 446-9222

National Association of Black Women Entrepreneurs
P.O. Box 1375
Detroit, MI 48231
(313) 559-9255

National Association of Minority Women in Business
906 Grand Avenue, Suite 200
Kansas City, MO 64106
(816) 421-3335

National Association of Negro Business and Professional Women
1806 New Hampshire Avenue, N.W.
Washington, DC 20009
(202) 483-4206

National Association of Professional Asian-American Women
P.O. Box 494
Washington Grove, MD 20880

The National Coalition of 100 Black Women
38 W. 32nd Street, Suite 1610
New York, NY 10001
(212) 947-2196

Organization of Pan Asian American Women
P.O. Box 39128
Washington, DC 20016
(202) 429-6824

Local Groups

Florida

Florida Women's Alliance
404 Ingraham Avenue
Lakeland, FL 33801
(813) 688-4060

Network of Executive Women
P.O. Box 320834
Tampa, FL 33629
(813) 251-9172

Women Business Owners of North Florida
P.O. Box 16445
Jacksonville, FL 32216

Georgia

Atlanta Women's Network
P.O. Box 95293, Executive Park
Atlanta, GA 30347

Black Women Entrepreneurs
2990 Stone Hogan Connection, S.W.
Atlanta, GA 30331
(404) 344-1729

Georgia Executive Women's Network
5108 Victor Trail
Norcross, GA 30071
(404) 840-0039

Louisiana

Capital Area Network
P.O. Box 3935
Baton Rouge, LA 70821
(504) 926-2666

Professional Women's Exchange
P.O. Box 12264
Alexandria, LA 71301
(318) 487-2061

The first woman producer to win an Oscar was Julia Phillips in 1974 for The Sting. The film won seven Oscars.

Professional Women's Network
P.O. Box 12712
Alexandria, LA 71315
(318) 487-8975

Maryland

Washington Alliance of Business Women
Kranton Financial Services
3 Bethesda Metro Center, Suite 900
Bethesda, MD 20814

Massachusetts

The Boston Club
1698 Massachusetts Avenue
Cambridge, MA 02138
(617) 354-4666

New Jersey

Forum of Executive Women
147 Lansdowne Avenue
Haddonsfield, NJ 08033
(609) 428-5105

New York

Financial Women's Association of New York
215 Park Avenue South, Suite 2010
New York, NY 10003
(212) 533-2141

Rochester Women's Network
39 Saginaw Drive
Rochester, NY 14623
(716) 271-4182

Pennsylvania

Philadelphia Women's Network
513 Valmore Road
Fairless Hills, PA 19030
(215) 946-2773

Canada

Referrals
171 Westmoreland Avenue
Toronto, Ontario M6H 3A1
(416) 531-1924

Fast Fact: Business Schools for Women

While some argue that all-women business schools poorly prepare women to participate in the male-dominated arena of business, others say the single-sex environment is more condusive to asking questions and exploring issues. The nation's only two management schools for women:

Simmons Graduate School of Management
409 Commonwealth Avenue
Boston, MA 02215
(617) 536-8390

Smith Management Program
Smith College
Northampton, MA 01063
(413) 585-3060

THE 20 BEST-PAID WOMEN IN CORPORATE AMERICA

1. Turi Josefsen
Executive vice president
U.S. Surgical Corporation, $26.7 million

2. Rena Rowan
Executive vice president, design
Jones Apparel Group, $6.72 million

3. Marion Sandler
Chair and CEO
Golden West Financial Corporation, $6.44 million

4. Sandra Kurtzig†
Chair, ASK Group, $3.6 million

5. Jill Barad
President and COO, Mattel, $3.46 million

6. Linda Wachner
Chair, president, and CEO
Warnaco Group, $3.16 million

7. Sherry Lansing
Chair, Paramount Motion Picture Group, $3 million*

8. Jane Shaw
President and COO, Alza, $2.31 million

9. Lucie Salhaney
Chair, Fox Broadcasting Company, $1.5 million

10. C. F. St. Mark
President, logistics systems and business services
Pitney Bowes, $1.18 million

11. Ellen Gordon
President and COO
Tootsie Roll Industries, $1.09 million

12. Brenda Lynn
Executive vice president, loan production
Plaza Home Mortgage Corporation, $1.03 million

13. Kay Koplovitz
President and CEO, USA Network, $1 million*

14. Babette Heimbuch
President and COO
FirstFed Financial Corporation, $989,161

15. Patricia DeRosa
Executive vice president,
Gap Division, The Gap, $868,191

16. Nina McLemore†
Senior vice president, corporate development
Liz Claiborne, $839,472

17. Carol Bartz
Chair, president, and CEO, Autodesk, $821,042

18. Laurel Cutler
Executive vice president and worldwide director of marketing planning
Foote, Cone & Belding Communications, $779,576

19. Sally Frame Kasaks
Chair and CEO, Ann Taylor, $753,077

20. Carol Bernick
Executive vice president and assistant secretary
Alberto-Culver, $693,494

All figures include salary, bonuses, exercised stock options, and other compensation. Excluded are women in private companies and on Wall Street.

* Estimated
† Left company in 1993

Source: Working Woman, January 1994

Sarah Tilghman Hughes was the first woman federal judge to swear in a U.S. president, in 1963.

In households headed by persons under age 45, more than 75% of wives are working.

SKILLED TRADES AND OTHER MANUAL OCCUPATIONS

•Within the skilled trades, women remain concentrated in a few traditionally female categories such as dressmakers, textile sewing machine operators, and electrical and electronic equipment assemblers.
•Although the presence of women in the skilled trades has not grown recently, these jobs are in many ways more desirable than traditional women's work because they are more likely to command higher wages, provide a wider variety of work schedules, and offer greater benefits and job security than positions in other sectors.

WOMEN IN THE SKILLED TRADES, BY OCCUPATION

	% in 1983	% in 1992
Precision production, craft, repair		
Mechanics and repairers	3.0	3.1
Construction trades	1.8	1.9
Mining and drilling	2.3	0.8
Precision production	21.5	23.7
Operators, fabricators, laborers		
Machine operators, assemblers, and inspectors	42.1	39.7
Transportation and material moving operations	7.8	8.8
Handlers, equipment cleaners, helpers, and laborers	16.8	18.0

Source for above: Department of Labor, Women's Bureau

RECOMMENDED READING

Directory of Non-Traditional Training and Employment Programs Serving Women (Washington, D.C.: U.S. Department of Labor, Women's Bureau, 1991).

APPRENTICESHIP AND JOB TRAINING RESOURCES

Apprenticeship and Nontraditional Employment for Women
P.O. Box 2490
Renton, WA 98056
(206) 235-2212

Boston Tradeswomen Network
P.O. Box 255
Dorchester, MA 02122
(617) 288-3710

Century Freeway Women's Employment Program
2610 Industry Way, Suite B
Lynwood, CA 90262
(213) 639-9181

Chicago Women in the Trades
37 S. Ashland Avenue
Chicago, IL 60607
(312) 942-1444

Cleveland Hard Hatted Women
4209 Lorain Avenue
Cleveland, OH 44113
(216) 961-4449

Coal Employment Project
17 Emory Place
Knoxville, TN 37917
(412) 883-4927

Coalition of Labor Union Women
15 Union Square
New York, NY 10003
(212) 242-0700

Electrical Women's Round Table
P.O. Box 292793
Murfreesboro, TN 37229
(615) 890-1272

enTrade
2830 Ninth Street
Berkeley, CA 94710
(510) 649-6270

Florida Tradeswomen Network
1009 Citrus Isle
Fort Lauderdale, FL 33325
(305) 764-1128

Georgia Women in Trades
6335 Riverdale Road
Riverdale, GA 30274
(404) 997-6881

Kansas City Tradeswomen
4115 Blue Parkway
Kansas City, MO 64130
(816) 831-2719

Milwaukee Women in the Trades
3509 Whitnall Avenue
Milwaukee, WI 53207
(414) 769-8524

Minnesota Women in the Trades
550 Rice Street; Women's Building
St. Paul, MN 55103
(612) 228-9955

National Association of Women in Construction
327 South Adams
Fort Worth, TX 76104
(817) 877-5551

Network of Women in Trade and Technical Jobs
c/o Wentworth Institute
550 Huntington Avenue
Boston, MA 02115

New York Tradeswomen
P.O. Box 870, Peck Slip
New York, NY 10272
(212) 227-2981

Nontraditional Employment for Women
243 W. 20th Street
New York, NY 10011
(212) 627-6252

North East Women in Transportation
c/o Women Unlimited
280 State Street
Augusta, ME 04330
(207) 623-7576

Northern New England Tradeswomen
RR 2 Box 66-17, Emerson Falls
St. Johnsbury, VT 05817
(802) 748-3308

Operating Engineers Women's Support Group
335 Haddon Road
Oakland, CA 94606
Beth at (510) 835-2511, Carla at (510) 636-1134, or Lisa at (510) 769-0340

Professional Women in Construction
342 Madison Avenue, Room 451
New York, NY 10173
(212) 687-0610

Rhode Island Tradeswomen Network
66 Academy Street
Danielson, CT 06239
(203) 774-4731

Rocky Mountain Tradeswomen Network
7270 Wolff
Westminster, CO 80030

Sacramento Tradeswomen
1551 36th Street
Sacramento, CA 95816
(916) 456-5555

TOP/WIN
2300 Alter
Philadelphia, PA 19146
(215) 551-1808

Trade Union Women of African Heritage
530 W. 23rd Street, Suite 4051
New York, NY 10011
(212) 547-5696

Trades Mentor Network
115 Battery Street
Seattle, WA 98121
(206) 461-8408

Tradeswomen
P.O. Box 2622
Berkeley, CA 94710
(510) 649-6160

Wider Opportunities for Women
1325 G Street N.W., Lower Level
Washington, DC 20005
(202) 638-3143

A working woman has a 55% chance of finding romance on the job.

Women & Employment
601 Delaware Avenue
Charleston, WV 25301
(304) 345-1298

Women At Work
78 Marengo Avenue
Pasadena, CA 91101
(818) 796-6870

Women Can/Women Can II
828 South Wabash, Suite 200
Chicago, IL 60605
(312) 922-8530

Women Empowering Women
2830 Ninth Street
Berkeley, CA 94710
(510) 649-6265

Women in Machining
1176 Main Street
Springfield, MA 01103
(413) 781-6900

Women in Nontraditional Occupations
c/o New Haven Women's Center
614 Orange Street
New Haven, CT 06511
(203) 772-2710

Women in Skilled Trades
362 22nd Street
Oakland, CA 94612
(510) 891-9393

Women in the Building Trades
555 Armory Street
Jamaica Plain, MA 02130
(617) 524-3010

Women in the Trades
1044 Mississippi Boulevard
Memphis, TN 38126
(901) 942-4653

Women in Trades and Technology
Hinds Community College
3925 Sunset Drive
Jackson, MS 39213
(601) 366-1405

Women in Trades Fair
700 Third Avenue, Suite 940
Seattle, WA 98104
(206) 684-0390

Women Unlimited
280 State Street
Augusta, ME 04330
(207) 623-7576

Women Working Technical
Bergen County Technical School
280 Hackensack Avenue
Hackensack, NJ 07601
(201) 343-6000, x270

Women's Maritime Association
1916 Pike Place #12, Box 743
Seattle, WA 98101

Women's Project
2224 Main Street
Little Rock, AR 72206
(501) 372-5113

Women's Work
P.O. Box 5852
Tacoma Park, MD 20913
(301) 422-2062

Job Corps Regional Offices

Region I
One Congress Street
Boston, MA 02114
(617) 565-2166

Region II
201 Varick Street
New York, NY 10014
(212) 337-2282

Region III
3535 Market Street
Philadelphia, PA 19104
(215) 596-6301

Region IV
1371 Peachtree Street, N.E.
Atlanta, GA 30367
(404) 347-3178

Region V
230 South Dearborn Street
Chicago, IL 60604
(312) 353-1572

Region VI
525 Griffin Street
Dallas, TX 75202
(214) 767-2567

Region VII
911 Walnut Street
Kansas City, MO 64106
(816) 426-3661

Region VIII
1961 Stout Street
Denver, CO 80294
(303) 844-4807

Region IX
71 Stevenson Street
San Francisco, CA 94105
(415) 744-6658

Region X
1111 Third Avenue
Seattle, WA 98101
(206) 442-1133

Bureau of Apprenticeship and Training Regional Offices

Region I
One Congress Street, 11th Floor
Boston, MA 02114
(617) 565-2288

Region II
Federal Building
201 Varick Street, Room 602
New York, NY 10014
(212) 337-2313

Region III
Gateway Building, Room 13240
3535 Market Street
Philadelphia, PA 19104
(215) 596-6417

Region IV
1371 Peachtree Street, N.E.
Room 418
Atlanta, GA 30367
(404) 347-4405

Region V
230 South Dearborn Street, Room 758
Chicago, IL 60604
(312) 353-7205

Region VI
Federal Building, Room 502
525 Griffin Street
Dallas, TX 75202
(214) 767-4993

Region VII
1100 Federal Office Building
911 Walnut Street
Kansas City, MO 64106
(816) 426-3856

Region VIII
U. S. Custom House
721-19th Street, Room 476
Denver, CO 80202
(303) 844-4791

Region IX
71 Stevenson Street
Federal Building, Room 715
San Francisco, CA 94105
(415) 744-6580

Region X
1111 Third Avenue, Room 925
Seattle, WA 98101
(206) 553-5286

RE-ENTERING THE JOB MARKET—RECOMMENDED READING

Back to Work: How to Re-Enter the Working World, Nancy Schumann and William Lewis (New York: Barron's Educational Series, 1985).

Congratulations! You've Been Fired: Sound Advice for Women Who've Been Terminated, Pink-Slipped, Downsized or Otherwise Unemployed, Emily Koltnow and Lynn S. Dunow (New York: Fawcett/Columbine, 1990).

Re-Entering: Successful Back-to-Work Strategies for Women Seeking a Fresh Start, Eleanor Berman (New York: Crown, 1980).

Returning to the Job Market: A Woman's Guide to Employment Planning (Washington, D.C.: American Association of Retired Persons, 1992).

Working Smart: A Woman's Guide to Starting a Career, Viviana Consoli (Glenview, Ill.: Scott, Foresman & Co., 1987).

Working women who are represented by unions earned 33% more than nonunion workers in 1991.

GENERAL JOB TRAINING AND CAREER COUNSELING

The following organizations offer training and advice across the spectrum of career opportunities and tend to be directed toward entering, or reentering, the workforce. If you have a specific field in mind, many of the industry-specific organizations listed in the Networking section offer programs and training directed toward the development of skills and opportunities particular to careers in those fields.

Private Groups

Black Women in Sisterhood for Action
P.O. Box 1592
Washington, DC 20013
(301) 460-1565

Black Women Organized for Educational Development
518 Seventeenth Street, Suite 202
Oakland, CA 94612
(510) 763-9501

CareerTrack
3080 Center Green Drive
Boulder, CO 80301
(303) 447-2323

Coalition on Women and Job Training
c/o Women Work!
1625 K Street, Suite 300
Washington, DC 20006
(202) 467-6346

Counseling Program
Center for the Education of Women
University of Michigan
330 East Liberty
Ann Arbor, MI 48104
(313) 998-7210

Information and Career Advisory Network (I CAN)
Women's Center
133 Park Street, N.E.
Vienna, VA 22080
(703) 281-2657

National Seminars Group
National Businesswomen's Leadership Association
6901 W. 63rd Street
Shawnee Mission, KS 66202
(913) 432-7755

The Nontraditional Employment Training Project
Wider Opportunities for Women
1325 G Street, N.W., Lower Level
Washington, DC 20005
(202) 638-3143

Women Employed
22 West Monroe, Suite 1400
Chicago, IL 60603
(312) 782-3902

State Employment Service Offices

State employment service offices provide help finding jobs and offer other services such as career counseling.

Alabama: (205) 261-5364
Alaska: (907) 465-2712
Arizona: (602) 542-4016
Arkansas: (501) 371-1683
California: (916) 322-7318
Colorado: (303) 866-6180
Connecticut: (203) 566-8818
Delaware: (302) 368-6911
District of Columbia: (202) 639-1115
Florida: (904) 488-7228
Georgia: (404) 656-0380
Hawaii: (808) 548-6468
Idaho: (208) 334-3977
Illinois: (312) 793-6074
Indiana: (317) 232-7680
Iowa: (515) 281-5134
Kansas: (913) 296-5317
Kentucky: (502) 564-5331
Louisiana: (504) 342-3016
Maine: (207) 289-3431
Maryland: (301) 383-5353
Massachusetts: (617) 727-6810
Michigan: (313) 876-5309
Minnesota: (612) 296-3627
Mississippi: (601) 354-8711
Missouri: (314) 751-3790
Montana: (406) 444-4524
Nebraska: (402) 475-8451
Nevada: (702) 885-4510
New Hampshire: (603) 224-3311
New Jersey: (609) 292-2400
New Mexico: (305) 841-8437

New York: (518) 457-2612
North Carolina: (919) 733-7522
North Dakota: (701) 224-2842
Ohio: (614) 466-2421
Oklahoma: (405) 521-3652
Oregon: (503) 378-3212
Pennsylvania: (717) 787-3354
Puerto Rico: (809) 754-5326
Rhode Island: (401) 277-3722
South Carolina: (803) 737-2400
South Dakota: (605) 773-3101
Tennessee: (615) 741-0922
Texas: (512) 463-2820
Utah: (801) 533-2201
Vermont: (802) 229-0311
Virginia: (804) 786-7097
Virgin Islands: (809) 776-3700
Washington: (206) 753-0747
West Virginia: (304) 348-9180
Wisconsin: (608) 266-8561
Wyoming: (307) 235-3611

WOMEN AND WORK—GENERAL READING

Breaking with Tradition: Women and Work, The New Facts of Life, Felice N. Schwartz (New York: Warner Books, 1992).

Hardball for Women: Winning at the Game of Business, Pat Heim with Susan K. Golant (Los Angeles: Lowell House, 1992).

The Minority Career Guide, Michael F. Kastre, Nydia Rodriguez Kastre, and Alfred G. Edwards (Princeton, N.J.: Peterson's, 1993).

The Smart Woman's Guide to Career Success, Janet Harter (Hawthorne, N.J.: Career Press, 1993).

The Smart Woman's Guide to Interviewing and Salary Negotiations, Julie Adair King (Hawthorne, N.J.: Career Press, 1993).

The Smart Woman's Guide to Resumes and Job Hunting, Julie Adair King and Betsy Sheldon (Hawthorne, N.J.: Career Press, 1993).

What Color Is Your Parachute?, Richard Nelson Bolles (Berkeley, Calif.: Ten Speed Press, 1994).

What Mona Lisa Knew: A Woman's Guide to Getting Ahead in Business by Lightening Up, Barbara Mackoff (Los Angeles: Lowell House, 1990).

When Can You Start? The Complete Job Search Guide for Women of All Ages, the staff of Catalyst (New York: Macmillan, 1981).

The Women's Job Search Handbook, Gerri Bloomberg and Margaret Holden (Charlotte, Vt.: Williamson, 1991).

Work of Her Own: How Women Create Success and Fufillment Off the Traditional Career Track, Susan Wittig Albert (New York: G.P. Putnam's, 1992).

Work, Sister, Work: How Black Women Can Get Ahead in Today's Business Environment, Cydney Shields and Leslie C. Shields (New York: Fireside, 1994).

Burnita S. Matthews was the first woman to serve as a federal district judge, in 1949. Matthews was appointed by President Harry S. Truman and presided over the 1957 bribery trial of teamster union chief Jimmy Hoffa.

The Tony Award is named after Antoinette Perry, an actress and theatrical director. Formally known as the American Theatre Wing Institute Antionette Perry Award, it is the first award named after a woman.

CHILD CARE
CHILD CARE
CHILD CARE

CHILD CARE

CHILD CARE
CHILD CARE
CHILD CARE
CHILD CARE
CHILD CARE
CHILD CARE
CHILD CARE
CHILD CARE
CHILD CARE
CHILD CARE
CHILD CARE
CHILD CARE
CHILD CARE
CHILD CARE
CHILD CARE
CHILD CARE

THE FAMILY AND MEDICAL LEAVE ACT

Over the past 25 years the American family and workforce have undergone dramatic changes. First, changing cultural standards have resulted in large numbers of women entering the workforce. Second, the rising cost of living has made two incomes a necessity in many areas of the country. (Also, the number of single-parent families is rapidly growing.) Finally, with America's aging population, more workers are finding the need to take time off from work to attend to the medical needs of elderly parents.

With these new demands comes a growing conflict that forces many to choose between job security and family responsibilities. The landmark Family and Medical Leave Act of 1993 provides the American worker with a right to take unpaid, job-protected leave for meeting family health needs and for the worker's own illness. Employee rights include:

- Workers who have been employed for one year and have worked at least 1,250 hours (a minimum of 25 hours a week) can take up to 12 weeks of unpaid leave in any 12-month period for the birth or adoption of a child; acquiring a foster child; the serious illness of a child, spouse, or parent; and the serious illness of the employee.
- The right to take leave applies equally to male and female workers who are employed by a company with 50 or more workers.
- Leave can be taken intermittently or on a schedule that reduces the usual number of hours per workday or workweek, to care for a child, spouse, or parent, or because of the employee's illness. Intermittent or reduced leave schedules because of the birth of a child, adoption, or foster care are subject to employer approval.
- The employer maintains any preexisting health insurance for the duration of the leave and at the level and under the same conditions coverage was provided prior to commencement of the leave.
- The employee must be restored to the original or an equivalent position with equivalent benefits, pay, and all other terms and conditions of employment.

For information on additional requirements and exclusions, contact your regional branch of the Department of Labor's Women's Bureau (see pp.57–9).

For information about enforcement of the Family and Medical Leave Act, or to file a complaint about a violation, contact:

Wage and Hour Division, Employment Standards Administration.
Department of Labor
200 Constitution Avenue
Washington, DC 20210
(202) 219-8305

Source: Women's Bureau, Department of Labor

Mother's Day was started in 1907 by Anna Jarvis.

STATES AND JURISDICTIONS WITH FAMILY LEAVE LAWS

Child care tops the list of special help sought by employees who transfer from one job to another; 16% ask for it, compared with 14% who want help finding schools and 13% seeking a new job for their spouse.

Although all states are governed at a minimum by the requirements of the federal Family and Medical Leave Act, most states also have their own laws, some of which provide greater benefits than federal law. This map shows which states have their own laws, and who they cover. The table that follows shows specific requirements under various state laws. (The 16 states that have no additional laws governing family and medical leave are not included here.)

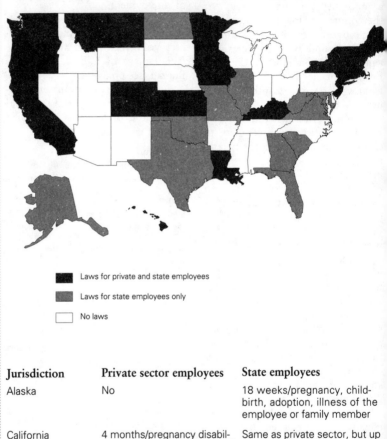

Laws for private and state employees

Laws for state employees only

No laws

Jurisdiction	Private sector employees	State employees
Alaska	No	18 weeks/pregnancy, childbirth, adoption, illness of the employee or family member
California	4 months/pregnancy disability, childbirth, adoption, illness of family member	Same as private sector, but up to 1 year/pregnancy, childbirth, adoption
Colorado	Reasonable period/pregnancy, childbirth, adoption	Same as private sector

Jurisdiction	Private sector employees	State employees
Connecticut	16 weeks/childbirth, adoption, foster care, illness of the employee or family member; "reasonable leave of absence"/pregnancy disability	24 weeks/childbirth, adoption, illness of the employee or family member; "reasonable period"/disability resulting from pregnancy, childbirth
Delaware	No	6 weeks/adoption
District of Columbia	16 weeks/childbirth, adoption, foster care, illness of the employee, family member, or person sharing mutual residence and committed relationship	Same as private sector
Florida	No	6 months/childbirth, adoption, illness of family member
Georgia	No	12 weeks/childbirth, adoption, serious health condition of the employee or family member
Hawaii	4 weeks/childbirth, adoption, illness of family member, "reasonable period"/ disability resulting from pregnancy, childbirth	Same as private sector
Illinois	No	1 year/childbirth, adoption, illness of family member or household resident
Iowa	8 weeks/disability resulting from pregnancy, childbirth	Same as private sector, plus accrued sick leave for disability resulting from pregnancy, childbirth
Kansas	Reasonable period/ disability resulting from pregnancy, childbirth	Same as private sector
Kentucky	6 weeks/adoption	Same as private sector
Louisiana	4 months/disability resulting from pregnancy, childbirth; 6 weeks/normal pregnancy, childbirth	Same as private sector
Maine	10 weeks/childbirth, adoption, illness of the employee or family membe	Same as private sector

7% of childcare applicants submitted to Trustline, a state background-check service in California, have flunked.

75% of women with children over six years old have jobs.

Jurisdiction	Private sector employeesr	State employees
Maryland	No	12 weeks/childbirth, adoption, acquiring a foster child, illness of family member or legal dependent, or to care for a child under 14 during school vacation
Massachusetts	8 weeks/childbirth, adoption	Same as private sector
Minnesota	6 weeks/childbirth, adoption; same sick leave terms for employee illness apply to leave for the illness of a child; 16 hours/school conferences or classroom activities related to an employee's child	Same as private sector
Missouri	No	No leave required; however, if an employer permits leave for childbirth, adoptive parents entitled to the same
Montana	Reasonable period/ pregnancy and paid pregnancy disability	Same as private sector, plus sick leave for illness of the employee or family member, and 15 days of paid sick leave following childbirth, adoption
New Hampshire	Unspecified period (based on doctor's certification)/ disability resulting from pregnancy or childbirth	Same as private sector
New Jersey	12 weeks/childbirth, adoption, illness of family member	Same as private sector
New York	No leave required; however, if an employer permits leave for childbirth, adoptive parents entitled to same	Same as private sector
North Dakota	No	2 or 4 months (depends on eligibility)/childbirth, adoption, illness of family member
Oklahoma	No	12 weeks/pregnancy, childbirth, adoption, illness of a child or legal dependent

Jurisdiction	Private sector employees	State employees
Oregon	12 weeks/childbirth, adoption, illness of family member; reasonable period/pregnancy, pregnancy disability	Same as private sector
Puerto Rico	8 weeks/pregnancy, childbirth (4 weeks preceding and 4 weeks after childbirth; 12 additional weeks for postnatal complications after the 4-week period from the date of childbirth)	Same as private sector
Rhode Island	13 weeks/childbirth, adoption, illness of the employee or family member	Same as private sector
South Carolina	No	6 months/pregnancy, disability due to maternity, illness of the employee; 6 weeks/adoption; 8 days/illness of a family member
Tennessee	4 months/pregnancy, childbirth	Same as private sector, plus 30 days/adoption
Texas	No	6 weeks of any combination of accrued paid leave and leave without pay/normal childbirth, adoption; accrued paid sick leave balance/pregnancy that prevents employee from performing duties, or for the illness of the employee or family member
Vermont	12 weeks childbirth, adoption, serious illness of the employee or family member	Same as private sector
Virginia	No	6 weeks/childbirth, adoption
Washington	12 weeks/childbirth, adoption, terminal illness of child	Same as private sector
West Virginia	No	12 weeks/childbirth, adoption, illness of family member or dependent
Wisconsin	6 weeks/childbirth, adoption; 2 weeks/illness of the employee; 2 weeks/illness of family member, legal dependent; no more than 10 weeks for any combination of leave	Same as private sector

"Ask your child what he wants for dinner only if he's buying."—Fran Lebowitz

Up until 1900, less than 20% of all women over 14 were in the paid labor force at any one time.

Less than 2% of private sector companies and 9% of government agencies offer employer-sponsored day-care.

In Japan, the law guarantees unpaid child-care leave of up to one year for working parents of both sexes.

TEMPORARY DISABILITY INSURANCE FOR FAMILY LEAVE

These jurisdictions have temporary-disability-insurance laws that provide partial salary replacement for non-work-related disabilities, including childbirth and pregnancy-related conditions.

Jurisdiction	Amount of benefits
California	Minimum of $50; maximum $336/week, based on schedule
Hawaii	58% of average weekly wage; maximum set each year ($323 in 1993)
New Jersey	2/3 average weekly wage; maximum $304
New York	50% of weekly wage; maximum $170
Puerto Rico	65% of average weekly wage; maximum $113, minimum $12
Rhode Island	4.2% of total wages in one quarter; maximum $374 plus dependant allowance

Source: Women's Bureau, Department of Labor

FEDERAL PROGRAMS TO ASSIST FAMILIES WITH DEPENDENT CARE NEEDS

Child Care and Development Block Grants provide support to families through federal funding to states, Native American tribes, and territories. To qualify, individuals must be working or attending job-training or educational programs, have a child under age 13, and have a total family income of less than 75% of the state's median income for a family of the same size.

The At-Risk Child Care Program is designed to provide childcare assistance to low-income working families who are at risk of becoming welfare recipients in the absence of financial assistance for child care. The program is administered by states, and families must contribute to the cost of care based on a sliding fee scale developed by the state.

The Child and Dependent Care Tax Credit is available to all families who incur dependent care expenses while working, looking for work, or attending school full-time, regardless of the gross income of the family. To qualify, parents must have a child under 13 living at home.

Earned Income Credit is a cash refund available to employees with earned incomes of less than $23,050 in 1993 dollars and dependents under age 19 (or 24 if they are in school full-time). There is no age requirement for dependents who are permanently and totally disabled.

The Family and Medical Leave Act provides employees with up to 12 weeks per year of unpaid leave for childcare. For details see Family and Medical Leave Act, p. 135.

Source: Business and Professional Women's Foundation

FLEXIBLE TIME AND LEAVE BENEFITS

This study found no differences by gender, age, or dependent care responsibilities in the benefits granted to workers. Instead, benefits offered are largely dependent on income.

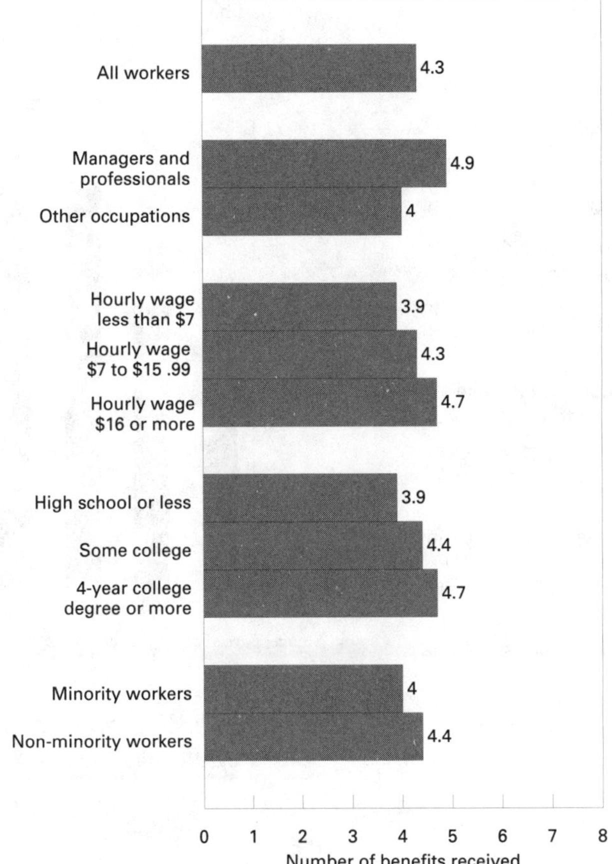

Source: Families and Work Institute, 1993

Pregnant employees who work for family-responsive companies are more satisfied with their jobs (73% as opposed to 41%), feel sick less often, miss less work (2.1 days as compared to 3.4), spend more uncompensated time working, work later in their pregnancies, and are more likely to return to their jobs, according to studies.

Pope John Paul II issued an apostolic letter in November of 1988 titled "On the Dignity of Women;" in it he defined a woman's role in the church and society as two vocations: "virginity and motherhood."

Women employed full-time outside the home do 70% of the housework; full-time housewives do 83%.

LEAVE AND BENEFITS—RESOURCES

Leave Policies

Association of Junior Leagues
660 First Avenue
New York, NY 10016
(212) 683-1515

Institute for Women's Policy Research
1400 Twentieth Street, N.W., Suite 104
Washington, DC 20036
(202) 785-5100

International Foundation on Employee Benefit Plans
P.O. Box 69
Brookfield, WI 53008
(414) 786-6700

National Council of Jewish Women
53 West 23rd Street, 6th Floor
New York, NY 10010
(212) 645-4048

Benefits

Employee Benefit Research Institute
2121 K Street, N.W., Suite 600
Washington, DC 20037
(202) 775-6356

Employers Council on Flexible Compensation
927 Fifteenth Street, N.W., Suite 1000
Washington, DC 20005
(202) 659-4300

MOTHERS IN THE WORKPLACE

Mothers Working within a Year of Childbirth
This graph shows the percentage of women in the workforce aged 18–44 who had had a child within a year of the survey.

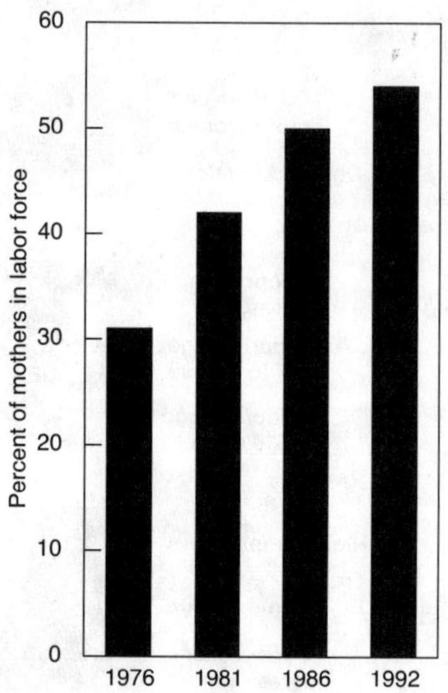

Source: Bureau of the Census, 1992

Fast Fact: Working Women and Dependent Care

Today, the typical woman can expect to spend 17 years caring for children and 18 years caring for older family members. Nine out of 10 women will be caregivers of children or parents or both. The majority of these women will also be employed, and their employment decisions will be influenced and altered by the availability and affordability of dependent care options.

Source: Business and Professional Women's Foundation

EDUCATION LEVELS OF WORKING MOTHERS

This graph shows the education levels of women aged 15–44 who have given birth in the last year and reentered the labor force.

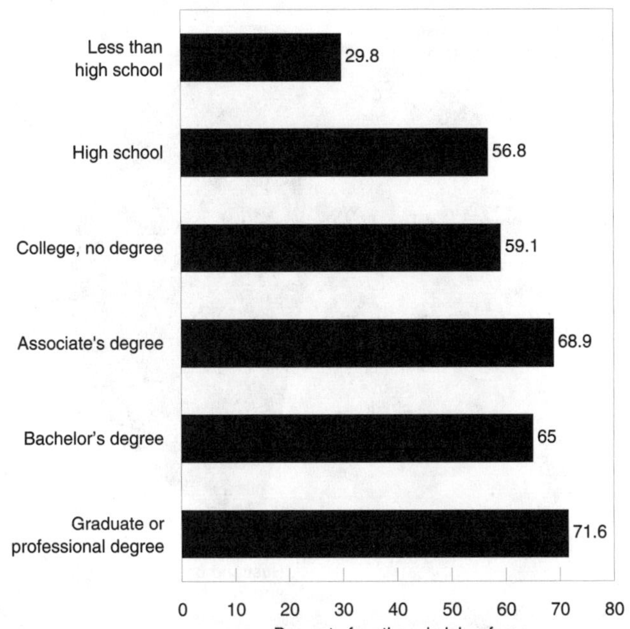

(Data from July 1991–June 1992)
Source: Fertility Statistics Branch, Bureau of the Census, 1992

Felice Schwartz's famous "Mommy Track" article appeared in *The Harvard Business Review* in January of 1989.

"Whenever I date a guy, I think, is this the man I want my children to spend their weekends with?"—Rita Rudner, stand-up comic

SIX RULES FOR MAKING THE MOMMY TRACK WORK

1. Define your objectives. Decide what you're willing to do, what kind of career path you want, and what kind of salary you'll take.
2. Older is better. The further along in your career you are, the more likely it is that you will be in a position to negotiate the terms of a new job, or of your cutback and eventual reentry.
3. Find family-friendly supervisors and companies. A recent Families and Work Institute study of supervisors at a large high-tech company found that the supervisors who had problems with parental-leave plans and productivity after the leave were those who were unsupportive of work/family options. (Not surprisingly, most of the supervisors with supportive attitudes were female.)
4. Have a plan. Do your homework; offer a specific proposal. Look for departments that are cutting back and say, "I can do this job in less time if you move me into the position part-time." Consider telecommuting, a compressed workweek, or job sharing. Is there a lateral move you can make that offers more flexibility?
5. Use the track as a career experiment. Many successful women look back and realize that their mommy-track years gave them a badly needed chance to take stock of long-held professional goals and then change direction.
6. Don't stay away too long. Most women who have achieved a high level of competence say that up to two years is a manageable absence—especially if you keep in touch with your former colleagues or network within the industry.

Source: Barbara Kantrowitz and Pat Wingert, Working Mother (February 1993), reprinted by permission

WORKING MOTHERS ON THE RISE

Fathers' behavior toward their children is linked to the way they themselves are treated on the job, according to a University of Illinois study.

These two charts show the shift in two-parent family employment patterns over the last 20 years.

June 1992

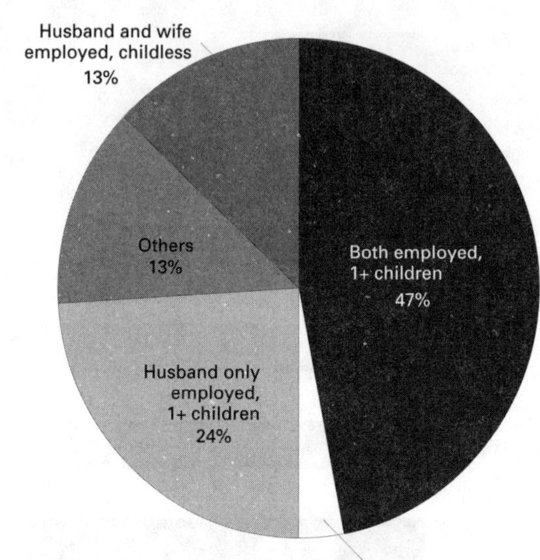

"Parenthood: that state of being better chaperoned than you were before marriage."—Marcelene Cox

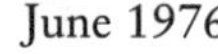
June 1976

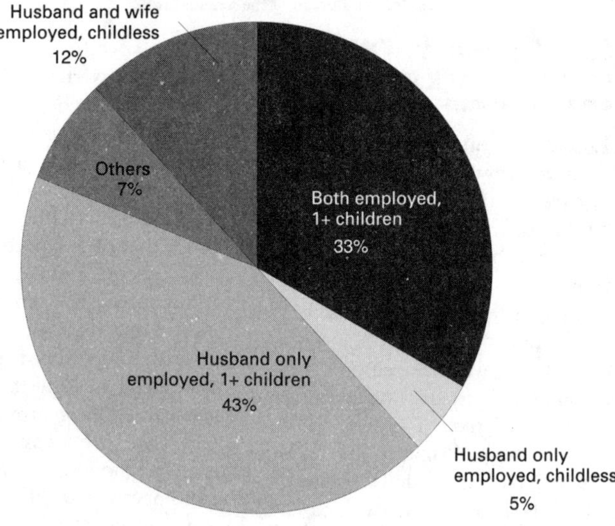

Source: Bureau of the Census

MOTHERS AND JOB SHIFTS

Mothers who work for flexible bosses are more than seven times less likely to want to quit and nearly four times as likely to say they love their jobs than mothers who work for inflexible bosses.

Reasons Mothers Take a Job Shift

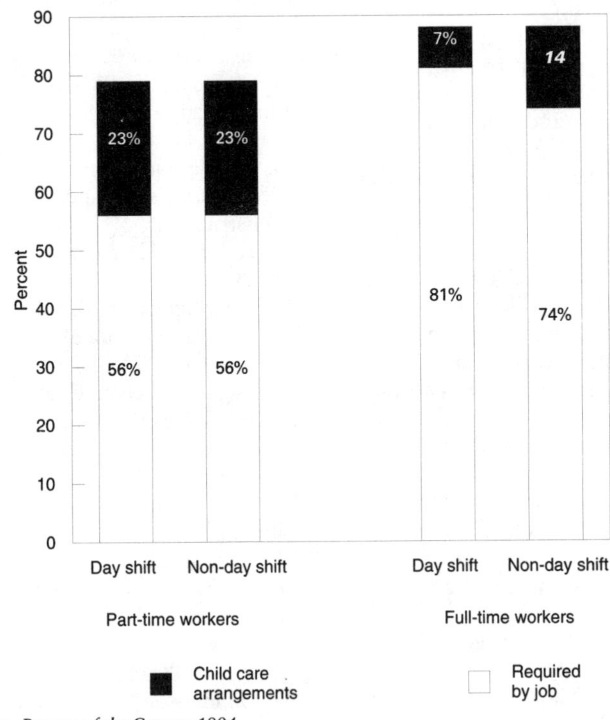

Source: Bureau of the Census, 1994

Work Shifts among Mothers

This graph compares the work schedules of the principal jobs held by employed mothers with children under 15.

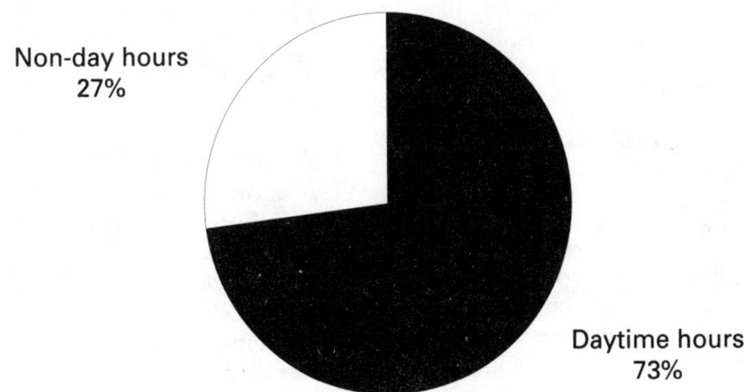

Source: Bureau of the Census, 1991

Laws in Virginia, Florida, North Carolina, and New York guarantee women the right to breast-feed in public.

Of the nation's 6 million employers, 5,600 provided some form of child care assistance in 1992.

UNICEF'S MOTHER-FRIENDLY WORKPLACES

UNICEF has identified a number of businesses whose work environments encourage and promote mother-friendly policies. The following companies, large and small, offer such incentives as private rooms for breast-feeding, lactation counselors, on-site infant care, and flexible hours.

Aerospace Corporation, El Segundo, California
Aid Association for Lutherans, Milwaukee, Wisconsin
American Academy of Pediatrics, Chicago
Amoco Corporation, Chicago
Aveda Corporation, Minneapolis
Essence Magazine, New York
First National Bank of Chicago
John Hancock Mutual Life Insurance Company, Boston
Kinder, Lydenberg, Domini, & Company, Cambridge, Massachusetts
KPMG Peat Marwick, Los Angeles
Los Angeles Department of Water and Power
NCR Corporation, Dayton, Ohio
The Partnership Group, Philadelphia
Patagonia, Ventura, California
White Dog Cafe, Philadelphia
Work/Family Directions, Boston

Source: UNICEF

WORKING MOTHER'S HUNDRED BEST PLACES TO WORK

This list, created by Working Mother magazine, is based on pay, opportunities for advancement, child care, and family-friendly benefits. Starred companies are among the ten best employers for working mothers.

Aetna Life & Casualty
Allstate Insurance
American Airlines
*American Telephone & Telegraph
Amoco Corporation
Arthur Andersen & Company
Baptist Hospital of Miami
*Barnett Banks
Bausch & Lomb
Baxter International
BE&K Engineering and Construction
Ben & Jerry's Homemade
Beth Israel Hospital (Boston)
Bright Horizons Children's Center
The Bureau of National Affairs
Leo Burnett U.S.A.
Burroughs Wellcome Company
Calvert Group
Champion International Corporation
Cigna Companies
Citibank
CMP Publications
Colgate-Palmolive Company
Consolidated Edison Company of New York
*Corning Incorporated
Dayton Hudson Corporation
Dow Chemical
DuPont
Eastman Kodak
Exxon
Fannie Mae (Federal National Mortgage Association)
*Fel-Pro Incorporated
Frontier Cooperative Herbs
G.T. Water Products
Gannett Company
*Glaxo
Hallmark Cards
Hanna Andersson
Helene Curtis
Hewitt Associates
Hewlett-Packard Company
Hoechst Celanese
Hoffmann–La Roche
Home Box Office
Honeywell
Household International
*International Business Machines Corporation

John Hancock Mutual Life Insurance Company
*Johnson & Johnson
SC Johnson Wax
Lancaster Laboratories
Levi Strauss & Company
Lincoln National Corporation
Lotus Development Corporation
LucasArts Entertainment Company
Lutheran General Hospital (Park Ridge, Illinois)
Marquette Electronics
Marriott Corporation
Mattel Toys
MBNA America Bank
Mentor Graphics Corporation
Merck & Company
3M (Minnesota Mining and Manufacturing)
Morrison & Foerster
Motorola
Mutual of New York
*NationsBank Corporation
Neuville Industries
Nike
Northern States Power Company
Northern Trust Corporation
NYNEX
Official Airline Guides
Patagonia
Phoenix Home Life Mutual Insurance Company
Pitney Bowes
Polaroid Corporation
The Prudential Insurance Company of America
Quad/Graphics
The Quaker Oats Company
Riverside Methodist Hospital (Columbus, Ohio)
*The St. Paul Companies
The St. Petersburg Times
SAS Institute
Schering-Plough Corporation
The Seattle Times Company
Silicon Graphics
Syntex Corporation
Tom's of Maine
Toyota Motor Manufacturing, U.S.A.
The Travelers
United States Hosiery Corporation
United Technologies
UNUM Life Insurance
The USA Group
US West
Wegmans Food Markets
Work/Family Directions
*Xerox Corporation

Source: © Milton Moskowitz and Carol Townsend, Working Mother magazine (Oct. 1993); reprinted with permission

FATHER-FRIENDLY COMPANIES

Child magazine and the Families and Work Institute have identified ten companies that have made a significant effort to support paternity leave, childbirth training for fathers, flexible and comprehensive on-site day care, and other father-friendly policies. The ten best are:

American Telephone & Telegraph
Apple Computer
Ben & Jerry's Homemade
DuPont
Eastman Kodak
John Hancock Financial Services
Los Angeles Department of Water and Power
Peabody & Arnold
Sacramento County Sheriff's Department
Tom's of Maine

Source: Child magazine and the Fatherhood Project of the Families and Work Institute

FLEXIBLE WORK SCHEDULES—RESOURCES

Association of Part-Time Professionals
Crescent Plaza, Suite 216
7700 Leesburg Pike
Falls Church, VA 22043
(703) 734-7975

New Ways to Work
149 Ninth Street
San Francisco, CA 94103
(415) 552-1000

Work in America Institute of Scarsdale
700 White Plains Road
Scarsdale, NY 10583
(914) 472-9600

Only 13% of all Russian women of childbearing age use contraceptives, as opposed to 50 to 60% in most other countries.

FAMILY LIFE: WHO DOES WHAT IN TWO-WAGE FAMILIES?

Two-thirds of all mothers employed full-time would like to work fewer hours so that they can devote more time to their families, says a 1987 Cornell study.

This table lists the average hours men vs. women devote to household chores and child care when both parties are wage earners with family responsibilities.

Workdays, hours devoted to	No children		Children	
	Female	Male	Female	Male
Chores	2.41	1.73	2.60	2.00
Children	—	—	3.75	2.59
Days off, hours devoted to				
Chores	5.31	4.39	5.36	4.67
Children	—	—	9.20	7.01

Source: Families and Work Institute, 1993

FATHERS AS DAYCARE PROVIDERS FOR PRESCHOOLERS

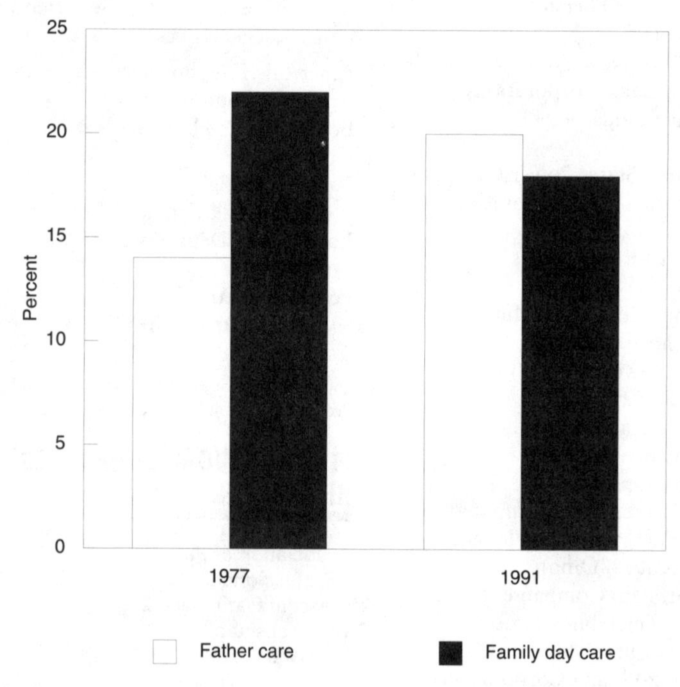

Source: Bureau of the Census, 1994

RESOURCES FOR PARENTS

Parent Action
2 North Charles Street, Suite 960
Baltimore, MD 21202
(410) 727-3687
(National membership organization that represents and supports the concerns of parents)

Parents' Agenda
Child Care Action Campaign
330 Seventh Avenue, 17th Floor
New York, NY 10001
(212) 239-0138

WORK AND FAMILY—RESOURCES

Administration for Children, Youth and Families
U.S. Department. of Health and Human Services
200 Independence Avenue, S.W.
Suite 600
Washington, DC 20201
(202) 401-9200

Business and Professional Women's Foundation
2012 Massachusetts Avenue, N.W.
Washington, DC 20036
(202) 293-1200

Center on Work and Family
Boston University
1 University Road
Boston, MA 02215
(617) 353-7225

Child Care Action Campaign
330 Seventh Avenue, 17th Floor
New York, NY 10001
(212) 239-0138

The Conference Board
Work and Family Information Center
845 Third Avenue
New York, NY 10022
(212) 759-0900

Families and Work Institute
330 Seventh Avenue
New York, NY 10001
(212) 465-2044

Family Resource Coalition
200 S. Michigan Avenue, Suite 1520
Chicago, IL 60604
(312) 341-0900

Mothers on the Move, An Alliance of Entrepreneurial Mothers
P.O. Box 64033
Tucson, AZ 85728
(602) 628-2598

NOW Legal Defense and Education Fund
99 Hudson Street, 12th Floor
New York, NY 10013
(212) 925-6635

Work and Family Clearinghouse
Women's Bureau
U.S. Department of Labor
200 Constitution Avenue, N.W.
Washington, DC 20210
(800) 827-5335

Working Woman
230 Park Avenue, 7th Floor
New York, NY 10169
(800) 234-9675

Zero to Three
2000 Fourteenth Street North,
Suite 380
Arlington, VA 22201
(703) 528-4300

FATHERS AND CHILD CARE

•Only 15% of children under age 5 in 1988 were cared for by their fathers while their mothers worked outside the home. By 1991, however, that figure rose to 20%.
•Fifty-six percent of preschoolers with jobless fathers are cared for by their fathers, as are 20% of kids whose fathers work full-time.
•Two percent of black preschoolers, 9% of white preschoolers, and 10% of Hispanic preschoolers in single-parent homes are cared for by their fathers while their mothers work.

Source: Bureau of the Census

Federal funding for maternal and child health has decreased 23.4% in the past 10 years.

82% of American women give the federal government a grade of C or lower for passing laws that protect and help mothers and families; 28% say the government scores an F.

MARIAN WRIGHT EDELMAN— VIOLENCE AND AMERICA'S CHILDREN

Marian Wright Edelman is the president of the Children's Defense Fund, a private nonprofit organization devoted to the support of children and their needs. This essay was written as the introduction to CDF's publication The State of America's Children Yearbook, 1994.

The ugly, malignant tumor of violence devouring American communities has spread to younger and younger children. The murder of babies and young children has become routine not only in Bosnia but in Boston and Baltimore. Twenty-five American children—the equivalent of a classroomful—are killed by guns every two days in our spiritually sick nation.

Escalating violence against and by children and youth is no longer coincidence. It is the cumulative, convergent, and heightened manisfestation of a range of serious and too long neglected problems. Epidemic child and family poverty, increasing economic inequality, racial intolerance and hate crimes; pervasive drug and alcohol abuse and violence in our homes and popular culture; and growing numbers of out-of-wedlock births and divorces have all contributed to the disintegration of the family, community, spiritual values, and supports all children need. Add to these crises easy access to deadlier and deadlier firearms; hordes of lonely and neglected children and youths left to fend for themselves by absentee parents in all race and income groups; gangs of inner-city and minority groups relegated to the cellar of American life without education, jobs or hope; and political leadership over the 1980s that paid more attention to foreign than domestic enemies and to the rich than the poor, and you face the social and spiritual disintegration of American society that confronts us today.

Never before has our country seen or permitted the epidemic of gun death and violence that is turning our communities into fearful armed camps and sapping the lives and hopes of our children. Never have we seen such a dangerous domestic arms race.

Never has America permitted children to rely on guns and gangs rather than parents and neighbors for protection and love, or pushed so many onto the tumultuous sea of life without life vests of nurturing families and communities, challenged minds, job prospects, and hope.

Never have we exposed children so early and relentlessly to cultural messages glamorizing violence, sex, possessions, alcohol, and tobacco with so few mediating influences from responsible adults. Never have we let children grow up listening to violent rap instead of nursery rhymes, worrying about guns and drugs rather than grades and dates, and dodging bullets instead of balls.

Robert Kennedy asked why "we seemingly tolerate a rising level of violence that ignores our common humanity and our claims to civilization alike. We calmly accept," he said, "newspaper reports of civilian slaughter in far-off lands. We glorify killing on movie and television screens and call it entertainment. We make it easy for men of all shades of sanity to acquire whatever weapons and ammunition they desire.... Some Americans," he continued, "who preach nonviolence abroad fail to practice it here at home. Some who accuse others of inciting riots have by their own conduct incited them. Some look for scapegoats, others look for conspiracies, but this much is clear: violence breeds violence, repression brings retaliation, and only a cleansing of our whole society can remove this sickness from our soul."

We did not heed him then. Instead we tolerated the violent deaths of over a million and a quarter fellow citizens in a silent American holocaust. Will we heed him now and give our children back their childhoods, safety, and futures, their sense of security and hope, their ability to trust adults to protect, guide, love, and value them? Will we stop the domestic and global arms race and teach our children that power means character and service and the peaceful rather than violent resolution of conflict? Will we rebuild our families, reinvest in our communities, and give every American a healthy start, a fair start, and a safe start? Will we fundamentally change our personal and national priorities? Will America's dream die on your and my watch?

The first step toward change is to recognize that there is no easy, single, or quick solution to the gun violence, family disintegration, poverty, and racism we have permitted to cumulate, escalate, permeate, and imprison our culture and national life over many years. But there are achievable solutions that will require simultaneous and sustained personal, collective, and private- and public-sector leadership. America is fighting a potentially fatal sickness whose cure requires the intensive care of every American—president, parent, youth, professional, and citizen alike. Together we must counter the cultural cacophony of racism, greed, selfishness, and gun violence, and rebuild our frayed family, community, and economic life. Business as usual won't do any more than marginal or cosmetic political gestures will.

Adults must stop our hypocrisy and break the code of silence about the breakdown of spiritual values and parental and community responsibility for our children. I believe adults have no right to ask children to do what we are not doing or to assume sole or primary responsibility for problems we adults have created. It is adults who have taught children to look for meaning outside rather than inside themselves, taking them, in Dr. King's words, "to judge success by the index of our salaries or the size of our automobiles, rather than by the quality of our service and relationship to humanity."

And it is adults who have to stand up and be adults and accept our responsibility to morally guide, parent, protect, and invest in the young. Recognize that it is the most important calling you have. What you do every day, what you say, and how you act will do more to shape the future of America than any other factor.

The most important step each of us can take to end the violence that is tearing our country apart is to change our selves, our hearts, our personal priorities, and our neglect of any of God's children, and add our voice to those of others in a new movement that is bigger than our individual efforts to put the social and economic underpinnings under all American children.

Do not be overwhelmed or give up because problems seem so hard or intractable. Millions of children are still beating the odds every day and staying in school and becoming law-abiding citizens despite the violence and poverty and drugs and family decay all around them. And so you and I can keep on keeping on until we change the odds for all American children by making the violence of guns, poverty, preventable disease, and family neglect un-American.

"Being a mother is a noble status, right? Right. So why does it change when you put 'unwed' or 'welfare' in front of it?"—Florynce Kennedy, civil rights lawyer

Several new Barbie computer games were released in 1994, including one in which the character must find her way through a mall to meet Ken for a date, another in which she searches for "fashion treasures" to wear to the Fantasy Ball, and a third in which she aspires to become the hottest supermodel.

CHILD-CARE ARRANGEMENTS

Child-Care Choices for Single and Married Mothers

This chart shows the range of child-care options chosen by both single and married working women for children up to age 14 (including preschoolers). Percentages do not add up to 100% because the figures include child-care options for a range of ages and not all apply for all children.

Child Care Method	% married couples	% single mothers
Care in child's or another's home	19.8	15.1
By father	13.3	2.2
By grandparent	5.8	10.1
By other relative	3.6	7.4
By non-relative	8.6	11.2
Organized child-care facilities	8.9	8.1
Child/group care center	6.2	5.5
Nursery school/preschool	2.7	2.6
Kindergarten/grade school	54.7	55.4
Child cares for self	1.4	3.7
Mother cares for child at work	5.0	1.0
Other arrangements	0.5	0.7

Source: Bureau of the Census

Family Income Spent on Child Care

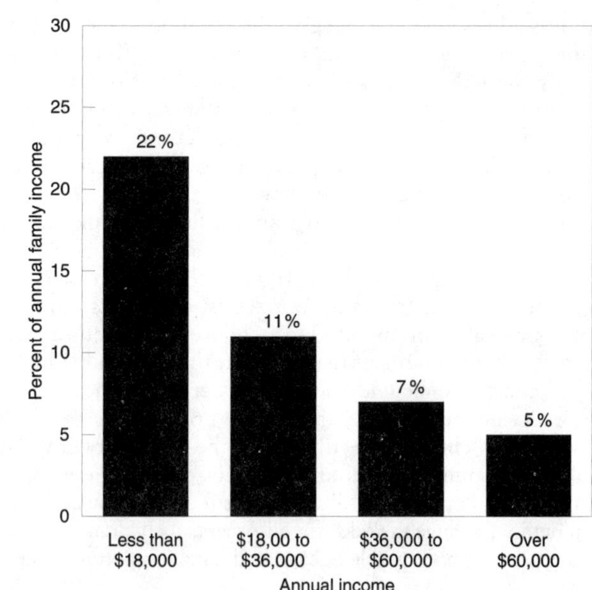

Source: Bureau of the Census, 1991

CHILD CARE AND POVERTY

This graph shows the percentage of income spent on child care by families below the poverty line, as opposed to those above.

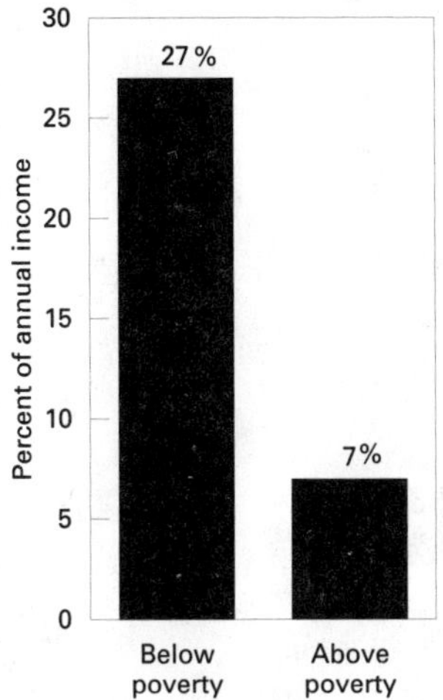

Source: Bureau of the Census, 1991

LATCH-KEY KIDS

Age of Children in Self-Care

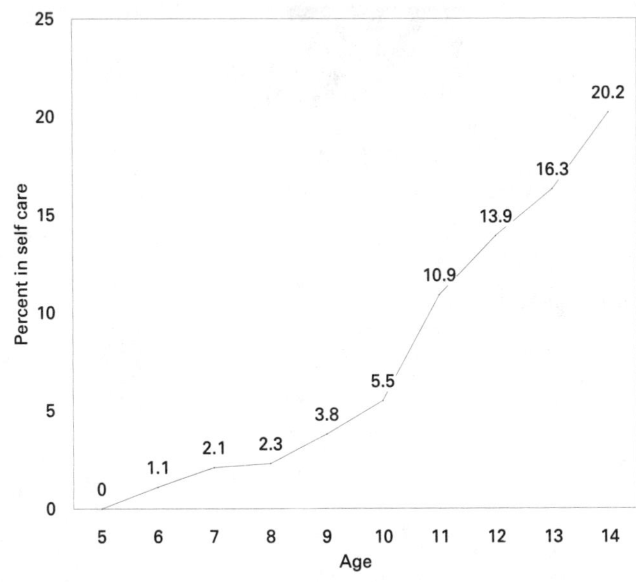

(Data from 1991)

The average number of children in an American family is 2.2, while the average number of children in a family on welfare is 1.9, according to the Coalition for the Homeless.

82% of the American public believes that it is best for young children to be cared for by one or both parents or by extended family members.

Who Leaves Their Kids the Keys?
This graph shows the percentage of children reported to be in self-care while their mothers are at work, broken down by characteristics of family or mother.

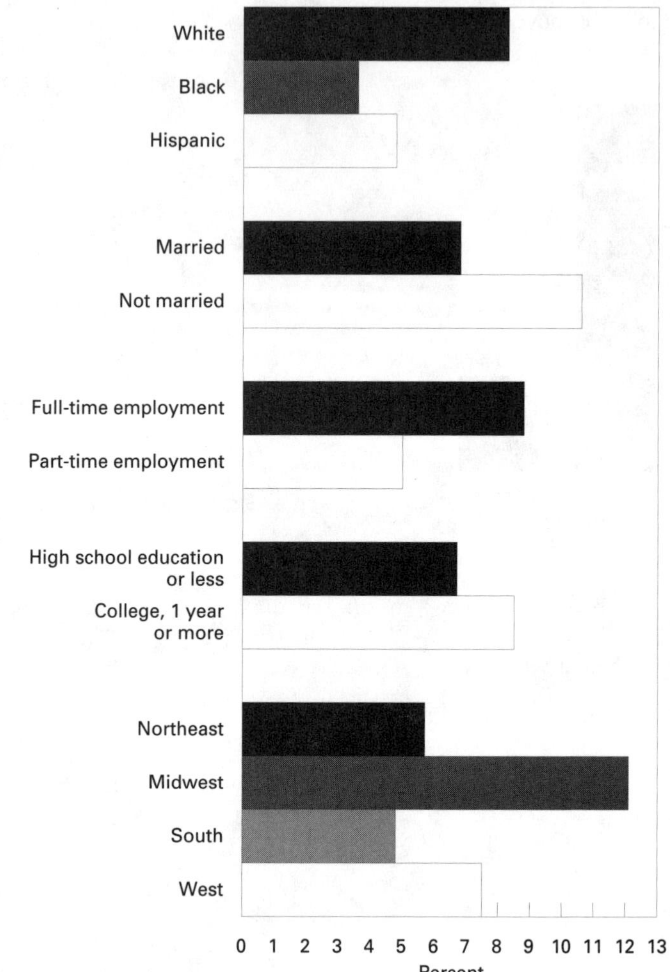

Source for above: Bureau of the Census, 1994

CHILD-CARE TAX CREDIT

Parents who pay for child care can claim the dependent care tax credit on their federal income taxes, thereby reducing their overall child care expenses. On average, parents pay $2,500 per year, per child, for full-time child care.

Who can claim the credit? If you pay someone to care for your child under the age of 13 (or for a spouse or other dependent who is incapable of self-care) so that you can work or look for work, you can claim the credit. In most cases, married couples can claim the credit only for expenses incurred in order to enable both spouses to work or look for work. If you are divorced from the father of your child, you can claim the credit only if you are the custodial parent.

What kind of child care is covered? Child-care centers, baby-sitters, family-day-care homes, after-school centers, nursery schools, and in-home caregivers. If you hire a provider to work in your home, you must comply with all laws regarding employees, including minimum-wage provisions.

How does the credit work? Each year you can claim the credit against expenses of up to $2,400 for the care of one child or dependent, and up to $4,800 for the care of two or more. You may not, however, claim care expenses that exceed your income, or, in the case of married couples, exceed the income of the lower-earning spouse. You cannot claim credit for expenses that have been reimbursed directly or indirectly by your employer.

What tax forms do you need to claim the dependent care tax credit? Fill out and attach Form W-10 (Dependent Care Provider's Identification and Certification) to your tax form along with Schedule 2441, the Dependent Care Tax Credit. If you are married and living with your spouse, you must file a joint return in order to claim the credit.

What about state credits and deductions? More than half the states, plus the District of Columbia, also offer credits or deductions for dependent care expenses.

Source: Child Care Action Campaign

GUIDELINES FOR HIRING A NANNY

Questions to ask candidates:

- Why do you like to take care of children?
- What would your typical day on the job be like?
- What would you do with children on a rainy day?
- What would you do if the children were crying and would not stop?
- How would you handle it when a child misbehaves?
- Have you ever toilet-trained a child?
- Under what circumstances would you hit the child? (You should not hire anyone who would hit your child under any circumstances.)
- How much television do you watch?
- How do you feel about reading books to my child?
- Do you drive?
- Do you smoke?
- Do you have training in cardiopulmonary resuscitation and first aid?

Also:

- Interview the candidates in person and take notes.
- Ask for at least two references of employers who had children your child's age. Ask the former employer about the nanny's strengths and weaknesses. Would they hire her again?
- Watch the nanny hold or talk with your child. Is the nanny gentle and responsive?
- Don't hire anyone on the spot.

Source: Child Care Council of Westchester

Choice Nanny Franchise Systems reported a 33% increase in business nationally after Zoë Baird's nanny problems.

While African-American women make up 19% of single women in the U.S., 59% of all single mothers are African-American.

"A mother is not a person to lean on, but a person to make leaning unnecessary."—Dorothy Canfield Fisher

HOUSEHOLD EMPLOYEES

Anyone considered an employee is someone on whom you owe tax. According to the federal government, an employee is technically anyone who performs services if you, as an employer, can control what is done and how it will be done. It does not matter whether the person works full- or part-time, permanently, or on a temporary basis. A household worker is an employee who performs domestic services in a private home, including baby-sitters, companions for the elderly or infirm, maids, caretakers, nurses, housekeepers, cooks, butlers, family chauffeurs, and maintenance personnel. Baby-sitting that is performed in the caretaker's home does not establish an employer-employee relationship, because the caretaker controls when and how the work is performed. Also, independent contractors, self-employed persons, and representatives of an agency or au pair program who work in or around the home are not considered to be employees.

For important tax information related to hiring a baby-sitter or other household employee, request a copy of *Hiring Someone to Work in Your Home*, available from:

The Women's Bureau
Department of Labor
200 Constitution Avenue, N.W.
Washington, DC 20210
(800) 827-5335

Source: Women's Bureau, Department of Labor

NANNY SCHOOLS

All of these schools offer placement services.

American Nanny College
4650 Arrow Highway, A-10
Montclair, CA 91763
(714) 624-7711

Delta College
Nanny Training Program
University Center, MI 48710
(517) 686-9417

DeMarge College
Certified Professional Nanny Program
3608 Northwest 58th
Oklahoma City, OK 73112
(405) 947-1534

English Nanny and Governess School
30 South Franklin Street
Chagrin Falls, OH 44022
(216) 247-0600

Nannys and Grannys
6440 West Coley Avenue
Las Vegas, NV 89102
(702) 364-4700

Northwest Nannies Institute
11830 Southwest Kerr Parkway
Lake Oswego, OR 97035
(503) 245-5288

Sullivan College
Professional Nanny Program
P.O. Box 33-308
Louisville, KY 40232
(502) 456-6504

Vermont School for Nannies
207-232 Skitchewaung
Springfield, VT 05156
(802) 885-3556

Vincennes University
Professional Nanny Program
1002 North First Street
Vincennes, IN 47591
(812) 885-6820

Source: American Council of Nanny Schools

AU PAIR AGENCIES

The following agencies have been authorized by the federal government to bring au pairs into the United States.

American Heritage Association
Flavia Hall
P.O. Box 147
Marylhurst, OR 97036
(503) 635-3702

American Institute for Foreign Study
102 Greenwich Avenue
Greenwich, CT 06830
(203) 869-9090

American Scandinavian Student Exchange
250 North Coast Highway
Laguna Beach, CA 92651
(714) 494-4100

Ayusa International
One Post Street, Suite 700
San Francisco, CA 94104
(415) 434-8788

Educational Foundation for Foreign Study
1 Memorial Drive
Cambridge, MA 02142
(617) 225-3838

Exploring Cultural and Educational Learning/Au Pair Registry
2098 Oak Haven Place
Sandy, UT 84093
(801) 944-5900

World Learning
1015 Fifteenth Street, N.W., Suite 1100
Washington, DC 20005
(202) 408-5380

Interexchange Au Pair
161 Sixth Avenue, #902
New York, NY 10013
(212) 924-0446

Source: United States Information Agency

TEN BEST STATES FOR CHILD CARE

Experts have identified ten states as having done an impressive job of providing quality child care for their citizens. Hawaii, for example, is rated highly because it provides after-school care in every elementary school, while Maryland and Massachusetts impose strict guidelines for adult-child ratios in child-care facilities (three to one, as opposed to Idaho, which is the most lax, with a ratio of twelve to one).

Vivian Cadden, a board member of the Child Care Action Campaign, working with a panel of child-care experts, employed the following criteria to select the ten best states listed below: caretaker-child ratio and group size; availability of child care; health and safety standards (including immunization requirements, and monitoring and inspections); and state commitment to quality, quantity, and affordability of child care.

California
Colorado
Connecticut
Hawaii
Maryland
Massachusetts
Minnesota
Vermont
Washington
Wisconsin

Source: Vivian Cadden and Working Mother (February 1993)

CHOOSING CHILD CARE

Child Care Action Campaign recommends that the following factors be considered when choosing the best arrangement for you and your child.

Licensing. State licensing generally assures the basic health and safety of a facility (though it may not guarantee the quality you are looking for). Check your state's licensing standards and ask prospective child-care facilities if they comply. If a facility is not licensed, find out why.

Quality. Some high-quality center-based programs have been accredited by the National Association for the Education of Young Children. Even

85% of employed African-American mothers, 78% of Latina mothers, and 70% of white mothers work full time.

The percentage of married women who hold a job and whose youngest child is between ages 6 and 18 rose from 49.2% in 1970 to 74.7% in 1990.

if a center has not been accredited, key elements of quality to look for include: staff structure and training; interactions between children and staff; cleanliness; safety; and adequate age-appropriate equipment. Visit the program and talk to other parents. Never enroll your child in a center or family-day-care home where you are not welcome to drop in unannounced.

Optimal staff-to-child ratios. Family day care: 1 adult to 5 children, including the caregiver's own (no more than 2 infants under one year). Day-care centers: 1 adult to every 3 or 4 infants or toddlers; 4 to 6 two-year-olds; 7 or 8 three-year-olds; 8 or 9 four-year-olds; 8 to 10 five-year-olds; 10 to 12 after-school children. The total size of the group should be no more than twice the staff-child ratio.

Training. There are no consistent standards for child-care staff training. Qualified staff may have college degrees in early childhood education or a child development associate's credential. If caregivers at a prospective facility do not have such formal training, ask if the program provides in-service training for staff. Firsthand observation is the most reliable means of assessing a caregiver's ability to care for your child. Ask about staff turnover.

Adult-to-child and child-to-child interactions. Watch to see if the children are busy, happy, and absorbed in their activities. Are the adults interested, loving, and actively involved with the children?

Cleanliness. Watch to see if teachers or other adults wash their hands frequently, especially after diaper changing. Do children wash before eating and after going to the toilet? Are the facilities, toys, and equipment cleaned regularly?

Play equipment. A variety of interesting, age-appropriate play materials and equipment should be provided. Look for books, blocks of all sizes, wheel toys, balls, puzzles, plants, science materials, small manipulative materials, musical toys, housekeeping toys, and large climbing equipment appropriate to the age group.

Safety and emergency procedures. There should be an emergency plan clearly posted near the telephone, including phone numbers for a doctor, ambulance, fire department, police, etc. Smoke detectors should be installed and fire extinguishers readily available and in working order. Staff should be trained to deal with emergencies.

Price of care. The price for family day care ranges from $10 to $120 per child per week. In centers, care for infants (under 2 years) usually costs between $20 and $200 per week; rates range from $25 to $170 per week for preschoolers. In-home caregivers must be paid at least the minimum wage, and parents are responsible for social security and other taxes.

Location. When possible, choose a child-care center close to your home or work. Sometimes a center en route to work, near the school that an older child attends or near a relative, can be a good choice.

Source: Child Care Action Campaign

CONSORTIUM DAY-CARE CENTERS

An alternative to an employer-owned day-care center is a consortium center. Through consortium centers, groups of employers can share the costs and benefits of establishing and operating dependent-care centers, an especially attractive option for small employers.

Source: Business and Professional Women's Foundation

HOW TO EVALUATE AN INFANT/TODDLER CENTER

This checklist may be of help in choosing a day-care center for an infant or toddler.

Basic information
- Hours are suitable
- Fees are affordable
- Program is licensed

Physical space/safety
- Building safe, clean, well maintained
- Room light, well ventilated
- Space designed for active and quiet play
- Separate area for diapering
- Separate area for napping
- Fire alarm/smoke detectors, fire extinguishers/alternate exits
- Hazardous supplies out of reach
- Window guards/gates on stairs, covers on radiators, caps on electrical sockets

Staff
- Director accessible and responsive
- Enough adults to provide individual attention

Caregivers
- Are comfortable with physical aspects of care
- Respond promptly to signs of distress
- Talk directly to infants and toddlers
- Set limits consistently and gently
- Work well with each other
- Allow children to explore, giving help when needed

Program
- Scheduling is flexible to meet individual needs
- Appropriate materials are easily accessible
- Equipment for babies includes:
  soft toys
  rattles
  mobiles
  squeeze toys
  cardboard books
- For toddlers, there should also be:
  push and pull toys
  riding toys
  instruments
  crayons
  water play

Parent involvement
- System for daily communication with staff
- Scheduled parent/caregiver meetings
- Parents welcome in the center any time

Source: Child Care Action Campaign

Fast Fact: Child-Care Workers

With 24 million children under age 13 in need of day care, and spaces in licensed centers for only 6 million, the demand for child care far outweighs supply. The scarcity of quality child care is worsened by the employment situation of child-care workers, who leave the profession at a high rate due to low wages, few or no benefits, and the low status of the profession. Day-care centers average about a 40% staff turnover per year—only gas station attendants and dishwashers leave their jobs more frequently. In 1992 the average hourly pay for child-care workers was $5.35 per hour, or $9,363 annually, half of what other comparably educated women earn and one-third of what comparably educated men earn.

Source: Business and Professional Women's Foundation

20% of women in a recent survey consider their parents to be their best friends.

CHILD CARE AT WORK

How to Start a Discussion about Introducing Child Care in Your Company

- Talk to other employees about their child-care problems
- Find out what other employers are doing about child care
- Speak to your union representative about the possibility of establishing in-house child-care facilities
- Look for allies within your company—an affirmative action committee, employee assistance program, task force on women's issues, or a labor-management work/family committee, for example
- Encourage other employees to let managers know about their child-care problems
- Work through the company newsletter, take advantage of the suggestion box, and make questions about child care part of company surveys

Source: Child Care Action Campaign

Fast Fact: The Work and Family Clearinghouse

The Labor Department's Work and Family Clearinghouse is a useful source for women trying to implement child- and elder-care policies in their workplaces. Written materials and telephone discussions are among the services provided. A resource kit is also available to assist employers and others interested in the full range of work and family programs.

To obtain guidelines and information for your employer on off- or on-site centers, family day care, resources and referrals, flexible leave policies, maternity leave, financial assistance, public-private partnerships, and more, contact:

The Work and Family Clearinghouse
Women's Bureau
U.S. Department of Labor
200 Constitution Avenue, N.W.
Washington, DC 20210
(800) 827-5335

WORKPLACE CHILD CARE—RESOURCES

In addition to the Work and Family Clearinghouse, many other organizations offer assistance to companies that want to start a child-care program.

Association of Junior Leagues
Director of Public Policy
825 Third Avenue
New York, NY 10022

Catalyst
290 Park Avenue
New York, NY 10002
(212) 777-8900

Childcare Action Campaign
99 Hudson Street, Room 1233
New York, NY 10013
(212) 335-9595

Childcare Law Center
625 Market Street, Suite 915
San Francisco, CA 94105
(415) 415-5498

Childcare Systems
329 W. Main Street
Lansdale, PA 19446

Conference Board
845 Third Avenue
New York, NY 10022

National Association of Childcare Resource and Referral Agencies
2116 Campus Drive, S.E.
Rochester, MN 55904
(507) 287-2020

Work and Family Information Center
Council of Labor Union Women
15 Union Square
New York, NY 10003

CHILD-CARE RESOURCES AND REFERRALS—STATE NETWORKS

ALABAMA
Alabama Association for Child Care Resource and Referral Agencies
309 N. 23rd Street
Birmingham, AL 35203
(205) 252-1991

ALASKA
Alaska Child Care Resource and Referral Alliance
P.O. Box 10339
Anchorage, AK 99510
(907) 279-5024

CALIFORNIA
California Child Care Resource and Referral Network
809 Lincoln Way
San Francisco, CA 94122
(415) 661-1714

COLORADO
Colorado Child Care Resource and Referral Network
5675 S. Academy Boulevard
Colorado Springs, CO 80906
(719) 540-7252

FLORIDA
Florida Child Care Resource and Referral Network
1282 Paul Russell Road
Tallahassee, FL 32301
(904) 656-2272

ILLINOIS
Illinois Child Care Resource and Referral System
100 W. Randolph, Suite 16-206
Chicago, IL 60601
(312) 814-5524

INDIANA
Indiana Association for Child Care Resource and Referral
4460 Guion Road
Indianapolis, IN 46254
(317) 299-2750

IOWA
Iowa Commission of Children, Youth and Families
Department of Human Rights
Lucas Building
Des Moines, IA 50319
(515) 281-3974

MAINE
Maine Association of Child Care Resource and Referral Agencies
P.O. Box 280—WHCA
Milbridge, ME 04658
(207) 546-7544

MARYLAND
Maryland Child Care Resource Network
608 Water Street
Baltimore, MD 21202
(310) 752-7588

MASSACHUSETTS
Massachusetts Office for Children
10 West Street, 5th Floor
Boston, MA 02111
(617) 727-8900

MICHIGAN
Michigan Community Coordinated Child Care (4C) Association
2875 Northwind Drive, #200
East Lansing, MI 48823
(517) 351-4171

MINNESOTA
Minnesota Child Care Resource and Referral Network
2116 Campus Drive, S.E.
Rochester, MN 55904
(507) 287-2497

NEW HAMPSHIRE
New Hampshire Association of Child Care Resource and Referral Agencies
99 Hanover Street, P.O. Box 448
Manchester, NH 03105
(603) 668-1920

NEW JERSEY
Statewide Clearinghouse/Division of Youth and Family Services
Capitol Center
50 E. State Street, CN 717
Trenton, NJ 08625
(609) 292-8408

NEW YORK
New York State Child Care Coordinating Council
237 Bradford Street
Albany, NY 12206
(518) 463-8663

"I think we're seeing in working mothers a change from 'Thank God, it's Friday' to 'Thank God, it's Monday.' If any working mother has not experienced that feeling, her children are not adolescent."—Ann Diehl in Vogue, January 1985

Single parents experience greater anxiety, more career setbacks, and a sense that their bosses do not trust them, according to a Boston University study.

"Parenthood remains the greatest single preserve of the amateur."
—Alvin Toffler

NORTH CAROLINA
North Carolina Child Care Resource and Referral Network
700 Kenilworth Avenue
Charlotte, NC 28204
(704) 376-6697

OHIO
Ohio Child Care Resource and Referral Association
92 Jefferson Avenue
Columbus, OH 43215
(614) 224-0222

OREGON
Oregon Child Care Resource and Referral Network
325 13th Street, N.E., #206
Salem, Oregon 97301
(503) 585-6232

SOUTH CAROLINA
South Carolina Child Care Resource and Referral Network
2129 Santee Avenue
Columbia, SC 29205
(803) 254-9263

TEXAS
Texas Associaton of Child Care Resource and Referral Agencies
4029 Capitol of Texas Highway S., Suite 102
Austin, TX 78704
(512) 440-8555

VERMONT
Vermont Associaton of Child Care Resource and Referral Agencies
Early Childhood Programs/
Vermont College
Montpelier, VT 05602
(802) 828-8675

VIRGINIA
Virginia Child Care Resource and Referral Network
3701 Pender Drive
Fairfax, VA 22030
(703) 218-3730

WASHINGTON
Washington State Child Care Resource and Referral Network
P.O. Box 1241
Tacoma, WA 98401
(206) 383-1735

WISCONSIN
Wisconsin Child Care Improvement Project
315 W. Fifth, Box 369
Hayward, WI 54843
(715) 634-3905

Source: National Association of Child Care Resource and Referral Agencies

CHILD CARE RESOURCES

REFERRALS, PLACEMENT, INFORMATION

American Council of Nanny Schools
Delta College
University Center, MI 48710
(517) 686-9417

Child Care Action Campaign
330 Seventh Avenue, 17th Floor
New York, NY 10001
(212) 239-0138

Child Care Aware
2116 Campus Drive, S.E.
Rochester, MN 55904
(800) 424-2246

International Child Resource Institute
1810 Hopkins Street
Berkeley, CA 94707
(510) 644-1000

National Association of Child Care Resource and Referral Agencies
1319 F Street, N.W., Suite 606
Washington, DC 20004
(202) 393-5501

National Association for Family Day Care
725 Fifteenth Street, N.W., Suite 505
Washington, DC 20005
(800) 359-3817

POLICY AND RESEARCH

Center for Parenting Studies
Wheelock College
200 The Riverway
Boston, MA 02215
(617) 734-5200

Child Care Action Campaign
330 Seventh Avenue, 17th Floor
New York, NY 10001
(212) 239-0138

Child Care Law Center
22 Second Street, 5th Floor
San Francisco, CA 94105
(415) 495-5498

The Children's Foundation
725 Fifteenth Street, N.W., Suite 505
Washington, DC 20005

National Association for the Education of Young Children
1509 Sixteenth Street, N.W.
Washington, DC 20036
(202) 424-2460

National Coalition to End Racism in America's Child Care System
22075 Koths
Taylor, MI 48180
(313) 295-0257

CHILD CARE — RECOMMENDED READING

Child Care Choices: Balancing the Needs of Children, Families, and Society, Edward F. Zigler and Mary E. Lang (New York: Free Press, 1991).

The Complete Guide to Choosing Childcare, National Association of Child Care Resource and Referral Agencies (New York: Random House, 1990).

Hard Choices: How Women Decide about Work, Career and Motherhood, Kathleen Gerson (Berkeley: University of California Press, 1985).

The Politics of Parenthood: Child Care, Women's Rights and the Myth of the Good Mother, Mary Frances Berry (New York: Viking, 1993).

The Preschool Years: Family Strategies That Work—From Experts and Parents, Ellen Galinsky and Judy David (New York: Times Books, 1988).

Who Cares for America's Children? Child Care Policy for the 1990s, Cheryl D. Hayes, John L. Palmer, and Martha Zaslow, eds. (Washington, D.C.: National Academy Press, 1990).

73% percent of all two-parent families would have one parent stay home with the children "if money were not an issue."

HEALTH
HEALTH
HEALTH

HEALTH

HEALTH
HEALTH
HEALTH
HEALTH
HEALTH
HEALTH
HEALTH
HEALTH
HEALTH
HEALTH
HEALTH
HEALTH
HEALTH
HEALTH
HEALTH
HEALTH

THE WOMEN'S HEALTH INITIATIVE

The scientific neglect of women's health began to be recognized nationally in 1989, when a government investigation revealed that research into women's health had long lagged behind that into men's: only 14% of the budget for the National Institutes of Health (NIH), for instance, was being spent on women's health issues. In an attempt to rectify this, in 1993 Dr. Bernadine Healy, the first female director of the NIH, launched the Women's Health Initiative, a project intended to establish the most statistically valid profile of women's health ever developed.

The 45 hospitals associated with the Women's Health Initiative will study the prevention of cardiovascular disease, cancer, and osteoporosis—the most common causes of death, disability, and impaired quality of life in postmenopausal women. Women can enroll in any of the trial's three components: one will evaluate the effect of low-fat diets on the prevention of breast and colon cancer as well as coronary heart disease; the second will examine the effect of hormone replacement therapy on prevention of breast cancer; and the third will evaluate the effect of calcium and vitamin D on prevention of osteoporosis and colon cancer.

Women who want to participate in the Women's Health Initiative can contact the following hospitals or call the NIH hotline at (800) 549-6636.

(*Starred programs will recruit primarily minority populations.)

University of Alabama, Birmingham*
Birmingham, AL
(205) 375-7575

University of Arizona Family and Community Medicine Center*
Tucson, AZ
(602) 321-7440

University of California, Davis, School of Medicine
Sacramento, CA
(916) 734-0130

University of California, San Diego*
La Jolla or Chula Vista, CA
(619) 622-5770 or (619) 498-4980

Emory University School of Medicine*
Decatur, GA
(404) 473-8600

Northwestern University Medical School
Chicago, IL
(312) 908-0895

University of Iowa
Iowa City or Bettendorf, IA
(319) 335-6628 or (800) 348-4692

Brigham and Women's Hospital
Boston, MA
(617) 278-0782

University of Minnesota Hospital and Clinics
Minneapolis, MN
(612) 336-5743

University of Medicine and Dentistry of New Jersey
Newark, NJ
(201) 982-4001

State University of New York, Buffalo
Buffalo, NY
(716) 829-3128

Bowman Gray School of Medicine
Winston-Salem, NC
(919) 716-7056

University of Pittsburgh
Pittsburgh, PA
(412) 624-3598

Memorial Hospital
Pawtucket, RI
(401) 729-2865

University of Tennessee, Memphis
Memphis, TN
(901) 767-4200

Fred Hutchinson Cancer Research Center
Seattle, WA
(206) 667-6550

Source: Office of Research on Women's Health

On average, women live 4 years longer than men, 7 years longer in developed countries and 2 years longer in developing countries.

Elizabeth Blackwell was the first woman to receive a medical degree, in 1849.

HEALTH CARE VISITS

Women in America are living longer than at any other time in history, and yet life expectancy at birth for women in this country ranks sixteenth among industrialized nations.

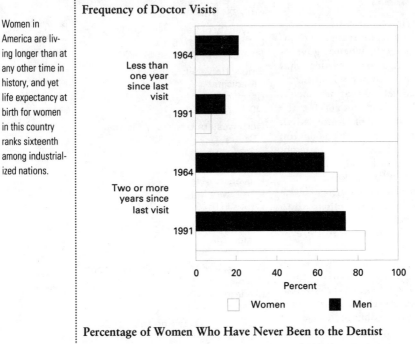

Frequency of Doctor Visits

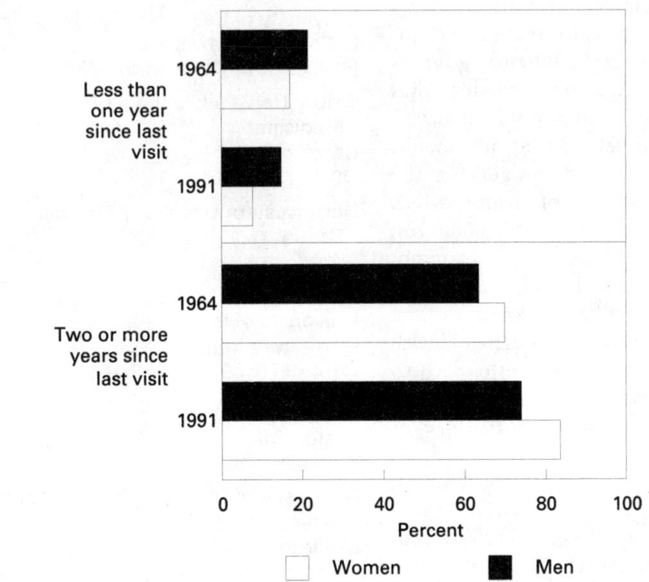

Percentage of Women Who Have Never Been to the Dentist

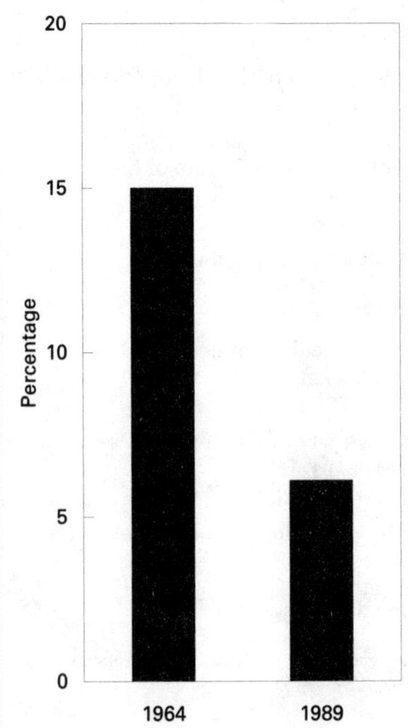

Source for above: Department of Health and Human Services

LIFE EXPECTANCY

Changes in Longevity Since 1900

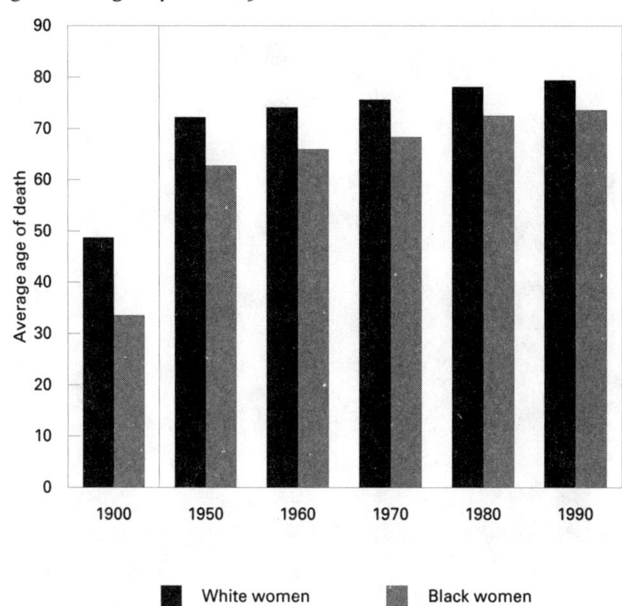

The ratio of suicide attempts by girls to that of boys is 4 to 1; however boys and men are more likely to succeed.

International Life Expectancies

These figures represent life expectancy at birth, from 1989.

Country	Women	Men
Japan	82.5	76.2
France	81.5	73.1
Switzerland	81.3	74.1
Netherlands	81.1	73.7
Canada	80.6	73.7
Spain	80.3	73.6
Sweden	80.1	74.2
Hong Kong	80.1	74.3
Norway	80.0	73.3
Italy	79.9	73.3
Australia	79.6	73.3
Greece	79.4	74.3
United States	78.6	71.8
England & Wales	78.4	72.9
Puerto Rico	77.2	69.1
Kuwait	75.8	72.5
Chile	75.7	70.0
Poland	75.5	66.7
Cuba	75.3	72.2
Romania	72.3	66.4

Source for above: Department of Health and Human Services

20% of all breast cancers are not discernible on mammograms.

DEATH RATES AMONG GROUPS OF WOMEN

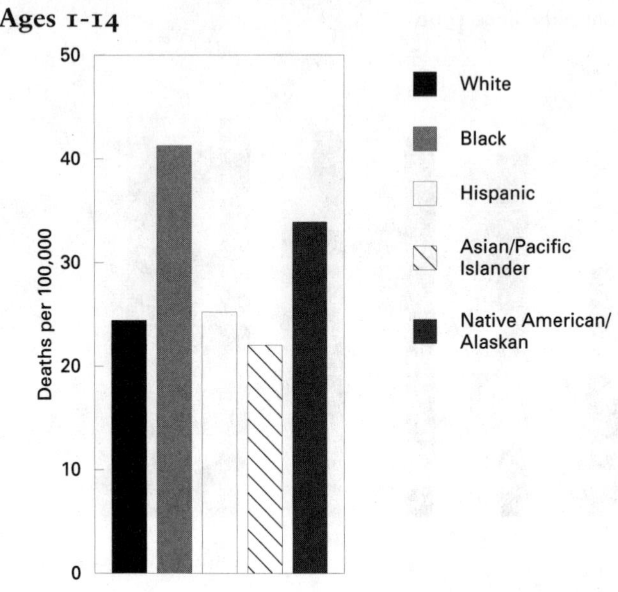

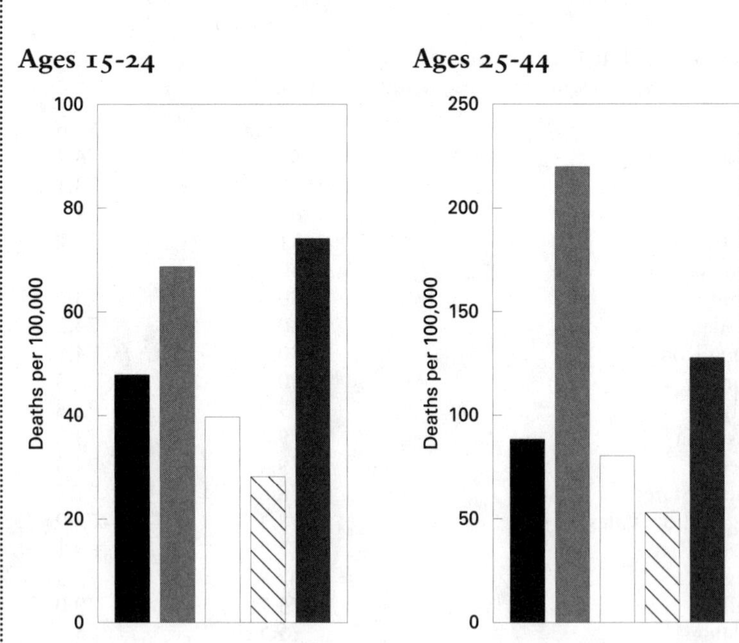

Ages 45-64

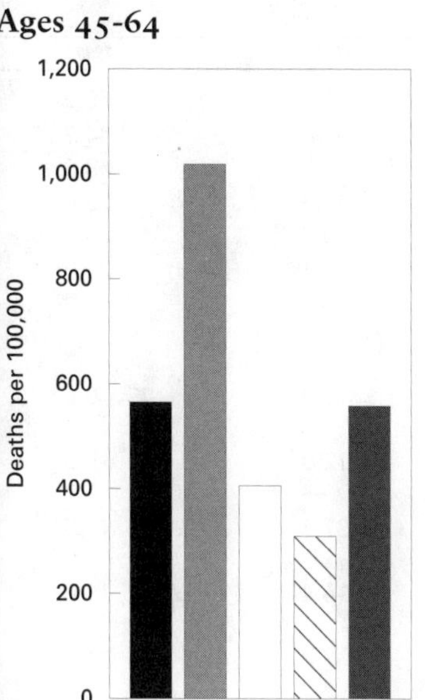

Ages 65-74

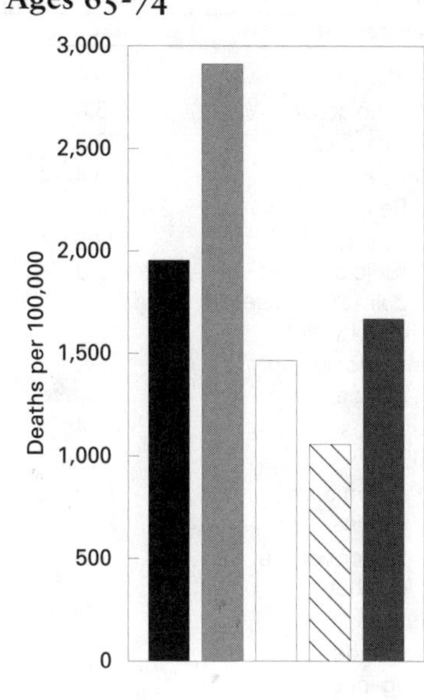

During the eight years of the Vietnam War, 54,000 Americans died. This year alone, around 45,000 women will die of breast cancer.

Ages 75-84

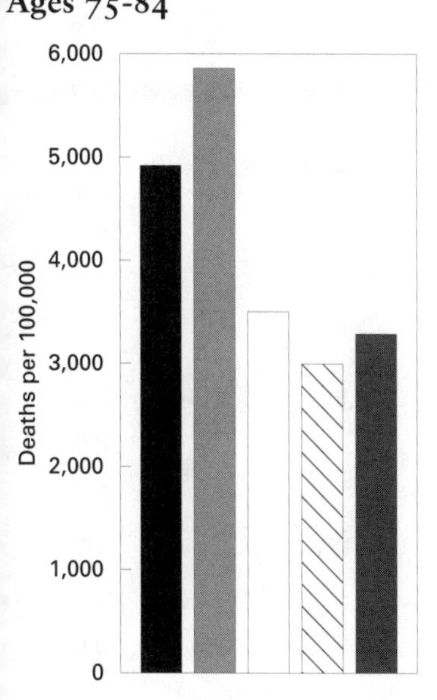

Ages 85+

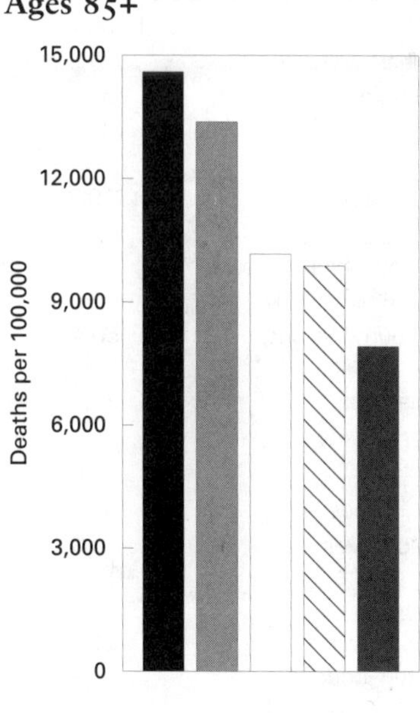

A significantly higher proportion of women executives, professionals, and administrative workers will die of breast cancer than will blue-collar workers.

DEATH: CAUSES AND RATES

WHITE WOMEN

*Cause of death**	*1950*	*1970*	*1990*
All causes	645.0	501.7	369.9
Heart disease	223.6	167.8	344.2
Stroke	79.7	56.2	68.6
Cancer	119.4	107.6	23.8
Respiratory	4.6	10.1	26.5
Breast	22.5	23.4	22.9
Chronic obstructive pulmonary disease (emphysema)	2.8	5.3	10.6
Pneumonia and influenza	18.9	15.0	10.6
Diabetes	16.4	12.8	9.5
AIDS	—	—	1.1
Unintentional injuries	30.6	27.2	17.6
Motor vehicle crashes	0.6	14.4	11.0
Suicide	5.3	7.2	4.8
Homicide	1.4	2.2	2.8
Drug-induced	—	—	2.5
Alcohol-induced	—	—	2.8

BLACK WOMEN

*Cause of death**	*1950*	*1970*	*1990*
All causes	1,106.7	814.4	581.6
Heart disease	349.5	251.7	168.1
Stroke	155.6	107.9	42.7
Cancer	131.9	123.5	137.2
Respiratory	4.1	10.9	27.5
Breast	19.3	21.5	27.5
Chronic obstructive pulmonary disease (emphysema)	—	—	10.7
Pneumonia and influenza	50.4	29.2	13.7
Diabetes	22.7	30.9	25.4
AIDS	—	—	9.9
Unintentional injuries	38.5	35.3	20.4
Motor vehicle crashes	10.3	13.8	9.3
Suicide	1.7	2.9	2.4
Homicide	11.7	15.0	13.0
Drug-induced	—	—	3.4
Alcohol-induced	—	—	7.7

** These figures are for deaths per 100,000*
Source: Department of Health and Human Services

DIET AND CANCER

Research is showing the importance nutrition plays in preventing cancer. According to the National Cancer Institute, evidence indicates that women may reduce their cancer risk by observing these nutrition guidelines:

1. **Maintain desirable weight.** Women who are 40% or more overweight increase their risk of colon, breast, gallbladder, ovary, and uterine cancers. Your doctor can recommend a diet and exercise regimen to help maintain appropriate weight and body fitness.
2. **Eat a varied diet, including vegetables and fruits.** A varied diet eaten in moderation offers the best hope for lowering the risk of cancer. Studies have also shown that daily consumption of fresh vegetables and fruits is associated with decreased risk of lung, bladder, esophagus, colorectal, and stomach cancers.
3. **Eat more high-fiber foods.** High-fiber diets, including whole grain cereals, breads, and pasta, as well as vegetables and fruits, are a good substitute for fatty foods and may reduce the risk of colon cancer.
4. **Cut down on total fat intake.** A diet high in fat may be a factor in the development of certain cancers, particularly breast and colon.
5. **Limit consumption of alcohol or don't drink at all.** Heavy use of alcohol, especially when accompanied by cigarettes or chewing tobacco, increases the risk of cancers of the mouth, larynx, throat, esophagus, and liver.
6. **Limit consumption of salt-cured, smoked, and nitrite-cured foods.** These forms of food preserving seem to be associated with a higher incidence of esophagus and stomach cancers.

Source: National Cancer Institute

More than half of cervical cancer cases occur among African-American women, and the resulting mortality rate is three times as high as for whites.

CANCER DEATH RATES BY TYPE OF CANCER

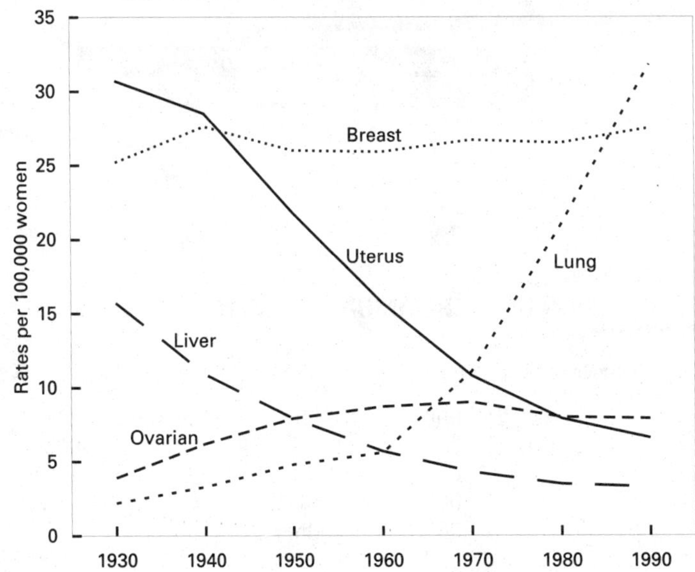

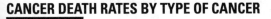

Source: American Cancer Society

CANCER SURVIVAL RATES

While the incidence of lung cancer in men has been declining in recent years, the rate among women has continued to rise.

Women's Cancer Survival Rates by Race, 1983–89

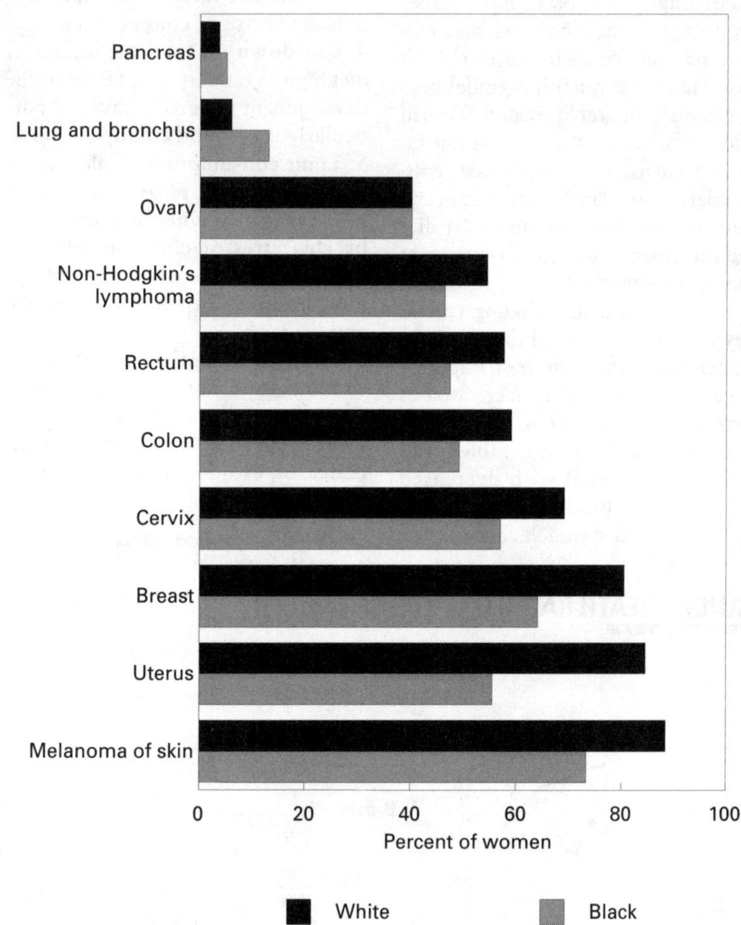

MOST COMMON CANCERS AMONG WOMEN

Forms of cancer with the highest incidence, from 1993.

Breast	182,000	Melanoma of the skin	15,000
Colon and rectum	74,000	Pancreas	14,000
Lung	72,000	Bladder	13,200
Uterus	46,000	Leukemia	12,400
Ovary	24,000	Kidney	10,600
Lymphoma	23,500	Oral	9,800

Source: American Cancer Society

WOMEN'S CANCER CENTERS AND RESOURCES

National Organizations

Susan G. Komen Breast Cancer Foundation	Occidental Tower, 5005 LBJ Freeway, Suite 370, LB 74, Dallas, TX 75244	(800) 462-9273 or (214) 450-1777 (offices)	Education, advocacy
Evelyn H. Lauder Breast Center, Iris Cantor Diagnostic Center, Memorial Sloan-Kettering	205 E. 64th Street, New York, NY 10021	(212) 639-5200	Patient services
National Alliance of Breast Cancer Organizations	1180 Avenue of the Americas, 2nd floor, New York, NY 10036	(212) 719-0154	Advocacy
National Breast Cancer Coalition	Washington, DC	(800) 935-0434 or (202) 296-7477	Advocacy
Reach to Recovery Program, American Cancer Society	1599 Clifton Road, N.E., Atlanta, GA 30329	(800) 227-2345	Support
Strang-Cornell Breast Center	428 E. 72nd Street, New York, NY 10021	(212) 794-0077	Patient services
Women's Comprehensive Cancer Screening Program, Duke Comprehensive Cancer Center	Duke University Medical Center, P.O. Box 3814, Durham, NC 27710	(919) 684-3785	Patient services, education/ information
Women's Health Initiative	National Institutes of Health, Office of Disease Prevention, Building No. 1, Room 260, 9000 Rockville Pike, Bethesda, MD 20892	(800) 549-6636	Research

A study of more than 100 women found that women who exercise moderately 3 times a week or take estrogen supplements after menopause stand a better chance of protecting themselves from heart disease than women who do neither.

Y-Me National Organization for Breast Cancer Information and Support	18220 Harwood Avenue, Homewood, IL 60430	(708) 799-8338 or (708) 799-8228 (24-hour hotline)	Support

No proven screening exam exists for ovarian cancer, which kills approximately 13,000 women each year.

State-Wide Organizations

Alabama	Woman to Woman	Gasden, AL	(205) 543-8896	Education/information, support
Arkansas	Anchorage Women's Breast Cancer Support Group	Anchorage, AK	(907) 261-3151	Advocacy, education/information, support
California	Phillips Cancer Support House	Fort Smith, AR	(501) 782-6302	Education, support
California	Bay Area Black Women's Health Project	Oakland, CA	(510) 533-6923	Advocacy, education/information
California	Breast Cancer Action	P.O. Box 460185, San Francisco, CA 94146	(415) 922-8279	Advocacy, education/information
California	Women's Cancer Resource Center	3023 Shattuck Avenue, Berkeley, CA 94705	(415) 548-9272	Advocacy, education/information, support
California	Survivors Support Group	Los Angeles, CA	(213) 294-7195	Education/information, support
Connecticut	Women Together	Danbury, CT	(203) 790-9151 or (203) 790-6568	Education/information, support
Delaware	Looking Ahead	Wilmington, DE	(302) 652-5433	Education/information, support
Florida	Just Us	Miami, FL	(305) 387-7549	Advocacy, education/information, support
Hawaii	Breast Cancer Support Group	Queen's Medical College, Honolulu, HI		Education/information, support
Idaho	Idaho Breast Cancer Coalition	Boise, ID	(208) 386-2764	Advocacy, education/information
Illinois	Cancer Support Network	Bloomington, IL	(309) 828-9296	Education/information, support

Kansas	Victory in the Valley	Witchita, KS	(316) 262-4040 or (800) 657-7202	Education/information, support
Louisiana	Louisiana Breast Cancer Task Force	Harvey, LA	(504) 368-2493	Advocacy, education/information, support
Maine	The HOPE Group	South Paris, ME	(207) 827-3753	Support
Maryland	Advocacy Committee for Breast Cancer Survivors	Bethesda, MD	(301) 718-7293	Advocacy, education/information
Massachusetts	Women's Community Cancer Project	c/o The Women's Center, 46 Pleasant Street, Cambridge, MA 02139	(617) 354-9888	Education, advocacy, support
Massachusetts	Valley's Women's Health Project (lesbians and their families)	Amherst, MA	(413) 548-9431	Advocacy, education/information, support
Michigan	"EXPRESSIONS" for Women	East Grand Rapids, MI	(616) 957-3223	Advocacy, education/information, support
Missouri	Breast Cancer Network	Mid-America Cancer Center, Springfield, MO	(417) 885-2565 or (800) 432-2273	Advocacy, education/information, support
New Jersey	Breast Cancer Resource Center	Princeton, NJ	(609) 497-2126	Education/information, support
New Jersey	Montclair-North Essex YWCA Woman's Center	Montclair, NJ	(201) 746-5400	Support
New Mexico	New Mexico Breast Cancer Coalition	Albuquerque, NM	(505) 268-2899	Advocacy, education/information
New York	Brass Ears	Binghamton, NY	(607) 648-3871	Education/information, support
New York	SHARE, Self-Help for Women with Breast Cancer	19 W. 44th Street, Suite 415, New York, NY 10036	(212) 719-0364 (office); hotlines: (212) 382-2111 (English), (212) 719-4454 (Spanish), (212) 296-7108 (Chinese)	Advocacy, education/information, support

The U.S. government appropriated $132 million for breast cancer research to the National Cancer Institute in 1992, a gain of almost 50% over 1991 spending.

For information on gynecological cancers and clinical trials in your area, contact the Society of Gynecologic Oncology, 401 N. Michigan Avenue, Chicago, IL 60611, or call (312) 644-6610.

New York	The Long Island 1 in 9 Breast Cancer Action Coalition	East Meadow, NY	(516) 357-9622	Advocacy
North Carolina	The Charlotte Organization for Breast Cancer Education	Charlotte, NC	(704) 846-2190	Advocacy, education/information
Ohio	Cancer Family Care	Cincinnati, OH	(513) 731-3346	Education/information, support
Pennsylvania	Linda Creed Breast Cancer Foundation	Philadelphia, PA	(215) 955-4354	Advocacy, education/information, support
Rhode Island	The HOPE Center for Life Enhancement	Providence, RI	(401) 454-0404	Education/information, support
South Dakota	Friends Against Breast Cancer	Sioux Falls, SD		Education/information, support
South Dakota	Native American Women's Health Education Resource Center	Lake Andes, SD	(605) 487-7072	Advocacy, education/information
Tennessee	The Breast Concerns and Mastectomy Support Group	Nashville, TN	(615) 665-0628	Advocacy, education/information, support
Texas	Rosebuds	Joan Gordon Center, Houston, TX	(713) 685-2729 or (713) 668-2996	Education/information, support
Vermont	Breast Cancer Action Group	Burlington, VT	(802) 863-3507	Advocacy, education/information
Virginia	Virginia Breast Cancer Foundation	Richmond, VA	(804) 740-3446	Advocacy, education/information
Washington, DC	Greater Washington Coalition for Cancer Survivorship	Washington, DC	(202) 364-6422	Education/information, support
Washington, DC	Mary-Helen Mautner Project for Lesbians with Cancer	Washington, DC	(202) 332-5536	Advocacy, education/information
Wyoming	Support Group	Riverton, WY	(307) 856-7457	Support

CANCER READING LIST

Breast Cancer Journal: A Century of Petals, Juliet Wittman (Golden, Col.: Fulcrum Publishers, 1993).

Breast Implants: Everything You Need to Know, Nancy Bruning (Alameda, Calif.: Hunter House, 1992).

Cancer as a Woman's Issue, Midge Stocker, ed. (Chicago: Third Side Press, 1991).

Coping with Chemotherapy, Nancy Bruning (2nd ed.; New York: Ballantine, 1986).

Dr. Susan Love's Breast Book, Susan Love (Reading, Mass.: Addison-Wesley, 1990).

Everyone's Guide to Cancer Therapy, Malin Dollinger, Ernest H. Rosenbaum, and Greg Cable (Toronto: Somerville House Books, 1991).

"Mammography Screening: A Decision-Making Guide," Maryann Napoli (1990; available from Center for Medical Consumers, 237 Thompson St., New York, 10012).

Nutrition for the Chemotherapy Patient, Janet L. Ramstack and Ernest H. Rosenbaum (Palo Alto, Calif.: Bull Publishing, 1991).

One in Three: Women with Cancer Confront an Epidemic, Judith Brady, ed. (Pittsburgh: Cleis Press, 1991).

The Politics of Cancer, Samuel Epstein (New York: Anchor Books, 1979).

The Power Within: True Stories of Exceptional Patients Who Fought Back with Hope, Wendy Williams (New York: Harper & Row, 1990).

Understanding Breast Cancer Risk, Patricia T. Kelly (Philadelphia: Temple University Press, 1991).

The Unfortunate Experiment: The Full Story Behind the Inquiry into Cervical Cancer Treatment, Sandra Coney (Aukland, New Zealand: Penguin Books, 1988).

What Every Woman and Her Doctor Could Discuss About Ovarian Cancer, Ezra M. Greenspan (1990; available from the Chemotherapy Foundation, 183 Madison Ave., New York, NY 10016).

Women's Cancers: How to Prevent Them, How to Treat Them, How to Beat Them, Kerry McGinn and Pamela Haylock (Alameda, Calif.: Hunter House, 1993).

"Education is the key to prevention. Women need to know what makes us healthy, what keeps us healthy, and what we can do to get healthy and stay that way."—M. Joycelyn Elders, M.D., Surgeon General

For every 100 women alive today, at least 11 will have breast cancer at some point between birth and age 85.

PROFILES OF SELECTED CANCERS

	Uterine	Cervical	Ovarian
Description of Organ	The uterus is a hollow, pear-shaped organ located in a woman's lower abdomen between the bladder and the rectum. Also the location of conception and menstruation.	The cervix is the narrow, lower portion of the uterus where it opens into the vagina, which leads to the outside of the body.	Ovaries are located in the pelvis, one on each side of the uterus; one ovary releases an egg each menstrual cycle. Also, the body's main source of female hormones.
Statistics	31,000 new cases each year; 5,700 deaths	13,500 new cases; 4,400 deaths	22,000 new cases; 13,300 deaths
Symptoms	Abnormal bleeding after menopause. Occurs primarily after menopause.	No symptoms in early cases, but can be detected in a Pap smear; in later cases, abnormal bleeding between periods, after sexual intercourse, douching, or pelvic exam. Increased vaginal discharge. Pain is NOT a symptom.	Swelling, bloating, or discomfort in the lower abdomen. May cause loss of appetite, gas, indigestion, nausea, and weight loss.
Diagnosis	Physical exam including pelvic exam to feel for abnormalities; biopsy; D and C (dilation and curettage—to get tissue to examine).	Pelvic exam; Pap smear; Schiller test (apply iodine solution to the cervix; healthy cells turn brown, abnormal cells turn white or yellow). Also: colposcopy using an instrument like a microscope to look at the cervix; biopsy; D and C.	Physical and pelvic exam; ultrasound; CAT scan; lower GI series; intravenous pyelogram. In order for the pathologist to examine the tumor tissue, ovary must be completely removed.
Treatment	Depends on many factors but includes surgery, radiation, chemotherapy, hormone therapy. Discuss with doctor.	Depends on many factors but includes surgery, radiation, chemotherapy. Discuss with doctor.	Depends on many factors but includes surgery, radiation, chemotherapy. Discuss with doctor.
Risk factors	Early menarche, late menopause, history of infertility, failure to ovulate, tamoxifen or unopposed estrogen therapy, obesity.	Early age of first intercourse, multiple sex partners, cigarette smoking, certain sexually transmitted diseases.	Older age (most prevalent in women over 60), no childbearing, breast cancer.

Source: National Cancer Institute

STATE-BY-STATE RATES OF BREAST AND UTERINE CANCERS

These numbers are based on estimated new cases for 1993. The total of new breast cancer cases in the U.S. was 182,000, with 44,500 of uterine cancer.

State	Population rank	Breast cancer rank	Breast cancer cases	Uterine cancer rank	Uterine cancer cases
Alabama	22	22	27,000	17	900
Alaska	48	50	200	48	50
Arizona	23	25	2,400	28	500
Arkansas	33	30	1,800	28	500
California	1	1	18,500	1	4,600
Colorado	26	30	1,800	32	350
Connecticut	27	23	2,600	25	550
Delaware	46	41	600	41	125
Dist. of Columbia	49	41	600	33	250
Florida	4	3	11,300	4	2,600
Georgia	11	12	4,400	11	1,000
Hawaii	40	47	425	41	125
Idaho	42	43	550	39	175
Illinois	6	7	8,700	6	2,200
Indiana	14	14	4,300	11	1,000
Iowa	30	26	2,300	30	400
Kansas	32	29	1,900	29	450
Kentucky	24	23	2,600	21	750
Louisiana	21	21	2,800	18	850
Maine	39	36	900	36	225
Maryland	19	18	3,400	20	800
Massachusetts	13	10	5,100	11	1,000
Michigan	8	9	6,800	8	1,700
Minnesota	20	20	3,100	22	700
Mississippi	31	32	1,700	25	550
Missouri	15	15	4,100	16	950
Montana	44	45	500	41	125
Nebraska	36	34	1,300	33	250
Nevada	38	39	800	38	200
New Hampshire	41	36	900	26	225
New Jersey	9	8	6,900	9	1,600
New Mexico	37	36	900	38	200
New York	2	2	15,600	2	3,500
North Carolina	10	11	5,000	10	1,300
North Dakota	47	47	425	44	100
Ohio	7	6	8,800	6	2,200
Oklahoma	28	27	2,100	22	700
Oregon	29	28	2,000	25	550
Pennsylvania	5	4	10,700	3	2,700
Rhode Island	43	35	950	38	200
South Carolina	25	26	2,300	22	700
South Dakota	45	43	550	44	100
Tennessee	17	17	3,500	11	1,000
Texas	3	5	9,000	5	2,300
Utah	34	40	750	33	250
Vermont	50	46	450	46	75
Virginia	12	12	4,400	11	1,000
Washington	16	19	3,300	24	600
West Virginia	35	33	1,400	30	400
Wisconsin	18	16	3,600	18	850
Wyoming	51	49	300	46	75

Source: American Cancer Society

70% of African-American and Latina women have never had a mammogram.

CERVICAL CANCER

Cervical cancer outranks all other cancers combined in women in developing countries.

An estimated 4,400 deaths from cervical cancer and 5,700 from uterine cancer in general occurred in 1992.

Cervical Cancer Facts

- Around 4,400 women die from cervical cancer each year.
- Health officials estimate that 90% of these deaths could be prevented if more women had Pap tests.
- Approximately 20% of all cancers in women are cervical cancer.
- Cervical cancer is one of the most frequent types of female cancer and the third most prevalent gynecologic cancer.
- 50,000 women develop an early form of cervical cancer every year.
- 85% of women age 20–80 who have never had a Pap smear account for a disproportionate 37% of the cervical cancer deaths.

If it is detected in its earliest, preinvasive states, cancer of the cervix is nearly 100% preventable. The Pap test is the most reliable way to determine whether a cancerous or precancerous condition exists.

Who Should Have a Pap Test?

- Women who are over 18.
- Women of all ages who are sexually active. (A series of abnormal Pap tests may be an early indication of certain sexually transmitted diseases.)
- Women over 65, particularly if there is no history of prior exams. Medicare covers one exam every three years. More frequent tests may be covered if determined to be medically necessary.
- Women whose mothers took DES (diethylstilbestrol), a drug prescribed between 1941 and 1971 for pregnant women in danger of experiencing miscarriage.

Pap Smears

Since the perfection in the 1950s of the Pap smear (named after Dr. George Papanicolaou), cervical cancer death rates have dropped dramatically in the U.S.

Today, as a general rule the American Cancer Society recommends that all women over 18, as well as sexually active teenagers, receive a Pap smear once a year three years in a row. With normal findings, the test may then be performed less frequently. However, if you are part of a high risk group (see Profiles of Selected Cancers, pp. 180–1), your doctor may recommend that you test more than once a year.

In recent years, however, some women have lost confidence in the Pap test due to reports of inaccurate results. As a result, recent federal regulations have tightened the standards clinical labs are required to meet and instituted inspection and certification of labs, a move that should improve the accuracy of the tests. To ensure yourself a valid test, ask your doctor if your Pap test will be evaluated using the Bethesda System for reporting, which experts have described as the most accurate means of interpreting Pap smear data. You can also ask if the lab is accredited by the American Society of Cytology or the College of American Pathologists.

Source: Department of Health and Human Services

Fast Fact: Endometrial Cancer

Cancer of the uterus is the most common gynecological cancer, occurring in around 31,000 women each year. A common symptom of endometrial cancer is abnormal vaginal bleeding, often near or during menopause. The best way to evaluate whether this cancer is present is through a pelvic exam, a Pap smear, and sampling cells lining the uterus.

CERVICAL CANCER RATES

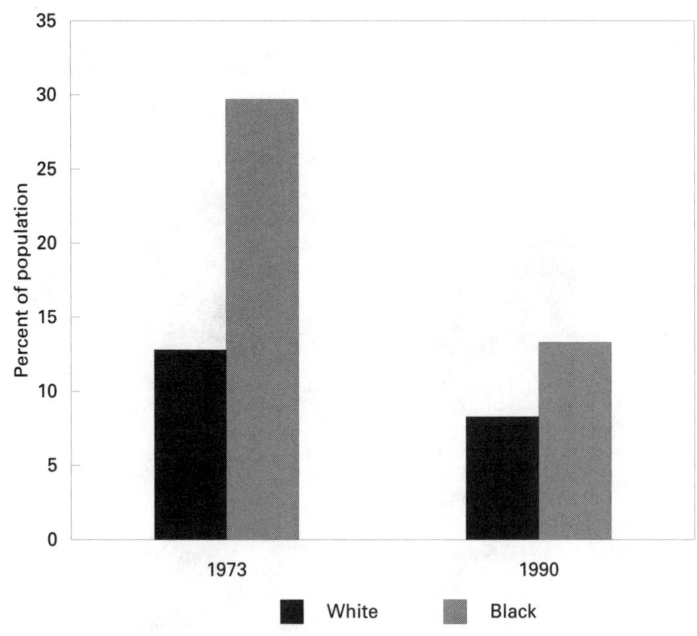

Source: Department of Health and Human Services

Because of Pap test detection, the death rate from uterine cancer had decreased more than 70% over the past 40 years.

SURVIVAL RATES FOR CERVICAL CANCER

For women who develop full cervical cancer, survival rates are not good. These numbers were derived from studies conducted from 1983–1989.

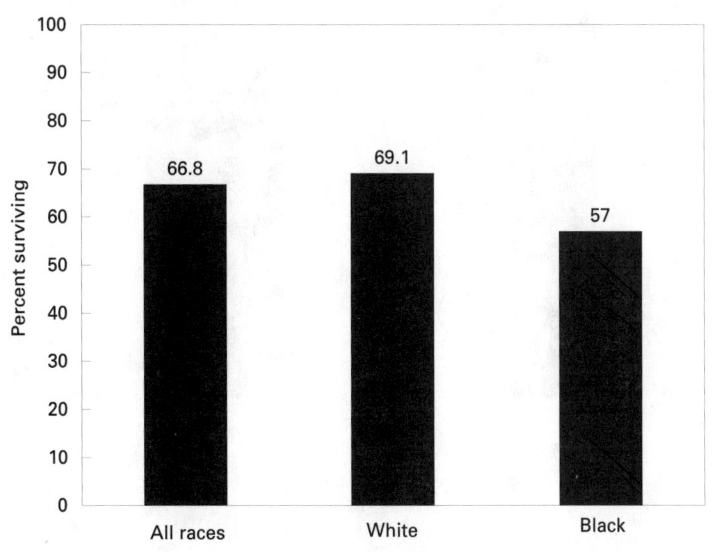

Source: Department of Health and Human Services

SCREENING TESTS: CERVICAL AND BREAST CANCERS

The incidence of breast cancer is lower for black women than for white women, but death rates from breast cancer are higher for black women.

Annual Exams for Breast and Cervical Cancer

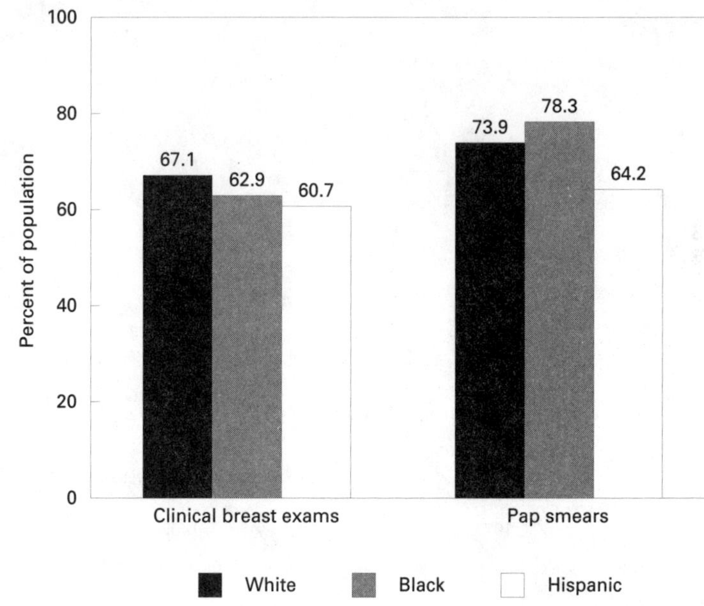

Tests for Cervical Cancer by Age and Group

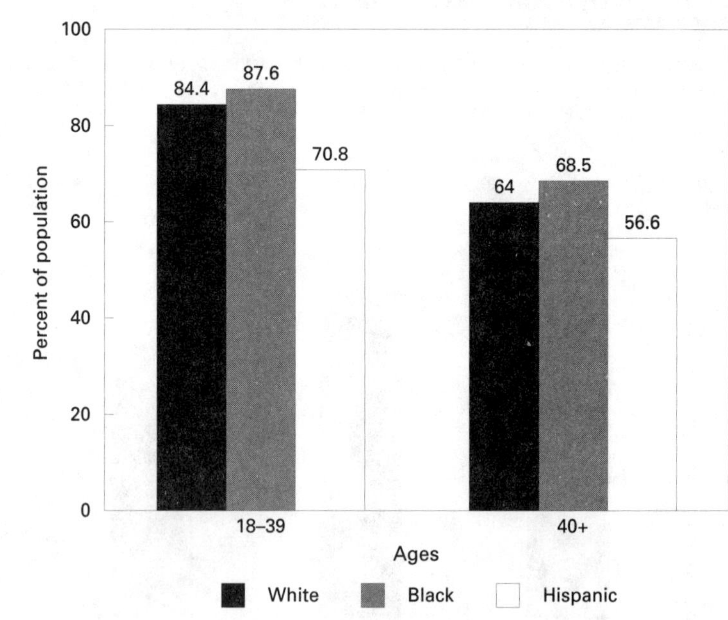

(Data from 1987)
Source: National Health Interview Survey

KEY FACTS ABOUT BREAST CANCER

- •Breast cancer kills one American woman every 12 minutes.
- •One in eight American women will develop breast cancer during her lifetime.
- •More than forty thousand women will die of breast cancer in 1995.
- •The incidence of breast cancer has doubled in the past thirty years. In women ages 30–34, the incidence has tripled; in women ages 35–39, it has quadrupled.
- •Breast cancer ranks second only to lung cancer as the leading cause of cancer deaths among women.
- •All women are at risk. More than 70% of those who develop breast cancer have no known risk factors.
- •Mammography is detection, not prevention; 20% of all breast cancers are not discernible on mammograms.

Source: Breast Cancer Action

CHANCES OF DEVELOPING BREAST CANCER

By age 25:	1 in 19,608
By age 30:	1 in 2,525
By age 35:	1 in 622
By age 40:	1 in 217
By age 45:	1 in 93
By age 50:	1 in 50
By age 55:	1 in 33
By age 60:	1 in 24
By age 65:	1 in 17
By age 70:	1 in 14
By age 75:	1 in 11
By age 80:	1 in 10
By age 85:	1 in 9
Ever:	1 in 8

Source: National Cancer Institute

RISK FACTORS FOR BREAST CANCER

The following risks are listed in very rough order of importance:

- •Women over the age of 40, with risk increasing with age
- •Personal or family history of breast cancer
- •Born in North America or Northern Europe
- •Never had children, or late age of first live birth (over 30)
- •Higher education and socioeconomic status
- •Large doses of radiation to the chest
- •Early age at menarche or late age at menopause
- •Ovaries not removed before menopause
- •Live in an urban environment, or in the northern U.S.
- •Never married or given birth
- •Heavy postmenopausal weight
- •History of primary cancer in endometrium or ovary
- •Cancer incidence rates correlate with variations in diet, especially fat intake, although a causal role has not been firmly established

Breast cancer risk factors appear to be more useful in providing clues to the development of cancer than in identifying prevention strategies. Since adult women may not be able to alter their personal risk factors in any practical sense, the best opportunity for reducing mortality is through early detection.

Source: American Cancer Society

Only about 30% of women have had a mammogram to detect breast cancer, a disease responsible for around 45,000 deaths each year.

54% of all white women are first diagnosed with readily treatable Stage I breast cancer, while only 42% of black women are diagnosed at this early stage nationwide.

BREAST SELF-EXAMINATION

Steps for Self-Exams

Here's what you should do to check for changes in your breasts:

1. Stand in front of a mirror that is large enough to let you see your breasts clearly. Check both breasts for anything unusual. Check the skin for puckering, dimpling, or scaliness. Look for any discharge from the nipples.

Do steps 2 and 3 to check for any change in the shape or contour of your breasts. As you do these steps, you should feel your chest muscles tighten.

2. Watching closely in the mirror, clasp your hands behind your head and press your hands forward.

3. Next, press your hands firmly on your hips and bend slightly toward the mirror as you pull your shoulders and elbows forward.

4. Gently squeeze each nipple and look for a discharge.

5. Raise one arm. Use the flat part of the fingers of your other hand to check the breast and the surrounding area—firmly, carefully, and thoroughly. Some women like to use lotion or powder to help their fingers glide easily over the skin. Feel for any unusual lump or mass under the skin.

Feel the tissue by pressing your fingers in small, overlapping areas. To be sure you cover your whole breast, take your time, and follow a definite pattern: lines, circles, or wedges.

Some women repeat step 5 in the shower. Your fingers will glide easily over soapy skin, so you can concentrate on feeling for changes underneath.

6. It's important to repeat Step 5 while you are lying down. Lie flat on your back, with one arm over your head and a pillow or folded towel under the opposite shoulder. This position flattens the breast and makes it easier to check. Check each breast and the area around it very carefully using one of the patterns described above.

Alternative Patterns of Self-Exam

Some research suggests that many women do BSE more thoroughly when they use a pattern of up-and-down lines or strips. Other women feel more comfortable with another pattern. The important thing is to cover the whole breast and to pay special attention to the area between the breast and the underarm, and to the underarm itself. Check the area above the breast, up to the collarbone and all the way over to your shoulder.

Lines: Start in the underarm area and move your fingers downward little by little until they are below the breast. Then move your fingers slightly toward the middle and slowly move back up. Go up and down until you cover the whole area.

Circles: Beginning at the outer edge of your breast, move your fingers slowly around the whole breast in a circle. Move around the breast in smaller and smaller circles, gradually working toward the nipple. Don't forget to check the underarm and upper chest areas, too.

Wedges: Starting at the outer edge of the breast, move your fingers toward the nipple and back to the edge. Check your whole breast, covering one small wedge-shaped section at a time. Be sure to check the underarm area and the upper chest.

Source: National Cancer Institute

STAGES OF BREAST CANCER

The most important factor in deciding how to treat breast cancer is the stage of the cancer. Stage is determined based on the size of the tumor and on whether the cancer is only in the breast or has spread to other organs. The stages can be summarized as follows:

•Carcinoma in situ is very early breast cancer. Cancer cells are found in only a few layers of cells. Because it has not invaded nearby tissue, the cancer is called noninvasive.

•Stage I and stage II are early stages of breast cancer, but the cancer has invaded nearby tissue. Stage I means that cancer cells have not spread beyond the breast and the tumor is no more than about an inch across. Stage II means that cancer has spread to underarm lymph nodes and/or the tumor in the breast is 1 to 2 inches across.

•Stage III means that the tumor in the breast is more than 2 inches across, the cancer is more extensive in the underarm lymph nodes, or it has spread to other lymph node areas or to other tissues near the breast. This stage of breast cancer is also called locally advanced cancer.

• Stage IV is metastatic cancer. Then cancer has spread from the breast to other organs of the body.

• Recurrent cancer means the disease has reappeared, even though the patient's treatment has seemed to be successful. Even when a tumor in the breast seems to have been completely removed or destroyed, the disease sometimes returns because undetected cancer cells have remained in the area after treatment or because the disease had already spread before treatment.

When the cancer returns only in the breast area, it is called a local recurrence. If the disease returns in another part of the body, it is called metastatic breast cancer (or distant disease).

Source: National Cancer Institute

Fast Facts: Cancer

Colorectal Cancer

Cancer of the colon or anus is one of the most common cancers women face: the American Cancer Society estimates that 77,000 women will be diagnosed with one form or the other each year, and that almost 30,000 will die. As part of an annual pelvic exam, women over the age of 40 should have a digital rectal exam and a check for hidden blood. All women over 50 are advised to have a baseline flexible sigmoidoscopy.

Source for above: Women's Comprehensive Cancer Screening Program, Duke University Medical Center

Skin Cancer

Sun exposure is a major factor in the development of basal and squamous cell skin cancers, an incidence that increases for those living closer to the equator. More than 700,000 cases are diagnosed each year in the U.S. and almost all are related to exposure to ultraviolet radiation.

Source: American Cancer Society

The 5-year survival rate for localized breast cancer has risen from 78% in the 1940s to 93% today.

Women who have small breast cancers that have not spread to the underarm lymph nodes or elsewhere have a 10-year survival rate of more than 90%.

CHOOSING A MAMMOGRAPHY FACILITY

In the past the only standard of performance for clinics administering mammograms was a voluntary one, but starting in the fall of 1994, the Food and Drug Administration will enforce strict new guidelines. These will require each of the nation's 12,000 mammography facilities to pass inspection and become accredited, have specialized equipment and specially trained technicians, keep complete records of performance, and undergo annual audits.

Currently most mammograms cost between $50 and $150. Some health insurance plans cover the cost, as does Medicare in some instances; community health services and some employers provide them free or at low cost. Your doctor, local health department, or chapter of the American Cancer Society may be able to direct you to low-cost programs in your area.

Source: National Cancer Institute

BENIGN BREAST CONDITIONS

A variety of lumps and abnormalities found in women's breasts are not cancerous. Indeed an estimated 50% of all women have irregular or "lumpy" breasts, and many doctors believe that nearly all women have some benign changes beginning at age 30. These include normal changes that occur during the monthly cycle — increased lumpiness, tenderness, and swelling — as well as benign lumps than can appear in the breast at any time. The latter category includes:

•**Cysts:** Fluid-filled sacs that often enlarge and become tender just before menstruation.
•**Fibroadenomas:** Solid, round, rubbery, movable lumps, usually painless, that are benign but should be removed anyway.
•**Lipomas:** Single, painless lumps sometimes found in older women; they, too, should be removed to be sure they aren't dangerous.
•**Intraductal papillomas:** Small wart-like growths in the lining of a duct near the nipple, which can produce bleeding from nipple.
•**Mammary duct ectasia:** Inflammation of the ducts that causes thick discharge from nipple; can be painful without treatment.
•**Mastitis:** Inflammation, generally in breastfeeding women, in which breast is red, lumpy, and painful.
•**Traumatic fat necrosis:** Painless, round lumps, sometimes with red-looking skin, caused by a bruise or blow to breasts; occasionally appears in women with larger breasts or older women.
•**Breast calcification:** Calcifications are small calcium deposits in the breast that can be detected only by mammography. One variety, macrocalcifications, represent degenerative changes in the breasts and are considered benign; biopsies are not required. They are found in about 50% of women over the age of 50 and in about 10% of younger women. Microcalcifications, on the other hand, are tiny specks of calcium in the breast. When many are found in one area, they may indicate a small cancer and should be treated.

Source: National Cancer Institute

BREAST CANCER TREATMENT CHART

The following chart lists procedures and considerations associated with the range of treatment for early-stage breast cancer.

Type	Procedure	Advantages	Disadvantages
Lumpectomy with radiation	Removes only the lump, followed by radiation; some lymph nodes may also be removed for testing; following surgery, external radiation administered to breast and surrounding area and "booster" radiation given to biopsy site—5 days a week for 5 weeks.	Breast is not removed; generally little deformity of surrounding tissue; appears to be as effective for early-stage breast cancer as more serious treatments.	Lumpectomy may change breast shape for small-breasted women with large lumps; scar tissue may make exams more difficult; arm may swell; radiation may cause skin to react as if sunburned, may cause tiredness, may increase risk of infection if white blood cell count drops—treatment usually requires daily visits for about 5 weeks.
Partial or segmental mastectomy	Removes tumor plus wedge of normal tissue surrounding it; some or all underarm lymph nodes may also come out.	Little chance of losing muscle strength or of arm swelling among women with large breasts; preserves most of breast, at least for large-breasted women.	Will noticeably change shape of smaller breasts; chance of arm swelling in these cases.
Total or simple mastectomy	Removes all of the breast, at times with a few lymph nodes, at times followed by radiation.	Chest muscles not removed and arm strength not diminished; breast reconstruction easier; most lymph nodes remain so swelling of arm less likely.	Breast removed; since lymph nodes aren't always removed, cancer may not be discovered if it has spread.
Modified mastectomy	Removes the breast, underarm lymph nodes, and lining over chest muscles; sometimes smaller of two chest muscles also removed.	Keeps chest muscles and muscle strength under arm; swelling less likely, or relatively mild; breast reconstruction easier than radical mastectomies; survival rates equal to radical treatment if done in early stages.	Breast is removed; arm may swell.

Every 12 minutes, a woman dies of breast cancer.

Type	Procedure	Advantages	Disadvantages
Radical mastectomy	Removes breast, chest muscles, all underarm lymph nodes, some additional fat and skin.	Cancer can be completely removed if it hasn't spread.	Removes entire breast and chest muscles, leaving long scar and hollow chest area; may cause swelling, loss of muscle strength, and discomfort in arm; breast reconstruction difficult.

Recent studies have also shown that women with early-stage breast cancer may benefit from adjuvant (additional) therapy, which involves chemotherapy or hormone therapy after primary treatment, even if underarm lymph nodes show no sign of cancer. Cancer may return in about 30% of cases in which no cancer shows up in the lymph nodes, but adjuvant therapy may prevent or delay the return.

Source: National Cancer Institute

MAMMOGRAPHY: HOW THE EXPERTS DIVIDE

While no one disputes the fact that mammograms save the lives of women older than 50, major medical organizations have not been able to agree on whether or not younger women should have routine mammograms. In light of this debate, the National Cancer Institute has chosen not to offer a standard guideline at all, suggesting only that doctors provide women with detailed written information on which they can base their own decisions. The current recommendations from major organizations are as follows:

Recommendation	Organizations
Have the first mammogram at age 40, with one or two until age 50 and annual mammograms thereafter.	American Cancer Society, American College of Radiologists, American College of Obstetricians and Gynecologists, American Women's Association, and many advocacy and support groups for women with breast cancer
Have the first mammogram in the 50s, followed by one every year or two thereafter.	American College of Physicians, the American College of Family Practice, the U.S. Preventive Services Task Force, the National Women's Health Network, the National Center for Medical Consumers

JOYCELYN ELDERS—WOMEN'S HEALTH AS A NATIONAL PRIORITY

Joycelyn Elders was named U.S. Surgeon General by President Bill Clinton after serving as the chief health officer in Arkansas. During her tenure she has earned a reputation as an outspoken advocate of health care reform. This speech was delivered on February 9, 1994.

The current recognition of women's health as a national priority is rooted in a reaction to the longstanding biases toward women both as participants in research protocols and recipients of health care services. Data has identified several barriers to achieving optimal health for women by the year 2000, including: limited research on women's health issues; limited access to appropriate health information; insufficient data on the health status of minority women; and limited awareness by health care providers of the gender–cultural environment of women. Likewise, many American women forgo needed health care due to lack of adequate insurance.

For far too long we have had a health system that simply does not work well for everybody—particularly for women and children. It doesn't work for the uninsured—the 39 million people with no health insurance. It doesn't work as well for people who are employed by small businesses and pay 35% more for the same health coverage as people who work for larger companies. It doesn't work for the people who lose their jobs. When the job goes, the health coverage goes—and unless a spouse has family coverage, the family's health security goes too.

And our current health system most certainly does not work well (when it works at all) for the working poor. These are the people with part-time jobs, or the kind of jobs that don't offer health coverage, or the kind of jobs that don't allow them to earn enough to keep a roof over their heads, pay their expenses, feed their families, *and* pay the high cost of health care.

The people of this nation are tired of this old system, which works well for some but not others. People have asked for change—and we, all of us together as a nation—are going to make some changes. There could be no better time to discuss women's health than in the context of health care reform. Women's health and preventive care must be at the core of any new health plan because women are increasingly the victims of life-threatening illnesses, yet still at the bottom of the research agenda, and because women are more likely to use the personal health system than men, but less likely to have insurance.

I want to go back to those 39 million uninsured people again. . . . I want to talk about those 85% because almost two-thirds of them are women and children (15 million women and 9.5 million children). Women make up a larger portion of the people who hold part-time jobs, clerical jobs, sales jobs, and jobs in domestic service and caregiving fields that too often don't offer health insurance. The result is that many women must rely on their spouses for health insurance, and risk being dropped if they are divorced or widowed.

These are just some of the reasons that women's health is and should be at the core of health reform. But there are some even more compelling reasons. Women in America are living longer than at any other time in history, and yet life expectancy at birth for women in this country ranks sixteenth among industrialized nations. Women of color and disadvantaged women have a life expectancy that is even shorter than the national average. (The average life expectancy for white American women is 78 years, and 74 years for blacks.) Women are also dying at disproportionate rates in their 60s, 50s, sometimes even in their 40s—due to cardiovascular disease, cancer, diabetes, lupus, and other chronic diseases. And now, women are dying in their 30s and 20s with AIDS, and as victims of violence.

HIV infection and AIDS are among the newer challenges to women's health. Women are the fastest growing group of persons with AIDS—cases have been increasing at a rate of 25% per year. A decade ago, AIDS was not even listed as a cause of death among women, but by 1991, AIDS was the fifth leading cause of death among women aged 25–44.

Violence against women—spouse abuse, elder abuse, rape, abuse of female children, and even homicide—is also increasing in all categories. In addition, too many women are suffering the devastating health effects of poverty, the most pervasive chronic disease of all, and the effects of poverty have taken their toll on the health of women and their children. Many women have no reliable source of income, and even among women who are employed, there are great disparities between their incomes and those of their male counterparts. Women represent over 51% of the population and account for over 45% of the workforce—yet the median income of men in 1990 was about twice that of women ($20,000, vs. $10,070 for women). Even when a woman works full time, she earns only 70 cents to every dollar earned by a man.

Economic well-being is intrinsically linked to physical and mental health. And in its absence, poverty takes a vicious toll on the lives and health of its victims. The number of children in this country who live in poverty is scandalous. And children live in poverty because their families live in poverty—their mothers live in poverty. Nearly six times as many women lead single-headed households as men. In 1992 there were over two million children living in families headed by single women. And we know that women bear the major responsibility for the health needs of children—of uninsured children. There has to be a full-scale attack on poverty and its effect on women, or we will never fully succeed in improving the health of women.

But what of the diseases that plague women and lower their quality of life? Many of the conditions that lead to excess morbidities and premature death among women are preventable. We can do something about this—but women need to know that they can do something. . . .

The prevention messages are simple, yet so valuable. They are about changing behaviors and reducing risks. I talk a lot about prevention—and with good reason. Because more than half of all premature deaths, one-third of all acute disabilities, and two-thirds of all chronic disabilities in this country could be prevented.

These conditions affect us all, but they have a particular effect on the health and lives of women. I'm talking about teen pregnancy, tobacco use, drug and alcohol abuse, violence, HIV infection, and AIDS. I'm talking about our high rate of infant mortality, and low-birth-weight babies, born all too often to many poor and disadvantaged women in this country. I'm talking about our high rate of chronic diseases of mid-life and later years.

We know that prevention works, and we know that we could significantly decrease these high morbidity and mortality rates if we could get a better handle on a few risk factors. These risk factors include: poor or inadequate diet; late or no prenatal care; lack of exercise; use of tobacco, alcohol, and other drugs; violent and abusive behavior; unsafe sexual practices/behaviors; lack of seatbelt use; inadequate screening for conditions like breast and cervical cancer.

When we look at the leading causes of death among women—heart disease, cancers, stroke, and diabetes—we realize that many women don't even know they are at risk. Every year there are just about as many women dying with heart disease as there are men. Yet you can go almost anywhere in this country and ask what the leading cause of death among American women is, and somebody won't know the answer. They will tell you breast cancer, diabetes, stroke—but a lot of women don't know they are at high risk for disabling and life-threatening heart disease. And if you don't know you are at risk, then you may not do all you could to be healthy—you may not take the precautions or seek out the preventive services that could reduce illness, disability, frailty in later life, and premature death.

As I've said, education is the key to prevention. Women need to know what makes us healthy, what keeps us healthy, and what we can do to get healthy and stay that way. But education is only the first step. Once a knowledge base is established, women must have access to the health services they need.

Breast cancer, for example, will strike one in nine women in the U.S. Today 2.6 million women have breast cancer and 46,000 women will die with the disease this year. Our best weapon against death from breast cancer is early diagnosis and treatment. In fact, we can reduce death from breast cancer by about one-third this way—but you've got to have access to preventive screening and treatment for it to work. Still, in 1990, only 43% of women over the age of 50 had had a mammogram in the past two years. This is very serious, because these are women whose risk is increasing. Just last year women earning less than $10,000 a year were 30% less likely to have had a mammogram in the past year.

Some of the most common mental disorders—major depression and anxiety disorders—affect almost twice as many women as men. Women of color and poor, less educated, and unemployed women are all more likely to experience depression. We must improve access to mental health services for women.

We even need to improve our track record with the most basic service to women—prenatal care. Only about 75% of American women receive prenatal care in their first trimester of pregnancy. That is an embarrassingly low rate for an industrialized country. And it is worse for women of color and disadvantaged women. Late or no prenatal care is linked to low birth weight, infant mortality, high rates of pregnancy-related complications, and even maternal death. Behind every one of those numbers is a child or a mother who shouldn't have to die, or be deformed, or suffer just because the system doesn't work for everyone.

Access to preventive and primary care has been a problem for a long time. We have seen over the years that lack of access to these services has had a major impact on the health and quality of life of women, and consequently our children and families. I believe that women's health needs to be addressed seriously and comprehensively in order to optimize the health and well-being of American women.

As our nation debates the issue of improving health care in general, I urge women to participate fully in the process of public dialog, of forming public consensus, and of putting into place policies that will change the health care system to secure health services for all Americans. This will have a great impact on women's health. Let us collectively work toward a goal of health for American women that is both the absence of disease and the presence of well-being.

7.5 million women have chronic bronchitis, a disease more common in whites than blacks.

LUNG CANCER

•Lung cancer kills more women (and indeed more Americans) than any other kind of cancer—over 50,000 each year and climbing. That rate is up 440% over the last 35 years, according to the American Cancer Society.
•Lung cancer is a particularly deadly form of cancer — around 80% of all women who develop it will die from it.
•Cigarettes are responsible for almost 80% of all lung cancer in women, with those who smoke two or more packs a day experiencing lung cancer mortality rates up to 25 times greater than nonsmokers.
•Thanks to significantly lower smoking levels, women develop and die from lung cancer at less than half the rate of men.
•If a woman has a long history of smoking, she should ask her doctor to perform a chest X ray to screen for lung cancer.

Sources: American Cancer Society; Duke University Medical Center Women's Cancer Prevention Program

Nearly 30% of Native American women smoke, compared to around 23% of African-American and 10% and 13% respectively for Asian-American and Latina women.

SMOKING AMONG WOMEN

The two following graphs show the decline in smoking among women. The first charts the average number of years individual female cigarette smokers over 18 have been smoking since 1965, while the second shows the prevalence of smoking as an age-adjusted percentage of the over-25 female population since 1974.

Smoking History of the Average Female Smoker

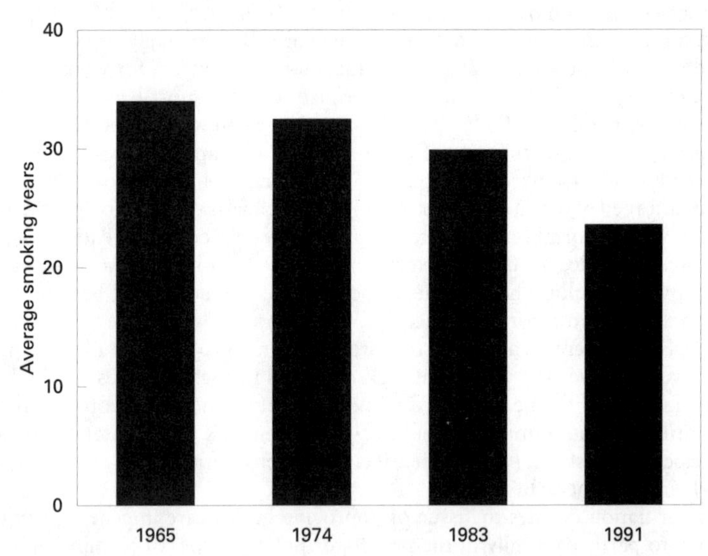

Percentage of Women Who Smoke

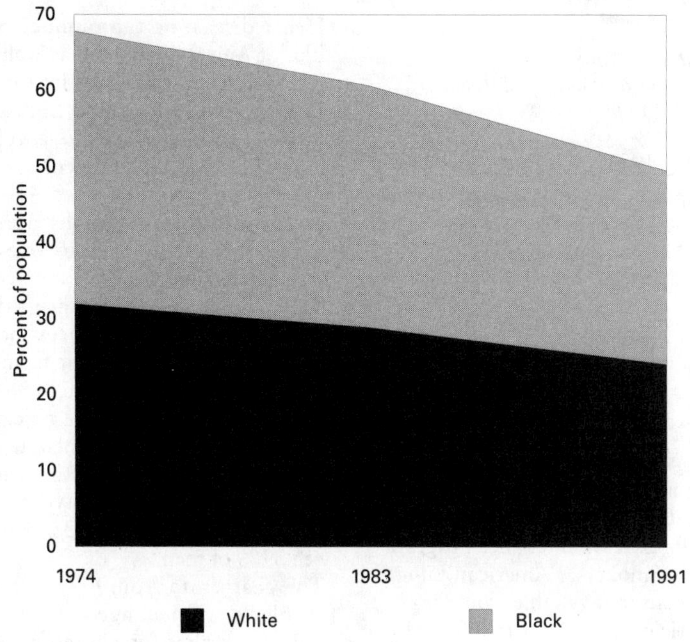

Source for above: Department of Health and Human Services

One in four American women smokes cigarettes.

While breast cancer claims about 45,000 women's lives each year, lung cancer is responsible for the deaths of around 50,000.

SMOKING AS A RISK FACTOR FOR CORONARY HEART DISEASE

•Smoking even up to 4 cigarettes a day is connected with doubling the risk of coronary heart disease, and smoking 5 to 14 each day triples it.

•Smoking is probably the most important risk factor for heart disease in women because it reduces a woman's two best protectors—estrogen and HDL.

•The number of cigarettes smoked each day is positively correlated with the risk of fatal coronary heart disease, nonfatal heart attack, and angina.

•Tobacco use during pregnancy can interfere with healthy fetal development. Babies born to smokers are more likely to be low in birth weight, born prematurely, have lower scores on standard tests of physical functions, and die within the first year of life.

•The absolute effect of smoking is signficantly increased when added to other risk factors.

Source: National Council on Alcoholism and Drug Dependence

Women who smoke cigarettes while they're on the Pill dramatically increase their risk of heart disease and stroke, particularly if they are over 35.

Smoking lowers fertility by 1/4 to 1/3 and increases the chances of miscarriage to 10 times that of nonsmokers.

SMOKING—RESOURCES AND READING

ORGANIZATIONS

Action on Smoking and Health
2013 H Street, N.W.
Washington, DC 20006
(202) 659-4310

American Lung Association
1740 Broadway
New York, NY 10019
(800) 586-4872

International Network of Women Against Tobacco
American Public Health Association
1015 Fifteenth Street, N.W.
Washington, DC 20005
(202) 789-5689

READING

"A Lifetime of Freedom from Smoking: A Maintenance Program for Ex-Smokers," American Lung Association (available from the American Lung Association, 1740 Broadway, New York, NY 10019).

"Clearing the Air: How to Quit Smoking . . . And Quit for Keeps," National Cancer Institute (available from the National Cancer Institute, Building 31, Room 10A24, 9000 Rockville Pike, Bethesda, MD 20892).

Women Smokers Can Quit, Sue F. Delany (Evanston, Ill.: Women's Healthcare Press, 1989).

WOMEN AND HEART DISEASE

•Heart disease is the number-one killer of American women as well as men. While cancer in all its forms takes the lives of around 233,000 women each year, cardiovascular disease kills 485,000 women.

•One in nine women aged 45–64 has some form of heart disease or stroke; this ratio soars to one in three beyond age 65.

•While more men develop heart disease, in many circumstances more women who are afflicted die from it. At older ages, for instance, women who have heart attacks are twice as likely as men to die from them within a few weeks. And for all ages, 39% of women who have heart attacks die within a year compared with 31% of men.

•The death rate from heart attack for black women aged 35–74 is about twice that for white women, and three times that for women of other races.

•Because heart attack has been perceived as more of a male phenomenon, women have often been excluded from studies about heart disease. As a result, little is known about the differences in female and male symptoms and general heart conditions.

•Despite the fact that heart disease ranks so high on the mortality list, death rates from heart attack, stroke, and other related afflictions are declining. Those rates among women declined 25.6% from 1979 to 1989, while stroke dropped 31.4% for the same period.

Source: American Heart Association

THE AMERICAN HEART ASSOCIATION'S CHECK-UP CHECKLIST

Sixteen elements that affect the health of your heart should be discussed with your doctor:

1. Age
2. Race
3. Family history of heart disease, diabetes, cancer, or other diseases
4. Blood pressure
5. Blood cholesterol, plus HDL and LDL cholesterol if appropriate
6. Blood triglycerides
7. Glucose tolerance (for women concerned about diabetes)
8. Ideal weight for age, height, body type
9. Smoking behavior
10. Alcohol consumption
11. Response to stressful situations
12. Satisfaction with work and family life
13. Oral contraceptives
14. Estrogen replacement therapy (for postmenopausal women)
15. Dietary changes
16. Exercise routines

Source: American Heart Association

Helen Brooke Taussig became the first woman president of the American Heart Association in 1965.

HEART ATTACK INCIDENCE

The following chart is based on estimated annual figures.

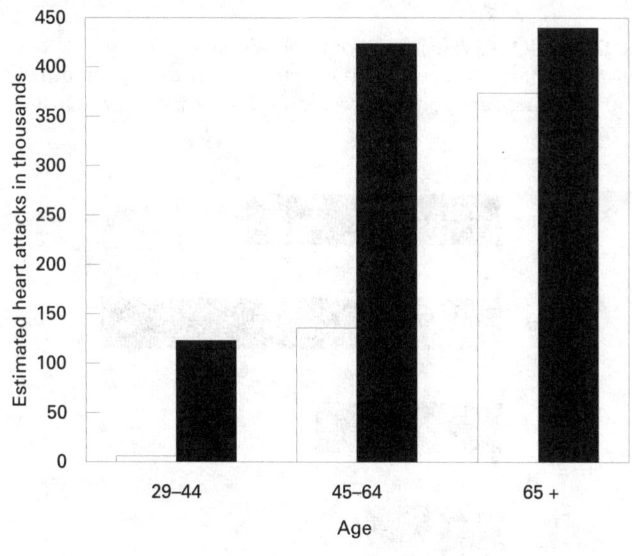

Source: Framingham Heart Study

Obesity, a major factor in heart disease, affects nearly 44% of black women and around 42% of some Hispanic groups, compared to 27% of the total U.S. population.

HEART ATTACK SURVIVOR MORTALITY

Death Rates Among Women and Men

These figures apply to women and men aged 35–94 who survived an initial heart attack for 30 days and were then tracked for about 20 years.

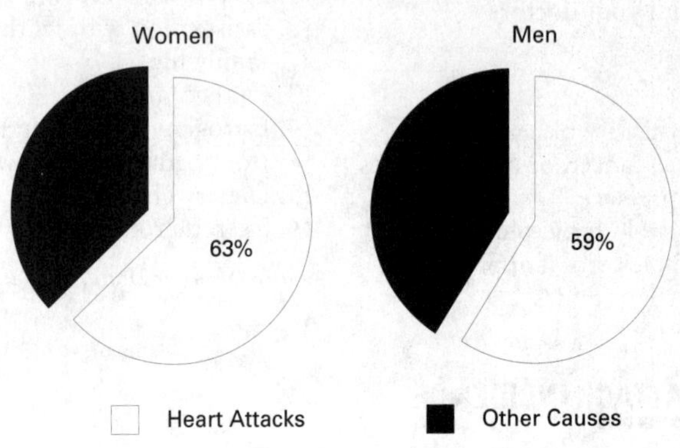

Source: National Heart, Lung and Blood Institute

Annual Death Rates Among Groups of Women

The following chart shows the fatal effects of heart disease on different ethnic groups of American women, aged 45 and older (and age adjusted), from 1988–90.

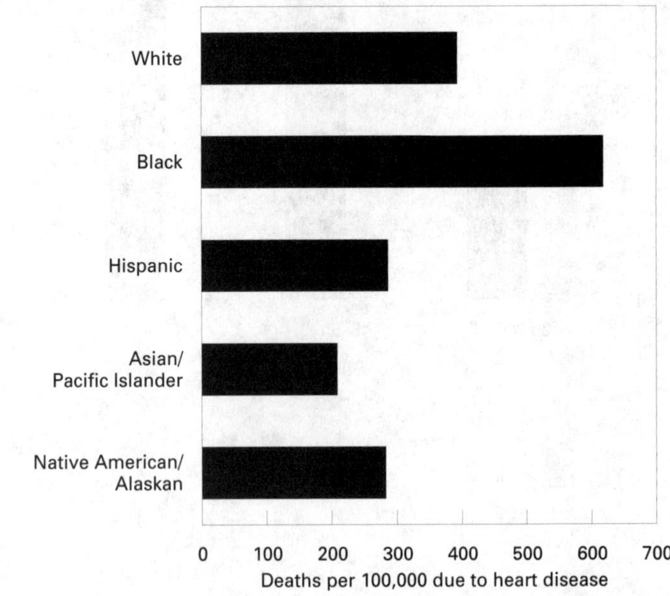

Source: Department of Health and Human Services

Heart Disease Death Rates Since 1950

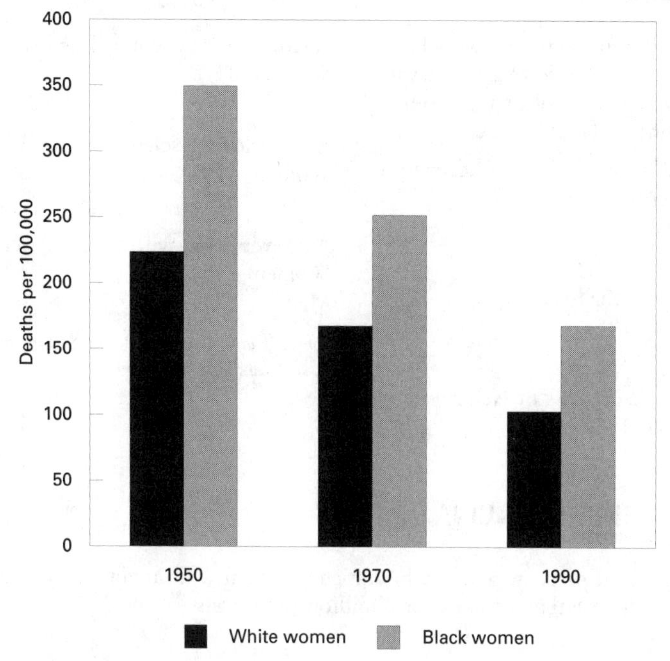

Source: Department of Health and Human Services

Heart Disease Compared to Other Major Causes of Death

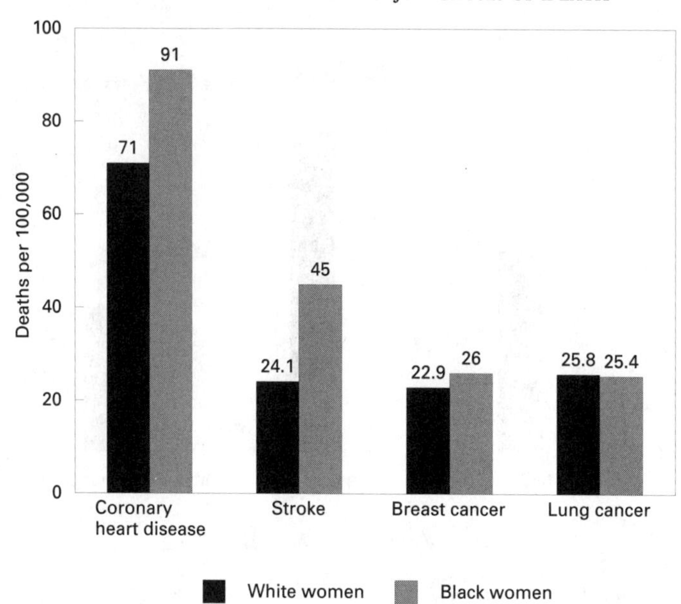

(Data based on 1989 mortality)
Sources: National Center for Health Statistics and the American Heart Association

All cardiovascular diseases combined claim more than 485,000 women's lives annually, while all forms of cancer combine to kill about 233,000, according to the American Heart Association.

1.5 million women have cerebrovascular disease, which is more common in blacks than whites.

LEVELS OF TRUST IN NEWS SOURCES ABOUT HEART DISEASE

Ten million women have heart disease, six million of whom are under age 65.

The following data shows whether women and men have a high level of trust for the following sources' reporting on heart disease:

A TV talk show like *Oprah* or *Donahue*
Women 15%
Men 9%

A story in the local paper
Women 18%
Men 15%

An article in *Time* or *Newsweek*
Women 47%
Men 45%

A story on the evening TV news
Women 31%
Men 26%

An article by a scientist
Women 51%
Men 58%

A conversation with your physician
Women 75%
Men 77%

Source: National Science Board, Science and Engineering Indicators, 1993

PREVALENCE OF ANGINA

Age-adjusted percentage of both women and men with angina, a symptom of heart disease that afflicts over 3 million Americans.

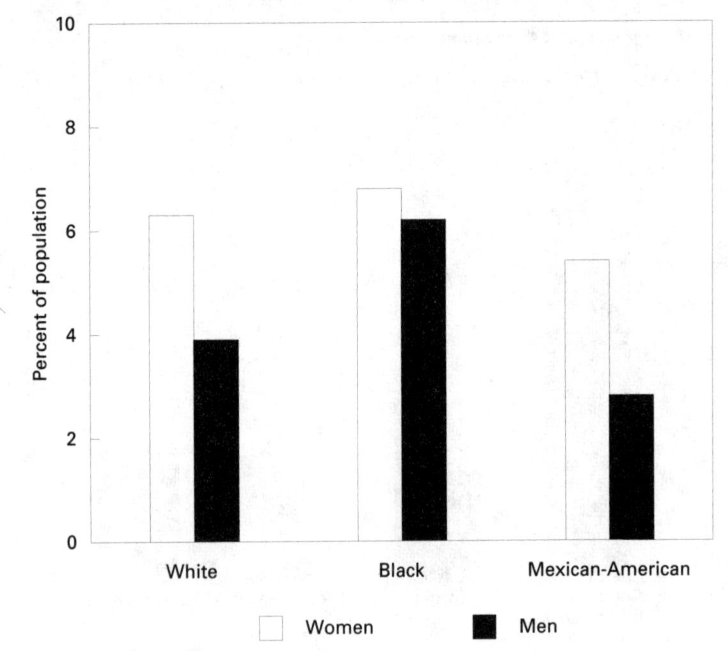

Source: American Heart Association

HIGH BLOOD PRESSURE

The most common chronic condition in women and the largest form of heart disease is hypertension or high blood pressure. This condition affects over half of American females from 55–64 and around 67% over 65. In addition, a larger number of women than men die of high blood pressure—around 57% of the total deaths from hypertension.

Women with diabetes have twice the risk of death from coronary heart disease as those without it.

High Blood Pressure Rates

The figures in the following chart are based on an estimated percentage of women with hypertension among Americans aged 18–74.

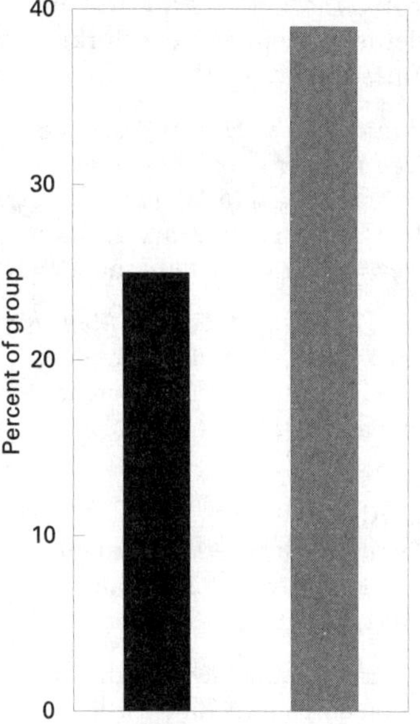

Hypertensives are defined as persons with a systolic level ≥140 and/or a diastolic level ≥90 or who report using antihypertensive medication.

Source: National Health and Nutrition Examination Survey, National Center for Health Statistics

High Blood Pressure Among Women

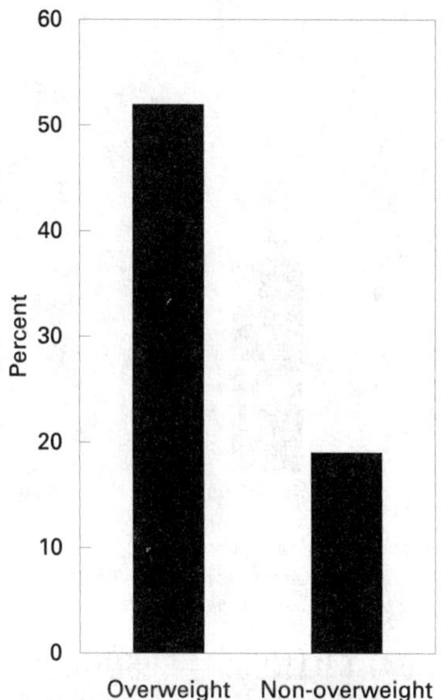

Source: National Health and Nutrition Examination Survey, National Center for Health Statistics

More than 38% of African-American women have hypertension, compared to about 27% of all U.S. women.

STROKE DEATH RATES

Stroke is the third largest cause of death among both women and men, although its incidence is about 19% higher for men than for women.

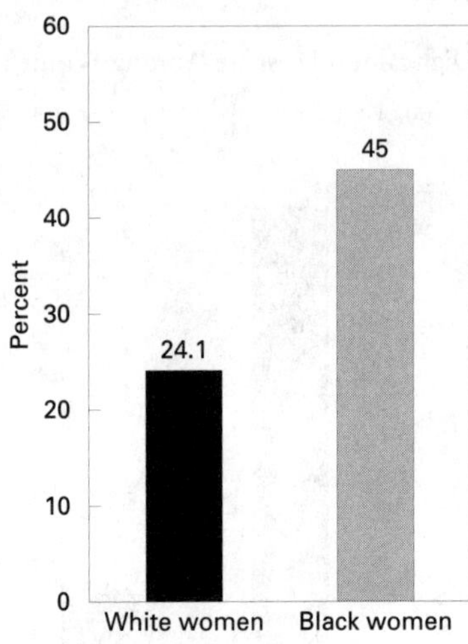

(Data is based on 1989 mortality)
Sources: National Center for Health Statistics and the American Heart Association

HEART ILLNESS—RESOURCES AND READING

ORGANIZATIONS

The American Heart Association
7320 Greenville Avenue
Dallas, TX 75231
(800) 242-8721

National Heart, Lung, and Blood Institute
Information Center
P.O. Box 30105
Bethesda, MD 20824
(301) 951-3260

READING

The Female Heart: The Truth About Women and Coronary Heart Disease, Marianne J. Legato and Carol Colman (New York: Simon & Schuster, 1991).

"The Healthy Heart Handbook for Women," National Institutes of Health (available from the National Heart, Lung and Blood Institute, Box 30105, Bethesda, MD 20824).

The Woman's Heart Book: The Complete Guide to Keeping Your Heart Healthy and What to Do If Things Go Wrong, Frederick Pashkow and Charlotte Libove (New York: Dutton, 1993).

Women and Heart Disease: What You Can Do to Stop the #1 Killer of American Women, Carol and Diethrich Cohan (New York: Times Books, 1992).

Women, Take Heart: A Leading Cardiologist's Breakthrough Program to Help Women Combat Heart Disease, Richard Helfant (New York: G. P. Putnam, 1993).

Yale University School of Medicine Heart Book, Barry L. Zaret, M.D., Marvin Moses, M.D., Lawrence S. Cohen, M.D. (New York: Hearst Books, 1992).

Newsletters

Harvard Heart Letter (available from P.O. Box 420234, Palm Court, FL 32142).

Heartline (available from the Coronary Club, 95000 Euclid Avenue, E4-15, Clevelend, OH 44195).

DRUG ABUSE

Drug Use Among Women, as of 1992

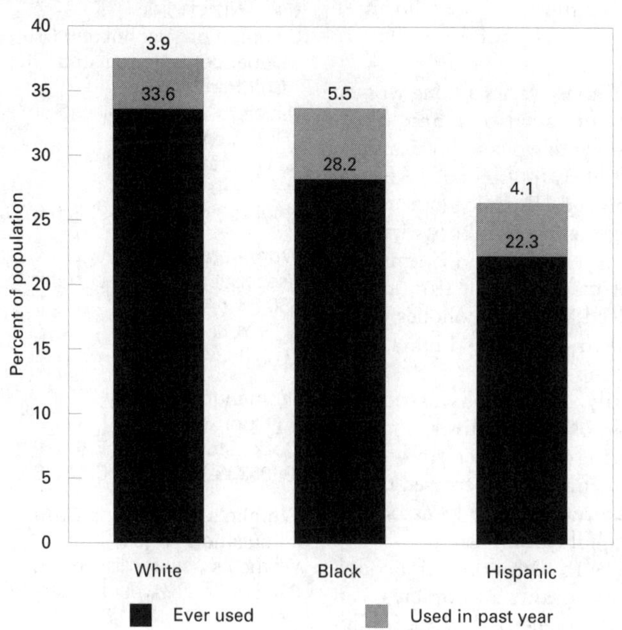

Drug Use Overall, as of 1992

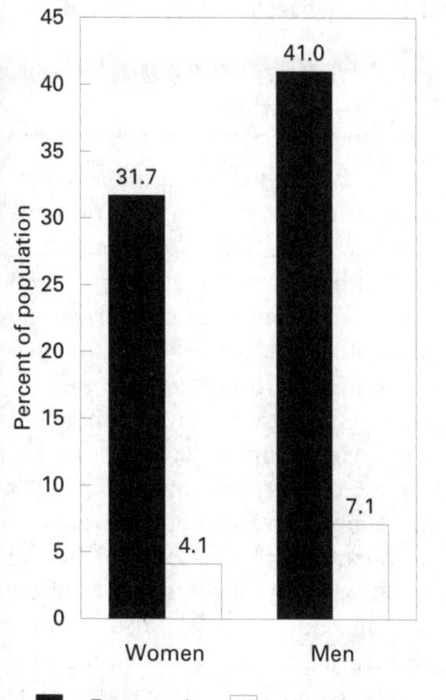

Source for above: Substance Abuse and Mental Health Services Administration

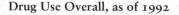

Fast Fact: Drug Treatment for Pregnant Addicts

One of the most difficult problems facing drug-addicted pregnant women is finding treatment for their addiction. Many programs are reluctant to accept pregnant women; as the National Council on Alcoholism and Drug Dependence points out, there are tremendous fears among service providers about liability problems associated with treating pregnant addicted women. In New York City, out of 78 drug treatment programs surveyed, 54% refused admission to pregnant addicts and 87% refused to take pregnant crack-addicted women on Medicaid.

Source: National Council on Alcoholism and Drug Dependence

Women tend to mix alcohol with other drugs more commonly than do men.

Most alcohol and drug treatment centers do not provide child care or adequate alternatives for female patients, a situation that is a major deterrent to women seeking treatment.

Native American women aged 15 to 34 are 36 times more likely than white women to have cirrhosis of the liver. And while black women overall tend to drink less than white women, they are still over 6 times more likely to develop cirrhosis.

While equal proportions of black and white women drink heavily, more black women (46%) are likely to abstain from alcohol altogether than are white women (34%).

While nearly one third of the estimated 10 million alcoholics in America are women, less than a quarter of the patients at publicly funded alcohol treatment centers are women. At drug treatment centers the figure is about 30%.

ALCOHOL

Drinking and Women

- Roughly a third of those who abuse alcohol or are alcohol-dependent are women.
- Alcohol abuse varies among women of different racial or ethnic backgrounds: white women, for example, are more likely to drink than African-American and Hispanic women.
- Among heavy drinkers, women equal or surpass men in the number of problems that result from drinking. Indeed, female alcoholics die at rates 50 to 100 times higher than male alcoholics.
- Typically, drinking is associated with cirrhosis of the liver, a condition that is more severe in women than in men. But an increased risk of breast cancer may also be associated with alcohol consumption.
- Exposure to high doses of alcohol, as well as cocaine and opiates, can disrupt the menstrual cycle, inhibit ovulation, and lead to an early menopause.
- Women who drink heavily or are alcoholic are more likely to become victims of alcohol-related aggression such as date rape.

Sources: National Council on Alcoholism and Drug Dependence; Substance Abuse and Mental Health Services Administration

Alcohol Consumption Among Women

Moderate drinking among women 18 and over, as defined here, consists of fewer than 60 drinks per month, and heavy drinking consists of more.

Do not drink	Drink Moderately	Drink Heavily
40%	55%	5%

Source: National Council on Alcoholism and Drug Dependence

WOMEN AND SUBSTANCE ABUSE—RESOURCES

ORGANIZATIONS

Coalition on Alcohol and Drug Dependent Women and Their Children
National Council on Alcoholism and Drug Dependence
12 W. 21st Street, 8th Floor
New York, NY 10010
(800) 423-4673 or (212) 206-6770

Woman to Woman
Association of Junior Leagues
660 First Avenue
New York, NY 10016
(212) 683-1515

Women for Sobriety
P.O. Box 618
Quakerstown, PA 18951
(800) 333-1606 or (215) 536-8026

Women's Alcohol and Drug Education Project
Women's Action Alliance
370 Lexington Avenue, Suite 603
New York, NY 10017

The Last to Know, Bonnie Friedman, dir. (available from New Day Films, 22 Riverside Drive, Wayne, NJ 07470).

Fast Fact: Women and Alcoholism

On the whole, women drink less than men, and those who do drink consume less and have fewer alcohol-related health problems. Yet women appear to be more susceptible to the physical consequences of drinking—to be precise, they get drunk much more quickly than men. If a man and a woman of similar weight drink the same amount, for instance, 30% more alcohol will enter the woman's bloodstream. This seems to be the result partially of the relative difference in body sizes, but also because women may lack the same quantity of a crucial stomach enzyme that processes alcohol.

Source: National Council on Alcoholism and Drug Dependence

HIV/AIDS FACTS

•HIV (Human Immunodeficiency Virus), which causes AIDS (Acquired Immune Deficiency Syndrome), is passed on by sexual contact, contaminated needles, and infected blood. Babies can also contract it from their mothers during pregnancy or childbirth; indeed more than 2,000 children in the U.S. are infected.
•Around 1 million people are currently infected with AIDS in the U.S.
•Over the last seven years, the percentage of U.S. women who have contracted HIV from heterosexual sex has risen from 11% to 34%.
•At least 40% of people with HIV worldwide are women, of whom about 80% are mothers; by the year 2000, 60% are expected to be women and children.
•Around a third of pregnant women with AIDS will pass the disease on to their newborns.
•Men who are diagnosed with HIV live up to six times longer than women.
•There is no cure for AIDS, although therapies have been developed to treat its infections. The drugs AZT, ddI in combination with AZT, and ddI have been approved for the treatment of HIV, but they do not prevent the spread of the disease. Sexual partners should be tested.

Source: American Foundation for AIDS Research

MANIFESTATIONS OF AIDS

People with AIDS are very susceptible to many life-threatening diseases and to certain forms of cancer. Before AIDS develops (when people are HIV positive) there are no symptoms or manifestations of the disease. When people are first infected with the virus—when they are HIV positive but have not developed the advanced stage of HIV infection known as AIDS—many do not have any symptoms, while others come down with a flu-like illness for a short time. More persistent or severe effects may not resurface with adults until AIDS fully develops, a period that can last for over 10 years (or 2 years for children). Then manifestations can include weight and appetite loss, lack of energy, fevers and sweats, yeast infections (oral or vaginal), skin rashes, pelvic inflammatory disease, cervical cancer, and memory loss, among other things. Later people become vulnerable to a range of opportunistic infections such as Kaposi's sarcoma, lymphomas, pneumonia, and other bacterial infections; manifestations include coughing, seizures, shortness of breath, dementia, severe or persistent diarrhea, fever, vision loss, severe headache, wasting, extreme fatigue, nausea, vomiting, loss of coordination, coma, abdominal cramps, or pain and difficulty swallowing.

Source: National Institute of Allergy and Infectious Diseases

SHOULD YOU BE TESTED?

Have you:

•had more than one sexual partner?
•had sex (vaginal, anal, or oral) without using a condom?
•had sex with anyone without knowing about their past sexual behavior?
•used sex toys without a condom?
•used, or are using, IV drugs?
•had sex with a man who has a history of:
 bisexuality
 IV drug use
 hemophilia
 sexually transmitted disease?
•received a blood transfusion between 1978 and 1985?

If you answered yes to any of these questions, consider getting tested for the virus that causes AIDS.

Source: National Consumers League

14% of the Native American population with AIDS is female; 5% of the white population with AIDS is female.

The majority of women who are substance abusers have current or childhood histories of physical or sexual abuse.

HIV CLINICAL TRIAL INFORMATION

In the 10 years of the AIDS epidemic, nearly 133,000 Americans have died of the disease. In that same time, more than 404,000 women have been lost to breast cancer.

Studies have shown that a woman diagnosed with HIV has a shorter survival time than a man. But until recently, women were systematically excluded from nearly all clinial trials of experimental treatments for fear of fetal injury if they became pregnant. The result is that very little research has been done on the course of HIV in women, although it may be quite different than the much-studied male version; instead of the path taken in men, for instance, HIV in women often appears as an aggressive yeast or pelvic inflammatory infection, or as rapidly developing cervical cancer.

Recently, however, clinical trials have begun including women. This means that women can now gain access to new treatments not available to the public. Clinical trials are also the safest and fastest way to help discover a treatment that works. Women who are HIV positive can volunteer to be involved in these studies, but must meet the specific requirements of the trial. To find out more about trials in which women can participate, call the AIDS Clinical Trials Information Service at (800) 874-2572.

Sources: Sex Information and Education Council of the U.S.; National Institute of Allergy and Infectious Diseses

Around 26% of girls aged 12–17 have used illicit drugs, compared to nearly 24% of boys. Crack use is also higher among girls, with the ratio of boys to girls standing at 8.8 to 10.

SOURCES OF AIDS AMONG WOMEN

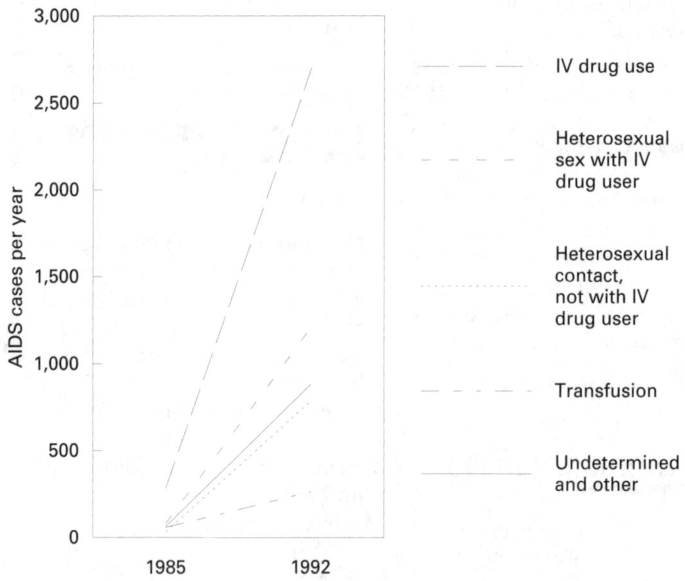

(Hemophilia/coagulation disorder was responsible for 1 case in 1981 and 3 in 1992, a level too slight to record on this graph.)

AIDS CASES AMONG WOMEN

AIDS by Race

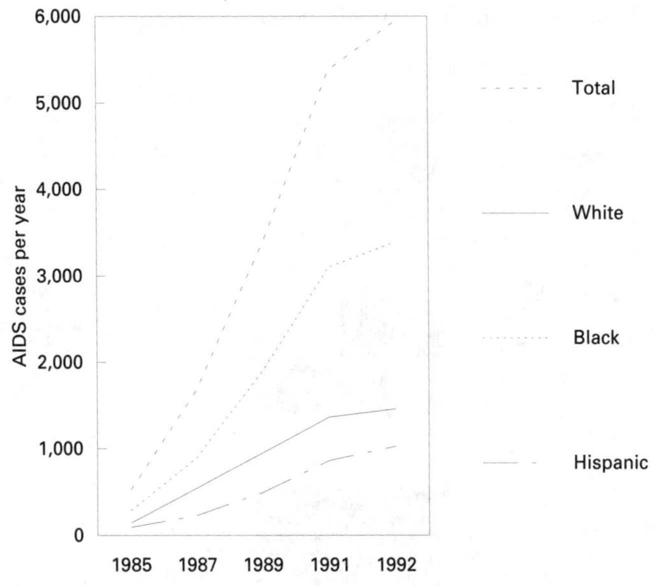

AIDS by Age for 1992

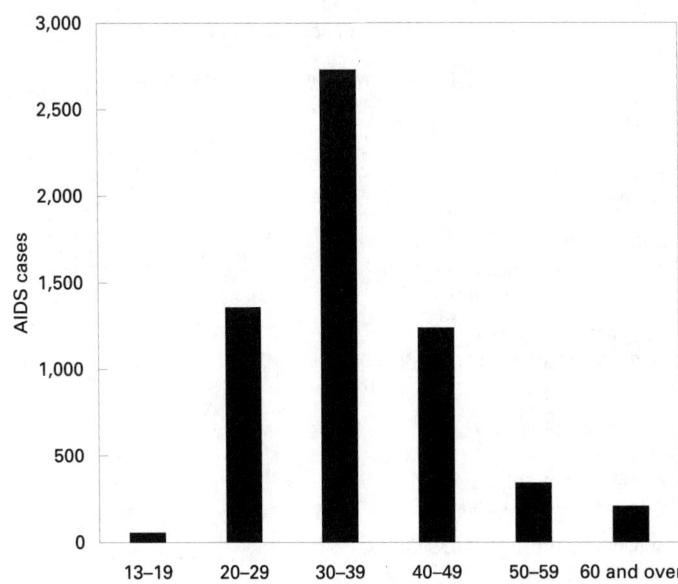

Source for above: Department of Health and Human Services, 1992

More than one million women worldwide became infected with HIV in 1993. By the year 2000, more than 13 million will have been infected, and about 4 million of them will have died.

Women of color account for 73% of women with AIDS in the U.S.

THE EFFECT OF AIDS ON SEXUAL BEHAVIOR

By the end of the decade, as many women as men will be diagnosed with AIDS worldwide, predicts the Centers for Disease Control.

This graph shows the number of unmarried women aged 15–44 who have changed their sexual behavior since hearing of HIV/AIDS. (The terms "white" and "black" in this sample do not include Hispanic women.)

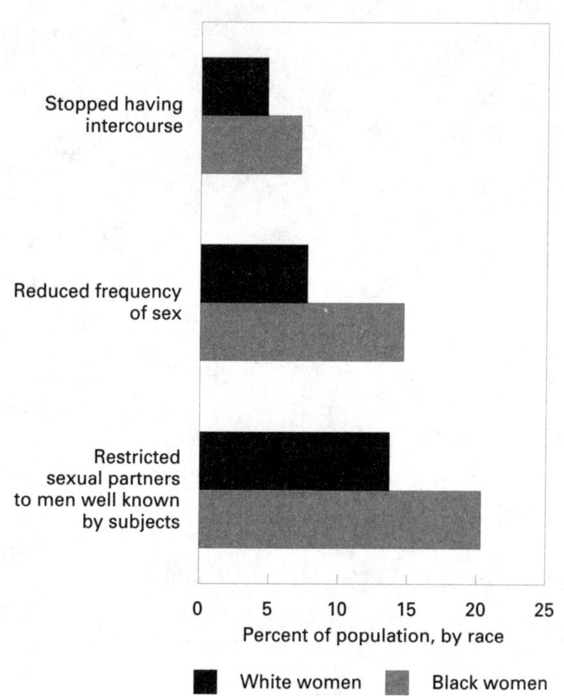

Source: Department of Health and Human Services

AIDS HOTLINES

The National AIDS Hotline is recognized as the most authoritative organization to answer questions about AIDS.

AIDS Clinical Trials Hotline
(800) 874-2572 or (800) 243-7012 (deaf access)

National AIDS Hotline
(800) 342-2437 (English),
(800) 344-7432 (Spanish),
or (800) 243-7889 (deaf access)

National Native American AIDS Line
(800) 283-2437

Project Inform National Hotline
(AIDS treatment information)
(800) 822-7422

AIDS/HIV—RESOURCES

National Organizations

American Indian AIDS Institute
333 Valencia Street, Suite 200
San Francisco, CA 94103
(415) 626-7639

Association for Women's AIDS Research and Education
San Francisco General Hospital
Building 90, Ward 95
955 Potrero
San Francisco, CA 94110
(415) 476-4091

Center for Women Policy Studies
National Resource Center on Women and AIDS
2000 P Street, N.W., Suite 508
Washington, DC 20036
(202) 872-1770

Hispanic AIDS Forum
c/o APRED
270 Park Avenue
New York, NY 10017
(212) 870-1902 or 870-1864

Lesbian and Gay Rights AIDS Project
American Civil Liberties Union
132 West 43rd Street
New York, NY 10036
(212) 944-9800 x545

National AIDS Clearinghouse
Centers for Disease Control
P.O. Box 6003
Rockville, MD 20849
(800) 458-5231 or (800) 243-7012 (deaf access)

National Institute of Allergy and Infectious Diseases
National Institutes of Health
Bethesda, MD 20892
(301) 496-5717

National Minority AIDS Council
300 I Street, N.E., Suite 400
Washington, DC 20002
(202) 544-1076

National Native American AIDS Prevention Center
1433 E. Franklin Avenue, #3A
Minneapolis, MN 55404
(800) 283-2437

Local Resources

HIV Early Intervention Program
T.H.E. (To Help Everyone) Clinic for Women
3860 W. Martin Luther King Boulevard
Los Angeles, CA 90008
(213) 295-6571

Women's AIDS Network
P.O. Box 6182
San Francisco, CA 94101
(415) 864-4376 x2007, calling for clarification

Chicago Women's AIDS Project
5249 North Kenmore
Chicago, IL 60640
(312) 271-2242

Women's AIDS Project
The Kupuna Network
4611 South Ellis Avenue
Chicago, IL 60653
(312) 536-3000

Boston Women's AIDS Information Project
464 Massachusetts Avenue
Boston, MA 02118
(617) 859-8689

Community Health Awareness Group
3028 East Grand Boulevard
Detroit, MI 48202
(313) 872-2424

HIV/AIDS Program
Chicanos Latinos Unidos en Servicio
220 South Robert Street, Suite 103
Saint Paul, MN 55107

Women and AIDS Resource Network
30 Third Avenue, Suite 512
Brooklyn, NY 11217
(718) 596-6007

People of Color Against AIDS Network
1200 S. Jackson, Suite 25
Seattle, WA 98144
(206) 322-7061

United AmerIndian Center
AIDS/HIV Education Awareness Program
409 N. Broadway
Green Bay, WI 54303
(414) 437-2161

Women are the fastest growing group of persons with AIDS, with cases increasing at a rate of 25% per year. A decade ago, AIDS was not even listed as a cause of death among women.

98% of heterosexual transmission of HIV is from men to women; only 2% is from women to men.

In New York City, AIDS is the leading cause of death among women between the ages of 25 to 34.

AIDS/HIV—RECOMMENDED READING AND FILMS

Advice for Life: A Woman's Guide to AIDS Risk and Prevention, Chris Norwood (National Women's Health Network, 1987).

AIDS: Allie's Story, 14 min. video from ABC's 20/20 (available from AIMS Media, 6901 Woodley Avenue, Van Nuys, CA 91406).

"Me First! Medical Manifestations of HIV in Women," New Jersey Women and AIDS Network (available from New Jersey Women and AIDS Network, 5 Elm Road, #112, New Brunswick, NJ 08901).

"Minority Women and AIDS: A Dialogue," proceedings of the 1987 Minority Women and AIDS Conference (available from Women in Crisis, 133 West 21st Street, 11th Floor, New York, NY 10011).

Triple Jeopardy: Women and AIDS (London: Panos Institute, 1992; available from the Panos Institute, 9 White Lion Street, London N1 9PD, England).

"Women and AIDS," Women's AIDS Network (available in English and Spanish from the San Francisco AIDS Foundation, P.O. Box 426182, San Francisco, CA 94142).

Women and AIDS: A Survival Kit, 22 min. video (1989; available from University of California Extension Media Center, 2176 Shattuck Avenue, Berkeley, CA 94709).

FACTS ABOUT SEXUALLY TRANSMITTED DISEASES

- Health problems caused by sexually transmitted diseases (STDs) tend to be more severe and more frequent for women than for men.
- Many STDs cause no symptoms, particularly among women—although someone who is infected may still pass along the disease.
- STDs can spread into the uterus and fallopian tubes to cause pelvic inflammatory disease, which in turn is a major cause of both infertility and ectopic pregnancy.
- Cervical cancer has also been associated with STDs.
- Experts believe that having STDs other than AIDS increases one's risk of becoming infected with AIDS.
- In pregnant women, STDs are associated with spontaneous abortion, premature birth, and infection in the newborn. These diseases can be passed from mother to baby before or during birth, and some may cause a baby to be permanently disabled or even die; infection in the newborn occurs in 30–70% of cases with infants born to acutely infected mothers.
- Nearly 2/3 of all STDs occur in people younger than 25.
- Most STDs can be cured if diagnosed and treated early.

Source: National Institute of Allergy and Infectious Diseases

PREVENTING SEXUALLY TRANSMITTED DISEASES

The best way to prevent sexually transmitted diseases (STDs) is to avoid sexual intercourse. But if you decide to be sexually active, there are things that can be done to protect yourself:

- Be direct about asking a new sex partner whether he or she has been exposed to an STD or has any unexplained symptoms.
- Learn to recognize physical symptoms of STDs such as sores, rashes, or discharges, especially in the genital area.
- Don't have sex if your partner shows signs of these conditions, and urge him or her to get medical attention.
- Use condoms during intercourse; condoms are the best way to prevent the spread of these STDs, although diaphragms also reduce the risk of transmission for some of these infections.

Source: National Institute of Allergy and Infectious Diseases

CITIES WITH THE HIGHEST CHLAMYDIA RATES AMONG WOMEN

	Cases per 100,000
1. Newark, NJ	2,113.4
2. Honolulu, HI	2,033.1
3. Atlanta, GA	1,168.1
4. Minneapolis, MN	1,077.1
5. Indianapolis, IN	1,052.2
6. Richmond, VA	1,047.8
7. St. Louis, MO	1,014.1
8. Baltimore, MD	1,005.4
9. Philadelphia, PA	984.1
10. Portland, OR	954.7
11. Columbus, OH	923.0
12. Kansas City, MO	919.6
13. Oklahoma City, OK	883.6
14. Boston, MA	847.7
15. Norfolk, VA	855.3

Source: Centers for Disease Control

CHLAMYDIA RATES AMONG WOMEN

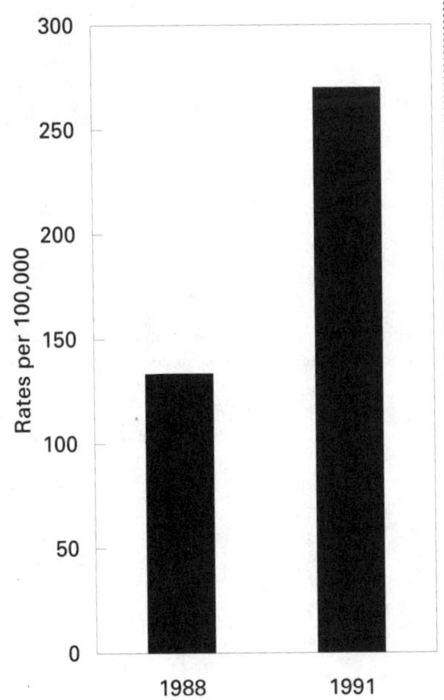

Source: Centers for Disease Control

Prenatal transmission resulted in over half a million pediatric AIDS cases worldwide in 1991.

Genital herpes cases increased from 15,000 in 1966 to 125,000 in 1989.

MAJOR SEXUALLY TRANSMITTED DISEASES

One in four women is infected with an STD by the age of 21.

One-third of sexually active teens use contraception; one-fourth of those use condoms.

Disease	Incidence	Symptoms	Complications	Treatment
Chlamydia	The most common of all STDs, it is responsible for around 4 million new cases each year.	Many people have few or no symptoms of this infection (1 in 3 women have none), although some may find abnormal genital discharge and burning with urination. Chlamydia is easily confused with gonorrhea because the symptoms are similar.	Pelvic inflammatory disease is a serious complication of chlamydia, and infertility can also result. Inflamed rectum and conjunctivitis can result as well. Pregnant women may also pass the infection to their newborns, who may develop pneumonia or conjunctivitis.	A seven-day course of antibiotics and a follow-up visit to a doctor. All sex partners should be tested and treated.
Genital herpes	Affects an estimated 30 million Americans, with around 500,000 new cases annually.	Symptoms can include vaginal discharge, itching and burning sensations, and painful blisters or open sores in genital area, around the anus, and on the buttocks or thigh. Sores usually disappear within 2 to 3 weeks, but virus remains in body and lesions can recur. Number and pattern of recurrences often change over time.	Can be transmitted to babies if an outbreak is taking place during birth, with untreated infections in newborns resulting in mental retardation and death.	There is no cure; symptoms can be alleviated with acyclovir, a prescription antiviral drug.
Genital warts (venereal warts)	These highly contagious warts infect 500,000 Americans each year.	Small, hard, painless bumps in and around the vaginal area, near the anus, and possibly in the mouth; if untreated, may grow and develop a fleshy, cauliflower-like appearance.	Scientists believe that the virus that causes gential warts may also cause certain genital cancers. They may also cause problems during pregnancy.	Either a topical drug applied to the skin, freezing the warts, or injecting a type of interferon. Surgery is also possible for large warts.

Disease	Incidence	Symptoms	Complications	Treatment
Gonorrhea	Around 1.5 million new cases of this highly contagious disease each year in this country.	Most women have no symptoms. Those that do occur include discharge from vagina and painful or difficult urination. The most serious and common complications occur in women, including, in the later stages, pelvic inflammatory disease, abdominal pain, bleeding between periods, vomiting, fever, ectopic pregnancy, and infertility.	If it is not treated it can spread to the bloodstream and infect joints, heart valves, and the brain. The disease can be passed to a newborn infant during delivery.	Penicillin, although several resistant strains of the disease have appeared, which must be treated with other antibiotics. Whatever course of antibiotics is adopted, a follow-up visit to a doctor is necessary. All sex partners should be tested and treated.
Syphilis	Over 130,000 cases in 1990 with the number rising dramatically in recent years.	The first symptom—a chancre sore that usually appears around the vagina—is very mild and can be overlooked. Untreated, infection may produce a transient rash, serious involvement of heart and central nervous system, blindness, mental disorders, and eventual death. Full course of disease can take years.	Pregnant women are likely to pass syphilis to their unborn children, who may be born with serious mental and physical problems as a result, or may die.	Penicillin remains the most common treatment.
Trichomoniasis	Affects 2–3 million Americans a year.	Often occurs without symptoms; when they do appear, symptoms include heavy yellow-green or gray vaginal discharge, discomfort during intercourse, vaginal odor, painful urination, itching and irritation of genital area, and, more rarely, lower abdominal pain.	Data associates trichomoniasis with increased risk of HIV; it may also cause delivery of low-birth-weight babies.	Both partners should be treated with metronidazole.

Sexually transmitted diseases caused more death and illness in women worldwide in 1992 than AIDS did in men, women, and children combined, *Worldwatch* magazine reported.

GONORRHEA RATES

84% of American women are not concerned about contracting a sexually transmitted disease.

This graph is based on figures for women from 1990–92.

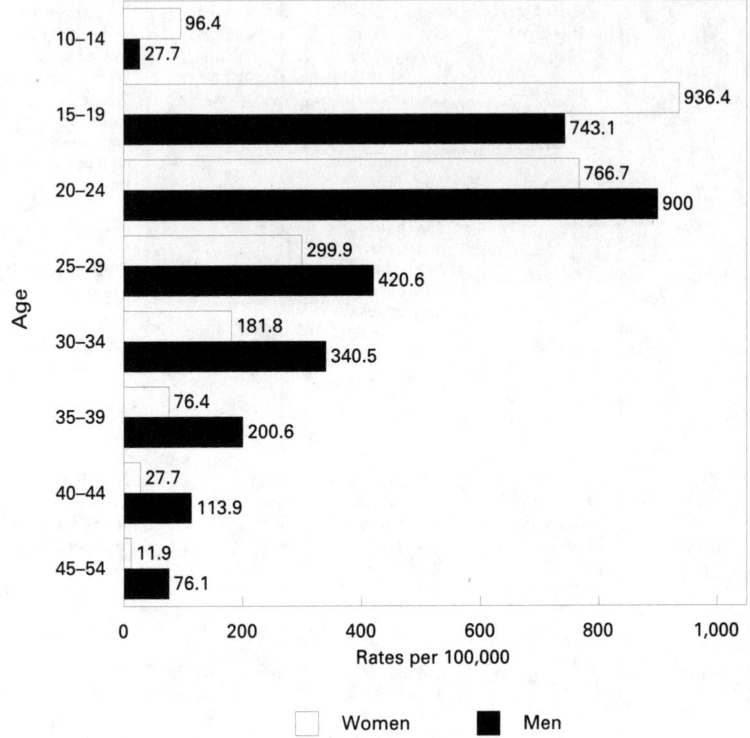

Source: National Institute of Allergy and Infectious Diseases

SYPHILIS RATES

This graph is based on figures for women from 1990–92.

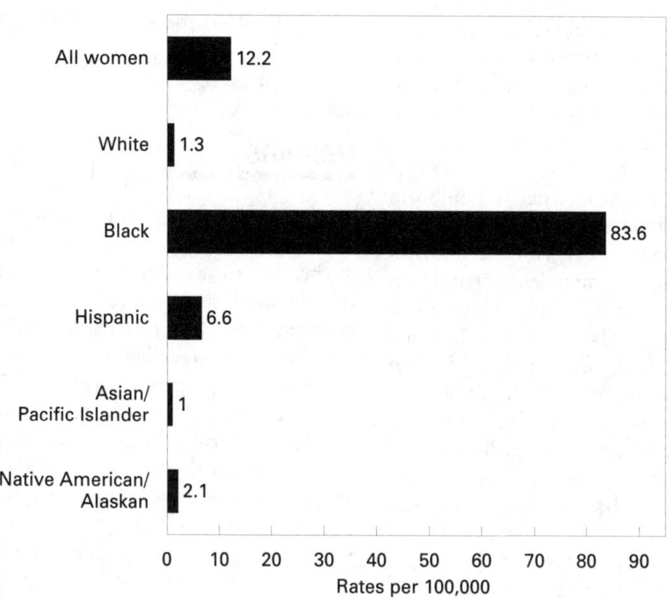

Source: Division of STD/HIV Prevention, Centers for Disease Control

Traditional healers throughout sub-Saharan Africa promote the idea that a man infected with a sexually transmitted disease should have sex with a virgin to cure himself.

SEXUALLY TRANSMITTED DISEASES—RESOURCES AND READING

American Social Health Association
P.O. Box 13827
Research Triangle Park, NC 27709
(800) 227-8922 or (919) 361-8400

Herpes Resource Center
P.O. Box 13827
Research Triangle Park, NC 27709
(919) 361-8488

National Institute of Allergy and Infectious Diseases
National Institutes of Health
Bethesda, MD 20892
(301) 496-5717

Planned Parenthood
810 Seventh Avenue
New York, NY 10019
(212) 603-4600 or (800) 248-7797

The Truth About Herpes, Stephen Sack, M.D. (available from the Herpes Resource Center, P.O. Box 13827, Research Triangle Park, NC 27709).

STD HOTLINES

National Herpes Hotline
(919) 361-8488

National STD Hotline
(800) 227-8922

PELVIC INFLAMMATORY DISEASE

The most serious and common complication of sexually transmitted diseases among women is pelvic inflammatory disease (PID), a term used to describe infections of the uterus, fallopian tubes, and ovaries. Untreated, PID can lead to infertility, ectopic pregnancy, chronic pelvic pain, and other serious health problems.

•Each year more than 1 million American women experience an acute episode of PID. More than 100,000 of that number become infertile—approximately 20% of women who have PID. In addition, a large proportion of the 70,000 ectopic pregnancies each year are the result of PID—indeed, a women who has had the disease has a six- to tenfold greater risk.

•The major symptoms of the disease are lower abdominal pain and abnormal vaginal discharge, as well as fever, pain in the right upper abdomen, painful intercourse, and irregular menstrual bleeding. Certain forms of PID, however, produce minor or no symptoms, even though they can seriously damage reproductive organs.

•The two most common sexually transmitted diseases to cause PID are chlamydia and gonorrhea.

•Sexually active teenagers are more likely to develop PID than older women—more than three times as likely as women from 25–29— although in all age groups, the more sexual partners a women has, the greater her risk of developing PID.

•Diagnosing PID can be difficult, so if a women thinks she might have a sexually transmitted disease she should be tested; early treatment may prevent the development of PID. To prevent the diseases that cause PID, doctors recommend the use of a barrier contraceptive such as a diaphagm or a condom.

•PID is treated by administering at least two antibiotics. All sexual partners, even those without symptoms, should also be treated to ensure that the cause of the infection is stamped out.

Source: National Institute of Allergy and Infectious Diseases

FIBROIDS

•Fibroid tumors are benign growths that appear outside, inside, or within the wall of the uterus. When they remain small they generally produce no symptoms, although larger growths can cause pain, a feeling of heaviness, bleeding between periods, longer periods, excessive flow, frequent or painful urination, and dizziness or weakness; large tumors can also cause problems conceiving or carrying a pregnancy to term.

•Women may be able to limit painful fibroids by altering their intake of estrogen, or, in more extreme cases, through surgery. Nevertheless, in around 10% of cases the fibroids return.

•Fibroids affect around 30% of all women by the time they reach 35, although they occur more commonly among black women.

•Although of unknown cause, fibroids seem to be related to estrogen production. So they tend to grow more actively when women are taking birth control pills or menopausal estrogens.

Sources: National Cancer Institute; National Women's Health Network

DES

Risks

An estimated 4.8 million American women received a powerful synthetic hormone known as DES from 1941 to 1971, despite reports from as early as 1953 that it was ineffective for this purpose. Studies have shown that the 2.4 million daughters of women who took DES are now facing a series of medical problems ranging from cancer to reproductive difficulties. The following risks are faced by DES daughters:

•A rare vaginal cancer develops in around one of every 1,000 DES daughters, with the greatest risk occuring from ages 15–22.

•Twice the rate of abnormal cervical cells are found in DES daughters, a condition that can be pre-cancerous.

•Permanent impairment of the immune system has been found to be a greater risk for DES-exposed mothers as well as their offspring.

•Up to half of all DES daughters will have some kind of reproductive difficulty, including infertility, ectopic pregnancy, miscarriage, and premature delivery. (Nevertheless, about 80% of these women will indeed be able to have a baby.)

Precautions for DES Daughters

Women whose mothers took DES should alert their doctors to that fact and be sure to schedule regular check-ups throughout their lives. They should also take certain precautions, particularly during pregnancy:

•Since DES daughters have three to five times more ectopic pregnancies than other women, when one of these women first suspects she is pregnant, she should have a blood test and perhaps ultrasound to confirm that the pregnancy is indeed located in the uterus; if not, she will have to have immediate surgery.

•Since miscarriage in the second trimester is about twice as frequent among DES daughters, these women should have their entire pregnancies treated as high-risk; this means patients should have frequent exams and learn to monitor for possible early contractions. Bed rest and labor-stopping medications may also need to be considered.

Source: DES Action USA

DES—RESOURCES

American Cancer Society
1599 Clifton Road, N.E.
Atlanta, GA 30329
(404) 320-3333

DES Action USA
West Coast office:
1615 Broadway, Suite 510
Oakland, CA 94612
(415) 465-4011

East Coast office:
L.I.J. Medical Center
New Hyde Park, NY 11040
(516) 775-3450

National Cancer Institute
Department of Health and Human Services, Building 31, Room 10-A24
9000 Rockville Pike
Bethesda, MD 20892
(800) 422-6237

HYSTERECTOMIES

•Over half a million women in the U.S. underwent a hysterectomy in 1992, making it the second most common form of major surgery (after cesarean sections).

•One out of every three women can expect to have a hysterectomy by the time she reaches 60.

•The hysterectomy rate in the U.S. varies significantly according to geography and race, with rates running higher in the South and Midwest; likewise the operation is performed more commonly on black women than white, and on women of lower socio-economic status.

•In response to the high number of questionable hysterectomies, California passed a law in 1987 requiring written and verbal informed consent from patients before the operation can be performed.

•The most common conditions that result in hysterectomies in this country are endometriosis, fibroid tumors, dysfunctional uterine bleeding, uterine prolapse, and chronic pelvic pain.

•Despite its high frequency, high cost, and the availability of alternatives, there have been few studies examining hysterectomy in detail.

Source: House Subcommittee on Aging

There are 2.4 million DES daughters in the U.S. DES was also used in other countries, and on U.S. military bases worldwide.

Only 41% of commercial health insurance firms typically cover reversible methods of birth control.

Gynecologists earned over $2.1 billion in the U.S. performing hysterectomies.

6 million women have asthma, which is more common in blacks than whites.

HYSTERECTOMIES—RESOURCES AND READING

ORGANIZATIONS

HERS (Hysterectomy Educational Resources and Services)
422 Bryn Mawr Avenue
Bala-Cynwyd, PA 19004
(215) 667-7757

National Women's Health Network
1325 G Street, N.W.
Washington, DC 20005
(202) 347-1140

READING

All About Hysterectomy, Harry C. Huneycutt, M.D., and Judith L. Davis (New York: Reader's Digest Press, 1977)

Coping with a Hysterectomy, Suzanne Morgan (New York: Dial Press, 1982)

How to Avoid a Hysterectomy, Lynn Payer (New York: Pantheon Books, 1987)

Hysterectomy: Before and After, Winnifred Cutler (New York: Harper and Row, 1988)

The No-Hysterectomy Option, Herbert A. Goldfarb, M.D., and Judith Greif, M.S., RNC (New York: John Wiley & Sons, 1990)

No More Hysterectomies, Vicki Hufnagel, M.D. (New York: Plume, 1988).

ENDOMETRIOSIS

Endometriosis is a perplexing disease affecting women in their reproductive years. This condition develops when tissue like the endometrium, which lines the uterus and is shed each month, is found outside the uterus, in other areas of the body. In these locations the endometrial tissue forms growths or tumors, which can cause pain, infertility, and other problems.

While infertility affects about 30–40% of women with endometriosis, the growths are generally not cancerous—they are a normal type of tissue outside the normal location, often in the ovaries, fallopian tubes, and other parts of the abdomen. Like the normal lining of the uterus, endometrial growths build up tissue each month, break down, and cause bleeding. Unlike the lining of the uterus, however, this tissue has no way to leave the body; the result is internal bleeding, inflammation, and formation of scar tissue, among other problems.

The most predictable symptoms of endometriosis include:

- Pain before and during periods (usually worse than normal pain)
- Pain during or after sex
- Infertility
- Heavy or irregular bleeding.

Fatigue is also common, as are the following conditions when associated with periods:

- Painful bowel movements
- Lower back pain
- Diarrhea and/or constipation
- Intestinal upset

The causes of endometriosis are unknown, and the diagnosis is generally considered uncertain without a special surgical procedure called laparoscopy. Once the condition is definitely diagnosed, treatment can begin, although no sure cure has yet been found. Nothing is certain to stop the pain short of menopause.

Source: Endometriosis Association

ENDOMETRIOSIS—RESOURCES AND READING

ORGANIZATIONS

Endometriosis Association
8585 North 76th Place
Milwaukee, WI 53223
(800) 992-3636 or (800) 426-2363 (Canada)

Endometriosis Treatment Program
St. Charles Medical Center
2500 N.E. Neff Road
Bend, OR 97701
(800) 446-2177 x7563

READING

Living with Endometriosis, Kate Weinstein (Reading, Mass.: Addison-Wesley, 1987).

Overcoming Endometriosis: New Help from the Endometriosis Association, Mary Lou Ballweg and the Endometriosis Association (New York: Congdon and Weed, 1987).

What Women Can Do About Chronic Endometriosis, Judith Sachs (New York: Dell Publishing, 1991).

TOXIC SHOCK SYNDROME

Toxic Shock Syndrome (TSS) is a disease that begins with virus-like symptoms—heachache, vomiting, sudden high fever (102° or higher), and diarrhea—but within 48 hours may lead to falling blood pressure severe enough to cause kidney failure. Other symptoms include a rash that looks like sunburn, dizziness, muscle aches, and fainting or near fainting when standing up.

No one is sure just how the bacteria that causes toxic shock enters the bloodstream, but the disease generally strikes women who have been using tampons. If you have any of the symptoms listed above and are using a tampon, remove it and contact a doctor immediately.

The risk of toxic shock can be minimized by:

- not using tampons at all
- alternating tampon use with feminine pads
- using a tampon with the minimum absorbency needed, since the risk of TSS is related to absorbency: the higher the absorbency, the greater the risk

Source: Women's Health Network

URINARY TRACT INFECTIONS

The causes of urinary tract infections (UTIs) are not clearly established, although for many women, sexual intercourse seems to precipitate an infection. Women who use diaphragms are also more likely to develop a UTI than other women. Symptoms of urinary tract infections include:

- Frequent urge to urinate, although often without success
- Painful, burning sensation during urination, and sometimes even when not urinating
- Feeling bad all over; tired, shaky, and washed out
- Uncomfortable pressure above the pubic bone
- Cloudy, milky, or even reddish urine

UTIs are treated with antibacterial drugs, and various drugs are also available to relieve the pain. In addition, a heating pad or warm bath may help, and most physicians suggest that drinking plenty of water assists in cleansing the urinary tract of harmful bacteria. It is also best to avoid coffee, alcohol, and spicy foods.

Many doctors suggest preventive steps that a woman can take to avoid UTIs, including:

- Drink plenty of water every day (some doctors also suggest cranberry juice)
- Don't put off urinating when you feel the need
- Wipe from front to back to prevent bacteria from around the anus from entering the vagina or urethra
- Cleanse the genital area before intercourse
- Empty the bladder shortly before and after intercourse
- Avoid feminine hygiene sprays and scented douches

Source: National Institute of Diabetes and Digestive and Kidney Diseases

About four out of five women who have a urinary tract infection get another within 18 months.

The rate of urinary tract infections gradually increases in women as they age.

WORKPLACE HEALTH HAZARDS

Only a small number of workplace hazards have been studied for their effects on reproduction. This list indicates only the most commonly known hazards.

Chemical	Workers Affected	Effect of Exposure
Aromatic hydrocarbons (benzene, toluene, xylene)	Chemical workers, lab workers, refinery workers, painters, electronic and semiconductor workers, general manufacturing, auto workers (10,000,000)	Menstrual problems, contaminated breast milk, infertility or sterility, leukemia, hepatic blood, damage to nervous system, irregular heartbeat, nose and throat irritation, muscle fatigue, skin rash, vomiting, upset stomach, anemia, birth defects
Video display terminals (VDTs)	Office and other clerical workers (10,000,000)	Miscarriage, neck and back injuries, carpal tunnel syndrome, eyestrain, headaches
Vinyl chloride and other vinyl compounds	General manufacturing, plastics workers, clothing and textile workers, auto workers (2,325,000)	Miscarriage, menstrual problems, birth defects, cancer, neurotoxicity, liver damage, cardiovascular damage, bone disease
Manganese and manganese compounds	Battery makers, glass and pottery workers, pharmaceutical workers, steel workers, waste water treaters, solderers and welders, smelters, plumbers, painters, artists and jewelers, typesetters, auto workers, general manufacturing, paint manufacturers (1,550,000)	Decreased fertility, contaminated breast milk, central nervous system disorders, lower back fatigue, vomiting, coughing, tight chest
Lead and lead compounds	Battery makers, glass and pottery workers, plumbers, painters, smelters, artists and jewelers, typesetters, solderers and welders, auto workers, general manufacturing, paint manufacturers (1,500,000)	Miscarriage, menstrual problems, infertility or decreased fertility, chromosome damage, contaminated breast milk, birth defects, damage to the nervous system, kidney damage, anemia, deterioration of motor skills, behavioral disorders, brain damage, headaches, fatigue, weakness, gastrointestinal disorders

Chemical	Workers Affected	Effect of Exposure
Ionizing radiation (X-rays, gamma rays)	Hospital and health care workers, lab workers, nuclear workers, food workers, dental personnel (1,320,000)	Infertility or decreased fertility, chromosome damage, premature birth, birth defects, cancer, leukemia, anemia
Boron and boric acid	Wood processors, textile workers, glass and pottery workers, leather workers, chemical workers, artists and jewelers, printers, painters, steel workers, electrical workers (1,000,000)	Contaminated breast milk, damaged ovaries, infertility, birth defects, eye, nose and throat irritation, skin irritation, respiratory irritation, possible kidney and liver damage
Extreme heat	Auto workers, food workers, laundry workers, steel workers, glass and pottery workers, foundry workers, truck drivers (1,000,000)	Miscarriage, birth defects, cardiovascular stress, damage to nervous system
Infectious agents (cytomegalovirus, herpes simplex virus, mumps, rubella, syphilis, toxoplasmosis, varicella virus)	School teachers, hospital workers, flight attendants, poultry, meat, and fish handlers, animal lab workers, dishwashers, sales clerks (1,000,000)	Miscarriage, birth defects, health effects associated with the infectious disease
Pesticides	Workers involved in manufacture of, use of, or exposure to pesticides (chemical workers, farm workers, exterminators, food workers, general manufacturing, office workers) (1,000,000)	Decreased fertility and miscarriage, contaminated breast milk, menstrual problems and infertility, birth defects, cancer, neurotoxicity, death with large exposure, stuttered speech, loss of memory, abdominal pain, nervousness, sleep disturbance

Source: Coalition of Trade Union Women

Black women aged 45 to 64 are twice as likely to die from diabetes as white women the same age.

There is a federal law to protect people with AIDS from discrimination, but only 11 cities in the U.S. protect a woman from losing her job, home, and children because she is a lesbian.

Heart disease kills over half a million women annually.

WORKPLACE HAZARDS—RESOURCES AND READING

ORGANIZATIONS

Association of Occupational and Environmental Clinics
1010 Vermont Avenue, N.W., # 513
Washington, DC 20005
(202) 347-4976

Coalition of Trade Union Women
15 Union Square
New York, NY 10003
(212) 242-0700

National Birth Defects Center
30 Warren Street
Boston, MA 02135
Pregnancy/Environmental Hotline: (617) 787-4957 or, in Massachusetts, (800) 322-5014

Occupational and Environmental Reproductive Hazards Clinic and Education Center
University of Massachusetts Medical Center
55 Lake Avenue North
Worcester, MA 01655
(508) 856-2818

Occupational Safety and Health Administration
200 Constitution Avenue, N.W.
Washington, DC 20210
(202) 219-8151

Utah Department of Health
Family Health Services Division
44 Medical Drive
Salt Lake City, UT 84113
Pregnancy riskline: Utah (800) 822-2229 or Montana (800) 521-2229

READING

"Is Your Job Making You Sick?" CLUW Handbook on Workplace Hazards (available from Coalition of Labor Union Women, 15 Union Square, New York, NY 10003).

Hazardous Inheritance: Workplace Dangers to Reproductive Health, Margaret Lazarus and Renner Wunderlich, dirs. (1989; video available from Cambridge Documentary Films, P.O. Box 385, Cambridge, MA 02139).

LUPUS

•Lupus is a chronic disorder of the immune system that occurs ten times more frequently in women than in men. Affecting around one in 500 Americans, it also strikes blacks, Chinese, and some Native American groups more widely than Caucasians.

•Lupus can cause inflammation of various parts of the body, especially the skin, joints, blood, and kidneys. For most people it is a mild disease affecting only a few organs, although for others it may cause more serious problems, including death.

•Although most patients do not experience all of these symptoms at one time, the warning signs of lupus include (from the most common to the least):

Achy joints
Fever over 100° F
Swollen joints (arthritis)
Prolonged fatigue
Skin rashes
Anemia
Kidney involvement
Pain in the chest on deep breathing
Butterfly-shaped rash across face
Photosensitivity
Hair loss
Fingers turning white and/or blue in cold
Seizures
Mouth ulcers

•The cause of lupus is not known, but since lupus occurs most commonly in young females, doctors believe that female sex hormones, particularly estrogen, may influence the immune system, making women more susceptible to the development of the disease.

•Currently there is no cure for lupus, although early diagnosis and treatment can signficantly help control the disease. General treatment guidelines are as follows:

•Patients should rest regularly when lupus is active, and should increase

activity when the disease is in remission in order to increase strength and joint flexibility.
•Photosensitive patients should use sunscreens to prevent rashes, or treat rashes with cortisone creams.
•Sufferers with achy joints can take aspirin or aspirin-like drugs.
•Cortisone drugs can help patients with more severe organ involvement.
•Patients should call a doctor if they have a fever over 100°.

Source: Lupus Foundation of America

LUPUS—RESOURCES

The American Lupus Society
3914 Del Amo Boulevard, Suite 922
Torrance, CA 90503
(800) 331-1802 or (310) 542-8891

Lupus Foundation of America
4 Research Place, Suite 180
Rockville, MD 20850
(800) 558-0121 or (301) 670-9292

OSTEOPOROSIS

Facts

•Osteoporosis is a condition characterized by low bone mass and structural deterioration of bone tissue, leading to an increased likelihood of hip, spine, and wrist fractures.
•Between a half and a third of all postmenopausal women over 50 have osteoporosis or porous bones, a condition responsible for more than 1.5 million factures annually.
•Osteoporosis afflicts women at significantly higher rates than men—spinal osteoporosis, for instance, is eight times more common among women, and hip fracture is twice to three times more likely.
•The symptoms of osteoporosis are nonexistent; indeed it is often called the "silent disease" because people may not know they have it until their bones become so weak that a sudden strain, bump, or fall causes a bone to fracture or reveals a seriously deteriorated vertebra.
•Collapsed vertebrae associated with osteoporosis may initially be felt or seen in the form of severe back pain, loss of height, or spinal deformities such as stooped posture.

Risk Factors for Osteoporosis

•Menopause before age 45
•A family history of fractures in elderly women
•Use of certain medications, particularly corticosteriods
•Chronically low calcium intake
•Thin and/or small bones
•Caucasian or Asian
•Inactive lifestyle
•Cigarette smoking
•Excessive use of alcohol
•Advanced age
•Heavy caffeine consumption

Prevention Guidelines for Osteoporosis

Because women are much more susceptible than men, the prevention of osteoporosis has received much attention among women. Medical experts agree that the disease is highly preventable, and believe that building strong bones, especially before age 35, and maintaining a healthy lifestyle may be a woman's best defense against developing the disease. To help prevent bone loss, doctors recommend the following guidelines for women:
•Eat a balanced diet rich in calcium. (See Some Calcium-Rich Foods, p. 245.)
•Exercise regularly, especially weight-bearing activities.
•Don't smoke, and limit alcohol intake.
•Ask your doctor about estrogen replacement therapy if you have had an early or surgically induced menopause.

Source: National Osteoporosis Foundation

Nearly half of all women develop osteoporosis by age 70.

A woman's risk of hip fracture is equal to her combined risk of breast, uterine, and ovarian cancer.

One in four women, as opposed to one in eight men, will be clinically depressed at some time in her life.

Around 40% of women are seriously depressed each week, compared with 26% of men.

RATES OF OSTEOPOROSIS IN WOMEN

Age Group	Rate
45–49	17.9%
50–54	39.2
55–59	57.7
60–64	65.6
65–69	73.5
75+	89.0

Source: National Institutes of Health

OSTEOPOROSIS—RESOURCES AND READING

ORGANIZATIONS

National Arthritis and Musculoskeletal and Skin Disease Information Clearinghouse
Box AMS
9000 Rockville Pike
Bethesda, MD 20892
(301) 495-4484

National Institute of Aging
National Institute of Health
Bethesda, MD 20892
(301) 496-4000

National Osteoporosis Foundation
1150 17th Street, N.W., Suite 500
Washington, DC 20036
(202) 223-2226

READING

"Boning Up on Osteoporosis" (available from National Osteoporosis Foundation/Aging, 2100 M Street, N.W., Suite 602, Washington, DC 20037).

"The Older Person's Guide to Osteoporosis" (available from National Osteoporosis Foundation/Aging, 2100 M Street, N.W., Suite 602, Washington, DC 20037).

"Osteoporosis," a Medicine for the Layman publication (available from Clinical Center Communications, National Institutes of Health, 9000 Rockville Pike, Building 10, Room 1C255, Bethesda, MD 20892).

"Osteoporosis," Scientific Workshop: Research Directions in Osteoporosis (1987; available from the NIAMS Information Clearinghouse, Box AMS, Bethesda, MD 20892).

"Osteoporosis: Cause, Treatment, Prevention" (1986; available from the NIAMS Information Clearinghouse, Box AMS, Bethesda, MD 20892).

Osteoporosis: The Silent Thief, William A. Peck and Louis V. Avioli (Glenview, Ill.: Scott Foresman, 1988).

Preventing Osteoporosis: Dr. Kenneth H. Cooper's Preventive Medicine Program, Kenneth H. Cooper, M.D. (New York: Bantam Books, 1989).

WOMEN AND MENTAL HEALTH

- Women's risk for most types of depression exceeds that for men by two to one; they also suffer more from phobias and panic disorders, and have a nine-to-one edge on both life-threatening eating disorders and multiple personality or disassociative disorders.
- Schizophrenia in women, which has been found to occur at the same rate as in men, occurs differently and responds differently to treatment than it does in men.
- Women attempt suicide more often than men, although men are more apt to succeed. Men are more likely to use guns, while women use pills or other methods that are slower and therefore treatable.
- While most men define themselves by accomplishments, women tend to define themselves by relationships; consequently, the loss of a relationship (i.e. a death in the family) may cause depression and anxiety.
- Forty percent or more of American women are survivors of sexual or physical abuse, a situation that has serious mental health consequences.

Indeed the large majority of seriously mentally ill women in treatment have past histories of physical and sexual abuse.

•Post-traumatic stress disorder is more likely to be caused by rape than by any other traumatic event, including combat.

•Sixty-four percent of female psychiatric inpatients are abused as adults (e.g., as battered women).

•Seventy-five percent of the U.S. population living in poverty are women and children, conditions that create a much greater risk for mental health problems.

•Recent studies have linked bulimia with major depression; substance abuse, panic disorders, agoraphobia, and kleptomania have also been shown to be connected.

•Through suicide, depression is the seventh or eighth greatest cause of death in the U.S., and second among adolescents and young adults.

•With appropriate treatment, around 80% of even the most serious depressions can be successfully alleviated.

Sources: American Psychological Association; Menninger Clinic; National Institute of Mental Health; Substance Abuse and Mental Services Administration

SERIOUS MENTAL ILLNESS

This graph reflects the balance of men and women with serious mental illness from 1989.

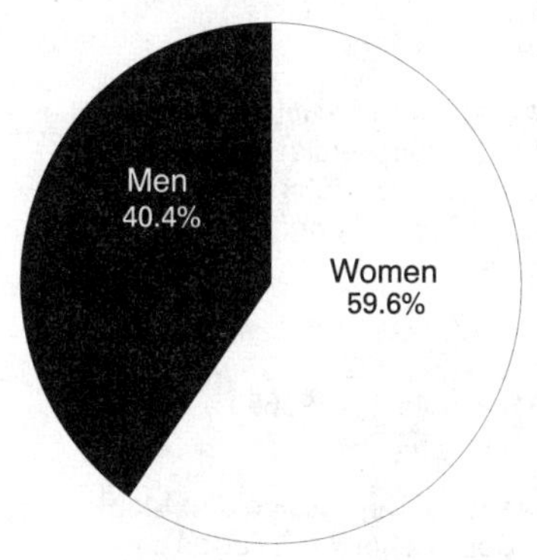

Source: National Institute of Mental Health

MENTAL HEALTH REFERRALS

For a referral to a qualified therapist in your area, contact the following associations:

American Association for Marriage and Family Therapy
1100 17th Street, N.W., 10th Floor
Washington, DC 20036
(800) 374-2638

American Association of Sex Educators, Counselors and Therapists
435 N. Michigan Avenue, Suite 1717
Chicago, IL 60611
(312) 644-0828

American Psychiatric Association
1400 K Street, N.W.
Washington, DC 20005
(202) 682-6000

American Psychological Association
750 First Street, N.E.
Washington, DC 20002
(202) 336-5700

National Association of Social Workers
750 First Street, N.E.
Washington, DC 20002
(202) 408-8600

Only about a quarter of the addicts enrolled in drug- and alcohol-abuse treatment programs are women. Many women addicts are deterred from treatment programs because they emphasize aggressive confrontation of the problem rather than encouragement and support.

Mental health treatments available to women are limited because many medications for treating mental disorders have not been adequately tested on women.

Women are twice as likely as men to develop panic disorder.

MENTAL HEALTH—RESOURCES

American Institute of Stress
124 Park Avenue
Yonkers, NY 10703
(914) 963-1200

American Self-Help Clearinghouse
St. Clares-Riverside Medical Center
Denville, NJ 07834
(201) 625-7101 or (201) 625-9053 (deaf access)

Depression After Delivery
P.O. Box 1282
Morrisville, PA 19067
(215) 295-3994

National Depressive and Manic Depressive Association
730 North Franklin Street, Suite 501
Chicago, IL 60610
(312) 642-0049

National Foundation for Depressive Illness
P.O. Box 2257
New York, NY 10116
(212) 505-7777 or (800) 248-4344 (for recorded information about symptoms of depression)

National Mental Health Association
1021 Prince Street
Alexandria, VA 22314
(703) 684-7722

Recovery
82 North Dearborn Street
Chicago, IL 60610
(312) 337-5661

The Women's Program
Menninger Clinic
Box 829
Topeka, KS 66601
(903) 273-7500

Women's Programs Office
American Psychological Association
750 First Street, N.E.
Washington, DC 20002
(202) 336-6044

MENTAL HEALTH—RECOMMENDED READING

In a Different Voice: Psychological Theory and Women's Development, Carol Gilligan (Cambridge: Harvard University Press, 1982).

The Lavender Couch: A Consumer's Guide to Psychotherapy for Lesbians and Gay Men, Marny Hall (Boston: Alyson Publications, 1985).

A New Approach to Women and Therapy, Miriam Greenspan (New York: McGraw-Hill, 1983).

Toward a New Psychology of Women, Jean Baker Miller (rev. ed.; Boston: Beacon Press, 1986).

Trusting Ourselves: The Sourcebook on Psychology for Women (New York: Atlantic Monthly Press, 1990).

Women and Madness, Phyllis Chesler (New York: Avon Books, 1972).

Women and Mental Health, Elizabeth Howell and Joan P. Bean, eds. (New York: Basic Books, 1981).

Women and Psychotherapy: A Consumer Handbook, Federation of Organizations for Professional Women (available from the Federation of Organizations for Professional Women, 2000 P Street, N.W., Suite 403, Washington, DC 20036).

STRESS

•Job stress is considered by many authorities to be one of the major adult health problems today.
•Studies of occupational stress make it clear that it is those who are bossed rather than those who do the bossing who suffer more work-relat-

ed illness. Secretaries, for instance, suffer the second highest rate of stress-related diseases, a situation that can be attributed to a heavy workload with little say over how and when the work is done. Likewise, female clerical workers experience coronary heart disease at twice the rate of other working women.

•Built-in stress will be found in the fact that women in all job descriptions earn far less than their male counterparts even when those positions and experiences are identical.

Sources: American Institute of Stress; Framingham Heart Study; National Institute of Mental Health

STRESS—RECOMMENDED READING

The Female Stress Syndrome: How to Recognize and Live with It, Georgia Witkin-Lanoil (New York: Newmarket, 1984).

Gender and Stress, Rosalind C. Barnett, Lois Biener, Grace K. Baruch, eds. (New York: Free Press, 1987).

Lives in Stress: Women and Depression, D. Bella, ed. (Beverly Hills, Calif.: Sage Publishing, 1982).

Women Under Stress, Donald Roy Morse and W. Lawrence Furst (New York: Van Nostrand Rheinhold, 1982).

WOMEN AND EATING DISORDERS

No one knows for sure how many people overeat or exercise compulsively, but estimates place as much as 25% of the entire population of the U.S. in this group. Of that number, the overwhelming majority are women; for example, 90% of the victims of anorexia and bulimia are female. While the rate for anorexia runs around 0.5% of all women between 10 and 30, up to 10% of deaths among teenage girls may result from the illness.

Research into eating disorders suggests that:

•50% of fourth-grade girls diet because they think they are too fat.

•90% of high school junior and senior women diet, although only about 10% are overweight.

•14% of college-aged women vomit at least once in a while to control weight.

•8% of college-aged women use laxatives at least once in a while to control weight.

•40% of college-aged women follow diets of 800 calories a day or less. Semi-starvation is 1,200 calories a day, while the average normal-weight woman eats 1,800–2,200 calories a day. After two years, 95% of dieters regain their lost weight plus 10 extra pounds. After five years, 98% have followed the same path.

Source: Anorexia Nervosa and Related Eating Disorders

The onset of eating disorders among women occurs by age 20 in 86% of all cases.

DANGER SIGNALS OF EATING DISORDERS

Anorexia

Anorexia nervosa is a disorder in which preoccupation with dieting and thinness leads to excessive weight loss. The behavioral symptoms of anorexia include:

- dissatisfaction with appearance; believing that body is fat even while severely underweight
- serious depression
- refusing to eat, except for small amounts of a few "safe" foods
- dieting even when underweight
- maintaining less than 85% of medically healthy weight
- studying recipes and cookbooks with fascination
- shopping for groceries and cooking for others, but refusing to eat
- obsessing about meal plans and keeping calorie journals
- compulsively weighing and measuring food

Only half of all people with eating disorders report being cured, and 6% of all serious cases end in death.

The ratio of girls suffering from eating disorders as compared to boys is 9 to 1.

- eating in ritualistic ways
- combining foods and condiments strangely
- exercising compulsively
- withdrawing from relationships and becoming socially isolated
- insisting they are fat even when they are alarmingly thin
- denying anything is wrong, becoming sullen, angry, or defensive when others express concern

The physical consequences of prolonged dieting associated with anorexia include:

- hunger, cravings, preoccupation with food, and in many cases, binge eating
- dry, scaly skin, which may be yellow or gray
- dull, brittle, thin hair
- loss of muscle as well as fat; person may look like a skeleton covered only with skin
- loss of menstrual periods, and sometimes fertility
- loss of sexual desire
- icy hands and feet; person is cold when others are warm
- downy fuzz on face, limbs, and body

Bulimia

Bulimia nervosa involves frequent episodes of binge eating, almost always followed by purging and intense feelings of guilt and shame. The behavioral symptoms of bulimia include:

- eating large amounts of food quickly
- secretively gobbling "forbidden goodes"
- preferring high-fat, high-sugar binge foods
- trying to undo binges by vomiting, exercising, fasting, or abusing laxatives and diuretics (water pills)
- usually dieting when not binging
- obsession with exercise
- sometimes shoplifting, binge spending, abusing alcohol, using street drugs, or jumping from one sexual relationship to another

The physical consequences of bulimia include:

- weight fluctuations because of alternating diets and binges
- swollen glands in neck under jaw
- loss of tooth enamel
- broken blood vessels in face and bags under eyes
- upset of body's fluid/mineral balance leading to rapid or irregular heartbeat and possible heart attack
- dehydration, fainting spells, tremors, blurred vision
- loss of or irregular menstrual periods
- laxative dependency, damage to bowels
- indigestion, cramps, abdominal discomfort, bloating, gas, constipation
- liver and kidney damage in some cases
- internal bleeding, infection
- death; heart attack and suicidal depression are the major risks

Compulsive Eating and Binge Eating

Compulsive eaters and overweight binge eaters experience uncontrolled eating, which they sometimes keep a secret. The behavioral symptoms include:

- binge eating, or nibbling and snacking over several hours
- may or may not overeat at mealtime
- usually not overeating in front of other people
- preferring high-sugar, high-fat "comfort foods"
- dieting, making themselves hungry, then eating and feeling out of control
- eating not just to satisfy physical hunger but also to relieve stress and numb painful feelings
- not compensating for overeating by vomiting, exercising, fasting, or abusing laxatives and diuretics

The physical consequences of compulsive eating include:

- weight gain; sometimes obesity
- increased risk of high blood pressure, clogged blood vessels, heart attack, and stroke
- increased risk of some cancers
- increased risk of bone and joint problems
- increased risk of diabetes

Sources for above: American Anorexia and Bulimia Association; Anorexia Nervosa and Related Eating Disorders

EATING DISORDERS—RESOURCES AND READING

Organizations

American Anorexia/Bulimia Association
418 E. 76th Street, Suite 3B
New York, NY 10021
(212) 734-1114

Anorexia Nervosa and Related Eating Disorders
P.O. Box 5102
Eugene, OR 97405
(503) 344-1144

Center for the Study of Anorexia and Bulimia
1 W. 91st Street
New York, NY 10024
(212) 595-3449

Foundation for Education about Eating Disorders
5238 Duvall Drive
Bethesda, MD 20816
(301) 229-6904

National Anorexic Aid Society
Harding Hospital
445 E. Granville Road
Worthington, OH 43085
(614) 436-1112

National Association of Anorexia Nervosa and Associated Disorders
P.O. Box 7
Highland Park, IL 60035
(708) 831-3438

National Eating Disorders Organization
Harding Hospital
445 E. Granville Road
Worthington, OH 43085
(614) 436-1112

Overeaters Anonymous
P.O. Box 92870
Los Angeles, CA

The Renfrew Center
475 Spring Lane
Philadelphia, PA 19128
(800) 736-3739

Reading

Anorexia and Bulimia: Anatomy of a Social Epidemic, Richard Gordon (Cambridge, Mass.: Basil Blackwell, 1990).

Breaking Free from Compulsive Eating, Geneen Roth (New York: New American Library, 1986).

Controlling Eating Disorders with Facts, Advice and Resources (Phoenix: Oryx Press, 1992).

The Famine Within, 90 min. video, Katherine Gilday (1990; available from Direct Cinema, P.O. Box 10003, Santa Monica, CA 90410).

Fasting Girls: The Surprising History of Anorexia Nervosa, Joan Brumberg (Cambridge: Harvard University Press, 1988).

Fat Is a Feminist Issue, Susie Orbach (New York: Berkeley Publishers, 1982).

Feeding the Hungry Heart: The Experience of Compulsive Eating, Geneen Roth (New York: New American Library, 1983).

The Hungry Self: Women, Eating and Identity, Kim Chernin (New York: Times Books, 1985).

My Name is Caroline, Caroline Miller (New York: Doubleday, 1988).

The Obsession: Reflections on the Tyranny of Slenderness, Kim Chernin (New York: Harper & Row, 1981).

A Parent's Guide to Anorexia and Bulimia, Katherine Byrne (New York: Schocken Books, 1987).

Surviving an Eating Disorder, Michele Siegel, Judith Brisman, Margot Weinshel (New York: Harper & Row, 1988).

When Food's a Foe, Nancy J. Kolodny (Boston: Little, Brown, 1987).

Up to 5% of college women are bulimic.

2 million Americans use diet pills, most of them women.

In a study of patients diagnosed with anorexia, researchers found a 7% death rate.

ALTERNATIVE TREATMENTS

	Amenorrhea	Anemia	Anxiety	Benign breast disease
Therapies				
Acupuncture	xxx		xx	xx
Alexander technique			xx	
Aromatherapy			x	
Bach flower remedies			xx	
Biochemic tissue salts	xx		x	
Biofeedback	xx		xxx	
Chiropractic				
Clinical ecology	xx	xx	xxx	xxx
Dance therapy			xxx	
Herbal medicine	xxx		xxx	xxx
Homeopathy	xxx		xxx	xx
Hypnotherapy	xx		xxx	
Massage			xxx	
Meditation/ visualization	xx		xxx	
Megavitamin therapy	xx	xxx	xx	
Naturopathy	xx	xx	xx	xxx
Osteopathy	xx		x	
Psychotherapy			xxx	
Reflexology	xx		xx	x
Shiatsu			xx	
Spiritual healing	xx		xx	x
Yoga				

xxx—**excellent results** xx—**worth a try**
x—**useful as adjunct to other therapies, orthodox or alternative**

Cancer	Cervical erosion	Chlamydia	Cystitis	Depression
X				XX
				XX
X	X		XX	XX
			XX	XX
				X
			XXX	X
				XX
XX	XX	X	XXX	XX
XX	XX	X	XXX	XX
XX				XXX
XX	XX			XX
XXX	XX		X	XXX
XXX	X		XX	XX
XXX	XX		XXX	XXX
			XX	XX
XXX				XXX
	X		XX	XX
				X
XXX				XX
			XX	XX

On average, every woman born in Russia has 4 or 5 abortions during her childbearing years.

Dorothy Brown, M.D., was the first black woman surgeon in the United States—and the first American state legislator to attempt to legalize abortion, in 1967.

Therapies	Dysmenorrhea	Endometriosis	Fibroids	Hot Flashes
Acupuncture	xxx	xx	xxx	
Alexander technique	x			
Aromatherapy	x			
Bach flower remedies				
Biochemic tissue salts	x			
Biofeedback				
Chiropractic				
Clinical ecology	x	xx	xxx	
Dance therapy	x			
Herbal medicine	xx	xxx	xxx	xxx
Homeopathy	xx	xxx	xx	xxx
Hypnotherapy	xx	xx		
Massage	x			
Meditation/ visualization	xx	xxx	xx	x
Megavitamin therapy	x	xxx		xxx
Naturopathy	xx	xxx	xxx	xxx
Osteopathy	x			
Psychotherapy	x			
Reflexology	x	xx	x	
Shiatsu	x	x		
Spiritual healing			xx	
Yoga	xxx			

xxx—**excellent results** xx—**worth a try**
x—**useful as adjunct to other therapies, orthodox or alternative**

Infertility	Osteoporosis	Pelvic inflammatory disease	Postnatal depression	Pre-eclamptic toxemia
XXX			XX	
			X	
			X	
			X	
				XXX
XXX			XX	
			XX	
XXX	XX	XXX	XX	
XXX	XXX	XXX	XX	X
XX			XX	XX
			XX	
XX		XX	XX	X
XXX	XXX		XXX	X
XXX	XXX		XXX	XX
XX			X	
			XXX	
X			XX	
XXX			XXX	
			XXX	

Source: Alternative Health Care for Women

In unhappy marriages, women are 3 times more likely to be depressed than men.

More than half of American women use their obstetrician-gynecologist as their primary physician.

ALTERNATIVE HEALTH CARE

Guidelines for Alternative Therapy

While traditional medicine remains the treatment of choice for most women, for certain conditions many turn to a range of alternative therapies, from acupuncture and psychotherapy to aromatherapy and herbal medicine. Because alternative therapies are so diverse and some have no training canon, as does traditional medicine, it can be difficult to find the right practitioner. To ensure that you get a good therapist, follow the tips below:

•Ask your doctor to recommend someone. G.P.s are often very interested in alternative therapies, and many of them have tried one or several themselves. In any case, it is a good idea to let your doctor know if you are having some form of alternative treatment.

•Ask friends, neighbors, or colleagues to recommend someone they have found to be helpful.

•Select a practitioner who is registered with one of the alternative professional organizations—at the moment this is your only safeguard that the practitioner you are going to has attained a certain professional standard.

•If you have a particular complaint, such as endometriosis, contact one of the self-help organizations to see which therapies might be helpful.

•Join or form a self-help group to find out what approaches are useful for what problem (if there is a branch of the American Holistic Medical Association in your area, this would be a good group).

•When you contact a practitioner, see if he or she has treated your condition before. See if you can speak to people who have been treated to find out how satisfied they were.

•Don't expect miracles. Sometimes the best any practitioner can do is to help you live with your condition.

•Don't expect an instant cure. Most alternative therapies are gentle and take a while to work. The longer you've had a complaint, the longer it will take to obtain relief.

•Find out beforehand how much you can expect to pay.

•Avoid practitioners who claim to have the only answer. A combination of approaches, orthodox and alternative, often works best.

•Avoid any practitioner who blames you entirely for your illness.

•Look for someone you like and get along with, and who will listen to you and involve you in your treatment.

•Do remember that orthodox medicine may be what is appropriate in your particular case. Alternative therapies seem to work best for chronic ailments, self-limiting illnesses, and illnesses with a strong psychological component.

Source: Alternative Health Care for Women

ALTERNATIVE HEALTH—RESOURCES AND READING

ORGANIZATIONS

The American Holistic Medical Association/Foundation
2727 Fairview Avenue East
Seattle, WA 98102
(206) 322-6842

The Foundation for Advancement in Cancer Therapy
Box 1242 Old Chelsea Station
New York, NY 10113
(212) 741-2790

The International Association of Holistic Health Practitioners
3419 Thom Boulevard
Las Vegas, NV 89106
(712) 873-4542

READING

Alternative Health Care for Women, Patsy Westcott and Leyardia Black (Rochester, Vt.: Thorsons Publishing Group, 1987).

WOMEN'S HEALTH ORGANIZATIONS AND RESOURCES

General Resources

ACCESS
25 Taylor Street, #702
San Francisco, CA 94102
(415) 441-4434

Boston Women's Health Book Collective
240A Elm Street
Somerville, MA 02144
(617) 625-0271

Center for Medical Consumers
237 Thompson Street
New York, NY 10012
(212) 674-7105

CHOICE Hotline
(215) 985-3300

Coalition for the Medical Rights of Women
25 Taylor Street, Suite 702
San Francisco, CA 94102
(800) 376-4636 or (415) 567-2674

Every Woman's Center
University of Masschusetts
Wilder Hall
Amherst, MA 01002
(413) 545-0883

Federation of Feminist Health Centers
633 E. 11th Street
Eugene, OR 97401
(503) 344-0966

Health House
420 Lake Avenue
St. James, NY 11780
(516) 862-6743

Jacobs Institute of Women's Health
409 12th Street, S.W.
Washington, DC 20024
(202) 863-4990

Menninger Clinic: The Women's Program
5800 S.W. Sixth Avenue
P.O. Box 829
Topeka, KS 66601
(800) 351-9058

National Women's Health Network
1325 G Street, N.W.
Washington, DC 20005
(202) 347-1140

National Women's Health Resource Center
2440 M Street, N.W., Suite 325
Washington, DC 20037
(202) 293-6045

New Bedford Women's Center
252 County Street
New Bedford, MA 02740
(508) 996-3343

Planned Parenthood
810 Seventh Avenue
New York, NY 10019
(212) 603-4600 or (800) 248-7797

Rhode Island Women's Health Collective
90 Printery Street
Providence, RI 02904
(401) 861-0030

Santa Fe Health Education Project
P.O. Box 577
Santa Fe, NM 87504
(505) 982-3236

Women's Health Education Project
2271 Second Avenue
New York, NY 10035
(212) 987-0066

Women's Health Resource Center
Brigham and Women's Hospital
850 Boylston Street and Route 9
Chestnut Hill, MA 02167
(800) 522-8765

Women's Self-Help Center
2838 Olive Street
St. Louis, MO 63103
(314) 531-2003

Organizations for Women of Color

Caribbean Women's Health Association
2725 Church Avenue
Brooklyn, NY 11226
(718) 826-2942

Hispanic Health Council
98 Cedar Street, #3A
Hartford, CT 06106
(203) 527-0856

"Books have been written by men physicians.... One would suppose in reading them that women possess but one class of physical organs, and that these are always diseased. Such teaching is pestiferous, and tends to cause and perpetuate the very evils it professes to remedy."—Mary Ashton Livermore, What Shall We Do with Our Daughters? (1883)

"It is an undoubted fact that meat spoils when touched by menstruating women."
—British Medical Journal (1878)

84% of all women have a standard source of health care and 58% identify a physician's office as that source.

Institute on Black Chemical Abuse
2616 Nicollet Avenue South
Minneapolis, MN 55408
(612) 871-7878

Minnesota Indian Women's Resource Center
2300 Fifteenth Avenue, S.
Minneapolis, MN 55404
(612) 728-2000

National Asian Women's Health Organization
440 Grand Avenue, Suite 208
Oakland, CA 94610
(510) 208-3171

National Association for Sickle Cell Disease
4221 Wilshire Boulevard, Suite 360
Los Angeles, CA 90010
(213) 936-7205

National Black Women's Health Project
1237 Ralph David Abernathy Boulevard, S.W.
Atlanta, GA 30310
(404) 758-9590, (800) 275-2947, or
(202) 835-0117 (public policy office)

National Coalition of Hispanic Health and Human Services Coalition
1501 16th Street, N.W.
Washington, DC 20036
(202) 387-5000

National Latina Health Organization
P.O. Box 7567
Oakland, CA 94601
(415) 565-7667

National Minority AIDS Council
300 I Street, N.E., Suite 400
Washington, DC 20002
(202) 544-1076

Native American Women's Health Education Resource Center
P.O. Box 572
Lake Andes, SD 57356
(605) 487-7072

Office of Minority Health Resource Center
Department of Health and Human Services
P.O. Box 37338
Washington, DC 20013
(800) 444-6472

Women of All Red Nations
4511 N. Hermitage
Chicago, IL 60640

Periodicals

Best of Health: A Quarterly Newsletter for Black Women
P.O. Box 40-1232
Brooklyn, NY 11240

Feelin' Good Health Magazine for Black Women
5601 Slauson Avenue, Suite 281
Culver City, CA 90230
(213) 649-3320

FEMINIST HEALTH CENTERS

The groups on this list form a loose-knit network of clinics and health information projects run by and/or for women. The kinds of services will vary from clinic to clinic, but all share an alternative medical focus that concentrates on the needs of women and tries to empower women to take a larger role in their own health care.

California

Berkeley Women's Health Center
2908 Ellsworth
Berkeley, CA 94705
(510) 843-6194

Buena Vista Women's Services
2000 Van Ness Street, #406
San Francisco, CA 94109
(415) 771-5000

Chico Feminist Women's Health Center
330 Flume Street
Chico, CA 95928
(916) 891-1911

Lesbian Health Project
8240 Santa Monica Boulevard
West Hollywood, CA 90046
(213) 650-1508

Lyon Martin Women's Health Services
1748 Market Street, Suite 201
San Francisco, CA 94102
(415) 565-7667

North Country Clinic for Women and Children
785 18th Street
Arcata, CA 95521
(707) 822-2841

Redding Feminist Women's Health Center
1901 Victor Avenue
Redding, CA 96002
(916) 221-0193

Sacramento Feminist Women's Health Center
Folsom Boulevard, Suite A
Sacramento, CA 95816
(916) 451-0621

Santa Cruz Women's Health Center
250 Locust Street
Santa Cruz, CA 95060
(408) 427-3500

Wholistic Health for Women
Progressive Health Services
8240 Santa Monica Boulevard
West Hollywood, CA 90046
(213) 650-1508

Womancare
2850 6th Avenue, Suite 311
San Diego, CA 92103
(619) 298-9352

Women's Choice Clinic
4415 Sonoma Highway
Santa Rosa, CA 95405
(707) 575-8212

Women's Choice Clinic
2930 McClure Street
Oakland, CA 94609
(510) 444-5676

Colorado

Boulder Valley Women's Health Center
2855 Valmont
Boulder, CO 80301
(303) 442-5160

Connecticut

Women's Health Services
911 State Street
New Haven, CT 06511
(203) 777-4781

Florida

Gainesville Women's Health Center
720 N.W. 23rd Avenue
Gainesville, FL 32609
(904) 377-5055

Georgia

Feminist Women's Health Center
580 14th Street, N.W.
Atlanta, GA 30318
(404) 874-7551

Illinois

Chicago Women's Health Center
3435 N. Sheffield
Chicago, IL 60657
(312) 935-6126

Iowa

Cedar Rapids Clinic for Women
4089 21st Avenue, S.W., Suite 211
Cedar Rapids, IA 52404
(319) 390-4342

Emma Goldman Clinic for Women
227 N. Dubuque Street
Iowa City, IA 52240

Maine

Mabel Wadsworth Women's Health Center
334A Harlow Street
Bangor, ME 04402
(207) 947-5337

Massachusetts

Fenway Community Health Center
7 Haviland Street
Boston, MA 02115
(617) 267-0900

Montana

Blue Mountain Women's Clinic
1916 Brooks, #136
Missoula, MT 59801
(406) 721-1646

New Hampshire

Concord Feminist Health Center
38 South Main Street
Concord, NH 03301
(603) 225-2739

New York

Community Health Project
Lesbian Health Program
208 W. 13th Street
New York, NY 10014
(212) 675-3559

Two-thirds of women in the U.S. have had only one Pap smear in their lifetime.

If all women in the U.S. aged 40 to 49 followed the American Cancer Society/ National Cancer Institute guidelines, the mammography industry would gross at least $1 billion a year.

St. Marks Women's Health Collective
9 Second Avenue
New York, NY 10003
(212) 228-7482

Womancap
25 5th Avenue, #1A
New York, NY 10003
(212) 529-8489

The Women's Alternative Clinic at SUNY Purchase
735 Anderson Hill Road
Purchase, NY 10583
(914) 251-6386

OHIO

Center for Choice II
16 North Huron
Toledo, OH 43604
(800) 589-6005 or (419) 255-7769

OREGON

Portland Feminist Women's Health Center
1020 N.E. 2nd Avenue
Suite 200
Portland, OR 97232
(503) 233-0808

Eugene Feminist Women's Health Center
633 East 11th Street
Eugene, OR 97401
(503) 342-5940

PENNSYLVANIA

Elizabeth Blackwell Health Center for Women
1124 Walnut Street
Philadelphia, PA 19107
(215) 923-7577

VERMONT

Southern Vermont Women's Health Center
187 North Main Street
Rutland, VT 05701
(802) 775-1946

WASHINGTON

Aradia Women's Health Center
1300 Spring Street
Seattle, WA 98104
(206) 323-9388

Cedar River Clinic, A Feminist Women's Health Center
4300 Talbot Road S., #403
Renton, WA 98055
(206) 255-0471

45th Street Clinic
1629 North 45th Street
Seattle, WA 98103
(206) 633-3350

Yakima Feminist Women's Health Center
106 East E Street
Yakima, WA 98901
(509) 575-6422

DISTRICT OF COLUMBIA

Washington Free Clinic
1156 Wisconsin Avenue, N.W.
Washington, DC 20007
(202) 667-1106

Source: Federation of Feminist Women's Health Centers

FEMINIST WOMEN'S HEALTH CARE—READING LIST

How to Stay Out of the Gynecologist's Office, Federation of Feminist Women's Health Centers (Hollywood: Women to Women Publishers, 1991).

A New View of a Woman's Body, Federation of Feminist Women's Health Centers (West Hollywood, Calif.: Feminist Health Press, 1991).

Self-Help Home Remedies, Chico Feminist Women's Health Center (Chico, Calif.: Chico Feminist Women's Health Center, 1976).

Taking Our Bodies Back, 33 min. film, Margaret Lazarus and Renner Wunderlich (1974; available from Cambridge Documentary Films, P.O. Box 385, Cambridge, Mass. 02139).

Woman-Centered Pregnancy and Birth, Federation of Feminist Women's Health Centers (Pittsburgh and San Francisco: Cleis Press, 1984).

A Woman's Book of Choices: Abortion, Menstrual Extraction, and RU-486, Rebecca Chalker and Carol Downer (New York: Four Walls Eight Windows, 1992).

WELL-BEING
WELL-BEING
WELL-BEING

WELL-BEING

WELL-BEING
WELL-BEING
WELL-BEING
WELL-BEING
WELL-BEING
WELL-BEING
WELL-BEING
WELL-BEING
WELL-BEING
WELL-BEING
WELL-BEING
WELL-BEING
WELL-BEING
WELL-BEING
WELL-BEING
WELL-BEING

MARIANNE WILLIAMSON—WOMEN'S SELF WORTH

Marianne Williamson, best-selling author of A Woman's Worth and A Return to Love, delivered this speech at an Estée Lauder luncheon in December 1993.

I think that women have been hiding out for a very long time. Not only have we been consigned a place where our deepest feelings and passions were not considered relevant, but I think that in many ways we have conspired with those attitudes, helped to create them by not recognizing the importance of our deepest feelings and our most authentic selves. Basically our attitude towards cosmetics and clothes is, "Give me a place to hide. Be the mask. You do it for me." You know, "I can find the makeup that looks right or the clothes that look right and then I can just go in there and hide, and I won't have to deal with who I am."

Interestingly enough, that can work, until about the age of 35. You can be really bitter, mad, even mean, and still look gorgeous if you're 25 or 30. You hit about 35, and that anger becomes a hardness on your face that no make-up can hide. You hit the age of 35 and who you really are starts to show as never before. Now, the good news is, when we like who we are, we get more beautiful with age. If we like who we are—and that's the space that we really want to hold for ourselves now—it is not that we are hiding our age, but that we are celebrating our age. . . .We want to show that it's very beautiful being 40, it's beautiful being 50, it's beautiful being 60.

And the truth of the matter is, when it comes to this thing of age, until you're 40 you don't even begin to have it figured out yet. It's like building a lasagna. You spend time working on the pasta, you spend time working on the sauce, you spend time getting the cheese together, and then you're ready to build the lasagna because all the elements are finally there.

So in our 20s we're working on one thing, and around 30 we're working on another, and in your mid-30s we're working on another, around 40 we're just about to get to the point we could put it together, and people start saying, "It's over!" This is when we're just beginning to feel, "Now I can know who I am because I am all those things: I am those things I concentrated on in my 20s, I am those things I concentrated on in my 30s, I am all those things." We're beginning to integrate, and then we can begin to truly shine, and in shining, truly serve. . . . And that's what has got to happen, women getting together and recognizing our interests. It's not that we've been oppressed by men; we have been oppressed by a thought system that we ourselves have conspired in. We have to take responsibility for our own shift in consciousness before anyone else is going to shift theirs.

Listen, if we don't all get there, none of us will get there. Anyone who opens a window for themselves is opening a window that all of us can rush through. People sometimes ask me, what is the advice you give to women? I don't give advice to women; I salute women. We don't need another person telling us how we should look, we need another person telling us how beautiful we are. We don't need to be told what to do, we need to recognize that the way we are is fine.

So now we're looking inside, to find out who we really are, and one of the reasons that we don't want to look at who we really are is because there's a lot of pain in there based on what we've been through. We've been through the marriages, we've been through the divorces, we've been through the relationships, we've been through those things that feel like failure to us. . . . I think there's something important about honoring everything that we've been through. We've been through what we've been through, our so-called failures as well as our successes, and our greatest education has been our life experience. But we live in a society that does not honor life experience, a society that says if you see lines, that's bad! We must show that we're not hiding, we are expressing; we are transforming, bringing a greater beauty to the faces we have.

The lie is our problem. The lies in the air, the illusions in the air, but we're coming together in a different way now. We must come together to support each other in all of this. Products, clothes, these things are fine; we want to feel good when out there. But ultimately what we're all learning is that our power to work effectively in the outer world comes from our finding our juice, our passion, our serenity, our intelligence, our feelings in the inner world. And that is why there is not anything that cosmetics can do for us if we have not done some of it for ourselves.

The fact that we are growing up is not something to mourn, it's something to celebrate. The fact that we are now adults—when a woman is 35, a woman is 40, this is not the time to hide. It's time to celebrate that we have matured. Because the truth of the matter is, if there's any reason for this country to think, "Oh, well maybe things will be okay," it's because of the women, and the feminine consciousness of maturity, responsibility, and care for the culture.

So for those of you who are under 35, that's great. But for those of you that are 35 and 40 and 50 and 60, all I can say is, isn't the world lucky that we're here?

WOMEN AND WEIGHT

Recommended Weights for Women Aged 25 and Over

Height	*Weight in pounds (in indoor clothing)*		
	Small Frame	***Medium Frame***	***Large Frame***
4'10"	96–104	101–13	109–25
4'11"	99–107	104–16	112–28
5'0"	102–10	107–19	115–31
5'1"	105–13	110–22	118–34
5'2"	108–16	113–26	121–38
5'3"	111–19	116–30	125–42
5'4"	114–23	120–35	129–46
5'5"	118–27	124–39	133–50
5'6"	122–31	128–43	137–54
5'7"	126–35	132–47	141–58
5'8"	130–40	136–51	145–63
5'9"	134–44	140–55	149–68
5'10"	138–48	144–59	153–73

Source: Metropolitan Life Insurance Company

47% of normal-weight women want to be thinner, and 16% of those who are already underweight want to be thinner than they are, according to surveys.

Overweight in America
By sex and age

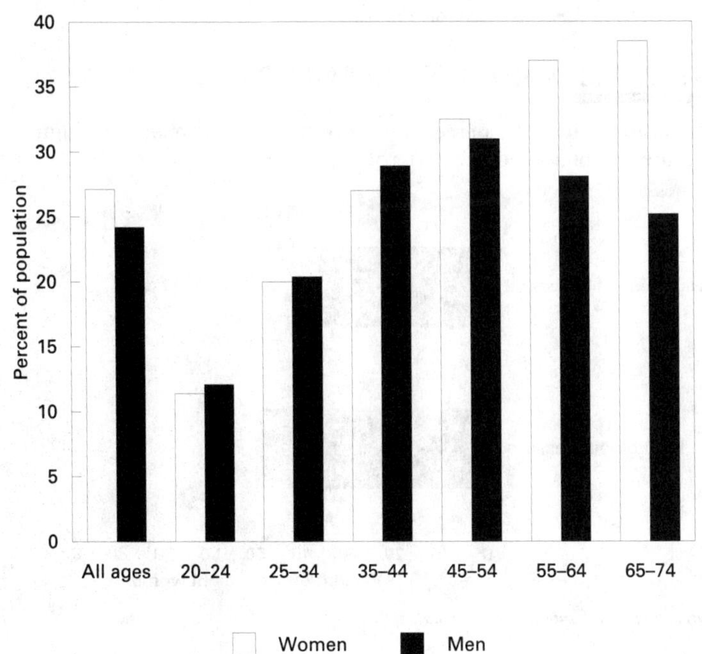

Source: National Center for Health Statistics

An estimated 8 million women were enrolled in Weight Watchers in 1989.

Overweight Women by Race

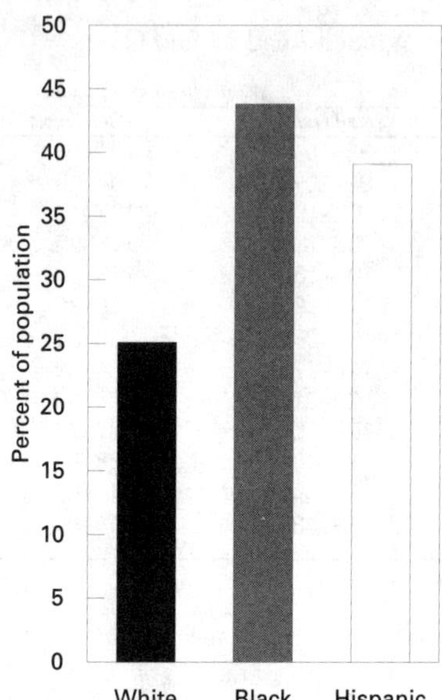

Source: National Center for Health Statistics

OVERWEIGHT AND ITS HEALTH DANGERS

This graph shows the percentage of overweight women with high blood pressure and high blood cholesterol.

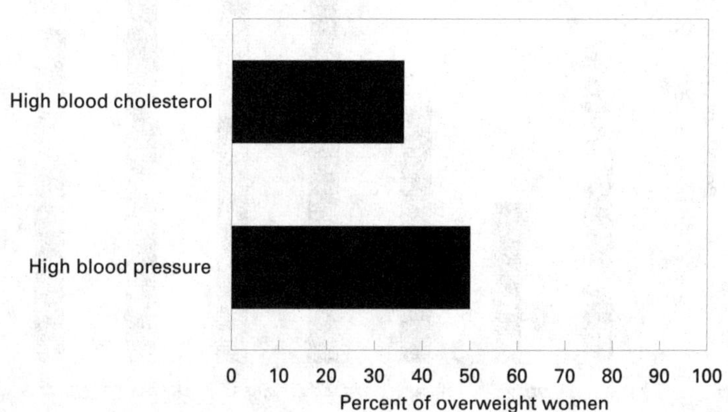

Source: National Center for Health Statistics

NUTRITION

Heart disease and osteoporosis afflict many women, but good nutrition can go a long way toward preventing their onset.

95% of dieters fail on diets and gain their weight back.

Recommended Daily Dietary Allowances for Women Aged 19–50

Vitamins	
A	80 mg
D	1 mg (19–24), .5 mg (25–50)
E	8 mg
K	6 mg (19–24), 6 mg (25–50)
C	6 mg
Thiamine	1.1 mg
Riboflavin	1.3 mg
Niacin	15 mg
B_6	1.6 mg
Folate	8 mg
B_{12}	.2 mg

Minerals	
Calcium	1,200 mg (19–24), 800 mg (25–50)
Phosphorus	1,200 mg (19–24), 800 mg (25–50)
Magnesium	280 mg
Iron	15 mg
Zinc	12 mg
Iodine	15 mg
Selenium	5.5 mg

Source: National Academy of Sciences and the National Research Council

SOME CALCIUM-RICH FOODS

Calcium has been shown to help prevent osteoporosis, a dangerous bone disease that afflicts many older women. For more information about osteoporosis, see pp. 223–4.

	Calories	Calcium (milligrams)
Cheddar cheese, cut pieces (1 oz.)	115	204
Swiss cheese (1 oz.)	105	272
Low-fat (2%) cottage cheese (1 cup)	205	155
Skim milk (1 cup)	85	302
Plain low-fat yogurt (8 oz.)	145	415
Baked custard (1 cup)	305	297
Atlantic sardines, canned in oil, drained, including the bones (3 oz.)	175	371
Raw oysters, meat only (1 cup)	160	226
Collard greens, cooked, drained, from frozen (1 cup)	60	357
Turnip greens, cooked, drained, from frozen (1 cup)	50	249
Refried beans, canned (1 cup)	295	141
Molasses, cane, blackstrap (2 tbsp.)	85	274

Source: Human Nutrition Information Service

Researchers in Finland determined that if Barbie were real, she would have so little body fat that she would probably not menstruate.

CHOLESTEROL

Cholesterol is a fatlike substance present in all animal foods. Dietary cholesterol, as well as saturated fat, raises blood cholesterol levels in many people, which in turn increases their risk for heart disease. A total cholesterol level below 200 is desirable, with one between 200 and 239 considered borderline, and levels of 240 and above viewed as high.

Studies show that women's cholesterol runs higher than men's from ages 20 to 24 and again from age 45 up. Before age 45, the total blood cholesterol level of women averages below 220, but between 45 and 55 it rises to between 223 and 246. In 1989 an estimated 55 million adult women had serum cholesterol levels of 200 or higher, including more than 60% of white females and 54% of black females.

As many as 80% of 10- and 11-year-old girls don't eat normally because they want to be thin, according to *Healthy Weight Journal.*

High Cholesterol Among Women

Estimated percentage of American women with serum cholesterol over 240.

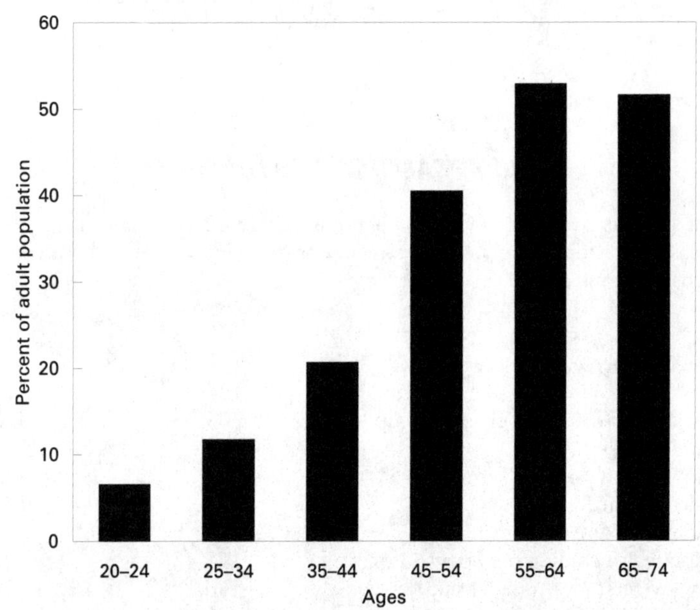

Source for above: Food and Drug Administration

FAT

Saturated fat is found mainly in foods that come from animals, although a few vegetable fats, such as coconut oil, cocoa butter, palm kernel oil, and palm oil, are also high in this kind of fat. Saturated fat boosts your blood cholesterol level more than anything else in your diet.

Unsaturated fat actually helps to lower cholesterol levels when it is used in place of saturated fat. One type is polyunsaturated fat, which is found in many cooking and salad oils, such as safflower, corn, soybean, cottonseed, sesame, and sunflower oils. Another type is monounsaturated fat, which is found in olive and canola oils.

Figure Out Your Fat Intake
Experts recommend that no more than 30% of total calories come from fat. Since food labels list fat in grams, to find out what your total gram intake of fat should be, multiply your daily calories by 0.30 (30%) and divide by 9 (the number of calories in a gram of fat).

Source: Food and Drug Administration

Fat women earned $6,710 less than thin women in 1993, were 10% more likely to have income's below the poverty level, had completed a third of a year less schooling, and were 20% less likely to be married.

FAT IN SELECTED FOODS

	Fat content (grams)
Bread (1 slice)	1
Doughnut (1 medium, 2 oz.)	11
Bagel (1)	2
Vegetables, leafy raw (1 cup)	trace
French fries (10)	8
Fruit, raw or canned (1/2 cup)	trace
Avocado (1/4 whole)	9
Skim milk (1 cup)	trace
Low-fat yogurt, plain (8 oz.)	4
Natural cheddar cheese (1 1/2 oz.)	14
Process cheese (2 oz.)	18
Ricotta, part skim (1/2 cup)	10
Ground beef, lean, cooked (3 oz.)	16
Chicken, with skin, fried (3 oz.)	13
Egg (1)	5
Mayonnaise (1 tsp.)	11
Chocolate bar (1 oz.)	9

Source: Human Nutrition Information Service

White and black women were asked to react to pictures of women of various sizes in a Harvard study. White women overwhelmingly rated the heavy models as less intelligent and much less successful in their jobs. Weight was much less of a factor in the black women's ratings.

The average woman wants to lose 31 pounds to reach an ideal weight of 133, according to the American Journal of Public Health.

CHOLESTEROL IN SELECTED FOODS

To stay within the desirable range, some health authorities recommend that dietary cholesterol be limited to an average of 300 milligrams or less per day.

	Cholesterol content (in milligrams)
Liver (3 oz., cooked)	331
Egg (1 yolk)	213
Beef or chicken (3 oz., cooked)	76
Whole milk (1 cup)	33
Skim milk (1 cup)	4

Source: Human Nutrition Information Service

AMOUNT OF SALT IN SELECTED FOODS

Some health authorities say that sodium intake should be limited to no more than 3,000 milligrams a day, although others say no more than 2,400 milligrams. One teaspoon of salt provides about 2,000 milligrams of sodium.

	Salt content (in milligrams)
Bread (1 slice)	110–75
Tomato juice, canned (3/4 cup)	660
Vegetable soup, canned (1 cup)	820
Milk (1 cup)	120
Yogurt, plain (8 oz.)	160
Processed cheese (2 oz.)	800
Tuna, canned, water-packed (3 oz.)	300
Ham, lean, roasted (3 oz.)	1,020
Salad dressing (1 tbsp.)	75–220
Soy sauce (1 tbsp.)	1,030
Dill pickle (1 medium)	930
Potato chips, salted (1 oz.)	130

Source: Human Nutrition Information Service

ADDED SUGARS IN SELECTED FOODS

To avoid getting too many calories from sugars, try to limit your added sugars to six teaspoons a day if you eat about 1,600 calories, 12 teaspoons at 2,200 calories, or 18 teaspoons at 2,800 calories.

	Added sugars (in teaspoons)
Muffin (1 medium)	1
Angel food cake (1/12 tube cake)	5
Fruit, canned in juice (1/2 cup)	0
Fruit, canned in heavy syrup (1/2 cup)	4
Milk, plain (1 cup)	0
Low-fat fruit yogurt (8 oz.)	7
Chocolate shake (10 fl. oz.)	9
Syrup or honey (1 tbsp.)	3
Gelatin dessert (1/2 cup)	4
Cola (12 fl. oz.)	9

Source: Human Nutrition Information Service

SAMPLE MENU FOR HEALTHY WOMEN

Based on traditional American cuisine, this menu outlines a suggested diet, limiting salt and fat intake, for women 25 to 49 years old.

Breakfast
- Bagel, plain (1/2 medium)
- Cream cheese, low-fat (1 tsp.)
- Cereal, shredded wheat (1 cup)
- Banana (1 small)
- Milk, 1% (1 cup)
- Orange juice (3/4 cup)
- Coffee (1 cup) with milk 1% (1 oz.)

Lunch
- Minestrone soup, canned, low-sodium (1/2 cup)
- Roast beef sandwich:
- Whole wheat bread (2 slices)
- Lean roast beef, unseasoned (3 oz.)
- American cheese, low-fat and low-sodium (3/4 oz.)
- Lettuce (1 leaf)
- Tomato (3 slices)
- Mayonnaise, low-fat and low-sodium (2 tsp.)
- Apple (1 medium)
- Water (1 cup)

Dinner
- Salmon (3 oz.)*
- Vegetable oil (1 tsp.)
- Baked potato (1/2 medium)*
- Margarine (1 tsp.)
- Green beans (1/2 cup), seasoned with margarine (1/2 tsp.)*
- Carrots (1/2 cup), seasoned with margarine (1/2 tsp.)*
- White dinner roll (1 medium)
- Margarine (1 tsp.)
- Ice milk (1/2 cup)
- Iced tea, unsweetened (1 cup)

Snack
- Popcorn (2 cups)*
- Margarine (1 tsp.)

Calories	1,831
Total fat†	30%
Saturated fat†	8.7%
Cholesterol	156mg
Protein†	18%
Total carbohydrates†	52%
Simple carbohydrates††	37%
Complex carbohydrates††	63%
Sodium	1,415 mg

100% recommended daily allowance met for all nutrients except zinc, 93%

*No salt is added in recipe preparation or as seasoning; all margarine is low-sodium.
†As a percentage of calories.
††As a percentage of overall carbohydrates.

Source: National Heart, Lung, and Blood Institute

NUTRITION—RESOURCES AND READING

ORGANIZATIONS

The Food and Nutrition Information Center
National Agricultural Library
10301 Baltimore Boulevard, Room 304
Beltsville, MD 20705
(301) 504-5719

National Center for Nutrition and Dietetics
The American Dietetic Association
216 West Jackson Boulevard, Suite 800
Chicago, IL 60606

READING

Calories and Weight: The USDA Pocket Guide, U.S. Department of Agriculture (Washington, D.C.: U.S. Department of Agriculture).

Coaches Guide to Nutrition and Weight Control, Patricia A. Eisenman, Stephen C. Johnson, and Joan E. Benson (Champaign, Ill.: Leisure Press, 1990).

The Columbia Encyclopedia of Women's Nutrition, Carlton Fredericks (New York: Putnam, 1989).

Dr. Jean Mayer's Diet and Nutrition Guide, Jean Mayer and Jeanne Goldberg (New York: Pharos Books, 1990).

Everywoman's Guide to Nutrition, Judith E. Brown (Minneapolis: University of Minnesota Press, 1990).

In Rhode Island, the U.S. Court of Appeals found that a 329-pound woman had been discriminated against by her former, and prospective, employers because her obesity was perceived to limit her activities.

No greater tendency to overeat has been found during pregnancy than at other times, nor does there seem to be a connection between food cravings and binges, according to an Oxford University study.

Jane Brody's Nutrition Book, Jane Brody (New York: Bantam, 1987).

A Lowfat Lifeline for the 90's: How to Survive in a Fat-Filled World, Valerie Parker (Lake Oswego, Oreg.: Lowfat Publications, 1990).

The Mount Sinai School of Medicine Complete Book of Nutrition, Victor Herbert and Genell Subak-Sharpe, eds. (New York: St. Martin's Press, 1990).

Nutrition, Weight Control, and Exercise, Frank I. Katch and William D. McArdle (Philadelphia: Lea & Febinger, 1988).

Personal Nutrition, Marie Boyle and Eleanor Whitney (St. Paul, Minn.: West Publishing, 1989).

The Restaurant Companion, Hope Warshaw (Chicago: Surrey Books, 1990).

The Tufts University Guide to Total Nutrition, Stanley Gershoff with Catherine Whitney (New York: Harper & Row, 1990).

AMERICAN COLLEGE OF SPORTS MEDICINE'S EXERCISE GUIDELINES

These recommendations about the quantity and quality of exercise apply to healthy adults and are geared toward developing and maintaining cardio-respiratory fitness, body composition, muscular strength, and endurance.

Frequency of training—Three to five days a week.
Intensity of training—60–90% of maximum heart rate, or 50–85% of maximum oxygen uptake or maximum heart-rate reserve.
Duration of training—20 to 60 minutes of continuous aerobic activity. Duration is dependent on the intensity of the activity; thus, lower intensity activity should be conducted over a longer period of time.
Mode of activity—Any activity that uses large muscle groups, can be maintained continuously, and is rhythmic and aerobic in nature.
Resistance training—Strength training of a moderate intensity, sufficient to develop and maintain fat-free weight. At least two days a week, one set of 8–12 repetitions of 8–10 exercises that condition the major muscle groups is the recommended minimum.

Source: American College of Sports Medicine

ENERGY EXPENDITURES

These projections are based on a 150-pound person; lighter-weight women will use fewer calories.

Activity	Calories per hour
Lying down or sleeping	80
Sitting	100
Driving an automobile	120
Standing	140
Domestic work	180
Walking, 2½ mph	210
Bicycling, 5½ mph	210
Gardening	220
Golf	250
Bowling	270
Walking, 3¾ mph	300
Swimming, ¼ mph	300
Square-dancing, volleyball, roller-skating	350
Tennis	420
Skiing, 10 mph	600
Squash and handball	600
Bicycling, 13 mph	660
Running, 10 mph	900

Source: National Institutes of Health

TOP ATHLETIC AND FITNESS ACTIVITIES

This list shows the most popular physical activities among American working women, ranked according to the percentage of women who participate in each.

Athletic activities	Fitness activities
1. Bowling (33%)	1. Walking (85%)
2. Tennis/racket sports (20%)	2. Bicycling (63%)
3. Golf (17%)	3. Aerobics/jazzercize (61%)
4. Volleyball (17%)	4. Swimming (50%)
5. Softball/baseball (16%)	5. Jogging/running (33%)

Source: Women's Sports Foundation

"Nobody can make you feel inferior without your consent."—Eleanor Roosevelt

WOMEN NAMED SPORTS ILLUSTRATED'S SPORTSMAN OF THE YEAR

Sports Illustrated has been naming a Sportsman of the Year since 1954, and in that time six women have received the honor.

1972 Billie Jean King, tennis
1976 Chris Evert, tennis
1983 Mary Decker, track
1984 Mary Lou Retton, gymnastics
1987 Judi Brown King, track, and Patty Sheehan, golf (two of "Eight Athletes Who Care" awarded the honor)

ASSOCIATED PRESS WOMEN ATHLETES OF THE YEAR

Multiple winners of this award, voted by AP sports editors, include: Babe Didrikson (six); Chris Evert (four); Patty Berg and Maureen Connolly (three); and Tracy Austin, Althea Gibson, Billie Jean King, Nancy Lopez, Alice Marble, Martina Navratilova, Wilma Rudolph, Kathy Whitworth, and Mickey Wright (two each).

1931	Helene Madison, swimming
1932	Babe Didrikson, track
1933	Helen Jacobs, tennis
1934	Virginia Van Wie, golf
1935	Helen Wills Moody, tennis
1936	Helen Stephens, track
1937	Katherine Rawls, swimming
1938	Patty Berg, golf
1939	Alice Marble, tennis
1940	Alice Marble, tennis
1941	Betty Hicks Newell, golf
1942	Gloria Callen, swimming
1943	Patty Berg, golf
1944	Ann Curtis, swimming
1945	Babe Didrikson Zaharias, golf
1946	Babe Didrikson Zaharias, golf
1947	Babe Didrikson Zaharias, golf
1948	Fanny Blankers-Koen, track
1949	Marlene Bauer, golf
1950	Babe Didrikson Zaharias, golf
1951	Maureen Connolly, tennis
1952	Maureen Connolly, tennis
1953	Maureen Connolly, tennis
1954	Babe Didrikson Zaharias, golf
1955	Patty Berg, golf
1956	Pat McCormick, diving
1957	Althea Gibson, tennis
1958	Althea Gibson, tennis
1959	Maria Bueno, tennis
1960	Wilma Rudolph, track
1961	Wilma Rudolph, track
1962	Dawn Fraser, swimming
1963	Mickey Wright, golf
1964	Mickey Wright, golf
1965	Kathy Whitworth, golf
1966	Kathy Whitworth, golf
1967	Billie Jean King, tennis
1968	Peggy Fleming, skating

"In contrast to males, for whom identity development is the outcome of increasing experience and separation and gained autonomy, the female personality develops through attachments to others."—Carol Gilligan, Making Connections

1969	Debbie Meyer, swimming
1970	Chi Cheng, track
1971	Evonne Goolagong, tennis
1972	Olga Korbut, gymnastics
1973	Billie Jean King, tennis
1974	Chris Evert, tennis
1975	Chris Evert, tennis
1976	Nadia Comaneci, gymnastics
1977	Chris Evert, tennis
1978	Nancy Lopez, golf
1979	Tracy Austin, tennis
1980	Chris Evert Lloyd, tennis
1981	Tracy Austin, tennis
1982	Mary Decker Tabb, track
1983	Martina Navratilova, tennis
1984	Mary Lou Retton, gymnastics
1985	Nancy Lopez, golf
1986	Martina Navratilova, tennis
1987	Jackie Joyner-Kersee, track
1988	Florence Griffith Joyner, track
1989	Steffi Graf, tennis
1990	Beth Daniel, golf
1991	Monica Seles, tennis
1992	Monica Seles, tennis
1993	Cheryl Swoopes, basketball

WOMEN IN THE TRACK AND FIELD HALL OF FAME

The Track and Field Hall of Fame, located in Indianapolis, has been enshrining athletes since 1974. The dates in parentheses after the honorees' names are the years of induction.

Roxanne Anderson (1991)
Dee Boekman (1976)
Alice Coachman (1975)
Mildred (Babe) Didrikson (1974)
Mae Faggs (1976)
Barbara Ferrell (1988)
Evelyne Hall (1988)
Doris Brown Heritage (1990)
Nell Jackson (1989)
Mildred McDaniel (1983)
Edith McGuire (1979)
Madeline Manning (1984)
Betty Robinson (1977)
Wilma Rudolph (1974)
Jean Shiley (1993)
Helen Stephens (1975)
Wyomia Tyus (1980)
Stella Walsh (1975)
Martha Watson (1987)

WOMEN IN THE INTERNATIONAL TENNIS HALL OF FAME

The following women players have been named to the Tennis Hall of Fame in Newport, Rhode Island. For athletes to be eligible, they must be five years' removed from being a "significant factor" in competitive tennis. The year of induction is in parentheses.

Juliette Atkinson (1974)
Tracy Austin (1992)
Maud Barger-Wallach (1958)
Pauline Betz Addie (1965)
Molla Bjurstedt Mallory (1958)
Louise Brough Clapp (1967)
Mary Browne (1957)
Maria Bueno (1978)
Mabel Cahill (1976)
Maureen Connolly Brinker (1968)
Allison Danzig (1968)
Charlotte (Lottie) Dod (1983)
Dorothy Douglass Chambers (1981)
Shirley Fry Irvin (1970)
Althea Gibson (1971)
Evonne Goolagong Cawley (1988)
Ellen Hansell (1965)
Darlene Hard (1973)
Doris Hart (1969)
Ann Hayden Jones (1985)
Gladys Heldman (1979)
Hazel Hotchkiss Wightman (1957)
Helen Hull Jacobs (1962)
Billie Jean King (1987)
Suzanne Lenglen (1978)
Alice Marble (1964)
Kathleen McKane Godfree (1978)
Elizabeth Moore (1971)
Angela Barrett Mortimer (1993)
Betty Nuthall Shoemaker (1977)
Margaret Osborne duPont (1967)
Mary Outerbridge (1981)
Sarah Palfrey Danzig (1963)
Ellen Roosevelt (1975)
Dorothy Round Little (1986)
Elizabeth Ryan (1972)

Eleanora Sears (1968)
Margaret Smith Court (1979)
May Sutton Bundy (1956)
Bertha Townsend Toulmin (1974)
Virginia Wade (1989)
Marie Wagner (1969)
Helen Wills Moody Roark (1959)

THE GOLF HALL OF FAME

Founded in 1950, the Women's Golf Hall of Fame was absorbed into the Ladies Professional Golf Association's Hall of Fame in 1967. To qualify for inclusion, an athlete must have won at least 30 official events including two major championships, or have won 35 official events with one cham-pionship, or have won 40 official events. The year of induction is in parentheses.

	Career victories
Patty Berg (1951)	57
Pat Bradley (1991)	30
JoAnne Carner (1982)	42
Babe Didrikson Zaharias (1951)	31
Sandra Haynie (1977)	42
Betty Jameson (1951)	10
Nancy Lopez (1987)	47
Carol Mann (1977)	38
Betsy Rawls (1960)	55
Patty Sheehan (1993)	31
Louise Suggs (1951)	50
Kathy Whitworth (1975)	88
Mickey Wright (1964)	82

FITNESS—RESOURCES AND READING

ORGANIZATIONS

American Alliance for Health, Physical Education, Recreation and Dance
1900 Association Drive
Reston, VA 22091
(703) 476-3450

Melpomene Institute for Women's Health Research
1010 University Avenue
St. Paul, MN 55104
(612) 642-1951

Women's Sports Foundation
Eisenhower Park
East Meadow, NY 11554
(800) 227-3988

READING

The Bodywise Woman: Reliable Information about Physical Activity and Health, Melpomene Institute for Women's Health Research (New York: Prentice-Hall, 1990).

Stretch and Strengthen: A Safe, Comprehensive Exercise Program to Balance Your Muscle Strength, Judy Alter (Boston: Houghton Mifflin, 1992).

SPAS

For more information about these spas, contact your local travel agent or call SPA-Finders at (800) 255-7727 or (212) 924-6800.

Women-Only Spas
The following spas have programs designed specifically for women:

Cal-A-Vie, Vista, California
Elizabeth Arden's Main Chance, Phoenix, Arizona
The Golden Door, Escondido, California
The Greenhouse, Arlington, Texas
Green Mountain at Fox Run, Ludlow, Vermont
The Kerr House, Grand Rapids, Ohio
The Wooden Door, Milwaukee, Wisconsin

Health and Weight-Loss Spas
Cooper Wellness Center, Dallas, Texas
Duke University Diet and Fitness Center, Durham, North Carolina
Hilton Head Health Institute, Hilton Head, South Carolina
National Institute of Fitness, St. George, Utah
Structure House, Durham, North Carolina

Around 30% of American women have lied about their age, according to a recent study.

For 99% of women, the risk of fatal cancer is not increased by hair dyes.

91% of women in a recent survey were satisfied with their levels of self-esteem.

SKIN CANCER

Skin cancer is the most prevalent of all cancers. Estimates vary on its occurrence, but evidence suggests that approximately 700,000 Americans develop skin cancer every year. Its principal cause is almost universally accepted by medical experts to be overexposure to sunlight, especially when it results in sunburn and blistering.

Types of Skin Cancer

The three main types of skin cancer are basal cell, squamous cell, and melanoma.

•Basal cell carcinoma usually occurs in people who have light hair and fair complexions, who sunburn readily, and who do not tan. Appearing as a small, shiny, fleshy nodule on exposed parts of the body, basal cell carcinoma grows slowly. When diagnosed and treated promptly, it has a high cure rate.

•Squamous cell carcinoma, which typically develops on the face, ears, lips, and mouth of fair-skinned persons, usually starts out as a red, scaly, plate-like patch or nodule. Though it can spread to other parts of the body, it also carries a high cure rate when detected and treated early.

•Melanoma, the most dangerous form of skin cancer, usually shows up as a dark brown or black mole-like lesion with irregular edges. Sometimes the growths may turn red, blue, and white. The most common sites are the upper back in men and women and the chest and lower legs of women.

Skin-Cancer Prevention Tips

•Limit sun exposure beginning early in life.

•Do not sunbathe or visit tanning parlors, and limit sun exposure during the hours of 10 A.M. to 3 P.M. When going into the sun, wear protective clothing such as a hat, long-sleeved shirt, and sunglasses.

•Use sunscreen lotions to reduce the amount of ultraviolet light reaching the skin. Sunscreens offering the best protection are those with the highest "sun protection factor" number on the label, such as 15 and higher.

•Examine your skin regularly for signs of skin cancer. If there are changes that make you suspicious, call the doctor right away.

Detection

Skin cancer is almost totally curable if caught in the early stages, and periodic self-exams are helpful to aid in early recognition of any lesions. The following is a suggested method of self-examination that will ensure that no area of the body is neglected. To perform your examination you will need a full-length mirror, a hand mirror, and a brightly lit room.

•Examine your body front and back in the mirror, then right and left sides, arms raised.

•Bend elbows and look carefully at forearms, upper arms, and palms.

•Next, look at backs of the legs and feet, including soles and spaces between toes.

•Examine back of neck and scalp with the help of a hand mirror, parting hair (or using blow dryer) to lift and give you a close look.

•Finally, check back and buttocks with hand mirror.

Sources: American Academy of Dermatology; National Institute on Aging

BAD HABITS AND A GOOD APPEARANCE

According to plastic surgeons, the following habits should be avoided if you value your appearance:

Smoking
•Constricts the small blood vessels of your face, reducing the supply of oxygen to delicate facial tissues and leaving you with a grayish "smoker's face"
•Contributes to lines on face and around eyes
•Stains your teeth

Drugs
•Cause acne flare-ups
•Suppress circulation to your skin, causing it to lose its natural color and look gray and tired
•Contribute to nasal problems
•Cause facial lines and wrinkles
•If the drugs are steroids, cause fluid retention that results in a distortion of your face

Drinking
•Dehydrates your skin by drawing water away from its surface
•Increases broken capillaries
•Causes blood vessels to expand, increasing the redness of your skin
•Lowers your physical reaction time, contributing to accidents (facial damage in accidents is a leading cause of facial disfigurement)

Source: Facial Plastic Surgery Information Service

SUNBURN AND SKIN CANCER: WHO IS AT RISK?

With the connection well established between skin cancer and excessive exposure to sunlight, women need to be vigilant about avoiding sunburn. How skin reacts to the sun, however, varies greatly from person to person. Whether someone burns or tans depends on a number of factors, including skin type, the time of year, and the amount of sun exposure received recently. The skin's susceptibility to burning has been classified on a five-point scale, as follows:

•Type I (extremely sensitive)—always burns, never tans
•Type II (very sensitive)—burns easily, tans minimally
•Type III (sensitive)—burns moderately, tans gradually to a light brown
•Type IV (minimally sensitive)—burns rarely, tans well to a dark brown
•Type V (not sensitive)—never burns

Source: American Academy of Dermatology

"You'd be surprised how much it costs to look this cheap."
—Dolly Parton

There are 1,192 brands of shampoo, 814 brands of conditioner, and 473 brands of hairspray currently on the market.

BEAUTY PRODUCT USE AMONG TEENAGERS

	Total users 12-19 (millions)	% of users who started by age 13	% of users who started by age 15
Blusher	9.4	71.6	92.6
Eye shadow	8.3	72.5	93.4
Fragrance	12.1	86.4	96.0
Hair conditioner	12.4	94.1	97.3
Lip gloss	9.2	84.9	95.5
Mascara	9.2	63.6	92.5
Medicated skin care	8.0	66.2	88.9

Source: TEEN/Simmons Custom Market Study, Cosmetic Insiders Report (June 1993)

"I cannot and will not cut my conscience to fit this year's fashions."—Lillian Hellman

LEADING COSMETIC COMPANIES

Company	1992 sales
1. Proctor & Gamble	$4.6 billion
2. Estée Lauder	2.6 billion
3. Colgate/Mennen	1.61 billion
4. Revlon	1.6 billion
5. Bristol-Myers Squibb	1.5 billion
6. Avon Products	1.4 billion
7. Cosmair/L'Oreal	1.4 billion
8. Unilever	1.36 billion
9. Alberto-Culver	1.07 billion
10. Helene Curtis	1.02 billion
11. Mary Kay Cosmetics	1.01 billion
12. Gillette Company	970 million
13. Schering-Plough	821 million
14. Warner-Lambert	624 million
15. Benckiser USA	548 million
16. Amway	505 million
17. Johnson & Johnson	479 million
18. Carter-Wallace	347 million
19. Maybelline	342 million
20. Sanofi/YSL	335 million
21. Wella	270 million
22. Neutrogena	267 million
23. Merle Norman	248 million
24. Nexxus	240 million
25. Tsumura	159 million

Source: Cosmetics Insiders Report (June 1993)

TOP-SELLING WOMEN'S PERSONAL-CARE PRODUCTS

Product (company)	1992 sales
1. Avon (Avon Products)	$3,662 million
2. L'Oreal (L'Oreal)	2,933 million
3. Estée Lauder (Estée Lauder)	1,100 million
4. Nivea (Beiersdorf)	908 million
5. Oil of Olay (Procter & Gamble)	750 million
6. Tampax (Tambrands)	663 million
7. Maybelline (Maybelline)	289 million
8. Neutrogena (Neutrogena)	267 million
9. o.b. (Johnson & Johnson)	265 million
10. Playtex (Playtex Family Products)	210 million

Source: Financial World (Sept. 1, 1993)

EXPENDITURES ON PERSONAL CARE

This graph shows the average annual expenditures by women and men on personal-care services, including haircuts, manicures, massages, etc.

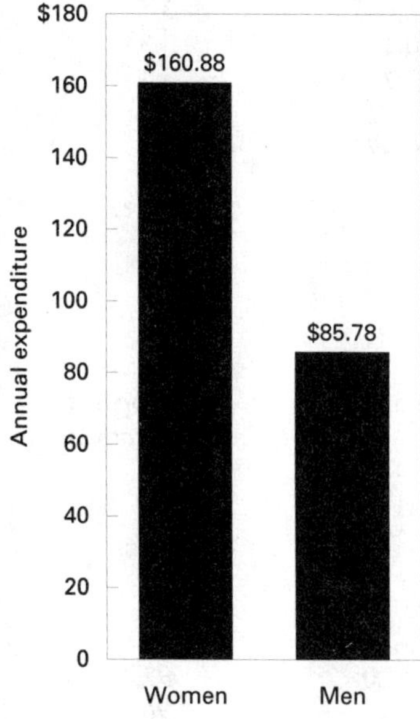

(Data from 1992)
Source: Unpublished BLS data, Consumer Expenditure Interview Survey

CONSUMERISM—READING

Cosmetics Buying Guide, Andrew Schemen and David L. Severson (Yonkers, N.Y.: Consumer Reports Books, 1993).

THE POLITICS OF BEAUTY—READING

Backlash: The Undeclared War Against American Women, Susan Faludi (New York: Crown, 1991).

The Beauty Myth, Naomi Wolf (New York: William Morrow, 1991).

Who Stole Feminism?, Christina Hoff Sommers (New York: Simon & Schuster, 1994).

Fast Fact: The Beauty Myth

Naomi Wolf's best-selling book The Beauty Myth brought into focus the idea that society puts pressure on women to diet, use makeup, dress up, and work out in ways that are demeaning. These male-driven forces, Wolf contended, ultimately keep women at a disadvantage in spite of the progress of the women's movement. Her more recent book, Fire with Fire, calls for a more tolerant acceptance of women's individual choices in matters of beauty and appearance, among other issues.

A group called the Barbie Liberation Organization, composed of performance artists in New York City, switched the voice chips of more than 300 talking GI Joe and Barbie dolls in 1993 and smuggled them back into stores to protest stereotypes.

The Barbie doll was introduced by Mattel in 1959. Her creator, Ruth Handler, later invented the first breast prosthesis for mastectomy patients.

TOP TEN PLASTIC-SURGERY PROCEDURES

	Total	% of all plastic surgery
Tumor removal	502,567	33.2
Hand surgery	138,233	9.1
Lacerations	135,494	8.9
Eyelid surgery	59,461	3.9
Scar revision	52,647	3.5
Nose reshaping	50,175	3.3
Liposuction	47,212	3.1
Collagen injections	41,623	2.7
Face-lift	40,077	2.6
Breast reduction	39,639	2.6

(Data from 1992)
Source: American Society of Plastic and Reconstructive Surgeons

TOP TEN AESTHETIC PROCEDURES

	Total	% performed on women
Eyelid surgery	59,461	85
Nose reshaping	50,175	72
Liposuction	47,212	87
Collagen injections	41,623	94
Face-lift	40,077	93
Breast augmentation	32,607	100
Retin-A treatment	23,520	92
Chemical peel	19,049	96
Tummy tuck	16,810	93
Dermabrasion	13,457	76

(Data from 1992)
Source: American Society of Plastic and Reconstructive Surgeons

PLASTIC SURGEONS' FEES

	Average fee
Face-lift	$4,156
Tummy tuck	3,618
Buttock lift	3,084
Nose reshaping (primary open rhinoplasty)	2,997
Breast augmentation	2,754
Breast reduction	2,325
Cheek implants	1,895
Chemical peel (full face)	1,634
Liposuction (any single site)	1,622
Dermabrasion	1,551
Eyelid surgery (both uppers)	1,514
Collagen injections (per 1 cc injection)	266

(Data from 1992)
Source: American Society of Plastic and Reconstructive Surgeons

SELECTING A PLASTIC SURGEON

What to Look for When Interviewing a Plastic Surgeon
During a preliminary discussion of your procedure, your plastic surgeon should:
- Answer all of your questions thoroughly in language you can understand.
- Ask about your motivations and expectations, discuss them with you, and solicit your reaction to her recommendations.
- Offer alternatives where appropriate, without pressuring you to consider unnecessary procedures.
- Welcome questions about professional qualifications, experience, costs, and payment policies.
- Make clear not only the risks of surgery but the possible variations in outcome. If the surgeon shows you photographs of other patients, or uses computer imaging to show you possible results, it should be clear that there is no guarantee that your results will match these.
- Make sure the final decision is *yours.*

Warning signals:
- Doesn't have hospital privileges for your procedure
- Certified in unrelated specialty
- Completed residency in unrelated specialty
- Unwilling to answer your questions
- Impatient or arrogant manner
- Unprofessional office or personal appearance
- Pressures you to add unnecessary procedures

How to Find a Plastic Surgeon
Good sources and qualifications:
- Recommendation from a friend who had similar procedure
- Recommendation from family doctor or operating-room nurse
- Listed by American Society of Plastic and Reconstructive Surgeons
- Has privileges to do your procedures at accredited hospital
- Certified by American Board of Plastic Surgery
- Completed residency in a specialty related to your procedure

Poor sources:
- Yellow Pages listing
- Other advertising
- Media mention
- General physician referral service
- Recommendation by "just anyone"

Source: Plastic Surgery Research Foundation

PLASTIC SURGERY—RESOURCES AND READING

ORGANIZATIONS

American Society of Plastic and Reconstructive Surgeons
444 E. Algonquin Road
Arlington Heights, IL 60005
(800) 635-0635

Facial Plastic Surgery Information Service
1110 Vermont Avenue, N.W., Suite 220
Washington, DC 20005
(800) 332-3223

READING

The Complete Book of Cosmetic Surgery: A Candid Guide for Men, Women, and Teens, Elizabeth Morgan (New York: Warner Books, 1988).

Plastic Surgery: The Kindest Cut, John Camp (New York: Henry Holt, 1989).

72% of women would not give up their pets if they were allergic to them, as opposed to 42% of men.

16 million TV viewers tune into the Miss America Pageant every year.

BREAST IMPLANTS

Since breast implants first came on the market thirty years ago, an estimated one million women in the U.S. have had these devices surgically inserted to enlarge or reshape their breasts, or for reconstruction following breast cancer surgery. Most are filled with a silicone gel, although about 10% contain saline (salt water).

Until recently, both gel-filled and saline implants were available to virtually any woman who wanted them. An impassioned debate on the safety of silicone implants, however, has changed all that. As of April 1992, the Food and Drug Administration ordered restrictions on the use of silicone implants while extensive studies of their safety are carried out; the same highly restricted studies of saline-filled implants are now under way as well. The devices are now primarily available only to a limited number of women who choose breast reconstruction because of disease, injury, or other disorders; only a very few elective implants will be allowed. The tightly controlled studies of these implants will evaluate the risks as well as the psychological benefits.

Most women with silicone-gel-filled breast implants do not experience serious problems. If you are not having problems, there is no reason to have the implants removed. However, you should have regular checkups, and if you have any breast discomfort, changes in size or shape, or symptoms that you think may be related to your implants, see your doctor.

Although the effects of breast implants are not yet clearly established, the Food and Drug Administration and some plastic surgeons say that silicone-gel implants can:

•Rupture at an unknown rate, leaking silicone into the body and causing inflammation
•Cause loss of sensation in the breasts, as well as inflammation and hardening of breasts
•Interfere with the detection of breast cancer
•Trigger a skin disease called aclero-derma, along with arthritis-like diseases that can cause severe pain and swelling of the joints

It is not known whether implants are associated with the development of connective-tissue and immune-related disoders, although some people have suggested that may be the case. Still, women should be aware of the symptoms of these disorders:

•joint pain and swelling
•skin tightness, redness, or swelling
•swollen glands or lymph nodes
•unusual and unexplained fatigue
•swollen hands and feet
•unusual hair loss

Source: Food and Drug Administration

BREAST IMPLANTS—RESOURCES

Command Trust Network
P.O. Box 17082
Covington, KY 41017

Food and Drug Administration
Breast Implant Information, HFE-88
5600 Fishers Lane
Rockville, MD 20857
(301) 443-3170

The Problem Reporting Program
12601 Twinbrook Parkway
Rockville, MD 20852

COSMETIC BREAST SURGERY

Varieties of Cosmetic Breast Surgery

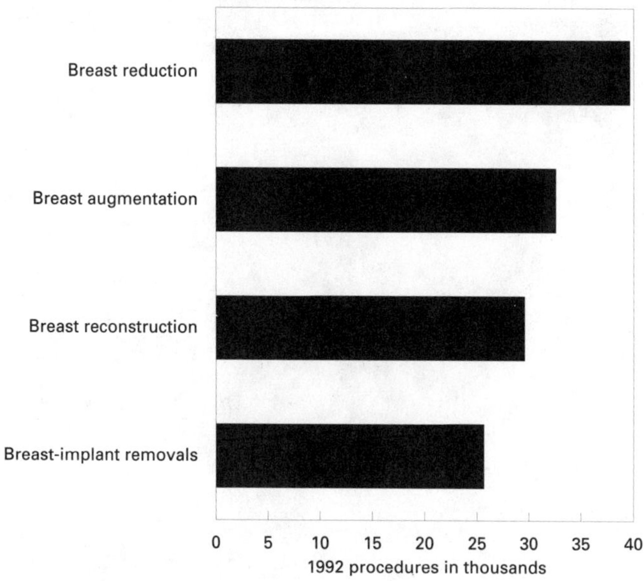

Breast Implants

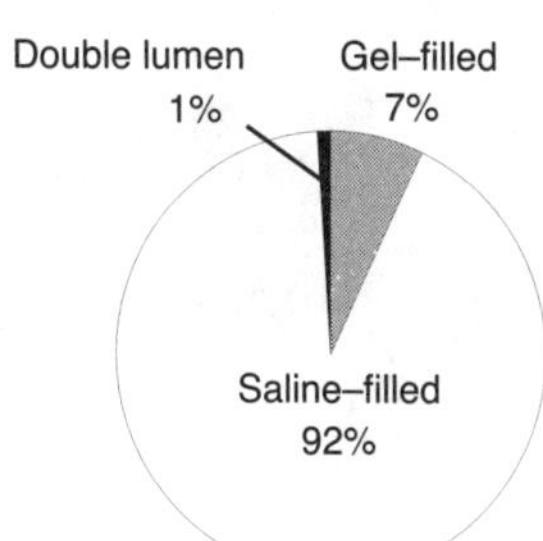

Breast Implant Removal

The following reasons were given for implant removal by women who had implants for breast augmentation:

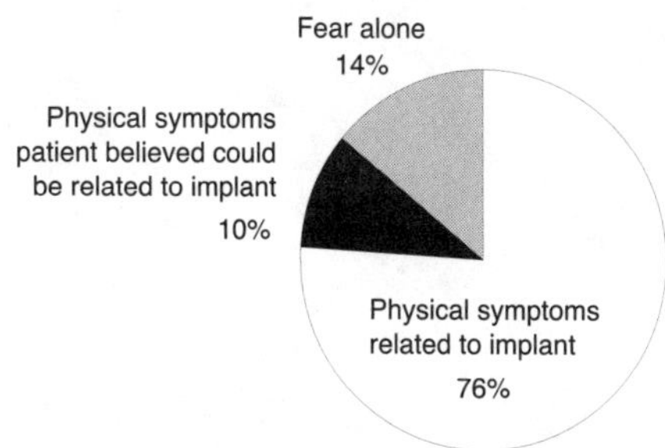

(Data from 1992)
Source for above: American Society of Plastic and Reconstructive Surgeons

85% of women in a California study were afflicted with body-image disorder.

FERTILITY

THE MENSTRUAL CYCLE

For some women, cycles recur fairly regularly every 28 days, as the chart below shows. But the number of days in each cycle can vary from woman to woman, from 21 to 35 days.

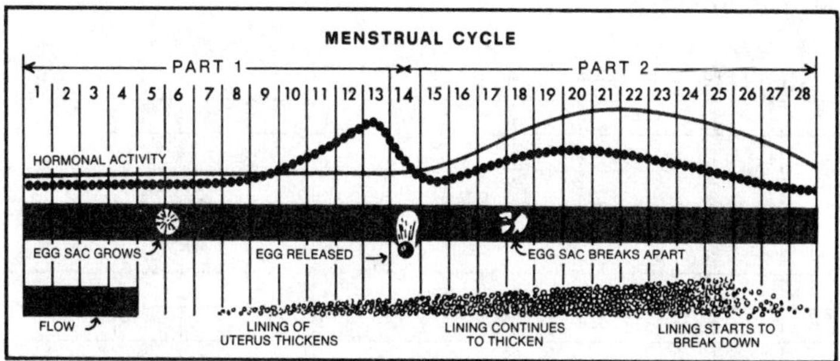

Source: Planned Parenthood Federation of America

A belief in supernatural interaction following menopause is found in Indian villages in Mexico where the ceremonial priestess is often a woman who is past the menstrual cycle.

MENSTRUATION—RECOMMENDED READING

Menstrual Health in Women's Lives, Alice J. Dan and Linda L. Lewis, eds. (Urbana, Chicago: University of Illinois Press, 1992).

Menstruation, Health and Illness, Diana Taylor (New York: Hemisphere Publishing, 1991).

The Wise Wound: Myths, Realities, and Meanings of Menstruation (rev. ed.), Penelope Shuttle and Peter Redgrove (New York: Grove Weidenfeld, 1988; Bantam, 1990).

PREMENSTRUAL SYNDROME

Premenstrual Syndrome (PMS) refers to a large number of physical and emotional symptoms that occur over the weeks prior to a woman's menstrual period. The exact cause of PMS is unknown, although some researchers assert that it results from hormonal imbalance; others, however, believe poor diet, vitamin deficiencies, and poor metabolism may be responsible.

PMS is unusual in that the number and severity of symptoms will vary from woman to woman, with no one experiencing all the symptoms mentioned here:

- Tension
- Mood swings
- Depression, sadness, pessimism
- Cravings
- Irritability
- Headaches
- Panic attacks
- Fatigue, insomnia
- Changes in appetite
- Visual disturbances
- Crying
- Changes in sex drive
- Weight gain, bloating
- Backaches
- Adverse reactions to oral contraceptives
- Ordinarily pain-free menstrual periods
- Increased premenstrual sensitivity to alcohol
- Pregnancy complications, including miscarriage, toxemia, and postpartum depression.
- Symptoms beginning with puberty and worsening with age
- Absense of symptoms during last six months of pregnancy
- Symptoms occurring or becoming more severe after tubal ligation or hysterectomy

Sources: National Mental Health Association

The Yoruba believe that menopausal women are actually pregnant but that witchcraft is preventing the pregnancy from continuing to its normal conclusion.

MENSTRUAL DIARY

Men exhibit significantly higher irritability tendancies during their wives' menstrual periods than the women themselves, a recent study discovered.

In both the Plains Cree and Winnebago Indian cultures, women can become shamans only after the menopause.

Some women want to keep track of their moods and physical feelings during their monthly cycles, a process that can be facilitated by maintaining a diary like the following:

MONTH →

DAY ↓

	1	2	3	4	5	6	7	8	9	10	11	12
1												
2												
3												
4												
5												
6												
7												
8												
9												
10												
11												
12												
13												
14												
15												
16												
17												
18												
19												
20												
21												
22												
23												
24												
25												
26												
27												
28												
29												
30												
31												

Indicate each day of your menstruation with an M or other such mark in the appropriate square. Indicate each day on which you experience the following symptoms by using the letters from this key:

D—Depression
P—Pain (backache or headache)
F—Fatigue
T—Tension, irritability, or anxiety
BT—Breast tenderness
B—Bloated feeling

Source: Alternative Health Care for Women

PMS—RESOURCES AND READING

Organization
PMS Access
P.O. Box 9326
Madison, WI 53715
(800) 222-4767

Reading
"For an Improved Lifestyle" (available from Madison Pharmacy Associates, P.O. Box 9326, Madison, WI 53715).

PMS: A Positive Program to Gain Control, Stephanie DeGraff Bender (available from Madison Pharmacy Associates, P.O. Box 9326, Madison, WI 53715).

PMS: The Premenstrual Syndrome, Lorna Peterson (Phoenix: Oryx Press, 1985).

Premenstrual Syndrome Examined Through a Feminist Lens, Esther R. Rome (1983; available from Boston Women's Health Book Collective, P.O. Box 192, W. Somerville, MA 02144).

"Premenstrual Syndrome: The Odds Are Almost Even" (available from Madison Pharmacy Associates, P.O. Box 9326, Madison, WI 53715).

Self Help for Premenstrual Syndrome, Dr. Michelle Harrison (New York: Random House, 1985).

MENOPAUSE

What to Expect During Menopause
•Hot flashes—The earliest and most common sign of menopause, these can be as mild as a light blush or severe enough to wake you from a sound sleep.
•Moods and depression—While some women may feel more emotional during menopause, or may seem that way to others, some women may not.
•Vaginal dryness—Lower estrogen levels cause the tissues of the vagina to become thinner, drier, and less elastic, developments that can make sexual intercourse uncomfortable. Interest in sex can change also; some women can experience stronger sex drives and others weaker.

Health Risks of Menopause
•Osteoporosis—For women, the loss of estrogen around the time of menopause means that they may lose bone mass faster and thus become more vulnerable to osteoporosis. Weight-bearing exercise, calcium, vitimin D, and estrogen can help reduce the risk of fractures.
•Cardiovascular disease—Heart disease alone causes half of all deaths in women older than 50 and may be connected to the loss of estrogen that comes with menopause. Eating low-fat, low-cholesterol food, not smoking, and exercising regularly may help.

Source: National Institute on Aging

TIPS FOR WOMEN HAVING HOT FLASHES

What You Can Do:
Hormone replacement therapy is the most effective remedy for hot flashes and bone loss but it's not for everyone. Here are some other suggestions.

Hot Flashes:
- Go somewhere that's cool (sleeping in a cool room may keep hot flashes from waking you up as often).
- Dress in layers that you can take off.
- Drink cold water or juice at the beginning of a flash.
- Use sheets and clothing that let your skin "breathe."

Source: National Institute on Aging

Women's periods stop altogether on average around age 50. However, menopause can occur anywhere from the 30s to the mid-50s.

The number of women aged 45 to 64 taking estrogen jumped nearly 30% between 1990 and 1993, from 5.8 million to 7.4 million.

Women in Ireland used to confine themselves to bed to await death in the belief that no role was possible for them following the end of their reproductive life.

HORMONE THERAPY: ESTROGEN AND PROGESTERONE

Advantages

•Prevents thinning of bones (osteoporosis)
•Relieves distressing symptoms of menopause, particularly hot flashes and vaginal dryness
•May protect against heart disease (addition of progesterone may negate this benefit)

Disadvantages

•Increases risk of endometrial cancer, except in women who have undergone a hysterectomy (addition of progesterone may decrease this risk)
•May accelerate growth of estrogen-dependent cancerous tumors; questionable effect on breast cancer
•Continuation or resumption of periods

Who Should Not Take Estrogen

•Anyone with known or suspected breast cancer; anyone with known or suspected estrogen-dependent cancerous tumor(s)
•Anyone who is or suspects she is pregnant
•Anyone with a history of blood clots associated with prior use of estrogen
•Anyone with undiagnosed abnormal genital bleeding
•Anyone with a history of stroke or heart attack

Possible Normal Side Effects

•Breast tenderness
•Fluid retention
•Nausea
•Slight weight gain
•Vaginal bleeding

Source: Yale University School of Medicine Heart Book

After menopause, women need 1,200 to 1,500 milligrams of calcium a day, compared with 1,000 to 1,200 before menopause.

ESTROGEN AND CARDIOVASCULAR DEATH RATES

Effect of estrogen use on cardiovascular death rates

Age	Deaths per 10,000	
	Nonusers of estrogen	Users of estrogen
50–59	16.2	4.5
60–69	39.1	11.8
70–79	150.8	61.7

Source: Department of Health and Human Services

MENOPAUSE—RESOURCES AND READING

ORGANIZATIONS

National Institute of Aging
9000 Rockville Pike
Bethesda, MD 20892
(301) 496-1752

Medical College of Pennsylvania
Center for the Mature Woman
3300 Henry Avenue
Philadelphia, PA 19129
(215) 581-6267

READING

The Change: Women, Aging and the Menopause, Germaine Greer (New York: Alfred A. Knopf, 1992).

Changing Perspectives on Menopause, Ann M. Voda, Myra Dinnerstein, Sheryl O'Donnell, eds. (Austin: University of Texas Press, 1982).

Choice Years: How to Stay Healthy, Happy and Beautiful Through Menopause and Beyond, Judith Paige and Pamela Gordon (New York: Random House, 1991).

Managing Your Menopause, Wulf H. Utian (New York: Prentice-Hall, 1990).

Menopause: A Self-Care Manual, rev. ed., Judy Costlow et al. (Santa Fe: Santa Fe Health, 1989

Menopause and Beyond, 60-min. film, Dr. Judy Seifer (1992; available from Focus International, 14 Oregon Drive, Huntington Station, NY 11746).

The Menopause Handbook, Susan F. Trien (New York: Ballantine, 1991).

Menopause, Naturally: Preparing for the Second Half of Life, Sadja Greenwood and Marcia Quackenbush (San Francisco: Volcano Press, 1989).

Natural Menopause: The Complete Guide to a Woman's Most Misunderstood Passage, Susan Perry and Katherine O'Harlan (Boston: Addison-Wesley, 1992).

Silent Passage, Gail Sheehy (New York: Random House, 1992).

Stay Cool Through Menopause: Answers to Most Frequently Asked Questions, Melvin Frisch (New York: Body Press-Perigee/Putnam, 1989).

What's Stopped Happening to Me? Gail Parent et al. (New York: Lyle Stuart/Carol, 1990).

Among the Sinkaietk, it is the common belief that death may occur in conjunction with, or as a result of menopause.

Every day 3,500 women enter menopause.

PREGNANCY RATES

These rates apply to women aged 15–44; the data, the most recent available, is from 1987.

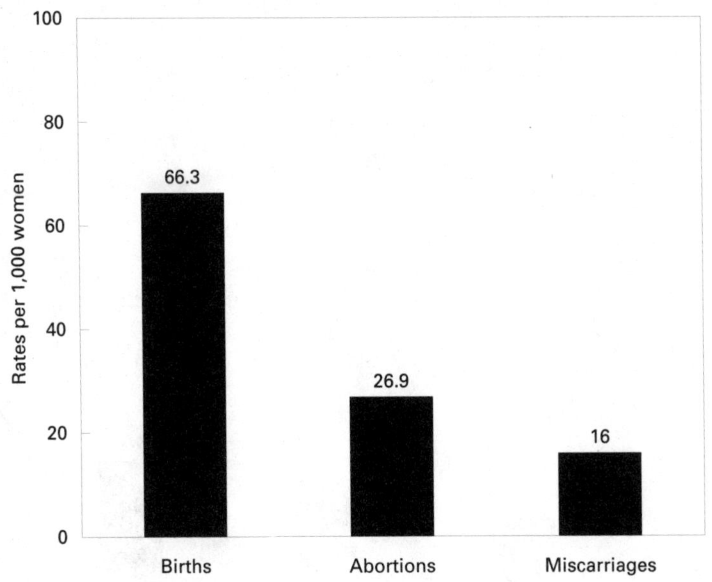

Source: Alan Guttmacher Institute

FERTILITY RATES

If the difference in infant mortality rates continues to widen, black babies will be three times as likely to die as white babies by the year 2000, warn federal health officials.

Women 18 to 34 years old in 1992 could expect to have an average of 2.1 children in their lifetime, a number just at the replacement level of fertility.

Fertility rates measure only full-term pregnancies that result in births.

Fertility Rates by Age Group

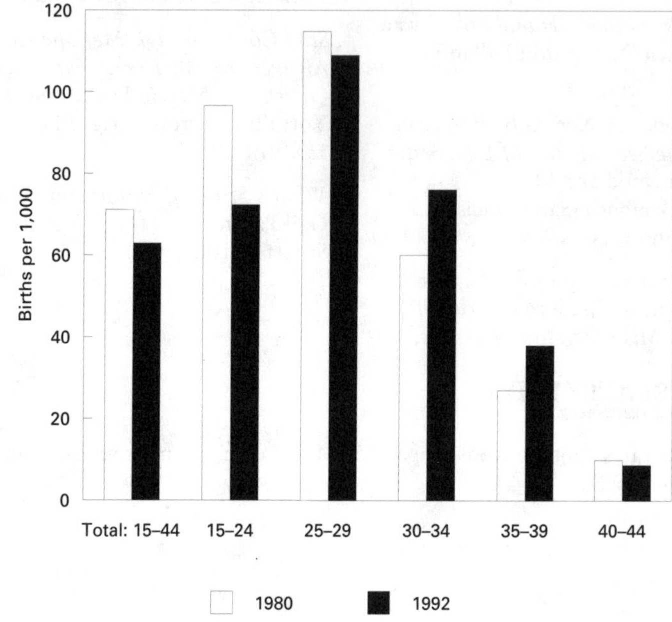

Increases in Fertility Among Women Over 30

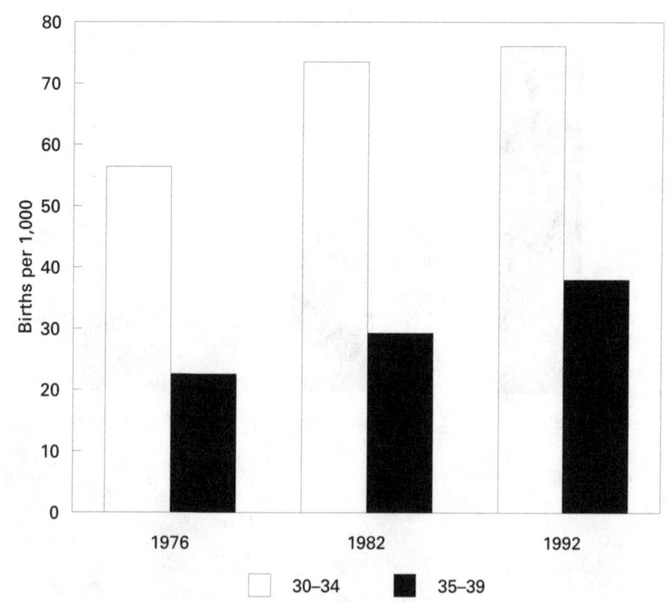

Source : Fertility of American Women, Bureau of the Census

CHILDLESSNESS ON THE RISE

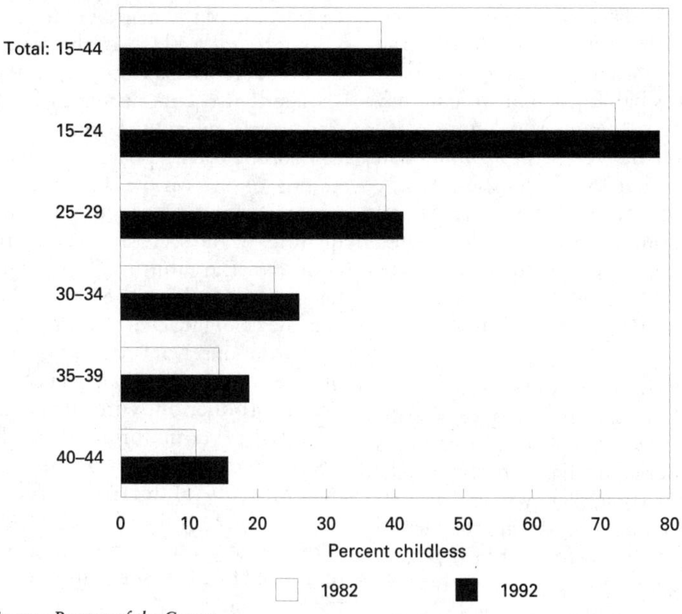

Source: Bureau of the Census

In 1988, about 1 in 12 American women aged 15 to 44 had an impaired ability to have children.

INTERNATIONAL FERTILITY RATES

Total fertility rate means the average number of births per woman.

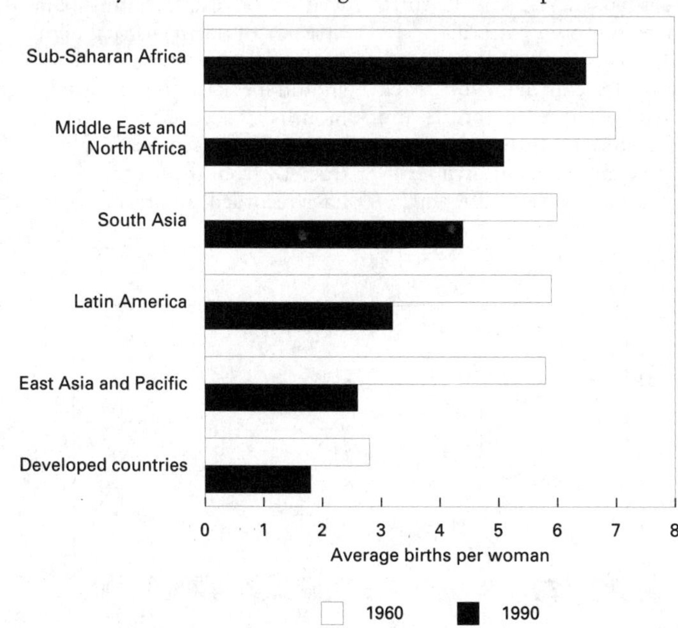

Source: United Nations

PREDICTING YOUR FERTILITY

There are days when a woman is fertile, days when she is infertile, and some days when fertility is unlikely but possible. In total, a woman may become pregnant from unprotected sex over the course of around eight days of her cycle—as long as five days before ovulation, the day of ovulation, and two days following. The temperature method, the calendar method, and the cervical-mucus method are ways to identify those fertile days.

The Temperature Method

The temperature method is based on the fact that a woman's body temperature is lower during the first part of the cycle, generally rising slightly with ovulation and remaining up during the second part until just before her next period. Recording each day's temperature, then, helps to indicate when ovulation has occurred. Technically, the method requires daily charting of the temperature your body registers when you're completely at rest. As each day's temperature is plotted, you will learn to recognize your own pattern.

The following chart, based on a 28-day cycle, can help you track your fertility. The temperatures and cycle-breakdown shown here are merely an example; your own fertility pattern may be very different.

The Cervical-Mucus Method

A more recently developed method for predicting when ovulation is about to take place is the mucus method. It is based on another change that occurs during the menstrual cycle, when the hormones that control the cycle's phases act on the glands of the cervix that produce mucus, changing the quality and quantity of the secretions during the course of the month. With proper instruction, many women can recognize the changing characteristics that signal the onset of fertility. In simplest terms, fertility is signaled by mucus production, with the height of fertility coinciding with the greatest production. But, as with other forms of fertility prediction, women should receive detailed instruction from a physician or fertility specialist before relying on it.

The Calendar Method

This method attempts to predict ovulation using a woman's menstrual history. It requires keeping a written record, counting from the first day of one menstrual period up to the first day of the next. Records should be kept for at least eight months to account for variation in cycles. To determine fertility, subtract 18 from the shortest cycle you have recorded, and regard that num-

Temperature chart

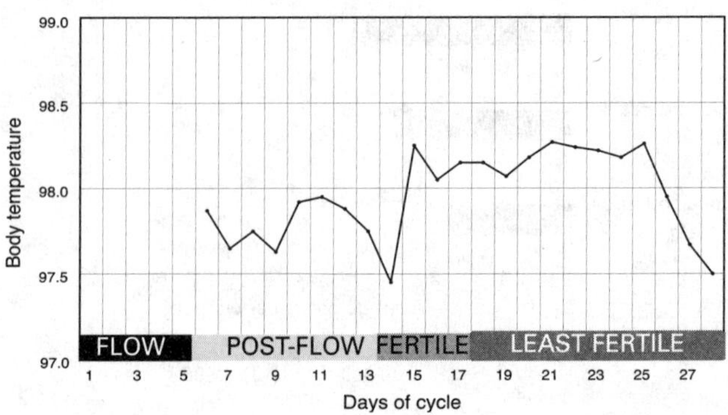

ber of days after the start of your cycle as the start of your potential period of fertility. (If the shortest cycle is 28 days, subtract 18; you'll then count ten days after the start of your cycle as the start of your fertile period.)

BIRTH CONTROL
These three methods of fertility prediction can also be used for birth control, but their effectiveness varies. Of the three, the calendar method is the least effective, with 20% of women who use it getting pregnant in a year. The temperature and mucus methods, although harder to learn and perform correctly, have a much lower failure rate—between 2–3%. Because of the difficulty of practicing these methods accurately, it is recommended that women receive detailed instruction from a physician and combine the systems for greater protection.

Sources: Planned Parenthood Federation of America; American College of Obstetricians and Gynecologists

FERTILIZATION TECHNIQUES

IN VITRO FERTILIZATION
In vitro fertilization (IVF) is a process in which an egg and sperm are combined in a laboratory dish, where fertilization occurs. The fertilized and dividing egg is then transferred into the woman's uterus.

The basic steps in an IVF treatment cycle are:

•Ovulation enhancement—drugs are used to induce the patient's ovaries to grow several mature eggs rather than the single egg that normally develops each month.
•Egg harvest—eggs are obtained by inserting a needle into the ovarian follicle and removing the fluid and the egg by suction.
•Fertilization—a defined number of sperm are placed with each egg in a separate dish containing IVF culture medium. The dishes are then placed in an incubator with a controlled temperature that is the same as the woman's body.
•Embryo transfer—after 48 hours, when pre-embryos usually consist of two to four cells each, they are ready to be placed into the woman's uterus.

Among all women undergoing IVF in the U.S. in 1988, the rate of pregnancies resulting in live birth was approximately 12% per treatment cycle.

GIFT
GIFT stands for gamete intrafallopian transfer, a process during which sperm and eggs are mixed and injected into one or both fallopian tubes, where fertilization can take place as it does in unassisted reproduction. Once fertilized, the egg or embryo travels to the uterus by natural processes. Patients with normal, healthy fallopian tubes are candidates for GIFT, which is most often used for couples with unexplained infertility or minimal endometriosis. Specialists generally agree that pregnancy rates are 5% to 10% higher for GIFT than for IVF.

QUESTIONS TO CONSIDER WHEN CHOOSING AN IVF/GIFT PROGRAM
Cost and Convenience
1. How much does the entire procedure cost, including drugs per treatment cycle?
2. How much do I pay if my treatment cycle is canceled before egg recovery? Before embryo replacement?
3. What are the costs for embryo freezing, storage, and transfer?
4. How much work will I miss? Will my husband miss work?
5. If I must have lodging, is there a low-cost place for me to stay? Do you help arrange this?
6. If I do not get pregnant, when do I make my next office visit for further evaluation and counseling?

The Georgeanna and Howard Jones Institute for Reproductive Medicine, the first in vitro fertilization clinic, opened on January 8, 1980.

Details about the Program

1. Does the program meet the American Fertility Society minimal standards?
2. Does the program report its results to the IVF Registry?
3. Is the program a member of the Society for Assisted Reproductive Technology?
4. How many doctors will be involved in my care?
5. Are one or more doctors board certified in reproductive endocrinology?
6. To what degree can my own doctor participate in my care?
7. What types of counseling and support services are available?
8. Whom do I call day or night if I have a problem?
9. Do you freeze embryos (cryopreservation)?
10. Is donor sperm available in your program? Donor eggs?
11. Do you have an age limit?

Success of the Program

1. When did this program perform its first IVF procedure? First GIFT procedure?
2. How may babies have been born from this program's IVF efforts? GIFT efforts?
3. In the past two years, how many treatment cycles have been initiated for IVF? For GIFT?
4. In the past two years, how many egg recovery procedures have been performed in the IVF program? GIFT program?
5. In the past two years, how many embryo transfer procedures have been completed in the IVF program?
6. In the past two years, how many pregnancies have resulted from IVF? From GIFT?
7. In the past two years, how many miscarriages have occurred from pregnancies initiated by IVF? By GIFT?
8. In the past two years, how many live births have occurred in your program from IVF? From GIFT?
9. How many ongoing pregnancies are there from IVF? From GIFT?
10. How many deliveries were twins or other multiple births?

Source: American Fertility Society

SPERM BANKS

The following have been accredited as human-semen cryobanks by the American Association of Tissue Banks:

Biogenetics Corporation
1130 Route 22 West
P.O. Box 1290
Mountainside, NJ 07092
(800) 637-7776

California Cryobank
1019 Gayley Avenue
Los Angeles, CA 90024
(310) 443-5244 or (800) 231-3373

Cryogenic Laboratories
2233 Hamline Avenue North
Roseville, MN 55113
(612) 636-3792

Genetic Semen Bank
University of Nebraska Medical Center
42nd and Dewey Avenue
Omaha, NE 68105
(401) 559-5070

Reproductive Resources
4720 I-10 Service Road
Suite 508
Metarie, LA 70001
(504) 454-7973 or (800) 227-4561

University of Texas
Southwestern Medical Center
Andrology and Reproductive Endocrinology Laboratory
Department OB/GYN
Dallas, TX 75235
(214) 688-2376

FERTILITY DRUGS

Drug	Function	Contraindications	Side Effects
Clomiphene (brand names Clomid, Seraphine)	Induces ovulation by chemically stimulating the pituitary gland to produce hormones that trigger the ovulation process	May not be appropriate for patients with large fibroid tumors, ovarian cysts, or liver problems	Vary in frequency and intensity with each patient; may include nausea, vomiting, visual problems, headache, insomnia, hot flashes, breast tenderness, heightened emotional sensitivity
Bromocriptine (brand name Parlodel)	Reduces pituitary's production of prolactine hormone while it is taken	May not be appropriate for patients with pituitary tumors larger than 1 cm	May include nausea, nasal stuffiness, dizziness, low blood pressure, headache
Human Menopausal Gonadotropin or HMG (brand name Pergonal)	Stimulates ovary to develop follicles. In addition, an injection of Human Chorionic Gonadotropin is required to trigger ovulation	May not be appropriate in cases of pituitary tumor, ovarian cysts, or ovarian or adrenal problems	20–40% possibility of multiple births; small risk of hyperstimulation syndrome; involves a great deal of emotional stress
Gonadotropin Releasing Hormone (GnRH)	Triggers normal pituitary hormonal activity so ovulation can occur	Because it is a natural hormone, no obvious contraindications	No known physical side effects; patient must carry pump and attached IV tubing for one or two weeks or until ovulation occurs

Source: National Women's Health Network

The national ultrasound bill is about $1 billion a year.

As a result of simultaneous in vitro fertilization, sisters Linda Schaper and Barbara Payne of Missouri gave birth to a set of triplets in January and February 1994, with Schaper having two babies and Payne having one.

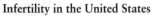

Ann Moore, one of the first participants in the Peace Corps, invented the Snugli infant carrier, drawing on her observations of the customs of mothers in West Africa.

INFERTILITY

Infertility in the United States

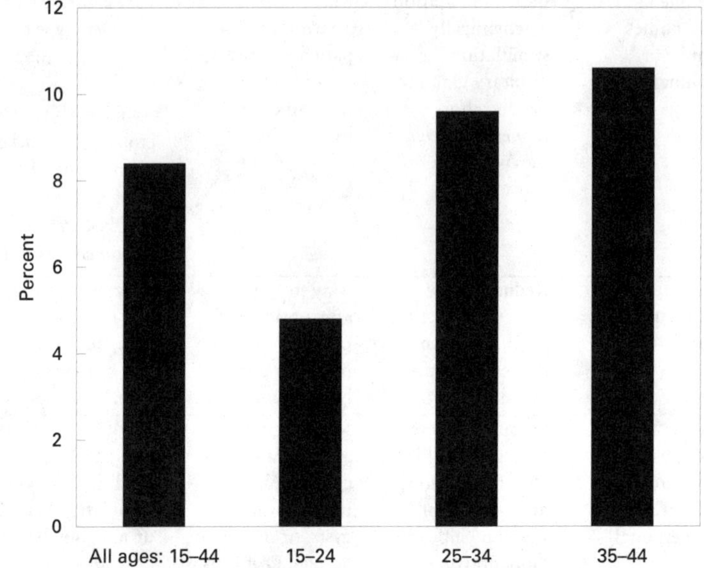

Infertility among Married Women

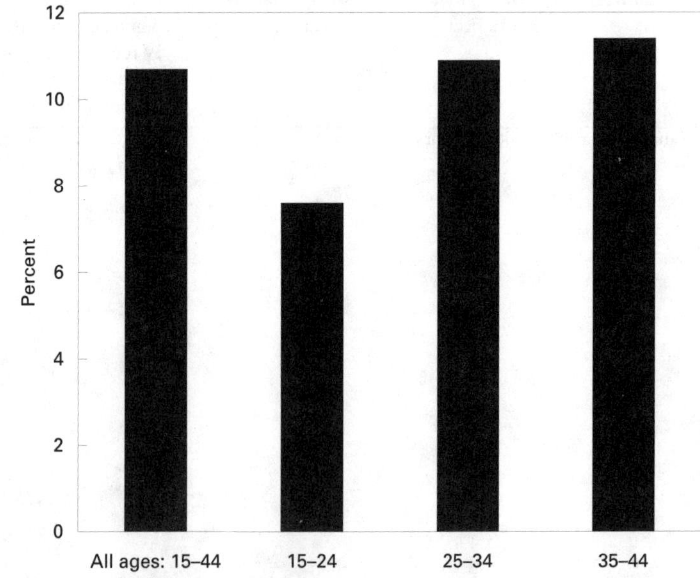

Source for above: National Center for Health Statistics

COMMON CAUSES OF INFERTILITY

•Almost 2.4 million American couples, or 15%, are infertile, a condition defined by the failure to achieve pregnancy within one year of unprotected intercourse.
•In approximately 40% of infertile couples, the male is either the sole cause or a contributing cause.
•A woman's failure to ovulate or produce sufficient progesterone accounts for approximately 25% of all infertility cases.
•Conditions within the cervix can contribute to infertility, although somewhat less than 5% of infertility problems are traceable solely to the cervix.
•Defects in the uterus are often detectable by a special X-ray. Problems revealed may include uterine scar tissue, polyps, fibroids, or an abnormally shaped uterine cavity. These conditions, which are seen in about 5% of infertile women, can interfere with secure implantation of the fertilized egg.
•Problems within the pelvis that can interfere with fertility include scar tissue or endometriosis. The latter is found in about 35% of infertile women who have no other diagnosable problem.
•Tubal and/or peritoneal factors account for about 25% of all infertility problems, open tubes being necessary for conception.
•In approximately 10% of couples seeking pregnancy, all tests are normal, and in a much higher percentage, only minor abnormalities are found. Many of these couples choose to undergo more intensive testing for problems involving the immune system, hormones, or infection.

Source: American Fertility Society

USE OF INFERTILITY SERVICES

Date of Most Recent Visit to Infertility Clinics

	1988	% of pop.
In the last year	1,346	2.3
In the last 3 years	2,392	4.1
In the last 5 years	3,123	5.4

(Numbers in thousands)
Source: National Center for Health Statistics

INFERTILITY— RESOURCES AND READING

ORGANIZATIONS

American Fertility Society
1209 Montgomery Highway
Birmingham, AL 35216
(205) 978-5000

Resolve
1310 Broadway
Somerville, MA 02144
(617) 623-0744
Resolve has local chapters nationwide serving the needs of the infertile population.

READING

Between Strangers: Surrogate Mothers, Expectant Fathers and Brave New Babies, Lori Andrews (New York: Harper & Row, 1989)

Designs of Life, Robert Lee Hotz (New York: Simon & Schuster, 1991).

From Infertility to In Vitro Fertilization, Geoffrey Scher, M.D., and Virginia Marriage (New York: McGraw-Hill, 1988).

STATE LAWS ON INFERTILITY INSURANCE

The following states have regulated insurance coverage to include in vitro fertilization (IVF), as of October 1991.

State	Date enacted	Mandate to cover	Mandate to offer	Diagnosis and treatment including IVF	Diagnosis and treatment excluding IVF	IVF only
Maryland	1985	x				x
Arkansas	1987	x				x
Texas	1987		x			x
Hawaii	1987	x				x
Massachusetts	1987	x		x		
Connecticut	1989		x	x		
Rhode Island	1989	x		x		
California	1989		x		x	
New York	1989	x			x	
Illinois	1991	x		x		

Source: American Fertility Society

CONTRACEPTION AMONG WOMEN

By Age

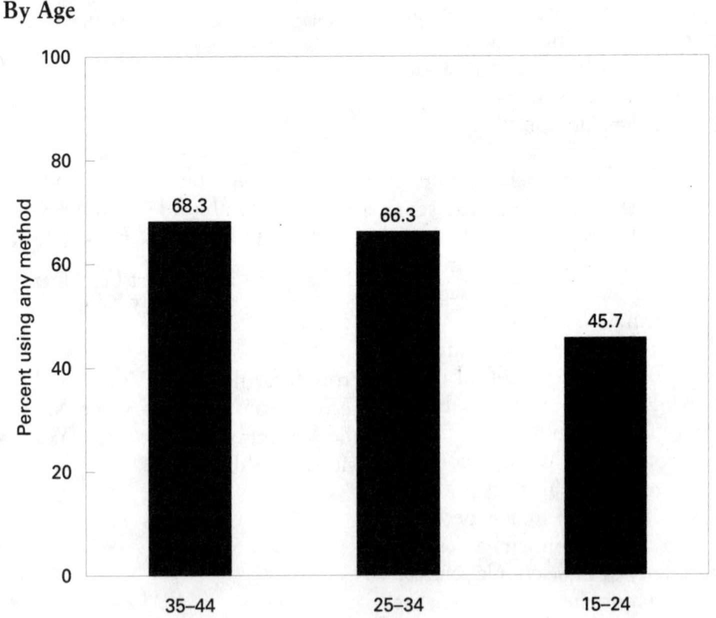

Source: National Center for Health Statistics

By Marital Status

Condoms
Pill
Tubal ligation
Rhythm*
Abortion
Vasectomy
I.U.D.
Diaphragm
Cream/jelly
None

0 5 10 15 20 25 30 35 40 45
Percent of group

Single Married Divorced

**The rhythm method was not statistically significant among divorced women in this study.*
Source: *Janus Report* *(New York: John Wiley & Sons, 1993)*

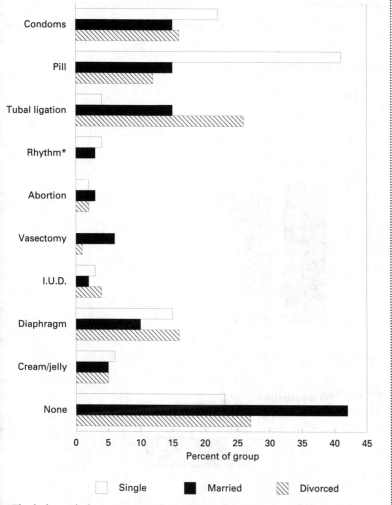

The Pill first became available in the U.S. in 1961.

CONTRACEPTION BY RACE

In classical Greece, where a woman was either "baby maker, prostitute, or slave," unwanted infants were routinely abandoned.

The following figures reflect the percentage of women who use any form of birth control at all.

By Race: Any Method

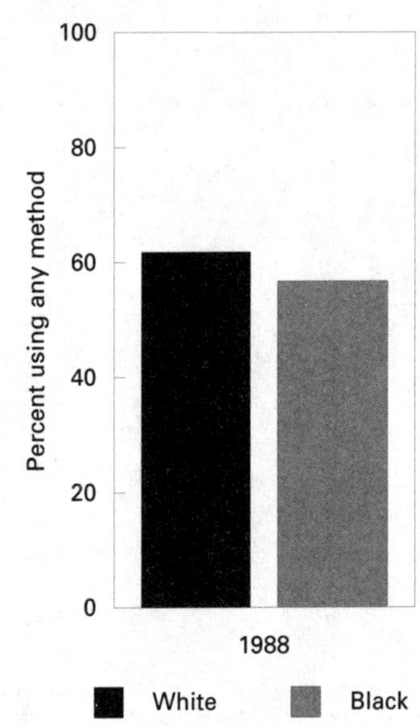

By Race: Which Method

These two bars show the breakdown for total contraceptive use, totalling 100%.

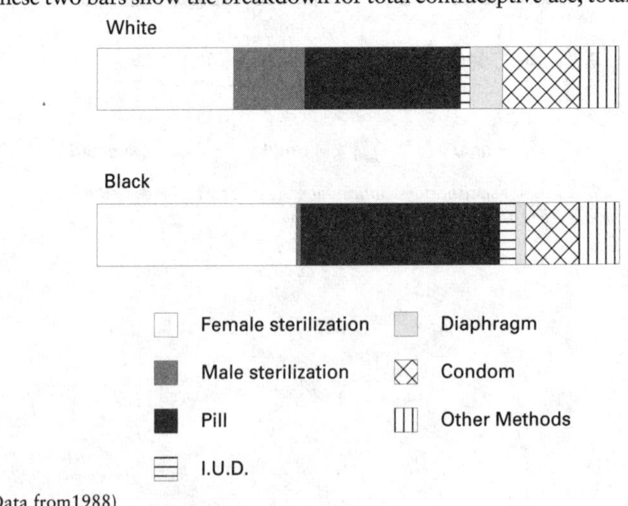

(Data from1988)

Source for above: National Center for Health Statistics

WOMEN OF COLOR AND CONTRACEPTION

Frequency of Birth Control Use

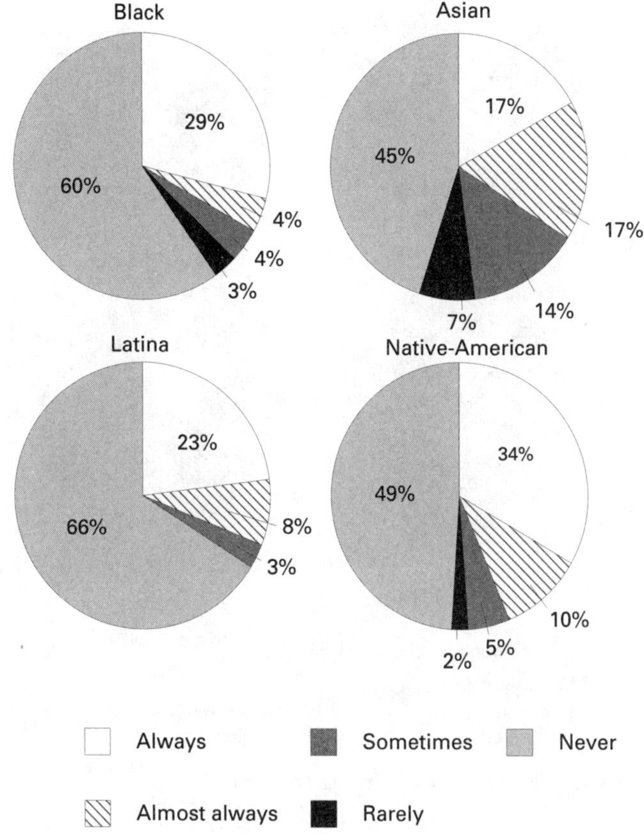

Women are more likely than men to get cellulite because one of estrogen's functions is to store extra fat on the thighs, hips, and buttocks.

Major Reasons for Not Using Birth Control

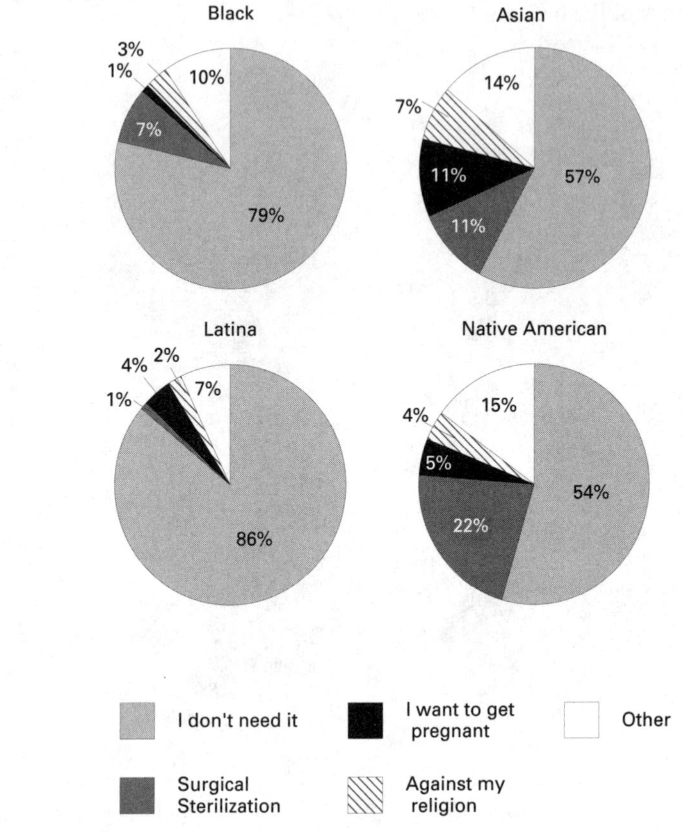

Source for above: Religious Coalition for Abortion Rights

SEX AND RELIGION: WHO USES CONTRACEPTION

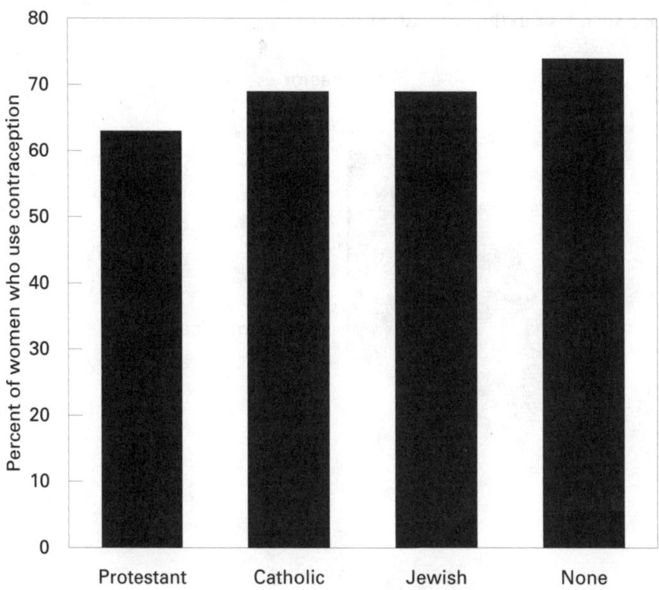

Source: Janus Report (New York: John Wiley & Sons, 1993)

CATHOLIC ATTITUDES TOWARD REPRODUCTION AND SEX

The 1992 Official Catholic Directory calculates that there are a total of 58 million U.S. Catholics, about 23% of the total U.S. population. Recent polls show:

•31% of Catholics feel abortion should be legal in all circumstances; 53% feel abortion should be legal in some circumstances; 13% feel it should be illegal in all circumstances.

•79% of Catholics disagree with the statement "using artificial means of birth control is wrong"; 19% agree.

•79% of Catholics think it is permissible to make up their own minds on such moral issues as birth control and abortion rather than always obeying official church teachings.

•60% of Catholics think that public education efforts to reduce the spread of AIDS among young people should focus more on encouraging them to practice safe sex rather than on abstaining from sex; 37% think public education efforts should focus more on abstinence.

Source: Catholics for a Free Choice

FREQUENCY OF FAMILY PLANNING VISITS

This graph shows the type of family planning visits by women who have had at least one such visit in the year surveyed.

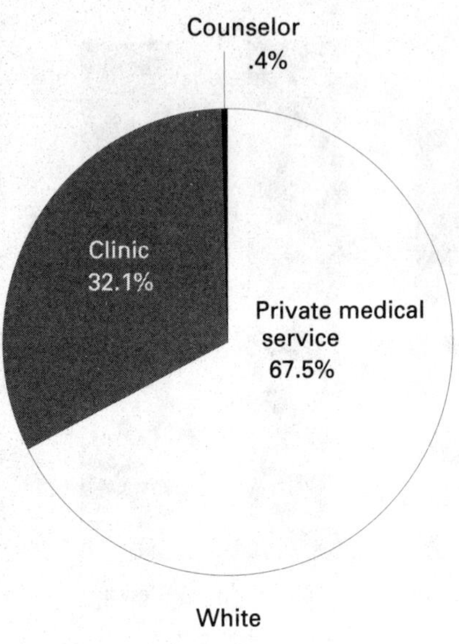

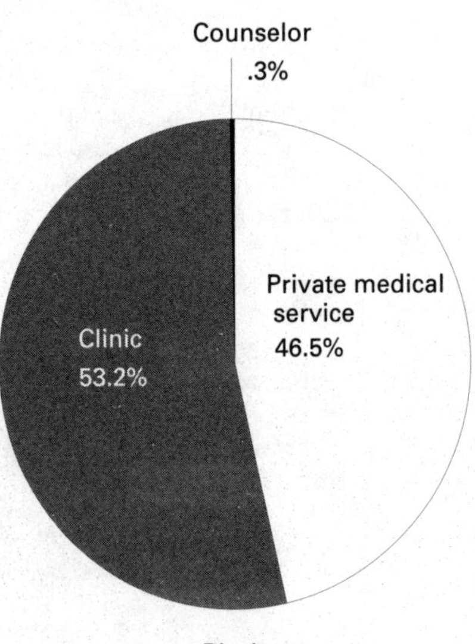

Source: National Center for Health Statistics

THE RISE OF FAMILY PLANNING IN THE THIRD WORLD

The following graph shows the percentage of married women using some form of contraception, by geographic region.

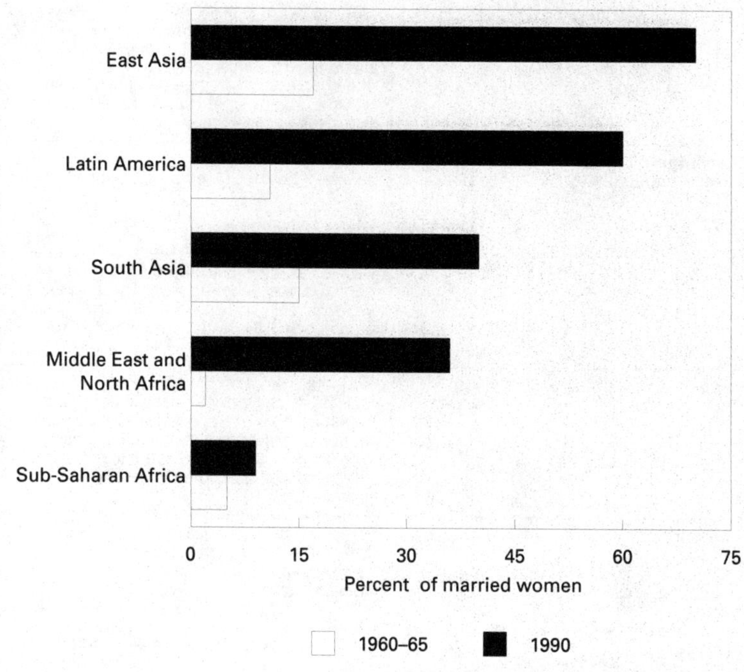

Source: United Nations

There would be an estimated 1.2 million additional unintended pregnancies each year if publicly funded women's health services did not exist.

"We thought it might be fun to have twins." — Sam Frustaci, whose wife gave birth to septuplets in 1985, the largest multiple birth in U.S. history.

CONTRACEPTIVE CHOICES

Type	Effectiveness	Helps protect against STDs*	Advantages
Pill	97%–99.9%	No	Nothing to put in place before intercourse; more comfortable and regular periods; less: acne, iron-deficiency anemia, premenstrual tension, rheumatoid arthritis; protects against ovarian and endometrial cancers, pelvic inflammatory disease, non-cancerous breast tumors, ovarian cysts; fewer tubal pregnancies
Diaphragm/ cervical cap	82%–94%	Yes	No major health concerns; can last several years
IUD	97%–99.2%	No	Nothing to put in place before intercourse; copper IUDs may be left in place for up to eight years; no daily pill; no effect on hormone levels in the body; IUDs with hormones may reduce menstrual cramps
Depo-Provera	99.7%	No	Protects against pregnancy for 12 weeks; no daily pill; nothing to put in place before intercourse; can be used while breastfeeding (six weeks after delivery); can be used by some women who cannot take the Pill; protects against cancer of the uterine lining, iron-deficiency anemia
Norplant	99.96%	No	Protects against pregnancy for five years; no daily pill; nothing to put in place before intercourse; can use while breastfeeding (six weeks after delivery); can be used by some women who cannot take the Pill
Sponge, foam, and over-the-counter forms	72%–97%	Yes	Easy to buy in drugstores, supermarkets, etc.; insertion is easy and may be part of sex play; sponge can be worn up to 30 hours
Condoms	88%–92%	Yes	Easy to buy in drugstores, supermarkets, etc.; can help relieve premature ejaculation; can be put on as part of sex play
Female condoms	74%–77%	Yes	Provides protection with uncooperative partners; can be put on as part of sex play
Sterilization (tubal sterilization and vasectomy)	99.6%–99.8%	No	Permanent protection against pregnancy; no lasting side effects; no effect on sexual pleasure; protects women whose health would be threatened by pregnancy
Periodic abstinence	80%–97%	No	No medical or hormonal side effects; calendars, thermometers, charts easy to get; most religions accept periodic abstinence
Abstinence	100%	Yes	No medical or hormonal side effects; some religions support abstinence for unmarried people

**Sexually transmitted diseases*
***Some family planning clinics charge according to income*

Problems	Cost**
Must be taken daily; rare but serious health risks, including blood clots, heart attack, and stroke—mostly for women over 35 who smoke; side effects include temporary irregular bleeding and other discomforts	$15–$25 monthly (often less at clinics) with $35–$125 exam by private doctor
Can be messy; some women have allergies to latex or spermicide; cannot use during vaginal bleeding or infection; increased risk of bladder infection with diaphragm; cervical cap is difficult for some women to fit and use	$13–$25 diaphragm or cap, $50–$125 examination, $8 kits of spermicidal jelly or cream
Temporary increase in cramps; spotting between periods; heavier and longer periods; increased chance of tubal infection, which may lead to sterility, for women with more than one sex partner, or whose partner has other partners; rarely, wall of uterus can be punctured	$150–$300 exam, insertion, and follow-up visit with private doctor
Side effects include irregular bleeding, weight gain, headaches, depression, and abdominal pain; side effects cannot be reversed until medication wears off (up to 12 weeks); may cause delay in getting pregnant after shots are stopped	$30–$75 per injection; $35–$125 exam by private doctor
Side effects include irregular bleeding and other minor discomforts; very slightly increased risk of serious health problems; rarely, infection at insertion site	$500–$750 exam, implants, insertion; $100–$200 removal
Can be messy; allergies; some brands may irritate vagina or penis; difficulty removing sponge (have clinician remove immediately if it shreds); cannot use sponge during vaginal bleeding; women who have had toxic shock syndrome must not use sponge; cannot use sponge after childbirth, abortion, or miscarriage until clinician approves	$8 applicator kits of foam and gel, $2–$4.50 refills, similar prices for films and suppositories, $3–$5 3-sponge pack
Allergies; loss of sensation; breakage	25¢ and up dry, 50¢ and up lubricated, $2.50 and up animal tissue
Not widely available; breakage	$2.50 each
Mild bleeding or infection right after operation; some people later regret not being able to have children; reaction to anesthetic; reversibility cannot be guaranteed; rarely, tubes reopen, allowing pregnancy to occur Tubal sterilization: Very rare injury to blood vessels or bowel Vasectomy: Infection or blood clot in or near the testicles; temporary bruises, swelling, or tenderness of the scrotum; sperm form small lumps near testicles	Tubal sterilization $1,000–$2,500, vasectomy $240–$520
Uncooperative partners; taking risks during "unsafe" days; poor recordkeeping; illness and lack of sleep affect body temperature; vaginal infections and douches change mucus; cannot use with irregular periods or temperature patterns	$5–$8 and up temperature kits (drugstores), free classes in health and church centers
Difficult for many people to abstain for long periods; people often forget to protect themselves against pregnancy or STDs when they stop abstaining	None

Source: Planned Parenthood Federation of America

According to *The Myths of Motherhood* by Shari Thurer, the popularity rating of female newscasters rises after they give birth.

The birth rate jumped from 51 to 60 for every 1,000 teenage girls between 1985 and 1990.

40,000 teenage girls drop out of school each year because of pregnancy.

27% of the "brightest" female high school students have had sexual intercourse, 20% of whom began before they were 14, according to a recent survey.

TEENAGE SEX, CONTRACEPTION, PREGNANCY, AND CHILDBEARING

Sex and Contraception

•Half of unmarried 15- to 19-year-old women and 60% of unmarried 15- to 19-year-old men reported in 1988 that they had had vaginal intercourse.
•Six in ten women aged 15 to 19 in 1988 who had coitus reported having had two or more sexual partners.
•One-third of teenage women use no contraceptive the first time they have sex.

Pregnancy

•Each year more than one million teenagers become pregnant. In 1988, the teenage pregnancy rate was 113 per 1,000 women aged 15 to 19.
•By age 18, one in four women will have been pregnant.
•Nearly 20% of teenagers who experience a premarital pregnancy will get pregnant again within a year. Within two years, more than 30% will have a repeat pregnancy.
•Eight in ten teenage pregnancies are unintended.
•Nonwhite teenagers have twice the pregnancy rate of white teenagers.
•Pregnancy rates of American teenagers are twice as high as rates in England, France, and Canada, three times as high as Sweden, and seven times as high as the Dutch rate.
•Four in ten teenage pregnancies (excluding miscarriages) end in abortion.

Childbearing

•About half of all teenage pregnancies end in births. In 1988, that meant that 10,588 babies were born to teenagers 14 and younger.
•Seventy-three percent of births to teenagers result from unintended pregnancies.
•Two-thirds of women under age 20 who gave birth in 1988 were unmarried—54% of whites and 91% of blacks.
•More than 90% of teenagers who give birth keep their babies.
•Teenage mothers are at a greater risk of socioeconomic disadvantage throughout their lives than those who delay childbearing until their twenties.

Source: Planned Parenthood Federation of America

FAMILY PLANNING RESOURCES FOR TEENAGE WOMEN

See also Abortion Resources, p. 304, Adoption Resources, pp. 306–7, and Pregnancy and Childbirth Resources, pp. 318–9.

Organizations

The Center for Population Options
1025 Vermont Avenue, N.W.,
Suite 200
Washington, DC 20005
(202) 347-5700

National Organization of Adolescent Pregnancy and Parenting
4421A East-West Highway
Bethesda, MD 20814
(301) 913-0378

Nurturing Network
P.O. Box 2050
Boise, ID 83701
(208) 344-7200 or (800) 866-4666

Parents Anonymous
520 S. Lafayette Park Place
Los Angeles, CA 90057
(213) 388-6685

Planned Parenthood Federation of America
810 Seventh Avenue
New York, NY 10019
(212) 541-7800

Preventing Adolescent Pregnancy
Girls, Inc.
30 E. 33rd Street
New York, NY 10016
(212) 689-3700

Reading

Teen Parenting: Your Baby's First Year—A How-to-Parent Book Especially for Teenage Parents (2 vols.), J. W. Lindsay (Buena Park, Calif.: Morning Glory Press, 1991).

FAMILY PLANNING—RESOURCES AND READING

ORGANIZATIONS

In addition to these national resources, please see Feminist Health Centers (pp. 236–8) and Women's Health Organizations and Resources (pp. 235–6) in the Health chapter.

National Family Planning and Reproductive Health Association
122 C Street, N.W., Suite 380
Washington, DC 20001
(202) 628-3533

Planned Parenthood Federation of America
810 Seventh Avenue
New York, NY 10019
(212) 603-4600 or (800) 230-7526

READING

Family Planning, Tim Parks (New York: Grove Weidenfeld, 1991).

How Not to Get Pregnant, Sherman J. Silber (New York: Warner Books, 1990).

Woman's Body, Woman's Rights and Wrongs: The Global Politics of Population Control and Contraceptive Choice, Linda Gordon (New York: Harper & Row, 1990).

In the Third World, 200,000 women die each year—1 every 3 minutes— as a result of the antiabortion policies of their own governments, reports the World Health Organization.

TOTAL BIRTHS TO UNMARRIED MOTHERS

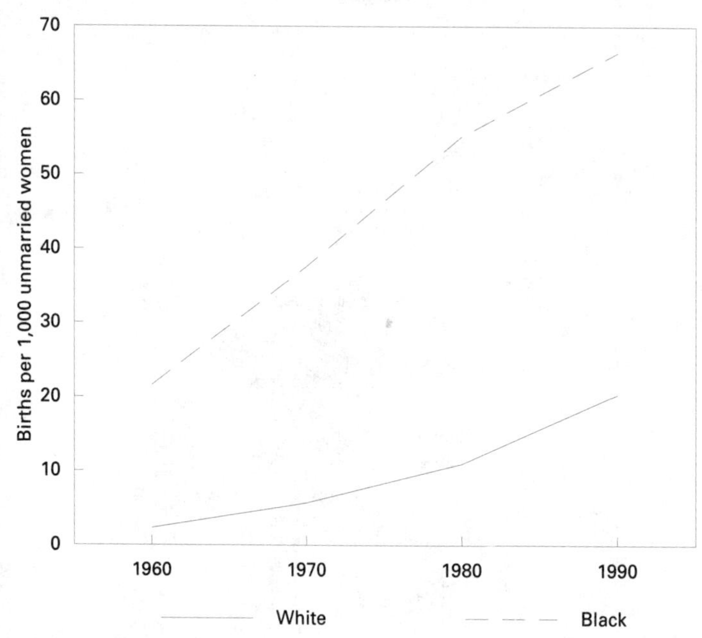

Source: National Opinion Research Center

In Sweden, it is considered unethical to feed infants anything other than human milk. For those women who cannot nurse, there are milk banks, just as there are blood banks.

Approximately 3.5 million lesbian and gay Americans have mothered or fathered children. Approximately 10,000 children are being raised by lesbians who conceived through artificial insemination.

PROFILE OF SINGLE MOTHERS

Age

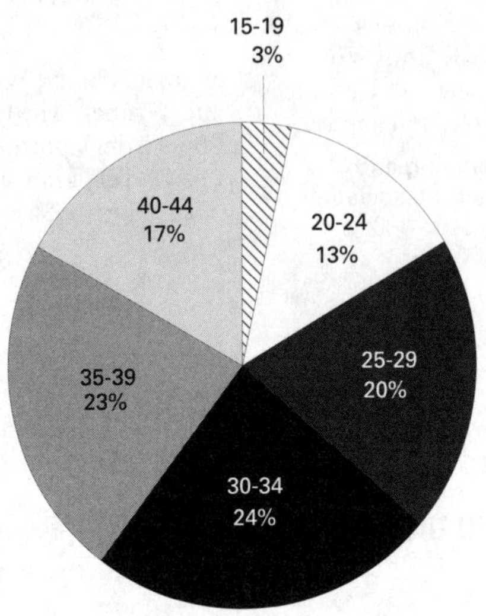

Race

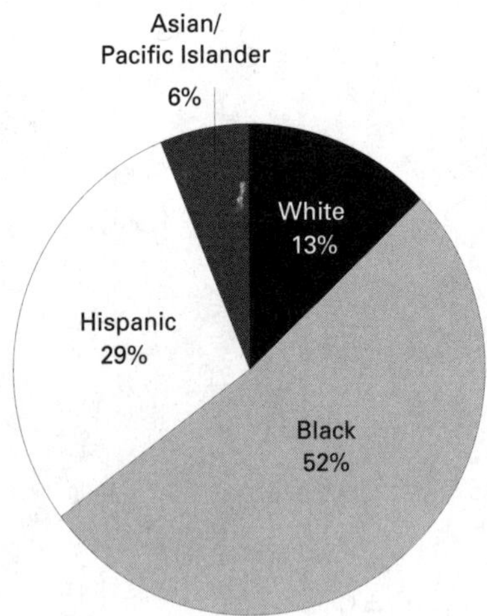

Education
Years of school completed*

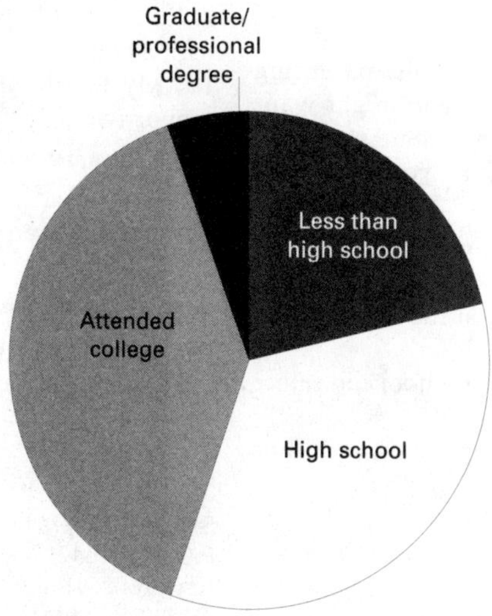

Region of Residence

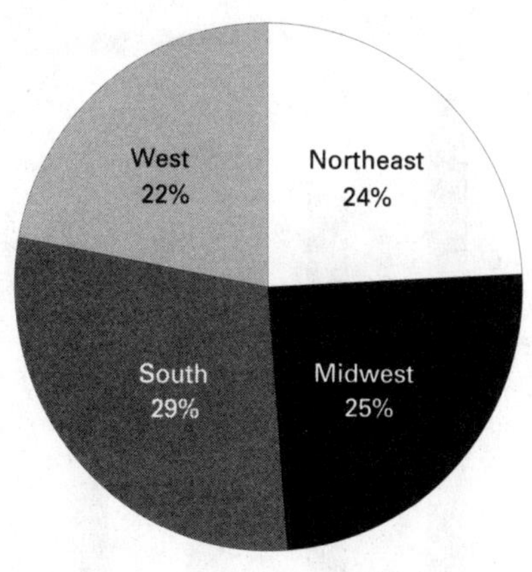

*Percentages do not appear here because all data is not exact.

Age ranges are 15 to 44 for above graphs; data is from 1992.
Source for above: Bureau of the Census

"Will your child learn to multiply before she learns to subtract?" —Children's Defense Fund poster.

54% of all pregnancies are unintended

SOME THOUGHTS FOR WOMEN CONSIDERING SINGLE MOTHERHOOD

Planned Parenthood suggests that if you're thinking about parenting without a partner, you might want to read through these statements and think about what your answers mean to you.

1. Loving my baby will get me through hard times.
2. I'm being pressured to keep the baby.
3. I'm willing to put school and career on hold.
4. I'll be more dependent on other people.
5. Money won't be a problem.
6. My baby will give me all the love I need.
7. I know someone who is always available and whom I can trust to take care of the child.
8. Having another child will strengthen my family.
9. I'll find a life partner more easily with a child.
10. My family and friends will be supportive.

Source: Planned Parenthood Federation of America

RESOURCES FOR SINGLE MOTHERS

The Nurturing Network
910 Main Street, Suite 360
P.O. Box 2050
Boise, ID 83701
(800) 866-4666

Single Mothers by Choice
P.O. Box 1642, Gracie Square Station
New York, NY 10028
(212) 988-0993

UNINTENDED PREGNANCIES: BIRTH VS. ABORTION

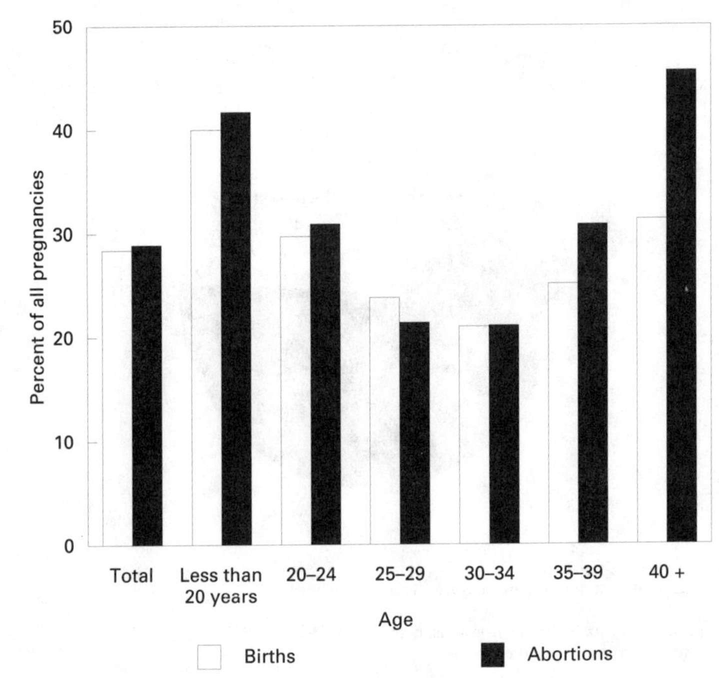

Source: Alan Guttmacher Institute

ABORTION STATISTICS

Legal Abortions

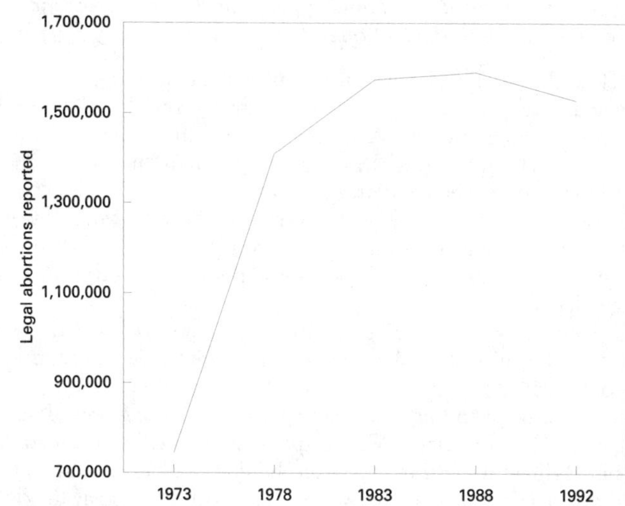

(Data from 1994)
Source: Allan Guttmacher Institute

Legal Abortions by Age

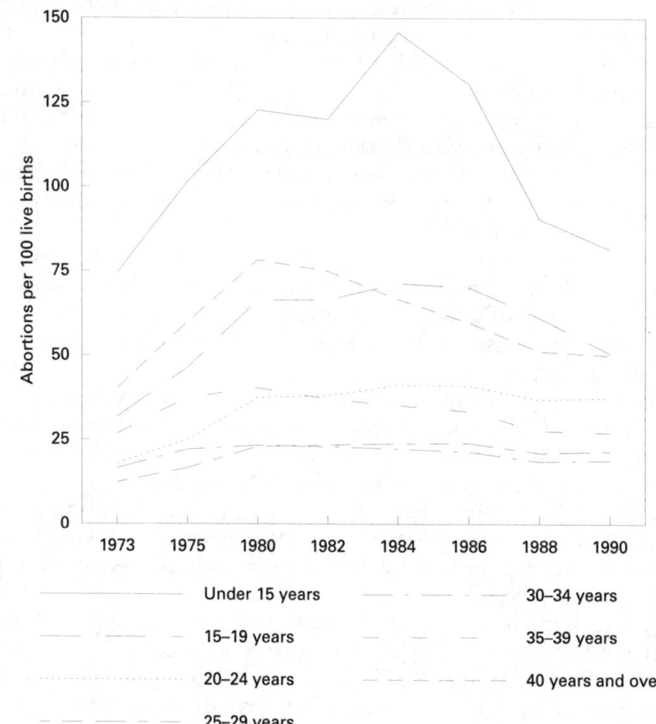

Source: National Center for Health Statistics, Health, United States, 1992

KATE MICHELMAN—ABORTION AND RESPONSIBILITY

President of the National Abortion and Reproductive Rights Action League, Kate Michelman addressed the changing needs of the pro-choice movement in the following speech to the National Press Club on January 11, 1994.

I look back at 25 years and our continuing struggle to hang on to *Roe* v. *Wade*: the marches, the court appeal, the violence at the clinics. I look back with a measure of anger that we've spent so many years fighting a battle that we shouldn't have to fight—the battle to give women in this country the simple right to the difficult choice of an abortion.

Our victories, when they came, were sweet—but fleeting. We still wake up the next morning to find the ground we've won slipping away. And we still watch women who most need our help—the poor, the rural, the young—denied their rights.

And all the while we run against a darkening shadow of too many women facing the difficult choice of an abortion, too many unintended pregnancies, too many unwanted children.

How do we respond to this crisis that spreads around us—that knows no color or neighborhood or class? We've spent the last 25 years leading the fight for one right—the right to choose an abortion. We had to make that fight. It was right to make that fight. Now we've got to begin leading the fight to make abortion less necessary.

We must wake the nation to the broader truth that reproductive freedom is not just whether or not to have an abortion. Genuine reproductive freedom requires the ability to make informed, responsible decisions about sexuality, contraception, abortion, pregnancy and childbirth.

Simply put, that means waking America up to the crisis in reproductive health care. Taking reproduction seriously. Making it a cornerstone of domestic policy. Convincing young adults of the risk and responsibility of sexual relations and pregnancy. Making healthy, strong, loving families a personal triumph. Cherishing all our children. Making the most vital family value the raising of children who are wanted and loved and have a real chance to be successful and happy.

Every time you hear about a desperate mother abandoning her baby, about a grim tale of abuse and neglect, or about a teenager who believed she couldn't get pregnant or get AIDS the first time she had sex—it means we have failed to take reproduction seriously, to instill values that makes families whole and society strong.

Changing attitudes will not come easily. It will take some sharp and painful debate. It will take a public that has shrunk from these issues to finally confront them, to wrestle with the crucial responsibilities involved with sexuality and reproduction. It's going to mean opening America's eyes, changing our perception, changing our very culture. It's going to mean changing America's mindset toward sexuality, women, and childbearing. It's going to mean facing the stark realities of teen pregnancy—and the terrible cost of continuing neglect.

It's going to mean reassessing and reordering our values. To take reproduction seriously. To teach responsibility. To value children. And it's going to mean understanding that the very soul of this country and the endurance of our freedoms depend on how we go about preparing our children to make the right choices to have them believe that theirs will be a better world.

If you're not convinced that we've failed to pass these values on to our children—all our children—then explain the tragic statistics of unintended pregnancies, teen pregnancies, infant mortality, and low-birth-weight babies. If you're satisfied that we have sound reproductive policies in America, then explain all the terrible gaps in public education—where we leave so many children to flounder with their own sexuality. Or the broken promises of health care that leave so many mothers and children at risk, uncertain about access, and fearful of cost. These are the pieces of society's neglect, the rusty fragments we once called values in this country.

It's not too late to pick up the pieces—and to weld them together into coherent national policies that guarantee every young person the education and access to contraception to make responsible choices, and guarantee every woman who chooses to have a child the right to proper care and respect. It's not too late to assemble reproductive policies that confront the grim truth that unless we prepare and nurture strong families and make every pregnancy wanted and secure, we will forfeit a just society.

If the nation's policies reflect the nation's values, then health care reform offers the greatest opportunity we've had in decades to make families stronger, women healthier and children whole. No right is as crucial to a woman's reproductive choice than her right to health care.

If health care offers security, education offers hope. We need to teach adolescents not just about sex and birth control but about human relations. The joy of love. The dilemma of choices. And the sobering responsibilities and economics of rearing a healthy family.

More than anything, it's going to take a more concerned nation—and more dedicated, involved parents. No amount of social drafting, no amount of money can make up the difference. America has to recognize the critical importance of reproductive health, and the risk of continued neglect, and how society gains from thoughtful, responsible childbearing decisions.

We must protect and secure reproductive choices—choices that today are not given equally, choices that make the difference between security and despair, and choices that are the measure of a truly just society.

FREDERICA MATHEWES-GREEN—ABORTION AND WOMEN'S RIGHTS

Frederica Mathewes-Green is the director of the Real Choices Program of the National Women's Coalition for Life and former vice president of Feminists for Life of America. She wrote the following essay for Sisterlife, the journal of Feminists for Life.

The abortion debate seems like an unresolvable conflict of rights: the right of women to control their own bodies, the right of children to be born. Can one both support women's rights and oppose abortion?

Truly supporting women's rights must involve telling the truth about abortion and working for it to cease. Many years ago I felt differently; in college I advocated the repeal of abortion laws, and supported my friends who traveled for out-of-state abortions. In those early days of feminism, women faced daunting obstacles. The typical woman was thought to be charmingly silly, prone to having parking lot fender-benders and then consoling herself with a new hat. Certainly not someone who should run a corporation—perhaps someone who should not even vote.

But the hurdles were not only political; we felt physically vulnerable, as rape statistics rose and women's bodies were exploited in advertising and entertainment. The external world's disparagement of our abilities was compounded by the extra cruelty that our bodies were at risk as well, from violence without and invasion within. For an unplanned pregnancy felt like an invader, an evil alien bent on colonizing one's body and destroying one's plans. The first right must be to keep one's body safe, private, and healthy; without that, all other rights are meaningless.

It is because I still believe so strongly in the right of a woman to protect her body that I now oppose abortion. That right must begin when her body begins, and it must be hers no matter where she lives—even if she lives in her mother's womb. The same holds true for her brother.

The average woman does not gain, but loses, when she has an abortion. She loses, first, the hundreds of dollars in cash she must pay to receive the surgery. Secondly, she must undergo a humiliating procedure, an invasion deeper than rape, as the interior of her uterus is crudely vacuumed to remove every scrap of life. Thirdly, she can lose her health. A woman's body is a delicately balanced ecology, not meant to have its natural, healthy processes disrupted by invasive machinery.

The most devastating loss of all is the loss of her own child. Abortion rhetoric paints the unborn as a parasite, a lump. But it is in fact her own child, as much like her as any child she will ever have, sharing her appearance, talents, and family tree. In abortion, she offers her own child as a sacrifice for the right to continue her life, and it is a sacrifice that will haunt her. Many women grieve silently after abortion, their sorrow ignored by a society that expects them to be grateful for the "freedom" to abort. A man who saw his wife gradually disintegrate after her abortion asks, "What kind of trade-off is that: gain control of your body, lose control of your mind?"

For all these losses, women gain nothing but the right to run in place. Abortion doesn't cure any illness; it doesn't win any woman a raise. But in a culture that treats pregnancy and child-rearing as impediments, it surgically adapts the woman to fit in. If women are an oppressed group, they are the only such group to require surgery in order to be equal. In Greek mythology,

Procrustes was an exacting host: if you were the wrong size for his bed, he would stretch or chop you to fit. The abortion table is modern feminism's Procrustean bed, one that, in a hideous twist, the victims actually march in the streets to demand.

If we were to imagine a society that supports and respects women, we would have to begin with preventing these unplanned pregnancies. Contraceptives fail, and half of all aborting women admit they weren't using them anyway. Thus, preventing unplanned pregnancies will involve a return to sexual responsibility. This means either avoiding sex in situations where a child cannot be welcomed, or being willing to be responsible for lives unintentionally conceived, perhaps by making an adoption plan, entering a marriage, or making faithful child-support payments. Using contraceptives is no substitute for this responsibility, any more than wearing a seat belt entitles one to speed.

Secondly, we need to make continuing a pregnancy and raising a child less of a burden. Most agree that women should play a part in the public life of our society; their talents and abilities are as valuable as men's, and there is no reason to restrict them from the employment sphere. But during the years that her children are young, mother and child usually prefer to be together. If women are to be free to take off these years in the middle of a career, they must have faithful, responsible men who will support them. Both parents can also benefit from more flexibility in the workplace: allowing parents of school-age children to set their hours to coincide with the school day, for example, or enabling more workers to escape the expenses of office, commute, and child care by working from home. We also must welcome women back into the work force when they want to return, accounting their years at home as valuable training in management, education, and negotiation skills.

Women's rights are not in conflict with their own children's rights; the appearance of such a conflict is a sign that something is wrong in society. When women have the sexual respect and employment flexibility they need, they will no longer seek as a substitute the bloody injustice of abortion.

Less than 1% of all abortion patients experience a major complication.

For every $1.00 spent by the federal government on abortions for poor women, $4.40 is saved in medical and welfare expenditures for an unintended birth.

ABORTION PROVIDERS

Type of facility	1985	1988	Percent change
Total	2,680	2,582	-4
Hospital	1,191	1,040	-13
Public	265	230	-13
Private	926	810	-13
Nonhospital facility	1,489	1,542	4
Clinics	837	885	6
less than 30 abortions	16	33	106
30–390 abortions	132	147	11
400–990 abortions	228	233	2
1,000 abortions or more	461	472	2
Physicians' offices	652	657	1
less than 30 abortions	154	181	18
30–390 abortions	498	476	-4

Source: Alan Guttmacher Institute

RU 486

In 1988, a drug called RU 486, in combination with a prostaglandin agent, was approved for use in France for the termination of pregnancies less than seven weeks old. RU 486 is 96% effective, with few women experiencing side effects more severe than those of a normal to heavy menstrual period. The current treatment is a four-step process that includes:

- Pregnancy test and physical examination
- Administration of RU 486 one week later (French abortion law requires this waiting period)
- Administration of prostaglandin two days later
- Follow-up examination to assure the procedure is complete.

RU 486 is not available in the U.S., although there is political pressure for its approval. For more information, contact:

National Women's Health Network
1325 G Street, N.W.
Washington, DC 20005
(202) 347-1140

Source: National Women's Health Network

WHY WOMEN HAVE ABORTIONS

This graph is based on the percentage of abortion patients reporting specific reasons that contributed to their decision.

Major Reasons for Abortion

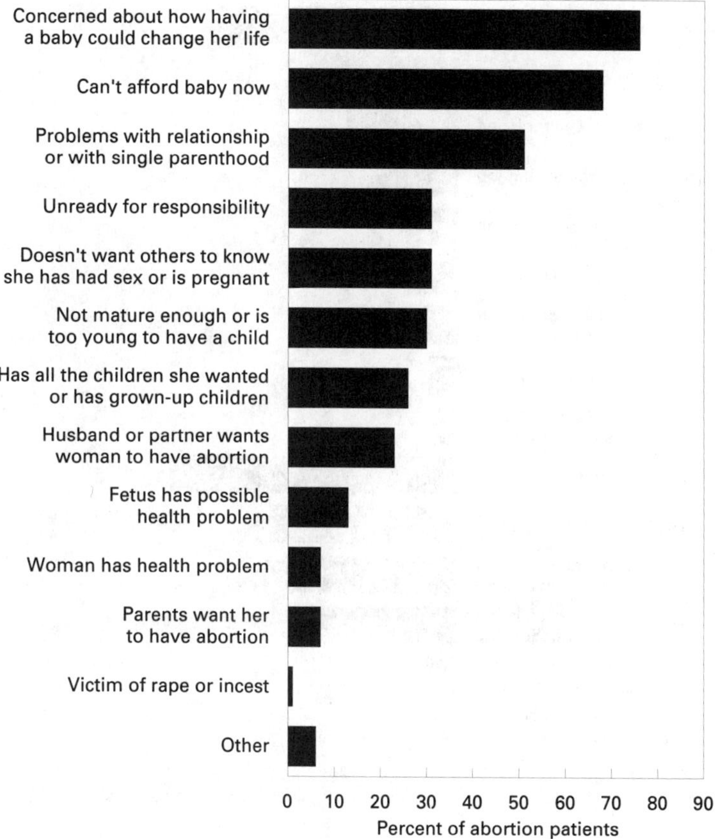

Detailed Explanations, Reasons for Abortions

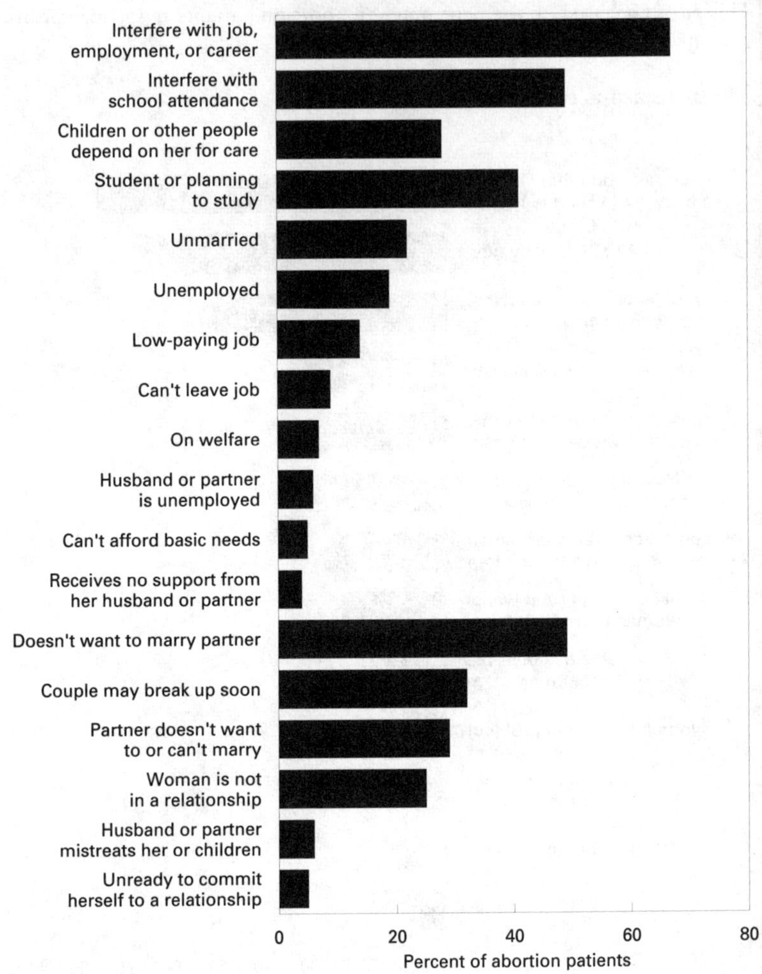

Source for above: Allan Guttmacher Institute

MORAL QUESTIONS: IS ABORTION MURDER?

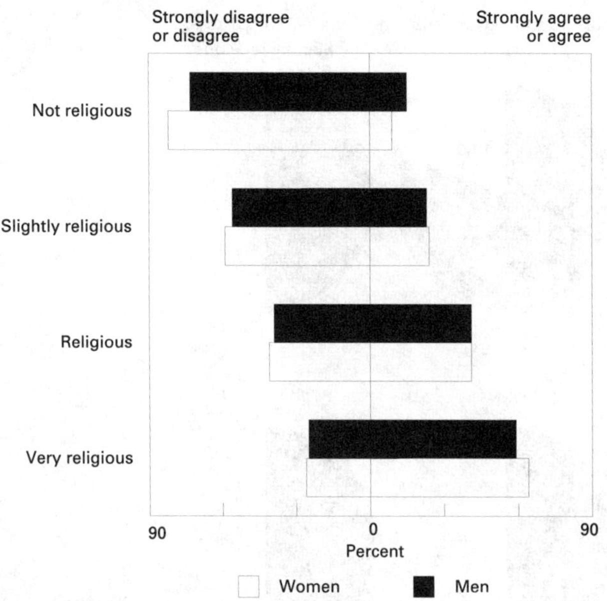

"The States are not free, under the guise of protecting maternal health or potential life, to intimidate women into continuing pregnancies." — Justice Harry A. Blackmun, in the 1973 majority opinion for Roe v. Wade, establishing the constitutional legality of abortion.

ABORTION: THINGS TO CONSIDER

Planned Parenthood suggests that you think about what these statements mean to you if you're considering an abortion.

1. No one is pressuring me to choose abortion.
2. I have strong religious beliefs against aboritons.
3. I look down on women who have abortions.
4. I'd rather have a child at another time.
5. I can afford to have another child.
6. I can afford to have an abortion.
7. I care about what other people will think.
8. I can handle the abortion experience.
9. I'll go before a judge if necessary.
10. I would do anything to end this pregnancy.

Source: Planned Parenthood Federation of America

ABORTION RATES AND RELIGIOUS FEELINGS

Women Who Have Had Abortions by Religious Feelings

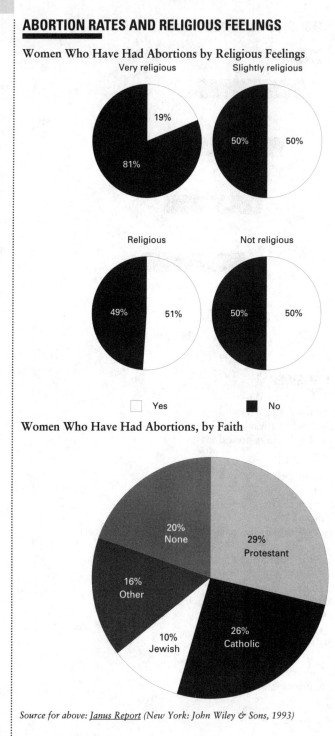

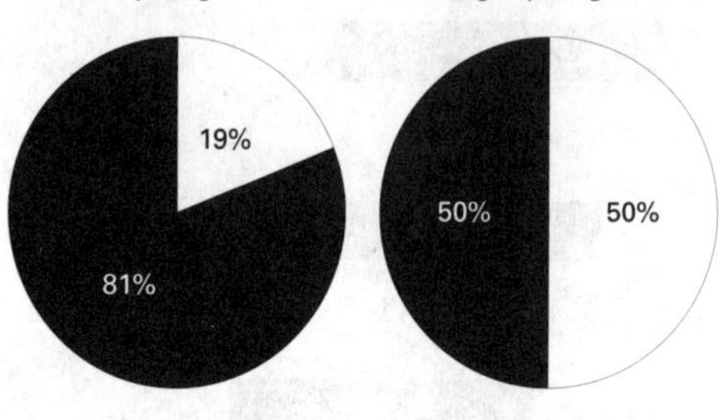

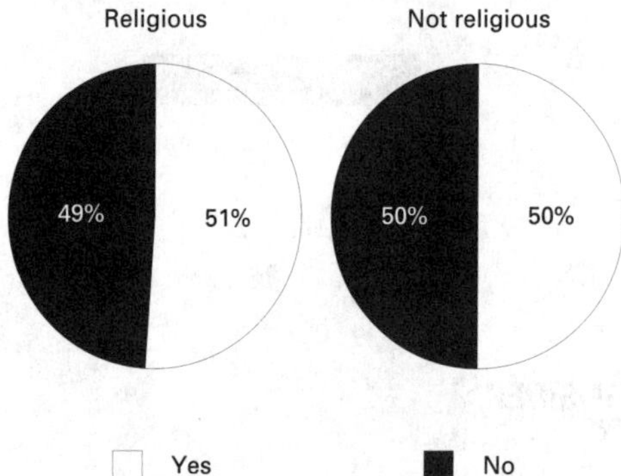

Women Who Have Had Abortions, by Faith

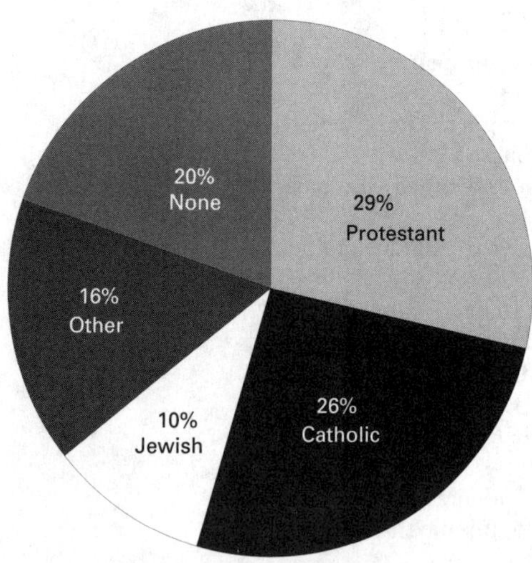

Source for above: Janus Report (New York: John Wiley & Sons, 1993)

PARENTAL CONSENT LAWS

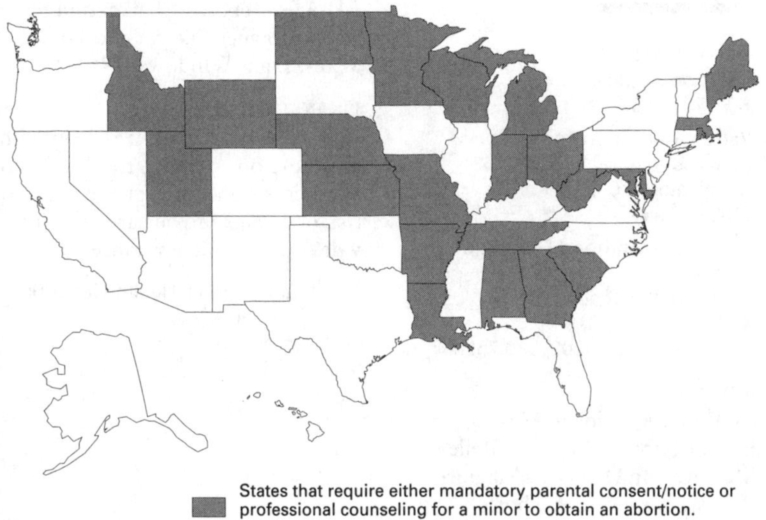

States that require either mandatory parental consent/notice or professional counseling for a minor to obtain an abortion.

Source: Planned Parenthood Federation of America

ABORTION SERVICES UNDER MEDICAID

All 50 states are required by federal law to provide funding for low-income women's abortions in cases of rape, incest, and life endangerment. However, not all 50 states comply with the federal regulations. The following chart shows states that go beyond federal requirements and provide additional funding.

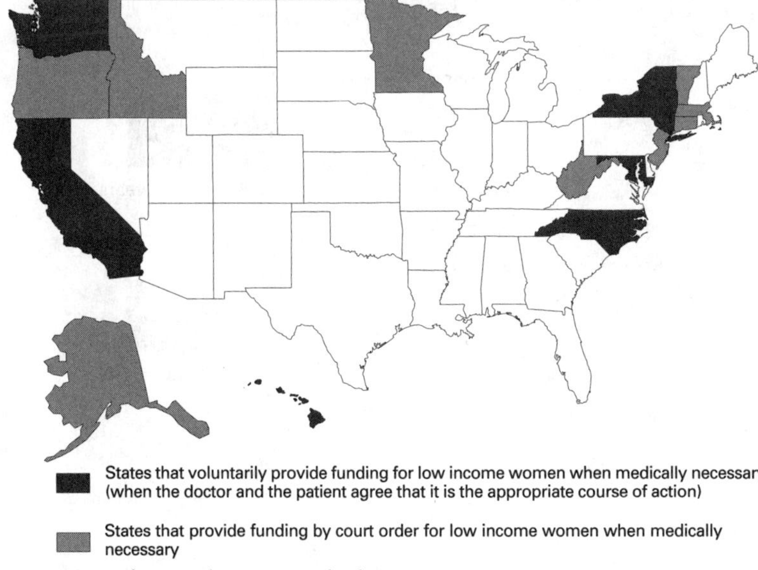

States that voluntarily provide funding for low income women when medically necessary (when the doctor and the patient agree that it is the appropriate course of action)

States that provide funding by court order for low income women when medically necessary

Source: Center for Reproductive Law and Policy

83% of all U.S. counties lacked a single abortion provider in 1988, although these counties were home to 31% of all women aged 15 to 44.

ABORTION—RESOURCES AND READING

ORGANIZATIONS

Abortion Hotline
(800) 772-9100

National Abortion Federation
1436 U Street, N.W., Suite 103
Washington, DC 20009
(202) 667-5881

Planned Parenthood Federation of America
810 Seventh Avenue
New York, NY 10019
(212) 541-7800 or (800) 230-7526

READING

Abortion: A Guide to Making Ethical Choices, Marjorie Reiley Maguire and Daniel C. Maguire (Catholics for a Free Choice).

A Woman's Book of Choices: Abortion, Menstrual Extraction, RU-486, Rebecca Chalker and Carol Downer (New York: Four Walls, Eight Windows, 1992).

FINANCIAL ASSISTANCE

If you need financial help with an abortion, contact the National Women's Health Network for a list of groups in your area that provide support and assistance:

National Women's Health Network
1325 G Street, N.W.
Washington, DC 20005
(202) 347-1140

ADOPTIONS IN THE U.S.

These bars cover unrelated children adopted by women 20–54 years of age.

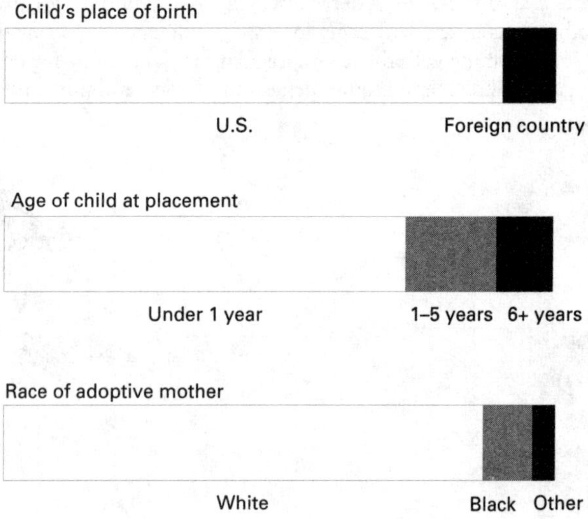

Child's place of birth

U.S. | Foreign country

Age of child at placement

Under 1 year | 1–5 years | 6+ years

Race of adoptive mother

White | Black | Other

Source: National Center for Health Statistics, 1987

ADOPTION FACTS

•Approximately half of adoptees in the U.S. are healthy infants, the remainder being older kids and children with special needs (physical, mental, or emotional disabilities, part of a sibling group, etc.).
•Around one-fifth of adoptees in the U.S. in 1987 were foreign-born children adopted by Americans.
•Around 40% of adoptions by people unrelated to the child are arranged by public agencies, 30% by private agencies, and 30% by private individuals.
•State laws governing adoptions vary widely. In general, the birth parent(s) sign(s) a consent to the adoption or a relinquishment of parental rights, although these are not legally binding prior to the birth of the child and can generally be revoked for a limited period of time after birth. The biological father usually must be notified of any adoption plan. Separately, the prospective adoptive parents must file a petition to adopt. After a period of court supervision, usually six months to one year, during which the adoptive parents have custody of the child, the adoption is finalized.
•A 1988 study confirmed that mothers who chose adoption for their babies ultimately received educational advantages, were more likely to delay marriage, were more likely to be employed and have a higher income, were less likely to be have a repeat out-of-wedlock pregnancy, and were less likely to abort if they had a repeat out-of-wedlock pregnancy.
•Pregnant teens who received counseling and information on adoption were almost seven times more likely to choose adoption.
•Only 1–2% of adopted adults search for their biological parents.

Source: National Council for Adoption

BASIC REQUIREMENTS FOR ADOPTION

Although there are few hard and fast rules about who can adopt, here are the basic requirements that most adoption agencies look at when they talk to people about adopting:

Marital status—Easier if married than single. If married, a minimum of three years of marriage is common.

Previous marriages—Generally, divorced persons are accepted so long as their current marriage is stable and the relationship good.

Age—The minimum age legally is usually 18. The outer limit for most agencies used to be 40, but some agencies will now consider persons who are older. There is a rule of thumb that there should be no more than 40 years' age difference between the age of the adopted child and the youngest parent.

Health—The health of the parents should be good. Some agencies have rules about obesity or underweight. A few agencies now prohibit placements with those who smoke, and some sectarian agencies prohibit placements with those who drink alcoholic beverages. All screen out drug abusers.

Religion—Sectarian agencies usually give priority to members of their faith groups, and some limit placements only to members of their faith groups. Persons with no particular religious preference or membership should first approach non-sectarian agencies.

Fertility status—Generally, infertile couples receive priority for placement of healthy babies; however, this guideline can be waived. For children with special needs or for international adoptions, fertile couples may apply.

95% of Glamour's surveyed readers believe that the best interests of the child should count for more in the rulings on adoption disputes; 81% of the readers believe that the biological father should not be able to claim his child if he was absent when she was up for adoption.

10 to 17% of all births in developed countries are outside of marriage.

Previous children—Most agencies will not place more than two children with any one family. If a family already has one child by birth or adoption, they may be selected for another child.

Employment policies—Generally, it is acceptable for both parents to work outside the home; however, some agencies ask one parent, usually the mother, to remain at home for the first six months with a baby.

Finances—The ability to pay any fee that is charged for placement is necessary; however, some agencies have sliding-scale fees or reduce flat fees, based on need. Chiefly, the desire is to see a family able to manage its income, budget well, and support all children, including the child the family desires to adopt.

Housing—The family home should be safe, clean, and able to accommodate the child.

Medical Records—Full medical background on adoptive parents will be required, whether infertile or fertile.

Background check—Those who adopt will be checked to be sure they have no criminal record.

Source: National Council for Adoption

CHOOSING AN ADOPTION AGENCY

- Always begin by calling the department or office in your state that licenses adoption agencies. Find out if the agency has a current license, when the agency was last visited by a representative of the department, if there are any unresolved complaints about it, and if there are any questions, including questions of a financial nature.
- Call to see if the agency is a member in good standing of one or more of the various organizations that work in the human services field.
- Check with various adoptive parent support groups to see what the reputation of the agency is.
- Ask the agency to provide you with a copy of the fee schedule for various services, including any costs related to an adoption that may be charged by others. Get a copy of the agency's written policy on refunds.
- Ask for a copy of the agency's most recent annual report.
- Ask for the names of some clients in your area that they have worked with or are working with. Talk to those individuals about their experiences with the agency.

Source: National Council for Adoption

ADOPTION—RESOURCES

Adoptive Families of America
3333 Highway 100 North
Minneapolis, MN 55422
(612) 535-4829

American Academy of Adoption Attorneys
P.O. Box 33053
Washington, DC 20033
(Write for a free directory)

Ask America Network
657 Mission Street, Suite 303
San Francisco, CA 94105
(415) 543-2275

Children Awaiting Parents
700 Exchange Street
Rochester, NY 14618
(716) 232-5110

Committee for Single Adoptive Parents
P.O. Box 15084
Chevy Chase, MD 20825

Independent Adoption Center
391 Taylor Boulevard, Suite 100
Pleasant Hill, CA 94523
(510) 827-2229

National Adoption Information Clearinghouse
1400 Eye Street, N.W., Suite 600
Washington, DC 20005
(202) 842-1919

National Council for Adoption
1930 17th Street, N.W.
Washington, DC 20009
(202) 328-1200

ADOPTION READING LIST

Adopting After Infertility, Patricia A. Johnston (Indianapolis: Perspective Press, 1992).

Adopting Children With Special Needs: A Sequel, Linda Dunn, ed. (North American Council on Adoptable Children).

Adoption: A Handful of Hope, Suzanne Arms (Berkeley: Celestial Arts, 1990).

The Adoption Lifecycle: Children and Their Families Through the Years, Elinor B. Rosenberg (New York: Macmillan, 1992).

The Adoption Resource Book (3rd ed.), Lois Gilman (New York: HarperCollins, 1992).

Family Bonds: Adoption and the Politics of Parenting, Elizabeth Bartholet (Boston: Houghton Mifflin, 1993).

Handbook for Single Adoptive Parents, Hope Marindin (Committee for Single Adoptive Parents).

How to Raise an Adopted Child, Judith Schaffer and Christina Lindstrom (New York: Crown Publishers, 1989).

The Open Adoption Book: A Guide to Adoption Without Tears, Bruce Rappaport (New York: Macmillan, 1992).

Self-Awareness, Self-Selection and Success: A Parent Preparation Guidebook for Special Needs Adoption, Flynn and Morton Hamm (North American Council on Adoptable Children).

To Love a Child: A Complete Guide to Adoption and Foster Parenting, Edward Wamer (Reading, Mass.: Addison-Wesley, 1992).

"There's a time when you have to explain to your children why they're born, and it's a marvelous thing if you know the reason by then." — Hazel Scott, jazz musician

The cost of prenatal care for a pregnant woman for 9 months is $600. The cost of medical care for a premature baby for one day is $2,500.

PRENATAL CARE

This is a partial list of preventive prenatal care services, one that reflects minimum recommendations for prenatal care. Physicians may add other services after considering a patient's medical history. The schedule for visits and the frequency of services are left to clinical discretion, except for those indicated at specific gestational ages.

First Prenatal Visit

Screening

History

Genetic and obstetric history
Dietary intake
Tobacco/alcohol/drug use
Risk factors for intrauterine growth retardation and low birth weight
Prior genital herpetic lesions

Laboratory/diagnostic procedures
Blood pressure
Hemoglobin and hematocrit
ABO/Rh typing
Rh(D) and other antibody screen
VDRL/RPR
Hepatitis B surface antigen
Urinalysis for bacteriuria
Gonorrhea culture
High-risk groups
- Hemoglobin electrophoresis
- Rubella antibodies
- Chlamydial testing
- Counseling and testing for HIV

Counseling

Nutrition
Tobacco use
Alcohol and other drug use
Safety belts
High-risk groups
- Discuss amniocentesis
- Discuss risks of HIV infection

Follow-Up Visits

Screening
Blood pressure
Urinalysis for bacteriuria

Screening tests at specific gestational ages

14–16 weeks:
- Maternal serum alpha-fetoprotein
- Ultrasound cephalometry

24–28 weeks:
- 50 g oral glucose tolerance test
- Rh(D) antibody
- Gonorrhea culture
- VDL/RPR
- Hepatitis B surface antigen
- Counseling and testing for HIV

36 weeks:
- Ultrasound exam

Counseling

Nutrition
Safety belts
Meaning of upcoming tests
High-risk groups
Tobacco use
Alcohol and other drug use

Source: U.S. Preventive Services Task Force

WEIGHT GAIN DURING PREGNANCY

Facts

•Most women should expect to gain about three or four pounds during the first three months and about a pound a week for the rest of their pregnancy. Total weight gain: 25 to 35 pounds.

•If you are underweight, you should gain 28 to 40 pounds.

•If your weight is normal, you should gain 25 to 35 pounds.

•If you are very heavy, you should gain 15 to 25 pounds. Pregnancy is not the time to diet to lose weight, no matter how heavy you are.

•A pregnant woman's weight gain is apportioned this way:
- Baby: 7 to 8 pounds
- Breast increase: 1 to 2 pounds
- Blood increase: 4 to 5 pounds
- Fat: 5 to 7 pounds
- Body fluid: 1 to 2 pounds
- Uterus increase: 2 to 5 pounds
- Placenta: 2 to 3 pounds
- Amniotic fluid: 2 to 3 pounds

Source: National Maternal and Child Health Clearinghouse

Weight Gain Over Nine Months

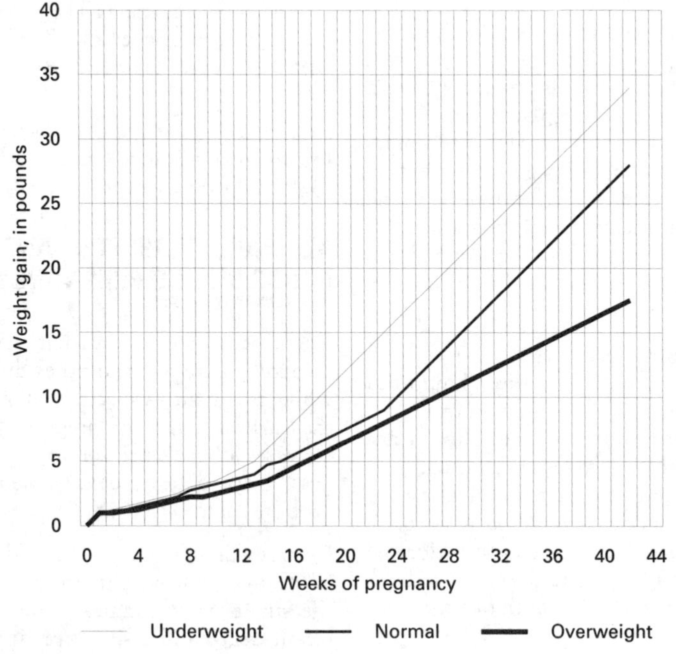

Source: National Maternal and Child Health Clearinghouse

"Making the decision to have a child—it's wondrous. It is to decide forever to have your heart go walking around outside your body."
—Elizabeth Stone

AMERICAN COLLEGE OF OBSTETRICIANS AND GYNECOLOGISTS' GUIDELINES FOR EXERCISE DURING PREGNANCY

Pregnancy and postpartum

1. Regular exercise (at least three times per week) is preferable to intermittent activity. Competitive activity should be discouraged.
2. Vigorous exercise should not be performed in hot, humid weather or when you have a fever.
3. Ballistic movements (jerky, bouncy motions) should be avoided. Exercise should be done on a wooden floor or a tightly carpeted surface to reduce shock and provide sure footing.
4. Deep flexion or extension of joints should be avoided because of connective tissue laxity. Activities that require jumping, jarring motions or rapid changes in direction should be avoided because of joint instability.
5. Vigorous exercise should be preceded by five minutes period of muscle warm-up. This can be accomplished by slow walking or stationary cycling with low resistance.
6. Vigorous exercise should be followed by a period of gradually declining activity that includes gentle stationary stretching. Because connective tissue laxity increases the risk of joint injury, stretches should not be taken to the point of maximum resistance.
7. Heart rate should be measured at times of peak activity. Target heart rates and limits established in consultation with a physician should not be exceeded.
8. Care should be taken to gradually rise from the floor in order to avoid lightheadedness from falling blood

The cost of drug treatment for an addicted mother for 9 months is $5,000. The cost of medical care for a drug-exposed baby for 20 days is $30,000.

Alcohol abuse by pregnant women is the leading known cause of mental retardation in newborns. Fetal alcohol syndrome strikes one to three of every 1,000 babies.

pressure. Some form of activity involving the legs should be continued for a brief period.
9. Liquids should be taken liberally before and after exercise to prevent dehydration. If necessary, activity should be interrupted to replenish fluids.
10. Women who have led sedentary lifestyles should begin with physical activity of very low intensity and advance activity levels very gradually.
11. Activity should be stopped and the physician consulted if any unusual symptoms appear.

Pregnancy only
1. Maternal heart rate should not exceed 140 beats per minute.
2. Strenuous activities should not exceed 15 minutes in duration.
3. Exercises that involve strong bearing down should be avoided.
4. No exercise should be performed while lying down flat on the back after the fourth month of pregnancy is completed.
5. Caloric intake should be adequate to meet extra energy needs not only of pregnancy, but also of the exercises performed.
6. Maternal rectal temperature should not exceed 99.6 degrees F.

Source: American College of Obstetricians and Gynecologists Resource Center

MISCARRIAGE READING LIST

Empty Arms: Coping After Miscarriage, Stillbirth and Infant Death, Ilse Sherokee (Maple Plain, Miss.: Wintergreen, 1990).

How to Prevent Miscarriages and Other Crises of Pregnancy, Stefan Semchyshyn (New York: Macmillan, 1989).

Miscarriage—A Shattered Dream, Ilse Sherokee (Wayzata, Minn.: Pregnancy and Infant Loss Center, 1985).

Miscarriage: Women Sharing from the Heart, Marie Allen and Shelly Marks (New York: John Wiley & Sons, 1993).

Preventing Miscarriage: The Good News, Jonathan Scher and Carol Dix (New York: Harper & Row, 1990).

Surviving Pregnancy Loss, Rochelle Friedman and Bonnie Gradstein (Boston: Little, Brown, 1982).

ALCOHOL, CIGARETTES, AND DRUGS DURING PREGNANCY

Scientific studies show that using alcohol, cigarettes, and other drugs while pregnant—especially during the earliest stages of pregnancy—increases a baby's risk for serious illness, birth defects, developmental problems, and even death.

Cigarette Smoking
With low birth weight standing as the single most common cause of infant death and disease, pregnant women who smoke should know that they are more likely than nonsmokers to have low-birth-weight babies (less than 5.5 pounds) and babies whose physical and intellectual growth is below normal. Smoking is also a major cause of miscarriages, complications during pregnancy, and premature deliveries.

Street Drugs
Marijuana, cocaine, heroin, and other narcotic drugs can be particularly damaging for a pregnant woman and her unborn baby. Using these drugs increases the risks of miscarriage, premature birth, and pregnancy complications. It also increases the newborn's risks for low birth weight, retarded growth, visual and coordination problems, and many serious medical problems that require intensive care. One of the most distressing effects is the severe withdrawal symptoms drugs produce in newborn babies. Infants exposed to these drugs are restless and jittery, experience

tremors, disturbed sleeping and feeding patterns, have a high-pitched cry, and are startled by even the slightest stimulation. These babies may also have a very difficult time bonding with their mothers.

Alcohol

A significant number of infants born to women who drink heavily during pregnancy (an average of five drinks per day) are born with fetal alcohol syndrome (FAS). This term is used to describe a pattern of malformation in children born to alcoholic mothers. Mental handicaps and hyperactivity are probably the most debilitating aspects of FAS; indeed, prenatal alcohol exposure is one of the leading causes of mental retardation in the Western world. Problems with learning, attention, memory, and problem solving are common, along with lack of coordination, impulsiveness, and speech and hearing impairments.

While research into the effects of alcohol on fetal development continues, doctors now recommend that women abstain from alcohol altogether during pregnancy. Recent evidence shows that the number of women who drink while pregnant is indeed declining. However, it appears that the rate of consumption in high-risk communities remains virtually unchanged.

Sources: Centers for Disease Control; Department of Health and Human Services

INCIDENCE OF FETAL ALCOHOL SYNDROME

Rates for the overall population, which aren't included in the following graph, have been reported at between 0.3 and 0.9 per 100,000.

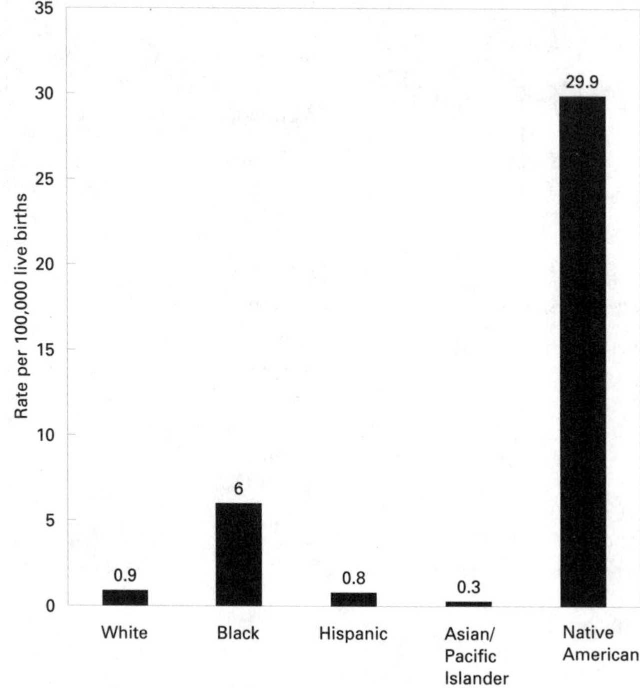

Source: Centers for Disease Control

The use of drugs such as cocaine is known to increase the risk of brain damage and stroke to the fetus.

THE BIRTH GAMBLE

This list shows the risk of maternal death (over a lifetime):

	Risk
Sub-Saharan Africa	1 in 20
Southeast Asia	1 in 40
Middle East and North Africa	1 in 80
South America	1 in 130
Central America and Caribbean	1 in 150
East Asia and Pacific	1 in 200
Industrialized countires	1 in 3,600

Source: UNICEF

INFANT MORTALITY RATES

U.S. Infant Mortality by Race

This chart and the chart below show the number of infants per 1,000 live births that die at less than one year. Race is determined here by race of child.

	White	Black
1950	26.8	43.9
1960	22.9	44.3
1970	17.8	32.6
1975	14.2	26.2
1980	11.0	21.4
1985	9.3	18.2
1990	7.7	17.0

Source: National Center for Health Statistics, Health, United States, 1992

International Infant Mortality

	Rate, 1989
Japan	4.59
Sweden	5.77
Finland	6.03
Singapore	6.61
Netherlands	6.78
Northern Ireland	6.90
Canada	7.13
Switzerland	7.34
France	7.54
Ireland	7.55
Norway	7.72
Australia	7.99
Spain	8.07
Austria	8.31
England and Wales	8.45
Belgium	8.64
Italy	8.80
Greece	9.78
United States	9.81
Israel	9.94
New Zealand	10.19
Cuba	11.08
Czechoslovakia	11.31
Costa Rica	13.90
Puerto Rico	14.27
Hungary	15.74
Poland	15.96
Chile	17.06
Kuwait	17.33
Romania	26.90

Source: UNESCO

States with Lowest Percentage of Low-Birth-Weight Live Births

	Percent
1978–80	
Oregon	5.07
Iowa	5.08
South Dakota	5.12
North Dakota	5.14
Minnesota	5.18
1983–85	
Alaska	4.80
North Dakota	4.80
Iowa	5.01
New Hampshire	5.01
Oregon	5.10
1988–90	
Alaska	4.91
Maine	4.96
New Hampshire	4.96
Minnesota	4.98
South Dakota	5.03

Source: National Center for Health Statistics, Health, United States, 1992

LOW-BIRTH-WEIGHT BIRTHS

Low birth weight is defined here as less than 2,500 grams.

All Women

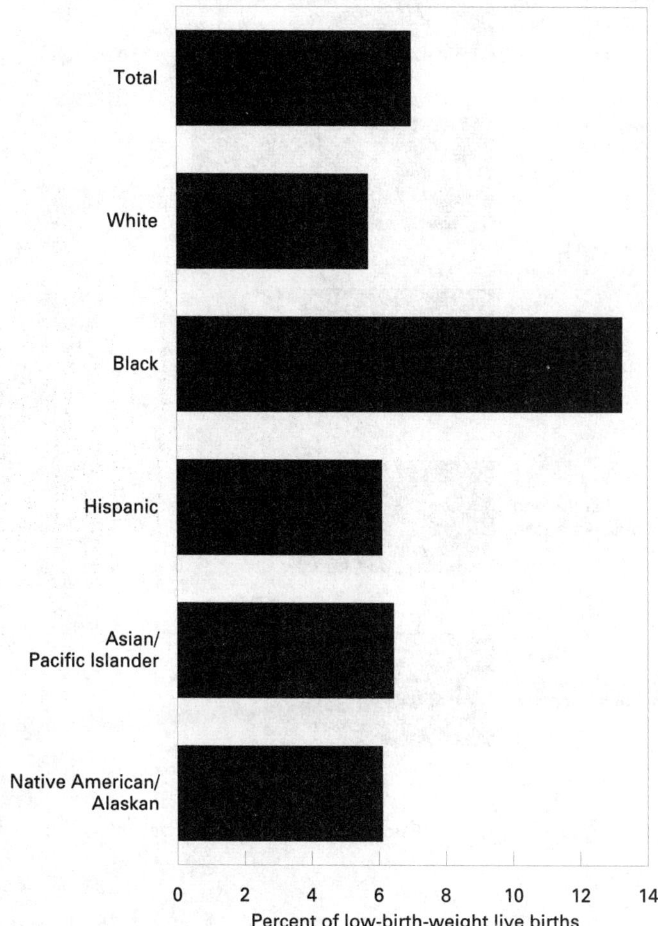

Hispanic

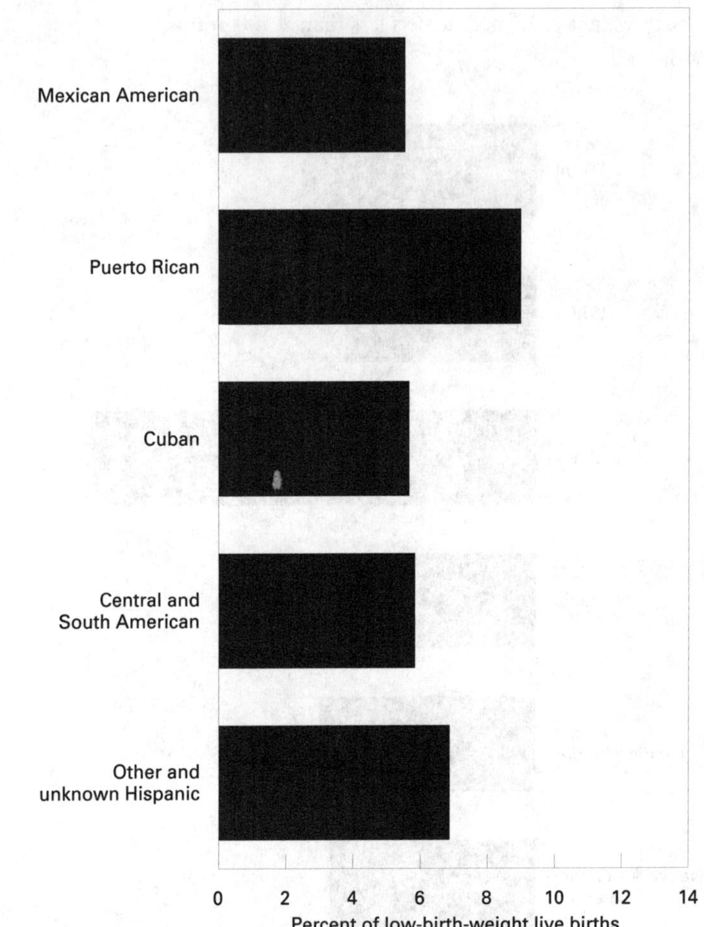
Mexican American
Puerto Rican
Cuban
Central and South American
Other and unknown Hispanic
0
2
4
6
8
10
12
14
Percent of low-birth-weight live births

Asian/Pacific Islander

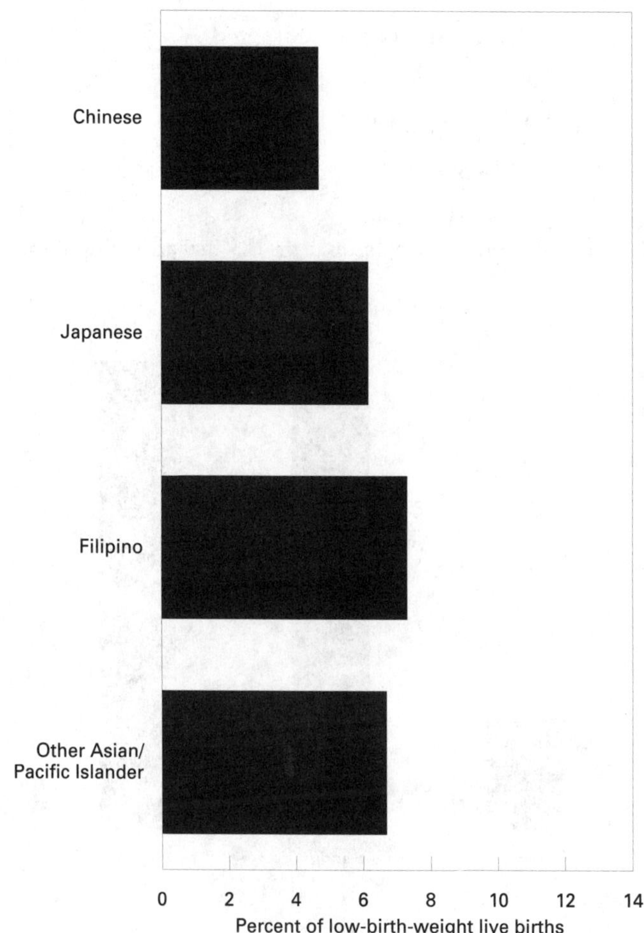

Source for above: National Center for Health Statistics, Health United States, 1992

CESAREAN SECTIONS

Half of the one million cesareans performed annually in the U.S. are estimated by experts to be not medically necessary.

Cesareans are the single most common form of major surgery performed in the U.S.

Cesarean Sections Performed in the U.S.

1980	1985	1991
614,000	875,000	931,000

Source: National Center for Health Statistics

C-Sections vs. All Deliveries

This graph shows the percentage of births in the U.S. that are Cesarean sections.

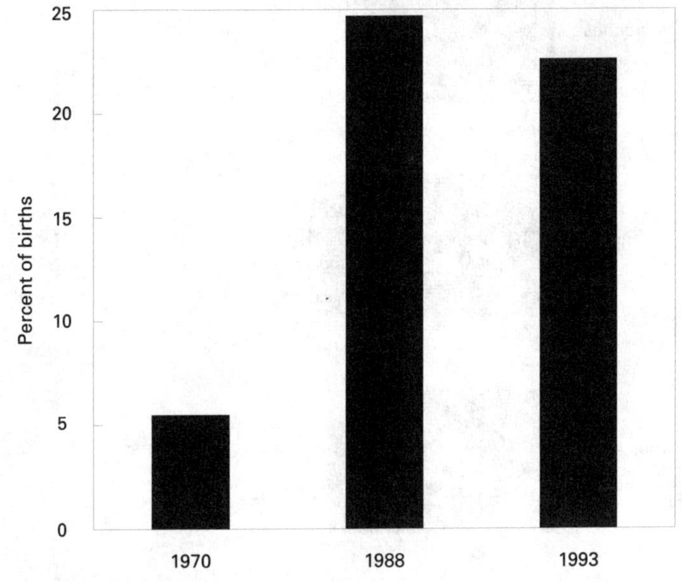

Source: Public Citizen

Cesarean Childbirth

Reasons for performing cesareans include:

- •Abnormalities of mother's birth canal
- •Abnormalities in position of the fetus, including breech position
- •Diabetes
- •Placenta previa (the placenta blocks the infant from being born)
- •Abruptio placentae (the placenta prematurely separates from the uterine wall and hemorrhage occurs)
- •Ruptured uterus
- •Presence of weak uterine scars from previous surgery or cesarean
- •Fetus too large for mother's birth canal
- •Rapid toxemia (a condition in which high blood pressure can lead to convulsions in late pregnancy)
- •Vaginal herpes infection
- •Pelvic tumors
- •Absence of effective uterine contractions after labor has begun
- •Prolapse of umbilical cord (the cord is pushed out ahead of the infant, compressing the cord and cutting off blood flow)

Source: National Institute of Child Health and Human Development

CESAREAN—RESOURCES AND READING

C/SEC
22 Forest Road
Framingham, MA 01701
(508) 877-8266

International Cesarean Awareness Network
P.O. Box 152
Syracuse, NY 13210
(315) 424-1942

International Childbirth Education Association
P.O. Box 20048
Minneapolis, MN 55420
(612) 854-8660

Women's Health Alert, Sidney M. Wolfe and the Public Citizen Health Research Group (Reading Mass.: Addison-Wesley Publishing, 1991). Of particular interest here are lists of cesarean rates by state and hospital.

BIRTH SUPPORT PROVIDERS

BIRTH SUPPORT OPTIONS

Obstetrician—Medical doctor certified in obstetrics and gynecology, trained in solving problems during pregnancy and dealing with complications during the birth process. Approach to the birth process differs from doctor to doctor. Always works out of a hospital, always covered by insurance.

Nurse-midwife—Registered nurse with two years experience in obstetrics and one to two years' schooling as a midwife. Takes on the role of helping the birth mother through a natural process using medical intervention only when absolutely necessary. Available in some hospitals, and in birthing centers with a physician backup in a nearby hospital. Most major health care providers cover the cost of a nurse-midwife.

Direct-entry midwife—Credentials based on experience and apprenticeship. Believes in completely natural childbirth—they are there to lend support. Not legal in some states and not likely to be covered by insurance.

Childbirth Assistant—Plans your day of labor, 2–3 prenatal visits, 2–3 postnatal visits, early labor support with continuity of care, client-directed consumer advocacy, and birth plan counseling.

Monitrice—A registered, licensed nurse providing clinical assessment skills and comfort measures for labor and birth.

Doula—Provides postpartum homehelp, including household tasks, new mother care, and sibling care. Some doulas also provide labor support.

Sources: National Association of Birthing Centers; National Association of Childbirth Assistants

WHO'S HELPING GIVE BIRTH

Attendant	1990	1991
Physician	3,948,270	3,892,053
Midwife	163,049	182,457
Other	30,709	31,123

Source: National Center for Health Statistics

BIRTHING LOCATIONS

BIRTH LOCATION OPTIONS

Hospital—The latest medical technology is available if anything goes wrong. Birth is treated as a medical process and the mother and baby as patients. Parents are sometimes separated from the baby or may only be with it for limited time periods. Always covered by insurance.

Birthing center—Health care team observes birth and provides support, calling in a doctor only for emergencies. Birthing takes place in a comfortable setting. Staff takes an active role in the birth process as well as in prenatal

About 60% of new mothers complain of feeling low after giving birth; 10% are sad enough to be classified as clinically depressed, according to the Journal of Affective Disorders.

care. The baby is never separated from its parents. Most major health-care providers cover the cost.

At-home birth—Setting is the most comfortable and relaxed, but mother must rely on local rescue squad in case of emergency. Mother must find birth assistant and organize the necessary supplies for the birth process. There is no family separation. Not likely to be covered under insurance.

Source: National Association of Birthing Centers

WHERE BABIES ARE BORN

Location	1990	1991
Hospital	4,109,634	4,640,153
Other	46,946	45,835

Source: National Center for Health Statistics

PREGNANCY AND CHILDBIRTH—RESOURCES

American Society for Psychoprophylaxis in Obstetrics (ASPO/Lamaze)
1101 Connecticut Avenue, N.W., Suite 700
Washington, DC 20036
(800) 368-4404

Healthy Mothers, Healthy Babies
409 12th Street, S.W., Room 523
Washington, DC 20024
(202) 638-5577

Informed Homebirth/Informed Birth and Parenting
P.O. Box 3675
Ann Arbor, MI 48106
(313) 662-6857

International Association of Parents and Professionals for Safe Alternatives in Childbirth
Route 1, Box 646
Marble Hill, MO 63764
(314) 238-2010

Maternity Center Association
48 E. 92nd Street
New York, NY 10128
(212) 369-7300

Midwives Alliance of North America
P.O. Box 175
Newton, KS 67114

National Association of Childbearing Centers
3123 Gottschall Road
Perkiomenville, PA 18074
(215) 234-8068

National Association of Childbirth Assistants
205 Copco Lane
San Jose, CA 95123
(408) 225-9167

National Maternal and Child Health Clearinghouse
8201 Greensboro Dr. Suite 600
Mclean, VA 22102
(703) 821-8955

National Perinatal Association
3500 E. Fletcher Avenue, Suite 525
Tampa, FL 33613
(813) 971-1008

Planned Parenthood Federation of America
810 Seventh Avenue
New York, NY 10019
(212) 541-7800

Positive Pregnancy and Parenting Fitness
51 Saltrock Road
Baltic, CT 06330
(800) 433-5523

Pregnancy Environmental Hotline
(617) 787-4957

Pregnancy RiskLine
(800) 822-2229

Reproductive Health Technologies Project
1601 Connecticut Avenue, N.W., Suite 801
Washington, DC 20009
(202) 328-2200

Resource Mothers
Women's Action Alliance
370 Lexington Avenue, Suite 603
New York, NY 10017
(212) 532-8330

PREGNANCY AND CHILDBIRTH— READING AND FILMS

Reading

American Red Cross Healthy Pregnancy, Healthy Baby Workbook (Washington, D.C.: American Red Cross, 1991).

A Child is Born (rev. ed.), Lennart Nilssen (New York: Delacorte Press, 1990).

The Complete Book of Pregnancy and Childbirth, Sheila Kitzinger (New York: Alfred A. Knopf, 1989).

A Good Birth, A Safe Birth: Choosing and Having the Childbirth Experience That You Want (3rd rev. ed.), D. Korte and R. Scaer (Boston: Harvard Common Press, 1992).

Mother To Be: A Guide to Pregnancy and Birth for Women With Disabilities, Judith Rogers and Molleen Matsumura (New York: Demos Publications, 1992).

The New Our Bodies Ourselves, Boston Women's Health Collective (New York: Simon & Schuster, 1992).

A New View of a Woman's Body, Federation of Feminist Women's Health Centers (New York: Simon & Schuster, 1981).

Nutrition During Pregnancy (Washington, D.C.: American College of Obstetricians and Gynecologists, 1992).

Peace of Mind During Pregnancy: An A–Z Guide to the Substances That Could Affect Your Unborn Baby, C. Kelley-Buchanan (New York: Dell 1988).

What to Expect When You're Expecting (rev. and expanded 2nd ed.), Arlene Eisenberg, Heidi E. Murkoff, and Sandee E. Hathaway, B.S.N. (New York: Workman, 1991).

Films

Birth of Amanda, 25 min. video, Laird Sutton (Multi-Focus, 1977).

Five Women: Five Births, 28 min. video, Suzanne Arms (Multi-Focus, 1978).

PREGNANCY AND CHILD-LOSS— RESOURCES AND READING

Organizations

The Compassionate Friends
P.O. Box 3696
Oak Brook, IL 60522
(708) 990-0010

SHARE
St. Joseph Health Center
300 First Capitol Drive
St Charles, MO 63301
(314) 947-6164

Sudden Infant Death Syndrome Alliance
10500 Little Patuxent Parkway
Suite 420
Columbia, MD 21044
(800) 221-7437

Reading

How to Go on Living After the Death of a Baby, Larry Peppers and Ronald Knapp (Atlanta: Peachtree Publishers, 1985).

Empty Arms: Coping After Miscarriage, Stillbirth and Infant Death, Ilse Sherokee (Maple Plain, Miss.: Wintergreen, 1990).

Women who take shorter maternity leaves are more likely to be depressed or anxious.

Breast-feeding burns 150 to 800 extra calories a day, depending on how often a mother nurses her baby.

A Silent Sorrow, Ingrid Kohn, M.S.W., and Perry-Lynn Moffit, M.D. (New York: Bantam Doubleday Dell, 1992).

POSTPARTUM DEPRESSION

One in ten new mothers experiences various degrees of postpartum depression, a condition that can occur within days of delivery or appear gradually, sometimes up to a year later. A woman suffering from postpartum depression may experience one or a combination of symptoms. All of the following symptoms, from the mildest to the most severe, are temporary and treatable.

- Nervousness, anxiety, panic
- Sluggishness, fatigue, exhaustion
- Sadness, depression, hopelessness
- Appetite and sleep disturbances
- Poor concentration, confusion, memory loss
- Overconcern for the baby
- Lack of interest in the baby
- Guilt, feeling of inadequacy or worthlessness
- Fear of harming the baby and/or yourself
- Exaggerated highs and/or lows
- Lack of interest in sex

Source: Depression After Delivery

POSTPARTUM—RESOURCES

Depression After Delivery
P.O. Box 1282
Morrisville, PA 19067
(800) 944-4773

Doulas of North America
1100 23rd Avenue East
Seattle, WA 98112

National Association of Postpartum Care Services
P.O. Box 1012
Edmonds, WA 98020
(206) 672-8011

BENEFITS OF BREASTFEEDING

- Facilitates the mother's postpartum recovery
- Reduces the incidence and severity of allergies and of ear and respiratory infections in infants
- Provides the most complete, easily digested, convenient, and economical source of nourishment for infants
- Creates a special closeness between mother and infant
- Enhances the mother's self-esteem and confidence
- May lessen the risk of breast cancer

Source: Healthy Mothers, Healthy Babies

BREASTFEEDING—RESOURCES, VIDEO AND READING

ORGANIZATIONS

American Society of Psychoprophylaxis in Obstetrics (ASPO/Lamaze)
1101 Connecticut Avenue, N.W., Suite 700
Washington, DC 20036
(800) 368-4404

Expanded Promotion of Breastfeeding Program
3333 K Street, N.W., Suite 701
Washington, DC 20007
(202) 298-7979

International Lactation Consultant Association
201 Brown Avenue
Evanston, IL 60202
(708) 260-8874

La Leche League International
9616 Minneapolis Avenue
Franklin Park, IL 60131
(708) 455-7730

National Center for Education in Maternal and Child Health
2000 15th Street N., Suite 701
Arlington, VA 22201
(703) 524-7802

National Healthy Mothers, Healthy Babies Coalition
409 12th Street, S.W.
Washington, DC 20024
(202) 863-2458

VIDEO

Best Start, For All the Right Reasons, 22 min. video (1989; available from Best Start, Inc., 3500 E. Fletcher Avenue, Suite 308, Tampa, FL 33613, [800] 277-4975).

READING

The Nursing Mother's Companion (rev. ed.), K. Huggins (Boston: Harvard Common Press, 1990).

The Womanly Art of Breastfeeding, La Leche League International (New York: New American Library, 1994).

LESBIAN MOTHERS—RESOURCES, FILM, AND READING

ORGANIZATIONS

Lesbian Mothers National Defense Fund
P.O. Box 21567
Seattle, WA 98111
(206) 325-2643

Momazons
P.O. Box 02069
Columbus, OH 43202
(614) 267-0193

FILM

Choosing Children: A Film About Lesbians Becoming Parents, 45 min. film, Debra Chasnoff and Kim Klausner (available from Frameline, 346 Ninth Street, San Francisco, CA 94103, [415] 703-8654).

READING

Considering Parenthood: A Workbook for Lesbians, Cheri A. Pies (San Francisco: Spinsters Ink, 1985).

SEXUALITY AND RELATIONSHIPS
SEXUALITY AND RELATIONSHIPS
SEXUALITY AND RELATIONSHIPS

SEXUALITY AND RELATIONSHIPS

SEXUALITY AND RELATIONSHIPS
SEXUALITY AND RELATIONSHIPS
SEXUALITY AND RELATIONSHIPS
SEXUALITY AND RELATIONSHIPS
SEXUALITY AND RELATIONSHIPS
SEXUALITY AND RELATIONSHIPS
SEXUALITY AND RELATIONSHIPS
SEXUALITY AND RELATIONSHIPS
SEXUALITY AND RELATIONSHIPS
SEXUALITY AND RELATIONSHIPS
SEXUALITY AND RELATIONSHIPS
SEXUALITY AND RELATIONSHIPS
SEXUALITY AND RELATIONSHIPS
SEXUALITY AND RELATIONSHIPS
SEXUALITY AND RELATIONSHIPS
SEXUALITY AND RELATIONSHIPS

GENERAL BOOKS ABOUT SEXUALITY—RECOMMENDED READING

Closer to Home: Bisexuality and Feminism, ed. Elizabeth R. Weise (Seattle: Seal Press, 1992).

The Complete Guide to Safer Sex, Ted McIlvenna (New York: Barricade Books, 1992).

Homosexuality/Heterosexuality: Concepts of Sexual Orientation, ed. David P. McWhirter, Stephanie A. Sanders, and June M. Reinisch (New York: Oxford University Press, 1990).

Human Sexuality, 4th ed., William Masters, Virginia Johnson, and Robert C. Kolodny (New York: Harper College, 1991).

The Kinsey Institute New Report on Sex: What You Must Know to Be Sexually Literate, June M. Reinisch and Ruth Beasley (New York, St. Martin's Press, 1991).

Sexual Interactions, 3rd ed., Elizabeth R. Allgeier and Albert R. Allgeier (Lexington, Mass.: D.C. Heath, 1991).

BOOKS BY WOMEN ON THE HISTORY OF SEX—RECOMMENDED READING

Sex in History, Reay Tannahill (Chelsea, Mich.: Scarborough House, 1982).

A Woman's History of Sex, Harriet Gilbert and Christine Roche (New York: Routledge Chapman & Hall, 1988).

SEX EDUCATION AND RESEARCH—RESOURCES

American Association of Sex Educators, Counselors, and Therapists
435 N. Michigan Avenue, Suite 1717
Chicago, IL 60611
(312) 644-0828

The Alan Guttmacher Institute
120 Wall Street
New York, NY 10005
(212) 248-1111

Kinsey Institute for Research in Sex, Gender, and Reproduction
313 Morrison Hall
Indiana University
Bloomington, IN 47405
(812) 855-7686

The National Coalition to Support Sexuality Education
c/o SIECUS
130 W. 42nd Street, Suite 2500
New York, NY 10036
(212) 819-9770

Planned Parenthood Federation of America
810 Seventh Avenue
New York, NY 10019
(212) 541-7800

Sex Information and Education Council of the U.S. (SIECUS)
130 W. 42nd Street, Suite 2500
New York, NY 10036
(212) 819-9770

SEX EDUCATION FOR KIDS—RECOMMENDED READING

Changing Bodies, Changing Lives: A Book for Teens on Sex and Relationships, rev. ed., Ruth Bell (New York: Random House, 1988).

Dr. Ruth Talks to Kids: Where You Came From, How Your Body Changes, and What Sex Is All About, Dr. Ruth Westheimer (New York: Macmillan Child Group, 1993).

Everybody's Doing It! How to

Research shows that female sexual response improves when women develop positive attitudes toward their bodies and raise their overall self-esteem.

There are no current nationwide research studies on sexual behavior, identity, or orientation.

Congress approved two national surveys of sexual behavior in the 1980s, but Sen. Jesse Helms and Rep. William Dannemeyer killed the proposals, saying that the studies would give unwarranted legitimacy to homosexuality.

Survive Your Teenagers' Sex Life and Help Them Survive It, Too, Andrea Warren and Jay Wiedenkeller (New York: Viking Penguin, 1993).

The Family Book About Sexuality, Mary Calderone and Eric W. Johnson (New York: HarperCollins, 1990).

A Kid's First Book About Sex, Joani Blank (Burlingame, Calif.: Down There Press, 1983).

The New Teenage Body Book, rev. ed., Kathy McCoy and Charles Wibblesman (Los Angeles: The Body Press, 1992).

MAJOR SURVEYS OF SEXUAL BEHAVIOR—RECOMMENDED READING

American Couples: Money, Work, Sex, Philip Blumstein and Pepper Schwartz (New York: William Morrow, 1983).

The Cosmo Report, Linda Wolfe (New York: Arbor House, 1981).

The Hite Report: A Nationwide Study on Female Sexuality, Shere Hite (New York: MacMillan, 1976; rev. ed., Dell, 1981).

The Janus Report on Sexual Behavior, Samuel S. Janus and Cynthia L. Janus (New York: John Wiley & Sons, 1993).

Love, Sex, and Aging: A Consumers Union Report, Edward M. Brecher and the Editors of Consumer Reports Books (Boston: Little, Brown, 1984).

The New Hite Report, Shere Hite (New York: Knopf, 1987).

SEX SURVEYS—DOES ANYONE TELL THE TRUTH?

Sex sells, and so do statistics about sex. But surveys of sexual behavior differ in their methods of data collection, and estimates of sexual behavior can vary significantly depending on who you ask, what you ask, how you ask, and why you ask.

Some of the issues that should be kept in mind about sex statistics:

- Most experts agree that women tend to underreport their experiences, while men tend to overreport them.
- Sex is an area of great privacy, so surveys asking about sexuality are usually met with much reticence. Since few people want to reveal anything about their sex lives, researchers often receive incomplete, inconsistent, or inaccurate responses.
- With sex research, as with all areas, imprecise wording of questions can produce poor data. The simple word "sex," for instance, can mean either intercourse alone or a range of acts.
- The source of a survey needs to be considered. Sex surveys are a favorite of magazines, but a sampling based on answers from a magazine's readers is far from a random sample and cannot be regarded as a gauge of anything but the opinions of those readers who chose to respond.
- Likewise, the sample base of more general studies needs to be taken into account; one report, for instance, has been criticized because the researchers distributed self-administered questionnaires through graduate students' and doctors' offices, creating a self-selected and biased sample.
- Older data should be regarded warily since it does not reflect changes that may have taken place in behaviors or in the willingness of people to speak honestly about their sexual lives.
- The methodology of a sex survey has a strong influence on the character and accuracy of the data obtained.

Such issues as whether the surveys are administered by a researcher or are filled out independently have a significant effect on how honest people are willing to be and how thoroughly they will respond to questions.

Sources: American Demographics; Library Journal; National Opinion Research Center; SIECUS

WOMEN'S FIRST SEXUAL EXPERIENCES

Age of First Sexual Experience

For this survey, women were asked how old they were when they first had sex with a man.

Age	Percent
Under 10	0.5
10–15	20.8
16–20	68.6
21–25	9.1
26–30	0.5
31+	0.1
Never have	0.5

Source: The Cosmo Report (New York: Arbor House, 1981)

Rise in Sexual Experience among Teenagers

This graph represents those women who reported being sexually experienced at ages 15 and at 17.

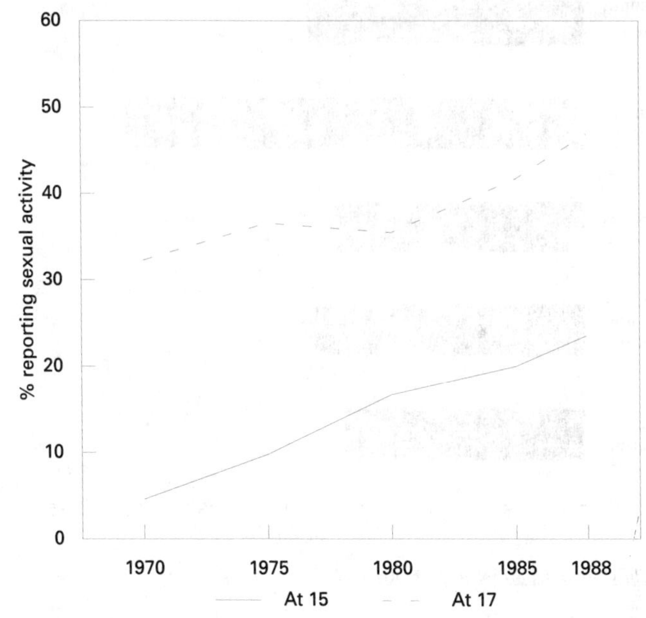

Source: National Opinion Research Center

Women who have a high sex drive are more likely to be amused by jokes than women with a lower sex drive, reports the Society for the Scientific Study of Sex.

25% of the women in a recent study by the *Journal of Sex and Marital Therapy* said they were dissatisfied with their sex lives.

Partner the First Time

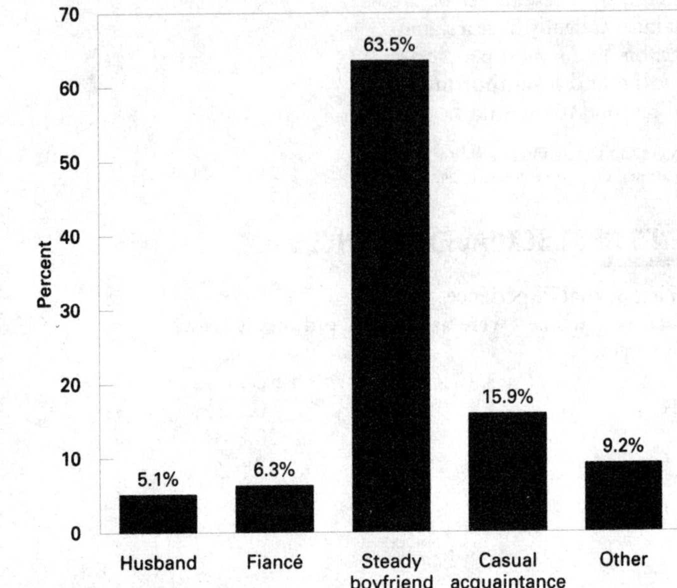

Source: *The Cosmo Report* *(New York: Arbor House, 1981)*

WOMEN'S REACTIONS TO THE FIRST TIME

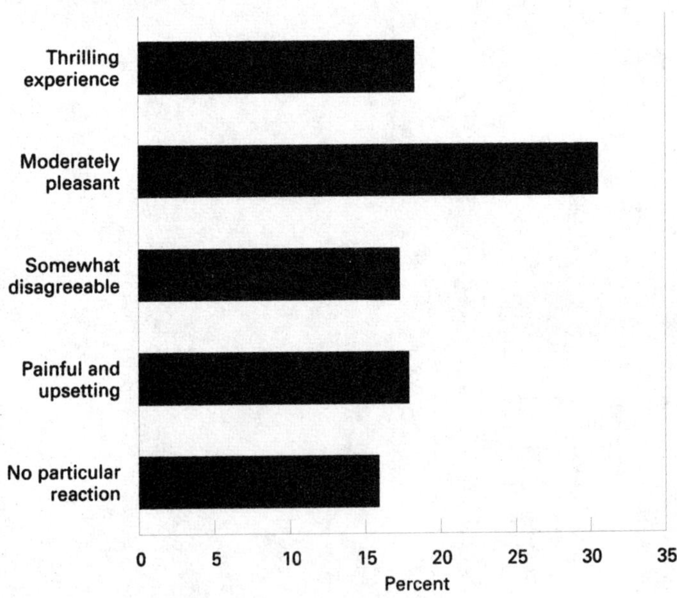

Source: *The Cosmo Report* *(New York: Arbor House, 1981)*

NUMBER OF SEXUAL PARTNERS

Total Number of Sexual Partners

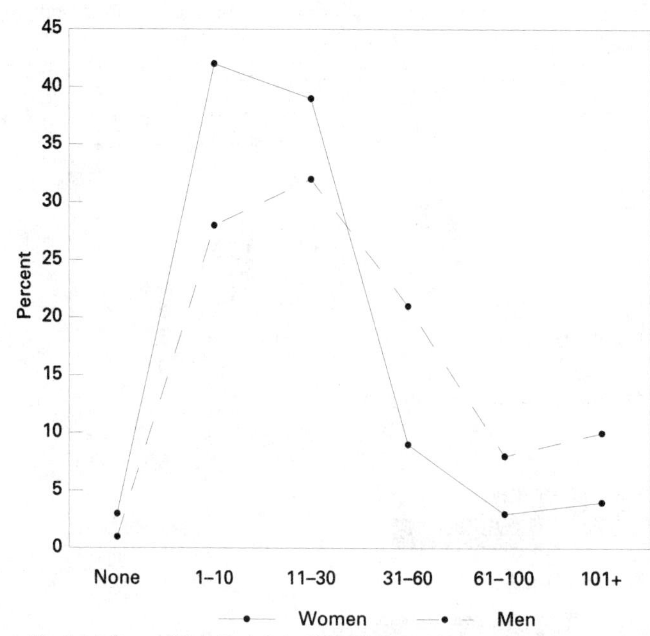

Source: *The Janus Report* *(New York: John Wiley & Sons, 1993)*

Recent Sexual Partners

Percentage of adults who have had two or more sexual partners over the following time spans.

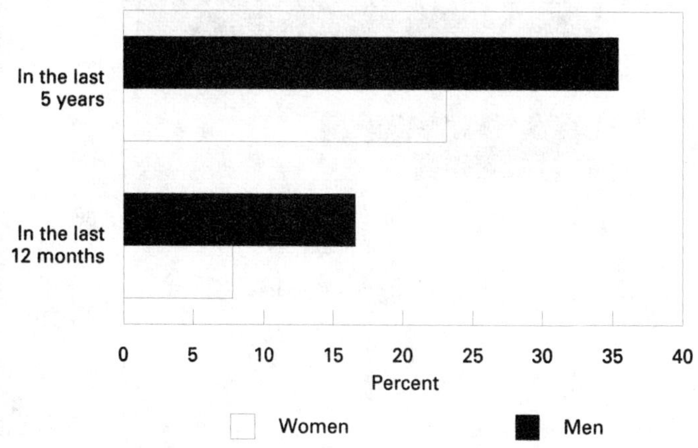

Source: National Opinion Research Center, General Social Survey, 1993

"A healthy sex life. Best thing in the world for a woman's voice."—Leontyne Price

74% of the women in a Ladies' Home Journal study in 1993 said that their husbands were "good" or "excellent" lovers.

FREQUENCY OF SEXUAL ACTIVITY

Frequency of Sexual Intercourse by Age

This chart shows the mean incidence of sexual intercourse in a year among adults.

Age	Women	Men
18–29	80.8	81.6
30–39	77.5	83.4
40–49	67.7	67.7
50–59	39.5	54.9
60–69	20.8	35.8
70+	4.6	15.3
Average	56.7	65.8

Source: National Opinion Research Center, General Social Survey 1993

Sexual Frequency: Married Couples

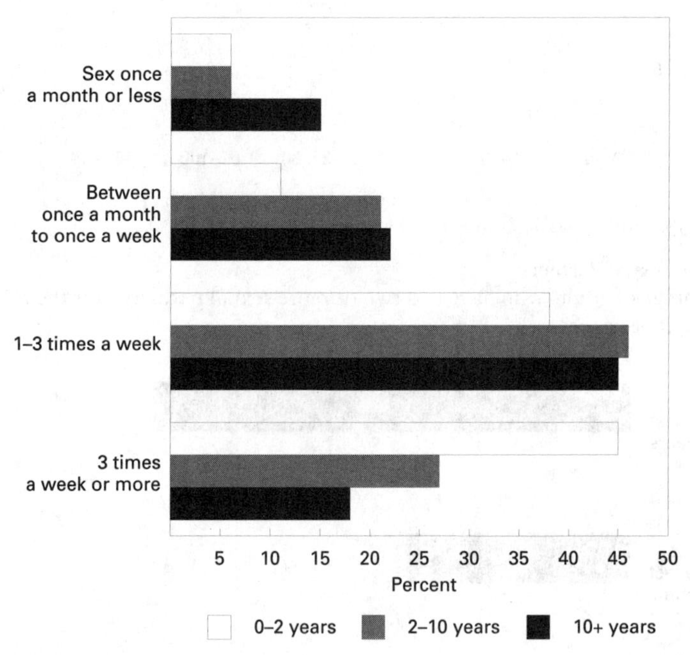

Sexual Frequency: Cohabiting Heterosexual Couples

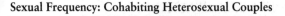

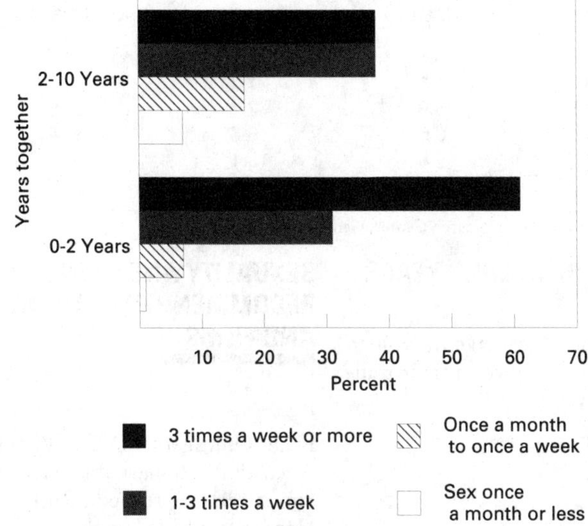

"Personally I know nothing about sex because I've always been married."—Zsa Zsa Gabor

Sexual Frequency: Cohabiting Lesbian Couples

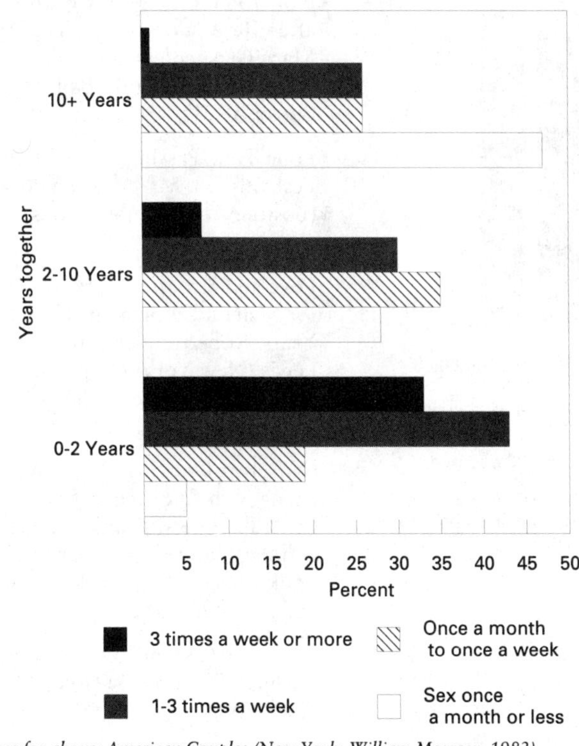

Source for above: American Couples (New York: William Morrow, 1983)

Unmarried couples who live together have sex more frequently than married couples. If couples live together before they marry, they continue to have sex more frequently after the marriage than couples who do not live together before marriage.

20% of married couples in their sixties still occasionally have sex outdoors.

ADULTS WHO AREN'T SEXUALLY ACTIVE

AGE	% WOMEN	% MEN	% MARRIED	% NOT MARRIED
18–29	11.9	15.5	2.2	19.5
30–39	5.7	7.1	1.7	16.0
40–49	10.5	5.9	2.7	25.9
50–59	24.0	10.6	6.6	53.4
60–69	41.7	17.6	15.1	74.5
70+	66.2	40.6	34.5	92.9

Source: National Opinion Research Center, General Social Survey, 1993

75% of men and women over the age of 60 feel their sex lives are as good as or better than ever.

SEX AND THE GOLDEN YEARS

The following percentage of women remain sexually active in their middle and late years.

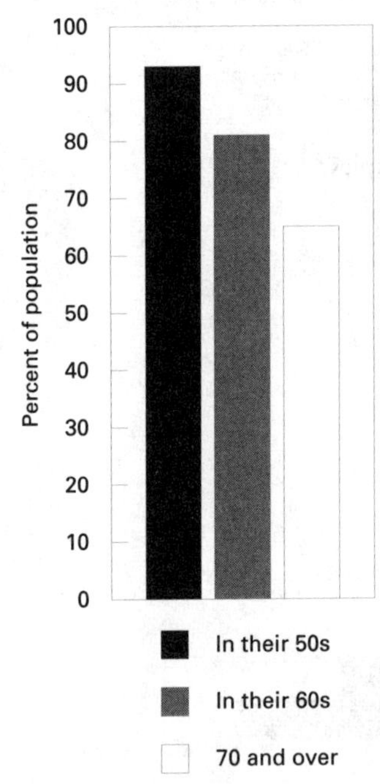

Source: Edward M. Brecher, Love, Sex and Aging: A Consumers Union Report (Boston: Little, Brown, 1984)

SEXUALITY AND AGING—RECOMMENDED READING AND FILMS

READING

Be an Outrageous Older Woman—A R.A.S.P. (Remarkable Aging Smart Person), rev. ed., Ruth Harriet Jacobs (Manchester, Ct.: Knowledge, Ideas, and Trends, 1993).

How to Find Love, Sex & Intimacy after 50: A Woman's Guide, Dr. Matti Gershenfeld and Judith Newman (New York: Ballantine Books, 1991).

Long Time Passing: Lives of Older Lesbians, ed. Marcy Adelman (Boston: Alyson Publications, 1986).

Love and Sex after Sixty: A Guide for Men and Women in Their Later Years, Robert Butler and Myrna Lewis (New York: Harper and Row, 1986; also available in large-print edition).

Ourselves Growing Older: Women Aging with Knowledge and Power, Paula B. Doress, Diana L. Siegel, and the Midlife and Older Women's Book Project (New York: Simon and Schuster, 1987).

Sex in the Golden Years, Deborah Edelman (New York: Donald I. Fine, 1992).

The Time of Our Lives: Women Write on Sex after 40, ed. Dena Taylor and Amber C. Sumrall (Freedom, Calif.: Crossing Press, 1993).

NEWSLETTERS

Conversations, ed. Carol B. Hittner (Conversations, P.O. Box 1071, Melbourne, FL 32902, [800] 477-9171).

Sex Over Forty, ed. E. Douglas Whitehead and Shirley Zussman (PPA, Inc., P.O. Box 1600, Chapel Hill, NC 27515, [919] 929-2148).

VIDEOS

Sex After 50, 90 min., Lonnie Barbach (1991; available from Focus International, 14 Oregon Drive, Huntington Station, NY 11746).

SEXUALITY AND WOMEN WITH SPECIAL NEEDS—RESOURCES AND READING

ORGANIZATIONS

American Foundation for the Blind
15 W. 16th Street
New York, NY 10011
(212) 620-2147 or (800) 232-5463

Project on Women and Disability
1 Ashburton Place, Room 1205
Boston, MA 02108
(617) 727-7440

Sexuality and Disability Training Center
Boston University Medical Center
88 E. Newton Street
Boston, MA 02118
(617) 638-7358

READING

Enabling Romance: A Guide to Love, Sex, and Relationships for the Disabled (and the People Who Care about Them), Erica Klein and Ken Kroll (New York: Crown Publishing, 1992).

Eyes of Desire: A Deaf Gay and Lesbian Reader, ed. Raymond Luczak (Boston: Alyson Publications, 1993).

Up Front: Sex and the Post-Mastectomy Woman, Linda Dackman (New York: Viking Penguin, 1990).

46% of the women in a 1993 Mademoiselle poll said that a man's penis size does make a difference to them.

About 10% of all women have never had an orgasm by any means, according to the Kinsey Institute.

46% of the women in a 1993 Ladies' Home Journal survey said they fake orgasms, with 8% faking frequently or always.

WOMEN'S ORGASMS

Orgasm at First Experience

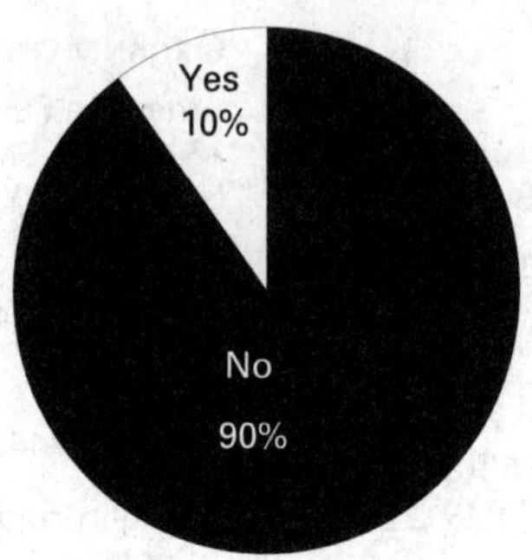

Source: The Cosmo Report (New York: Arbor House, 1981)

How Orgasms Are Achieved

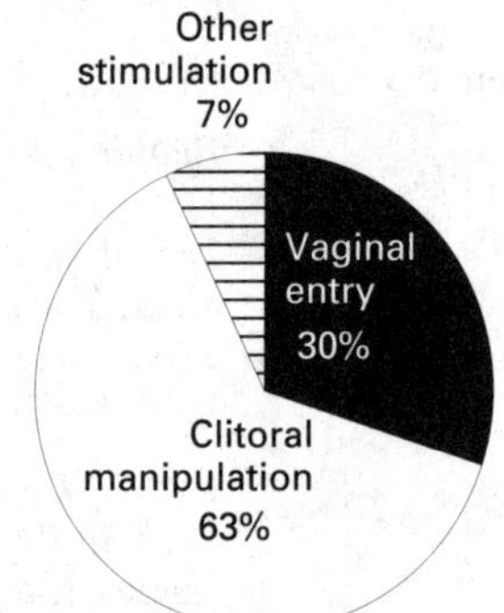

Source: The Cosmo Report (New York: Arbor House, 1981)

FREQUENCY OF ORGASM DURING LOVEMAKING

	ALWAYS	OFTEN	SOMETIMES	RARELY	NEVER
18–26	18%	39%	22%	8%	13%
27–38	16	51	18	9	6
39–50	14	52	22	7	5
51–64	21	44	22	10	3
65+	8	42	37	4	9

Source: The Janus Report (New York: John Wiley & Sons, 1993)

FACTORS INHIBITING ORGASM

In a study of 709 nurses—all heterosexual and capable of orgasm—researchers found that the following factors inhibited orgasm.

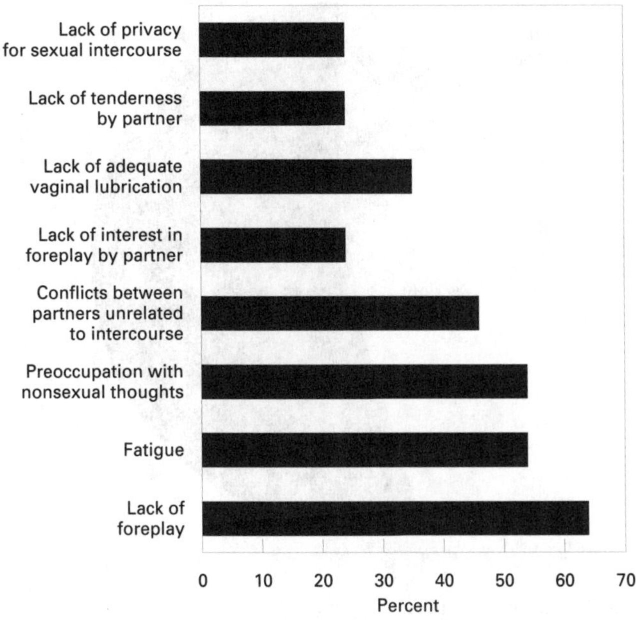

Source: Carol A. Darling, J. Kenneth Davidson, Sr., and Ruth P. Cox, "Female Sexual Response and the Timing of Partner Orgasm," Journal of Sex and Marital Therapy (vol. 17, no. 1, 1991)

"Love doesn't just sit there, like a stone, it has to be made, like bread; remade all the time, like new."
—Ursula K. Le Guin

FEMALE SEXUALITY AND ORGASM— READING AND FILMS

READING

Becoming Orgasmic: A Sexual Growth Program for Women, Julia Heiman and Joseph LoPiccolo (Englewood Cliffs, N.J.: Prentice-Hall, 1988).

For Each Other: Sharing Sexual Intimacy, Lonnie Barbach (New York: Doubleday, 1983).

For Yourself: The Fulfillment of Female Sexuality, Lonnie Barbach (New York: Doubleday, 1976).

A New View of a Woman's Body, Federation of Feminist Women's Health Centers Staff (West Hollywood, Calif.: Feminist Health Press, 1991).

The New Our Bodies, Ourselves: A Book by and for Women, rev. ed., Boston Women's Health Book Staff (New York: Simon & Schuster, 1992).

Women Discover Orgasm: A Therapist's Guide to a New Treatment Approach, Lonnie Barbach (New York: Free Press, 1980).

EDUCATIONAL VIDEOS (EXPLICIT)

Becoming Orgasmic, 44 mins., Julia Heiman and Joseph LoPiccolo (1992; available from the Sexuality Library, 938 Howard Street, Suite 101, San Francisco, CA 94103).

Selfloving, 60 mins., Betty Dodson (1991; available from the Sexuality Library; address above).

17% of the women in a 1993 Mademoiselle poll said they have had three or more one-night stands.

ORAL SEX

Women's Opinions of Oral Sex

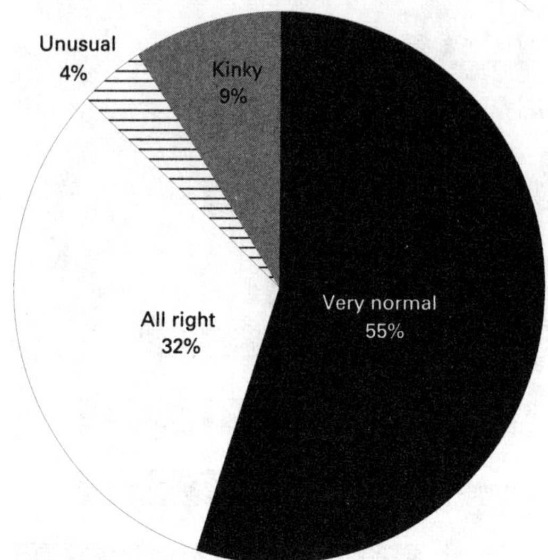

Source: The Janus Report (New York: John Wiley & Sons, 1993)

Oral Sex as the Favored Way to Orgasm

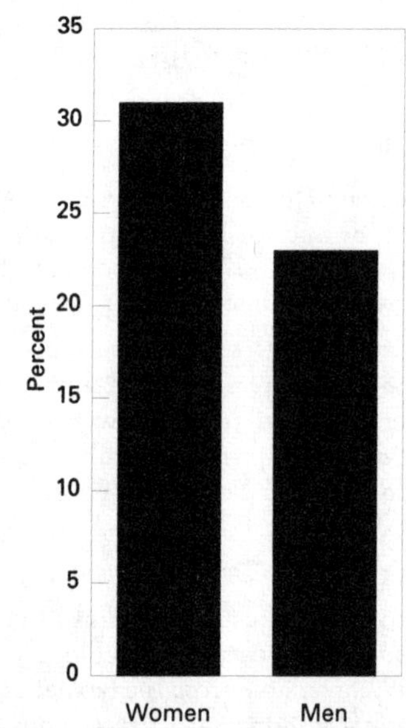

Source: Survey of Mademoiselle and Details readers, 1993

MASTURBATION

How Widespread Is Masturbation Among Women?

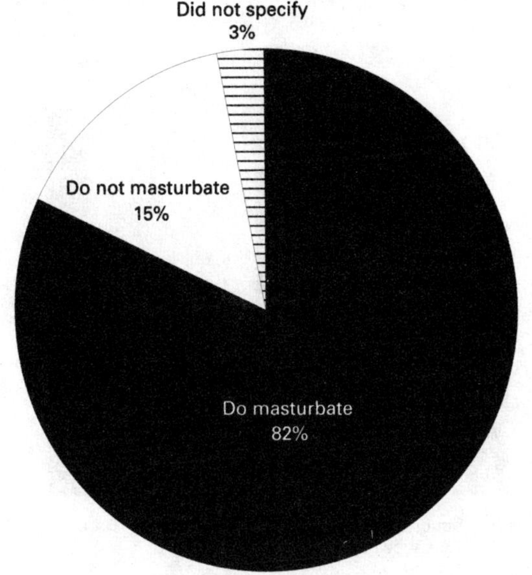

Source: *The New Hite Report,* © 1987 Shere Hite (reprinted by permission of Knopf)

"Until you've lost your reputation, you never realize what a burden it was or what freedom really is."—Margaret Mitchell

When Does Masturbation First Occur?

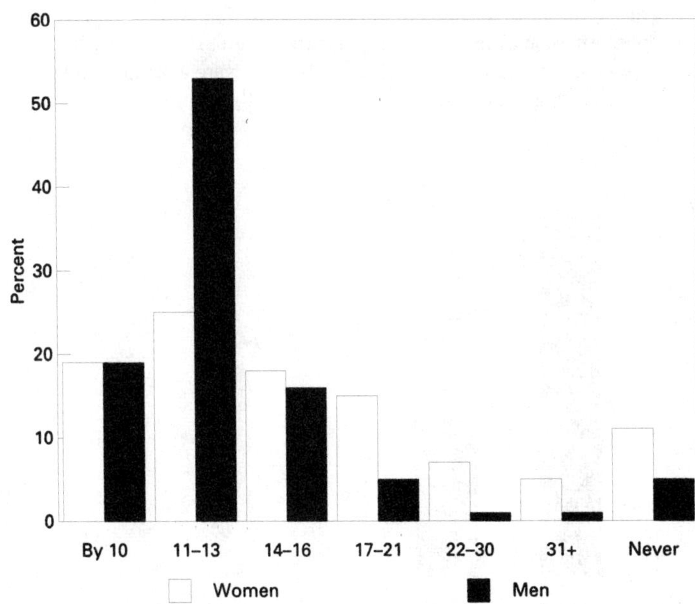

Source: *The Janus Report* (New York: John Wiley & Sons, 1993)

How Often Do People Masturbate?

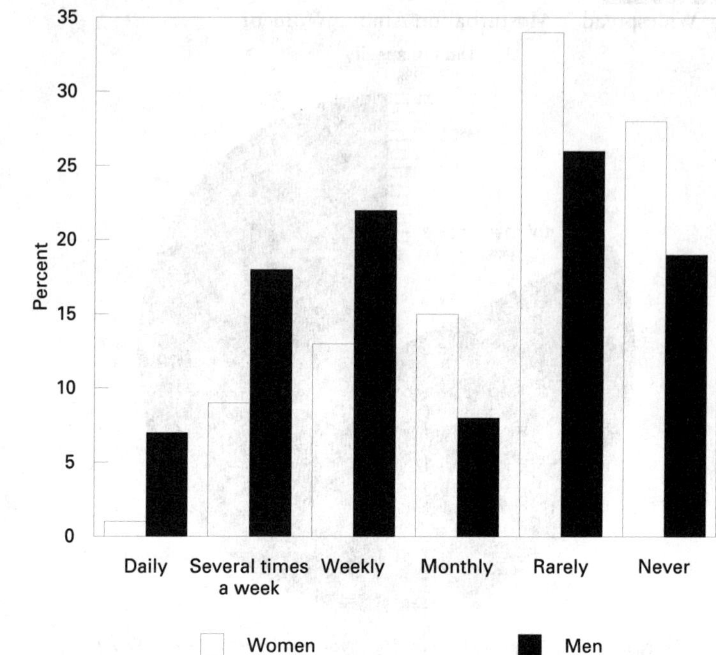

Source: The Janus Report (New York: John Wiley & Sons, 1993)

OTHER FORMS OF SEXUAL BEHAVIOR

Fetishism

Seven percent of women reported that they regularly engaged in fetishes in *The Cosmo Report* (1981). However, when women were asked in a different survey if they had dressed in special outfits for sex, the figure was much higher:

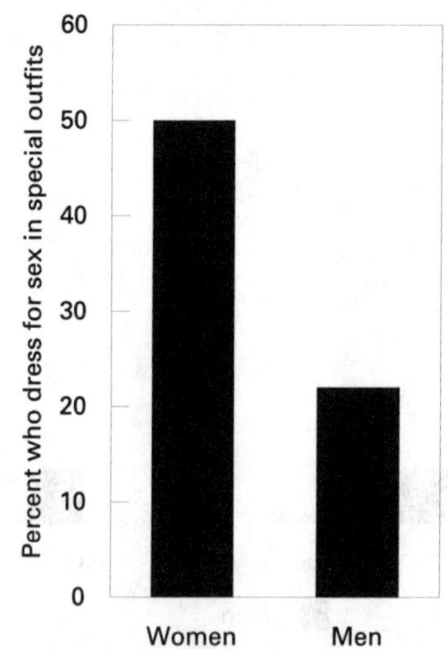

Source: Survey of Mademoiselle and Details subscribers, 1993

Anal Sex

Women who regularly participate in anal sex.

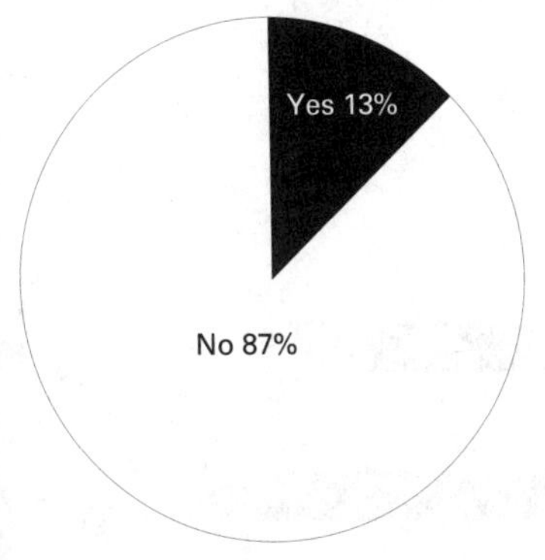

Source: The Cosmo Report (New York: Arbor House, 1981)

Sadomasochism and Bondage

Only 1.9% of women reported regularly participating in flagellation or other sadomasochistic behavior in a 1981 study (The Cosmo Report). When asked in a later survey if they had had "personal experience" with dominance or bondage, the percentage rose significantly.

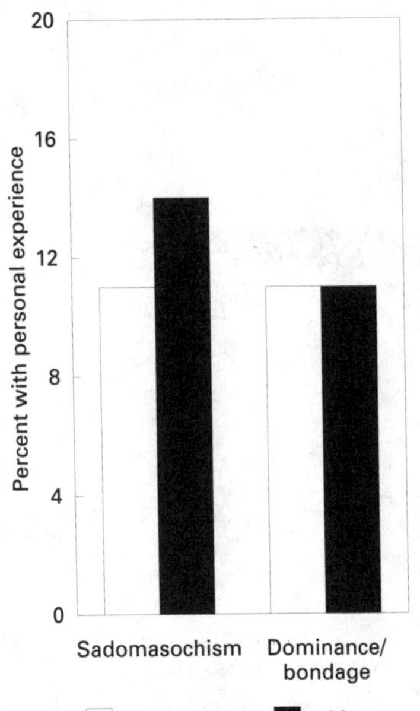

Source: The Janus Report (New York: John Wiley & Sons, 1993)

Group Sex

Percentage of people who report having had sex with two people at the same time.

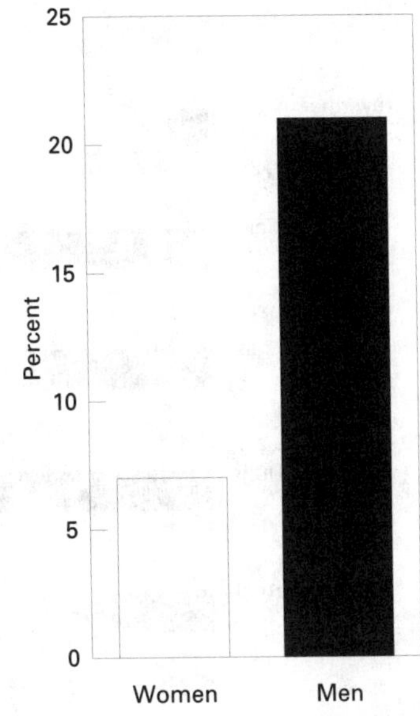

Source: Survey of Mademoiselle and Details subscribers, 1993

Orgies

Women gave these answers to the question, "Have you ever been to an orgy, sex club, or partner-swapping party?"

Never	83.5%
One time only	11.3%
Occasionally	4.2%
Often	1.1%

Source: The Cosmo Report (New York: Arbor House, 1981)

89% of the women in a 1993 Ladies' Home Journal survey said that the one sexual act they will not perform is anal sex.

Every year, 10 million men spend $3 billion at topless clubs, according to Gentlemen's Club magazine.

ATTITUDES TOWARD ALTERNATIVE SEXUAL BEHAVIOR

These graphs show women's and men's opinions about various sexual practices, whether they have participated in them or not.

Anal Sex

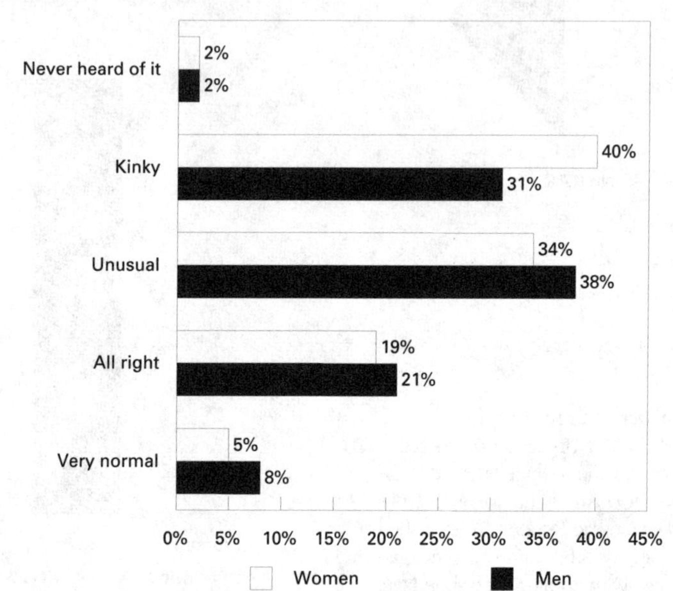

Sadomasochism

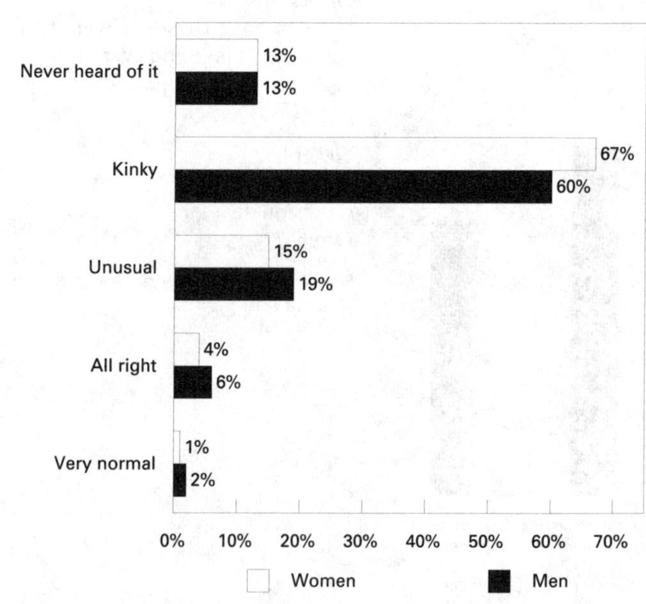

Dominance/bondage

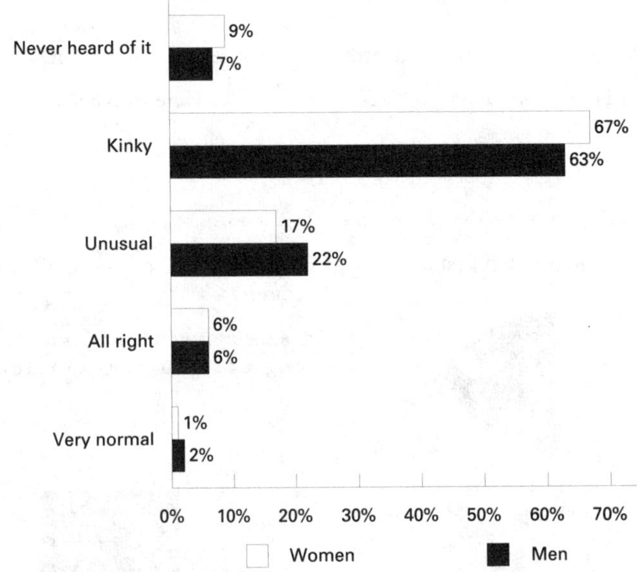

Source for above: The Janus Report (New York: John Wiley & Sons, 1993)

It is illegal for a husband to curse or swear during lovemaking in Willowdale, Oregon.

Fast Facts: Sexual Orientation

- Sexual orientation is the erotic, romantic, and affectional attraction to the same sex (homosexuality), to the opposite sex (heterosexuality), or to both (bisexuality).
- No single scientific theory about what causes sexual orientation has been suitably substantiated. Studies attempting to associate sexual orientation with genetic, hormonal, and environmental factors have so far been inconclusive.

Source: Sex Information and Education Council of the U.S. (SIECUS)

NOW did not adopt lesbian rights as an official part of its agenda until 1971.

The terms "heterosexuality" and "homosexuality" did not exist before 1890.

HOMOSEXUAL IDENTIFICATION AND EXPERIENCE

Sexual Orientation

These charts show how people identify their own sexual orientation.

	% Homosexual	% Bisexual	% Heterosexual
Women	2	3	95
Men	4	5	91

Source: The Janus Report (New York: John Wiley & Sons, 1993)

Women Who Have Had Lesbian Sex

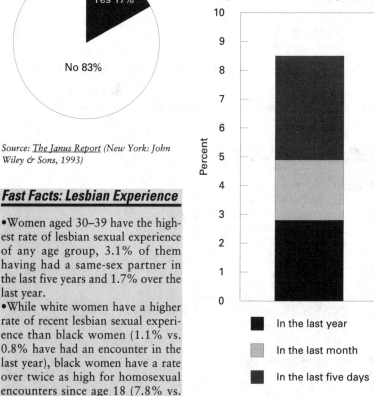

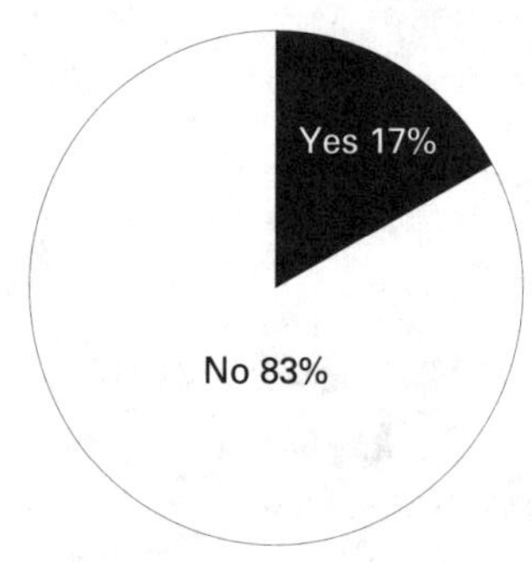

Source: The Janus Report (New York: John Wiley & Sons, 1993)

Fast Facts: Lesbian Experience

- Women aged 30–39 have the highest rate of lesbian sexual experience of any age group, 3.1% of them having had a same-sex partner in the last five years and 1.7% over the last year.
- While white women have a higher rate of recent lesbian sexual experience than black women (1.1% vs. 0.8% have had an encounter in the last year), black women have a rate over twice as high for homosexual encounters since age 18 (7.8% vs. 3.6%).

Source: National Opinion Research Center

How Common Are Lesbian Sexual Encounters?

Percentage of women who reported having sex with a same-sex partner.

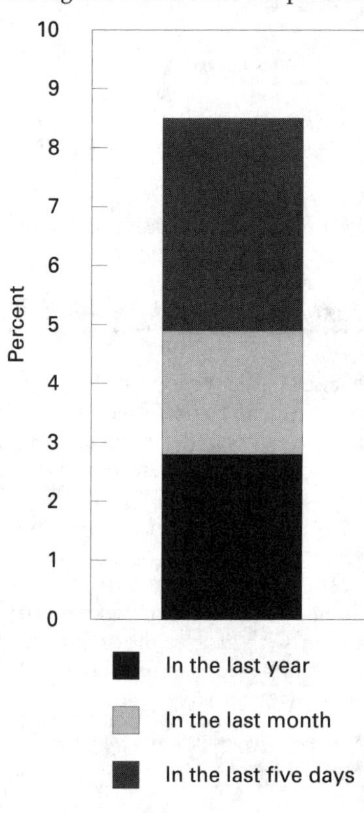

Source: Harris Poll, 1988

Fast Facts: P-FLAG

Parents, Families and Freinds of Lesbians and Gays (P-FLAG) was founded in 1981 by 25 parents concerned with society's attitude toward their lesbian, bisexual, and gay children. Today, P-FLAG represents more than 22,500 families. Local affiliates sponsor support groups in more than 340 communities in the U.S. and eleven countries. P-FLAG provides publications and reading lists; publishes *P-FLAGpole,* a quarterly newsletter; sponsors the Respect All Youth Project, the Family AIDS Support Project, and a speakers' bureau; and coordinates regional, national, and international conferences. Regional offices can be reached through the national headquarters:

P-FLAG
1012 14 Street, N.W., Suite 700
Washington, DC 20005
(202) 638-4200

LESBIAN SEXUALITY—RECOMMENDED READING

An Intimate Wilderness: Lesbian Writers on Sexuality, ed. Judith Barrington (Portland, Or.: Eighth Mountain Press, 1991).

Chicana Lesbians: The Girls Our Mothers Warned Us About, intro. Carla Trujillo (Berkeley, Calif.: Third Woman Press, 1991).

Historical, Literary, and Erotic Aspects of Lesbianism, Monika Kehoe (Binghampton, N.Y.: Harrington Park Press, 1986).

I Am Your Sister: Black Women Organizing Across Sexualities (Latham, N.Y.: Kitchen Table, Women of Color Press, 1986)

Lesbian Crossroads, interviews by Ruth Baetz (Tallahassee, Fla.: Naiad Press, 1988).

The Lesbian Erotic Dance: Butch, Femme, Androgyny, et al., JoAnn Loulan (San Francisco: Spinsters Ink, 1990).

Lesbian Passion: Loving Ourselves and Each Other, JoAnn Loulan (San Francisco: Spinsters Ink, 1987).

Looking at Gay and Lesbian Life, ed. Warren Blumenfeld and Diane Raymond (Boston: Beacon Press, 1992).

A Lure of Knowledge: Lesbian Sexuality and Theory, Judith Roof (New York: Columbia University Press, 1993).

Odd Girls and Twilight Lovers: A History of Lesbian Life in Twentieth-Century America, Lillian Fadermann (New York: Columbia University Press, 1991).

The Original Coming Out Stories, 2nd rev. ed., ed. Susan J. Wolfe and Julia Penelope (Freedom, Calif.: Crossing Press, 1989).

Sisters, Sexperts, Queers: Beyond the Lesbian Nation, ed. Arlene Stein (New York: New American Library, Dutton, 1993).

Testimonies: Lesbian Coming Out Stories, ed. Karen Barber and Sarah Holmes (Boston: Alyson Publications, 1994).

The American Psychiatric Association removed homosexuality from its list of disorders in 1973.

Karen Thompson won the right to care for her life partner, Sharon Kowalski, in a 1991 Minnesota court ruling. Kowalski had been severely disabled in an auto accident, and her parents had previously barred Thompson from seeing her.

MARTINA NAVRATILOVA— LESBIAN PRIDE COMES OUT OF THE CLOSET

Martina Navratilova is one of the greatest tennis players in history, with more singles titles overall than any woman player. The following is a speech she made at the Gay Pride March on Washington on April 4, 1993.

I'd like to welcome you and salute you for being here. What our movement for equality needs most, in my not so humble opinion, is for us to come out of the closet. We need to become visible to as many people as possible, so that we can finally shatter all those incredible myths that help keep us in the closet.

Let's come out and let all the people see what for the most part straight and square lives we lead. Let's come out and dispel the rumors and lies that are being spread about us. Let's come out and set everybody straight, so to speak.

Our goal is not to receive compassion, acceptance or, worse yet, tolerance, because that implies that we are inferior. . . . We are not to be tolerated, pitied, and endured. I don't want pity, do you? Of course not! Our goal must be equality across the board. We can settle for nothing less, because we deserve nothing less.

Labels, labels, labels—now, I don't know about you, but I hate labels. Martina Navratilova, the lesbian tennis player. They don't say Joe Montana, the heterosexual football player.

One's sexuality should not be an issue, one way or the another—one's sexuality should not become a label by which that human being should be identified. My sexuality is a very important part of my life, a very important part of my being, but it is still a very small part of my makeup, a very small part of what creates a whole human being. In any case, being a lesbian is not an accomplishment, it is not something I had to learn, study for or graduate in. It is what I am, nothing more and nothing less.

Now, I did not spend over 30 years of my life working my butt off trying to become the very best tennis player that I can be, to then be called Martina, the lesbian tennis player. Labels are for filing, labels are for bookkeeping, labels are for clothing, labels are not for people.

Being homosexual, bisexual, or heterosexual is not good or bad. It simply is.

So now we are here today so that one day, in the hopefully not too distant future, we will be referred to not by our sexuality but by our accomplishments and abilities—Melissa Etheridge, the incredible rock 'n' roller, Barney Frank, the congressman from Massachusetts, Dave Pallone, the baseball umpire, k.d. lang, "the best pipes in the business," as Roy Orbison called her, and Joe Zuniga, soldier, U.S. Army.

All these wonderful people and many more have come out of the closet. Each and every one had something to lose by that action, and each and every one could have made all kinds of excuses not to come out, but they didn't. So, now, I urge all of you who are still in the closet to throw away all of the excuses.

Instead, find all the wonderful reasons why you, too, should be out. Believe me, in the long run, the good will far outweigh the bad. Because if we want the world to accept us, we must first accept ourselves. If we want the world to give us respect, to not look at us with shame, we must first be willing to give ourselves respect. We must be proud of who we are and we cannot do that while we hide.

I believe the biggest, strongest weapon of our movement for equality is visibility, and the best way to get it is to come out. Yes, publicity of any kind—talk shows, articles, movies with positive gay characters —that all helps tremendously, but it is impersonal.

By coming out to our friends, family, employers, and employees, we make ourselves personal, touchable, real. We become human beings, and then we have the opportunity to show the world what we are all about—happy, intelligent, giving, loving people. We can show our moral strength, dignity, character.

We can share our joy and sorrow, our happiness and pain. We can just be. I urge you to be out, encourage your lovers and friends to come out. Come out, be proud and true to yourself, and as the song says, "Don't worry, be gay."

Half of all lesbian and gay youth report that their parents rejected them because of their sexual orientation.

More than a quarter of all lesbian and gay teenagers are forced to leave home because of conflicts with their families over their sexual identities.

20% of lesbian high school students experience verbal or physical assault in school.

FAMILIES OF LESBIANS AND BISEXUALS—RECOMMENDED READING

For Children and Adolescents

Heather Has Two Mommies, Leslea Newman (Boston: Alyson Publications, 1991).

When Someone You Know Is Gay, Susan and Daniel Cohen (New York: M. Evans & Company, 1989).

For Adult Children

Different Mothers: Sons and Daughters of Lesbians Talk About Their Lives, ed. Louise Rafkin (Pittsburgh: Cleis Press, 1990).

There's Something I've Been Meaning to Tell You: An Anthology about Lesbians and Gay Men Coming Out to Their Children, ed. Loralee MacPike (Tallahassee, Fla.: Naiad Press, 1989).

For Parents and Siblings

Different Daughters: A Book by Mothers of Lesbians, ed. Louise Rafkin (Pittsburgh: Cleis Press, 1987).

Homosexuality and Family Relations, ed. Frederick W. Bozett and Marvin B. Sussman (Binghampton, N.Y.: Haworth Press, 1990).

Now That You Know: What Every Parent Should Know About Homosexuality, rev. ed., Betty Fairchild and Nancy Hayward (New York: Harcourt, Brace, Jovanovich, 1989).

Parents Matter: Parents' Relationships with Lesbian Daughters and Gay Sons, Ann Muller (Tallahassee, Fla.: Naiad Press, 1987).

For Spouses

The Other Side of the Closet: The Coming-Out Crisis for Straight Spouses, Amity P. Buxton (Santa Monica, Calif.: IBS Press, 1991).

When Husbands Come Out of the Closet, Jean S. Gochros (Binghamton, N.Y.: Harrington Park Press, 1989).

TEENAGE LESBIANS AND BISEXUALS—RESOURCES AND READING

Organizations

The Hetrick-Martin Institute
401 West Street
New York, NY 10014
(212) 633-8920 or (212) 633-8926 (deaf access)

The Hetrick-Martin Institute is an educational, social service, and advocacy organization that offers services to lesbian, gay, and bisexual youth in New York City, and provides nationwide referrals.

Reading

Are You Still My Mother? Are You Still My Family? Gloria G. Back (New York: Warner Books, 1985).

Bridges of Respect: Creating Support for Lesbian and Gay Youth, rev. ed., Katherine Whitlock (Philadelphia: American Friends Service Committee, 1989).

Coming Out to Parents: A Two-Way Survival Guide for Lesbians and Gay Men and Their Parents, 2nd rev. ed., Mary V. Borhek (Cleveland: Pilgrim Press, the United Church Press, 1993).

Gay and Lesbian Youth, intro. Gilbert Herdt (Binghampton, N.Y.: Harrington Park Press, 1989).

SEXUAL ENHANCEMENT—RESOURCES RECOMMENDED BY SEXUALITY EXPERTS

For All Orientations

Reading

Good Vibrations: The Complete Guide to Vibrators, rev. ed., Joani Blank (Burlingame, Calif.: Down There Press, 1989).

Touching for Pleasure: A Twelve-Step Program for Sexual Enhancement, Adele P. Kennedy and Susan Dean (Chatsworth, Calif.: Chatsworth Press, 1990).

Educational Videos (explicit)

Complete Guide to Safe Sex, 90 mins., Laird Sutton (1988; available from Multi-Focus, 1525 Franklin Street, San Francisco, CA 94109).

Erotic Massage, 30 mins., Kenneth R. Stubbs and Louise-Andree Saulnier (1989; available from the Sexuality Library, 938 Howard Street, Suite 101, San Francisco, CA 94103).

For Heterosexual Women and Couples

Reading

Dr. Ruth's Guide for Married Lovers, Dr. Ruth Westheimer (New York: Warner Books, 1987).

The Intimate Male: Candid Discussions About Women, Sex, and Relationships, Linda Levine and Lonnie Barbach (New York: New American Library, Dutton, 1985).

More than Just Sex: A Committed Couple's Guide to Keeping Relationships Lively, Intimate, and Gratifying, Daniel Beaver (Boulder Creek, Calif.: Aslan, 1992).

The New Joy of Sex: A Gourmet Guide to Lovemaking for the Nineties, rev. ed., Alex Comfort (New York: Pocket Books, 1992).

The Perfect Fit: How to Achieve Mutual Fulfillment and Monogamous Passion through the New Intercourse, Edward Eichel and Philip Nobile (New York: Donald I. Fine, 1992).

Sexual Energy Ecstasy: A Practical Guide to Lovemaking Secrets of the East and West, David Ramsdale and Ellen Ramsdale (New York: Bantam, 1993).

What to Do When He Has a Headache: Renewing Desire and Intimacy in Your Relationship, Janet Wolfe (Westport, Ct.: Hyperion Press, 1993).

Educational Videos (explicit)

Behind the Bedroom Door series, 60 mins. each: Annie and Eric; James and Carol; Jim and Patti; Liz and Tom; Rod and Linda; Shane and Stacey (1993; series in which different couples "talk about their sex lives and demonstrate the activities they discuss"; available from the Sexuality Library, 938 Howard Street, Suite 101, San Francisco, CA 94103).

Sex: A Lifelong Pleasure, Dutch-produced series, including *Enjoying Sex,* 50 mins.; *Erection,* 70 mins.; *The Female Orgasm,* 60 mins.; *Harmony,* 65 mins. (1993; available from the Sexuality Library, address above).

For Lesbians

Reading

Lesbian Sex, JoAnn Loulan (San Francisco: Spinsters Ink, 1984).

The Lesbian Sex Book: A Guide for Women Who Love Women, Wendy Caster (Boston: Alyson Publications, 1993).

Lesbian S/M Safety Manual, ed. Pat Califia (Boston: Alyson Publications, Lace, 1988).

Susie Sexpert's Lesbian Sex World, Susie Bright (Pittsburgh: Cleis Press, 1991).

Sources: Journal of Sex and Marital Therapy; The Kinsey Institute New Report on Sex; the Sexuality Library; Society for the Scientific Study of Sex; Society for Sex Therapy and Research

"My reaction to porno films is as follows: After the first ten minutes, I want to go home and screw. After the first twenty minutes, I never want to screw again as long as I live."
—Erica Jong

"A woman's skin is overwhelmingly more sensitive to touch than a man's...anywhere on her body."
—Office Biology magazine

Among high school students, 81% of sexually active boys find sex pleasurable, compared to 59% of girls.

"Sexiness wears thin after a while and beauty fades, but to be married to a man who makes you laugh every day, ah, now that's a real treat."—Joanne Woodward

EROTICA FOR WOMEN—RECOMMENDED READING

Reading

Afterglow: More Stories of Lesbian Desire, ed. Karen Barber (Boston: Alyson Publications, 1993).

Bushfire: Stories of Lesbian Desire, ed. Karen Barber (Boston: Alyson Publications, 1991).

Erotic Interludes, ed. Lonnie Barbach (New York: HarperCollins, 1987).

Erotica: Women's Writing from Sappho to Margaret Atwood, ed. Margaret Reynolds (New York: Fawcett Books, 1991).

Forbidden Flowers, Nancy Friday (New York: Pocket Books, 1982).

Herotica Two: A Collection of Women's Erotic Fiction, ed. Susie Bright and Joani Blank (New York: New American Library, Dutton, 1992).

My Secret Garden, Nancy Friday (New York: Pocket Books, 1983).

Pleasures: Women Write Erotica, ed. Lonnie Barbach (New York: HarperCollins, 1985).

Slow Hand: Women Write Erotica, ed. Michele Slung (New York: HarperCollins, 1992).

The Unmade Bed: Sensual Writing on Married Love, ed. Laura Chester (New York: HarperCollins, 1992).

Periodicals

For Women (and Men) of All Orientations

Ecstasy: The Journal of Divine Eroticism (Box 862, Ojai, CA 93024).

frighten the horses: a document of the sexual revolution (Heat Seeking Publishing, 41 Sutter Street, Suite 1108, San Francisco, CA 94104).

Future Sex (1095 Market Street, Suite 809, San Francisco, CA 94103).

Libido: The Journal of Sex and Sensibility (Box 146721, Chicago, IL 60614).

TANTRA: The Magazine (Box 79, Torreon, NM 87061).

Yellow Silk: Journal of Erotic Arts (Box 6374, Albany, CA 94706).

For Lesbians

Black Lace (BLK Publishing, Box 83912, Los Angeles, CA 90083).

Brat Attack (Box 40754, San Francisco, CA 94140).

On Our Backs: Entertainment for the Adventurous Lesbian (526 Castro Street, San Francisco, CA 94114).

Sources: The Sexuality Library; Utne Reader; Whole Earth Review

ON-LINE DISCUSSION GROUPS ABOUT SEXUALITY

Electronic discussion groups listed as "open" are available to anyone with access to the on-line service provider or an Internet address; those listed as "private" require some form of permission or invitation to join.

BBS (Bulletin Board systems)
Many bulletin board systems specialize in sex-related topics, and some systems offer women-only forums. Magazines such as *Boardwatch* and *Online Access* provide up-to-date BBS listings.

CompuServe
Telephone/voice-mail: (614) 457-8600
E-mail: postmaster@compuserve.com
Open and private conferences are available; for sexuality information and professional advisory service, choose GO HSX.

Echo
Telephone/voice-mail: (212) 255-3839
E-mail: horn@echo.panix.com
LOVE is an open conference, SEX is private.

GLIB BBS
Telephone/voice-mail: (703) 379-4568
Bulletin board specializing in lesbian and gay issues.

Usenet Newsgroups
Access via Internet, commercial providers, or local BBS systems
There are many open (and generally explicit) conferences among the ALT.SEX newsgroups; some discussion participants use an anonymous server to protect against any private e-mail responses to their public newsgroup postings.

WELL
Telephone/voice-mail: (415) 332-4335
E-mail: info@well.sf.ca.us
Open conferences include COUPLES, EROS, GAY, SEXUALITY, and SINGLES; WOW (Women on Well) is private.

Sources: Future Sex; Utne Reader

SEX ADDICTION

Definition

Sex and Love Addicts Anonymous defines sex addiction as "an obsessive/compulsive pattern, either sexual or emotional (or both), in which relationships or activities have become increasingly destructive to all areas of one's life—career, family, and sense of self-respect."

Helplines

Sexual Addiction Access Helpline
(800) 362-2644

Sexual Compulsives Anonymous Information Line
(212) 439-1123

Support Organizations*

Sex Addicts Anonymous
National Service Organization
P.O. Box 70949
Houston, TX 77270
(713) 869-4902

Sex and Love Addicts Anonymous
The Augustine Fellowship
P.O. Box 119
New Town Branch
Boston, MA 02258
(617) 332-1845

Sexaholics Anonymous
P.O. Box 300
Simi Valley, CA 93062
(805) 581-3343

Co-dependents of Sex Addicts
Minnesota Co-SA
P.O. Box 14537
Minneapolis, MN 55414
(612) 537-6904
For spouses, lovers, and other relatives and friends of people with sex addiction problems

*All of these groups have local affiliates throughout the U.S.

SEX COUNSELING AND THERAPY—RESOURCES AND READING

Organizations

American Association of Sex Educators, Counselors, and Therapists
435 N. Michigan Avenue, Suite 1717
Chicago, IL 60611
(312) 644-0828
Non-profit interdisciplinary educational organization providing professional certification and nationwide referrals.

Masters & Johnson Institute
One Campbell Plaza (59th and Arsenal)
St. Louis, MO 63139
(314) 781-2224 or (900) 933-6868 (information, $3.99 per minute)
Institute providing psychotherapy, consultation, and couples therapy for sexual distress. Information Line is a 24-hour consultation service staffed by professional therapists and sex educators.

Reading

The Illustrated Manual of Sex Therapy, 2nd ed., Helen Singer Kaplan (New York: Brunner-Mazel, 1987).

Women and Sex Therapy, ed. Ellen Cole and Esther D. Rothblum (Binghamton, N.Y.: Harrington Park Press, 1988).

"I consider promiscuity immoral. Not because sex is evil, but because sex is too good and too important."—Ayn Rand

87% of the women in Shere Hite's 1987 study said they have their deepest emotional relationship with a woman friend.

EROTICA AND THE MARRIED LIFE

In a 1993 *Ladies' Home Journal* survey that drew responses from over 40,000 readers, 47% of the married women surveyed said they use erotic material at least occasionally to heighten lovemaking. Erotic videos and movies were the most popular choice, with 84% of the vote. Thirty-nine percent of wives who use erotic aids say they and their husbands use sex toys, and 34% choose sexy magazines.

Although more than half of all wives said they were satisfied with the frequency of lovemaking with their husbands, 42% said they wished they made love even more, and only 4% wanted less intimacy in the bedroom. However, 80% of all survey respondents said they enjoy making love outside the bedroom, and among these women, the living room (58%), outdoors (24%), and the car (23%) were the most popular places for passion.

Source: "The Love Life of the American Wife," Ladies' Home Journal (February 1993)

FRIENDSHIP AND COMMUNITY—RECOMMENDED READING

Between Women: Love, Envy, & Competition in Women's Friendships, Luise Eichenbaum and Susie Orbach (New York: Viking Penguin, 1989).

Community and the Politics of Place, Daniel Kemmis (Norman, Okla.: University of Oklahoma Press, 1991).

Friendships Between Women: A Critical Review, Pat O'Connor (New York: Guilford Press, 1992).

A Passion for Friends: Toward a Philosophy of Female Affection, Janice G. Raymond (Boston: Beacon Press, 1987).

Directory of Intentional Communities (available from Twin Oaks, Route 4, Box 169-U, Louisa, VA 23093).

The Secret Between Us: Competition Among Women, Laura Tracy (New York: Little, Brown, 1991).

RELATIONSHIP ISSUES—RECOMMENDED READING

The Dance of Anger: A Woman's Guide to Changing the Patterns of Intimate Relationships, Harriet G. Lerner (New York: Harper & Row, 1985).

Enabling Romance: A Guide to Love, Sex, and Relationships for the Disabled (and the People Who Care About Them), Erica Klein and Ken Kroll (New York: Crown Publishing Group, 1992).

Going the Distance: Finding and Keeping Lifelong Love, Lonnie Barbach and David L. Geisinger (New York: New American Library/Dutton, 1993).

Intimate Partners: Patterns in Love and Marriage, Maggie Scarf (New York: Random House, 1987).

Singing at the Top of Our Lungs: Women, Love, and Creativity, Claudia Bepko and Jo-Ann Krestan (New York: HarperCollins, 1993).

Too Good for Her Own Good: Searching for Self and Intimacy in Important Relationships, Claudia Bepko and Jo-Ann Krestan (New York: HarperPerennial, 1991).

Uncoupling: Turning Points in Intimate Relationships, Diane Vaughan (New York: Oxford University Press, 1986).

LESBIAN RELATIONSHIPS AND COMMUNITY—READING AND RESOURCES

READING

Alyson Almanac: A Treasury of Information for the Gay and Lesbian Community, 3d ed. (Boston: Alyson Publications, 1993).

Families We Choose: Lesbians, Gays, Kinship, Kath Weston (New York: Columbia University Press, 1991).

Gayellow Pages, national and New York/New Jersey editions (New York: Gayellow Pages, annual; available from P.O. Box 533, Village Station, NY 10014, [212] 674-0120).

A Legal Guide for Lesbian and Gay Couples, 7th ed., Hayden Curry, Denis Clifford, and Robin Leonard (Berkeley, Cal.: Nolo Press, 1993).

Lesbian Couples, Dorsey G. Green and Merilee D. Clunis (Seattle: Seal Press, 1988).

Loving Boldly: Issues Facing Lesbians, Esther D. Rothblum and Ellen Cole (Binghamton, N.Y.: Harrington Park Press, 1989).

On Intimate Terms: The Psychology of Difference in Lesbian Relationships, Beverly Burch (Champaign: University of Illinois Press, 1993).

Permanent Partners: Building Gay and Lesbian Relationships That Last, Betty Berzon (New York: Dutton, 1988).

Staying Power: Long-Term Lesbian Couples, Susan E. Johnson (Tallahassee, Fla.: Naiad Press, 1990).

Write From the Heart—Lesbians Healing from Heartache: An Anthology, Anita Pace et al. (Beverton, Or.: Baby Steps Press, 1992).

RESOURCES

Bay Area Bisexual Network
2404 California Street, Box 24
San Francisco, CA 94115
(415) 703-7977

Dignity USA
1500 Massachusetts Avenue, N.W., Suite 11
Washington, DC 20005
(202) 861-0017

Gay and Lesbian Advocates and Defenders
P.O. Box 218
Boston, MA 02112
(617) 426-1350

Lamda Legal Defense and Education Fund
666 Broadway
New York, NY 10012
(212) 995-8585

Lesbian Resource Center
1208 E. Pine
Seattle, WA 98122
(206) 322-3953

National Center for Lesbian Rights
1663 Mission Street
San Francisco, CA 94103
(415) 621-0674

National Gay and Lesbian Task Force
1734 14th Street, N.W.
Washington, DC 20009
(202) 332-6483

National Hate Crime Reporting Hotline
(800) 347-4283

Office of Lesbian and Gay Concerns
Unitarian Universalist Association
25 Beacon Street
Boston, MA 02108
(617) 742-2100 x461

In 1649 in the Massachusetts Bay Colony, Goodwife Norman and Mary Hammon were tried for lesbianism. Norman was found guilty and sentenced to "public acknowledgment." Hammon was acquitted.

Denmark was the first country in the world to legalize homosexual marriages, in 1989. Since then, over 2,000 gay and lesbian couples have married.

LESBIAN MARRIAGE

•The Hawaii Supreme Court recently found a law barring same-sex marriages to be a form of gender discrimination and, as such, a violation of the state's constitution. Calling marriage "a basic civil right," the court ruled 3-1 to strike down the state's requirement that couples be of different sexes. The case has now been sent back to a trial judge, who will hear Hawaii's attempt to prove a compelling state interest in the regulation.

•While no state government has legally recognized lesbian or gay unions, several states accord these couples certain of the protections and rights of marriage through domestic partnership programs. Even then, few of the traditional fringe benefits available to members of a heterosexual couple are extended to gay life-partners, including health care, insurance coverage, and standard inheritance rights.

Sources: Newsweek (May 17, 1993); Permanent Partners, Betty Berzon (New York: Dutton, 1988

38% of Woman's Day readers in 1986 would not choose the same spouse if they had it to do over again.

ELIGIBLE WOMEN AND MEN

This graph shows the ratio of unmarried men per 100 unmarried women, by age.

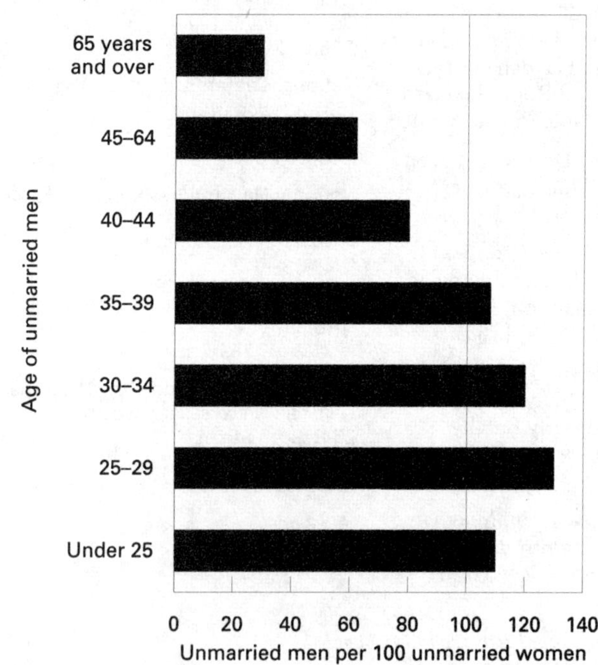

"Sometimes I wonder if men and women really suit each other. Perhaps they should live next door and just visit now and then."
—Katharine Hepburn

(Data from 1992)
Source: Bureau of the Census

THE RISE IN UNMARRIED COUPLES

This graph shows the number of unmarried-couple households, broken down the presence of children.

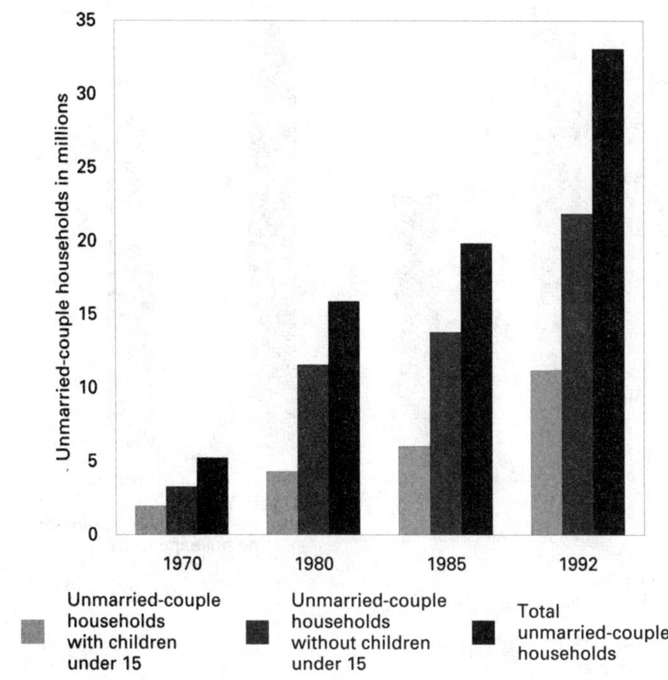

(Data from 1992)
Source: Bureau of the Census

There were approximately 27 million childless married couples in 1990, a 42% increase since 1970.

Unmarried men outnumber unmarried women in Japan, where the average age of marriage for women is 26, compared to 24 in the U.S.

INTERNATIONAL WOMEN HEADS OF HOUSEHOLDS

	% of households headed by women, in the 1980s
Grenada	45
Botswana	45
Saint Lucia	39
Norway	38
Jamaica	34
Austria	31
USA	31
Malawi	29
Zambia	28
Cuba	28
Poland	27
Sweden	27
Ghana	27
Rwanda	25
Australia	25
Canada	25
Puerto Rico	25
Switzerland	25
United Kingdom	25

(Data from 1991)
Source: UNICEF

"I had my career but never met Mr. Right. So at about age 30, I was ready to have a baby in my house instead of looking for someone from the outside to change my life."—Jane Wallace, formerly of the TV show West 57th, on choosing single motherhood

SINGLE AND MARRIED MOTHERS

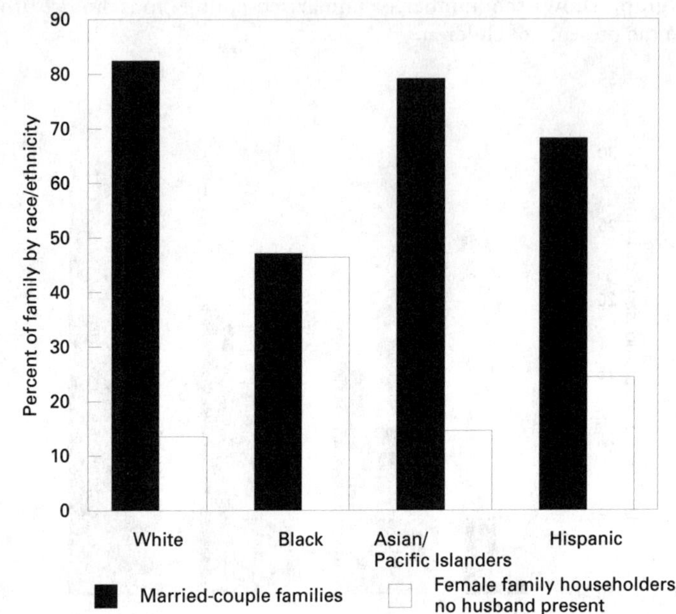

(Data from 1992)
Source: Bureau of the Census

The average length of a marital engagement in the U.S. is 14 months.

AGE OF FIRST MARRIAGE

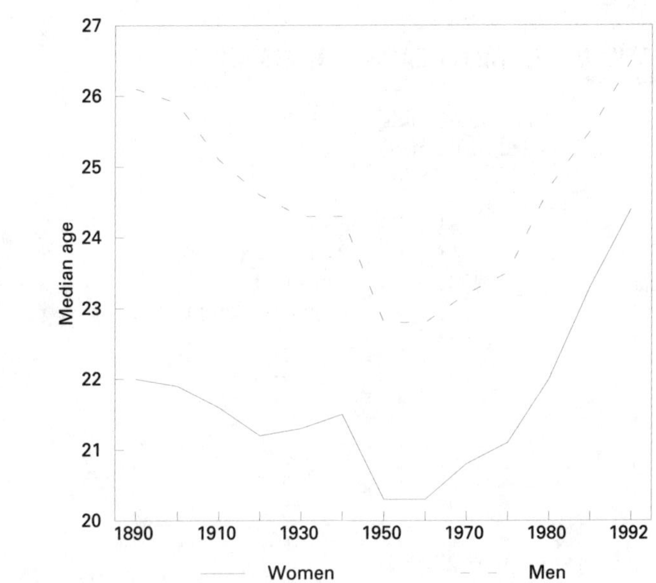

(Data from 1992)
Source: Bureau of the Census

MARRIAGE RATES SINCE 1921

This graph shows the rate of first marriages per 1,000 women aged 15–44, as well as remarriages among widowed and divorced women.

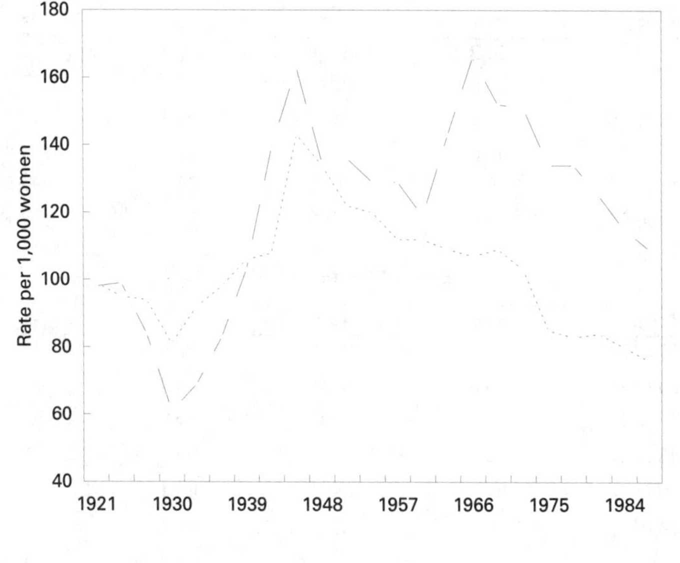

Source: National Center for Health Statistics

One-third of honeymooning American couples go to the Caribbean, according to a 1992 survey by American Demographics

Bridal market spending in the United States is an estimated $35 billion a year.

MARITAL STATUS AND INCOME LEVELS AMONG WOMEN

These numbers show the median income of women from 1992.

	ALL WOMEN	WHITE	BLACK	HISPANIC ORIGIN [1]
Total	$11,121	$11,389	$9,135	$8,610
Single, never married	$10,063	$10,792	$7,479	$7,584
Married, spouse present	$11,149	$11,073	$11,736	$9,002
Married, spouse absent	$ 9,997	$10,552	$8,175	$8,598
Divorced	$16,554	$17,046	$13,287	$12,201
Widowed	$9,781	$10,332	$6,909	$7,039

[1]Persons of Hispanic origin may be of any race

Source: Bureau of the Census

MARRIAGE AMONG WOMEN

The average cost of a formal wedding in the United States is $17,470, according to a study by Modern Bride.

The fastest-growing age group for new brides is 30 to 35.

More than one million couples take honeymoon trips each year in the U.S.

Marriage experience for women, by age, race, and Hispanic origin.

PERCENT EVER MARRIED—WHITE

Age	1975	1980	1985	1990
25 to 29	88.8	81.0	77.4	73.2
30 to 34	93.9	91.6	88.1	85.6
35 to 39	96.2	95.3	93.1	91.4
40 to 44	95.9	95.8	95.6	93.4
45 to 49	95.9	96.4	95.1	95.1
50 to 54	96.0	95.8	95.4	96.1

PERCENT EVER MARRIED—BLACK

Age	1975	1980	1985	1990
20 to 24	47.5	33.3	23.9	23.5
25 to 29	76.5	62.3	53.4	45.0
30 to 34	87.1	77.9	70.9	61.1
35 to 39	90.1	87.4	80.7	74.9
40 to 44	95.1	89.7	86.1	82.1
45 to 49	95.4	92.5	88.4	89.7
50 to 54	94.6	92.1	93.4	91.9

PERCENT EVER MARRIED—HISPANIC [1]

Age		1980	1985	1990
20 to 24	—	55.4	56.7	45.8
25 to 29	—	80.2	78.4	69.6
30 to 34	—	88.3	88.0	83.0
35 to 39	—	91.2	91.6	88.9
40 to 44	—	94.2	90.3	92.8
45 to 49	—	94.4	91.1	91.7
50 to 54	—	95.0	92.5	91.8

[1]Persons of Hispanic origin may be of any race.
Source: Bureau of the Census

HONEYMOON MEMORIES

While 47% of married women described their honeymoons as thrilling and 30% said the trips were very sexual, the downside weighs in as well. Ten percent called their honeymoons boring, 4% felt they were traumatic, and 4% said they were asexual. Responses among divorced women were significantly more negative, with 37% calling their honeymoons boring and 19% indicating that they were asexual. Only 5% of divorced men regarded them as boring, with an equal percentage describing them as asexual.

Source: The Janus Report (New York: John Wiley & Sons, 1993)

OPEN MARRIAGE

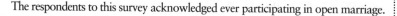

The respondents to this survey acknowledged ever participating in open marriage.

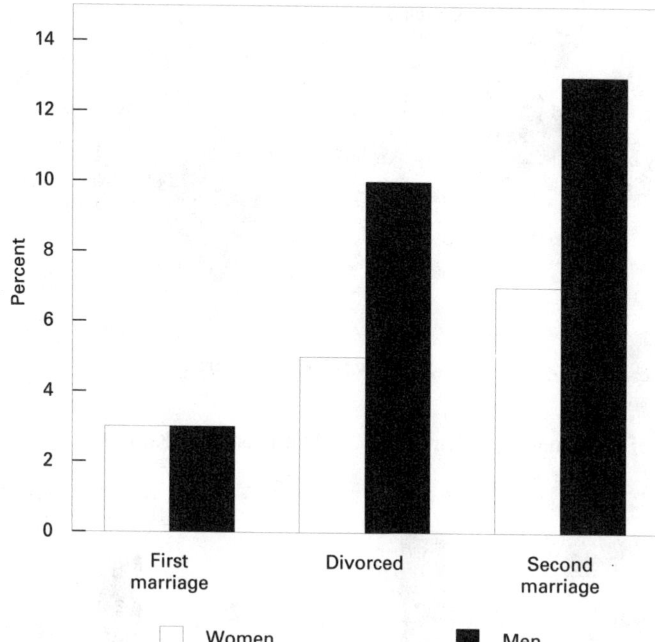

Source: The Janus Report (New York: John Wiley & Sons, 1993)

39% of married women lived with their husbands before they married them, as did 67% of divorced women.

INFIDELITY IN MARRIAGE

•Twenty-six percent of women admitted in a recent poll that they've cheated on their husbands, up from 21% ten years ago.

•Extramarital affairs are more exciting than marital sex, say 60% of those women who've looked outside of marriage for sex.

•Of those women who've been unfaithful, 33% met the other man at work.

•Seventy-eight percent of these women are now involved with another man.

•Wives who have commited adultery are more likely to report being dissatisfied with their marriages and to rate their husbands as poor lovers.

•Nonetheless, 47% of cheating wives say the experience has had a positive physical or emotional effect on their relationships with their husbands.

Source: Ladies Home Journal, February 1993

INTERRACIAL MARRIAGE

Interracial marriage in the U.S. increased by 266% from 1970 to 1992. The percentage was 0.6% the first of those years, and rose to 2.2% in 1992. Marriages between people of Hispanic ethnicity and other groups have also risen, from 1.3% in 1970 to 2.2% in 1993.

Source: Bureau of the Census

"When he's late for dinner, I know he's either having an affair or is lying dead in the street. I always hope it's the street."—Jessica Tandy, on her husband Hume Cronyn

EXTRAMARITAL AFFAIRS

Married Women Who Have Had Affairs

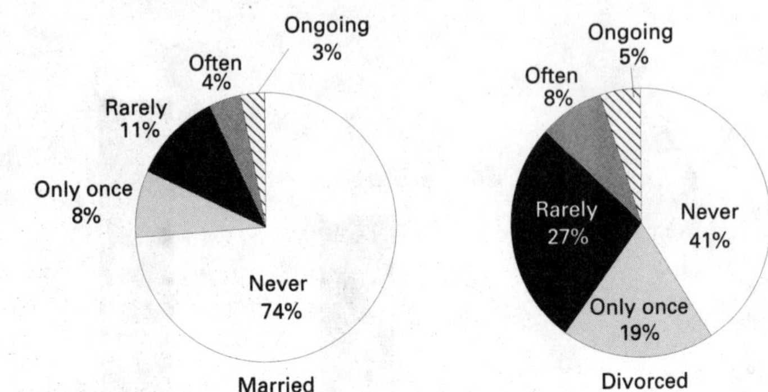

Source: The Janus Report (New York: John Wiley & Sons, 1993)

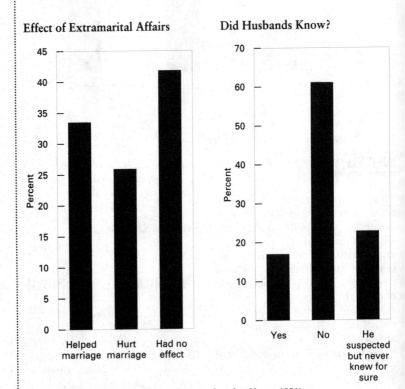

Effect of Extramarital Affairs

Did Husbands Know?

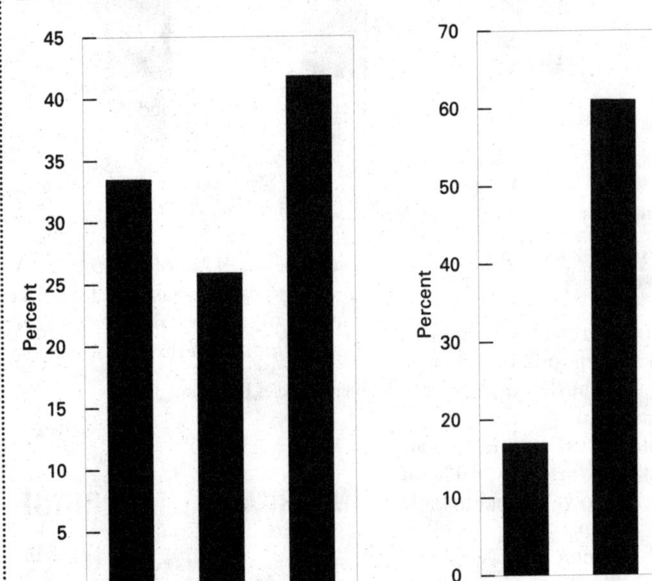

Source for above: The Cosmo Report (New York: Arbor House, 1981)

MARITAL RELATIONSHIPS—RECOMMENDED READING

For Better, For Worse: The Joys and Terrors of Five Couples Facing Parenthood, Susan Squire (New York: Doubleday, 1993).

Growing Older Together: A Couples' Guide to Understanding and Coping with the Challenges of Later Life, Barbara Silverstone and Helen Kandel Hyman (Westminster, Md.: Pantheon Books, 1992).

The Monogamy Myth: A New Understanding of Affairs and How to Survive Them, Peggy Vaughan (New York: Newmarket, 1989).

The Secrets of Happy Couples and How Their Marriages Thrive, Catherine Johnson (New York: Viking, 1992).

Second Honeymoon: A Pioneering Guide for Reviving the Midlife Marriage, Sonya Rhodes (New York: William Morrow, 1992).

When Partners Become Parents: The Big Life Change for Couples, Carolyn Pape Cowan and Philip A. Cowan (New York: Basic Books, 1992).

COUPLES PROGRAMS

Association for Couples in Marriage Enrichment
P.O. Box 10596
Winston-Salem, NC 27108
(910) 724-1526

Couple Communication
Interpersonal Communication Programs
7201 S. Broadway
Littleton, CO 80122
(303) 794-1764

National Marriage Encounter
4704 Jamerson Place
Orlando, FL 32807
(407) 282-8120

PAIRS—Practical Application of Intimate Relationship Skills
Falls Church, VA 22041
(800) 842-7470

HOW FULFILLING IS MARRIAGE?

Asked to react to the statement, "To be truly fulfilled, one must be married," 81% of surveyed women disagreed, compared to only 69% of men. Given the option of agreeing or disagreeing in varying degrees of strength, the largest discrepancy between the sexes came among those who strongly disagreed: 25% of women and 18% of men. Only 3% of women and 4% of men strongly agreed that marriage was the true road to fulfillment.

Source: Janus Report (New York: John Wiley & Sons, 1993)

COUPLES COUNSELING AND FAMILY THERAPY—READING AND RESOURCES

READING

Love Is Never Enough: How Couples Can Overcome Misunderstandings, Resolve Conflicts, and Solve Relationship Problems Through Cognitive Therapy, Aaron T. Beck (New York: Harper & Row, 1988).

Family Healing: Tales of Hope and Renewal from Family Therapy, Salvador Minuchin and Michael P. Nichols (New York: Free Press, 1992).

Rewriting Love Stories: Brief Marital Therapy, Patricia O'Hanlon Hudson and William Hudson O'Hanlon (New York: W.W. Norton, 1992).

Self-Delight in a Harsh World: The Main Stories of Individual, Marital, and Family Psychotherapy, James P. Gustafson (New York: W.W. Norton, 1992).

When Your Child Needs Help: A Parent's Guide to Therapy for

An Italian physicist has patented a condom that will play Beethoven if it breaks during use.

"Having family responsibilities and concerns just has to make you a more understanding person."—Sandra Day O'Connor

Children, Norma Doft with Barbara Aria (New York: Harmony Books, 1992).

Women and Power: Perspectives for Family Therapy, Thelma J. Goodrich, ed. (New York: W.W. Norton, 1991).

Women in Families: A Framework for Family Therapy, Monica McGoldrick, Carol M. Anderson, and Froma Walsh, eds. (New York: W.W. Norton, 1989).

RESOURCES

American Association for Marriage and Family Therapy
1100 Seventeenth Street, N.W.
Washington, DC 20036
(202) 452-0109 or (800) 374-2638 (referrals)

Institute of Marriage and Family Relations
6116 Rolling Road, Suite 306
Springfield, VA 22152
(703) 569-2400

National Institute of Relationship Enhancement
Center for Couples
4400 East-West Highway, Suite 28
Bethesda, MD 20814
(301) 986-1479

HOW TO TELL IF FAMILY THERAPY MIGHT BE OF HELP

If you or your family members experience many of these signs of distress, family therapy could be of assistance:

•Persistent feelings of dissatisfaction
•Problems with a child's behavior, school adjustment, or performance
•Sexual problems or concerns
•Unexplainable fatigue or difficulty sleeping
•Difficulties in talking with your fiancé, spouse, children, parents, other family members, friends, or co-workers
•Feelings of loneliness, moodiness, depression, sadness, failure, stress, or anxiety
•The need for tranquilizers, energizers, or sleeping aids
•Family stress due to chronic illnesses or illness in which stress plays a major role
•Problems with alcohol or drugs
•Frequent financial difficulties
•Difficulty in setting or reaching goals
•Drastic weight fluctuations or irregular eating patterns
•Work difficulties, frquent job changes, problems with co-workers
•Difficulties with anger, hostility, or violence

Source: American Association for Marriage and Family Therapy

FAMILY COMPOSITION

•Married-couple families accounted for more than 55% of all households in 1992; a majority of these couples did not have any children under 18 in the home.
•Single parents have risen to 10.5 million, up from 3.8 million in 1970.
•Only 47% of African-American family households are maintained by married couples. In contrast, 69% of Hispanic, 79% of Asian, Pacific Islander, and around 82% of white households were maintained by married couples.
•The average household size in 1992 was 2.62 persons, significantly smaller than a decade ago.
•About 60% of all persons living alone in 1992 were women, down from 67% in 1970.

(Data from 1992)
Source: Bureau of the Census

FAMILIES—RESOURCES

American Mothers
The Waldorf-Astoria
301 Park Avenue
New York, NY 10022
(212) 755-2359
Local networks, workshops

Families USA
1334 G Street, N.W.
Washington, DC 20005
(202) 737-6340
Advocates for affordable health and housing

Family Resource Coalition
200 S. Michigan Avenue, Suite 1520
Chicago, IL 60604
(312) 341-0900
Community-based parenting support groups nationwide

Families and Work Institute
330 Seventh Avenue
New York, NY 10001
(212) 465-2044
Policy development, national clearinghouse for information

National Council on Family Relations
3989 Central Avenue, N.W., Suite 550
Minneapolis, MN 55421
(612) 781-9331
Supports professionals who work with families

Parent Action
2 N. Charles Street, Suite 960
Baltimore, MD 21201
(410) 727-3687
Support and lobbying group

Single Parent Resource Center
141 W. 28th Street
New York, NY 10001
(212) 947-0221

MULTI-ETHNIC FAMILIES—RESOURCES

Association of MultiEthnic Americans
P.O. Box 191726
San Francisco, CA 94119
(510) 523-2632

Interracial Family Alliance
P.O. Box 16248
Houston, TX 77222
(713) 454-5018

Interracial-Intercultural Pride
P.O. Box 191752
San Francisco, CA 94119
(510) 653-1929

Pareveh, The Alliance for Adult Children of Jewish-Gentile Intermarriage
3628 Windom Place, N.W.
Washington, DC 20008

FAMILY LIFE—RECOMMENDED VIDEOS

Families in Trouble: Learning to Cope, 35 mins. (1991; available from Sunburst Communications, 39 Washington Avenue, Pleasantville, NY 10570).

A Kid's Guide to Families, 35 mins., Words, Inc. (1992; available from Learning Tree Publishing, P.O. Box 4116, Englewood, CO 80155).

A Kid's Guide to Family Changes, 40 mins., Words, Inc. (1993; available from Learning Tree Publishing, P.O. Box 4116, Englewood, CO 80155).

Let's Get a Move On! (A Kid's Video Guide to a Family Move), 30 mins., Jane Murphy and Karen Tucker (1991; available from KID-VIDZ, 618 Centre Street, Newton, MA 02158).

Our Families, Our Future, Roger Weisberg; Walter Cronkite, host (1993; available from *Our Families, Our Future*, P.O. Box 2284, South Burlington, VT 05407).

Teen Parent TV News, 28 mins., Lanita Duke (1993; available from Churchill Media, 12210 Nebraska Avenue, Los Angeles, CA 90025).

FAMILY ISSUES—RECOMMENDED READING

Family Dynamics

Between Sisters: Secret Rivals, Intimate Friends, Barbara Mathias (New York: Delacorte, 1992).

45% of women think they have closer relations with their siblings than their parents did with theirs.

"If you bungle raising your children, I don't think whatever else you do well matters very much."
—Jacqueline Kennedy Onassis

84% of women say they have people in their lives they regard as family who are not related by blood.

"Family life! The United Nations is child's play compared to the tugs and splits and need to understand and forgive in any family."
—May Sarton

Double Stitch: Black Women Write About Their Mothers and Daughters, Patricia Bell Scott, ed. (Boston: Beacon Press, 1991).

Family Bonds: Adoption and the Politics of Parenting, Elizabeth Bartholet (Boston: Houghton Mifflin, 1993).

The Father-Daughter Dance, Barbara Goulter and Joan Minninger (New York: Putnam, 1993).

Juggling: The Unexpected Advantages of Balancing Career and Home for Women and Their Families, Faye J. Crosby (New York: Free Press, 1991).

Loss of the Groundnote: Women Writing About the Loss of Their Mothers, Helen Vozenilek, ed. (San Diego, Calif.: Clothespin Fever Press, 1992).

Mother Daughter Revolution: From Betrayal to Power, Elizabeth Debold et al. (Reading, Mass.: Addison-Wesley, 1993).

Stories from the Motherline: Reclaiming the Mother-Daughter Bond, Finding Our Feminine Souls, Naomi Lowinsky (Los Angeles: Jeremy P.Tarcher, 1992).

Understanding Abusive Families, James Garbarino and Gwen Gilliam (New York: Free Press, 1984).

Women and Stepfamilies, Monica McGoldrick (Philadelphia: Temple University Press, 1990).

FAMILY AND SOCIETY

Black Families, Harrette Pipes McAdoo, ed. (Newbury Park, Calif.: Sage Publications, 1988).

Climbing Jacob's Ladder: The Enduring Legacy of African-American Families, Andrew Billingsley (New York: Simon & Schuster, 1988).

Contemporary Families: Looking Forward, Looking Back, Alan Booth, ed. (Minneapolis: National Council on Family Relations, 1991).

Embattled Paradise: The American Family in an Age of Uncertainty, Arlene Skolnick (New York: Basic Books, 1991).

The Family: A Social History of the Twentieth Century, John Harriss, ed. (New York: Oxford University Press, 1991).

New Families, No Families? The Transformation of the American Home, Frances K. Goldscheider and Linda J. Waite (Berkeley: University of California Press, 1991).

The Way We Never Were: American Families and the Nostalgia Trap, Stephanie Coontz (New York: Basic Books, 1992).

DIVORCE AND CUSTODY
DIVORCE AND CUSTODY
DIVORCE AND CUSTODY

DIVORCE AND CUSTODY

DIVORCE AND CUSTODY
DIVORCE AND CUSTODY
DIVORCE AND CUSTODY
DIVORCE AND CUSTODY
DIVORCE AND CUSTODY
DIVORCE AND CUSTODY
DIVORCE AND CUSTODY
DIVORCE AND CUSTODY
DIVORCE AND CUSTODY
DIVORCE AND CUSTODY
DIVORCE AND CUSTODY
DIVORCE AND CUSTODY
DIVORCE AND CUSTODY
DIVORCE AND CUSTODY
DIVORCE AND CUSTODY
DIVORCE AND CUSTODY

DIVORCE ON THE RISE

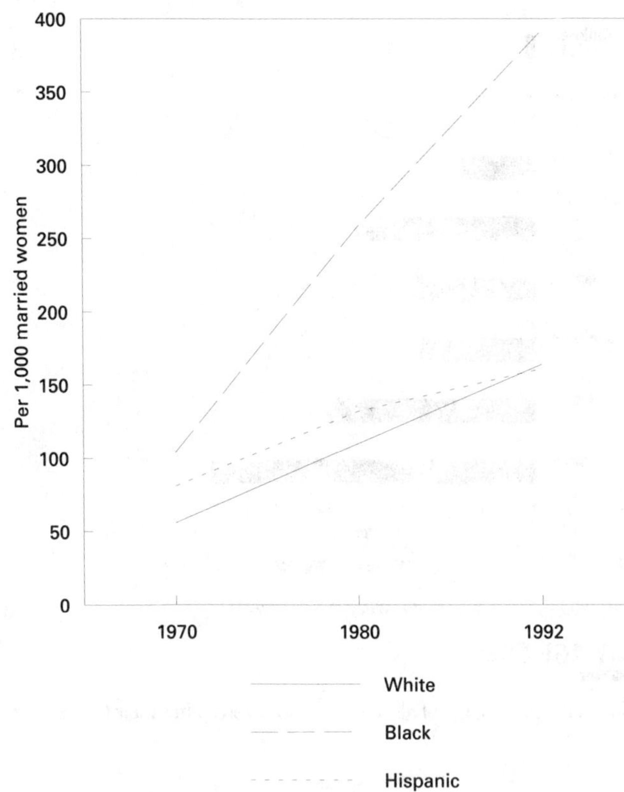

Source: Bureau of the Census

The percentage of marriages that end in divorce in the U.S. is among the highest in the world.

"I've given my memoirs far more thought than any of my marriages. You can't divorce a book."—Gloria Swanson

There were 1,351,000 one-parent family groups maintained by fathers in 1990.

Divorces that occur within the first 3 years of marriage account for 29.8% of all such splits.

WHY COUPLES DIVORCE

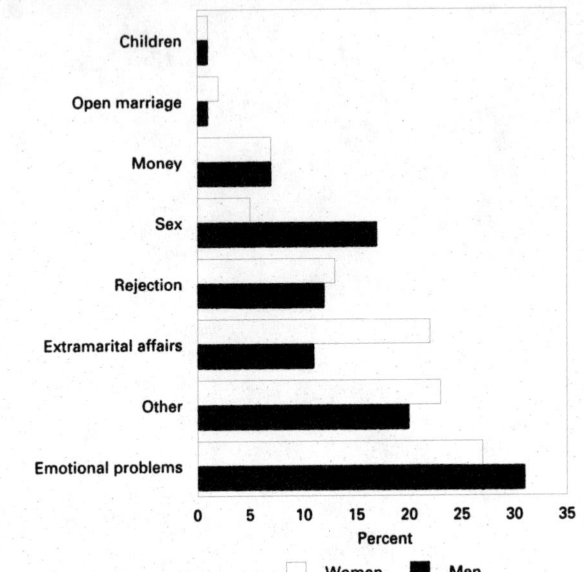

Source: The Janus Report (New York: John Wiley & Sons, 1993)

DIVORCE BY AGE GROUP

This graph shows the percentage of all women who divorce after their first marriage.

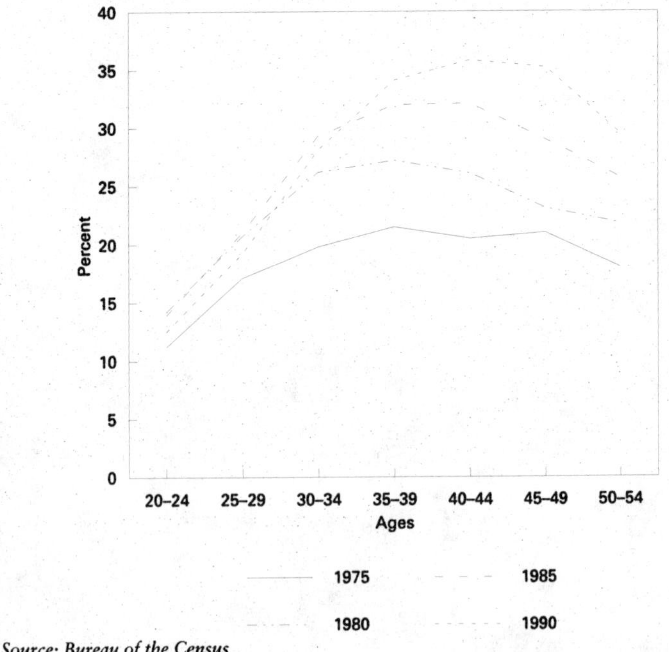

Source: Bureau of the Census

HOW MANY MARRIAGES END IN DIVORCE?

First Marriages

This chart shows the percentage of women whose first marriage ended or may end in divorce, among women 20–54.

Age	% ended in divorce by June 1990	% will end in divorce*
20–24	12.5	37.6
25–29	19.2	39.0
30–34	28.1	40.8
35–39	34.1	42.0
40–44	35.8	39.9
45–49	35.2	36.2
50–54	29.5	30.2

*This projection is based on the experience of women from 1985 to 1990.

Second Marriages

This chart shows the percentage of women whose second marriage ended or may end in divorce, among women 20–65 who have been married two or more times and whose first marriage ended in divorce.

Age	% ended in re-divorce by June 1990	% will end in re-divorce*
20–24	13.1	46.8
25–29	17.8	42.4
30–34	22.7	42.8
35–39	28.5	40.1
40–44	30.6	38.5
45–49	36.4	40.9
50–54	34.5	38.3
55–59	31.1	31.1
60–65	27.0	(X)

(X) Not applicable.
*This projection is based on the experience of women from 1985 to 1990.

Source for above: Bureau of the Census, 1992

3.1 million women between the ages of 15 and 65 have ended their first 2 marriages in divorce as of 1990.

The median duration of divorce before remarriage for all women who ended a first marriage and subsequently remarried is 2.5 years.

"I am a marvelous housekeeper. Every time I leave a man I keep his house."—Zsa Zsa Gabor

A divorcing stepparent in Virginia may sue for visitation and custody of stepchildren.

GROUNDS FOR DIVORCE, STATE BY STATE

	No fault sole ground	*No fault added to traditional*	*Incompatibility*	*Living separate and apart*	*Judicial separation or maintenance*	*Durational requirements*
Alabama		x	x	2 years	x	6 months
Alaska		x	x		x	None
Arizona	x				x	90 days
Arkansas		x		18 months	x	60 days
California	x				x	6 months
Colorado	x				x	90 days
Connecticut		x		18 months	x	1 year
Delaware	x					6 months
District of Columbia	x			1 year	x	6 months
Florida	x					6 months
Georgia		x		1 year		6 months
Hawaii	x			2 years	x	6 months
Idaho		x			x	6 weeks
Illinois		x		2 years	x	90 days
Indiana		x			x	6 months
Iowa	x				x	None
Kansas			x		x	60 days
Kentucky	x				x	180 days
Louisiana		x		6 months	x	None
Maine		x			x	6 months
Maryland		x		2 years	x	1 year
Massachusetts		x			x	None
Michigan	x				x	6 months
Minnesota	x				x	180 days
Mississippi		x				6 months
Missouri	x				x	90 days
Montana	x		x	180 days	x	90 days
Nebraska	x				x	1 year
Nevada			x	1 year	x	6 weeks
New Hampshire		x		2 years		1 year
New Jersey		x		18 months	x	1 year
New Mexico		x	x			6 months
New York		x		1 year	x	1 year
North Carolina				1 year	x	6 months
North Dakota		x			x	6 months
Ohio		x	x	1 year		6 months
Oklahoma		x			x	6 months
Oregon	x				x	6 months
Pennsylvania		x		1 year		6 months
Rhode Island		x		3 years	x	1 year
South Carolina		x		1 year	x	1 year
South Dakota		x			x	None
Tennessee		x		2 years	x	6 months
Texas		x		3 years		6 months
Utah		x			x	90 days

	No fault sole ground	No fault added to traditional	Incompatibility	Living separate and apart	Judicial separation or maintenance	Durational requirements
Vermont		x		6 months		6 months
Virginia		x		1 year	x	6 months
Washington	x				x	1 year
West Virginia		x		1 year	x	1 year
Wisconsin	x			1 year	x	6 months
Wyoming	x				x	60 days

Source: American Bar Association, Family Law Quarterly, vol. 27, no. 4 (1994), reprinted by permission

Fewer than 10% of divorce disputes go to trial.

DIVORCE MEDIATION AND ARBITRATION

Couples who have no significant conflict over money or other important areas may want to try divorce arbitration or mediation. Both methods, low-cost alternatives to regular divorce proceedings, can help divorcing parents and their children avoid some of the emotional trauma of the process.

Divorce arbitration is a procedure in which a neutral third party (an ex-judge or other expert) hears both sides and gives a decision, resolving such issues as child custody and visitation; the decision is either binding or non-binding, depending on what the concerned parties have decided. In mediation, the divorcing couple uses a trained and neutral third party who helps them agree on a voluntary, non-binding divorce settlement. Mediation is used in 38 states and is required in California for custody and visitation issues.

Sources: American Arbitration Association; The Children's Foundation; Judicial Arbitration and Mediation Services

RESOURCES

Academy of Family Mediators
1500 South Highway 100, Suite 355
Golden Valley, MN 55416
(612) 525-8670

American Arbitration Association
140 W. 51st Street
New York, NY 10020
(212) 484-4000

The Children's Foundation
725 15th Street, N.W.
Washington, DC 20005
(202) 347-3300

Judicial Arbitration and Mediation Services
345 Park Avenue, 8th Floor
New York, NY 10154
(212) 751-2700

A California court ordered a reduction in spousal support in 1993 for an ex-husband who resigned from a high-paying job to become a priest.

RECORD-KEEPING AND DIVORCE PREPARATION

If you have decided to get a divorce, you should begin planning and keeping records, even before you see an attorney. The records will help your attorney bargain more effectively and could serve as important evidence if your divorce should actually reach trial. The following checklist may help you with this process:

- Look over all mail and keep a list of the return addresses, especially those of insurance companies, credit card companies, banks, etc.
- Check over any income tax returns before signing them, and make copies of the return, attached schedules, etc.
- Obtain as much information as you can about family finances. Make copies whenever possible of:
  - bank statements
  - brokerage account statements
  - loan documents and statements
  - wills and trust agreements
  - mortgage applications
  - insurance policies

Married women average 744 work hours per year, but in the year after a separation the hours jump to 1,024.

any information about your husband's pension plan
appraisals
medical and dental plans
any financial statements relating to your husband's business

•Inventory safe-deposit boxes, if any, and keep a list of the contents
•Keep records (receipts and copies of statements) of general household and family expenses, including:

rent or mortgage payments
insurance premiums
all bills including utilities
medical and dental care
repairs
costs of transportation, education, and child care
food and clothing
any other expenses involving you and your children

Source: © NOW Legal Defense and Education Fund, reprinted by permission

DIVORCE PREPARATION: DO'S AND DON'TS

•Don't sign any blank forms or sign anything without reading it.
•Don't tie up your assets; you will need to have access to your funds for legal costs and other divorce-related expenses.
•Open an account of your own and put aside as much money as you can. Consider what other financial alternatives (such as loans from family, friends, or your bank) might be necessary to meet living expenses and legal fees.
•Have a complete checkup to make sure you are in good health.
•If you have a car, be sure that it is in good working order.
•Keep your personal papers, including all your financial documentation, in a safe place.
•If necessary, open up a safe-deposit box of your own to store your important papers and valuables, and a post office box to receive personal mail, including communications from your attorney.
•If you do not already have a credit card in your own name, apply for one.
•Stay in the home if you can. However, if your husband is abusing you or your children, contact a local battered-women's shelter and your attorney.
•If you plan to seek custody of your children, maintain close contact with them and continue to provide them with care and nurturance. If you must move out of your house, take the chidren with you if at all possible.
•Don't allow the divorce to run your life. If you have a job, don't give it up; you will need those regular paychecks. Maintain your relationships with friends and family; their companionship will help you keep up your spirits. Take care of your health, and try to stay calm and alert.
•Do not hurry the divorce process, especially if your husband is anxious to resolve it. You may be able to use time to your advantage. Do not be pressured into accepting unfair settlement terms at an early stage in the negotiation.
•If you are having trouble coping, turn to your friends, your family, support groups, therapists, and the entire network of resources that have knowledge and experience, and understanding of what you are going through. You don't have to grapple with it alone.

Source: © NOW Legal Defense and Education Fund, reprinted by permission

DIVORCE AMONG MOTHERS

First Marriages and Divorce among Mothers

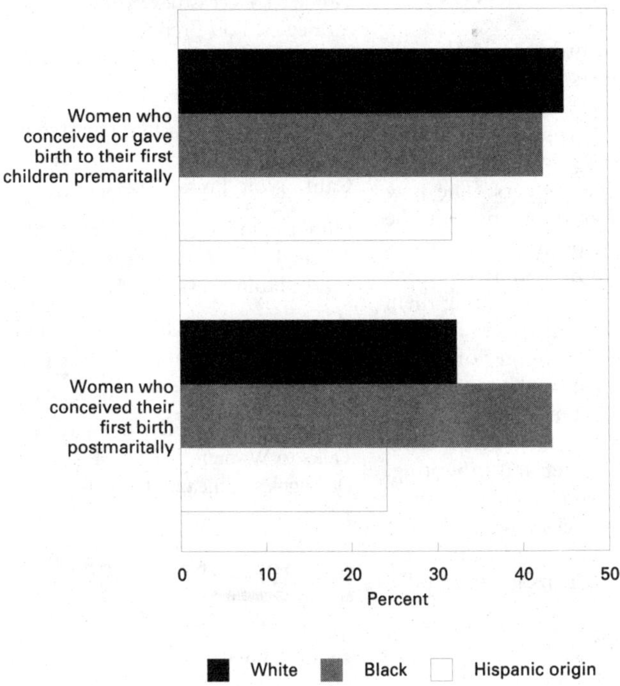

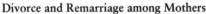

Divorce and Remarriage among Mothers

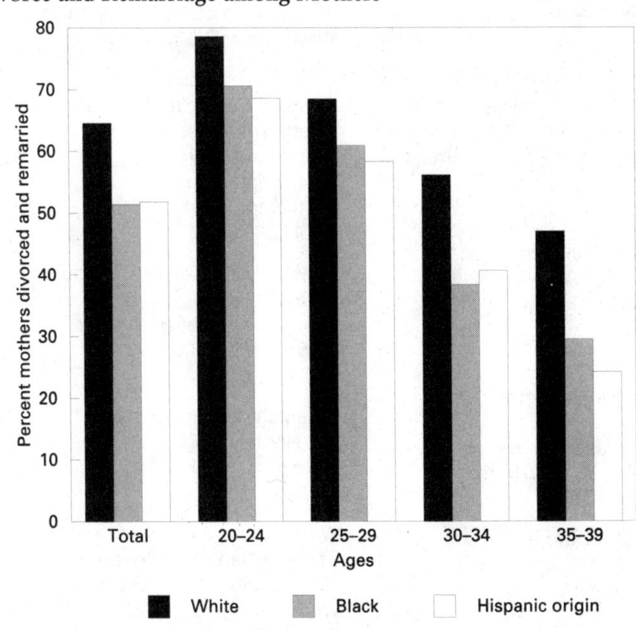

Source for above: Bureau of the Census, 1990

A sexual relationship between lawyer and client "may involve unfair exploitation of the lawyer's ability to represent the client competently," said the American Bar Association in a formal opinion in 1993.

Under Islamic law, a woman who accuses a man of rape must produce four male witnesses. If she can't, she may be jailed for adultery.

STRICT GUIDELINES FOR NEW YORK MATRIMONIAL LAWYERS

In an effort to protect emotionally vulnerable clients against unscrupulous matrimonial lawyers, the New York Court of Appeals has issued strict guidelines governing the conduct of divorce lawyers. The new guidelines, the most extensive in the nation, include prohibiting lawyers from engaging in sexual relations with clients while representing them and prohibiting divorce lawyers from attaching the homes of clients to collect payment without a judge's approval. The guidelines require divorce lawyers to provide their clients, at the outset and in writing, with information regarding their fees and the services covered by the refundable retainer, and to periodically send their clients itemized bills.

Source: The Matrimonial Strategist, reprinted with permission of Leader Publications

LEGAL RESOURCES

GENERAL

For information about attorneys who handle divorce and custody cases, check with your state bar association or the Martindale-Hubbel directory. You can also consult:

The American Academy of Matrimonial Lawyers
150 N. Michigan Avenue, Suite 2040
Chicago, IL 60601
(312) 263-6477

NEWSLETTERS

Fair$hare: The Matrimonial Law Monthly
c/o 225 Kingsland Terrace
South Orange, NJ 07079
(201) 763-6543

Matrimonial Strategist
New York Law Publishing Company
111 Eighth Avenue
New York, NY 10011
(212) 741-8300

BOOKS

Getting Your Share: A Woman's Guide to Successful Divorce Strategies, Lois Brenner (New York: New American Library–Dutton, 1991).

How to Do Your Own Divorce in California, Ed Sherman (Berkeley, Calif.: Nolo Press, 1994).

How to Do Your Own Divorce in Texas, Ed Sherman (Berkeley, Calif.: Nolo Press, 1994).

A New Yorker's Guide to Doing It Yourself, B. Alexandra (Berkeley, Calif.: Nolo Press, 1993).

You're Entitled: A Divorce Lawyer Talks to Women, Sidney M. DeAngeles (Chicago: Contemporary, 1989).

DIVORCE—RESOURCES

GENERAL

Clearinghouse on Pensions and Divorce
Pension Rights Center
918 16th Street, N.W., Suite 704
Washington, DC 20006
(202) 296-3776

National Center for Women and Retirement Research
Long Island University
Southampton Campus
Southampton, NY 11968
(516) 283-4809

NOW Legal Defense and Education Fund
99 Hudson Street, 12th Floor
New York, NY 10013
(212) 925-6635

Parents Without Partners
401 North Michigan Avenue
Chicago, IL 60611
(312) 644-6610

Women Work! The National Network for Women's Employment
1625 K Street, N.W., Suite 300
Washington, DC 20006
(202) 467-6346

SPECIAL INTEREST

American Association of Retired Persons
Social Outreach and Support Section
1909 K Street, N.W.
Washington, DC 20049
(202) 434-2277

Center for Battered Women's Legal Services
105 Chambers Street
New York, NY 10007
(212) 349-6009

Ex-Partners of Servicemen for Equality
P.O. Box 11191
Alexandria, VA 22312
(703) 941-5844

Older Women's League
730 11th Street, N.W.
Washington, DC 20001
(202) 783-6686

DIVORCE—RECOMMENDED READING

Adult Children of Divorce, Edward W. Beal, M.D., and Gloria Hochman (New York: Delacorte, 1991).

Divorce and Separation Legal Resource Kit, NOW Legal Defense and Education Fund (available from NOW Legal Defense and Education Fund, 99 Hudson Street, New York, NY 10013).

Divorced Families: Meeting the Challenge of Divorce and Remarriage, Constance R. Ahrons and Roy H. Rodgers (New York: W. W. Norton, 1989).

A Divorced Woman's Handbook: An Outline for Starting the First Year Alone, Jane Wilkie (New York: William Morrow, 1980).

The Dollars and Sense Guide to Divorce: The Financial Guide for Women, Judith Briles (New York: Ballantine, 1991).

The Encyclopedia of Marriage, Divorce, and Family, Margaret DiCanio (New York: Facts on File, 1989).

It's Not the End of the World, Judy Blume (New York: Dell, 1982).

Our Turn: The Good News About Women and Divorce, Dr. Christopher Hayes, Deborah Anderson, and Melinda Blau (New York: Pocket Books, 1993).

Second Chances: Men, Women, and Children, a Decade After Divorce, Judith S. Wallerstein and Sandra Blakeslee (New York: Ticknor & Fields, 1989; Boston: Houghton Mifflin, 1990).

Vicki Lansky's Divorce Book, Vicki Lansky (New York: New American Library–Dutton, 1991).

Women and Divorce: Turning Your Life Around (Southampton, N.Y.: National Center for Women and Retirement Research, 1993).

Your Pension Rights at Divorce: What Women Need to Know, 2nd ed. (Washington, D.C.: Pension Rights Center, 1994).

Between 1% and 2% of marriages ending each year are annulments. The average length of marriage before annulment is 1.2 years.

Divorced women and the minor children in their households experience a 33% decline in their standard of living after the divorce. Their former husbands experience a 13% rise in their standard of living.

ALIMONY CRITERIA, STATE BY STATE

	Statutory list of factors	Marital fault not considered	Marital fault relevant	Standard of living	Status as custodial parent
Alabama			x		
Alaska	x	x		x	x
Arizona	x	x		x	x
Arkansas		x			
California		x			
Colorado	x	x		x	x
Connecticut	x		x	x	x
Delaware	x	x		x	x
District of Columbia			x		
Florida	x		x	x	
Georgia	x		x	x	
Hawaii	x	x		x	x
Idaho	x		x		
Illinois	x	x		x	x
Indiana		x			x
Iowa	x	x		x	x
Kansas		x			
Kentucky	x	x		x	
Louisiana	x		x		x
Maine			x		
Maryland	x		x	x	
Massachusetts	x		x	x	x
Michigan (N/A)					
Minnesota	x	x		x	x
Mississippi			x		
Missouri	x		x	x	x
Montana	x	x		x	x
Nebraska		x			
Nevada	x	x			
New Hampshire	x		x	x	x
New Jersey		x			
New Mexico		x			
New York	x	x			x
North Carolina		x	x		
North Dakota			x		
Ohio	x	x		x	x
Oklahoma		x			
Oregon	x	x		x	x
Pennsylvania	x		x	x	x
Rhode Island	x		x	x	
South Carolina			x		
South Dakota			x		
Tennessee	x		x	x	x
Texas		x			

	Statutory list of factors	Marital fault not considered	Marital fault relevant	Standard of living	Status as custodial parent
Utah			x		
Vermont	x	x		x	x
Virginia	x		x	x	
Washington	x	x		x	
West Virginia			x		
Wisconsin	x	x			
Wyoming			x		

Source: American Bar Association, Family Law Quarterly, vol. 27, no. 4 (1994), reprinted by permission

A divorcing wife in California may have access to the financial records of her husband's company for ascertaining her alimony and share of community property. The discovery rights of a wife from her spouse's corporation are "at least as great" as those of a shareholder, ruled a state court.

TYPES OF SETTLEMENTS

	Child support only	*Alimony only*	*Child support and alimony*
Total	1,131	264	124
Current Marital Status			
Divorced	620	195	99
Married	506	64	22
Widowed	5	5	3
Race/ethnicity			
White	1,041	243	109
Black	80	11	8
Hispanic origin	46	10	15
Age			
15 to 17 years	—	—	—
18 to 29 years	134	12	11
30 to 39 years	596	50	47
40 years and over	400	202	66
Years of school completed			
Less than 12 years	58	57	4
High school: 4 years	543	85	49
College: 1 to 3 years	265	57	47
4 years or more	265	65	25
Year of Divorce			
1980 and later	920	152	110
1975 to 1979	170	42	12
1970 to 1974	38	26	2
Before 1970	3	45	—
Income in 1989			
Without income	23	7	—
With income	1,108	257	124
$1 to $999 or loss	24	6	4
$1,000 to $1,999	27	11	—
$2,000 to $3,999	62	7	—
$4,000 to $5,999	46	29	—
$6,000 to $7,999	49	21	12
$8,000 to $9,999	46	19	10
$10,000 to $11,999	49	27	2
$12,000 to $14,999	120	17	15

Numbers do not all add to totals because of rounding

Source: Bureau of the Census, 1991

The percentage of women awarded alimony or maintenance payments (14%) is not significantly different from what it was in the 1920s.

PROPERTY DIVISION IN DIVORCE, STATE BY STATE

	Community property	Only marital property divided	Statutory list of factors	Nonmonetary contributions	Economic misconduct considered	Special contribution to education
Alabama		x				
Alaska			x	x	x	x
Arizona	x		x			x
Arkansas		x	x	x		
California	x		x	x	x	x
Colorado		x	x	x	x	
Connecticut		x	x	x	x	x
Delaware			x	x	x	
District of Columbia		x	x	x	x	
Florida		x	x	x	x	x
Georgia		x				
Hawaii			x	x	x	
Idaho	x		x			
Illinois		x	x	x	x	
Indiana		x	x	x	x	
Iowa		x	x	x		x
Kansas			x		x	
Kentucky		x	x	x	x	x
Louisiana	x					
Maine		x	x	x		
Maryland		x	x	x		
Massachusetts			x	x		
Michigan (N/A)						
Minnesota		x	x	x	x	
Mississippi						
Missouri		x	x	x		
Montana			x	x	x	
Nebraska		x		x		
Nevada	x					
New Hampshire			x	x	x	x
New Jersey		x	x	x		x
New Mexico	x					
New York		x	x	x	x	x
North Carolina		x	x	x	x	x
North Dakota				x		
Ohio		x	x	x	x	x
Oklahoma		x				
Oregon				x		
Pennsylvania		x	x	x	x	x
Rhode Island		x	x	x	x	x
South Carolina		x	x		x	x
South Dakota				x	x	
Tennessee		x	x	x	x	x
Texas	x				x	
Utah					x	
Vermont			x	x	x	x
Virginia		x	x	x		x

	Community property	Only marital property divided	Statutory list of factors	Nonmonetary contributions	Economic misconduct considered	Special contribution to education
Washington	x		x			
West Virginia		x	x	x	x	x
Wisconsin	x		x	x		x
Wyoming			x			

Source: American Bar Association, Family Law Quarterly, vol. 27, no. 4 (1994), reprinted by permission

The number of midlife divorced women tripled between 1982 and 1992, and their average income dropped to less than $11,000 one year after divorce.

PROPERTY SETTLEMENTS IN DIVORCE

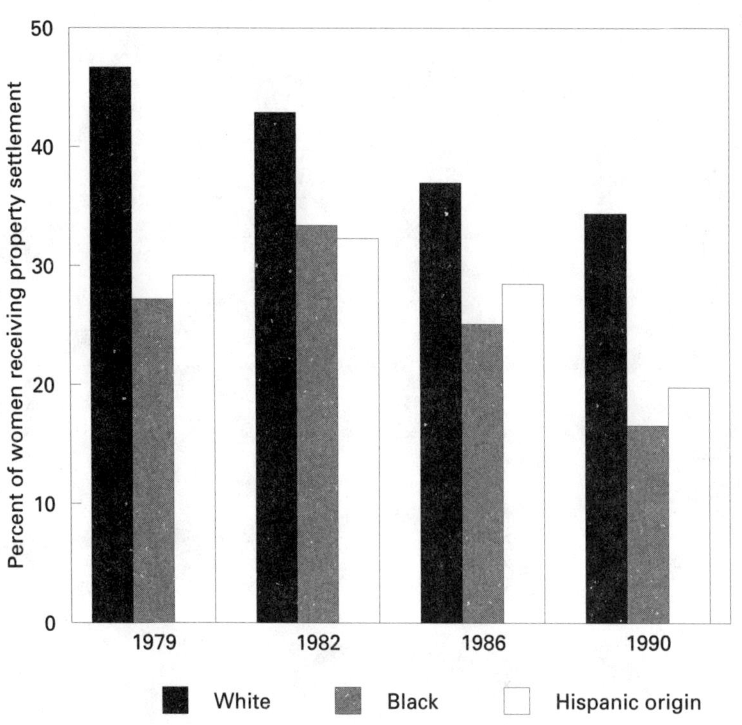

Source: Bureau of the Census, 1991

Under traditional English law, at marriage a woman became femme covert, or hidden within the male. In most places this meant that a husband was entitled to legal possession of everything his wife owned.

"Divorce is the one human tragedy that reduces everything to cash."
—Rita Mae Brown

CUSTODY CRITERIA, STATE BY STATE

	Statutory guidelines	Children's wishes	Joint custody laws	Cooperative parent	Domestic violence	Health	Attorney or guardian ad litem for child
Alabama	x		x				
Alaska	x	x	x	x	x	x	x
Arizona	x	x	x	x	x	x	x
Arkansas							
California	x	x	x		x		x
Colorado	x	x	x	x	x	x	x
Connecticut		x	x				x
Delaware	x	x				x	x
District of Columbia	x	x			x	x	x
Florida	x	x	x		x		x
Georgia	x	x	x				x
Hawaii	x	x			x		x
Idaho	x	x	x		x	x	
Illinois	x	x	x	x	x	x	x
Indiana	x	x	x				x
Iowa	x	x	x	x	x	x	x
Kansas	x	x	x	x	x	x	
Kentucky	x	x	x		x		x
Louisiana	x	x	x		x		
Maine	x	x			x		x
Maryland			x		x		x
Massachusetts			x		x		x
Michigan	x	x	x	x	x		x
Minnesota	x	x	x		x		x
Mississippi	x		x				
Missouri	x	x	x		x		x
Montana	x	x	x		x		x
Nebraska	x	x	x			x	x
Nevada	x	x	x		x		x
New Hampshire	x	x	x		x		x
New Jersey	x	x	x	x	x	x	x
New Mexico	x	x	x	x	x	x	x
New York		x	x				x
North Carolina		x	x				
North Dakota	x	x			x	x	x
Ohio	x	x	x		x	x	x
Oklahoma	x	x	x		x		
Oregon	x		x		x		x
Pennsylvania			x	x	x		x
Rhode Island			x		x		x
South Carolina		x	x				
South Dakota		x	x				x

	Statutory guidelines	Children's wishes	Joint custody laws	Cooperative parent	Domestic violence	Health	Attorney or guardian ad litem for child
Tennessee		x	x				
Texas		x	x		x	x	x
Utah	x	x	x				x
Vermont	x		x		x		x
Virginia	x		x			x	x
Washington	x	x			x	x	x
West Virginia		x	x		x		
Wisconsin	x	x	x	x	x	x	
Wyoming		x			x	x	

Source: American Bar Association, Family Law Quarterly, vol. 27, no. 4 (1994), reprinted by permission

A woman's homosexual activity outside her marriage constitutes adultery, ruled a South Carolina Court in barring an award of alimony.

GAY AND LESBIAN CHILD-CUSTODY AND VISITATION

•Conflict over child custody and visitation brings more lesbians and gay men into courtrooms in this nation than any other issue. Decisions on custody and visitation are made on a state-by-state, judge-by-judge basis.

•Eleven states have laws that say sexual orientation is irrelevant in custody disputes.

•Courts in eleven other states have based rulings on the presumption that lesbians and gay men are unfit for custody of their children solely on the basis of sexual orientation.

•Trial courts in Nevada, Virginia, and Kentucky have ruled that homosexuality in and of itself renders a parent unfit to have custody of her or his child.

•In appellate courts in California, Indiana, Massachusetts, and Arkansas, homosexuality is not grounds for depriving parents custody of their children.

•Studies show that there is no correlation between a parent's sexual orientation and that of the child. The incidence of same-sex orientation among children of homosexuals occurs as frequently and in the same proportion as in the general population.

Source: National Gay and Lesbian Task Force

RESOURCES

Custody Action for Lesbian Mothers
P.O. Box 281
Narberth, PA 19072
(215) 667-7508

National Center for Lesbian Rights
870 Market Street, Suite 570
San Francisco, CA 94102
(415) 392-6257

Fast Facts: Joint Custody

•In joint-custody situations, only 6 to 7% of parents are delinquent in making child-support payments, compared with 45 to 75% in sole custody cases.

•In a survey of 200 families, 85 to 90% of joint custody families described the arrangement as "highly satisfactory."

•Joint custody can make it possible for mothers to work.

•Sixty-two percent of parents decided on joint custody in between the time they filed for divorce and their final appearance in court; 24% agreed to joint custody with the help of their attorney; 5.8% accepted joint custody arrangements that were facilitated through court mediation.

•Sixty percent of joint custodians contribute "extras" (camp, music lessons, allowances, car payments and repairs, extra medical) compared to 20% in sole custody situations.

•Child-snatching by non-custodian parents is highly prevalent in sole-custody situations but is virtually nonexistent under joint custody.

Source: The Joint Custody Association

"No longer is the female destined solely for the home and the rearing of family and only the male for the marketplace and the world of ideas."
—Majority opinion in a 6–3 Supreme Court ruling that laws barring alimony for men are unconstitutional

90.2% of fathers with joint custody pay the child support they owe, compared to 79.1% with visitation privileges and 44.5% without visitation or joint custody.

"I couldn't believe the ridicule and bias I took for suggesting that it is in the best interest of our children to be raised in an intact family."
—Dan Quayle, on the *Murphy Brown* backlash

CHILD CUSTODY & SUPPORT—RESOURCES

SUPPORT

The Association for Children for Enforcement of Support
723 Phillips Avenue, Suite J
Toledo, OH 43612
(800) 537-7072

Children of Divorce and Separation
P.O. Box A
Glenside, PA 19038
(800) 366-8786

The Children's Foundation
725 15th Street, N.W., Suite 505
Washington, DC 20005
(202) 347-3300

Children's Rights Council
220 I Street, N.E.
Washington, DC 20002
(202) 547-6227

Committee for Mother and Child Rights
210 Ole Orchard Drive
Clear Brook, VA 22624
(703) 722-3652

Find Dad
(800) 729-6667
This is a private collection agency that will retain a percentage of any past due child support that they collect on your behalf. If they fail to collect, nothing is owed to them.

Grandparents United for Children's Rights
137 Larkin Street
Madison, WI 53705
(608) 238-8751

Mothers Without Custody
P.O. Box 27418
Houston, TX 77227
(800) 457-6962

National Center on Women and Family Law
799 Broadway, Room 402
New York, NY 10003
(212) 674-8200

CUSTODY

Child Custody Evaluation Services of Philadelphia
P.O. Box 202
Glenside, PA 19038
(215) 576-0177

Custody Action for Lesbian Mothers
P.O. Box 281
Narberth, PA 19072
(215) 667-7508

The Joint Custody Association
10606 Wilkins Avenue
Los Angeles, CA 90024
(213) 475-5352

National Gay and Lesbian Task Force
1734 14th Street, N.W.
Washington, DC 20009
(202) 332-6483

POVERTY IN THE SINGLE-PARENT FAMILY

For children, the best anti-poverty policy is a two-parent family. The poverty rate in such families is low (7.8%) compared with children in families headed by mothers (32%), and the duration of poverty is generally short. This is because a two-parent family potentially has two wage earners and the capacity to minimize child-care costs by staggering work hours. In addition, the presence of a male worker makes it more likely that one of the parents will have a job that pays substantially more than minimum wage and provides health insurance.

Source: The Association for Children for Enforcement of Support

CUSTODY—RECOMMENDED READING

Child Custody: A Complete Guide for Concerned Mothers, M. Takas (New York: Harper & Row, 1987).

Child Custody Legal Resource Kit, NOW Legal Defense and Education Fund (available from NOW Legal Defense and Education Fund, 99 Hudson Street, New York, NY 10013).

Child Custody Practice and Procedure, Linda D. Elrod (Deerfield, Ill.: Clark Boardman Callaghan, 1993).

Child Support Legal Resource Kit, NOW Legal Defense and Education Fund (available from NOW Legal Defense and Education Fund, 99 Hudson Street, New York, NY 10013).

Humanizing Child Custody Disputes: The Family's Team, Gordon B. Plumb and Mary E. Lindley (Springfield, Ill.: Charles C. Thomas, 1990).

Mothers Without Custody, Geoffrey L. Greif and Mary S. Pabst (Lexington, Mass.: Lexington Books, 1988).

Parent v. Parent: How You and Your Child Can Survive the Custody Battle, Stephen P. Herman (New York: Pantheon, 1990).

Sharing the Children: How to Resolve Custody Problems and Get on with Your Life, Robert E. Adler (New York: Farrar, Straus & Giroux, 1988).

Understanding Child Custody, Susan N. Terkel (New York: Franklin Watts, 1991).

CONDITIONS AMONG SINGLE-PARENT FAMILIES

A 1991 study focusing on child-support enforcement showed that during the first year of the breakup:
- 55% of mothers reported that their children missed regular health checkups
- 36% reported that their children did not get medical care when they became ill
- 32% reported that their children went hungry
- 37% reported that their children lacked appropriate clothing
- 26% reported having to leave their children unsupervised while they went to work

In the first year after a father failed to support his children:
- 48% moved in with friends or family to avoid homelessness
- 10% became homeless

When earnings proved insufficient:
- 87% of interviewees borrowed from family or friends
- 47% used a food bank
- 44% sought help from their church
- 26% sought help from a local charity

A majority of families were eventually forced to apply for government assistance, 91% within the first year after the father left. Of these:
- 52% received food stamps
- 41% received Medicaid
- 40% received funds from the Aid for Families with Dependent Children program

Source: The Association for Children for Enforcement of Support

Mia Farrow received sole custody of the children she parented with Woody Allen based on a finding of his "self-absorption," "lack of judgment," and "serious parental inadequacies."

Fathers in the U.S. owe mothers $24 billion in unpaid child support.

Millions of mothers never get a court order requiring child support, and even among those who do, only about half get the full amount they are entitled to.

CHILD SUPPORT GUIDELINES, STATE BY STATE

	Income share	*Percent of income*	*Extraordinary medical formula*	*Child care formula*	*Post-majority support*
Alabama	x				x
Alaska		x			
Arizona	x				
Arkansas		x			
California	x		x	x	
Colorado	x		x	x	x
Connecticut	x				
Delaware			x	x	
District of Columbia (N/A)					
Florida	x				
Georgia		x			
Hawaii					x
Idaho	x		x	x	
Illinois		x			x
Indiana	x		x	x	x
Iowa	x		x	x	
Kansas	x		x	x	
Kentucky	x				
Louisiana	x		x	x	
Maine	x		x	x	
Maryland	x		x	x	
Massachusetts (N/A)					
Michigan	x		x	x	
Minnesota		x			
Mississippi		x			
Missouri	x				x
Montana			x	x	
Nebraska	x				
Nevada		x	x	x	
New Hampshire		x			
New Jersey	x		x	x	
New Mexico	x		x	x	
New York		x	x	x	
North Carolina	x		x	x	
North Dakota		x			
Ohio	x				
Oklahoma	x				
Oregon	x		x	x	
Pennsylvania	x				
Rhode Island	x				
South Carolina	x				x
South Dakota	x				
Tennessee		x			x
Texas		x			
Utah	x		x	x	
Vermont	x		x	x	
Virginia	x		x	x	
Washington	x		x	x	x

	Income share	Percent of income	Extraordinary medical formula	Child care formula	Post-majority support
West Virginia			x	x	
Wisconsin		x			
Wyoming	x				

Source: American Bar Association, Family Law Quarterly, vol. 27, no. 4 (1994), reprinted with permission

WOMEN AWARDED CHILD SUPPORT

This chart breaks down how much money women receive from child support in relation to their total money incomes; the right-hand columns show child support received by women with incomes below the poverty line.

	ALL WOMEN		WOMEN BELOW POVERTY LINE	
	Money income	*Child support income*	*Money income*	*Child support income*
Average	$16,171	$2,995	$5,047	$1,889
Current marital status				
Married	14,469	2,931	(N/A)*	(N/A)*
Divorced	19,456	3,322	5,581	2,112
Separated	14,891	3,060	4,917	1,717
Widowed	(NA)*	(N/A)*	(N/A)*	(N/A)*
Never married	9,495	1,888	4,543	1,553
Race/ ethnicity				
White	16,632	3,132	5,010	1,972
Black	13,898	2,263	5,174	1,674
Hispanic origin	14,758	2,965	4,958	1,824
Number of own children present from absent father				
One	15,799	2,425	4,450	1,697
Two	17,465	3,527	5,336	2,046
Three	14,863	4,509	5,747	2,252
Four or more	12,217	3,226	(N/A)	(N/A)
Age				
18 to 29	9,938	1,961	4,589	1,515
30 to 39	17,006	3,032	5,962	2,167
40 and over	20,668	3,903	4,173	2,316

*Base is too small a sample size
Data from 1989
Source: Bureau of the Census

Experts say that unpaid child support is one of the main reasons that more than one in five American children live in poverty.

Any person seeking a renewal of a license from a Illinois licensing agency must now certify that he or she is not more than thirty days delinquent in complying with a child support order.

Only one in four U.S. families today is a nuclear family, with two married parents and one or more children.

In Sri Lanka, more than half of the plantation workers are women, and on average they earn more money than the men. However, 70% of the women workers' wages are paid to their husbands.

REASONS FOR NON-AWARD OF CHILD SUPPORT

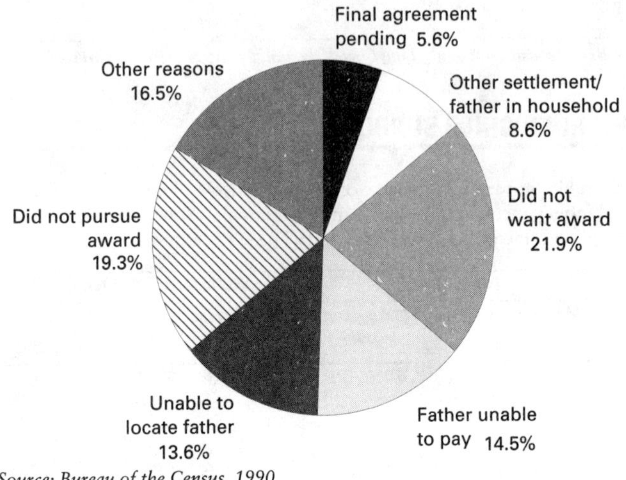

Source: Bureau of the Census, 1990

FAILURE TO PAY CHILD SUPPORT

•Fifty-eight percent of the ten million women with children under age 21 were awarded support in 1989. Still, only half received the full amount owed to them and a quarter received nothing.
•Of the 12.8 million cases handled by the child support enforcement system, only 18% were collected on in 1990.
•The average amount in overdue child support payments as of 1992 stood at $12,000 per parent. The total uncollected child support amounted to nearly $27 billion.
•The average annual child support payment in 1989 was $2,995.
•Approximately 75% of all parents who are overdue in child support payments can afford to make the payments.

Source: Find Dad

Fast Fact: Child-Support Orders

To collect child support you must first have a court order based on a divorce, dissolution, establishment of paternity, legal separation, or other types of order. All states have a child support enforcement agency that is federally funded and *must* help you collect support if your children are under 18, or if you applied for help before the child turned 18, for a maximum fee of $25.

Source: The Association for Children for Enforcement of Support

GERALDINE JENSEN—FEDERALIZING CHILD SUPPORT

Geraldine Jensen is the founder and president of the Association for Children for Enforcement of Support (ACES), the nation's largest grass-roots child-support advocacy group. This nonprofit organization, founded in 1984, lobbies for changes in child-support regulations, including the federalization of support enforcement that Jensen advocates in this essay.

A mother who once had to choose between buying Nike and Reebok now has to make a choice between feeding her children or keeping the house warm in the winter. Non-payment of child support, the leading cause of childhood poverty, has reached epidemic proportions in the United States. Adequate and regular child-support payments will not solve all of the problems of family break-up, but it will prevent our children from living in poverty.

Since 1975, state governments have been responsible for establishing paternity, establishing child support orders, and for enforcing orders. Unfortunately, the state child-support system is failing the children. Forty-five percent of the children who need child-support orders established do not have them. Only 19.3% of the families who have turned to government agencies receive payments.

For children born in 1975, the year in which the state child-support enforcement agencies were created by Congress, little happened to help collect support. When these children were nine years old, Congress enacted the 1984 Child Support Amendments. This law gave the states one more chance to improve by promising wage withholding if a person fell a month behind in payments, and allowed bonds to be posted to ensure payments and liens to be placed on property. However, the laws were not enforced by the state government child-support agencies.

When the children were 13 years old, Congress acted again to give the states yet another chance and passed the 1988 Family Support Act to strengthen the existing child-support laws. The provisions of this law included income withholding at the time of divorce or when paternity is established, along with child-support guidelines. In 1993, state officials and members of Congress asked for one last chance for the states to prove that they can do it. The children born in 1975 were 18 years old; their "chance" was gone. Millions of children who have not received child support have spent their childhood living in poverty because the current state government system has failed to follow these families and failed to enforce child support. Mothers in single-parent families, spending most of their time and energy working two or more part-time jobs just to make ends meet, are also forced to spend precious time fighting these many state bureaucracies.

We have lost a whole generation to poverty because of a "broken system"—one that is different in each state, and one in which judges review cases one at a time in a slow, antiquated process designed for the fifteenth century, when divorce or having children outside marriage was unusual.

The unusual has become the usual. Today, most children will spend part of their lives in single-parent households and will need child-support payments to be protected from poverty. It is time to federalize the child-support enforcement system. We must make children as important as taxes by using the IRS system of payroll tax collection to collect child support. We must have a modern, efficient, national computer system to locate absent parents and to act as a national child-support registry. We must have a child-support assurance program, so that the children who do not have both parents living in their home are protected from poverty the same way children whose parents die are protected under Social Security. This is the least we should do for our children. Anything less is just too little, too late.

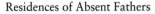

A California program uses computers to track down deadbeat parents and collect child support. It has collected over $11 million from in-state parents, and plans to go nationwide, where officials expect to collect up to $103 million for California clients alone.

ABSENT FATHERS

Absent fathers who lived in the same state as their children and who were supposed to pay child support had a payment rate in 1989 of 81.1%, while fathers who resided in a different state had a rate of 65.6%. Those fathers whose residence was overseas or unknown had a payment rate of 46.6%.

Residences of Absent Fathers

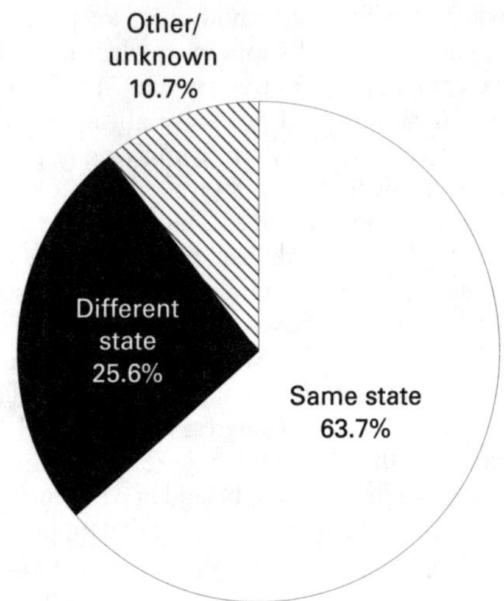

Source: Bureau of the Census, 1990

ENFORCING CHILD-SUPPORT ORDERS

It is not uncommon for an absent father to relocate to another town, state, or even country and fail to notify the custodial parent or authorities of his new address.

•To obtain or enforce an order for child support, you must know where the absent father lives or works. Your local office of child support enforcement can help you find the address.

•Establish a good working relationship with your case worker or attorney. Provide them with any information you think may be helpful to your case, including such background data about the missing father as: full name, nicknames, place and date of birth, prior addresses, employment history, schools attended, military experience, criminal record, and hobbies.

•The custodial mother can conduct an independent search using telephone and other directories, labor unions, high school or college alumni placement offices, former employers, professional associations, and even private detectives. The post office has a change-of-address notification service and an address correction service that can sometimes provide a current residential address.

•The Veterans Administration can access files listing the addresses of individuals who receive compensation, pensions, and education benefits.

•The Department of Defense and the National Personnel Record Center retain current military and civilian duty station addresses for over five million individuals.

•The Selective Service System has draft registration records, including current address information, for all males who meet the age eligibility requirements. (Names and addresses of those men reaching age 26 are dropped from the active files).
•Next to a missing father's name, his social security number is the most important element needed to locate him. By knowing his social security number, an address search can be made through an agency's records using the Federal or State Parent Locator Service (FPLS or SPLS).
•Custodial parents can look for such documents as old insurance policies, state and federal income tax returns, medical records, loan applications, and bank statements to find an absent parent's social security number.
• An authorized person can request the Social Security Administration (SSA) to conduct a search of its own records for the social security number. The SSA can quickly pick up the number 20% of the time. The remaining 80% of requests must be processed by hand, and while that can take up to two months, numbers are found for 50% of these cases.
• The FPLS can now access Internal Revenue Service records containing joint income tax returns to locate the absent parent's social security number. (The joint return must have been filed within the past three years, and no subsequent return can have been filed with another spouse.)

Source: The Children's Foundation Clearinghouse

DEADBEATS ON TV

Custodial parents in Contra Costa County, California, have banded together to produce a public access television show on deadbeat parents. The show features pictures of the negligent parents (the great majority of them fathers), their height, weight, race, last known occupation, last known locale, and number of minor children. If viewers know of deadbeat parents hiding assets, they are asked to turn them in. Delinquent parents are notified in advance of the show, and in some cases have negotiated payment schedules to avoid being mentioned on air.

GOVERNMENT ASSISTANCE—CHILD SUPPORT ENFORCEMENT

Of the ten million women with children from absent fathers in 1991, 2.9 million had at some time contacted a government agency for assistance in obtaining child support. Approximately one million women received aid in locating the father, establishing paternity, or establishing support obligations; a similar number received assistance in enforcing the support order or obtaining collection.

Source: Bureau of the Census

REGIONAL BRANCHES OF THE OFFICE OF CHILD SUPPORT ENFORCEMENT
For assistance in locating an absent father, the following regional and state offices may be of assistance.

Region I: Connecticut, Maine, Massachusetts, New Hampshire, Rhode Island, Vermont

Regional Office
Office of Child Support Enforcement/DHHS,
JFK Federal Building, Room 2303
Boston, MA 02203

State agencies nationwide collected money in only 18.7% of their child-support cases in 1992.

Clyde Hunt of Mount Clemens, Michigan, was charged in June 1994 with attempted murder when he allegedly laced his infant son's milk with bug poison because he didn't want to pay child support.

Connecticut
Bureau of Child Support Enforcement
Department of Human Resources
1049 Asylum Avenue
Hartford, CT 06105
(203) 566-3053

Maine
Division of Support Enforcement and Recovery
Bureau of Income Maintenance
Department of Human Services
State House, Station 11
Augusta, ME 04333
(207) 289-2886

Massachusetts
Child Support Enforcement Unit
Department of Revenue
141 Portland Street
Cambridge, MA 02139
(617) 727-4200

New Hampshire
Office of Child Support Enforcement Services
Division of Human Services
Health and Human Services Building
6 Hazen Drive
Concord, NH 03301
(603) 271-4427

Rhode Island
Bureau of Family Support
Department of Human Services
77 Dorrance Street
Providence, RI 02903
(401) 277-2847

Vermont
Office of Child Support Services
103 South Main Street
Waterbury, VT 05676
(802) 241-2319

Region II: New Jersey, New York, Puerto Rico, Virgin Islands

Regional Office
Office of Child Support Enforcement
Federal Building, Room 4048
26 Federal Plaza
New York, NY 10278
(212) 264-2890

New Jersey
Department of Human Services
Bureau of Child Support and Paternity Programs
CN 716
Trenton, NJ 08625
(609) 588-2361

New York
Office of Child Support Enforcement
New York State Department of Social Services
P.O. Box 14, 1 Commerce Plaza
Albany, NY 12260
(518) 474-9081

Puerto Rico
Child Support Enforcement Program
Department of Social Services
Box 3349
San Juan, PR 00902
(809) 722-4731

Virgin Islands
Paternity and Child Support Division
Department of Justice
GER Building, 2nd Floor
48B-50C Krondprans Gade
St. Thomas, VI 00802
(809) 774-5666

Region III: Delaware, District of Columbia, Maryland, Pennsylvania, Virginia, West Virginia

Regional Office
Office of Child Support Enforcement
P.O. Box 8436
3535 Market Street, Room 4119 MS/15
Philadelphia, PA 19101
(215) 596-1396

Delaware
Division of Child Support Enforcement
Department of Health and Social Services
P.O. Box 904
New Castle, DE 19720
(302) 421-8357

District of Columbia
Bureau of Paternity and Child Support Enforcement
Department of Human Services
425 I Street, N.W., 3rd Floor, Suite 3013
Washington, DC 20001
(202) 724-5610

Maryland
Child Support Enforcement Administration
Department of Human Resources
311 West Saratoga Street
Baltimore, MD 21201
(301) 333-3981

Pennsylvania
Bureau of Child Support Enforcement
Department of Public Welfare
P.O. Box 8018
Harrisburg, PA 17105
(717) 787-3672

Virginia
Division of Support Enforcement Program
Department of Social Services
8007 Discovery Drive
Richmond, VA 23229
(804) 662-7108

West Virginia
Child Advocate Office
Department of Human Services
1900 Washington Street East
Charleston, WV 25305
(304) 348-3780

Region IV: Alabama, Florida, Georgia, Kentucky, Mississippi, North Carolina, South Carolina, Tennessee

Regional Office
Office of Child Support Enforcement
101 Marietta Tower, Suite 821
Atlanta, GA 30323
(404) 331-5733

Alabama
Division of Child Support
Department of Human Resources
50 Ripley Street
Montgomery, AL 36130
(205) 242-9300

Florida
Office of Child Support Enforcement
Department of Health and Rehabilitative Services
1317 Winewood Boulevard, Building 3
Tallahassee, FL 32399
(904) 488-9900

Georgia
Office of Child Support Recovery
Department of Human Resources
878 Peachtree Street, N.E., Room 529
Atlanta, GA 30309
(404) 894-5087

Kentucky
Division of Child Support Enforcement
Cabinet for Human Resources
275 E. Main Street, 6th Floor East
Frankfort, KY 40621
(502) 564-2285

Mississippi
Child Support Division
Department of Human Services
P.O. Box 352
507 East Capital Street
Jackson, MS 39205
(601) 354-6844

North Carolina
Child Support Enforcement Section
Division of Social Services
Department of Human Resources
100 East Six Forks Road
Raleigh, NC 27603
(919) 571-4120

South Carolina
Child Support Enforcement Division
Department of Social Services
P.O. Box 1469
Columbia, SC 29202
(803) 737-5870

Tennessee
Child Support Services
Department of Human Services
400 Deadrick Street
Citizens Plaza Building, 12th Floor
Nashville, TN 37219
(615) 741-1820

Region V: Illinois, Indiana, Michigan, Minnesota, Ohio, Wisconsin

Regional Office
Office of Child Support Enforcement
105 W. Adams Street, 20th Floor
Chicago, IL 60603
(312) 353-4237

Illinois
Division of Child Support Enforcement
Department of Public Aid
201 South Grand Avenue East
Springfield, IL 62762
(217) 524-4602

Indiana
Child Support Enforcement Division
142 W. Washington Street, Room W-360
Indianapolis, IN 46204
(317) 232-4894

7.3 million children lived with stepfamilies in 1990.

Stepchildren make up 16% of the children in married-couple families.

30% of divorced adults cite physical abuse as the reason for their divorce.

Michigan
Office of Child Support
Department of Social Services
P.O. Box 30037
Lansing, MI 48909
(517) 373-7570

Minnesota
Office of Child Support Enforcement
Department of Human Services
444 Lafayette Road, 4th Floor
St. Paul, MN 55155
(612) 296-2499

Ohio
Office of Child Support
Department of Human Services
State Office Tower, 27th Floor
30 E. Broad Street
Columbus, OH 43266
(614) 752-6561

Wisconsin
Division of Economic Support
Bureau of Child Support
1 W. Wilson Street, Room 382
P.O. Box 7935
Madison, WI 53707
(608) 266-1175

Region VI: Arkansas, Louisiana, New Mexico, Oklahoma, Texas

Regional Office
Office of Child Support Enforcement
1200 Main Tower Building, Suite 1700
Dallas, TX 75202
(214) 767-9648

Arkansas
Division of Child Support Enforcement
Arkansas Social Services
P.O. Box 3358
Little Rock, AR 72203
(501) 682-8417

Louisiana
Support Enforcement Services Program
Office of Eligibility Determination
Department of Social Services
P.O. Box 94065
Baton Rouge, LA 70804
(504) 342-4780

New Mexico
Child Support Enforcement Division
Department of Human Services
P.O. Box 25109, PERA Building, Room 530
Santa Fe, NM 87504
(505) 827-7200

Oklahoma
Child Support Enforcement Unit
Department of Human Services
P.O. Box 53552
Oklahoma City, OK 73125
(405) 424-5871 x2874

Texas
Child Support Enforcement Division
Attorney General's Office
P.O. Box 12017
Austin, TX 78711
(512) 463-2181

Region VII: Iowa, Kansas, Missouri, Nebraska

Regional Office
Office of Child Support Enforcement
Federal Building, Room 515
Kansas City, MO 64106
(816) 426-5159

Iowa
Child Support Recovery
Iowa Department of Human Services
Hoover Building, 5th Floor
Des Moines, IA 50319
(515) 281-5580

Kansas
Child Support Enforcement Program
Department of Social and Rehabilitation Services
Biddle Building
300 S.W. Oakley Street
Topeka, KA 66606
(913) 296-3237

Missouri
Division of Child Support Enforcement
Department of Social Services
P.O. Box 1527
Jefferson City, MO 65102
(314) 751-4301

Nebraska
Child Support Enforcement Office
Department of Social Services
P.O. Box 95026
Lincoln, NE 68509
(402) 471-9390

Region VIII: Colorado, Montana, North Dakota, South Dakota, Utah, Wyoming

Regional Office
Office of Child Support Enforcement
Federal Office Building
1961 Stout Street, Room 1185
Denver, CO 80294
(303) 844-5646

Colorado
Division of Child Support Enforcement
Department of Social Services
1575 Sherman Street
Denver, CO 80203
(303) 866-5994

Montana
Child Support Enforcement Division
Department of Social and Rehabilitation Services
P.O. Box 5955
Helena, MT 59604
(406) 444-4614

North Dakota
Child Support Enforcement Agency
Department of Human Services
P.O. Box 7190
Bismarck, ND 58507
(701) 224-3582

South Dakota
Office of Child Support Enforcement
Department of Social Services
700 Governors Drive
Pierre, SD 57501
(605) 773-3641

Utah
Office of Recovery Services
Department of Social Services
120 N. 200 West, 4th Floor
Salt Lake City, UT 84145
(801) 538-4401

Wyoming
Child Support Enforcement Section
Division of Public Assistance and Social Services
Department of Family Services
Hathaway Building
Cheyenne, WY 82002
(307) 777-6948

Region IX: Arizona, California, Hawaii, Nevada, Guam,

Regional Office
Office of Child Support Enforcement
50 United Nations Plaza
Mail Stop 351
San Francisco, CA 94102
(415) 556-4415

Arizona
Child Support Enforcement Administration
Department of Economic Security
222 W. Encanto Boulevard
P.O. Box 6123—Site Code 776C
Phoenix, AZ 85005
(602) 252-0236

California
Child Support Program Branch
Department of Social Services
744 P Street, Mail Stop 9–010
Sacramento, CA 95814
(916) 654-1556

Hawaii
Child Support Enforcement Agency
Department of the Attorney General
P.O. Box 1860
Honolulu, HI 96805
(808) 587-3698

Nevada
Child Support Enforcement Program
Nevada State Welfare Division
2527 North Carson Street, Capital Complex
Carson City, NV 89710
(702) 885-4082

Guam
Office of the Attorney General
Child Support Enforcement Unit
Pacific News Building, Suite 701
194 Hernan Cortez Avenue, 2nd Floor
Agana, Guam 96910
(671) 475-3360

Region X: Alaska, Idaho, Oregon, Washington

Regional Office
Office of Child Support Enforcement
2201 Sixth Avenue, M/S RX–70
Seattle, WA 98121
(206) 442-2775

People who say that their marriages are distressed are 50 times more likely to be depressed than people who report themselves happily married.

California developed the first "no-fault" divorce law in 1969.

Alaska
Child Support Enforcement Division
Department of Revenue
550 West 7th Avenue, Suite 310
Anchorage, AK 99501
(907) 263-6270

Idaho
Bureau of Child Support Enforcement
Department of Health and Welfare
Statehouse Mail, 5th floor
Boise, ID 83720
(208) 334-5711

Oregon
Recovery Services Section
Adult and Family Services Division
Department of Human Resources
P.O. Box 14506
Salem, OR 97310
(503) 378-5439

Washington
Revenue Division
Department of Social and Health Services
P.O. Box 9162
Olympia, WA 98504
(206) 586-3520

Source: The Children's Foundation Clearinghouse

RETIREMENT YEARS
RETIREMENT YEARS
RETIREMENT YEARS

RETIREMENT YEARS

RETIREMENT YEARS
RETIREMENT YEARS
RETIREMENT YEARS
RETIREMENT YEARS
RETIREMENT YEARS
RETIREMENT YEARS
RETIREMENT YEARS
RETIREMENT YEARS
RETIREMENT YEARS
RETIREMENT YEARS
RETIREMENT YEARS
RETIREMENT YEARS
RETIREMENT YEARS
RETIREMENT YEARS
RETIREMENT YEARS
RETIREMENT YEARS

INCOMES OF AGING WOMEN

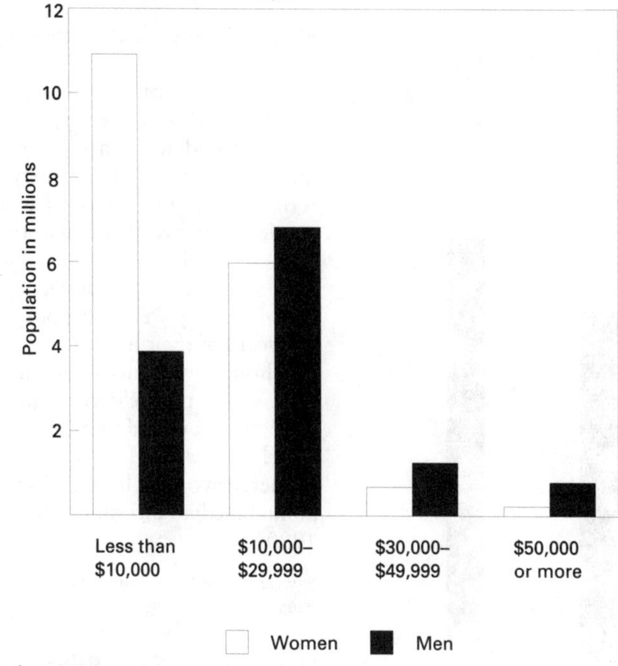

(Data from 1992)
Source: Bureau of the Census

"Old age is no place for sissies."
—Bette Davis

In North America, female life expectancy rose from 72 in 1950 to 78 in 1985.

MARITAL STATUS OF AGING AMERICANS

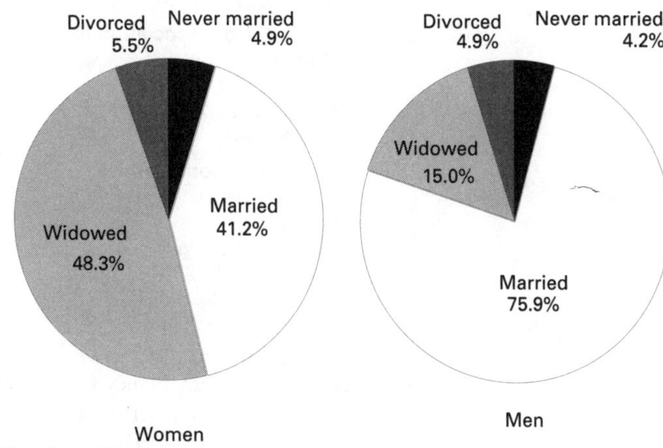

(Data from 1992)
Source: Bureau of the Census

The national poverty rate for women 65 and over is almost twice that for men.

In Africa, female life expectancy rose from 39 in 1950 to 55 in 1985.

WOMEN IN THE AGING POPULATION

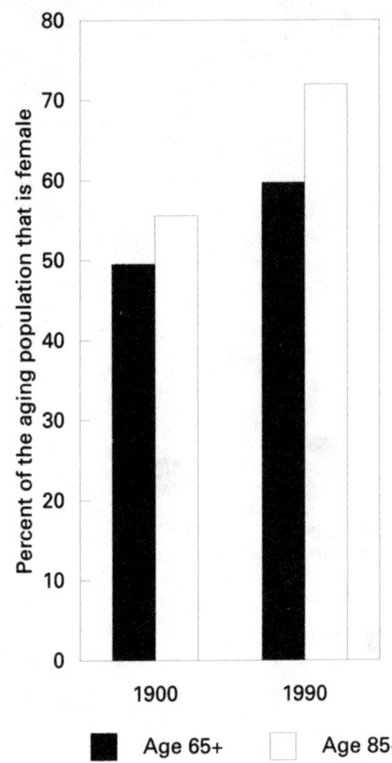

Source: Office of Research on Women's Health, National Institutes of Health

MARRIAGE, POVERTY, AND RETIREMENT

•Marital status is the most significant predictor of whether women will have a comfortable retirement or a life ending in poverty.
•A widowed woman is four times more likely to live in poverty after retirement than a married woman; single or divorced women are five times more likely.
•Eighty percent of widows now living in poverty were not poor before the death of their husbands.
•Although women made up only 58% of the total elderly population in 1990, they made up 74% of the elderly poor.
•Elderly women living alone had annual median incomes of $9,513 in 1990.

Source: Business and Professional Women's Foundation

WIDOWS—RESOURCES

ORGANIZATIONS

American Association for Counseling and Development
5999 Stevenson Avenue
Alexandria, VA 22304

Inter-National Association for Widowed People
P.O. Box 3564
Springfield, IL 62708
(217) 787-0886

Widowed Persons Service
American Association of Retired Persons
1909 K Street, N.W.
Washington, DC 20049

READING

Letting Go With Love: The Grieving Process, Nancy O'Connor (Apache Junction, Ariz.: La Mariposa Press, 1984).

On Your Own, Alexandra Armstrong and Mary R. Donahue (Chicago: Dearborn, 1993).

A Second Start: A Widow's Guide to Financial Survival at a Time of Emotional Stress, Judith N. Brown and Christina Baldwin (New York: Simon and Schuster, 1986).

Survival Handbook for Widows (And for Relatives and Friends Who Want to Understand), Ruth Loewinsohn (Des Plaines, Ill.: AARP and Scott, Foresman, 1984).

The Widow's Guide to Life: How to Adjust/How to Grow, Ida Fisher and Byron Lane (Englewood Cliffs, N.J.: Prentice-Hall, 1981).

To Live Again: Rebuilding Your Life After You've Become a Widow, Genevieve Ginsburg (Los Angeles: Jeremy P. Tarcher, 1987).

"Final Details," American Association of Retired Persons (Washington, D.C., 1990).

"On Being Alone," American Association of Retired Persons (Washington, D.C., 1988).

GRANDPARENTS—RESOURCES

AARP Grandparent Information Center
601 E Street, N.W.
Washington, DC 20049
(202) 434-2296

Coalition for Grandparents Parenting Grandchildren
2420 Bowditch Street
University of California
Berkeley, CA 94720
(510) 643-7538

Fast Fact: Grandparents Raising Their Grandchildren

The number of grandparents raising their grandkids is on the rise. According to the Census Bureau, an estimated one million children are cared for solely by a grandparent, a number that represents an increase of 40% over the last decade. The phenomenon, which is not specific to any socioeconomic or ethnic group, is the result of a variety of issues, including teen pregnancy, abuse, divorce, and AIDS.

D.C. Kinship Care Coalition
Childrens Hospital
Department of Social Work
111 Michigan Avenue, N.W.
Washington, DC 20010
(202) 884-5214

National Coalition of Grandparents
137 Larkin Street
Madison, WI 53705
(608) 238-8751

Northwest Coalition of Grandparents
Tacoma-Pierce County Health Department
3629 South D Street
Tacoma, WA 98408
(206) 591-6490

R.O.C.K.I.N.G.
(Raising Our Children's Kids: An Intergenerational Network of Grandparenting)
P.O. Box 96
Niles, MI 49120
(616) 683-9038

"Second Chance" Coalition
St. Petersburg Free Clinic
863 Third Avenue North
St. Petersburg, FL 33701
(813) 821-1200

Women live an average of 5 to 7 years longer than men.

African-American centenarians Sarah and A. Elizabeth Delany made national bestseller lists with their book *Having Our Say* in 1994.

HOUSING AND OLDER WOMEN

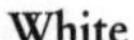

"Most women are worried when they get wrinkles, but I don't give a damn."—Zsa Zsa Gabor

How the Elderly Live

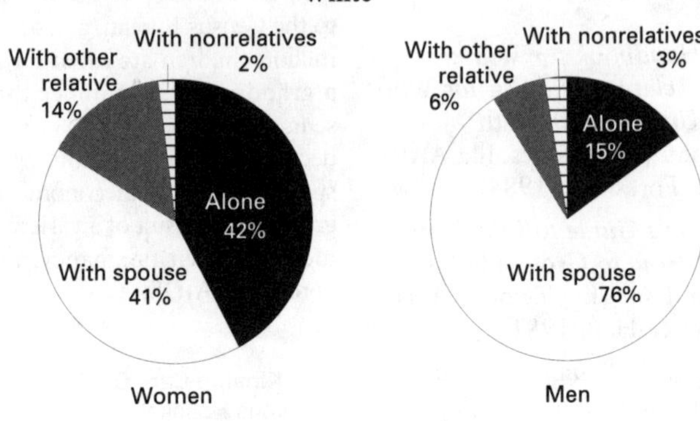

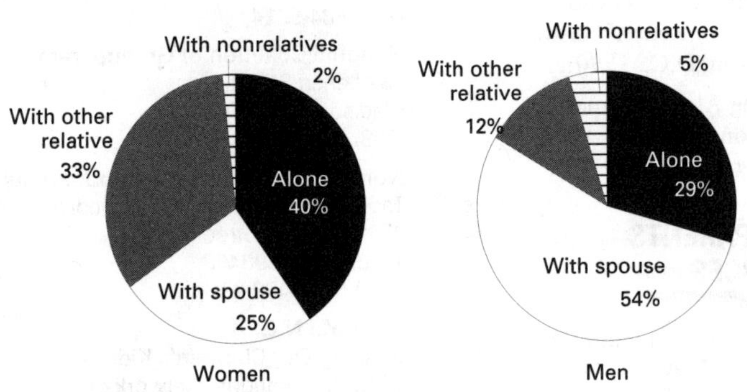

(Data from 1992)
Source: Bureau of the Census

Nursing Home and Home Care Residents

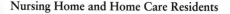

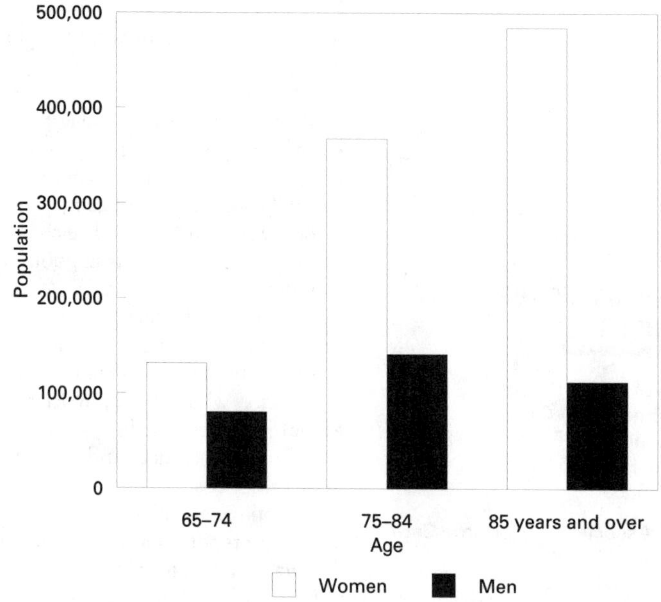

(Data from 1985 [most recent available])
Source: National Center for Health Statistics

42% of women over 65 and 16% of men over 65 lived alone in 1990.

Women make up 60% of the aging population, and outnumber men two to one in the over-75 age group, where health care costs are highest.

CAREGIVERS

Those who give care to the elderly can be spouses, adult children, other relatives, or friends.

•There are three to seven million caregivers in the United States, and approximately 70% of them are female.
•Nearly 37% of women over 18 can expect to be caregivers during their lifetime.
•About 48% of caregivers provide help to a spouse and 34% assist a parent.
•Nearly two million women care for children and parents simultaneously.
•Approximately 1/3 of caregivers live with their parents because their parents require assistance.
•Mainly owing to caregiving responsibilities for both children and elders, women spend an average of 11.5 years out of the paid labor force.

Source: Older Women's League, 1989 National Long Term Care Survey

HOME CARE

What Is Home Care?
Home care is a service for recovering, disabled, or chronically ill persons who need treatment and/or assistance with daily activities. Generally, home care is appropriate whenever a person needs assistance that cannot easily be provided solely by family or friends on an ongoing basis. Some of the people one might expect to be part of a home care team are:
•Physician
•Social worker
•Registered nurse
•Licensed vocational nurse
•Therapy specialist
•Dietician
•Home care aides
•Helpers/companions
•Volunteers (social visits, meal services, transportation, etc.)

A lifetime of drinking at least one cup of coffee a day decreases bone density in the hips and lower spine, thereby increasing the likelihood of hip fractures late in life, according to a recent study.

70% of the residents of nursing homes are women over 65.

The Cost of Home Care
The average expense per home care visit in 1993 was:

Nurse	$84
Therapist	$77
Home health aide	$46
Homemaker	$44
Other	$75
Average	$66

Source: National Association for Home Care

THE ELDERLY AT HOME—RESOURCES

Children of Aging Parents
Woodbourne Office Campus
1609 Woodbourne Road, Suite 302-A
Levittown, PA 19057
(215) 945-6900

National Association for Home Care
519 C Street, N.E.
Washington, DC 20002
(202) 547-7424

National Association of Meal Programs
204 E Street, N.E.
Washington, DC 20002
(202) 547-6157

National Shut-In Society
P.O. Box 986, Village Station
New York, NY 10014
(212) 222-7699

NURSING HOMES

Choosing a Nursing Home
Some important things to look for, think about, and ask when choosing a nursing home:

- Do you see handrails in hallways and other critical places?
- Are phones and large-print notices placed so that wheelchair-bound residents can make use of them?
- Are walking areas wide and clear?
- How often are fire drills held?
- Are the rooms, bathrooms, public areas, kitchens, and nurses' stations clean?
- Does staff interact with residents in a warm and friendly manner?
- Are residents doing things or just sitting in a lounge or the hallways? You might want to ask them how they keep occupied or what they like doing at the facility.
- Is there an out-of-doors area where residents can walk or sit, and is it used?
- How does the nursing home deal with problems between roommates?
- Is food appetizing and of good quality?
- Does the equipment—wheelchairs, therapy devices—appear in good condition?
- Will your family doctor be able to care for you or your family member in the facility? If you don't have your own doctor, who will the physician be?
- What is the fee schedule, what services are not included, and what will these things cost?
- Can you see a copy of the last inspection report? Note especially if the facility failed to meet any areas of the health code.

Source: New York State Department of Health

Nursing Home Ombudsman
If you need information on a particular nursing home, you can turn to your state's nursing home ombudsman office. You should also call them if you need to file a complaint against a specific facility. For a list of state ombudsmen, contact:

Administration on Aging
Department of Health and Human Services
330 Independence Avenue, S.W.
Washington, DC 20201
(202) 619-0724 (general information) or
(202) 619-0641 (publications)

HOUSING—RESOURCES

American Association of Homes for the Aging
901 E Street, N.W., Suite 500
Washington, DC 20004
(202) 783-2242

National Citizens' Coalition for Nursing Home Reform
1224 M Street, N.W., Room 301
Washington, DC 20005
(202) 393-2018

National Institute of Senior Housing
c/o National Council on the Aging
409 Third Street, S.W., Second Floor
Washington, DC 20025
(202) 479-6677

Nursing Home Information Service
National Council of Senior Citizens
925 15th Street, N.W.
Washington, DC 20005
(202) 347-8800

Fast Fact: Elderhostel

Created to provide travel and learning opportinities to people over the age of 60, Elderhostel consists of a network of over 1,900 educational and cultural institutions in the U.S., Canada, and 47 countries overseas. The organization is founded on the belief that retirement does not mean withdrawal from activity, but rather an opportunity to enjoy new challenges. For additional information and a catalog, contact:

Elderhostel
P.O. Box 1751
Wakefield, MA 01889

"I am at an age where my back goes out more than I do."
—Phyllis Diller

INCOME SOURCES FOR OLDER AMERICANS

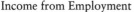

The U.S. retirement system has been referred to as a three-legged stool, with Social Security, individual savings, and employer-sponsored pension plans as the legs. The following graphs show how many Americans receive income from the three systems.

Income from Employment

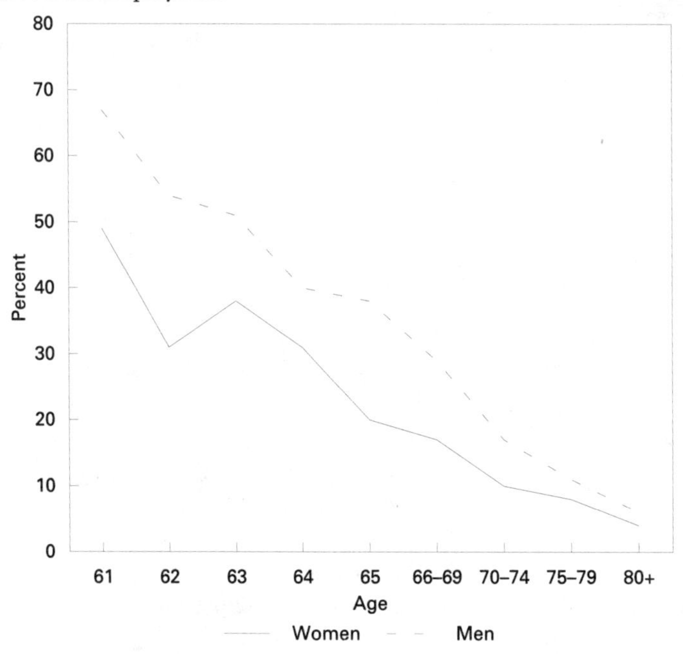

Margaret Skeete, listed in the Guinness Book of Records as the oldest American, died May 8, 1994, at the age of 115.

Income from Social Security

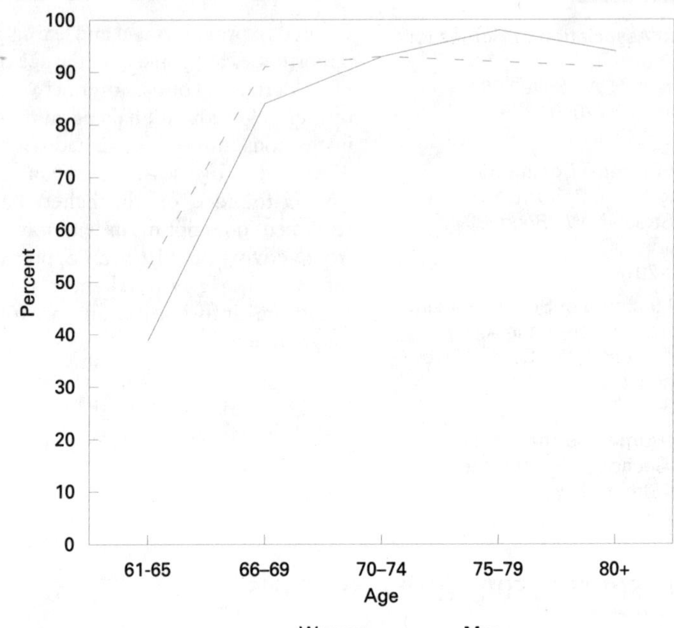

Income from Pensions

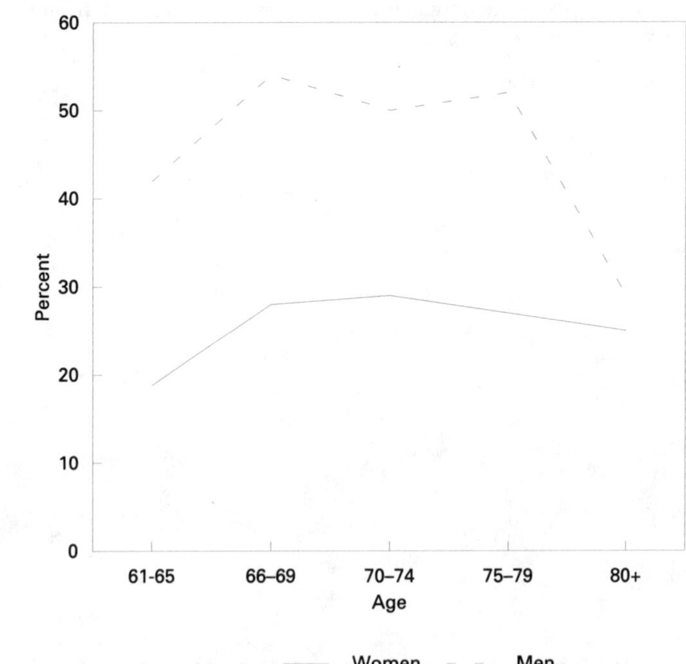

Source for above: Social Security Bulletin, 1991 Annual Statistical Supplement

WOMEN AND SOCIAL SECURITY BENEFITS

Although the Social Security system is intended to provide a reasonable level of financial support for the retirement years, women often do not enjoy this benefit at the level men do. The primary reason for lower benefits is the generally lower earnings women receive; this difference can be explained by the wage gap, occupational segregation, and the years out of the labor force that women often spend tending to family responsibilities—years when their Social Security accounts are not being credited. Women, in fact, on average spend 11.5 years out of the work force, compared to one year for men, and their benefits are therefore considerably lower.

The three forms of Social Security benefits available are:

•Worker benefits, which are paid to a retired or disabled worker based on his or her own earnings;
•Spousal benefits, which are paid to the spouse of a retired or disabled worker and which equal one-half of the spouse's worker benefit; and
•Survivor's benefits, which are paid to certain members of a deceased worker's family, based on the worker's earnings.

Dual Entitlement
Married women who are in the paid labor force and earn Social Security credits in their own right generally face the greatest inequities in the system because of "dual entitlement." A worker whose retirement worker benefit is lower than her benefit as a spouse is considered to be "dually entitled"; since that worker cannot receive the full amount of both benefits, she collects the higher of the two benefits. But because women's benefits are usually lower than men's, a "dually entitled" woman can find that her benefits are not any different than if she had never been employed.

Applying for Social Security Benefits
About three months before you would like to start receiving your benefits, call the Social Security Administration's toll free number—(800) 772-1213. Then apply at any Social Security office. You will need:
•Your Social Security card, or a record of your number
•Your birth certificate
•Your marriage certificate, if signing up on a spouse's record
•Your most recent W-2 form, or your tax return if self-employed

Source: Business and Professional Women's Foundation

Fast Fact: Substance Abuse

Alcohol and drug problems plague older women and men just as they do young people. For assistance in rehabilitating older or hanicapped persons experiencing either of these problems, contact:

Hopedale Hall
P.O. Box 267
Hopedale, IL 61747
(800) 354-7089 or
(800) 344-0824 (in Illinois)

The number of mid-life divorced women tripled between 1982 and 1992, reducing their average income to less than $11,000 one year after divorce.

The median monthly Social Security check for women in 1992 was $561.

SOCIAL SECURITY BENEFITS

Monthly Benefits

These figures represent the average monthly Social Security benefit as of December 1991, for all workers.

Retired worker	$542
Full benefits (retired at age 65+)	687
Reduced benefit (retired at age 62–64)	487
Disabled worker	485
Wives of retired or disabled workers	312
Husband retired	330
Husband disabled	217
Widows	$573
Non-disabled, aged 60+	585
Disabled, aged 50–64	409
Entitlement based on care of children	432

Source: Social Security Bulletin, Annual Statistical Supplement, 1992

Monthly Benefits: Women vs. Men

These figures reflect the median family Social Security benefits, comparing women to men by age.

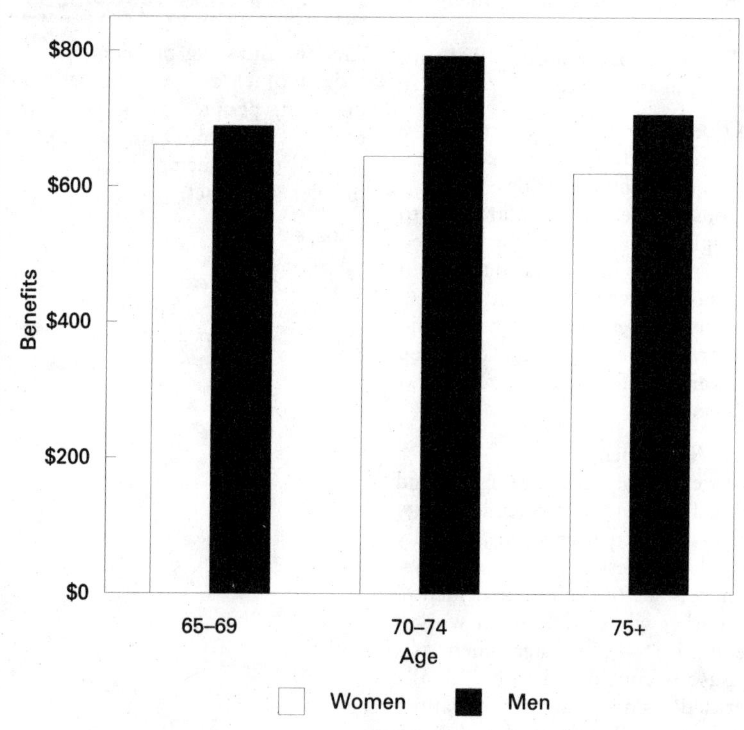

Source: Social Security Bulletin, Annual Statistical Supplement, 1991

BENEFICIARIES OF SOCIAL SECURITY

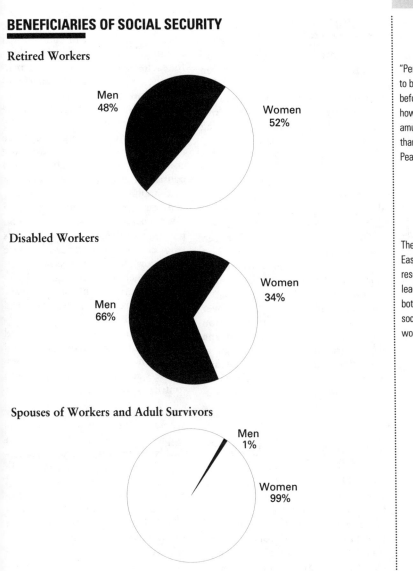

Retired Workers

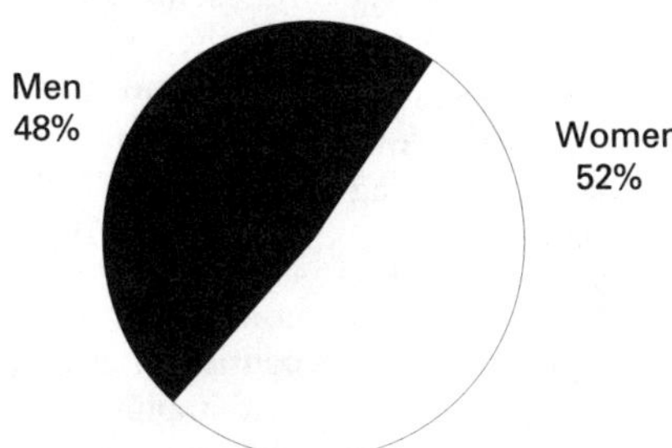

Disabled Workers

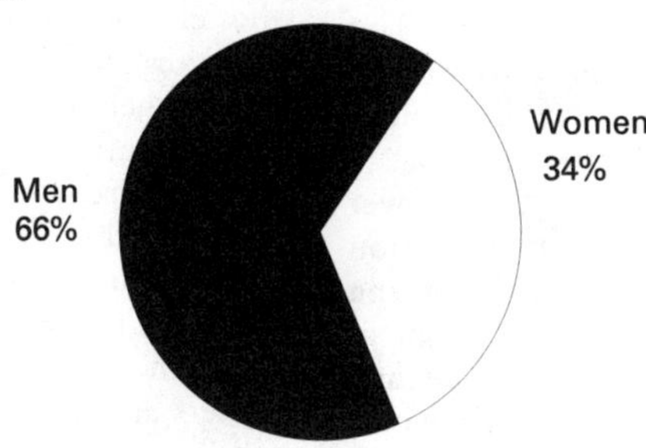

Spouses of Workers and Adult Survivors

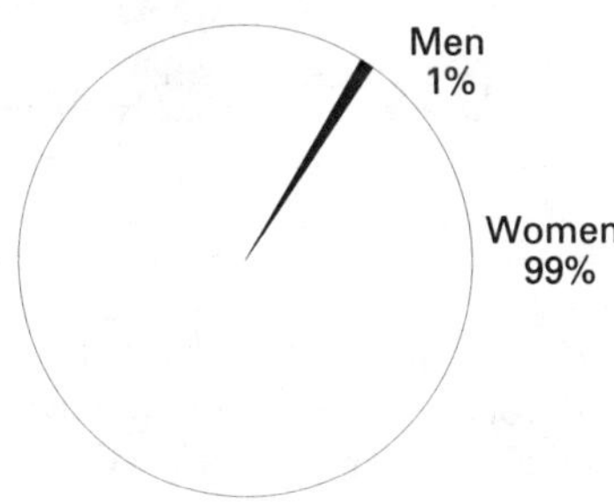

Source: National Council of Senior Citizens

"Perhaps one has to be very old before one learns how to be amused rather than shocked."—Pearl Buck

The Bemba of East Africa reserve many leadership roles, both political and social, for older women.

When asked to identify their single greatest economic concern, a female group of "affluent, aging baby boomers" said "paying for my children's education" most often, while the men said "providing adequate resources for retirement years."

PENSIONS

•Only 10% of women receive any benefits at all from private pension plans.
•Of full-time workers, only 46% are covered by private pension plans, including 43% of full-time working women and 50% of men.
•The average annual pension for women over 65 was $5,220 in 1989, compared to $8,649 for men.
•Only 13% of workers earning less than $10,000 annually have benefits that include a pension plan, and only 41% of those earning between $10,000 and $20,000 have one. This is of special importance to women since more than 2/3 of working women earned less than $20,000 in 1988.
•In businesses with 100 or fewer employees, only 24% have pension coverage, yet 45% of working women are employed by such companies. Women also make up more than 2/3 of all part-time employees, concentrated mostly in lower-paying occupations, and these jobs, too, can be excluded from pension plans.

KINDS OF PENSION PLANS

Defined benefit plans promise to pay a specific benefit at retirement. The benefit is usually calculated on a percentage of the employee's average earnings multiplied by her years of work under the plan. The most common method of payment is a lifetime monthly pension starting at retirement age. Some plans also pay benefits in the form of a lump sum.

Advantages: The employer promises to pay a specific pension benefit at retirement and is obligated to set aside sufficient funds to ensure that it can be paid.

Disadvantages: Mergers, acquisitions, or other financial or organizational shifts may result in the dissolution of a defined benefit plan.

Defined contribution plans promise that the employer will contribute a certain amount per year to the plan for each employee, although the benefit the employee receives at retirement is not specified. The contribution is usually a percentage of the worker's earnings that year, with each employee holding a separate account. Some require employee contributions. The benefit received consists of whatever money has been paid in plus the investment earnings.

Advantages: Essentially tax-deferred savings arrangements, they are good for younger workers and individuals who change jobs frequently since employees can take their pension benefits with them upon changing jobs.

Disadvantages: The amount available at retirement is uncertain and employees bear the risk of investment performance. Also, they tend to provide fewer benefits to low and middle-income workers, since these workers are less likely to be able to contribute to the plans.

Cash balance plans are basically hybrids of the above two. Each participant has an individual account that is credited with a yearly addition. Interest is credited at a rate specified in the plan and is unrelated to the investment earnings of the trust fund. When the worker leaves the job, the amount of the lump sum distribution is equal to the account balance.

Advantages: More generous benefits for those who retire at earlier ages or switch employers with some frequency.

Disadvantages: Higher costs and benefits for younger, short-service employees and lower costs and benefits for older, long-service employees.

Keogh plans are pension plans for the self-employed and are subject to the same limits on contributions and benefits as are private pension plans.

Individual Retirement Accounts can be started by all employed individuals and their spouses. Individuals may contribute the lesser of $2,000 or 100% of their annual wages to an IRA. Income tax on the contributed money is deferred if:

—The contributor (and, for joint filers, the spouse) is not eligible to participate in an employer-sponsored retirement plan; or

—The contributor has adjusted gross income below $25,000, or $40,000 for joint filers.

Source: Business and Professional Women's Foundation

Fast Fact: Planning Your Finances

The Pre-Retirement Education Planning Program (PREP) is an activity of the National Center for Women and Retirement Research designed to encourage women to look ahead to their financial future and to provide them with the information, skills, and motivation they need to plan effectively. The PREP program consists of four workbooks that can be used by individuals or groups of women. Topics include taking control of your finances, social and emotional concerns, health, employment, and retirement issues.

For more information, contact:
The National Center for Women and Retirement Research
Long Island University
Southampton Campus
Southampton, NY 11968
(800) 426-7386

REVIEWING YOUR RETIREMENT PLANS

- Your retirement plan is only as safe as the safety of your investments. There are no guarantees.
- Annuities are not actually retirement plans, but they are tax-deferred and can be a good supplement to your retirement plan.
- If your IRA is not tax-deductible, consult with your tax preparer before making further IRA contributions.
- Retirement plans have early withdrawal penalties. In most cases if you withdraw funds before age 59½, you can expect a 10% penalty and you will be taxed on the money withdrawn. You may be able to borrow from your retirement plan, but check with your CPA or pension plan consultant first.
- Most retirement plans require you to begin taking money out shortly after you reach 70½ or you will be penalized.
- You may also be penalized if you withdraw funds from an annuity before age 59½, but you don't have to start withdrawing funds after you reach age 70½. This allows you to extend the tax deferral.
- Make sure you know how much you can contribute to your plan (or plans) each year. If you overfund, you could wind up paying a penalty.
- When it comes to the ins and outs of retirement planning, check with your CPA, tax preparer, or pension plan consultant. In this area of investing, they are important members of your team.

Source: Money Smart, Esther Berger (New York: Simon & Schuster, 1993)

By the year 2000, over 19 million women will be over the age of 65 with one common characteristic: many of them never planned for the financial implications of old age.

FRANCES LEAR—WOMEN AND THEIR MONEY: TAKING CONTROL

The following essay by Frances Lear, the founder of Lear Publishing, advocates that women take control of their financial security. Lear is now producing investment videos for women.

Finance is no longer a man's game. The myth, of course, is that "women don't know how to handle money," as if money has gender, or men have an innate talent for the business of money that women do not have. Personal finance has to do with judgment and instinct and the ability to learn, three characteristics that women have in abundance.

The issue is a critical one. In our society, money means freedom. Without control over their finances, women are missing a critical element in their quest for self-determination.

Women clearly have the basic skills necessary to intelligently control their finances. What many women do not have is comfort, confidence, and trust in handling money themselves, or in handing its care over to someone else. That's because generations of women have been taught that someone else (a man) should be caring for their finances. I am frequently told about women—even with substantial portfolios—who have not been taken seriously by brokers. Take a look at the boards of most banks—major or minor. Virtually all of them are populated by men. The glass ceiling is particularly devastating at the upper reaches of banks and brokerage houses.

The contemporary "liberated" woman was designed by women who did not understand money, or care a lot about money, or realize the proper place for money in a woman's life. Their mindset lives on. The baby-boomer generation, although they are making money, knows little about what to do with it. Their expertise is in charge cards, not saving, not sound investing, not making their money last as long as they do.

Most women leave their economic future to an internally programmed fantasy that a man will come to their rescue. It's true of women who are seventeen or forty-five, women in Seattle or Tampa, porn stars and art historians. He stands between a woman and her sight of the future. He hides reality. The danger in women's lives is economic, and lies in the seductiveness of the rescue fantasy, and the official feminist disregard of a woman's fiscal responsibility to herself.

A hankering for money, to some, lays a tinge of immorality upon a woman; and too many women confuse wages with self-worth. Asking a male boss for a raise may hark back to asking daddy for an allowance, but since women no longer put up with being infantilized by others, it is counter-productive to infantilize ourselves.

A critical first step in the empowerment process is creating role models for women. By establishing success stories, by showing women that other women are succeeding in the often arcane art of growing their money, we can start a cycle that will eventually lead to financial independence.

Taking control of our money—being responsible for it, understanding its preciousness—is the next macro move for women, and will be done by gaining needed knowledge and not by attempting to understand the rhetoric of the financial community that keeps us dependent. Saving and investing—safely—for our future may be the only way to predict it. Until women are taught to handle their finances, until they are encouraged to take responsibility for their own financial destiny, they will always be dependent on men.

PERSONAL FINANCE

A Woman's Financial Focus from 40 to 60

- Play financial catch-up, if necessary. Look at and understand all of your investment accounts. Consolidate, but don't keep all of your money in one place. Have at least one bank and one brokerage account.
- It's never too late to start saving. If you are just starting, put away as much as you can to make up for lost time.
- Make ongoing contributions to retirement plans. Two things will come into play: how much you can afford to put away on a regular basis and contribution limits. The annual maximum you can contribute in most retirement plans is $30,000. If you can save more, consider supplementing your retirement plan with a tax-deferred annuity.
- Evaluate your investments. Make the necessary changes so that your percentage of growth investments is approximately equal to your age. For instance, if you are fifty, you'll want to have half growth and half income investments.
- Know your tax bracket. If you're in a high bracket, consider shifting some of your income-producing investments to insured tax-free municipal bonds.
- If you don't own your own home, think about investing in real estate as an inflation hedge. Not only does it generally appreciate over time, it provides you with a tax deduction on interest and property tax payments.
- Reexamine your health, life, and disability insurance to make sure you have sufficient coverage.
- Make a will or establish a trust. If your gross estate is valued at less than $600,000, a will may be adequate. If it's more, think about establishing a trust. Talk to an attorney who specializes in estate planning before deciding.

A Woman's Financial Focus from 60 On

- Review and understand your retirement plan because retirement is just around the corner.
- Contact Social Security for an estimate of the benefits you can expect.
- Shift some of your growth investments into income-producing investments. You may need this additional income to supplement your Social Security and pension benefits.
- Know where all of your documents and important papers are.
- If your husband manages the finances, ask him to make a list of your bank accounts, brokerage accounts, and other financial assets. Also, ask him for the names and telephone numbers of the financial advisers with whom he works.
- Consider making lifetime gifts to your heirs to reduce the size of your estate. You can give up to $10,000 per person per year tax free to as many people as you wish. If you are married, the maximum increases to $20,000. Besides reducing the size of your taxable estate, you'll have the pleasure of seeing your loved ones enjoy your money while you are still alive.
- Make decisions concerning future financial and health care needs. Decide in advance who will make medical and financial choices for you should you become physically or mentally incapacitated, and execute the appropriate documents.
- Review your will or trust and see if it needs revision. Things may have changed substantially since it was first drafted. Make sure its provisions reflect your current wishes.

The Sixtysomething Generic Investment Plan: Shift a portion of your portfolio to income-producing investments, including tax-free municipal bonds, Treasury securities, and high-yielding common stocks. But don't move totally out of growth investments.

In a recent study, women detailed financial problems so severe that most said they have no prospects of retiring.

Your emphasis is on income and preservation of principal, but you still need to be concerned about inflation.

Source: Money Smart, Esther Berger (New York: Simon & Schuster, 1993)

TEST YOUR RETIREMENT IQ

Answer each question True or False. Score your IQ below.

1. A prudent woman will plan to replace 60% to 80% of her pre-retirement income after she retires.
2. Women's job mobility can devastate pension income even if all wages and pension plans are identical in all jobs.
3. By law, both spouses must agree in writing to whatever survivor's benefit is selected by the worker upon retirement.
4. Reforms effective in 1989 guarantee that future retirees will lose no more than half their pensions to "integration."
5. Unlike most traditional pensions, voluntary savings plans such as 401(k)s and IRAs are not guaranteed by the federal government.

Answers:

(1) False. As a class, women are more vulnerable to inflation than men, and begin retirement with incomes equal to only 60% of men's incomes, so they need to replace all of their pre-retirement income.
(2) True. A person who works for four different companies for ten years each may have about one-half the pension of one who worked 40 years for one employer, assuming identical wages and pension plans.
(3) False. The spouse must consent to the *waiver* of the survivor's benefit, but under certain circumstances the retiree alone has the right to decide if the benefit will be 50%, or higher if the plan offers a choice of options.
(4) False. Only credits earned after January 1, 1989, are covered by the reform; workers are subject to the old formula permitting up to 100% integration for all credits earned before then.
(5) True. The fund set up to insure most traditional pensions by federal law (the Pension Benefit Guaranty Corporation) does not cover voluntary savings plans.

Scoring: Give yourself one point for each correct answer.

5	You're a pension virtuoso.
4	A brush-up course may be all you need.
2–3	Like most, you've got a way to go.
0–1	It's time for a retirement planning seminar.

Source: Older Women's League

Fast Fact: Senior Sports

The U.S. National Senior Sports Classic is a biennial multi-sport athletic competition for adults over the age of 55. Over 150,000 athletes qualify at the local level in 47 states to compete in any of 18 sports. The competition is hosted by the U.S. National Senior Sports Organization, which promotes sports and fitness in mature adults.

For more information or to get involved, contact:

U.S. National Senior Sports Organization
14323 S. Forty Road, Suite N300
Chester Field, MO
(314) 878-4900

FIVE RULES FOR BUYING LIFE INSURANCE

1. Understand and know what your life insurance needs are before any purchase, and make sure that the company you choose can meet those needs.
2. Buy your life insurance from a company that is licensed in your state.
3. Ask about lower premium rates for non-smokers.
4. Inform your beneficiaries about the kinds and amounts of life insurance you own.
5. Check your coverage periodically, or whenever your situation changes, to be sure it meets your current needs.

Source: American Council of Life Insurance

SOCIAL SECURITY AND FINANCES—RESOURCES

ORGANIZATIONS

Clearinghouse on Pensions and Divorce
Pension Rights Center
918 16th Street, N.W., Suite 704
Washington, DC 20006
(202) 296-3776

National Committee to Preserve Social Security and Medicare
2000 K Street, N.W., Suite 800
Washington, DC 20006
(202) 822-9459

National Pension Lawyer Referral Service
Pension Rights Center
918 16th Street, N.W., Suite 704
Washington, DC 20006
(202) 296-3776

National Senior Citizens Law Center
1815 H Street, N.W., Suite 700
Washington, DC 20006
(202) 887-5280

Social Security Administration
Office of Public Inquiries
6401 Security Boulevard
Baltimore, MD 21235
(301) 594-1234

U.S. Department of Labor
Office of Pension and Welfare
200 Constitution Avenue, N.W.
Washington, DC 20210

Womoney
Sharon Rich, Ed.D.
76 Townsend Road
Belmont, MA 02178
(617) 489-3601

READING

"Financing Your Future: Women and Retirement Income" (Washington, D.C.: Business and Professional Women's Foundation, 1992).

"Focus Your Future: A Woman's Guide to Retirement Planning," American Association of Retired Persons (Washington, D.C.: AARP, 1993).

Money Smart, Esther M. Berger with Connie Church Hasbun (New York: Simon and Schuster, 1993).

"The Social Security Book: What Every Woman Absolutely Needs to Know," American Association of Retired Persons (Washington, D.C.: AARP, 1991).

Social Security Manual, William W. Thomas III, ed. (Cincinnati: National Underwriter Company, 1993).

Women & Money, Frances Leonard (Reading, Mass.: Addison-Wesley, 1991).

OLDER WOMEN—RESOURCES

ORGANIZATIONS

Advocacy Center for Older Women Workers
474 Center Street
Newton, MA 02158
(617) 244-3304

American Association of Retired Persons Women's Initiative
1909 K Street, N.W.
Washington, DC 20049
(202) 434-2277

A widowed woman is four times more likely, and a single woman five times more likely, to live in poverty after retirement than a married woman.

"It's true some wines improve with age. But only if the grapes were good in the first place."
—Abigail van Buren ("Dear Abby")

Ex-Partners of Servicemen/Women for Equity
P.O. Box 11191
Alexandria, VA 22312
(703) 941-5844

Gray Panthers
2025 Pennsylvania Avenue, N.W., Suite 821
Washington, DC 20006
(202) 466-3132

Legal Counsel for the Elderly
601 E Street, N.W.
Building A, 4th Floor
Washington, DC 20049
(202) 434-2124

Legal Services for the Elderly
130 W. 42nd Street, 17th Floor
New York, NY 10036
(212) 595-1340

National Academy of Elder Law Attorneys
655 N. Alvernon Way, Suite 108
Tucson, AZ 85711
(602) 881-4005

National Caucus and Center on Black Aged
1424 K Street, N.W., Suite 500
Washington, DC 20005
(202) 637-8400

National Center for Women and Retirement Research
Long Island University
Southampton Campus
Southampton, NY 11968
(800) 426-7386

National Council on Aging
409 Third Street, S.W.
Washington, DC 20024
(202) 479-1200

Older Women's League
666 11th Street, N.W., Suite 700
Washington, DC 20001
(202) 783-6686

Select Committe on Aging
U.S. House of Representatives
Washington, DC 20515

Special Committee on Aging
U.S. Senate
Washington, DC 20510

Reading

"The Complete Collection," American Association of Retired Persons Publications and A/V Programs (Washington, D.C.: AARP, 1993). This catalog lists over 250 publications on finances, health, housing, consumer information, crime prevention, retirement planning, and other important topics.

Lesbians Over 60 Speak for Themselves, M. Kehoe (New York: Haworth Press, 1989).

POLITICS
POLITICS
POLITICS

POLITICS

POLITICS
POLITICS
POLITICS
POLITICS
POLITICS
POLITICS
POLITICS
POLITICS
POLITICS
POLITICS
POLITICS
POLITICS
POLITICS
POLITICS
POLITICS
POLITICS

THE GENDER GAP

The "gender gap" refers to differences between women and men in their political attitudes and voting choices. Although the gender gap has historical roots, political differences between the sexes have increased in scope and shown greater persistence in recent years. A gap has been shown in voting behavior, party identification, and attitudes toward various public policy issues.

1992	%Women	%Men
Bill Clinton	45	37
George Bush	41	38
Ross Perot	17	21
1988		
George Bush	50	57
Michael Dukakis	49	42
1984		
Ronald Reagan	54	62
Walter Mondale	46	38
1980		
Ronald Reagan	47	53
Jimmy Carter	42	35
John Anderson	9	9
1976		
Jimmy Carter	48	53
1972		
Richard Nixon	62	63
1968		
Richard Nixon	43	43
1964		
Lyndon B. Johnson	62	60
1960		
John F. Kennedy	49	52
1956		
Dwight D. Eisenhower	61	53
1952		
Dwight D. Eisenhower	58	53

Sources: Gallup Polls; Center for the American Woman and Politics, Eagleton Institute of Politics, Rutgers University

VOTING THE ISSUES

Women more often support:
- Environmental protection measures
- Health care programs
- Efforts to achieve racial equality

Women are more often opposed to:
- Use of force in nonmilitary situations
- Growth of nuclear power

Sources: Gallup Polls; Center for the American Woman and Politics, Eagleton Institute of Politics, Rutgers University

GENDER PAY GAP IN CONGRESSIONAL STAFFS

A study of approximately 11,500 members of the personal staffs of congressional members found:

- Average annual pay for House employees:
  Male—$39,200
  Female—$32,000

- Pay for Senate employees:
  Male—$37,800
  Female—$30,400

- Percentage of congressional staffers who are women: 60%
- Percentage of House and Senate staff bosses who are women: 33%
- Percentage of women staffers holding clerical positions: 90%
- Congressional staff positions in which women earn as much or more than men: House legislative director and executive secretary
- Average salary for a congressional field manager:
  Male—$46,700
  Female—$40,500

- For every dollar men earn, women earn:
  in the House—82¢
  in the Senate—80¢
  nationally—71¢

Source: Gannett News Service

New Jersey gave women the right to vote on July 2, 1776. The law was revoked in 1807, in large part because women were not voting for the incumbents.

Republicans voting in favor of the Family and Medical Leave Act — congresswomen: 50%; congressmen: 25%.

THE GENDER GAP AND POLICYMAKERS

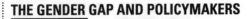

Issues Where Gender Differences Are Greatest

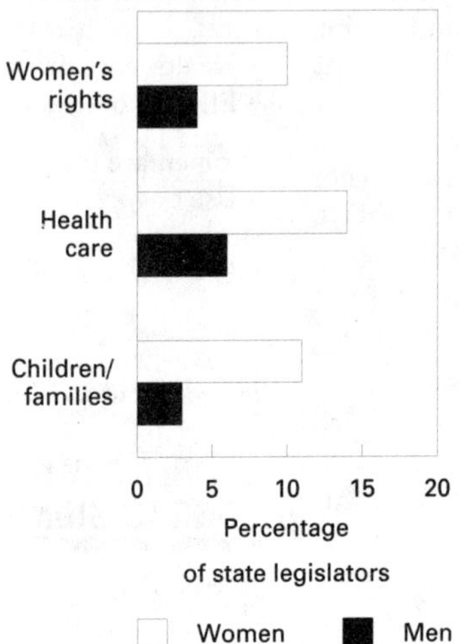

Positions Held by Female and Male Legislators on Selected Issues

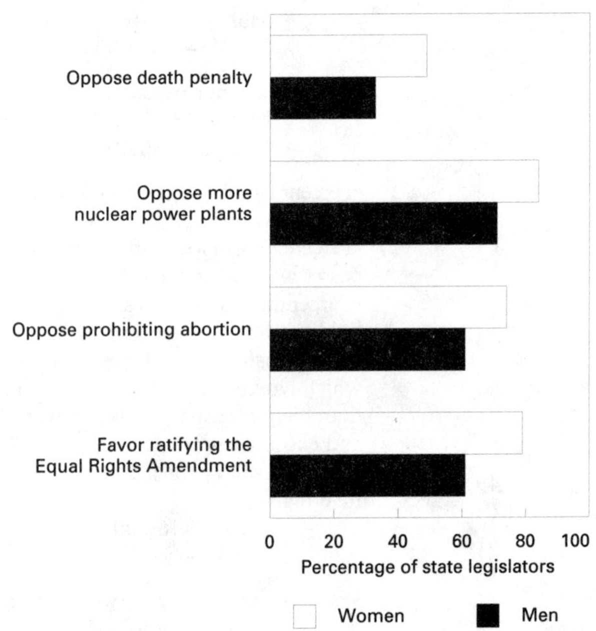

Source for above: Center for the American Woman and Politics, Eagleton Institute of Politics, Rutgers University

POLITICAL AFFILIATIONS

Party Identification

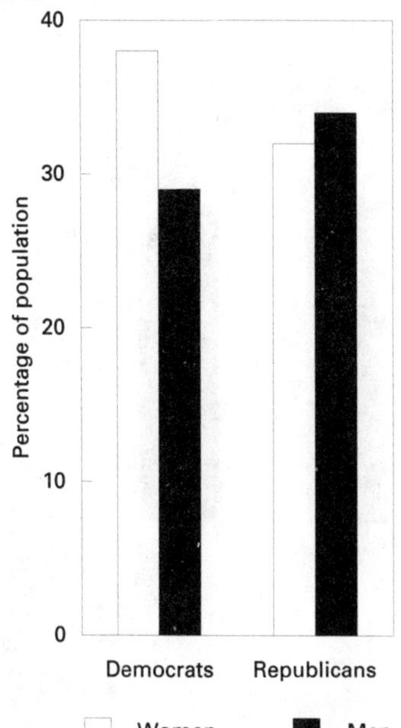

(Data from June 1992)
Source: CBS News/New York Times poll

VOTING PATTERNS

Voter Turnout by Race and Sex

Voter turnout is measured here as the percentage of the voting-age population that reported voting.

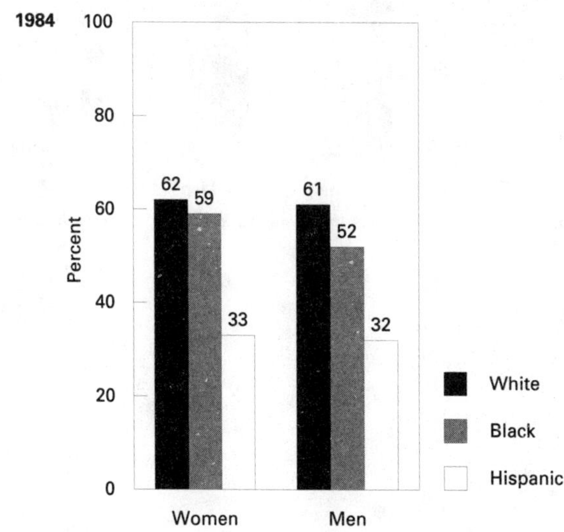

Marilyn Quayle, when asked why people think she's smarter than her husband, said, "He's blond."

Florence Harding was the first First Lady to vote for her husband for president, since his was the first election after women won suffrage.

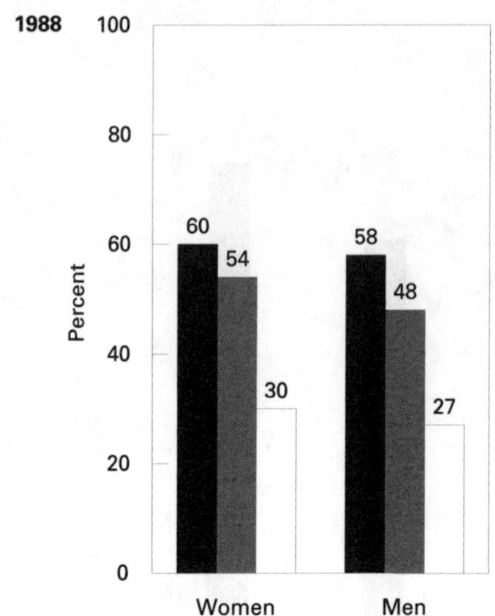

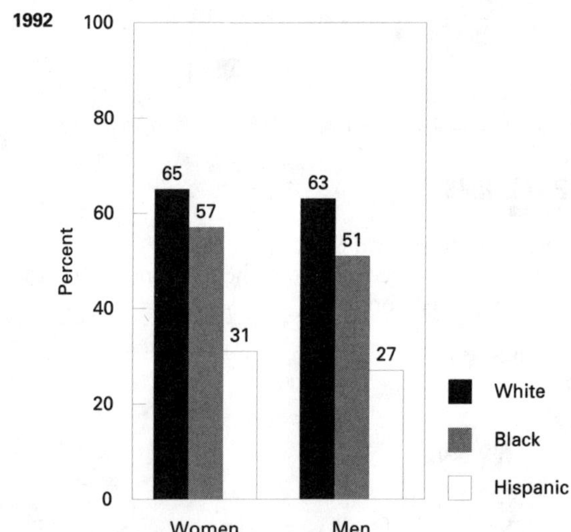

Source for above: Center for the American Woman and Politics, Eagleton Institute of Politics, Rutgers University

VOTER REGISTRATION

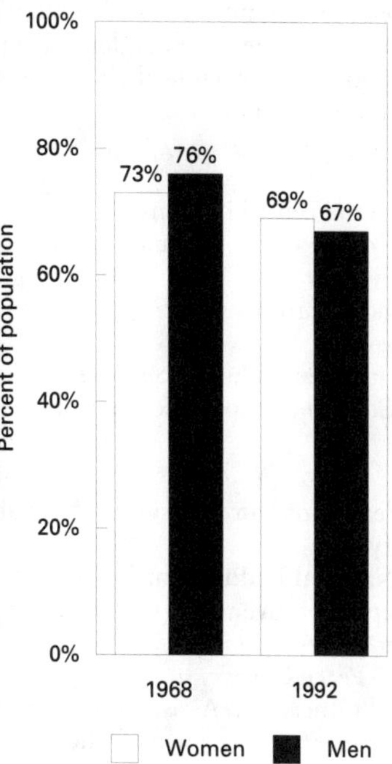

Source: Bureau of the Census

PRESIDENTIAL FIRSTS

First woman to run for president of the United States: Victoria C. Woodhull, suffragette, publisher, and stockbroker, ran in the presidential election of 1872 as a candidate of the Equal Rights Party, one of three third-party candidates running against Ulysses S. Grant and Horace Greeley. Grant won the election.

First woman to run for president as a major party candidate: Senator Margaret Chase Smith of Maine entered the 1964 Republican primary against fellow senator and victor Barry Goldwater of Arizona.

PRESIDENTIAL APPOINTMENT FIRSTS

First woman to hold a cabinet post in the U.S. government:
Frances Perkins was appointed by Franklin D. Roosevelt as secretary of labor. She served from March 1933 to July 1945.

Hazel R. O'Leary is the first woman and the first African American to serve as the U.S. secretary of energy.

Janet Reno is the first woman to serve as the U.S. attorney general.

Laura D'Andrea Tyson is the first woman to serve as the chair of the Council of Economic Advisors.

Marietta Peabody Tree became the first woman to attain the position of permanent ambassador to the U.N., in 1964.

The first woman appointed as counselor to the president was Anne Armstrong, appointed by Richard Nixon in 1973.

While Richard Nixon was courting his future wife, Pat, he would often drive her to her dates with other men, wait for her, and drive her home.

WOMEN PRESIDENTIAL APPOINTMENTS

Mary Louise Smith was elected the first woman chair of the Republican National Committee on September 16, 1974.

Fourteen women in American history have been appointed to head executive departments in the U.S. government. Eight of the 42 presidents (four Republicans and four Democrats) have appointed women to their cabinets. The current top women officials in the Clinton Administration:

Cabinet and Cabinet-Level Appointees

Madeline K. Albright	Ambassador to the United Nations
Carol M. Browner	Administrator of the Environmental Protection Agency
Hazel R. O'Leary	Secretary of the Department of Energy
Janet Reno	Attorney General
Donna E. Shalala	Secretary of Health and Human Services
Laura D'Andrea Tyson	Chair of the Council of Economic Advisors

Senior Clinton Appointees

37% of the Clinton administration's first 500 appointees were women.

Roberta Achtenburg	Assistant Secretary for Fair Housing and Equal Opportunity
Jane Alexander	Chair of the National Endowment for the Arts
Harriet C. Babbitt	Permanent Representative to the Organization of American States
Carol Bellamy	Director of the Peace Corps
Bonnie Cohen	Chief Financial Officer and Assistant Secretary of the Department of Interior for Policy Management and Budget
Lynn E. Davis	Under Secretary of State for International Security Affairs
Mary L. Good	Under Secretary for the Office of Technology in the Department of Commerce
Lorraine A. Green	Deputy Director of the Office of Personnel Management
Madeleine M. Kunin	Deputy Secretary of the Department of Education
Cassandra Pulley-Robinson	Deputy Administrator of the Small Business Administration
Joan Spero	Under Secretary of State for Economic and Agricultural Affairs
Sheila Widnall	Secretary of the Air Force in the Department of Defense

ELIZABETH DOLE—WOMEN IN PUBLIC LIFE

Elizabeth Dole, former secretary of labor and secretary of transportation, spoke at Radcliffe commencement exercises on June 11, 1993. She is now the president of the American Red Cross.

I have been asked to share some thoughts this afternoon on women in public policy—an interesting topic, because while there are more women in public leadership roles than in private, there are still relatively few. While there are greater opportunities for women in public leadership roles than in private, there are still relatively few. While there are great opportunities for women in government, there obviously remain impediments.

There are many ways to pursue the goal of involving women in shaping public policy. And there are many reasons to pursue this goal. In the first place, it's right. Too many of our number have felt the sting of discrimination. Secondly, women, I believe, have something very special to offer. And, thirdly, our workforce is changing. America must be able to welcome women and minorities into its leadership roles if we are to accommodate that change. Sixty-four percent of the new entrants to the workforce over the next 10 years will be women. If the public sector is to attract the best and the brightest, it must be able to attract and reward women.

When I was in law school at Harvard, only 24 of the 550 students were women. There were only a few women, at the time, who had made partner in major law firms. The private sector simply was not a strong option. Public policy beckoned as a rewarding alternative—a call to service, a chance to make a positive difference in people's lives.

There are some observations I could offer [women today] which might smooth the way a little. And I could summarize them this way: that our greatest obstacle—that we women are women in a world of men—is really an enormous opportunity.

Remember the question Henry Higgins asked in the film *My Fair Lady*, "Why can't a woman be more like a man?" Because I think it's important to learn the correct lesson from our successes, I believe that further gains do not depend on better answers to the question, "Why can't a woman be more like a man?" The question we should be asking now is, "Why can't a woman be more like a woman?"

I'd like to quote for you from a recent article in *Life* magazine: "Women," the article asserts, "are more committed than men to cushioning the hard corners of the country, to making it a safer place. Women want stricter law enforcement against drunk driving and illegal firearms and drug dealing. . . . It's not that men don't care about these issues. It's simply that women care more."

I don't know whether that's true. But perhaps our approach is different. Perhaps our involvement in public policy debates provides a leavening influence. Perhaps more women in public service would result in greater focus on cushioning corners for vulnerable Americans. If that's so, then it is doubly important that we women add our voices to the national debates, that we take our places at the tables of power, that we rise to the challenge of leadership when we believe that to be our calling.

So then, why can't a woman be more like a woman? In other words, progress for women in public policy and private life may indeed hinge on our ability to acknowledge and develop our skills and values as women. It may just be that those are the skills and values our country needs most at this moment.

I have been privileged during my years in public service to work with a number of successful women in public policy and I would like to pass along some of their observations, and some of my own, about drawing on our professional female advantages.

The first is to take full advantage of our trumpeted trait of flexibility—in fact to plan for the unexpected, and relish our ability to think on our feet. Rigid guidelines, set agendas, and line reporting responsibilities all help create the illusion of control in the current management environment. But perhaps a knack for flexibility is more important.

Another observation I have is that to succeed in the public arena, women must learn to trust their instincts. It's not just female intuition—it's a cognitive skill that we are perhaps more open to. Estimation skills are now being taught to children as they come up through elementary and secondary schools, and instinct is often times another word for it. It's an ability to take in a great deal of information and quickly reduce it to a rough but generally accurate picture. It's the soft route to hard data.

Yet too often we women allow ourselves to be intimidated into denying our instincts—whether it's a judgment of people, situations, or the heart of the policy question. The women in the audience have probably all had the experience of sitting across the table from someone—a man, let's say—with whom you disagree. Ask yourselves: how many times, in this situation, has your reaction been to question your own judgment rather than his—only to find out later that you were right on the money?

Over the ages, we women have perfected to a high art form this trait of second-guessing ourselves. Perhaps it stems from our early constant exposure to society's message that female traits and talents are inferior; but we have to get over it. It takes confidence to trust ourselves, and if we don't have confidence, our voices will be lost if ever they're heard.

The third common denominator I've seen among successful women leaders is a commitment to those who follow. About twenty years ago, a group of us formed an organization called "Executive Women in Government," which still flourishes today. Its purpose is twofold: to help younger women who want to follow into public service by giving them information and advice, and to make it easier for women in policy-making positions to relate to one another across government. Networking—women reaching out to other women—is a way of using our special opportunities to overcome obstacles. I have been helped many times in the stages of my career by women who were ahead of me. As a result, my door is always open to young women who are in need of a mentor, and I would encourage other women to do the same.

The final challenge for women is not to let others define success for us. Our lives are complicated, balancing personal and professional goals, loving our families while searching for individual fulfillment. And every woman must find her own answers—answers that are right for her. Women must allow ourselves, and each other, the freedom to choose. Women across America are discovering that feeling in as many ways as there are women—some through public service, some in the world of business or as lawyers and doctors, and some as wives, mothers, and volunteers. No one can or should tell us where we will find that feeling, or how we will come to define our own success. These are decisions we alone can make for ourselves.

In the fairy tales we were read as children, once having been rescued by the prince, the "female lead" lives happily ever after. That was the theme in Cinderella, Snow White, and Sleeping Beauty. But now perhaps we need to read our daughters a new bedtime story—with a heroine who isn't a princess, but a woman who sees that there are things that need to be changed to make life better for herself and others. A woman who is not a victim, and who doesn't need a rescuer. We need a tale about a woman whose talents and abilities are valued and admired, a woman who uses those talents to succeed. A woman who is committed, who feels passionately about her life's decisions. Such a story would not be a fairy tale—there are thousands of examples. And if each of us continues to ask the right question, "Why can't a woman be more like a woman?" there will be hundreds of thousands more tomorrow.

WOMEN IN THE U.S. CONGRESS

Patricia Schroeder, a Democrat from Colorado, was first elected to the U.S. House of Representatives in 1972. She is the longest-serving congresswoman to date.

A total of 163 (107D, 56R) women have served in the U.S. Congress to date (including delegates): 22 in the Senate (14D, 8R) and 144 (95D, 49R) in the House of Representatives. This compares to almost 1,800 men who have served in the Senate since 1789. Three women have served in both the House and Senate: Barbara Boxer (D-CA), Margaret Chase Smith (R-ME), and Barbara Mikulski (D-MD).

WOMEN IN CONGRESS SINCE 1917

Congress	Dates	Senate	House	Total
65th	1917–19	1 (1R)		1(1R)
75th	1937–39	2 (1D, 1R)*	6 (5D, 1R)	8 (6D, 2R)
85th	1957–59	1 (1R)	15 (9D, 6R)	16 (9D, 7R)
95th	1977–79	2 (2D)	18 (13D, 5R)	20 (15D,5R)
103rd	1993–95	7 (5D, 2R)	48 (36D,12R)**	55 (41D,14R)

* A total of three women served in the Senate this year (2D, 1R), but no more than two served at any one time.

** Includes a Democratic delegate from Washington, D.C.

Margaret Chase Smith, a Maine politician, served 4 terms in the House of Representatives and another 4 terms in the Senate.

WOMEN IN THE 103RD CONGRESS

Leadership roles in this Congress are held by Senator Barbara Mikulski (D-MD), who is assistant floor leader, and Rep. Barbara Kennelly (D-CT), who is chief deputy whip. No standing Congressional committees are chaired by women.

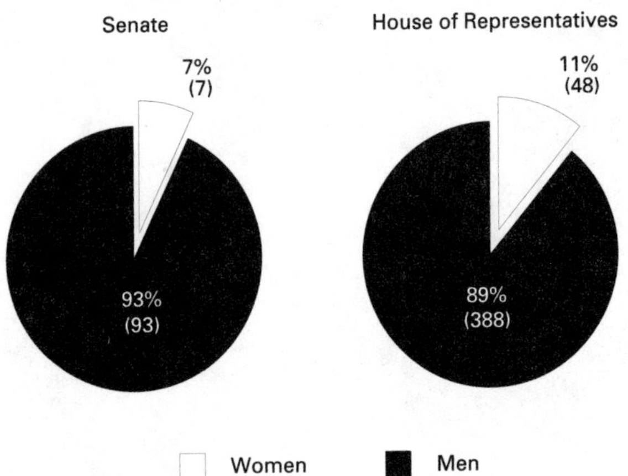

Women of Color in Congress

Fourteen women of color served in the 103rd Congress in 1993, a record that more than doubled the number who served in 1991:

African American
Rep. Corrine Brown (D-FL)
Rep. Eva Clayton (D-NC)
Rep. Barbara-Rose Collins (D-MI)
Rep. Cardiss Collins (D-IL)
Rep. Eddie Bernice Johnson (D-TX)
Rep. Cynthia McKinney (D-GA)
Rep. Carrie Meek (D-FL)
Sen. Carol Moseley-Braun (D-IL)
Del. Eleanor Holmes Norton (D-DC)
Rep. Maxine Waters (D-CA)

Asian/Pacific-American
Rep. Patsy Takemoto Mink (D-HI)

Latina
Rep. Ileana Ros-Lehtinen (R-FL)
Rep. Lucille Roybal-Allard (D-CA)
Rep. Nydia Velazquez (D-NY)

Source: Center for the American Woman and Politics, Eagleton Institute of Politics, Rutgers University

FIRSTS FOR WOMEN OF COLOR

- Carol Moseley-Braun (D-IL), elected to the U.S. Senate in 1992, is the first African-American woman to win a major party Senate nomination and the first woman of color ever to serve in the U.S. Senate.
- Shirley Chisholm (D-NY) became the first African-American congresswoman. She was elected in 1968 and served until 1983.
- Lucille Roybal-Allard (D-CA) recently became the first Mexican-American congresswoman. She was elected in 1993.
- Ileana Ros-Lehtinen (R-FL) became the first Cuban-American (either female or male) and the first Hispanic woman elected to either house. She entered Congress after a special election in 1989, followed by two general election victories in 1990 and 1992.
- Patsy Takemoto Mink (D-HI) was the first Asian/Pacific Islander woman elected to the House. Serving from 1965–77, she was reelected in 1990 and 1992.
- Nydia Velazquez (D-NY), elected in 1992, is the first Puerto Rican congresswoman.

Source: Center for the American Woman and Politics, Eagleton Institute of Politics, Rutgers University

The first woman to wear pants on the House floor was Susan Molinari, a Republican from New York, in 1990.

CONGRESSIONAL CANDIDATES AND WINNERS

In 1973, the U.S. Senate had no women members for the first time since the first woman was elected to the Senate in 1932.

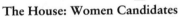

The Senate: Women Candidates and Winners

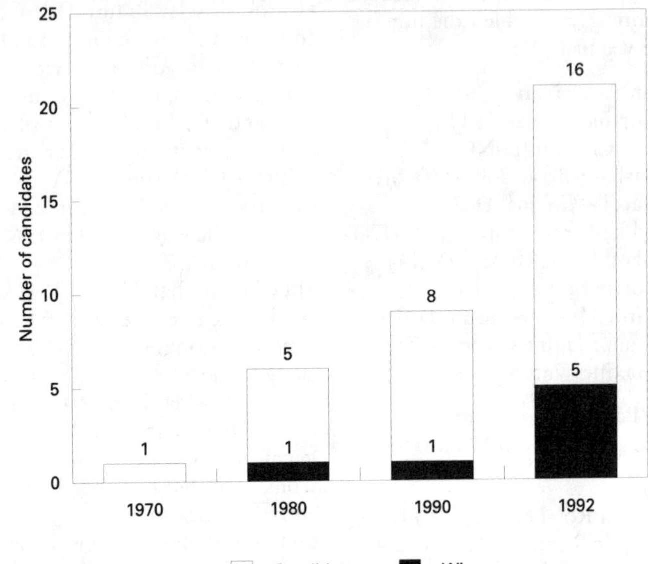

The House: Women Candidates

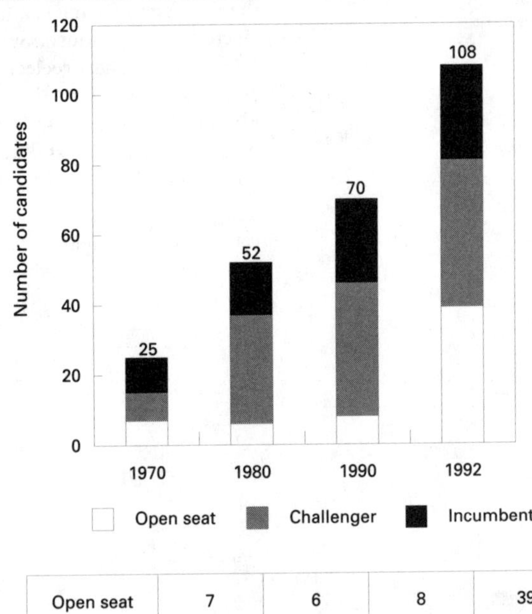

	1970	1980	1990	1992
Open seat	7	6	8	39
Challenger	8	31	38	42
Incumbent	10	15	24	27

The House: Women Winners

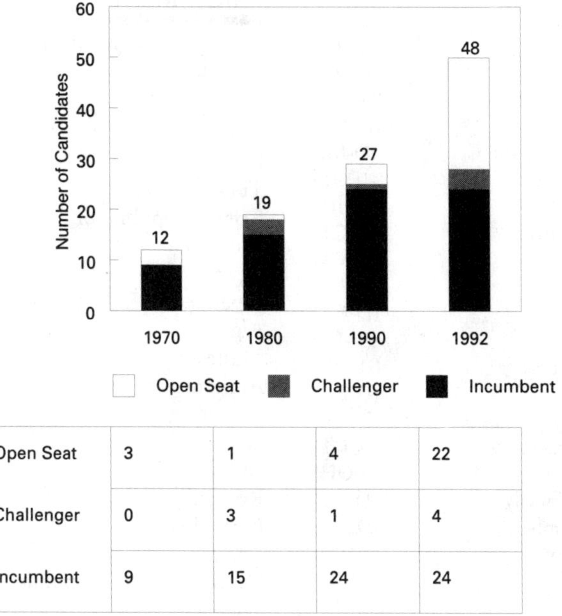

Open Seat	3	1	4	22
Challenger	0	3	1	4
Incumbent	9	15	24	24

Source for above: Center for the American Woman and Politics, Eagleton Institute of Politics, Rutgers University

Women constituted 13% of the House of Councilors and 2.3% of the House of Representatives in Japan in 1993.

CONGRESSIONAL FIRSTS

First woman elected to the House of Representatives:
Jeannette Rankin (R-MT) served from 1917 to 1919, and again from 1941 to 1942.

First woman elected to the Senate without having previously filled an unexpired congressional term:
Nancy Landon Kassebaum (R-KS) was elected in 1978. In 1992 Representative Barbara Mikulski (D-MD) became the first Democratic woman to win office this way.

First time in history that women have held both U.S. Senate seats from any state:
1993, when Barbara Boxer and Dianne Feinstein, both Democrats, won in California.

WOMEN IN THE SENATE

Member	Year first elected
Barbara Boxer (D-CA)	1992
Dianne Feinstein (D-CA)	1992
Kay Bailey Hutchison (R-TX)	1993 (special election)
Nancy Landon Kassebaum (R-KS)	1978 (reelected in 1984 and 1990)
Barbara Mikulski (D-MD)	1986 (reelected in 1992)
Carol Moseley-Braun (D-IL)	1992
Patty Murray (D-WA)	1992

Source: Center for the American Woman and Politics, Eagleton Institute of Politics, Rutgers University

The first black woman elected to Britain's Parliament was Diane Abbot, in 1987.

The first girl to be a page in Congress was appointed in 1970.

WOMEN IN THE HOUSE OF REPRESENTATIVES

Helen Bentley	(R-MD)
Corrine Brown	(D-FL)
Leslie Byrne	(D-VA)
Maria Cantwell	(D-WA)
Eva Clayton	(D-NC)
Barbara-Rose Collins	(D-MI)
Cardiss Collins	(D-IL)
Pat Danner	(D-MO)
Rose DeLauro	(D-CT)
Jennifer Dunn	(R-WA)
Karen English	(D-AZ)
Anna Eshoo	(D-CA)
Tillie Fowler	(R-FL)
Elizabeth Furse	(D-OR)
Jane Harman	(D-CA)
Eddie Bernice Johnson	(D-TX)
Nancy Johnson	(R-CT)
Marcy Kaptur	(D-OH)
Barbara Kennelly	(D-CT)
Blanche Lambert	(D-AR)
Marilyn Lloyd	(D-TN)
Jill Long	(D-IN)
Nita Lowey	(D-NY)
Carolyn Maloney	(D-NY)
Marjorie Margolies-Mezvinsky	(D-PA)
Cynthia McKinney	(D-GA)
Carrie Meek	(D-FL)
Jan Meyers	(R-KS)
Patsy Mink	(D-HI)
Susan Molinari	(R-NY)
Constance Morella	(R-MD)
Eleanor Holmes Norton	(D-DC)
Nancy Pelosi	(D-CA)
Deborah Pryce	(R-OH)
Ileana Ros-Lehtinen	(R-FL)
Marge Roukema	(R-NJ)
Lucille Roybal-Allard	(D-CA)
Lynn Schenk	(D-CA)
Patricia Schroeder	(D-CO)
Karen Shepherd	(D-UT)
Louise Slaughter	(D-NY)
Olympia Snowe	(R-ME)
Karen Thurman	(D-FL)
Jolene Unsoeld	(D-WA)
Nydia Velazquez	(D-NY)
BarbaraVucanovich	(R-NV)
Maxine Waters	(D-CA)
Lynn Woolsey	(D-CA)

Source: Center for the American Woman and Politics, Eagleton Institute of Politics, Rutgers University

INTERNATIONAL POLITICS: WOMEN MEMBERS OF PARLIAMENT

Countries where Parliament is still 95% male

	% Women
Pakistan	1
Kenya	1
Turkey	1
Korea, Republic of	2
Mongolia	2
Egypt	2
Japan	2
Algeria	2
Malta	3
Afghanistan	3
Yemen	3
Nepal	3
Albania	4
Romania	4
Barbados	4
Thailand	4
Central African Republic	4
Togo	4
Bahamas	4
Tunisia	4
Maldives	4
Argentina	5
Ivory Coast	5
Sri Lanka	5
Zaire	5

Regions with Higher Numbers of Women MPs

	% Women
Asia	13
Europe	13
Americas	12
Sub-Saharan Africa	9
Pacific	6
Arab States	4
World average	11

Source for above: UNICEF

CAROL MOSELEY-BRAUN—A POLITICIAN MAKES HER MARK

The first African-American woman to serve in the U.S. Senate, Carol Moseley-Braun (D-IL) spoke out against renewing a design patent for the United Daughters of the Confederacy during her first months in office. Her highly regarded speech on the floor of the Senate on July 22, 1993, excerpted here, turned the tide of Congressional support against the amendment and marked her as a strong new voice in the Senate.

The real bottom line with regard to this amendment and to the request for a design patent by the United Daughters of the Confederacy is that it is not needed. . . . They can continue to fundraise. They can continue to exist. They can continue to use the insignia. The only issue is whether or not this body is prepared to put its imprimatur on the Confederate insignia used by the United Daughters of the Confederacy.

I submit to you, Mr. President, and the Members who are listening to this debate, that the United Daughters of the Confederacy have every right to honor their ancestors and to choose the Confederate flag as their symbol if they like. However, those of us whose ancestors fought on a different side in the Civil War, or who were held, frankly, as human chattel under the Confederate flag, are duty bound to honor our ancestors as well by asking whether such recognition by the U.S. Senate is appropriate.

The United Daughters of the Confederacy did not require this action to either conduct the affairs of their organization or to protect their insignia against unauthorized use. This is not an issue about protecting the insignia of the United Daughters of the Confederacy, not is it an issue about whether or not they do good works in the community, nor is it an issue of whether or not the organization has the right to use the insignia. I think the answer in all those cases is they have a right to use whatever insignia they want, they have a right to organize in any way they want, they have a right to conduct whatever business they want. But at the same time it is inappropriate for this Senate, this U.S. Congress, to grant a special, extraordinary imprimatur, if you will, to a symbol which is as inappropriate to all of us as Americans as this one is.

I have heard the argument on the floor today with regard to the imprimatur that is being sought for this organization and for this symbol, and I submit this really is revisionist history. The fact of the matter is the emblems of the Confederacy have meaning to all Americans even 100 years after the end of the Civil War. Everybody knows what the Confederacy stands for. Everybody knows what the insignia means. That matter of common knowledge is not a surprise to any of us. When a former governor stood and raised the Confederate battle flag over the Alabama state capitol to protest the federal government support for civil rights and a visit by the attorney general at the time in 1963, everybody knew what that meant. Now, in this time, in 1993, when we see the Confederate symbols hauled out, everybody knows what it means.

So I submit, as Americans we have an obligation, number one, to recognize the meaning, not to fall prey to revisionist history on the one hand; and also really to make a statement that we believe the Civil War is over. We believe that as Americans we are all Americans and we have a need to be respectful of one another with regard to our respective histories, just as I would.

Whether we are black or white, Northerners or Southerners, all Americans share a common flag. The flag which is behind you right now, Mr. President, is our flag. . . . And to give a design patent that even our own flag does not enjoy to a symbol of the Confederacy seems to me just to create the kind of divisions in our society that are counterproductive, that are not needed.

So I come back to the point I raised to begin with. What is the point of doing this? Why would we give an extraordinary honor to a symbol which is counter to the symbol that we as Americans, I believe, all know and love, which would be a recognition of the losing side of the war, a war that I hope —while it is a painful part of our history—I hope as Americans we have all gotten past and we can say as Americans we come together under a single flag. And this organization, if it chooses to honor the losing side of the Civil War, that is their prerogative. But symbols are important. They speak volumes. And it is inappropriate for that organization to call on the rest of us, on everybody else, to give our imprimatur to the symbolism of the Confederate flag.

COUNTRIES WHERE WOMEN'S PRESENCE IN PARLIAMENT IS DECLINING

	%Women		%Decrease
	1975	1991	
Albania	33	4	-87
Hungary	29	7	-75
China	23	21	-8
Mongolia	23	2	-72
Bulgaria	19	9	-52
Poland	16	14	-12
Zaire	11	5	-54
Argentina	9	5	-44
Ivory Coast	9	5	-44
Barbados	8	4	-50
Korea, Rep.	6	2	-66
Kenya	4	1	-75
Pakistan	4	1	-75

Source: UNICEF

The year 1993 saw the election of several women prime ministers, including Kim Campbell (Canada), Hanna Suchocka (Poland), and Tansu Ciller (Turkey).

WOMEN GOVERNORS

Women Currently Serving as Governors

Joan Finney (D-KS)
Christine Todd Whitman (R-NJ)
Ann Richards (D-TX)
Barbara Roberts (D-OR)

In addition, 11 women serve as lieutenant governors among the 42 states that have such a position.

Mary Robinson was elected the first female president of Ireland on December 31, 1990.

Former Women Governors

	Years of service
Nellie Tayloe Ross (D-WY)	1925–27
Miriam "Ma" Ferguson (D-TX)	1925–27, 1933–35
Lurleen Wallace (D-AL)	1967–68
Ella Grasso (D-CT)	1974–80
Dixy Lee Ray (D-WA)	1977–81
Martha Layne Collins (D-KY)	1984–87
Madeleine Kunin (D-VT)	1985–91
Kay Orr (R-NE)	1987–91

STATEWIDE FIRSTS

First woman governor:
Nellie Tayloe Ross (D–WY) replaced her deceased husband and served from 1925 to 1927.

First woman governor elected in her own right:
Ella Grasso (D-CT) was elected in 1974 and re-elected in 1978.

First woman elected lieutenant governor:
Consuelo Bailey (R-VT) was elected in 1954.

First woman attorney general:
Pamela Fanning Carter of Indiana is the first African American woman attorney general and the only woman of color currently serving in that capacity; she was elected in 1992.

Wilma Mankiller was sworn in as the first female chief of the Cherokee Nation, the second largest tribe in the U.S., on December 5, 1985.

WOMEN IN STATEWIDE ELECTIVE EXECUTIVE OFFICES

Attorney General–8
Gale Norton (R-CO)
Bonney Campbell (D-IA)
Pamela Carer (D-IN)
Heidi Heitkamp (D-ND)
Frankie Sue Del Papa (D-NV)
Susan Loving (D-OK)
Jan Graham (D-UT)
Christine Gregoire (D-WA)

Secretary of State–11
March Fong Eu (D-CA)
Natalie Meyer (R-CO)
Pauline Kezer (R-CT)
Elaine Baxter (D-IA)
Joan Anderson Growe (D-FL-MN)
Judith Moriarty (D-MO)
Stephanie Gonzales (D-NM)
Cheryl Lau (R-NV)
Barbara Leonard (R-RI)
Joyce Hazeltine (R-SD)
Kathleen Karpan (D-WY)

State Treasurer–16
Jimmie Lou Fisher (D-AR)
Kathleen Brown (D-CA)
Gail Schoettler (D-CO)
Janet Rzewnicki (R-DE)
Lydia Justice Edwards (R-ID)
Marjorie O'Laughlin (R-IN)
Sally Thompson (D-KS)
Frances Jones Mills (D-KY)
Mary Landrieu (D-LA)
Kathi Gilmore (D-ND)
Dawn Rockey (D-NE)
Mary Ellen Withrow (D-OH)
Claudette Henry (R-OK)
Catherine Baker Knoll (D-PA)
Nancy Myer (R-RI)
Cathy Zeuske (R-WI)

Source: Center for the American Woman and Politics, Eagleton Institute of Politics, Rutgers University

WOMEN OF COLOR IN MAJOR STATE GOVERNMENT POSITIONS

Of the 72 women serving in statewide elective executive offices, four, or 5.6%, are women of color:

African-American
Pamela Carter (D-IN)
Attorney general

Asian/Pacific Islander:
March Fong Eu (D-CA)
Secretary of state

Cheryl Lau (R-NV)
Secretary of state

Latina
Stephanie Gonzales (D-NM)
Secretary of state

Source: Center for the American Woman and Politics, Eagleton Institute of Politics, Rutgers University

Fast Fact: First Couple to Run for Office

Dr. Genevieve Marcus and her husband, businessman Bob Smith, captured 8% of the vote in the 1990 California Democratic primary race for governor and lieutenant governor. Running as "co-governors" on a platform supporting full employment, child-care reform, and other social and environmental concerns, Smith and Marcus are the first married couple in the world to run for office.

Source: Equal Relationships Institute

BREAKDOWN OF STATE ELECTIVE OFFICES

By Sex and by Party

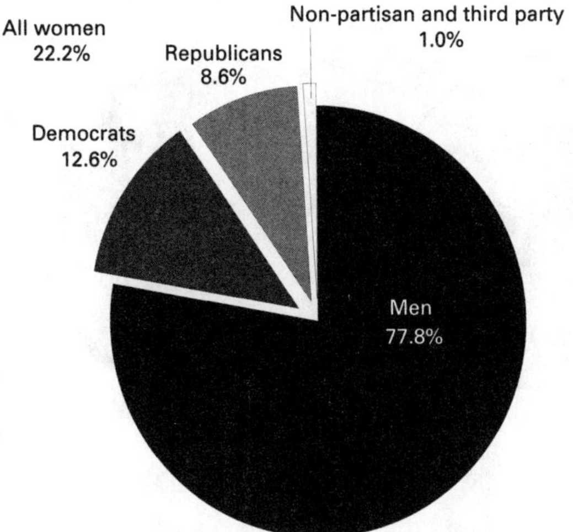

Source: Center for the American Woman and Politics, Eagleton Institute of Politics, Rutgers University

FIRSTS IN THE STATE LEGISLATURES

First Women Elected as State Legislators:
In 1894, Republicans Clara Cressingham, Carrie C. Holly, and Frances Klock were elected to the Colorado House of Representatives. In 1896, Democrat Martha Hughes was elected to the Utah State Senate.

WOMEN IN STATE LEGISLATURES

Since 1969, the number of women serving in state legislatures has increased five-fold. The following graphs illustrate the changing face of these state bodies.

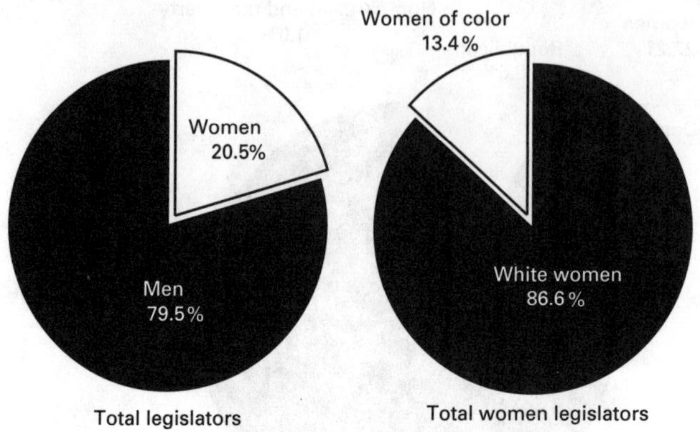

Women Officeholders

This graph shows the number of women officeholders, along with the percentage they represent of total legislators.

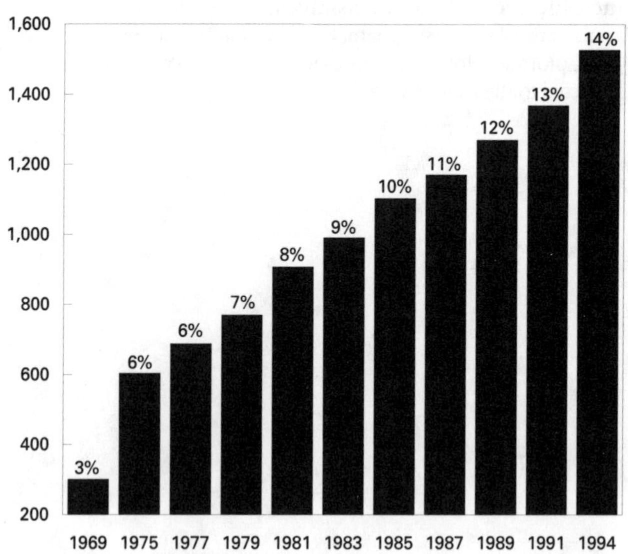

Party Affiliation of Women in State Legislatures

Democrats	61.0% (931)
Republicans	28.2% (583)
Non-partisans	0.7% (10)
Independents	0.1% (2)

(Data from 1993)

Eleanor Roosevelt was the first U.S. delegate to the United Nations, from 1945 to 1951.

Racial Breakdown of Women Legislators

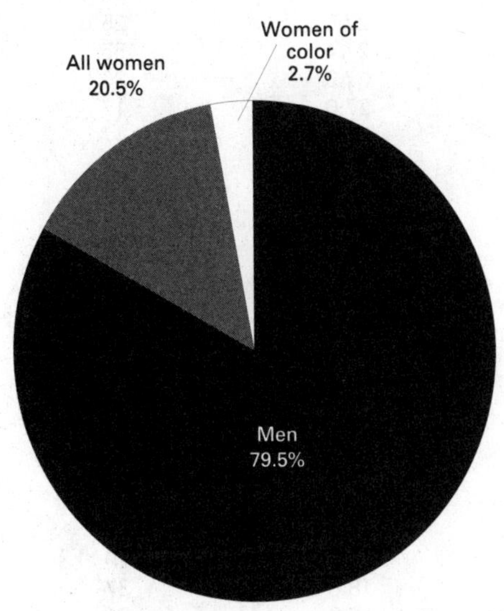

Total Legislators: 8,948

Women of color	(13.4% of women legislators)
African American	(153 legislators)
Asian/Pacific Islander	(18 legislators)
Latina	(27 legislators)
Native American	(6 legislators)

Source for above: Center for the American Woman and Politics, Eagleton Institute of Politics, Rutgers University

Adlai Stevenson gave an address at Smith College in 1955 encouraging the new graduates to participate in politics through the role of wife and mother rather than define themselves by a profession.

STATE RANKINGS OF WOMEN IN STATE LEGISLATURES, 1993

Rank/State	% Women	Total women	Legislators
1. Washington	39.5	58	147
2. Arizona	35.6	32	90
3. Colorado	35.0	35	100
4. Vermont	33.9	61	180
5. New Hampshire	33.5	142	424
6. Maine	31.7	59	186
7. Idaho	30.5	32	105
8. Kansas	29.1	48	165
9. Oregon	27.8	25	90
10. Minnesota	27.4	55	201
11. Wisconsin	27.3	36	132
12. Nevada	27.0	17	63
13. Connecticut	25.1	47	187
14. Rhode Island	24.7	37	150
15. Wyoming	24.4	22	90
16. Maryland	23.9	45	188
17. Hawaii	23.7	18	76
18. California	23.3	28	120
19. Illinois	23.2	41	177
20. Massachusetts	23.0	46	200
21. Alaska	21.7	13	60
22. Ohio	21.2	28	132
23. Nebraska	20.4	10	49
24. Michigan	20.3	30	148
25. Montana	20.0	30	150
26. South Dakota	20.0	21	105
27. New Mexico	19.6	22	112
28. Indiana	19.3	29	150
29. Missouri	18.8	37	197
30. North Carolina	18.2	31	170
31. Florida	17.5	28	160
32. Georgia	17.4	41	236
33. New York	16.6	35	211
34. West Virginia	16.4	22	134
35. North Dakota	16.3	24	147
36. Texas	16.0	29	181
37. Iowa	14.7	22	150
38. Delaware	14.5	9	62
39. Utah	13.5	14	104
40. South Carolina	12.9	22	170
41. New Jersey	12.5	15	120
42. Virginia	12.1	17	140
43. Tennessee	12.1	16	132
44. Mississippi	10.9	19	174
45. Pennsylvania	9.9	25	253
46. Arkansas	9.6	13	135
47. Oklahoma	9.4	14	149
48. Louisiana	7.6	11	144
49. Alabama	5.0	7	140
50. Kentucky	4.3	6	138

Source: Center for the American Woman and Politics, Eagleton Institute of Politics, Rutgers University

WOMEN IN LOCAL GOVERNMENT

Women Mayors

The percentage shown here is of the total number of mayors in the U.S.

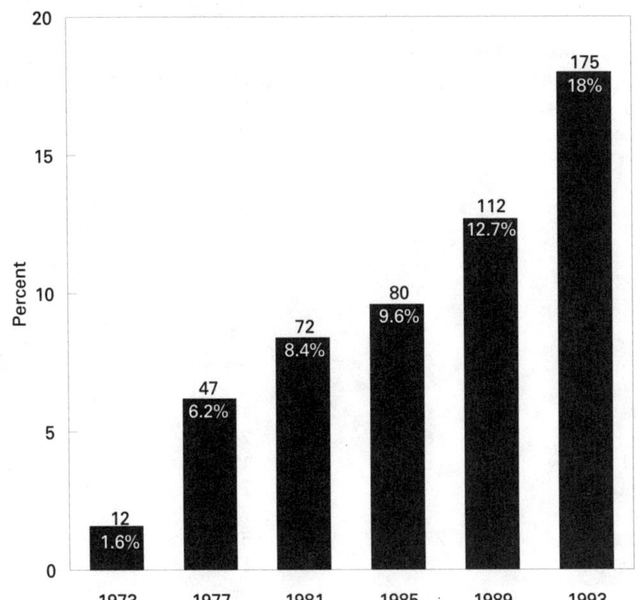

Sources: U.S. Conference of Mayors, and Center for the American Woman and Politics, Eagleton Institute of Politics, Rutgers University

Current Women Mayors Among the 100 Largest U.S. Cities

Rank by Size/City	Mayor (Party)	First year in office
6. San Diego, California	Susan Golding (R)	1993
11. San Jose, California	Susan Hammer (D)	1991
19. Washington, D.C.	Sharon Pratt Kelly (D)	1990
28. Fort Worth, Texas	Kay Granger (NP*)	1991
30. Portland, Oregon	Vera Katz (D)	1992
37. Virginia Beach, Virginia	Meyera Oberndorf (NP)	1988
43. Minneapolis, Minnesota	Sharon Sayles Belton (D)	1994
44. Tulsa, Oklahoma	M. Susan Savage (D)	1992
45. Cincinnati, Ohio	Roxanne Qualls (D)	1993
51. Wichita, Kansas	Elma Broadfoot (D)	1992
55. Tampa, Florida	Sandra Freedman (D)	1986
63. Las Vegas, Nevada	Jan Laverty Jones (NP)	1991
64. Corpus Christi, Texas	Mary Rhodes (NP)	1990
70. Lexington-Fayette, Kentucky	Pam Miller (D)	1990
75. Stockton, California	Joan Darrah (D)	1990
77. Shrevesport, Louisiana	Hazel Beard (R)	1990
88. Greensboro, North Carolina	Carolyn Allen (NP)	1987
90. Huntington Beach, California	Linda Moulton Patterson (NP)	1993

*NP indicates non-partisan

Source: Center for the American Woman and Politics, Eagleton Institute of Politics, Rutgers University

Wyoming passed the first women's suffrage law in 1869.

Cheryl Campbell Steadman and Marie Reynolds Garcia became the first female members of the Texas Rangers, an elite division of the Texas Department of Public Safety, in 1993.

95% of the top female appointees in local governments are white. However, African-American women are the fastest growing group in the American electoral process.

Eight wives of presidents did not serve as First Lady. Five died before their husbands became president, two married the presidents after their term of office, and one divorced her husband before he became president.

WOMEN MAYORS AND MUNICIPAL COUNCIL MEMBERS

State	1975	1985	% Increase
Alabama	85	281	230
Alaska	35	233	566
Arizona	39	87	123
Arkansas	160	365	128
California	220	465	111
Colorado	170	315	85
Connecticut	130	240	85
Delaware	22	57	159
Florida	174	311	19
Georgia	77	251	226
Hawaii	1	3	*
Idaho	45	141	213
Illinois	—	—	—
Indiana	—	—	—
Iowa	304	732	141
Kansas	165	445	170
Kentucky	—	—	—
Louisiana	65	183	182
Maine	87	243	179
Maryland	59	133	125
Massachusetts	48	217	352
Michigan	*	2,779	*
Minnesota	227	542	139
Mississippi	82	176	115
Missouri	—	—	—
Montana	57	110	93
Nebraska	83	241	190
Nevada	2	15	*
New Hampshire	39	113	190
New Jersey	213	451	112
New Mexico	33	86	161
New York	*	797	*
North Carolina	141	337	139
North Dakota	69	174	152
Ohio	*	1,129	*
Oklahoma	92	312	239
Oregon	175	344	97
Pennsylvania	—	—	—
Rhode Island	21	30	43
South Carolina	72	184	156
South Dakota	50	149	198
Tennessee	50	144	188
Texas	277	786	184
Utah	40	137	243
Vermont	44	87	98
Virginia	117	211	80
Washington	153	341	123
Washington, D.C.	3	7	*
West Virginia	120	202	68
Wisconsin	—	—	—
Wyoming	34	86	153
National	4,080	14,672	14.3

* Comparisons are invalid because number is too small or data are based on different assumptions

Source: Center for the American Woman and Politics, Eagleton Institute of Politics, Rutgers University

MAYORAL FIRSTS

First major city to elect a woman mayor:
Seattle, Washington, elected Bertha Landes in 1926.

First black woman to serve as mayor of a city with a population of over 100,000:
Loretta Glickman was elected mayor of Pasadena, California, in 1982.

NATIONAL POLITICAL ACTION COMMITTEES FOR WOMEN

There are almost fifty political action committees (PACs) and donor networks plus three party-affiliated fund-raising organizations that either give money predominately to women candidates or have a predominately female donor base (not including state affiliates of national organizations or issue PACs). The national organizations are:

EMILY's List
1112 16th Street, N.W., Suite 750
Washington, DC 20036
(202) 887-1957
Supports Democratic pro-choice women.

Hollywood Women's Political Committee
3679 Motor Avenue, Suite 300
Los Angeles, CA 90034
(310) 287-2803
Non-partisan; all members are women involved in the entertainment industry.

National Federation of Business and Professional Women's Clubs PAC
2012 Massachusetts Avenue, N.W.
Washington, DC 20036
Attn: Resource Center
(202) 293-1100
Non-partisan; supports women and pro-women candidates on the national level.

National Organization for Women PAC
1000 16th Street, N.W., Suite 700
Washington, DC 20036
(202) 331-0066
Non-partisan group that supports progressive female and male candidates on national, state and local levels.

National Women's Political Caucus
1275 K Street, N.W., Suite 750
Washington, DC 20005
(202) 898-1100
Non-partisan; supports candidates on national and state levels.

RENEW
(Republican Network to Elect Women)
1555 King Street, Suite 200
P.O. Box 507
Alexandria, VA 22313
(703) 836-2255
Supports Republican women on national, state, and local levels.

Susan B. Anthony
5310 North 26th Road
Arlington, VA 22207
(703) 534-3830
Non-partisan group that supports pro-life candidates on the national level.

WISH List (Women in the Senate and House)
210 W. Front Street
Red Bank, NJ 07701
(908) 747-4221
Supports Republican pro-choice women on national, state, and local levels.

Women's Campaign Fund
120 Maryland Avenue, N.E.
Washington, DC 20002
(202) 544-4484
Non-partisan; supports pro-choice women on national, state, and local levels.

Women's Council of the Democratic Senatorial Campaign Committee
430 South Capitol St., S.E.
Washington, DC 20003
(202) 224-2447
Supports Democratic pro-choice women candidates for the Senate.

The "Year of the Woman" in 1992 saw a 200% increase in Senate seats and a 68% increase in House seats for women. In real numbers, this translates into 4 Senate seats and 18 House seats.

Lyndon Johnson proposed to Lady Bird on their first date, and they were married two months later.

"The thing women have got to learn is nobody gives you power. You just take it."—Roseanne Arnold

Sylvia Rhone, CEO of EastWest Records, is the first woman and the first African-American woman to head her own record label.

NATIONAL PACS SUPPORTING LESBIAN AND GAY CANDIDATES

Gay and Lesbian Victory Fund
1012 14th Street, N.W.
Washington, DC 20005
(202) 842-8679

The Human Rights Campaign Fund
1012 14th Street, N.W.
Washington, DC 20005
(202) 628-4160

REGIONAL POLITICAL ACTION COMMITTEES

Ain't I A Woman Network/PAC
1501 Cherry Street
Philadelphia, PA 19102
(215) 248-1147

Alabama Solution
P.O. Box 370821
Birmingham, AL 35237
(205) 250-0205

Arkansas Women's Action Fund
1100 North University, Suite 109
Little Rock, AR 72207
(501) 663-1202

Capitol Power for Republican Women PAC
P.O. Box 20215
Alexandria, VA 22320

The Committee for the Election of Western New York Women
64 Tudor Place
Buffalo, NY 14222

Committee of 21
P.O. Box 19287
New Orleans, LA 70179
(504) 286-8867

Eleanor Roosevelt Fund of California
1001-158 Evelyn Terrace East
Sunnyvale, CA 94086
(408) 773-9791

First Ladies of Oklahoma
8364 S. Urbana Avenue
Tulsa, OK 74137

Focus 2020
P.O. Box 660
Huntsville, AL 35804

GWEN's List
13899 Biscayne Boulevard, Suite 154
North Miami Beach, FL 33181
(305) 947-9479

Harriet's List
P.O. Box 16361
Baltimore, MD 21210
(410) 377-5709

H.O.P.E. Chest
P.O. Box 1584
Mobile, AL 36633
(205) 432-7682

The Hope Chest
P.O. Box 21772
Columbus, OH 43221
(614) 451-9444

HOPE-PAC
3220 East 26th Street
Los Angeles, CA 90023
(213) 267-5853

Indiana Women's Political Network PAC
P.O. Box 88271
Indianapolis, IN 46208
(317) 283-2066

Latina PAC
915 L Street, Suite C, #222
Sacramento, CA 95814
(916) 395-7915

The Leader PAC
P.O. Box 7001
Fairfax Station, VA 22039
(202) 467-5522

Los Angeles African American Women's PAC
4102 Olympiad Drive
Los Angeles, CA 90043
(213) 295-2383

Los Angeles Women's Campaign Fund
1410 Ventura Boulevard, Suite 402
Sherman Oaks, CA 91423
(818) 990-7377

Marin County Women's PAC
3310 Paradise Drive
Tiburon, CA 94920
(415) 435-2504

Michigan Women's Campaign Fund
2600 W. Big Beaver
Troy, MI 48084
(313) 548-9563

Minnesota $$ Million
550 Rice Street
St. Paul, MN 55103
(612) 221-0441

Minnesota Women's Campaign Fund
550 Rice Street
St. Paul, MN 55103
(612) 222-1603

Missouri Women's Action Fund
1108 Hillside Drive
St. Louis, MO 63117
(314) 781-1081

PAC of the Woman's Democratic Club of Delaware
1222 Arundel Drive
Wilmington, DE 19808
(302) 998-5038

PAM's List
P.O. Box 43008
Upper Montclair, NJ 07043

Pennsylvania Women's Campaign Fund
P.O. Box 767
Hazleton, PA 18201
(717) 524-4713

Republican Women's PAC of Illinois
223 W. Jackson Boulevard, Suite 100
Chicago, IL 60606
(312) 939-7300

Sacramento Women's Campaign Fund
P.O. Box 162212
Sacremento, CA 95816
(916) 445-5598

Santa Barbara Women's Political Committee
P.O. Box 90618
Santa Barbara, CA 93190
(805) 682-6769

Task Force 2000 PAC
P.O. Box 36183
Houston, TX 77036
(713) 495-7539

VOW
5526 South Toledo Place
Tulsa, OK 74135

Women For:
8913 West Olympic Boulevard
Suite 103
Beverly Hills, CA 90211
(310) 657-7411

Women For: Orange County
21 Whitman Court
Irvine, CA 92715
(714) 854-8024

Women in the Nineties (WIN)
102 Woodmont Boulevard, Suite 360
Nashville, TN 37305
(615) 298-1250

Women Organizing Women PAC (WOW PAC)
P.O. Box 1652
New Haven, CT 06507
(203) 281-3400

Women's Investment Network (WIN-PAC)
3333 S.W. Arnold
Portland, OR 97219
(503) 246-6022

Women's Political Action Committee of N.J.
P.O. Box 170
Edison, NJ 08818
(908) 638-6784

Women's Political Committee
315 Conway Avenue
Los Angeles, CA 90024
(310) 446-4820

Women's Political Fund
P.O. Box 421811
San Francisco, CA 94142
(415) 861-5168

"There is no deodorant like success."—Elizabeth Taylor

When asked what they did for fun during a week, 47% of women in a *Redbook* poll said they read a book.

ELLEN MALCOLM—OVERCOMING THE CREDIBILITY GAP

Ellen Malcolm is president and founder of EMILY's List, a national political network that seeks to raise campaign funds for the election of pro-choice Democratic women. (Portions of the following essay originally appeared in the New York Times, August 8, 1992.)

The prospects for electing women to high office continue to be exhilarating. But as we look back on recent political successes, a pattern of personal attacks against female candidates emerges. Using familiar stereotypes, attackers tried to undercut the credibility of the women running for office, from New York to California. It's a pattern that will reemerge in 1994 and beyond.

Female candidates have to prove themselves again and again to voters and the press, long after their male opponents have established themselves. Whether these women are criticized for their fundraising skills or the management of their campaigns, it all boils down to "they can't win." Often these accusations are launched not in paid advertising but with behind-the-scenes sniping and whisper campaigns: for example, the opposing candidates' camp might give commentators an "inside" analysis to pass on to the public.

Time and time again I have been told in great confidential detail why a particular female candidate cannot win. Certainly men's campaigns are criticized, too, but not with the same level of minutiae as the women's. A recent example of this was the buzz in 1992 that Carol Moseley-Braun's Senate campaign in Illinois was (gasp!) disorganized. I have been in many campaigns, and few were models of efficiency. To trivialize Braun's campaign because junior staff people quit or the candidate was late for lunch is to set a standard of excellence that no campaign can meet.

Conventional wisdom, the nemesis of female candidates, often has it that a particular woman cannot raise money for her race. Early on in her race for the Senate, Barbara Boxer of California was considered a good candidate, but conventional wisdom, as divined by the pundits, pronounced that she could never compete financially with her male opponents. Men often have networks of large donors to tap. Female candidates like Boxer have successfully relied on small contributions from many people. And indeed Boxer's victory was made possible by thousands of checks for $25 and $100.

If a female candidate's political skills are proven, her detractors sometimes denounce her by attacking the people around her, especially the men with whom she is associated. In Pennsylvania's 1992 Senate race, Lynn Yeakel, the Democratic candidate, was criticized by an ally of her opponent for her father's record on civil rights in the 1960s. Several people across the country complained to me that Yeakel was not supportive of Israel. Their grounds? Yeakel's minister had made statements that were construed as anti-Israel. Yeakel's record as unequivocally committed to the integrity of Israel was deemed irrelevant in the face of the statements of her minister.

Perhaps any time a new political group breaks down barriers, questions arise about its members' ability to act on their own. Remember the concerns that John F. Kennedy, the first Roman Catholic president, would be influenced by the pope?

The antidote to attacks on female politicians' credibility is the women themselves. Women candidates are quite able to go toe-to-toe with their opponents; a record number did and won in 1992, and women will continue to win in the coming years.

The 1992 victories changed perceptions and helped future candidates fight negative stereotypes. If we keep fighting, we will begin to see enough women in high office to make our representative democracy truly representative.

GROUPS THAT SUPPORT WOMEN INVOLVED IN THE POLITICAL PROCESS

Organizations for Democratic Women

Democratic National Committee
Women's Outreach Desk
430 S. Capitol Street, S.E.
Washington, DC 20003
(202) 863-8000

The National Federation of Democratic Women
1 Plaza South, Suite 189
Tahlequah, OK 74464
(918) 456-1281

The Woman's National Democratic Club
1526 New Hampshire Avenue, N.W.
Washington, DC 20036
(202) 232-7363

Organizations for Republican Women

Republican National Committee
Office of the Co-Chairman
310 First Street, S.E.
Washington, DC 20003
(202) 863-8545

National Federation of Republican Women
124 N. Alfred Street
Alexandria, VA 22314
(703) 548-9688

The Women's National Republican Club
3 W. 51st Street
New York, NY 10019
(212) 582-5454

Non-Partisan Organizations

American Legion Auxiliary Girls' State/Girls' Nation
National Headquarters
777 N. Meridian Street
Indianapolis, IN 46204
(317) 635-6291
Offers a summer program for girls to learn about government.

Center for the American Woman and Politics
Eagleton Institute of Politics
Rutgers, The State University of New Jersey
New Brunswick, NJ 08901
(908) 828-2210
Offers intensive summer leadership program for women college students interested in politics.

Congressional Caucus for Women's Issues
2471 Rayburn Building
Washington, DC 20515
(202) 225-6740
Groups of congresspeople who provide resources on women's issues and advocate on behalf of women's rights.

The Fund for the Feminist Majority
1600 Wilson Boulevard, Suite 801
Arlington, VA 22209
(703) 522-2214
Offers internships to women college students or graduates.

National Woman's Party
144 Constitution Avenue N.E.
Washington, DC 20002
(202) 546-1210
Primary goal is passage of the Equal Rights Amendment.

National Women's Political Caucus
1275 K Street, N.W.
Washington, D.C. 20005
(202) 898-1100
A national, grassroots, bipartisan organization dedicated to increasing the number of women in elected and appointed office at every level.

The League of Women Voters

The League distributes information on candidates and issues, and actively encourages registration and voting. Its national headquarters are:

The League of Women Voters
1730 M Street, N.W.
Washington, DC 20036
(202) 429-1965

All local offices can be reached by writing to the League of Women Voters at the following addresses:

Alabama
3357 Cherokee Road
Birmingham, AL 35223
(205) 970-2389

Alaska
P.O. Box 423
Douglas, AK 99824

Women hold 10% of the seats in national legislatures worldwide, according to estimates by the Feminist Majority Report.

Dawn Steel, the former president of Columbia Pictures, was the first woman to head a major movie studio.

Arizona
7239 East Vista Drive
Scottsdale, AZ 85250
(602) 423-5440

Arkansas
The Executive Building
2020 W. Third, #501
Little Rock, AR 72205
(501) 376-7760

California
926 J Street, #1000
Sacramento, CA 95814
(916) 442-7215

Colorado
1410 Grant Street, #204-B
Denver, CO 80203
(303) 863-0437

Connecticut
1890 Dixwell Avenue, #113
Hamden, CT 06514
(203) 288-7996

Delaware
1800 N. Broom Street, Room 201
Wilmington, DE 19802
(302) 571-8948

District of Columbia
2025 Eye Street, N.W., #917
Washington, DC 20006
(202) 331-4122

Florida
540 Beverly Court
Tallahassee, FL 32301
(904) 224-2545

Georgia
1775 Peachtree Street, #233N
Atlanta, GA 30309
(404) 874-7352

Hawaii
49 S. Hotel Street, #314
Honolulu, HI 96813
(808) 531-7448

Idaho
514 E. Morton
Moscow, ID 83843

Illinois
332 S. Michigan Avenue, #1142
Chicago, IL 60604
(312) 939-5935

Indiana
740 E. 52nd Street, Suite 3
Indianapolis, IN 46205
(317) 925-8683

Iowa
4817 University Avenue, Suite 8
Des Moines, IA 50311
(515) 277-0814

Kansas
919 1/2 S. Kansas Avenue
Topeka, KS 66612
(913) 234-5152

Kentucky
Clauson Mouser Office Building
3033 Ring Road
Elizabethtown, KY 42701
(502) 769-0808

Louisiana
850 N. Fifth Street, #103
Baton Rouge, LA 70802
(504) 344-3326

Maine
335 Water Street
Augusta, ME 04330
(207) 622-0256

Maryland
200 Duke of Gloucester Street
Annapolis, MD 21401
(410) 269-0232

Massachusetts
133 Portland Street, Lower Level
Boston, MA 02114
(617) 523-2999

Michigan
200 Museum Drive, Suite 104
Lansing, MI 48933
(517) 484-5383

Minnesota
550 Rice Street, Suite 201
St. Paul, MN 55103
(612) 224-5445

Mississippi
P.O. Box 55505
Jackson, MS 39296
(601) 352-4616

Missouri
6665 Delmar, Room 204
St. Louis, MO 63130
(314) 727-8674

Montana
401 Ben Hogan Drive
Missoula, MT 59803

Nebraska
808 P Street, Suite 207
Lincoln, NE 68508
(402) 475-1411

Nevada
6 Savage Circle
Carson City, NV 89703

New Hampshire
207 North Main Street
Concord, NH 03301
(603) 225-5344

New Jersey
204 W. State Street
Trenton, NJ 08608
(609) 394-3303

New Mexico
440 Cerrillos Road, Suite G
Santa Fe, NM 87501
(505) 892-9766

New York
35 Maiden Lane
Albany, NY 12207
(518) 465-4162

North Carolina
801 Oberlin Road, Suite 325
Raleigh, NC 27605
(919) 839-5532

North Dakota
P.O. Box 5501
Fargo, ND 58105
(701) 232-6696

Ohio
YWCA Building
65 S. Fourth Street
Columbus, OH 43215
(614) 469-1505

Oklahoma
525 N.W. 13th Street
Oklahoma City, OK 73103
(405) 236-5338

Oregon
2659 Commercial Street, S.E., #220
Salem, OR 97302
(503) 581-5722

Pennsylvania
226 Forster Street
Harrisburg, PA 17102
(717) 234-1576

Puerto Rico
P.O. Box 13485
Santurce, PR 00908
(809) 722-3948

Rhode Island
P.O. Box 28678
Providence, RI 02908
(401) 453-1111

South Carolina
1314 Lincoln Street, #212
Columbia, SC 29201
(803) 771-0063

South Dakota
3611 Slaten Park Drive
Sioux Falls, SD 57103

Tennessee
1701 21st Avenue South, #425
Nashville, TN 37212
(615) 297-7134

Texas
1212 Guadelupe, #107
Austin, TX 78701
(512) 472-1100

Utah
3894 Highland Drive, Suite 8D
Salt Lake City, UT 84106
(801) 272-8683

Vermont
61 Pettingill Road
Essex, VT 05452

Virgin Islands
P.O. Box 638
St. Thomas, VI 00804

Virginia
900 S. Washington Street, Suite 311
Falls Church, VA 22046
(703) 237-1484

Washington
1411 4th Avenue, #803
Seattle, WA 98191
(206) 622-8961

West Virginia
1127 Montrose Drive
S. Charleston, WV 25303

Wisconsin
122 State Street, Suite 405
Madison, WI 53703
(608) 256-0827

Wyoming
P.O. Box 2862
Cheyenne, WY 82003

Kuwait is the only country that specifically denies women the right to vote.

"The worst part of success is to try to find someone who is happy for you."—Bette Midler

SEVEN SUGGESTIONS FOR WOMEN CANDIDATES FROM WOMEN POLITICAL LEADERS

•Do your research. Make sure you know what the voters think of you and what they know about you, as well as your opponent.

•Establish your persona. Voters want to get a personal sense of candidates, and it is up to you to paint a picture voters can simultaneously admire and like.

•Mobilize women. For women candidates of both parties, women activists are the key constituency. Emphasize women's equality.

•Stand for change. Address bread-and-butter concerns, particularly jobs, taxes, education, and crime.

•Defend your flank. Don't let your opponent steal from your base.

•Expect the worst. Opponents will use sleazy tactics to win; at such moments, women's campaigns must go on the attack and make sure every woman voter understands that she, too, is under attack.

•Aim for the best. Keep to the political high ground. Negative campaigning works worse for women candidates than for men, who are more readily forgiven.

Source: Political Woman (November 1993)

VIOLENCE AND SAFETY
VIOLENCE AND SAFETY
VIOLENCE AND SAFETY

VIOLENCE AND SAFETY

VIOLENCE AND SAFETY
VIOLENCE AND SAFETY
VIOLENCE AND SAFETY
VIOLENCE AND SAFETY
VIOLENCE AND SAFETY
VIOLENCE AND SAFETY
VIOLENCE AND SAFETY
VIOLENCE AND SAFETY
VIOLENCE AND SAFETY
VIOLENCE AND SAFETY
VIOLENCE AND SAFETY
VIOLENCE AND SAFETY
VIOLENCE AND SAFETY
VIOLENCE AND SAFETY
VIOLENCE AND SAFETY
VIOLENCE AND SAFETY

WOMEN AND VIOLENCE

•More than $2^1/_2$ million women annually are the victims of violent crime.
•Around a quarter of attacks on women involve the use of a weapon, and about a third of those involve a gun.
•About three out of four female victims of violence resist the actions of the offender, either physically or verbally.
•Roughly a third of women victims of violence are injured as a result of the crime.
•Approximately half of women victims of violent crime report the crime to the police.
•Women with lower incomes are subjected to the highest rates of violent crime.
•Women, the elderly in particular, are just as vulnerable as men to personal larceny such as purse snatching or pick-pocketing.
•Women commit about a quarter of all assaults against women.
•While the rate of violent crime committed against men has dropped since 1973, the rate of crimes against women has remained relatively constant. Still, except for rape, women are significantly less likely to experience violent crime than men.

Source: Department of Justice

Gun ownership is most strongly associated with homicide at the hands of a family member or intimate acquaintance.

THE VICTIM-OFFENDER RELATIONSHIP

This chart shows the percentage distribution of single-offender violent victimizations of women, by relationship of offender to victim, between 1987–91.

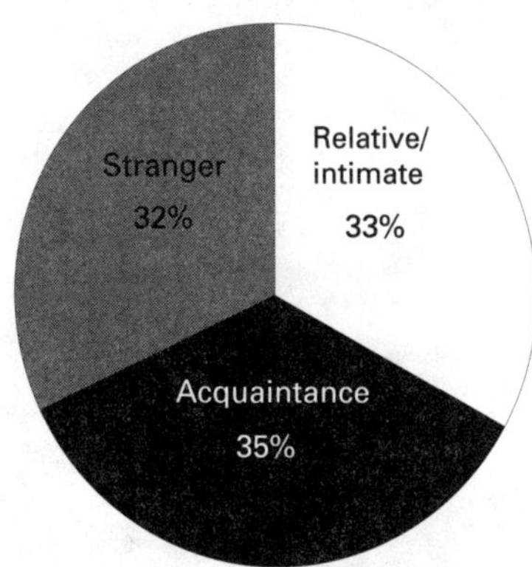

Relative/intimate	
Boyfriend/girlfriend	14.0%
Spouse	9.5%
Ex-spouse	4.0%
Brother/sister	1.3%
Child	1.3%
Parent	.8%
Other relative	2.0%

Source: Department of Justice

VICTIMIZATION

Half of all black female suicides and a quarter of white are believed to be connected to domestic violence.

Women's Victimization by Race

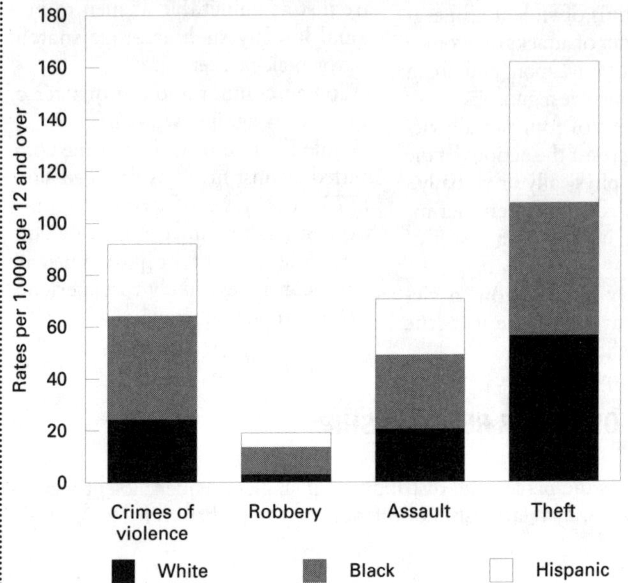

(Data from 1992)

Victimization by Age and Sex

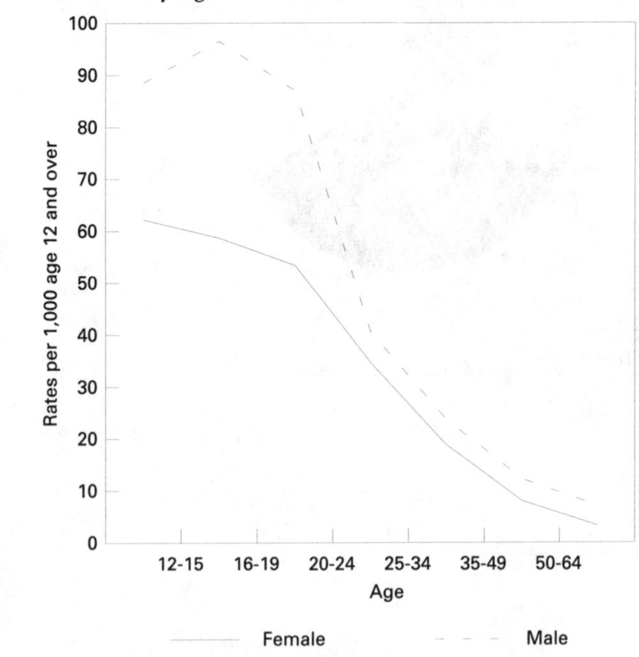

(Data from 1992)

Women's Victimization by Place of Residence

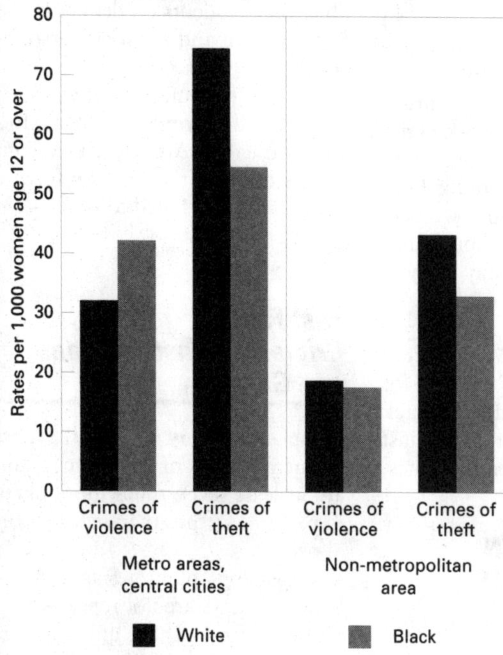

(Data from 1992)
Source for above: National Criminal Justice Reference Service

36% of female homicide victims were killed with handguns.

MURDER VICTIMS

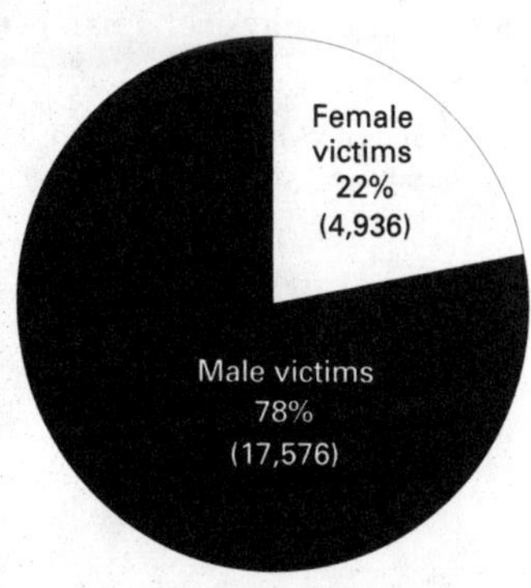

Total murder victims, 1992: 22,540
Source: Federal Bureau of Investigation, Uniform Crime Report, 1993

63% of homicide victims are men and 37% are women, according to a study by the *New England Journal of Medicine*; 51% of homicides occurred in the context of a quarrel or romantic triangle and 43% involved the use of handguns.

The "rule of thumb," which was in effect under English law until the late nineteenth century, affirmed legally that a man had a right to beat his wife so long as he used a rod no thicker than his thumb.

Of all women murdered in the U.S. during the first half of the 1980s, 52% were the victims of partner homicide.

CRIME AND RACE

•Black women are more than twice as likely to experience a robbery as white females. No significant difference, however, separates women of different races in regard to rape or assault.
•Hispanic women are more likely to be robbed than non-Hispanic women, including black women, although they and other women are equally likely to face other sorts of violent crime.
•Violent crime against women is primarily intra-racial; 90% of violent crime sustained by black women, for instance, is committed by black offenders, and 80% of crime against white women is committed by whites.

Source: Department of Justice

CAMPUS CRIME—TEN QUESTIONS STUDENTS SHOULD ASK

Legally, colleges are required to keep track of and publish annual reports of crime on their campuses. Prospective students also have the right to see copies of these reports. They may also want to ask the following questions about campus security:

1. During the past three years, how many assaults, burglaries, rapes, and homicides were committed on school grounds?
2. Are these statistics disseminated to parents and students each year?
3. Are campus security personnel trained professionals or semi-trained students?
4. What is the ratio of students living on school grounds to campus police and security personnel?
5. Does the college vigorously enforce underage drinking laws and outlaw illegal drug use?
6. Is a registration log kept of all dormitory visitors and guests?
7. Are security personnel stationed at the entrance of dormitories on a 24-hour basis?
8. Are single-sex dormitories available to all students on demand?
9. Do police and security personnel conduct regular foot patrols of the campus? Of dormitory hallways?
10. Do all dormitory doors lock automatically? Are there electronic alarms to warn the security force of doors that have failed to lock?

Source: Security on Campus

Fast Facts: Crimes Against Lesbians and Gays

•Lesbians and gay men are the most frequent victims of hate crimes, and are at least seven times more likely to be crime victims than heterosexual people.
•At least 75% of crimes against lesbians and gays are not reported.
•From 1991 to 1992, anti-gay and lesbian episodes increased 4% nationwide. In New York City, anti-gay and lesbian incidents involving injury requiring medical attention increased 41%.
•Twenty percent of lesbians experience verbal or physical assault in high school.

Sources: National Victim Center; Hetrick Martin Institute; SIECUS

CAMPUS CRIME—RESOURCES AND READING

ORGANIZATIONS

Campus Violence Prevention Center
Towson State University
Towson, MD 21204
(410) 830-2178

Security on Campus
618 Shoemaker Road
Gulph Mills, PA 19406
(215) 768-9330

READING

Avoiding Rape On and Off Campus, Carol Pritchard (Millburn, N.J.: American Focus Publishers, 1988).

Sexual Assault on Campus, Andrea Parrot (Lexington, Mass.: Lexington Books, 1993).

STOPPING MALE VIOLENCE—RESOURCES AND READING

NATIONAL ORGANIZATIONS

Ending Men's Violence: National Referral Directory
c/o Craig Norberg-Bohm
50 Wyman Street
Arlington, MA 02174

Men's Anti-Rape Resource Center
P.O. Box 73559
Washington, DC 20056
(202) 529-7239

REGIONAL ORGANIZATIONS

AMEND
777 Grant, Suite 600
Denver, CO 80203
(303) 832-6363

Emerge
18 Hurley Street
Cambridge, MA 02141
(617) 422-1550

READING

Stopping Rape: A Challenge for Men, Rus Ervin Funk (Philadelphia: New Society Publishers, 1993).

NATIONAL RESOURCES FOR VICTIMS

National Organization for Victim Assistance
1757 Park Road, N.W.
Washington, DC 20010
(202) 232-6682

National Victim Center
2111 Wilson Boulevard, Suite 300
Arlington, VA 22201
(703) 276-2880 (main office)
or (800) 877-3355 (referrals)

RAPE FACTS

- An estimated 683,000 adult American women are forcibly raped each year.
- One out of every eight adult women has been the victim of forcible rape.
- Rape is more likely to be committed against a woman by someone she knows than by a stranger.
- Less than 10% of all rapes involve more than one offender.
- Women raped by strangers are injured more often than women raped by someone they know.
- In 1991, only 52% of reported forcible rapes led to the arrest of the alleged perpetrator.
- Over half of all rape prosecutions are either dismissed before trial or result in an acquittal.
- Almost 25% of convicted rapists never go to prison; another 25% serve time in local jails where the average sentence is 11 months.

Sources: Department of Justice; National Victim Center; Committee on the Judiciary, U.S. Senate

The median time served in a U.S. prison for rape in 1989 was 41 months.

Half of rape victims in recent years were given no information about testing for HIV/AIDS.

Two in 10 rapes by strangers handled by the office of New York sex-crimes prosecutor Linda Fairstein in 1993 occurred at work or en route to or from work, and 1 in 10 acquaintance-rape cases was work-related.

98% of rape victims never see the arrest or prosecution of their attackers.

AVOIDING DATE RAPE

- Set sexual limits
- Do not give mixed messages; be clear
- Be independent and aware on your dates
- If things begin to get out of hand, be loud in protesting, leave, go for help
- Trust your gut-level feelings
- Be aware that alcohol and drugs are often related to acquaintance rape
- If you are unsure of a new acquaintance, go on a group or double date
- Have your own transportation, if possible
- Avoid secluded places where you are in a vulnerable position
- Be careful when you invite someone to your home or you are invited to his home

Source: Center for Women Policy Studies

WHO IS THE RAPIST?

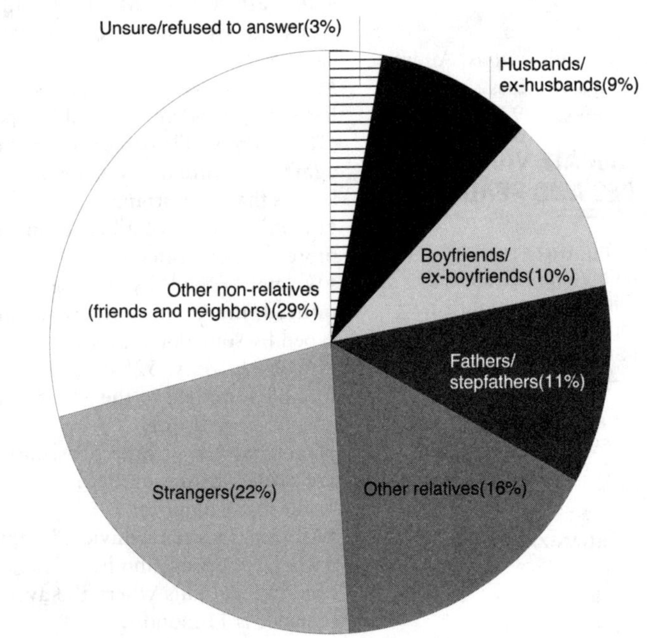

Source: National Victim Center

HOW WIDESPREAD IS RAPE?

This graph shows three different estimates of the number of forcible rapes per year, based on 1990 estimates.

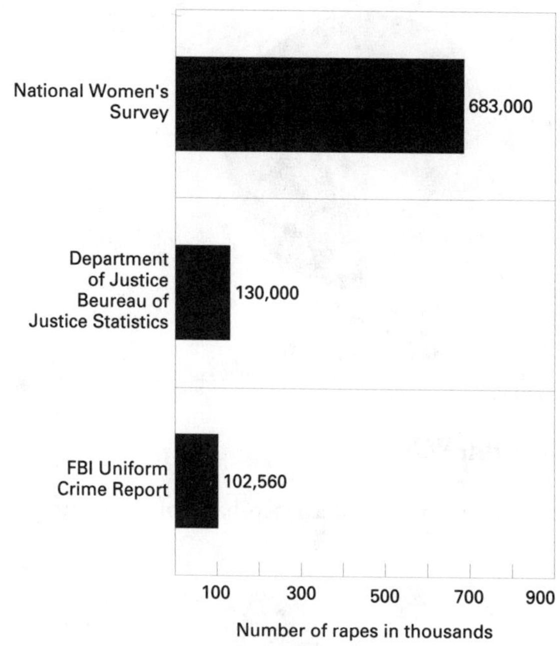

Source: National Victim Center

Andy Archambeau of Dearborn Heights, Michigan, was charged with breaking Michigan's anti-stalking law in May 1994 when he harassed a woman through e-mail.

RAPE REPORTING

To Report or Not to Report

This chart shows an estimated breakdown of how rape victims report the crime, or don't report it, to the police.

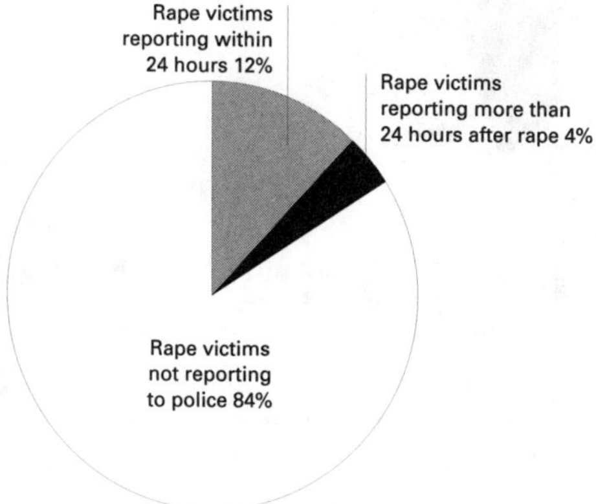

Marital rape is now a crime in all 50 states, although 30 states still have exemptions if simple force is used or if the woman is legally unable to consent due to physical or mental disability.

Rape Reporting and Victim Privacy
If there was a law prohibiting the news media from disclosing a rape victim's name and address, would you be:

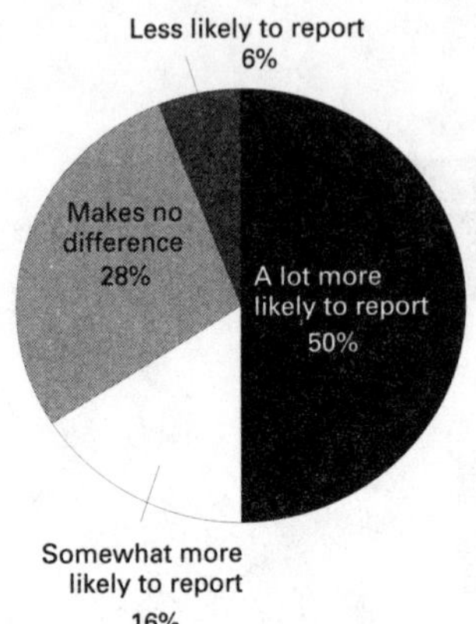

Source for above: National Victim Center

WHEN DOES RAPE HAPPEN?

This graph shows the variation from the average, based on figures from 1992.

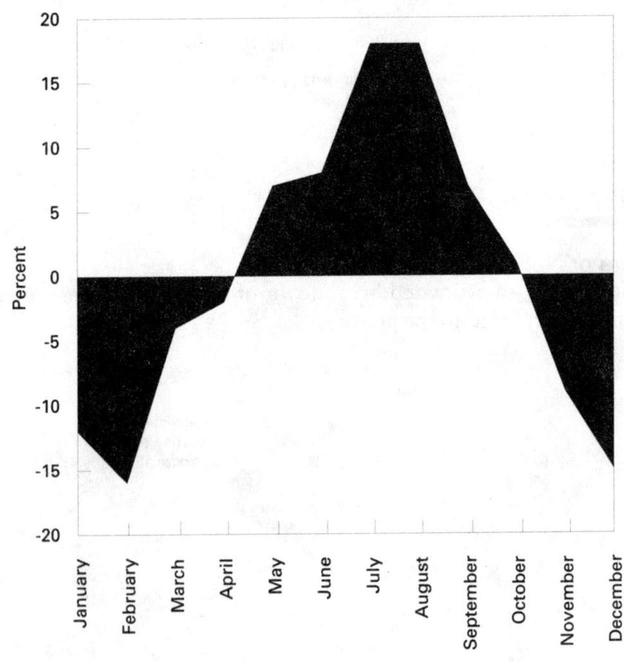

Source: Federal Bureau of Investigation, Uniform Crime Report, 1993

AGE AT THE TIME OF RAPE

This chart reflects the age of female rape victims at the time of the crime.

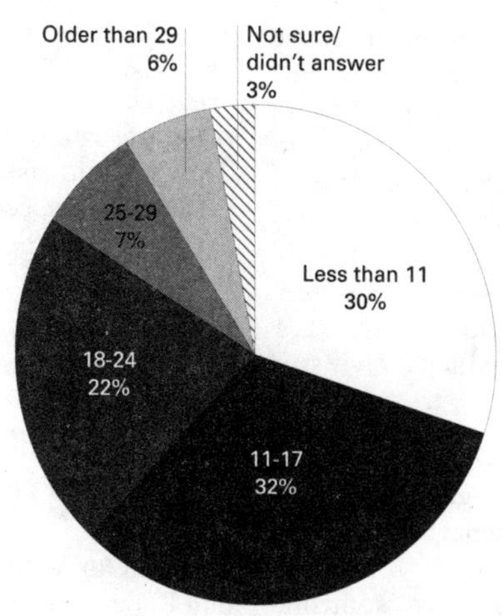

Source: National Victim Center

"That sister walking down the street is your mother, your daughter, your sister, your grandmother. Bitches are dogs and a hoe is a tool."—"Revolutionary Sister" by the Veldt, a funk-rock band

MENTAL HEALTH PROBLEMS AMONG RAPE VICTIMS

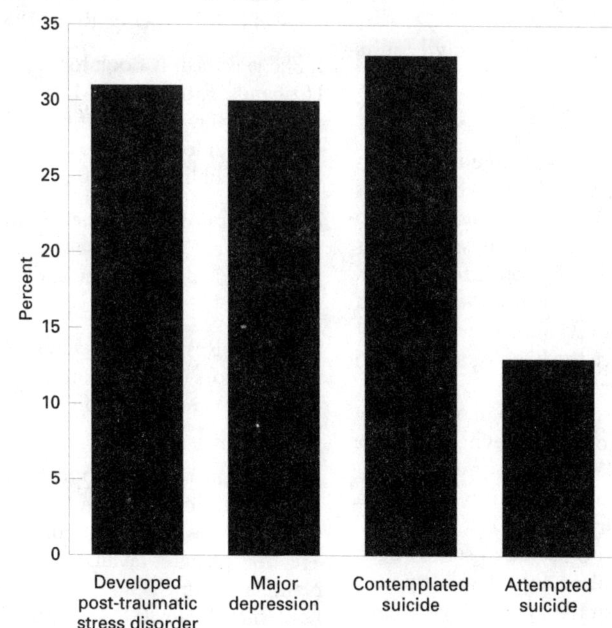

Source: National Victim Center

More than 70% of rape victims said they were concerned about their families' discovering that they were raped, and 65% said they were worried that they might be blamed for being raped.

Approximately 1,155,600 adult American women have been victims of 1 or more forcible rapes by their husbands.

CIVIL SUITS AND RAPE CASES

While it is possible for a sexual assault survivor to sue her assailant for monetary damages, suing is often futile unless the perpetrator has significant assets. Instead, women have found that under certain circumstances they can sue landlords, hotel owners, employers, or others, for neglecting security and therefore creating the conditions that allowed an assault to occur. Examples of situations in which a survivor might consider a civil suit include:

- A landlord fails to properly secure an apartment building.
- A parking lot owner doesn't fix broken lights in a lot.
- A moving company hires someone with a history of rape without an adequate background check.
- A hotel installs windows that can't be solidly locked.
- A nightclub fails to have security personnel protecting women's bathrooms.

The advantages of civil suits include:

- The survivor can sue for monetary damages.
- Most lawyers will take these cases on a contingency basis, which means that the survivor will not have to pay attorney's fees unless damages are won; consultations are also generally free. (This is not the case for a woman who wants to sue the rapist himself since the likelihood of recovering money is slim.)
- The survivor can decide whether the case will go to trial, when the case will be settled, and for how much.
- The standard of proof is lower in a civil lawsuit than in a criminal case.
- If the parties decide to settle out of court, a seal of confidentiality may be placed on the proceedings.

If a survivor believes she has cause to sue, she should contact a lawyer immediately—time is crucial because each state sets its own time limitations on filing these suits, some as short as 90 days. To find lawyers who may be able to help them, women should call their local rape crisis centers or the sexual assault programs run out of local hospitals. They should ask for referrals for lawyers who specialize in negligence actions, with specific experience in lack-of-security cases.

Sources: Madeline Bryer, J.D.; The Chronicle of Higher Education (August 7, 1991)

RAPE RESOURCES—BOOKS AND FILMS

Against Our Wills: Men, Women, and Rape (rev. ed.), Susan Brownmiller (New York: Bantam, 1988).

I Never Called It Rape: The Ms. Report on Recognizing, Fighting, and Surviving Date and Acquaintance Rape, Robin Warshaw (New York: Harper & Row, 1988).

If She Is Raped: A Book for Husbands, Fathers, and Male Friends, Alan W. McEvoy and Jeff B. Brookings (Holms Beach, Fla.: Learning Publishers, 1990).

The Politics of Rape: The Victim's Perspective, Diana Russell (Lanham, Md.: Madison Books, 1984).

Quest for Respect: A Healing Guide for Survivors of Rape, Linda Braswell (Ventura, Calif.: Pathfinder, 1992).

Rape in America: A Report to the Nation, National Victim Center and Crime Victims Research and Treatment Center (available from the National Victim Center, 2111 Wilson Boulevard, Suite 300, Arlington, VA 22201, (703) 276-2880).

Rape Culture, video/film, Mary Daly and Emily Culpepper (1983; available from Cambridge Documentary Films, P.O. Box 385, Cambridge, MA 02139, (617) 354-3677).

Sexual Assault: How to Defend Yourself, Dan Lena and Marie Howard (Hollywood, Fla.: Lifetime, 1990).

The Sexual Assault Survivor's Handbook for People with Developmental Disabilities, Nora J. Baladerian (Saratoga, Calif.: R & E Publishers, 1991).

Sexual Violence: Our War Against Rape, Linda Fairstein (New York: William Morrow, 1993).

Stopping Rape: Successful Survival Strategies, Pauline B. Bart and Patricia O'Brian (New York: Teachers College Press, 1985).

Surviving Sexual Violence, Liz Kelly (Minneapolis: University of Minnesota Press, 1989).

RAPE INFORMATION AND VICTIM ASSISTANCE—RESOURCES

For a nationwide listing of rape crisis centers, call the Washington, D.C., Rape Crisis Center Hotline at (202) 333-7273; through it you can gain access to the Sexual Assault and Child Sexual Abuse National Directory of Victim Survivor Services and Prevention Programs, which can give you the number of an organization in your area.

National Clearinghouse on Marital and Date Rape
2325 Oak Street
Berkeley, CA 94708
(510) 524-1582

National Coalition Against Sexual Assault
P.O. Box 21378
Washington, DC 20009
(202) 483-7165

National Victim Center
2111 Wilson Boulevard, Suite 300
Arlington, VA 22201
(703) 276-2880 (main office)
or (800) 877-3355 (referrals)

DOMESTIC VIOLENCE FACTS

- Every 15 seconds a woman is battered.
- An estimated 2 to 4 million American women are physically abused each year.
- Family violence kills as many women every five years as the total number of Americans who died in the Vietnam War.
- Between 15% to 25% of pregnant women are battered.
- More than half of all women will experience some form of violence from their spouse during marriage. More than one-third are battered repeatedly.
- Women are more likely to experience violence at the hands of a relative, intimate, or acquaintance than from a stranger. Indeed nearly two-thirds of female victims are related to or know their attackers, a rate nearly ten times greater than for males.
- Women are injured in the progress of violent crimes almost twice as frequently when the attacker is an intimate than when he is a stranger. Injured women are also more likely to require medical attention under these circumstances.
- From 22% to 35% of women who visit medical emergency rooms are there for injuries related to ongoing abuse.
- Up to 50% of all homeless women and children in this country are fleeing domestic violence.
- Women who leave their batterers are at a 75% greater risk of being killed by them than those who stay.
- Police are more likely to respond to a woman's call for help within five minutes if the offender is a stranger than if the attacker is known to the woman.

Sources: National Victim Center; National Coalition Against Domestic Violence

10% of Americans can imagine a situation in which they would approve of a husband slapping his wife's face, and 23% said they can imagine a situation in which they would approve of a wife slapping her husband's face, according to a Gallup poll.

There are 3 times as many animal shelters as battered women's shelters in the U.S.

Every 12 seconds, a man beats a woman.

TWELVE PREDICTORS OF DOMESTIC VIOLENCE

1. Grew up in a violent family
2. Tends to use force or violence to "solve" problems
3. Abuses alcohol or other drugs
4. Has poor self-esteem
5. Has strong traditional ideas about gender roles
6. Jealous of you and your relationships with friends and family members
7. Plays with guns, knives, or other lethal instruments
8. Expects you to follow his/her orders or advice
9. Experiences extreme mood changes
10. Gets angry in a way that makes you fearful
11. Treats you roughly
12. Makes you feel threatened

Source: National Coalition Against Domestic Violence

BATTERING—A TIMELINE OF RESPONSES

1850–1900—The Women's Christian Temperance Union and women suffragists protest the brutality of drunken husbands, fight for prohibition, and urge changes in divorce laws so that women can divorce for "mental cruelty."

1960s—The criminal justice system routinely screens out women's complaints of abuse.

1963—"The Wifebeater's Wife," a landmark study giving psychopathological profiles of battered women, is published.

1964—Refuge House, the first battered women's shelter, opens in London.

1970—The Journal of Marriage and Family cites family violence for the first time.

1971—The first rape crisis center opens in the U.S.

1973—The first battered women's shelter in the U.S. opens in St. Paul, Minnesota.

1974—A British study of 100 battered women found that 74 had been prescribed anti-depressant medication.

The first study of abusers is published, portraying batterers as essentially victims of "highly provocative" wives.

1975—Two formerly battered women open their apartment to battered women in Cambridge, Massachusetts, founding Transition House.

1976—Over 400 programs for battered women and rape victims exist in the U.S.

The International Tribunal on Crimes Against Women is held in Brussels.

Aegis, the first national newsletter on domestic violence, is created.

The first state coalitions of battered women's groups are established.

Casa Myrna Vazquez, the first battered women's shelter established by women of color, opens in Boston.

1977—Emerge, the first counseling program for men who batter, is founded.

1978—The National Coalition Against Domestic Violence forms.

1979—The Domestic Violence Prevention and Services Act passes the U.S. Senate.

1982—Women and Male Violence, a history of the battered women's movement by Susan Schechter, is published.

1985—The first support group for battered lesbians is formed in Seattle.

1987—Naming the Violence by Kerry Lobel, the first book about battering among lesbian couples, is published.

1988—The U.S. surgeon general declares wife abuse to be the leading health hazard to women.

1989—"Post-Traumatic Stress Syndrome" is identified in battered women by several experts on victims of trauma.

1990—Over 1,200 battered women's programs exist in the U.S.
1991—A dozen states have laws specifying mandatory or "pro-arrest" protocols for police in response to spouse abuse.
1992—Several states enact "anti-stalking" laws to protect victims who are relentlessly pursued by their abusers.

Source: Emerge: A Men's Counseling Service on Domestic Violence

LESBIAN BATTERING

The Difficulties Facing Victims

Although experts estimate that battering is as likely to occur in lesbian relationships as in heterosexual relationships, little protection exists for victims of lesbian domestic violence. Victims are often reluctant to report the battering and be identified as lesbians for fear of losing their jobs, families, friends, or children. They also fear that they will not receive appropriate treatment or counseling. Only a few cities, such as San Francisco, New York, Seattle, and Minneapolis, provide counseling services specifically for lesbian batterers and victims.

Additional problems include:

- Police officers often tend not to treat lesbian battering as a serious offense and frequently arrest both parties.
- While some states protect same-sex, non-related cohabitants from domestic abuse by providing temporary orders of protection, other states refuse to do so.
- Some judges dismiss charges of same-sex domestic violence.
- Even within the lesbian community, there is a reluctance to identify battering as a widespread problem.

Sources: NOW Legal Defense and Education Fund; National Coalition Against Domestic Violence

Resources

The National Center for Lesbian Rights
1663 Mission Street, Suite 550
San Francisco, CA 94103
(415) 621-0674

The National Coalition Against Domestic Violence
Lesbian Task Force
P.O. Box 18749
Denver, CO 80218
(303) 839-1852

Recommended Reading

Naming the Violence: Speaking Out About Lesbian Battering, Kerry Lobel (Seattle: Seal Press, 1986).

Violent Betrayal: Partner Abuse in Lesbian Relationships, Claire M. Renzetti (Thousand Oaks, Calif.: Sage, 1992).

There were approximately a million reported attacks on women in 1991 by their husbands or lovers, and another 3 million incidents of domestic violence that went unreported.

33% of women who come to the hospital emergency room in Peru are victims of domestic violence.

80% of Chilean women reported having suffered abuse by a male partner or relative; 63% reported that they were currently being abused.

LEGAL RESOURCES FOR BATTERED WOMEN

Two national organizations can provide special help to battered women and their lawyers. The first, the National Clearinghouse for the Defense of Battered Women, provides critical assistance, resources, and support to battered women who have killed or assaulted their abusers while attempting to protect themselves, or who are coerced into crime by their abusers. The second, the National Center on Women and Family Law, provides legal assistance and information to advocates, policymakers, and attorneys for low-income women. The center's National Battered Women's Law Project analyzes federal and state legislative developments, serves as an information clearinghouse, and produces manuals and other publications on legal issues facing battered women, among them, "Battered Women: The Facts," "Woman Battering: A Cause of Homelessness," and "Battered Women's Litigation Resource Packet." The organizations can be reached at the following addresses:

National Center for Women and Family Law
799 Broadway, Suite 402
New York, NY 10003
(212) 674-8200

National Clearinghouse for the Defense of Battered Women
125 S. 9th Street, Suite 302
Philadelphia, PA 19107
(215) 351-0010

NATIONAL ORGANIZATIONS AGAINST DOMESTIC VIOLENCE

Battered Women's Law Project
National Center on Women and Family Law
799 Broadway, Room 402
New York, NY 10033
(212) 674-8200

Center for the Prevention of Sexual and Domestic Violence
1914 N. 34th Street, Suite 105
Seattle, WA 98103
(206) 634-1903

Emerge: A Men's Counseling Service on Domestic Violence
18 Hurley Street, Suite 100
Cambridge, MA 02141
(617) 422-1550

Family Violence Prevention Fund
Building One, Suite 200
1001 Potrero Avenue
San Francisco, CA 94110
(415) 821-4553

Family Violence and Sexual Assault Institute
1310 Clinic Drive
Tyler, TX 75701
(903) 595-6600

National Clearinghouse for the Defense of Battered Women
125 S. 9th Street, Suite 302
Philadelphia, PA 19107
(215) 351-0010

National Coalition Against Domestic Violence
P.O. Box 18749
Denver, CO 80218
(303) 839-1852

National Council on Child Abuse and Family Violence
1155 Connecticut Avenue, N.W.
Suite 400
Washington, DC 20036
(202) 429-6695

National Family Violence HelpLine
(800) 222-2000

National Organization for Victim Assistance
1757 Park Road, N.W.
Washington, DC 20010
(202) 232-6682 (counseling and business) or (800) 879-6682 (information and referrals)

STATE COALITIONS AGAINST DOMESTIC VIOLENCE

Alabama
Alabama Coalition Against Domestic Violence
P.O. Box 4762
Montgomery, AL 36101
(205) 832-4842

Alaska
Alaska Network on Domestic Violence and Sexual Assault
419 6th Street, #116
Juneau, AK 99801
(907) 586-3650

Arizona
Arizona Coalition Against Domestic Violence
2345 E. Thomas, Suite 440
Phoenix, AZ 85016
(602) 224-9477

Arkansas
Arkansas Coalition Against Violence to Women and Children
7509 Cantrell Road, Suite 213
Little Rock, AR 72207
(501) 663-4668

California
Central California Coalition on Domestic Violence
619 13th Street
Modesto, CA 95354
(209) 575-7037

Northern California Coalition Against Domestic Violence
c/o Marin Abused Women's Services
1717 5th Avenue
San Rafael, CA 94901
(415) 457-2464

Southern California Coalition on Battered Women
P.O. Box 5036
Santa Monica, CA 90405
(213) 655-6098

Colorado
Colorado Domestic Violence Coalition
P.O. Box 18902
Denver, CO 80218
(303) 573-9018

Connecticut
Connecticut Coalition Against Domestic Violence
135 Broad Street
Hartford, CT 06105
(203) 524-5890

Delaware
Delaware Coalition Against Domestic Violence
c/o Child, Inc.
Philadelphia Pike
Wilmington, DE 19809
(302) 762-6110

District of Columbia
District of Columbia Coalition Against Domestic Violence
c/o Emergency Domestic Relations
111 F. Street, N.W.
Washington, DC 20001
(202) 662-9666

Florida
Florida Coalition Against Domestic Violence
P.O. Box 1201
Winter Park, FL 32790
(407) 628-3885

Georgia
Georgia Advocates for Battered Women and Children
250 Georgia Avenue, S.E., Suite 365
Atlanta, GA 30312
(404) 524-3847

Hawaii
Hawaii State Committee on Family Violence
P.O. Box 31107
Honolulu, HI 96820
(808) 595-3900 or (808) 532-3804

Idaho
Idaho Network to Stop Violence Against Women
5440 Franklin Boulevard, Suite 201
Boise, ID 83705
(208) 338-1323

Illinois
Illinois Coalition Against Domestic Violence
937 South Fourth Street
Springfield, IL 62703
(217) 789-2830

An American woman convicted of prostitution in Iran was flogged 80 times with a whip and was deported to the U.S. on May 5, 1994. This was the same week that a male American teenager was flogged in Singapore for vandalism, to much media attention.

"I've been a babe, and I've been a sister. Sister lasts longer."—Anna Quindlen

Indiana
Indiana Coalition Against Domestic Violence
c/o YWCA Women's Shelter
605 N. 6th Street
Lafayette, IN 47901
(317) 742-0075

Iowa
Iowa Coalition Against Domestic Violence
Lucas Building
First Floor
Des Moines, IA 50319
(515) 281-7284

Kansas
Kansas Coalition Against Sexual and Domestic Violence
P.O. Box 1341
Pittburgh, KS 66762
(316) 232-2757

Kentucky
Kentucky Domestic Violence Association
P.O. Box 356
Frankfort, KY 40602
(502) 875-4132

Louisiana
Louisiana Coalition Against Domestic Violence
P.O. Box 2133
Baton Rouge, LA 70821
(504) 389-3001

Maine
Maine Coalition for Family Crisis Services
P.O. Box 590
Sanford, ME 04073
(207) 324-1957

Maryland
Maryland Network Against Domestic Violence
167 Duke of Glouchester Street
Annapolis, MD 21401
(410) 839-5815

Massachusetts
Massachusetts Coalition of Battered Women's Service Groups
210 Commercial Street
Boston, MA 02109
(617) 248-0922

Michigan
Michigan Coalition Against Domestic Violence
P.O. Box 16009
Lansing, MI 48901
(517) 484-2924

Minnesota
Minnesota Coalition for Battered Women
1619 Dayton Avenue, #303
St. Paul, MN 55104
(612) 646-6177

Mississippi
Mississippi Coalition Against Domestic Violence
P.O. Box 333
Biloxi, MS 39533
(601) 435-1968

Missouri
Missouri Coalition Against Domestic Violence
311 Madison
Jefferson City, MO 65101
(314) 634-4161

Montana
Montana Coalition Against Domestic Violence
104 N. Broadway, #406
Billings, MT 9101
(406) 245-7990

Nebraska
Nebraska Domestic Violence Sexual Assault Coalition
315 S. 9th Street, Suite 18
Lincoln, NE 68508
(402) 476-6256

Nevada
Nevada Network Against Domestic Violence
2100 Capurro Way, Suite 21-I
Sparks, NV 89431
(702) 358-1171

New Hampshire
New Hampshire Coalition Against Domestic and Sexual Violence
P.O. Box 353
Concord, NH 03302
(603) 224-8893 or (800) 852-3388

New Jersey
New Jersey Coalition for Battered Women
2620 Whitehorse-Hamilton Square Road
Trenton, NJ 08690
(609) 584-8107

New Mexico
New Mexico State Coalition Against Domestic Violence
c/o La Casa, Inc.
P.O. Box 2463
La Cruces, NM 88004
(505) 526-2819 or (505) 525-3792

New York
New York State Coalition Against Domestic Violence
The Women's Building
79 Central Avenue
Albany, NY 12206
(518) 432-4864

North Carolina
North Carolina Coalition Against Domestic Violence
P.O. Box 51875
Durham, NC 27717
(919) 490-1467

North Dakota
North Dakota Council on Abused Women's Services
418 E. Rosser Avenue, Suite 320
Bismarck, ND 58501
(701) 255-6240 or (800) 472-2911

Ohio
Action Ohio Coalition for Battered Women
P.O. Box 15673
Columbus, OH 43215
(614) 221-1255

Ohio Domestic Violence Network
P.O. Box 5466
Cleveland, OH 44101
(216) 634-7501

Ohio Domestic Violence Network
65 South Fourth Street, Suite 302
Columbus, OH 43215
(614) 221-0023 or (800) 934-9840

Oklahoma
Oklahoma Coalition on Domestic Violence and Sexual Assault
2200 Classen Boulevard, Suite 1300
Oklahoma City, OK 73106
(405) 557-1210

Oregon
Oregon Coalition Against Sexual and Domestic Violence
2336 S.E. Belmont Street
Portland, OR 97214
(503) 239-4486

Pennsylvania
Pennsylvania Coalition Against Domestic Violence
6400 Flank Drive
Gateway Corporate Center, Suite 1300
Harrisburg, PA 17112
(800) 932-4632 or (717) 545-6400

Puerto Rico
Puerto Rico Coalition Against Domestic Violence
N-11 Calle 11
San Souci
Bayamon, PR 00619

Rhode Island
Rhode Island Council on Domestic Violence
324 Broad Street
Central Falls, RI 02863
(401) 723-3051

South Carolina
South Carolina Coalition Against Domestic Violence and Sexual Assault
P.O. Box 7776
Columbia, SC 29202
(803) 254-3699 or (803) 581-8313

South Dakota
South Dakota Coalition Against Domestic Violence and Sexual Assault
P.O. Box 595
Agency Village, SD 57262
(605) 698-3947

Tennessee
Tennessee Task Force Against Family Violence
P.O. Box 120972
Nashville, TN 37212
(615) 327-0805

Texas
Texas Council on Family Violence
8701 North Mopac Expressway,
Suite 450
Austin, TX 78759
(512) 794-1133

85% of women taken into custody in Pakistan are sexually abused.

For a series of articles on violence against women around the world, the Dallas Morning News won a Pulitzer Prize in 1994.

Utah
Citizens Against Physical and Sexual Abuse
P.O. Box 3617
Logan, UT 84321
(801) 752-4493

Vermont
Vermont Network Against Domestic Violence and Sexual Assault
P.O. Box 405
Montpelier, VT 05601
(802) 223-1302

Virginia
Virginians Against Domestic Violence
2850 Sandy Bay Road, Suite 101
Williamsburg, VA 23185
(804) 221-0990

Washington
Washington State Coalition Against Domestic Violence
200 W Street, S.E., Suite B
Tumwater, WA 98501
(206) 352-4029

West Virginia
West Virginia Coalition Against Domestic Violence
P.O. Box 85
307 Main Street
Sutton, WV 26601
(304) 765-2250

Wisconsin
Wisconsin Coalition Against Domestic Violence
1051 Williamson Street
Madison, WI 53703
(608) 255-0539

Wyoming
Wyoming Self-Help Center
341 East E Street, Suite 135A
Casper, WY 82601
(307) 235-2814

Source: National Coalition Against Domestic Violence

BATTERING—BOOKS AND FILMS

Defending Our Lives, 40 min. film, Margaret Lazarus and Renner Wunderlich (1993; available from Cambridge Documentary Films, P.O. Box 385, Cambridge MA 02139).

Ending the Violence: A Guidebook Based on the Experiences of One Thousand Battered Wives, Lee H. Bowker (Holmes Beach, Fla.: Learning Publications, 1986).

A Lamp in the Night: Domestic Violence from a Feminist Perspective, Margaret Minkel and Ruth K. Schutz (Rapid City, S.D.: M. Minkel, 1992).

They'll Find You Guilty, 30 min. film, Carol Jacobsen (1991; available from Carol Jacobsen, 1980 Alhambra, Ann Arbor, MI 48103, or call [313] 662-0776).

A GUIDE TO SELF-DEFENSE TRAINING

•Studies show that a physical self-defense response does not increase the level of physical injury and sometimes decreases the likelihood.
•Self-defense training can help you prepare responses that slow down, de-escalate, or interrupt an attack.
•Self-defense training, unlike the martial arts, does not require years of study to perfect.
•To find a self-defense class, check with your local rape crisis center, YMCA, YWCA, community college, or martial arts school. A good program is designed to adapt to every age and level of physical ability.
•Self-defense programs should include the following elements:

Women should be shown that they do not ask for, cause, invite, or deserve to be assaulted. Attackers are responsible for their attacks.

A woman's decision to survive the best way she can must be respected.

Options, techniques, and a way of analyzing situations should be offered.

Empowerment should be a goal of the program.

Source: The National Coalition Against Sexual Assault

BASIC SELF-DEFENSE STRATEGIES

•Stomp on your assailant's instep with your heel.
•Kick him in the shinbone and at the knee.
•Jab him in his solar plexus (the area of the stomach just below the sternum) with your umbrella, fist, or elbow.
•Poke him in the throat with your fingers or thumb.
•Box his ears or punch him in the temple.
•Grab his hair and double him over—strike forcibly on the back of his neck with your fist or elbow.
•Slam the heel of your hand up and under his nose, push in and up at the same time.
•Wrench his little finger.
•Strike his Adam's apple with the flat edge of your hand or your keys.
•If you have your keys held firmly, use them to cut your assailant's face and poke him.
•If the assailant is wearing glasses, try to fling them off.

Source: Security on Campus

PRECAUTIONS AGAINST VIOLENCE AND CRIME

In Your Home
•Secure your home with good lighting and effective locks—deadbolts where possible.
•Your home should always look and sound occupied.
•Have your phone near the bed, and keep emergency numbers near the phone.
•Keep your valuables out of window reach and visible view. Engrave them with special security numbers.
•Be aware of places where someone could hide.
•Use only your first initial and last name on your mailbox and in your phone book listing. If you live alone, add dummy names to the mailbox to create the illusion that others share your home.
•Require proper identification of all repair persons, utility workers, and delivery persons.
•Know your neighbors. Work out procedures for alerting each other in case of emergency.

In Elevators
•Stay at the front of the elevator, near the alarm button.
•If someone gets on of whom you are suspicious, push other buttons, so that the elevator will stop at all floors.
•Stay out of an elevator if someone suspicious is already on it.

On Public Transportation
•Sit near the driver or conductor, in a single seat or an outside seat.
•If followed after departing the subway or bus, head toward populated, well-lighted areas.

62% of Self magazine readers surveyed carry some form of self-protection, and 77% of the readers feel that gun-control laws should be stricter.

Tracey Thurman became the first wife to win a civil suit against her husband for physical abuse, in 1985.

In Automobiles

- Lock your car when entering and leaving.
- Park in well-lighted areas.
- Always have your keys ready as you approach the vehicle. Visually check to see if anyone is underneath or crouched beside the car, and check the front and back seats.
- Drive with doors locked and windows rolled at least three-quarters up.
- Put packages on the floor, out of view.
- Don't pick up hitchhikers.
- If your car is disabled: raise the hood, tie a white cloth to the aerial or door handle, stay in the car, and ask an interested motorist to call the police for you.

On the Street

- Whenever possible don't walk alone.
- Wear clothing that allows you freedom of movement.
- Walk on the outside of the sidewalk, facing traffic.
- Carry your purse and bundles under your arm. Always have one hand free.

If Approached

- Try to keep a minimum of two arm lengths between you and any stranger.
- Act alert and confident in public.
- Avoid conversation with strangers.
- Listen to your inner warning signals.
- Always keep your eye on someone close enough to grab you. If grabbed, yell "Fire," not "Help." It will attract attention quickly.

Sources: Chimera, Self-Defense for Women; National Institute of Mental Health, Violence and Traumatic Stress Branch

SELF-PROTECTION AND VICTIMS OF VIOLENT CRIME

Specific Forms of Self-Protection Taken by Victims

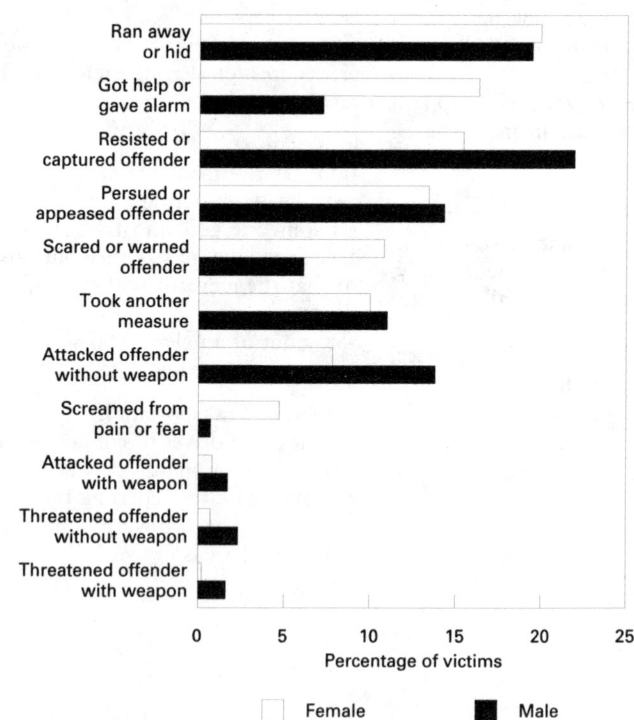

(Data from 1992)

Crimes in Which Victims Took Self-Protective Measures

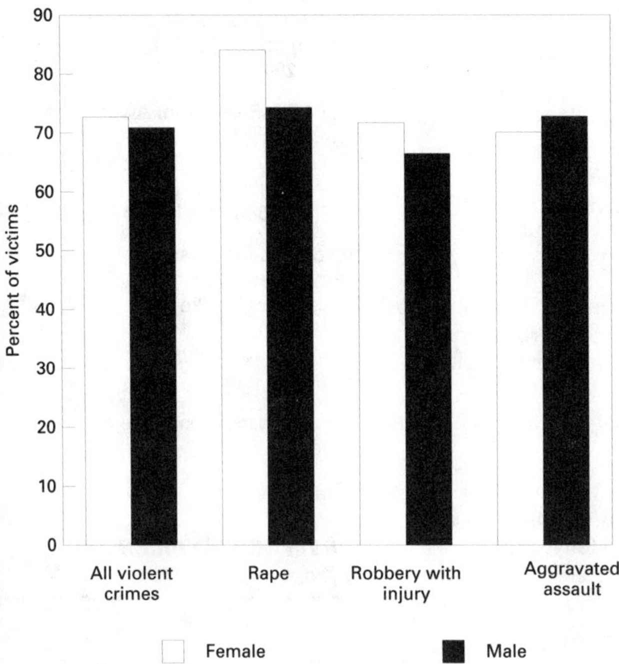

Source for above: National Criminal Justice Reference Service

Brazil has 84 all-female police stations to assist victims of violence.

Fast Fact: Dog Escort Program

Founded in 1981, Project Safe Run is a unique dog-escort program for female and elderly joggers. The dogs, acting as a strong deterrent to potential attackers, are available 24 hours a day to borrowers who fill out an application, complete a 15-minute training session on how to control the dog, and pay a $25 monthly donation. Chapter houses are located mainly in college towns. For additional information contact:

Project Safe Run Foundation
6920 Roosevelt Way, N.E., Suite 371
Seattle, WA 98115
(206) 727-1212 or (503) 345-8086

Of the 2,482 prisoners on death row in state prisons in 1991, 34 were women.

SELF-DEFENSE—RESOURCES AND READING

"Rape and Assault: Prevention Through Preparation" is an educational rape-prevention seminar for women in the workplace. Contact:
Al Marrewa/Powerflex USA
1015 Gayley Avenue, Suite 191
Los Angeles, CA 90024
(310) 475-2772

Self-Defense Seminar, 45 min. video (available from S.K. Productions, P.O. Box 290206, Wethersfield, CT 06129).

Self-Defense: Women Teaching Women, video/manual package (available from the Los Angeles Commission on Assaults Against Women, 6043 Hollywood Boulevard, Suite 200, Los Angeles, CA 90028).

Women's Self-Defense: A Complete Guide to Assault Prevention (available from the Los Angeles Commission on Assaults Against Women, 6043 Hollywood Boulevard, Suite 200, Los Angeles, CA 90028).

SELF-DEFENSE—ORGANIZATIONS

The American Women's Self-Defense Association
713 N. Wellwood Avenue
Lindenhurst, NY 11757
(516) 225-6262

Chimera*
Self-Defense for Women
59 E. Van Buren, #714
Chicago, IL 60605
(312) 939-5341

The Los Angeles Commission on Assaults Against Women
6043 Hollywood Boulevard, Suite 200
Los Angeles, CA 90028
(213) 462-1356

The National Rifle Association Women's Issues and Information
1600 Rhode Island Avenue, N.W.
Washington, DC 20036
(202) 828-6224

PrePARE (Protection, Awareness, Response, Empowerment)*
25 W. 43rd Street, Suite 2100
New York, NY 10036
(212) 719-5800 or (800) 442-7273

Resources for Personal Empowerment*
Model Mugging Program
P.O. Box 20316
New York, NY 10028
(800) 443-5425

*These organizations have regional offices.

Fast Facts: Women and Firearms

- The number of women who own firearms increased 53% from 1983 to 1986.
- Around 12 million women are estimated to legally own weapons in the U.S.
- Female gun purchasers buy firearms for self or home protection, according to 79% of surveyed U.S. gun dealers.
- Women prefer revolvers and pistols to shotguns and rifles, according to the same survey.

Source: Women and Guns, June 1992

JANET RENO—SUPPORTING CHILDREN AND COMBATING VIOLENCE AND NEGLECT

As attorney general of the U.S., Janet Reno is America's chief law enforcement official and head of the Justice Department. She is also the first woman to serve in that post, which she has held since her appointment in 1993. The full version of this speech, which touches on a range of concerns of importance to women, was delivered to the Women's Bar Association of the District of Columbia on May 26, 1993.

These last three months have been reminders to me of how wonderful public service is. . . . The opportunity to serve is one of the greatest opportunities that can be extended to any lawyer. And the opportunity to serve now is so extraordinary. But I think we have to use our ability to organize, our ability to get things done, our ability to be sensitive and to care, and to break through this mentality that seems to pervade so much of government, of gridlock, of stopping things, of stopping progress. Sometimes it's a nonpartisan issue. But let's just get to the common sense of the issue. Let's appreciate public service. Let's be valiant, good, loyal adversaries. But let's get things done as we do it.

A little over thirty years ago, I went home in the summer between my second and third year of law school to apply for a job at a law firm. They wouldn't give me a job because I was a woman. Fourteen years later they made me a law partner. And now I have become the attorney general.

Let us understand that with all our progress, if you had told me when I didn't get that job in that law firm that I would ever walk into this room in Washington, D.C., and see this many women lawyers around in this many positions, I wouldn't have believed it.

But let us also understand that out there and across America more women and children are living in poverty than any other group or category. More women and children are living in poverty in proportion to the population than ever in the history of America. And we've got to do something about that.

As we congratulate ourselves on where we have come and what we have become, let us understand that there are children who after school and in the evenings are unsupervised, and adrift and alone and fearful. And they are getting into trouble and they are being hurt. And we have to do something about that.

And let us first begin with ourselves and in our law firms, in our departments, in everything we do, let us say yes, we can go to law school. Yes, we can become attorney general of the United States. But, yes, we can put our families first and make a difference.

We can accomplish everything we need to do and still give us time to be with our families and to raise our children. We can still make the difference in their lives with quality time, if we put our children first.

Handguns kill 26,000 children every year.

One out of three girls and one out of five boys will be sexually abused by age 18.

CHILD ABUSE: FACTS AT A GLANCE

Victims

•Every 13 seconds, a child is abused.

•2.9 million cases of child abuse and neglect were reported in the United States in 1992.

•Approximately 53% of child victims are female, 46% male.

•1,261 children died of abuse or neglect in 1991—37% as a result of physical neglect, 58% as a result of physical abuse.

•About 95% of victims know the perpetrators.

Survivors

•Approximately 31% of women in prison say they were abused as children.

•About 95% of teenage prostitutes have been sexually abused.

•As many as 38% of all women have been sexually abused by the time they finish adolescence.

Perpetrators

•The typical child sex offender molests an average of 117 children, most of whom do not report the offense.

•An estimated 71% of offenders are under 35 years of age and knew their victim at least casually.

•Less than 4% of offenders over the age of 55 are sentenced to jail.

Source: Childhelp USA

PREVENTING ABUSE: TIPS FOR PARENTS

•Know where your child is at all times, who s/he is with, and what s/he is doing.

•Ask your child what happens when s/he is alone with babysitters, friends, etc.

•Encourage your child to tell you about any problems or questions s/he may have.

•Take the time to be an understanding listener.

•Discuss sexual abuse with your child, giving him/her clear and accurate information.

•Teach your child to say "no" to anyone who attempts to touch the private parts of their bodies or asks them to do anything that makes them feel uncomfortable, strange, or fearful.

•Instruct them to tell an adult what happened as soon as possible.

•Tell them to remember where and when the incident happened.

Source: National Council on Child Abuse and Family Violence

REPORTING SUSPECTED CHILD ABUSE

•Make a report as soon as you suspect that a child is being abused. Report the incident by telephone to your state or county child protective services office or child welfare department. Look in your telephone directory under "child abuse," or call one of the toll-free hotlines listed in Resources for Child-Abuse Prevention, p. 474.

•Be prepared to give the victim's name and address, what you believe is happening to the child, and the name and location of the alleged offender.

•Expect an investigation to be made of your report.

Source: National Committee for Prevention of Child Abuse

SEXUAL MOLESTATION OF WOMEN

Women who were sexually molested as children were surveyed for this study.

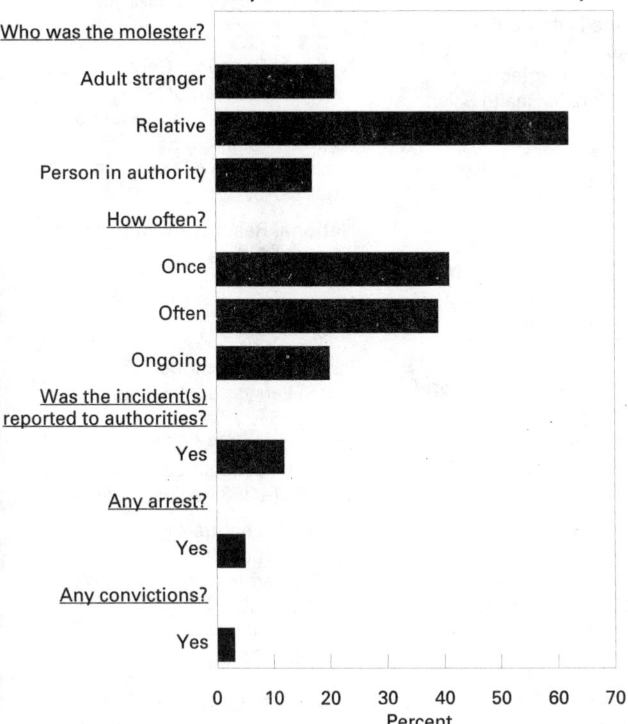

Source: The Janus Report (New York: John Wiley & Sons, 1993)

To find out if someone has ever been an inmate in the federal prison system, call the Bureau of Prisons at (202) 307-3126.

CHILD ABUSE—RECOMMENDED READING

Shifting the Burden of Truth: Suing Child Sexual Abusers—A Legal Guide for Survivors and Their Supporters, Joseph E. Crnich and Kimberly A. Crnich (Lake Oswego, Oreg.: Recollex Publishers, 1992).

The Silent Children: A Parent's Guide to the Prevention of Child Sexual Abuse, Linda Tschirhart Sanford (Fayetteville, N.Y.: Ed-U Press, 1980).

Something Happened and I'm Scared to Tell: A Book for Young Children Victims of Abuse, Patricia Kehoe (Santa Cruz, Calif.: Parenting Press, 1987).

When Your Child Has Been Molested, Kathryn B. Hagans and Joyce Case (Lexington, Mass.: Lexington Books, 1988).

Over 90% of women express their anger to a third person, not the person who angered them, according to a recent study.

CHILD-ABUSE PREVENTION—RESOURCES

C. Henry Kempe National Center for the Prevention and Treatment of Child Abuse and Neglect
University of Colorado Health Sciences Center
Department of Pediatrics
1205 Oneida Street
Denver, CO 80220
(303) 321-3963

Childhelp USA
6463 Independence Avenue
Woodland Hills, CA 91367
(818) 347-7280

Clearinghouse on Child Abuse and Neglect Information
3998 Fair Ridge Drive, Suite 350
Fairfax, VA 22033
(800) 394-3366

Covenant House Nineline
346 W. 17th Street
New York, NY 10011
(212) 727-4025 (administration) or
(800) 999-9999 (hotline)

Father Flanagan's Boys' Home
13940 Gutowski Road
Boys Town, NE 68010
(800) 448-3000 (hotline)

National Center on Child Abuse and Neglect
P.O. Box 1182
Washington, DC 20013
(202) 205-8586

National Child Abuse Hotline
(800) 422-4453

National Committee for the Prevention of Child Abuse
P.O. Box 2866
Chicago, IL 60690
(312) 663-3520

National Council on Child Abuse and Family Violence
1155 Connecticut Avenue, N.W.
Suite 400
Washington, DC 20036
(202) 429-6695

National Directory of Children, Youth, and Family Services
P.O. Box 1837
Longmont, CO 80502
(303) 776-7539

National Resource Center on Child Abuse and Neglect
American Humane Association
63 Inverness Drive E
Englewood, CO 80112
(800) 227-5242

National Resource Center on Child Sexual Abuse
107 Lincoln Street
Huntsville, AL 35801
(800) 543-7006

Parents Anonymous
520 S. Lafayette Park Place,
Suite 316
Los Angeles, CA 90045
(213) 388-6685 (in California) or
(800) 421-0353 (regional referrals)

Society's League Against Molestation
c/o Women Against Rape/Childwatch
P.O. Box 346
Collingswood, NJ 08108
(609) 858-7800

SURVIVORS OF SEXUAL ABUSE—RECOMMENDED READING

Breaking the Silence: Coming to Terms with Child Sexual Abuse, 52 min. video, Theresa Tollini (1983; available from New Day Films, 22-D Hollywood Avenue, Hohokus, NJ 07423, [201] 652-6590).

The Courage to Heal: A Guide for Women Survivors of Child Sexual Abuse, Ellen Bass and Laura Davis (New York: Harper & Row, 1988).

Daybreak: Meditations for Women Survivors of Sexual Abuse, Maureen Brady (Center City, Minn.: Hazelden, 1991).

Getting Through the Day: Strategies for Adults Hurt as Children, Nancy J. Napier (New York: W. W. Norton, 1992).

Secret Survivors: Uncovering Incest and Its Aftereffects, E. Sue Blume (New York: Ballantine, 1991).

SURVIVORS OF SEXUAL ABUSE—RESOURCES

Incest Survivors Anonymous
P.O. Box 5613
Long Beach, CA 90805

Incest Survivors Resource Network, International
P.O. Box 7375
Las Cruces, NM 88006
(505) 521-4260

Parents United
Daughters and Sons United
232 E. Gish Road, 1st Floor
San Jose, CA 95112
(408) 453-7611

Paul and Lisa
P.O. Box 348
Westbrook, CT 06498
(203) 399-5338

VOICES In Action (Victims of Incest Can Emerge Survivors)
P.O. Box 148309
Chicago, IL 60614
(312) 327-1500

ELDER ABUSE

Through physical abuse, negligence, psychological abuse, or financial exploitation, elder abuse is a problem of significant proportions. According to the National Council on Child Abuse and Family Violence, many more cases occur than are reported. Among the causes of elder abuse:

•Negative attitudes and dehumanizing stereotypes make older persons vulnerable to maltreatment.

•Adults who were once abused by their parents will frequently abuse their parents when they are old.

•Family members or caregivers may not be emotionally or financially capable of dealing with the severe impairments that accompany old age. Resentments, exhaustion, and/or guilt can be contributors to abusive behavior.

•Most elderly victims are dependent on the abuser for basic needs.

Source: National Council on Child Abuse and Family Violence

GOVERNMENT RESOURCES TO COMBAT ELDER ABUSE

Although each state has a different system to address elder abuse, the following are some of the agencies (federal, state, and local) that can help:

•Adult Protective Services—In most jurisdictions, either adult protective services, the area agency on aging, or the county department of social services receives and investigates allegations of elder abuse.

•Information and Referral—Every area agency on aging operates an information and referral line. The Eldercare Locator number, (800) 677-1116, assists long-distance caregivers to locate services in the community in which the elder lives.

•Law Enforcement—In states that have criminal statutes concerning elder abuse, it may be a requirement to report suspected abuse to a law enforcement agency.

•Long-Term Care Ombudsman Program—This federal program investigates and attempts to resolve nursing home complaints. Specific information is available at your state office for the aging.

Source: National Aging Resource Center on Elder Abuse

More than a million older women are victims of abuse each year. Twice as many women over age 65 are mugged at or near their homes as are younger women.

The murder rate for women aged 65 and older increased by 30% from 1974 to 1990, while the murder rate for men the same age dropped by 6%.

73% of women in prison are under 30 years of age.

54% of women in prison are women of color.

ELDER ABUSE—RESOURCES

American Public Welfare Association
810 First Street, N.E., Suite 500
Washington, D.C. 20002
(202) 682-0100

Elder Abuse Hotline
(800) 231-4024 (California only)

National Aging Resource Center on Elder Abuse
810 First Street, N.E., Suite 500
Washington, DC 20002
(202) 682-2470 or (202) 682-0100

National Committee for the Prevention of Elder Abuse
c/o Institute on Aging
Medical Center of Central Massachusetts
119 Belmont Street
Worcester, MA 01605
(508) 793-6166

National Council on Child Abuse and Family Violence
1155 Connecticut Avenue, N.W., Suite 400
Washington, DC 20036
(800) 222-2000

Philadelphia Elder Abuse Task Force
The Coalition of Advocates for the Rights of the Infirm Elderly
1315 Walnut Street, Suite 1000
Philadelphia, PA 19107
(215) 545-5728

WOMEN IN PRISON

A survey of state prison inmates found that:

- Women make up 5% of the total state prison population.
- Women inmates were more likely than men to test HIV-positive (3.3% to 2.1%). Hispanic women (6.8%) had higher HIV-positive rates than black women (3.5%) or white women (1.9%).
- Women were more likely than men to have used crack in the month before the offense (19% to 10%); 46% used no drugs during that same time period.
- Thirty-six percent of women committed their offense under the influence of drugs; 24% committed the offense in order to get money for drugs.
- Six percent entered prison pregnant.
- Women inmates were at least three times more likely than male inmates (43% to 12%) to have sustained physical or sexual abuse in their past.
- Thirty-one percent of women inmates received vocational training since entering prison.
- Among violent inmates, women (36%) were more likely than men (16%) to have victimized a relative or intimate.
- Violent women were also more likely than men (48% to 26%) to have committed a homicide.
- Seventy percent of violent female inmates had victimized men: 58% killed their victim, 18% robbed him, and 18% assaulted him.

Source: National Criminal Justice Reference Service

ARREST TRENDS

This chart shows the percentage change in arrests of women from 1983 to 1992.

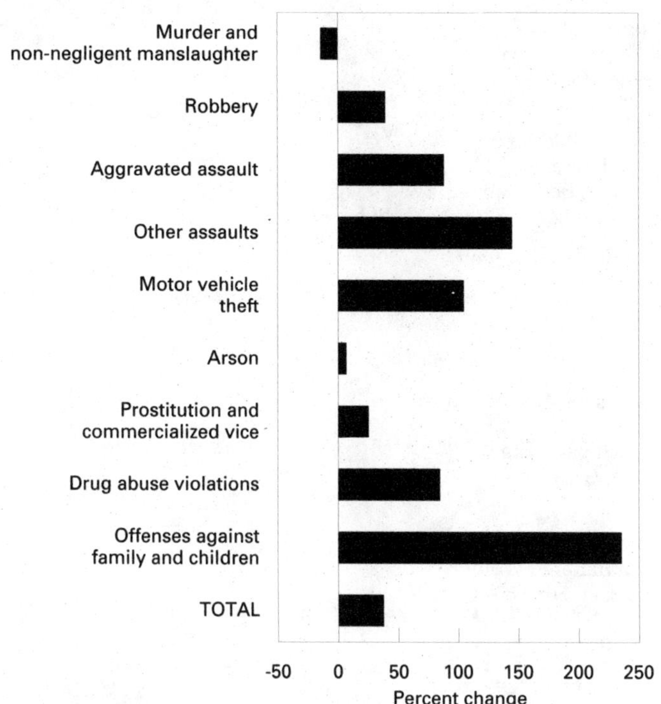

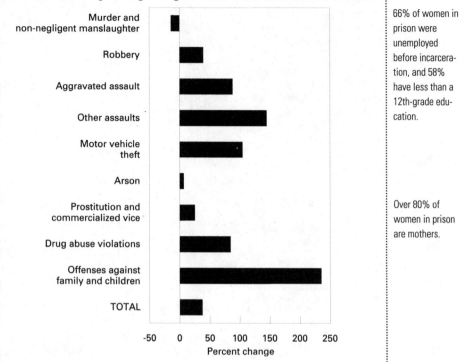

Source: Federal Bureau of Investigation, Uniform Crime Report, 1993

SENTENCE LENGTH

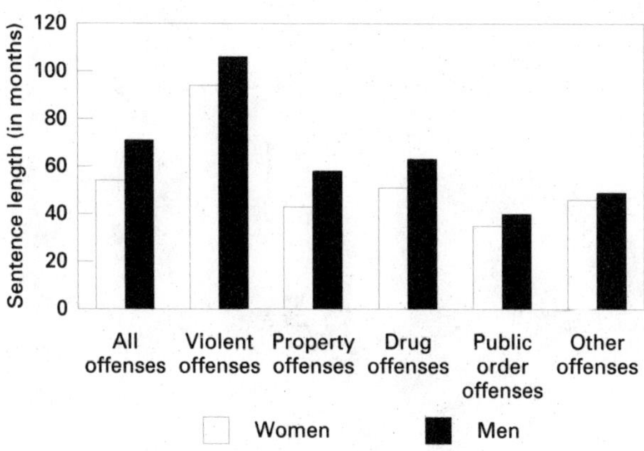

(Data from 1990)
Source: National Criminal Justice Reference Service

66% of women in prison were unemployed before incarceration, and 58% have less than a 12th-grade education.

Over 80% of women in prison are mothers.

WOMEN IN PRISON—RESOURCES

More than 52,000 children under age 18 had mothers who were in jail in 1989.

Aid to Imprisoned Mothers
599 Mitchell Avenue, S.W.
Atlanta, GA 30314
(404) 221-0092

The Center for Children of Incarcerated Parents
714 W. California Boulevard
Pasadena, CA 91105

Coalition to Support Women Prisoners at Chowchilla
P.O. Box 14844
San Francisco, CA 94114
(510) 530-6214 or (415) 861-4058

40% of female inmates incarcerated for murder or manslaughter had killed partners who repeatedly assaulted them. These women had sought police protection at least 5 times before resorting to homicide.

Legal Services for Prisoners with Children
474 Valencia Street, Suite 230
San Francisco, CA 94103
(415) 255-7036

The National Clearinghouse for the Defense of Battered Women
125 S. 9th Street, Suite 302
Philadelphia, PA 19107
(215) 351-0010

Prison Issues Committee
ACT/UP San Francisco
P.O. Box 14844
San Francisco, CA 94114

ACTIVISM

LIFETIME TELEVISION'S 100 IDEAS FOR CHANGE

Below is a list of a hundred ideas to make the world better for women and their families, suggested by Lifetime Television's largely female audience and listed in no particular order.

1. Accessible, affordable, and safe child-care options
2. Family-friendly workplaces
3. Increased attention to breast cancer prevention
4. A completely shattered glass ceiling
5. Preservation of the environment for the generations that will follow
6. Laws and services to protect victims of domestic violence
7. Affordable, quality health care
8. Parenting becomes a genderless job
9. More women involved in the political process
10. More research on women's health issues
11. The First Lady should be able to define her role as she sees fit
12. Opportunities and assistance for women to start small businesses
13. Teaching should be considered one of society's most respected careers
14. More strong, intelligent roles for women in entertainment
15. No stereotyping of women into "traditional" jobs
16. More women in leadership positions in all fields
17. An end to sexual harassment
18. Highlight women making positive changes in their communities
19. Similar household chore responsibilities for boys and girls
20. Recognition of the needs of women with AIDS
21. Women should not have to fear going out at night
22. Removal of the stigma surrounding mental illness
23. Violence should have no part in the debate over abortion
24. More public schools sensitive to the needs of families
25. Encourage self-esteem in children
26. Prenatal care for all prospective parents
27. Parking places for parents with babies
28. An end to gratuitous violence against female characters in entertainment
29. A criminal justice system more responsive to women
30. Feminism should not be thought of as a dirty word
31. Dolls with more realistic physical dimensions
32. Improved stalking laws
33. Family issues should not be pigeonholed as "women's issues"
34. An equal place for women in the military
35. Future generations should not have to bear the burden of an overwhelming debt
36. Recognition of the growing problems and special needs of children with AIDS
37. More job training to help women get off welfare
38. More education about drug and alcohol abuse in schools
39. More education about teen pregnancy
40. No discrimination against pregnant women in the workplace
41. A nationwide policy to enforce child support
42. No one should be denied the opportunity to pursue a college degree because of financial constraints
43. Discourage advertising billboards that objectify women
44. Put an economic value on the work of a homemaker
45. More respect for victims of sexual assault by the criminal justice system
46. Diet pills should not be readily available to girls under 18
47. Equal dry-cleaning prices for women and men
48. Girls should be encouraged to pursue careers in math and science
49. Stronger child abuse laws

The phrase "women's liberation" first appeared in Simone de Beauvoir's book *The Second Sex.*

Fed up with deteriorating work conditions, 150 women garment workers in New York City joined the Ladies Waist Makers Union and were locked out of their jobs in 1909. Other workers joined to form an uprising of 20,000, which ended with union contracts in 312 shops.

Kate Millett's controversial book Sexual Politics: A Surprising Examination of Society's Most Arbitrary Folly was originally submitted as a doctoral thesis, but soon became a national best-seller.

Susan B. Anthony gained public notoriety in 1872 when she was arrested for voting in a national election. She refused to pay the $100 fine because no women were allowed on the jury.

50. A better sense of personal responsibility among all Americans
51. Guns out of the schools and off the streets
52. Equal pay for equal work
53. Increased research and information on new and effective birth control methods
54. No more lewd mud flaps on trucks
55. Children should be taught about racial and religious tolerance at an early age
56. There should not be a beauty ideal
57. Classification of rape committed during wartime as a war crime
58. Consideration of child-related issues as a top national priority
59. Free alterations for women's clothing
60. Women should get more power over the remote control
61. Recognition of older females in all areas of entertainment
62. Girls called on in the classroom as much as boys
63. More ladies rooms in public institutions
64. Help for women "sandwiched" as primary caregivers to children and elderly
65. A crackdown on car dealers and auto mechanics who overcharge women
66. An end to verbal street harassment
67. Equal support for women's sports in schools
68. Celebration of the diversity of women
69. Emphasis on strengthening families
70. More changing tables in public bathrooms
71. An end to discrimination based on sexual orientation
72. Equal treatment of women by salespeople in the financial sector
73. Women should not be penalized by Social Security and pension laws
64. Better recognition of the needs of single mothers
75. Equal access to the armrest on airplanes and in movie theaters
76. Equal treatment of men and women in all aspects of divorce
77. Creation of fair adoption laws
78. The U.S. should help protect the rights of women and children in other countries
79. Similar educational opportunities and expectations for girls and boys
80. Tobacco companies should not market to young people
81. Increased awareness of date rape as a crime
82. No child should go to bed hungry
83. A change in the idea that "getting emotional" is negative
84. Women should not feel they are being judged for staying home and raising their children
85. Incorporate and encourage the arts in all levels of society
86. Equal-priced haircuts for men and women
87. Tougher enforcement of drunk driving laws
88. Greater emphasis on the benefits of good nutrition
89. Improve the nation's foster care system
90. More private areas for women to breastfeed in public places
91. Similar access to financial credit for women and men
92. A change in the perception that while older women look old, older men look distinguished
93. A change in the perception that all women are bad drivers
94. The option for women to volunteer for combat in the military
95. Dads calling the babysitter, too
96. Access to proper immunizations for all children
97. More female cartoon heroes
98. Support for "Take Our Daughters to Work Day" every year
99. More emphasis on prevention in health care
100. Make sure the "Year of the Woman" was not just one year

Source: Lifetime Television

ORGANIZING A RALLY

•**Purpose.** Who will be involved, who do you want to reach, and how will the rally help you achieve your goals?
•**Draw.** If the issue alone won't bring people to the event you may need a hook—a celebrity, musician, politician, or academic.
•**Budget.** How much will it cost, and where will the money come from?
•**Tone.** Create a sense of urgency. Keep the rally upbeat and empowering.
•**Logistics.** Schedule every task and make all assignments early.
•**Location.** Pick a site that will emphasize the number of your crowd, or one that has symbolic value. Ensure its accessibility, legality, and availability.
•**Pre-event publicity.** Inundate the media, put up posters, set up a telephone bank.
•**Building your network.** Get names, addresses, and phone numbers of all participants. Follow up.
•**Coalition building.** Weigh the pros and cons of organizing with other groups.
•**Follow-up.** Do a thorough postmortem on the event.

Source: Planned Parenthood Federation of America

ORGANIZING A LETTER-WRITING CAMPAIGN

For legislators, whether local, state, or federal, letters are the barometers that measure political pressure in the home district. A letter-writing campaign is a good way to ensure that your voice is heard when it comes time for representatives to make decisions that affect your rights.

•Remember that volume is the key to a successful campaign.
•Send personalized letters; they're more effective than form letters.
•Focus the campaign around your support or opposition to specific pieces of legislation.
•Tell people whom to target, and give them the information they need to write an informed letter.
•Make sample letters available.
•Alert as many people as possible to the need for letters. (This can be done by tabling, leafleting, or sending a letter to friends.)
•Make it easy for people to write letters on the spot.
•Send copies of the letters to your local newspaper.

Writing an Effective Letter
•Include your name and address; anonymous letters will be ignored.
•Keep the letters short and to the point.
•Cover only one subject per letter.
•Refer to the specifics of the bill; show your familiarity with the issue.
•Let the official know that you plan to monitor his or her record and publicize it in some way. Inform them that you vote.
•Address your politician properly. For the president and the U.S. Congress, write:

Senators:

The Honorable _____
U.S. Senate
Washington, DC 20510

Dear Senator ______,

Representatives:

The Honorable ________
U.S. House of Representatives
Washington, DC 20515

Dear Representative __________,

President Clinton
Office of the President
1600 Pennsylvania Avenue
Washington, DC 20500

Dear Mr. President,

Source: Planned Parenthood Federation of America

The first women's liberation conference was held on November 28–30, 1968, in Chicago. More than 200 women convened for the event.

"When I am alone I am not aware of my race or my sex, both in need of social contexts for definition."— Maxine Hong Kingston

It took 72 years to pass the constitutional amendment guaranteeing a woman's right to vote, making this the longest civil-rights campaign in U.S. history.

WHO TO CONTACT—CONGRESS AND THE WHITE HOUSE

For addresses and telephone numbers of Senate and House members:

Office of Records and Registration
1036 Longworth House Office Building
Washington, DC 20515
(202) 225-1300

White House Comments Line
(202) 456-1111

If you wish to have a copy of a bill and know its number, your representative may retrieve it for you, but you may also request it from the congressional document rooms:

House Document Room
B-18 Annex 2
Washington, DC 20515
(202) 255-3456

Senate Document Room
SH-B 04
Washington, DC 20510
(202) 224-7860

THE EQUAL RIGHTS AMENDMENT

The Equal Rights Amendment was written in 1921 by suffragist Alice Paul. Introduced in Congress every session since 1923, it passed in 1972 but failed to be ratified by the necessary 38 states by the July 1982 deadline. It was ratified by thirty-five states. The text of the proposed amendment reads:

Section 1. Equality of rights under the law shall not be denied or abridged by the United States or any state on account of sex.
Section 2. The Congress shall have the power to enforce, by appropriate legislation, the provisions of this article.
Section 3. This amendment shall take effect two years after date of ratification.

PENDING LEGISLATION

The Women's Health Equity Act of 1993 (H.R. 3075)
This act includes 32 pieces of legislation to improve health-care research and services for women, including AIDS research and prevention, federal environmental risk assessment for women, and RU-486 research.

Gender Equity in Education Act (H.R. 1793)
This omnibus package of nine bills is designed to facilitate enforcement of Title IX, prohibiting discrimination in federally funded educational institutions. The bills address a range of problems in schools, including sexual harassment, high female dropout rates, inequitable math/science training, and inadequate spending on female athletics.

The Economic Equity Act (H.R. 2790)
This act contains 23 pieces of legislation to promote workplace fairness, economic opportunity, improved child care, and economic self-sufficiency. The bills address issues such as unemployment insurance reform, tax incentives for family-friendly workplaces, pension reform, and uniform rules of child support enforcement.

Source: On the Issues: The Progressive Woman's Quarterly

PUBLIC SERVICE AND VOLUNTEERISM—RESOURCES

Big Brothers/Big Sisters of America
230 N. 13th Street
Philadelphia, PA 19107
(215) 567-7000
Volunteers work on a one-to-one basis with children in need.

General Federation of Women's Clubs
The Women's History and Resource Center
1734 N Street, N.W.
Washington, DC 20036
(202) 347-3168
Volunteer groups that address a wide range of community concerns.

Soroptimist International of the Americas
1616 Walnut Street, Suite 700
Philadelphia, PA 19103
(215) 732-0512
Provides financial and educational services to communities worldwide.

ACTIVISM—RECOMMENDED READING

Black Women in America: An Historical Encyclopedia, ed. Darlene Clark Hine (Brooklyn, N.Y.: Carlson Publishing, 1993).

Daughters of Feminists, Rose L. Glickman (New York: St. Martin's, 1993).

How to Make the World a Better Place for Women in Five Minutes a Day, Donna Jackson (New York: Hyperion, 1992).

Rights and Wrongs: Women's Struggle for Legal Equality, Susan Cary Nicholas, Alice M. Price, and Rachel Rubin (New York: Feminist Press, 1986).

Women Activists: Challenging the Abuse of Power, Anne Witte Garland (New York: Feminist Press, 1988).

The Women's Chronology: A Year-by-Year Record from Prehistory to the Present, James Trager (New York: Henry Holt, 1993).

The National Organization for Women was founded in 1966 as a result of the EEOC's failure to enforce Title VII of the Civil Rights Act of 1964; 28 women contributed $5 each to finance its organization.

EARLY WOMEN ACTIVISTS

Lucretia Mott (1793–1866)—held the Seneca Falls Women's Rights Convention, 1848; first president of the American Equal Rights Association, 1866

Sojourner Truth (c. 1797–1883), born Isabella Van Wagener—born a slave, became a public speaker; worked against slavery and for women's rights and suffrage

Dorothea Dix (1802–1887)—advocate for the mentally ill; key figure in establishment of hospitals for the mentally ill and developments in psychiatry

Elizabeth Cady Stanton (1815–1902)—organized the Seneca Falls Women's Rights Convention, 1848; author of the "Declaration of the Rights of Women," 1848; co-founder of the National Woman Suffrage Association

Susan B. Anthony (1820–1906)—co-founder of the National Woman Suffrage Association, 1869; one of the key forces behind women's suffrage legislation in 1920

Harriet Tubman (c. 1820–1913)—ran an underground railroad to help slaves escape, 1850

Clara Barton (1821–1912)—Civil War nurse; founder of the American Red Cross, 1882

Frances Willard (1839–1898)—co-founder of the Association for the Advancement of Women, 1873; co-founder of the Woman's Christian Temperance Union, 1874; worked for suffrage

Carrie Chapman Catt (1859–1947)—suffragist who helped form the League of Women Voters, 1920

Jane Addams (1860–1935)—founded the Women's International League for Peace and Freedom, 1915; won Nobel Peace Prize, 1931

Mary Anderson (1872–1964)—headed the Women's Bureau of the Department of Labor, 1918–1944

Rose Schneiderman (1882–1972)—organizer for the Women's Trade Union League, the International Ladies' Garment Workers Union, and the National American Woman Suffrage Association

Margaret Sanger (1883–1966)—birth control activist, first woman to open birth control clinic; founder of International Planned Parenthood, 1952

Alice Paul (1885–1977)—author of Equal Rights Amendment, 1923; first chair of national Woman's Party, 1942

Dr. Mae Jemison was the first African-American woman astronaut. She now focuses her efforts on health care and scientific projects related to women and people of color.

Senator Bob Packwood received more than $275,000 in donations from corporate interests and friends for his legal defense against sexual harassment charges.

Women runners passed a flaming torch in 1977 along 2,610 miles from Seneca Falls, N.Y., the site of the 1848 women's rights conference, to Houston, to open the federally-sponsored National Women's Conference.

THE WOMEN'S RIGHTS PROJECT

Human Rights Watch established the Women's Rights Project in 1990 to focus attention on the denial of women's rights worldwide; its aim is also to incorporate the women's rights campaign into the mainstream of human rights work. One of the project's two main goals involves documenting and challenging violence against women. The other focus of its work includes documenting and challenging systematic state-sanctioned discrimination against women in employment, education, property rights, and other areas that are crucial to the achievement of equality. Issues of concern and action include the use of violence against women as a method of tactical warfare, as well as the torture, extrajudicial killing, and detention without trial faced by women.

Source: Human Rights Watch

ORGANIZATIONS THAT FIGHT DISCRIMINATION AGAINST WOMEN

ACLU Women's Rights Project
American Civil Liberties Union
132 W. 43rd Street
New York, NY 10036
(212) 944-9800 x525
Seeks legal equality for women through litigation.

Center for Policy Alternatives
1875 Connecticut Avenue, N.W.,
Suite 710
Washington, DC 20009
(202) 387-6030
Non-profit, non-partisan group that promotes progressive public policy.

Clearinghouse on Women's Issues
P.O. Box 70603
Friendship Heights, MD 20813
(202) 362-3789 or (301) 871-6106
Disseminates educational information related to discrimination, emphasizing public policies affecting the economic and educational status of women.

Equal Rights Advocates
1663 Mission Street, Suite 550
San Francisco, CA 94103
(415) 621-0672
Nonprofit public-interest law center dedicated to equality for women.

National Federation of Business and Professional Women/USA
Office of Government Relations
20212 Massachusetts Avenue, N.W.
Washington, DC 20036
(202) 293-1100
Promotes economic and civil rights of working women.

National Organization for Men Against Sexism
54 Mint Street, Suite 300
San Francisco, CA 94103
(415) 546-6627
Pro-feminist men and women working toward equality of the sexes.

National Organization for Women
P.O. Box 96824
Washington, DC 20090
(202) 331-0066
Largest U.S. women's rights group, concerned with a broad spectrum of issues.

Women's Rights Project
Human Rights Watch
1522 K Street, N.W., Suite 910
Washington, DC 20005
(202) 371-6592
Documents and challenges state-sanctioned discrimination and violence against women worldwide.

EQUALITY ISSUES—RECOMMENDED READING

The Affirmative Action Handbook: A People's Guide to Starting and Defending Affirmative Action Programs
"Domestic Workers' Rights"
"Pregnancy Discrimination"
"Sex Discrimination in Employment"

These publications are available from:
Equal Rights Advocates
1663 Mission Street
San Francisco, CA 94103
(415) 621-0672

DISCRIMINATION IN CONSTRUCTION

Every federally funded construction project in the country with a value of $10,000 or more is required by executive order to establish affirmative-action plans for the hiring and training of women and minorities in the construction trades. According to the terms of the order (#11246), first issued in 1965 and amended in the late 1970s, the per-project goal for women is 6.9% of each craft, including carpenters, electricians, and laborers. Yet in the past 15 years no state has even come close to reaching that goal, and few contractors have been disciplined for their under-utilization of women or minorities.

Source: Equal Rights Advocates

ACTIVISM RESOURCES FOR WOMEN OF COLOR

Black Women Organized for Educational Development
518 17th Street, Suite 202
Oakland, CA 94612
(510) 763-9501
Provides educational seminars, a mentoring program, support groups, and a resource center for low-income women and women in transition.

Congressional Hispanic Caucus Institute
504 C Street, N.E.
Washington, DC 20002
(202) 543-1771
Offers educational programs and information for Hispanic college students.

Gabriela Network
(A U.S.–Philippine Women's Solidarity Organization)
P.O. Box 403
Times Square Station
New York, NY 10036
(718) 726-3902
Works to promote rights and leadership skills of Filippinas.

Mexican American Women's National Association
1101 Seventeenth Street, N.W., Suite 803
Washington, DC 20036
(202) 833-0060
Volunteer group that promotes educational and economic advancement of Latinas.

National Council of La Raza
810 First Street, N.E., Suite 300
Washington, DC 20002
(202) 289-1380
Runs the Poverty Project.

National Council of Negro Women
1667 K Street, N.W.
Washington, DC 20006
(202) 659-0006
Advocates for African-American women, children, and families, offering programs in education, career advancement, child care, teen pregnancy, drug abuse, and health.

Organization of Pan Asian American Women
P.O. Box 39128
Washington, DC 20016
All-volunteer group that focuses on the public policy concerns of Asian/Pacific Islander women.

"You can be up to your boobies in white satin, with gardenias in your hair and no sugar cane for miles, but you can still be working on a plantation."—Billie Holiday

Althea Gibson was the first African-American allowed to play in a major U.S. or international tennis tournament. She went on to become the top international player in both 1957 and 1958.

90% of campus rapes occurred when either the assailant, victim, or both were using alcohol.

The first lobotomy in the U.S. was performed in 1956, on a 63-year-old woman. It was believed to be a cure for the "mad housewife" syndrome.

THE VIOLENCE AGAINST WOMEN ACT (S. 11, H.R. 1133)

Background

Senator Joseph Biden first introduced the Violence Against Women Act in 1990 in response to escalating rates of violence against women (particularly rape and family violence). Statistics from 1991 showed that:

- 21,000 domestic crimes are reported to the police every week
- 1.1 million reported assaults are committed against women in their homes
- Unreported domestic crimes have been estimated at more than 3 million a year
- More than 2,000 women are raped and 90 murdered every week
- Women are six times more likely than men to be the victim of a violent crime committed by an intimate

Content

The Violence Against Women Act would provide for the first time a federal civil rights remedy aimed at violent gender-based crimes.

This wide-ranging bill is designed to provide funds for:

- Services to survivors of rape and battering, including rape crisis centers and battered women's shelters; victim's compensation; and a National Commission on Violence Against Women
- Interstate enforcement for orders of protection, and implementation of pro-arrest policies
- The creation of a federal civil rights remedy for crimes of violence committed because of the victim's gender
- Training for judges and law enforcement officials on gender and racial bias in the criminal justice system

Sponsors

Senator Joseph Biden, Representatives Patricia Schroeder, Louise Slaughter, Constance Morella, and Charles Schumer

Status

Passed the House in 1993 by voice vote. No action yet taken in the Senate. There are differences between the House and Senate versions of the bill, including appropriations for rape prevention programs, a toll-free hotline, and model educational programs for young people.

Sources: Senate Judiciary Committee; Congressional Caucus on Women's Issues; National Coalition Against Domestic Violence

COMBATING VIOLENCE AGAINST WOMEN—RESOURCES

National Clearinghouse for the Defense of Battered Women
125 S. Ninth Street, Suite 302
Philadelphia, PA 19107
(215) 351-0010
Legal resources for women facing criminal charges for defending themselves against their batterers or who are incarcerated.

National Coalition Against Domestic Violence
P.O. Box 34103
Washington, DC 20043
(202) 638-6388
Emphasizes political action, with lobbying campaigns, a newsletter, and mobilization.

National Organization for Victim Assistance
1757 Park Road, N.W.
Washington, DC 20010
(800) 879-6682 (information/referral) or
(202) 232-6682 (crisis counseling)
Direct services for victims.

National Victim Center
c/o INFOLINK
P.O. Box 17150
Fort Worth, TX 76102
Provides information and referrals, and runs a victim advocacy program.

Real Men
P.O. Box 1769
Brookline, MA 02146
(617) 499-6980
Group of educators and activists who encourage men to speak out against sexism; take direct actions, distribute literature, and raise funds for women's shelters.

Women's Action for New Directions
P.O. Box B
Arlington, MA 02174
(617) 643-6740
Works to reduce violence and militarism

EMILY HUME—A KID'S EYE VIEW OF SEXISM IN COMMERCIALS

Thirteen-year-old Emily Hume protested how women are portrayed in television commercials in this essay, which originally appeared in Advertising Age. Hume lives in River Forest, Illinois, where she attends Roosevelt Middle School.

What do Tony the Tiger, Cap'n Crunch, the Keebler Elves, Ronald McDonald, the Lego Maniac, and Toucan Sam all have in common?

They're all boys.

Boys are clearly favored in commercials. Almost all the cartoon characters, spokespeople, and actors you see in commercials are boys. And most commercials seem to be targeted to boys—especially toy commercials.

While some commercials, like the one for 2XL (a robot that asks questions), show boys getting all the questions right, other commercials for girls' toys, like Teen Talk Barbie, make comments like "Math class is tough!"

Many sexist commercials are for games. Some of the commercials I have spotted where a boy wins the game include Giggle Wiggle, Shark Attack, Shark Attack Bowling and Frog Soccer.

One example is a commercial for Giggle Wiggle. Four people are playing, two boys and two girls. At the end the boy wins and gleefully shouts, "I win! I win!" while clapping his hands.

My mouth fell open when I saw this commercial. Not only was this kid rude, but he sounded so annoying! I was really upset when I never saw a girl win in any commercials. I even saw a commercial where a dog wins the game!

I think it's these little things in commercials that can really make a person think, "Well if people are sexist in commercials, then I guess it's OK."

Well it's not! As a girl, I hear boys say sexist things all the time. Some boys even laugh when I tell them I like baseball.

I wish the tables could be turned for just one day so boys could see what it feels like to have sexist things said about them all the time.

I'm just sick of hearing things like, "You throw like a girl! You hit like a girl!" Well, I do throw and hit like a girl most likely because I am a girl! And I'm proud of it.

I talked to James Flinn, 11, a friend of mine. When asked about his thoughts on sexist commercials for games, he said, "Boys are too sensitive. If they see a cereal commercial with a girl in it they think, 'I can't buy that, it's for girls!'"

Guess Who? and Polar Dare are the only commercials I've seen in which a girl wins the game. In the Polar Dare commercial, after she wins the girl's reaction is a very surprised, "I win." She sounds aghast that she won. I'm not surprised that she's aghast because there are so many sexist commercials!

I hope that in the future ad companies will wise up and start to see that women have been neglected long enough! And we're not going to put up with it any more!

"Censorship, like charity, should begin at home; but unlike charity, it should end there."— Clare Boothe Luce

Activists drew skeleton heads and the words "Feed Me" on Calvin Klein ads featuring skinny supermodel Kate Moss in 1993.

MONITORING THE MEDIA FOR SEXISM AND VIOLENCE—RESOURCES

ORGANIZATIONS

Challenging Media Images of Women
P.O. Box 902
Framingham, MA 01701
Produces a newsletter for media watches.

Media Action Alliance
P.O. Box 391
Circle Pines, MN 55014
(612) 434-4343
Direct action and public education; also published newsletter.

Media Watch
P.O. Box 618
Santa Cruz, CA 95061
(408) 423-6355
Educational group that produces videos on media sexism.

National Coalition Against Pornography
800 Compton Road, Suite 9224
Cincinnati, OH
(513) 521-6227
Emphasizes stopping child and illegal pornography.

OTHER RESOURCES

Against Pornography, Diana E. H. Russell (Berkeley, Calif.: Russell Publications, 1993).

Challenging Media Images of Women (quarterly journal; available from Challenging Media Images of Women, P.O. Box 902, Framingham, MA 01701).

Don't Be a TV: Television Victim, 18 min. video, Media Watch (available from Media Watch, P.O. Box 618, Santa Cruz, CA 95061).

"Pornography and the Media: Images of Violence Against Women," Gail Dines, slide/lecture presentation (Dines represented by Lordly & Dame, 51 Church Street, Boston, MA 02116, [617] 482-3593).

"Sex, Power and the Media: Rethinking the Myths of America's Dream Girl," slide show (available from Media Watch, P.O. Box 618, Santa Cruz, CA 95061).

Still Killing Us Softly: Advertising Images of Women, Dr. Jean Kilbourne, 30 min. film (available from Cambridge Documentary Film, P.O. Box 385, Cambridge, MA 02139, [617] 354-3677).

Warning: The Media May Be Hazardous to Your Health, 36 min. video, Media Watch (available from Media Watch, P.O. Box 618, Santa Cruz, CA 95061).

ANTI-CENSORSHIP RESOURCES

National Coalition Against Censorship
275 Seventh Avenue
New York, NY 10001
(212) 807-6222
Supports First Amendment rights; organizes the Working Group on Women, Censorship, and "Pornography."

Fairness and Accuracy in Reporting (FAIR)
Women's Desk
130 W. 25th Street
New York, NY 10001
(212) 633-6700
Promotes equality of representation in the media; watchdog for negative media images.

SEXUAL ORIENTATION AND CIVIL RIGHTS LAW

A number of civil rights laws nationwide protect people on the grounds of sexual orientation as well as other issues.

•Eight states have civil rights laws, passed by the legislature and signed by the governor: Wisconsin, Connecticut, Massachusetts, Hawaii, New Jersey, Vermont, California, Minnesota.

•At least 14 states have executive orders.
•At least 75 cities/counties have civil rights ordinances.
•At least 41 cities/counties have council or mayoral proclamations banning discrimination in public employment.

Source: National Gay and Lesbian Task Force

"I think extreme heterosexuality is a perversion."—Margaret Mead

An $8.6 billion federal relief program for victims of the Los Angeles earthquake in January 1994 bans discrimination against lesbians and gay men in relief distribution, the first time federal legislation includes such a clause.

SODOMY LAWS IN THE U.S.

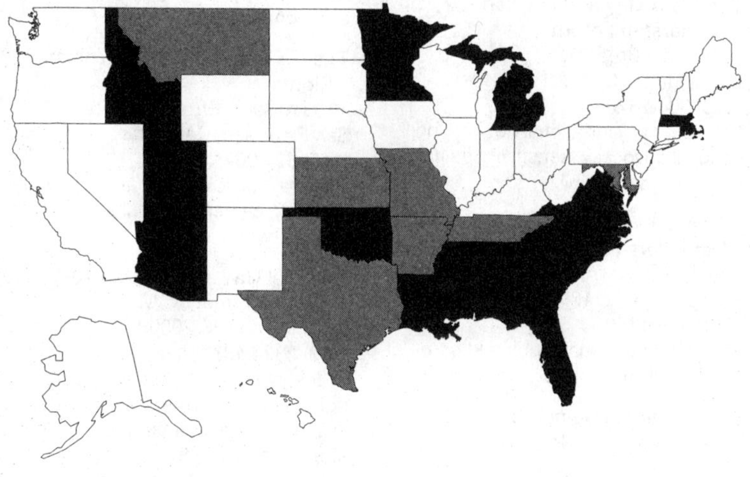

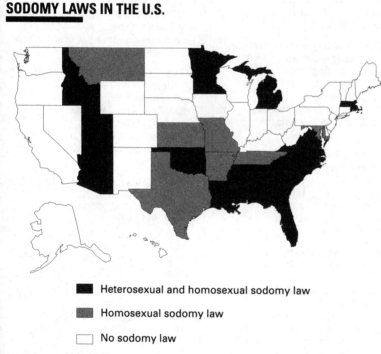

■ Heterosexual and homosexual sodomy law

■ Homosexual sodomy law

□ No sodomy law

(Data from 1993)
Source: National Gay and Lesbian Task Force Policy Institute

Only 20 cities and 5 counties have some form of health benefits for domestic partners as of 1992. Only 7 cities have citywide domestic partnership registration.

Stonewall, a gay bar in Greenwich Village, was raided by the police several times in the summer of 1969, but one night its gay and lesbian patrons fought back. The following week, the Gay Liberation Front was established, and the gay rights movement began.

ADVOCATES FOR LESBIAN AND BISEXUAL RIGHTS

Asian Lesbians of the East Coast/Asian Pacific Lesbian Network of New York
P.O. Box 850
New York, NY 10002
(212) 517-5598
A social and political organization that offers support groups for Asian Pacific lesbians.

Astraea
National Lesbian Action Foundation
666 Broadway, Suite 520
New York, NY 10012
(212) 529-8021

The Black Gay and Lesbian Leadership Forum
1219 S. La Brea
Los Angeles, CA 90019
(213) 964-7820
Promotes organizational networking, national advocacy, sensitivity training, and increased visibility.

Gay and Lesbian Advocates and Defenders (GLAD)
P.O. Box 218a
Boston, MA 02112
(617) 426-1350
Public interest legal group and home of the AIDS Law Project.

Human Rights Campaign Fund
Federal Advocacy Network
P.O. Box 1396
Washington, DC 20077
(202) 628-4160
Nation's largest lesbian and gay political group, promoting anti-discriminatory legislation through lobbying and its political action committee.

International Gay and Lesbian Human Rights Commission
520 Castro Street
San Francisco, CA 94114
(415) 255-8680
Monitors, documents, and exposes human rights violations against gays worldwide; also advocates direct action.

Lambda Legal Defense and Education Fund
666 Broadway, 12th Floor
New York, NY 10012
(212) 995-8585
Civil rights advocates.

The Lesbian Avengers
208 W. 13th Street
New York, NY 10011
(212) 967-7711 x3204
Direct action group with chapters nationwide.

Lesbian Mothers' National Defense Fund
P.O. Box 21567
Seattle, WA 98111
(206) 325-2643
Volunteer resource and support network dealing with legal, financial, and emotional issues.

The National Center for Lesbian Rights
1663 Mission Street, Suite 550
San Francisco, CA 94103
(415) 621-0674
National public interest law firm, legal resource center, and multicultural advocacy network.

National Gay and Lesbian Task Force
1734 14th Street, N.W.
Washington, DC 20009
(202) 332-6483
Oldest national gay and lesbian civil rights advocacy group, whose activities include lobbying, organizing, demonstrating, and educating.

NOW Legal Defense and Education Fund
99 Hudson Street, 12th Floor
New York, NY 10013
(212) 925-6635
See in particular their "Lesbian Rights" legal resource kit ($5).

P-FLAG: Parents, Families and Friends of Lesbians and Gays
1012 14th Street, N.W., Suite 700
Washington, DC 20005
(202) 638-4200
Nationwide group providing family support, public education, and civil rights advocacy.

HEALTH CARE QUESTIONS

As you evaluate various health care proposals, ask your elected representatives and advocates these key questions:

•Will this plan assure me access to comprehensive and affordable health services? Can I afford this plan?
•If I am unemployed or work part-time, am on welfare, or am divorced, will I be refused coverage?
•If I have a pre-existing condition, will I be covered?
•Will I be able to get basic care in my community? Will transportation, child care, and caregiving be covered?
•How will Medicaid and Medicare fit under this plan?

Source: Women Work! The National Network for Women's Employment

HALVING MATERNAL DEATHS

Each year 500,000 women die from causes related to pregnancy and childbirth, and 98% of these deaths occur in developing countries. Maternal mortality rates could be halved by:
•Paying special attention to the health and nutrition of the female child and to pregnant and lactating women
•Giving all couples information and services to prevent pregnancies that are too early, too closely spaced, too late, or too numerous
•Providing all pregnant women with access to prenatal care, trained attendants during childbirth, and referral facilities for high-risk pregnancies and obstetric emergencies
•Guaranteeing universal access to primary education.

Source: "Halving Maternal Deaths: A Strategy for the 1990s," address by James P. Grant, executive director, UNICEF (March 9, 1992)

FEMALE GENITAL MUTILATION

A practice in some countries in Africa, the Middle East, and Asia, female genital mutilation has been performed on an estimated 110 million women and girls. Female genital mutilation is the practice of removing parts of a woman's genitalia, in varying amounts depending on the tradition within a given culture. Female circumcision is the removal of the clitoral hood; excision is the removal of the clitoris itself; and infibulation includes removing the clitoris, scraping off the lips of both the inner and outer labia, and stitching shut the remaining genital orifice so that only a minute opening is left for the flow of urine and menses. These procedures are generally performed without anesthesia, primarily on young girls, usually by women.

Possible physical and psychological consequences can include:
•Stress and shock resulting from the pain
•Infection, which may spread to internal organs
•Painful intercourse
•Complications during childbirth
•The spread of AIDS (the blades used to perform the mutilations are often used on two or more girls in a row)
•A total inability to experience orgasm and to enjoy sexual relations.

Sources : Women's International Network News; off our backs (December 1993)

Reading and Resources

Women's International League for Peace and Freedom
1213 Race Street
Philadelphia, PA 19107
(215) 563-7110

Women's International Network News
187 Grant Street
Lexington, MA 02173
(617) 862-9431

A Nigerian woman facing deportation for herself and her two daughters was granted asylum in 1994 on the grounds that if deported, her children would have faced genital mutilation.

The National Women's Health Resource Center in Washington, D.C., gives Breast Cancer Awareness Awards. The winners for 1993 were Amy S. Langer, Caroline McMillian, and Ann W. Mulqueen.

Women's Rights Project
Human Rights Watch
1522 K Street, N.W., Suite 910
Washington, DC 20005
(202) 371-6592

off our backs
2423 18th Street, N.W.
Washington, DC 20009
(202) 234-8072

UNICEF
3 United Nations Plaza, Room 204
New York, NY 10017
(212) 326-7522

Possessing the Secret of Joy, Alice Walker (San Diego: Harcourt Brace Jovanovich, 1992).

Warrior Marks, film, Pratibha Parmar (1993; Women Make Movies, 462 Broadway, Suite 500, New York, NY 10013, [212] 925-0606).

ADVOCATES FOR HEALTH CARE REFORM

Breast Cancer Action
P.O. Box 460185
San Francisco, CA 94146
(415) 922-8279
Advocates political action and promotes research.

The Campaign for Women's Health
730 11th Street, N.W., Suite 300
Washington, DC 20001
(202) 783-6686
Monitors and responds to national health care initiatives that affect women.

Federation of Feminist Women's Health Centers
633 E. 11th Street
Eugene, OR 97401
(503) 344-0966
Works to secure reproductive rights and educate women about health care.

Lesbian Community Cancer Project
Pat Marker Place
1902 W. Montrose
Chicago, IL 60613
(312) 561-4662
Addresses the high rate of breast cancer through education and advocacy.

The National Breast Cancer Coalition
P.O. Box 66373
Washington, DC 20035
(202) 296-7477
Provides education programs and a national action network to promote policy changes.

The National Association of Child Advocates
1625 K Street, N.W., Suite 510
Washington, DC 20006
(202) 828-6950
Promotes maternal and child health care reform.

Native American Women's Health Education Resource Center
P.O. Box 572
Lake Andes, SD 57356
(605) 487-7073
Organizes a wide range of programs concerning domestic violence, AIDS and cancer prevention, and nutrition.

Public Voice for Food and Health Policy
1001 Connecticut Avenue, N.W., Suite 522
Washington, DC 20036
(202) 659-5930
Focuses efforts on safe and healthy foods.

Women's Community Cancer Project
c/o The Women's Center
46 Pleasant Street
Cambridge, MA 02139
(617) 354-9888
Advocacy and educational group.

Women's Health Action and Mobilization (WHAM)
P.O. Box 974
Canal Street Station
New York, NY 10013
(212) 713-5966
Activist group with an emphasis on education and public actions.

AIDS EDUCATION AND ADVOCACY GROUPS

The HIV Law Project
80 Fifth Avenue, Suite 1505
New York, NY 10011
(212) 645-8863
Provides legal representation and advocacy for low-income, HIV-positive people; promotes remedial legislation.

Lesbian AIDS Project
Gay Men's Health Crisis
129 W. 20th Street
New York, NY 10011
(212) 337-3532
Provides community and resource sharing and informational assistance.

Lesbian Caucus
AIDS Coalition to Unleash Power (ACT-UP)
135 W. 29th Street, 10th Floor
New York, NY 10001
(212) 564-2437
Direct action group.

The Names Project Foundation
310 Townsend Street, Suite 310
San Francisco, CA 94107
(415) 882-5500
Raises funds for direct services for people with AIDS through the AIDS Memorial Quilt.

Project Inform
1965 Market Street, Suite 220
San Francisco, CA 94103
(800) 822-7422 (hotline)
Disseminates information on new treatments, and runs outreach and advocacy programs.

AIDS ACTIVISM—RECOMMENDED READING

Latina AIDS Action Plan and Resource Guide, National Hispanic Education and Communications Projects (1990; available in Spanish and English from HDI Projects, 1000 16th Street,N.W., Room504, Wash., DC 20036 (202)452-0092).

PI Perspective (journal), *PI Briefing Paper* (newsletter) (available from Project Inform, 1965 Market Street, Suite 220, San Francisco, CA 94103).

Women, AIDS, and Activism, ACT-UP/New York Women and AIDS Book Group (Boston: South End Press, 1990).

Women AIDS, and Communities: A Guide for Action, Gerry Pearlberg (Metuchen, N.J.: Scarecrow Press, 1991).

Fast Fact: The Names Project's Quilt

Started by a group of friends in San Francisco, the Names Project's AIDS Memorial Quilt contains 25,246 panels (three by six feet), each memorializing a person who has lost his or her life to AIDS. When the quilt is exhibited with walkways, it covers the equivalent of 15 football fields. As of October 1993, the quilt has raised $1,298,382 for direct services for people with AIDS.

For more information about the AIDS Memorial Quilt, contact:

The Names Project Foundation
310 Townsend Street, Suite 310
San Francisco, CA 94107
(415) 882-5500

FREEDOM OF ACCESS TO CLINIC ENTRANCES ACT

This new law, which was enacted in May 1994, authorizes federal prosecutors to press criminal charges against abortion opponents who commit violent acts against abortion providers. Those convicted of violent acts, including bombings, shootings, vandalism, or assaults, will now face up to ten years in prison and $250,000 in fines. In addition, protestors who stage sit-ins, blockades, and other forms of civil disobedience against abortion clinics can have fines of up to $10,000 levied against them, along with six-month prison terms.

Source: Women Work! The National Network for Women's Employment

The percentage of college women drinking with the intent to get drunk has increased from 10% to 35% over the past 15 years. In addition, 60% of college women who acquired AIDS and other STDs were under the influence of alcohol while having intercourse.

400 protesters staged the first pro-choice civil disobedience rally on the steps of St. Patrick's Cathedral in New York City in 1989.

Of the two dozen pharmaceutical companies doing research on birth control in the 1960s and 1970s, only the Ortho Pharmaceutical Corporation remains.

VIOLENCE AGAINST ABORTION PROVIDERS

Violent Acts	***1977–83***	***1987***	***1990***	***1993***
Murder	0	0	0	1
Attempted murder	0	0	0	1
Bombing	8	0	0	1
Arson	13	4	4	8
Attempted bombing/arson	5	8	4	5
Invasion	68	14	19	14
Vandalism	35	29	26	73
Assault	11	5	6	7
Death threats	4	5	7	64
Kidnapping	2	0	0	0
Burglary	3	7	2	1
Stalking	0	0	0	140
Total	149	72	68	315
Disruption				
Hate mail and harassing calls	9	32	21	234
Bomb threats	9	28	11	15
Picketing	107	77	45	701
Total	125	137	77	950
Clinic blockades				
Number of incidents	0	2	34	46
Number of arrests	0	290	1,363	1,034

As of October 14, 1993. Numbers represent incidents reported to NAF; actual numbers may be higher.

Source: National Abortion Federation

Fast Fact: The Freedom of Choice Act

Now under consideration by Congress, the Freedom of Choice Act (FOCA) would establish as federal law a woman's basic right to an abortion before fetal viability. (A 24-week pregnancy is now the commonly accepted point of viability.) FOCA will not, however, guarantee abortion rights to minors, require states to use public funds for abortions (both will be state decisions), or address the question of what constitutes an undue burden on a woman's ability to have an abortion. (The latter concern arises from a Supreme Court ruling that upheld a woman's right to an abortion as long as constraints did not impose an "undue burden" on her.) FOCA has passed in the House Judiciary Committee but has not been brought to the floor for a vote; it is still in the Senate Judiciary Committee.

Organizations in support of FOCA include:
- National Abortion Rights Action League
- Planned Parenthood Federation

Groups that oppose the legislation include:
- National Black Women's Health Project
- National Campaign for Abortion and Reproductive Equity
- National Organization for Women

Source: Ms. (November/December 1993)

RU486: A CHRONOLOGY

RU486 is a pill that can be used for safe, effective early abortion as well as a "morning-after" pill. It may also be effective in treating breast cancer and several other serious diseases, although adequate tests have yet to be conducted.

Developed by the French firm Roussel Uclaf (whose parent company is Hoechst AG of Germany), RU486 has long been denied American women because its manufacturers, bowing to pressure from anti-abortion forces, have refused to market it in the U.S. Under the Clinton presidency, the political climate has begun to change, however, and American women are now closer than they have ever been to having access to this drug.

The history of RU486:

1983—Clinical trials on the use of RU486 as a method of early abortion begin in the U.S. at the University of Southern California.

1988—Anti-abortion forces threaten Hoechst AG with economic reprisal if RU486 is marketed in the United States. In March 1989 Hoechst informs abortion opponents that "it is not our intention to market or distribute RU486 outside of France." (RU486 had become available in France in 1988 after the French minister of health ordered Roussel Uclaf to return it to the market following the company's decision to withdraw the drug in the wake of anti-abortion pressure.)

June 1989—The U.S. Food and Drug Administration responds to pressure from anti-abortion congressmen by banning the importation of RU486 for personal use.

November 1990—Rep. Ron Wyden holds hearings on RU486 before the House Small Business Committee. Leading scientists testify that the import alert has hindered research on nonabortion uses of RU486, including its use as a possible treatment for breast cancer. Following these hearings, Rep. Wyden introduces legislation to remove the import alert.

February 1991—The American Association for the Advancement of Science (AAAS) endorses the testing and use of RU486. Having secured the support of AAAS, the Feminist Majority Foundation obtains endorsements of the drug from almost every scientific and medical organization in the country. In addition, the foundation collects over 3,000 petitions from individual scientists in support of RU486.

May 1991—New Hampshire becomes the first state in the nation to pass a resolution urging the commencement of clinical trials for RU486 in that state. Subsequent resolutions are passed in Hawaii, California, Maine, and Colorado, and are introduced in a dozen other states.

July 1992—In the first direct challenge to the FDA import alert on RU486, a pregnant American woman, Leona Benten, returns from Europe with a prescription of RU486. Customs officials seize the RU486 upon the arrival of Benten and Larry Lader of Abortion Rights Mobilization at Kennedy Airport. Despite a lower-court ruling on Benten's right to the drug, the Supreme Court refuses to order customs to return it to Benten, and refuses to order the FDA to overturn the import ban.

October 1992—A New England Journal of Medicine study concludes that RU486 is a safe, effective postcoital contraceptive, one that has fewer side effects and is easier to use than the current "morning-after" pill.

November 1992—Bill Clinton is elected president of the United States; during the campaign, Clinton had pledged his support for bringing RU486 to this country.

83% of U.S. counties have no identified abortion provider.

The National Right to Life Committee was established in 1970 in response to growing legislation to disallow many abortion restrictions.

The first March for Life was held in 1974, organized by Nellie Gray. In 1992, there were 70,000 demonstrators in the march.

December 1992—The FDA announces that a review of RU486 for U.S. distribution could be completed in as short a time as six months. FDA Commissioner David Kessler writes to Roussel Uclaf encouraging the company to submit an application to license RU486 in the U.S.
April 1993—Hoechst AG and Roussel Uclaf announce an agreement allowing the New York–based Population Council to test and manufacture RU486. However, Hoechst AG continues to prohibit Roussel Uclaf from selling RU486 to a U.S. distributor while an American manufacturer is established and gains FDA approval. These restrictions could delay making RU486 available for U.S. women by three or more years.
May 1993—A New England Journal of Medicine article reports that RU486, in combination with an oral prostaglandin in pill form, is now 99% effective in terminating pregnancy during the first nine weeks. This prostaglandin, already used in France, replaces an injection formerly used with RU486 and eases the administration of the drug.
September 1993—The Institute of Medicine releases a report recommending immediate submission to the FDA of a new drug application for the use of RU486 as a method of early abortion. They also call for expedited U.S. research on RU486 and other antiprogestins as contraceptives, and as possible treatments for endometriosis, some types of breast cancer, fibroid tumors, labor management, and meningiomas.
May 1994—Roussel Uclaf agrees to turn over RU486's patent rights and all technology to the Population Council for free. The non-profit council will find an American company to manufacture the pill and will conduct clinical trials in the fall of 1994. Roussel Uclaf, in return, rids itself of product liability claims and hopes to avoid boycott threats by anti-abortion groups.

Source: The Feminist Majority Foundation

RU486—RESOURCES

Abortion Rights Mobilization
175 Fifth Avenue
New York, NY
(212) 677-0412

The Feminist Majority Foundation
1600 Wilson Boulevard
Arlington, VA 22209
(703) 522-2214

National Women's Health Network
1325 G Street, N.W.
Washington, DC 20005
(202) 347-1140

PRO-CHOICE ORGANIZATIONS

Abortion Rights Mobilization
51 Fifth Avenue
New York, NY 10003
(212) 255-0682
Advocates legalization of RU486 in the U.S.

American Civil Liberties Union
Reproductive Freedom Project
132 W. 43rd Street
New York, NY 10036
(212) 944-9800 x618
Legal group that litigates abortion rights cases in the courts.

Catholics for a Free Choice
1436 U Street, N.W.
Washington, DC 20009
(202) 986-6093
Educational group that advocates social and economic programs for women, families, and children.

Center for Reproductive Law and Policy
120 Wall Street
New York, NY 10005
(212) 514-5534
Legal group that litigates abortion rights cases in court.

Committee to Defend Reproductive Rights
25 Taylor Street, #702
San Francisco, CA 94102
(415) 441-4434
Organizes and educates San Francisco Bay Area residents.

Fund for the Feminist Majority
1600 Wilson Boulevard, #704
Arlington, VA 22209
(703) 522-2214
Provides funding for pro-choice groups.

National Abortion Federation
1436 U Street, N.W., Suite 103
Washington, DC 20009
(202) 667-5881
Informational group with hotline referrals.

National Abortion Rights Action League
1156 15th Street, N.W.
Washington, DC 20005
(202) 973-3000
Largest organization to lobby specifically for reproductive rights.

National Family Planning and Reproductive Health Association
122 C Street, N.W., Suite 380
Washington, DC 20001
(202) 628-3535
Non-profit membership group involved in education, advocacy, networking, and grassroots mobilization.

The Native American Women's Health Education Resource Center
P.O. Box 572
Lake Andes, SD 57356
(605) 487-7073
Organizes programs on a wide range of health issues, including reproductive health.

Planned Parenthood Federation of America
810 Seventh Avenue
New York, NY 10019
(212) 541-7800
National network of health care providers; advocates for reproductive rights and provides educational resources.

Religious Coalition for Abortion Rights
100 Maryland Avenue, N.E., Suite 307
Washington, DC
(202) 543-7032
Emphasizes education and advocacy, and mobilizes clergy and women.

Voters for Choice
2000 P Street, N.W., Suite 515
Washington, DC 20036
(202) 822-6640
Provides technical assistance and funding to help elect pro-choice candidates.

PRO-LIFE ORGANIZATIONS

Black Americans for Life
419 Seventh Street, N.W., Suite 500
Washington, DC 20004
(202) 626-8833
Outreach group of National Right to Life Committee.

Eagle Forum
316 Pennsylvania Avenue, S.E.
Washington, DC 20003
(202) 544-0353
Membership group with emphasis on abortion, child care, censorship, and family issues.

Feminists for Life of America
811 E. 47th Street
Kansas City, MO 64110
(816) 561-4117
Regards abortion as anti-feminist by diverting male responsibility for fertility control and undermining women's autonomy.

Libertarians for Life
13424 Hathaway Drive
Wheaton, MD 20906
(301) 460-4141
Political libertarians opposing abortion as "the ultimate aggression."

National Right to Life Committee
419 Seventh Street, N.W., Suite 500
Washington, DC 20004
(202) 626-8833
Nation's largest pro-life group, with political action committee, educational programs, and outreach efforts.

National Women's Coalition for Life
P.O. Box 1553
Oak Park, IL 60304
(708) 848-5351
Offers educational information and referrals to local groups.

Canada passed a bill legalizing abortion and homosexuality in May 1969.

The March on Washington for Women's Lives in 1992 was the largest march and rally ever held in the capital, with 750,000 demonstrators.

The Nurturing Network
910 Main Street, Suite 360
P.O. Box 2050
Boise, ID 83701
(208) 344-7200
To encourage women with unplanned pregnancies to carry them full term, provides medical, financial, educational, and employment assistance.

Pro-Life Alliance of Gays and Lesbians
P.O. Box 33292
Washington, DC 20033
(202) 223-6697
Group for gays and lesbians who support the pro-life agenda.

REPRODUCTIVE RIGHTS—RECOMMENDED READING

Confessing Conscience: Churched Women on Abortion, Phyllis Tickle, ed. (Nashville, Tenn.: Abingdon Press, 1991).

Motherhood by Choice: Pioneers in Women's Health and Family Planning, Perdita Huston (New York: Feminist Press, 1992).

Population Policy and Women's Rights: Transforming Reproductive Choice, Ruth Dixon-Mueller (Westport, Conn.: Praeger, 1993).

Public Affairs Action Letter (Planned Parenthood Federation of America, subscription information: Jane Baldinger, 1120 Connecticut Ave., N.W., Suite 461, Washington, DC 20036).

Reproductive Rights and Wrongs: The Global Politics of Population Control and Contraceptive Choice, Betsy Hartmann (New York: Harper and Row, 1987).

Whose Life, Catherine Whitney (New York: William Morrow, 1991).

A Woman's Book of Choices, Rebecca Chalker and Carol Downer (New York: Four Walls, Eight Windows, 1992).

HOW TO BE AN ACTIVIST PARENT

Child Care

- Make inquiries about your state's licensing requirements for child care centers and family day care providers.
- Research the education, training, and turnover rates of your child care center's employees.

In Your Child's School

- Communicate with your child's teacher on a regular basis about how she or he is doing in school.
- Volunteer in your child's school.
- Organize community support for your neighborhood school.
- Participate in school improvement teams.
- Learn about your local school board.

In Your Workplace

- Learn about your employee benefits: flextime, child care benefits, health care that covers dependents, maternity/paternity leave beyond what is required by the Family and Medical Leave Act. Discuss these benefits with your human resources director.

In the Media

- Contact your local television network affiliate or cable company to express concern over programming with violent content. Check to see if they are complying with the Children's Television Act.

Source: Parent Action

PATRICIA IRELAND—AN ACTIVIST'S CONVERSION

Patricia Ireland, the president of the National Organization for Women, discusses women and activism.

It seems almost like yesterday. The shrill retort rings clear: "How can they expect me to teach calculus to girls!" All eyes turned to me as I felt myself shrinking in my seat. The outburst of my freshman calculus professor was in response to what I thought was a reasonable question about a math problem. I never asked another question, got a D in the class, and changed my major from math to education.

When I came of age in this society, women were expected to become first and foremost wives and mothers. I grew up hearing that I "could" become a teacher, so I could be there when my kids got home from school, and I would have "something to fall back on" if my husband should die or leave me. I had never even met a woman attorney until 1970. So I became a teacher. One year later, giving up my attempts to teach German in east Tennessee, I could not think of anything else in the world to be except what was then called a "stewardess."

Like so many women, I joined the feminist movement not because of any theoretical conversion, but because of the discrimination I faced. Working for Pan American Airlines for seven years, I learned that "women's work" meant long hours, low pay, and little respect. Airline advertising itself promoted sexual harassment: "We really move our tails for you" and "I'm Cheryl; fly me." The last straw came when I learned that the health benefits I got were worth less than the benefits the men got.

With advice from Dade County, Florida, NOW, I took my complaint about the discriminatory benefits to several federal agencies and to my own union. The practice was so blatantly illegal that it was soon changed. So I became an activist. I had discovered that I could fight back—and win.

I enrolled in law school to gain tools to fight discrimination. That year, *Ms.* made its first appearance. Today, *Ms.* continues. In the past two decades, I've seen similar growth in the National Organization for Women, and I now serve as NOW's president. (Pan Am, on the other hand, has gone bankrupt.)

When I became active, only 39% of women in the U.S. supported the idea of a women's rights movement. Today 78% say they are supporters of the women's movement, including 20% who say they are strong supporters. The gains of the past two decades have confirmed the strength of the entire women's movement.

As one organization in that movement, NOW has certainly had—and generated—its share of controversies. Some disputes revolved around strategies or tactics; others around the issues. Some remind me of how far we have come; others are still painfully current.

But I am proud that NOW took these stands and helped turn public opinion around. Such incidents remind us that today's radical issues often become tomorrow's givens. We must be willing to take heat to move the feminist agenda forward by advocating issues based not on existing politics, but on what women really need.

Change, even strongly desired change, is never easy. Communication between diverse communities and activists can be difficult and confusing. But such a process is crucial if we are to succeed in building the backlash to the backlash. We must empower more women to move into policy-making positions, not just in government but in all institutions—including NOW.

With the capture of the Supreme Court by the right (and with senators who had pledged to support women's rights voting to confirm each new and more conservative nominee) we learned again and bitterly that no one will fight for us the way we can fight for ourselves. But we've been developing our tactical repertoire for years.

The entire women's movement deserves credit for helping to transform righteous indignation into concerted political action. But we all know that our work is not finished. Like the rest of the feminist movement (and despite misperceptions of the extent of our resources), NOW's reach always exceeds our grasp. There are never enough hours in the day, monies in the till, staff in the Action Center, or activists in the field. But we at NOW believe that, working together, women have the strength and determination to change the balance of power in state legislatures, Congress, and even the White House. In this season of discontent, it will be women who can transform the national rage and demoralization into hope. We have been building toward this moment for 20 years.

FEDERAL CHILD SUPPORT BILLS

The following bills were submitted in the 103rd Congress:

House of Representatives
HR 915: "Child Support Economic Security Act," to improve collection of child support. Sponsor: Shroeder (2/16/93)
HR 1600: "Interstate Child Support Enforcement Act." Sponsor: Roukema (4/1/93)

Senate
S 434: "Child Support Tax Equity Act," to amend the Internal Revenue Code to permit a "bad debt" deduction for unpaid child support and require that the non-payer include the amount of these non-payments as income. Sponsor: Numerous (5/24/93)
S 689: To improve interstate enforcement of child support and parentage orders.Sponsors: Bradley, Feinstein, Glenn, Mitchell, Reid, Robb (4/1/93)

Source: Fairshare: The Matrimonial Law Monthly

CHILD CARE AND EDUCATION—RESOURCES

Child Care Action Campaign
330 Seventh Avenue, 17th Floor
New York, NY 10001
(212) 239-0138
Conducts and publishes research, serves as information clearinghouse.

Children's Defense Fund
25 E Street, N.W.
Washington, DC 20001
(800) 233-1200
Lobbies public officials to pass legislation ensuring children's rights; assists community activists.

The National Association of Child Advocates
1625 K Street, N.W., Suite 510
Washington, DC 20006
(202) 828-6950
Information exchange center for child advocacy groups; provides technical assistance in organizational development.

National Coalition to End Racism in America's Child Care System
22075 Koths
Taylor, MI 48180
(313) 295-0257
Educates and advocates for permanant homes for children.

Parent Action
2 N. Charles Street, Suite 960
Baltimore, MD 21201
(410) 727-3687
Lobbying group, formed by T. Berry Brazelton, to improve child care and parenting benefits.

CHILD ABUSE PREVENTION—RESOURCES

Organizations

American Humane Association, Children's Division
63 Inverness Drive East
Englewood, CO 80112
(303) 792-9900
Advocates for national standards, improved child welfare policies, and legislation.

Childhelp USA
6463 Independence Avenue
Woodland Hills, CA 91367
(818) 347-7280
Runs the National Campaign for the Prevention of Child Abuse and Neglect.

National Committee for Prevention of Child Abuse
P.O. Box 2866
Chicago, IL 60690
(312) 663-3520

VOICES in Action (Victims of Incest Can Emerge Survivors)
P.O. Box 148309
Chicago, IL 60614
(312) 327-1500

Hotlines

Childhelp USA/IOF Foresters National Child Abuse Hotline
(800) 422-4453

If the unpaid labor of women in the household were given economic value it would add an estimated one-third ($4 trillion) to the world's economic product, reported World Priorities in 1985.

Supreme Court Justice Ruth Bader Ginsburg founded the ACLU Women's Rights Project, and was involved in virtually all major gender cases that reached the Supreme Court in the 1970s.

Father Flanagan's Boys Home (Boys Town)
(800) 448-3000

National Directory of Hotlines and Crisis Intervention Centers
Covenant House Nineline
346 W. 17th Street
New York, NY 10011
(212) 727-4025

BREAST CANCER AND EXPOSURE TO PESTICIDES

The pesticide DDT may be one of the factors behind rising breast cancer rates. Women who had increased levels of DDE (a breakdown product of DDT) in their blood faced up to four times the risk of breast cancer, the study found. DDT was banned in the U.S. in 1972, but residue persists in the environment and moves up through the food chain to accumulate in milk and meat. Residues of DDT can be stored in the body's fatty tissues for decades.

Source: Journal of the National Cancer Institute (April 1993)

ENVIRONMENTAL ACTIVISM—RESOURCES

Mothers & Others for a Livable Planet
40 W. 20th Street
New York, NY 10011
(212) 727-4474
Publishes information concerning environmental issues.

Northwest Coalition for Alternatives to Pesticides
P.O. Box 1393
Eugene, OR 97440
(503) 344-5044
Provides information, policy development, assistance, and referrals.

Women's Environment and Development Organization
845 Third Avenue, 15th Floor
New York, NY 10022
(212) 759-7982
Coalition of grassroots environmental and health groups focusing on eliminating environmental hazards.

PESTICIDES—RECOMMENDED READING

"Children and Pesticides" (Eugene, Ore.: Northwest Coalition for Alternatives to Pesticides, 1990).

For Our Kids' Sake: How to Protect Your Child Against Pesticides in Food (New York: Mothers & Others for a Livable Planet, 1989).

"Guide to the Freedom of Information Act" (Eugene, Ore.: Northwest Coalition for Alternatives to Pesticides, 1990).

Pesticide Alert: A Guide to Pesticides in Fruits and Vegetables, Lawrie Mott and Karen Snyder (San Francisco: Sierra Club Books, 1987).

The Way We Grow: Good-Sense Solutions for Protecting Our Families from Pesticides in Food, Anne Witte Garland (New York: Berkley Publishing Group, 1993).

ADVOCATES FOR THE RIGHTS OF OLDER WOMEN

Gray Panthers
1424 16th Street, N.W., Suite 602
Washington, DC 20036
(202) 387-3111
Intergenerational activist group fighting agism, sexism, and homophobia.

National Council of Senior Citizens
1331 F Street, N.W.
Washington, DC 20004
(202) 347-8800
Coalition of seniors' clubs advocating increased Social Security benefits, better nutrition, and community employment projects, among other issues.

The Older Women's League (OWL)
730 Eleventh Street, N.W., Suite 300
Washington, DC 20001
(202) 783-6686
Multi-chapter group promoting a national agenda including universal health care, adequate Social Security benefits, and increased housing opportunities.

Women's Initiative
American Association of Retired Persons
601 E Street, N.W.
Washington, DC 20049
(202) 434-2400
Promotes a legislative agenda addressing the needs of older women.

OLDER WOMEN—RECOMMENDED READING

Building Public//Private Coalitions for Older Women's Employment: An OWL Handbook (Washington, D.C.: Older Women's League, 1987).

Employment Discrimination Against Older Women: A Handbook on Litigating Age and Sex Discrimination Cases (Washington, D.C.: Older Women's League, 1990).

Making Ends Meet: Midlife and Older Women's Search for Economic Self-Sufficiency Through Job Training and Employment (Washington, D.C.: Older Women's League, 1992).

Older Women as Caregivers: Responsive Community Programs Directory (Washington, D.C.: National Council of Negro Women, 1993).

The first independent radical women's newsletter, "Voice of the Women's Liberation Movement," was published in 1968. By 1971, there were over 100 such journals and newsletters.

APPENDICES

APPENDICES
APPENDICES
APPENDICES
APPENDICES
APPENDICES
APPENDICES
APPENDICES
APPENDICES
APPENDICES
APPENDICES
APPENDICES
APPENDICES
APPENDICES
APPENDICES
APPENDICES
APPENDICES
APPENDICES

SELECTED JUDICIAL AND LEGISLATIVE DECISIONS 1970–1994

1965

Griswold v. *Connecticut*—The U.S. Supreme Court struck down state laws prohibiting the use of contraceptives by married couples.

1970

Seidenberg v. *McSorley's Olde Ale House*—Sex discrimination in a public restaurant had no foundation in reason and violated the equal protection clause of the 14th Amendment, the Supreme Court ruled.

Congress initiated the first federal family planning program, Title X of the Public Health Services Act.

1971

Phillips v. *Martin Marietta*—The Supreme Court ruled that employers cannot refuse to hire women solely because they have small children unless fathers of small children are also denied employment.

Reed v. *Reed*—Unanimous Supreme Court decision that an Idaho law giving arbitrary preference to men as executors of estates could not be allowed to "stand in the face of the 14th Amendment" and was unconstitutional. This was the first time the court invoked the 14th Amendment to overturn a distinction based on sex. Ruth Bader Ginsburg argued the case.

1972

Eisenstadt v. *Baird*—By a vote of 6–1, the Supreme Court invalidated a Massachusetts law prohibiting the distribution of contraceptives to unmarried people, holding that the constitutional right to privacy extends to the reproductive decisions of both married and unmarried people.

Congress passed the Equal Employment Opportunity Act. This law empowered the Equal Employment Opportunity Commission to take legal actions in the federal courts to enforce Title VII of the Civil Rights Act of 1964.

The Equal Pay Act of 1963 was extended to cover executive, administrative, and professional personnel.

1973

Roe v. *Wade*—By a vote of 7–2, the Supreme Court invalidated a Texas law prohibiting abortions not necessary to save the woman's life. The Court held that the fundamental right to privacy extends to a woman's decision whether or not to have an abortion and that any other governmental interference with that right is subject to judicial scrutiny. The Court did, however, recognize two compelling state interests sufficient to justify restrictions on a woman's right to choose: states may regulate the abortion procedure after the first trimester of pregnancy in ways necessary to promote women's health; and after the point of fetal viability—approximately 24 to 28 weeks—a state may, to protect the potential life of the fetus, prohibit abortions not necessary to preserve the woman's life or health.

Doe v. *Bolton*—In a 7–2 vote, announced the same day as *Roe* v. *Wade*, the Court invalidated provisions of a Georgia law that required that any abortion be performed in a hospital; that a woman secure the approval of three physicians and a hospital committee before obtaining an abortion; and that a woman seeking to obtain an abortion be a resident of the state. The thrust of this ruling is to require that states not prohibit or substantially limit access to abortion.

Frontiero v. *Richardson*—The Supreme Court declared unconstitutional the government's practice of granting benefits to all married men serving in the armed forces, but not to servicewomen unless they could prove that they provided three-fourths of the family's support. Ruth Bader Ginsburg argued the case.

1974

Geduldig v. *Aiello*—The Supreme Court ruled that excluding pregnancy coverage from the list of compensable disabilities under the California Disability Plan did not constitute sex discrimination.

The Fair Housing Act of 1968 was extended by Congress to prohibit discrimination based on sex, in addition to the previously prohibited grounds of race, color, religion, and national origin.

The Educational Equity Act passed Congress. This authorized the secretary of Health, Education and Welfare to develop non-sexist curricula and non-discriminatory vocational and career counseling, sports education, and other programs designed to achieve equity for all students regardless of sex.

The Equal Credit Opportunity Act passed Congress. The act covered all agencies that regularly extend credit to individuals, banks, finance companies, department stores, credit card users, and government agencies. A woman's income or savings had to be counted as equal to a man's in determining eligibility for credit. Credit history of "family accounts" had to be extended to women as well as men. No one could be refused credit on account of sex or marital status.

1975

Taylor v. *Louisiana*—The Supreme Court declared it unconstitutional to deny women equal opportunity for jury service, thus striking down by an 8–1 vote the Louisiana statute that automatically excluded any woman from jury service unless she applied for it in writing.

Wimberly v. *Labor & Industrial Relations Commission of Missouri*—The Supreme Court ruled unconstitutional a state regulation denying pregnant women unemployment compensation.

Bigelow v. *Virginia*—By a vote of 7–2, the Supreme Court invalidated the application of a Virginia statute that prohibited the advertisement of abortion services.

Weinberger v. *Wiesenfeld*—The Supreme Court held unconstitutional a Social Security provision that gave widows with minor children monthly benefits based on their deceased husbands' contributions but denied similar benefits to widowers with minor children. Ruth Bader Ginsburg argued the case.

Stanton v. *Stanton*—By a vote of 8–1, the Supreme Court found unconstitutional a Utah law requiring divorced fathers to support sons until age 21 but daughters until only 18. Justice Harry Blackmun wrote, "No longer is the female destined solely for the home and the rearing of the family and only the male for the marketplace and the world of ideas. Women's activities are increasing and expanding."

Congress passed legislation opening U.S. military academies to women.

1976

Planned Parenthood of Central Missouri v. Danforth—By a vote of 6–3, the Supreme Court ruled that states cannot require a woman seeking an abortion to get consent from her husband. And it ruled 5–4 that states cannot force a single minor desiring an abortion to get permission from a parent. The decision struck down a Missouri law but upheld a provision requiring minors to get written consent from a judge before the operation can be performed.

Frank v. *Bowman Transportation Co.*—In a 5–3 decision, the Supreme Court ruled that workers who could prove they were denied jobs because of illegal discrimination were entitled to retroactive seniority and related benefits.

GE v. *Gilbert*—The Supreme Court ruled that employers could exclude pregnancy from sickness and accident disability insurance plans without violating federal prohibitions against sex discrimination.

1977

Maher v. *Roe, Beal* v. *Doe, Poelker* v. *Doe*—The Supreme Court ruled that neither the Constitution nor federal Medicaid law required states to pay for abortions that are not medically necessary.

Vorcheimer v. *Philadelphia*—Equally divided, the Supreme Court upheld a decision approving single-sex public high schools for academically superior boys and girls.

Carey v. *Population Services*—By a vote of 7–2, the Supreme Court invalidated a New York law prohibiting the sale or distribution of contraceptives to minors.

Satty v. *Nashville Gas Company*—The Supreme Court ruled that pregnant employees could be denied sick pay, although it also ruled that seniority rights could not be taken away from women who were on leave to give birth.

After 34 years of seeking veterans' status, World War II women pilots were granted veterans' benefits by an act of Congress.

1978

Los Angeles v. *Manhart*—The Supreme Court declared illegal an entrenched practice of American insurance companies, which used sex as a factor to determine premium rates for a wide range of insurance benefits.

Congress passed the Pregnancy Discrimination Act, which overturned the Supreme Court decision in *Satty* v. *Nashville Gas Company*. Employers could no longer discriminate against women on the basis of pregnancy.

1979

Colautti v. *Franklin*—The Supreme Court declared unconstitutional a Pennsylvania law that required a doctor performing an abortion to choose the abortion method most likely to save the life of a fetus that might be old enough to survive outside the womb.

Cannon v. *University of Chicago*—The Supreme Court ruled that an individual has the right to bring a private suit to uphold the anti-discrimination provisions of Title IX.

US Steelworkers of America and Kaiser Aluminum v. *Weber*—The Supreme Court upheld private voluntary affirmative action, which promotes the hiring and advancement of women and minorities in traditionally segregated job categories.

Bellitti v. *Baird*—By a vote of 8–1, the Supreme Court overturned a Massachusetts law that required parental consent or judicial approval for a minor to obtain an abortion.

1980

Harris v. *McRae, Williams v. Zbaraz*—The Supreme Court upheld the Hyde Amendment (originally passed in 1976), which prohibited the use of federal funds for abortions not necessary to preserve the woman's life. It also held that states participating in the Medicaid program are not required by Title X to fund medically necessary abortions for which federal funds are unavailable under the Hyde Amendment.

Trammel v. *U.S.*—The Supreme Court ruled unanimously that husbands or wives can, if they choose, testify against their spouse in a federal criminal trial.

1982

North Haven Board of Education v. *Bell*—By a vote of 6-3, the Supreme Court ruled that the law barring sex discrimination by schools and colleges receiving federal funding covered not only the students but the employees of those institutions.

1983

City of Akron v. *Akron Center for Reproductive Health*—By a vote of 6–3, the Supreme Court invalidated those provisions of a city ordinance that required physicians to give their patients anti-abortion information, including telling them that "the unborn child is a human life from the moment of conception"; required a 24-hour waiting period following these lectures; mandated that all abortions performed after the first trimester be performed in a hospital; required parental consent for a minor to obtain an abortion, without providing a procedure for waiver of the consent requirement; and required physicians to dispose of fetal remains in an unspecified "humane and sanitary manner."

Planned Parenthood Association of Kansas City, Mo. v. *Ashcroft*—The Supreme Court invalidated a provision of a Missouri statute, by a vote of 6–3, that required all second-trimester abortions to be performed in a hospital. By a vote of 5–4, the Court upheld requirements that a second physician be present during a post-viability abortion; that a minor woman obtain either parental consent or a judicial waiver; and that a pathology report be made for each abortion.

Simopoulos v. *Virginia*—By a vote of 8–1, the Supreme Court affirmed the criminal conviction of a physician for performing a second-trimester abortion outside a licensed hospital. Thus, the Court held that the Virginia restriction on abortions after the first trimester was necessary to promote the health of women obtaining abortions.

Christman v. *American Cyanamid*—American Cyanamid settled, before trial, a 1979 suit brought against its policy of excluding all fertile women from certain positions that exposed them to toxic substances, unless they provided proof of sterilization; the policy also involved demoting or transferring women who refused to be sterilized.

EQUAL RIGHTS AMENDMENT

The Equal Rights Amendment was written in 1921 by suffragist Alice Paul. Introduced in Congress every session since 1923, it passed Congress in 1972 but failed by three states to be ratified by the necessary 38 states by the July 1982 deadline. The text of the proposed amendment:

Section 1. Equality of rights under the law shall not be denied or abridged by the United States or any state on account of sex.

Section 2. The Congress shall have the power to enforce, by appropriate legislation, the provisions of this article.

Section 3. This amendment shall take effect two years after the date of ratification.

1984

Grove City v. *College Bell*—By a vote of 6–3, the Supreme Court accepted the Reagan Administration position that Title IX banned sex discrimination only in specific programs within an educational institution that directly received federal funding.

1985

National Gay Task Force v. *Oklahoma Board of Education*—The Supreme Court let stand a lower court decision striking down an Oklahoma law that permitted the firing of teachers for speaking in favor of lesbian and gay rights.

1986

Bowers v. *Hardwick*—By a vote of 6–3 the Supreme Court ruled that states could impose criminal penalties for a homosexual act—even though it was between consenting adults, in private.

Thornburgh v. *American College of Obstetricians and Gynecologists*—By a vote of 5–4, the Supreme Court invalidated provisions of a Pennsylvania statute requiring that physicians give their patients anti-abortion information; that detailed reports be filed about the woman obtaining an abortion; that physicians performing post-viability abortions use the "degree of care" required to preserve the life and health of any unborn child; and that a second physician be present at post-viability abortions without providing an exception for a medical emergency. This decision marked the first time that the court explicitly stated, "A woman's right to make that choice freely is fundamental."

Meritor Savings Bank v. *Vinson*—The Supreme Court affirmed in this case that sexual harassment on the job is sexual discrimination and a violation of Title VII of the Civil Rights Act of 1964.

Bazemore et al. v. *Friday et al.*—The Supreme Court affirmed two essential pay equity concepts: that past practices of discrimination can be used to analyze current systems of pay, and that statistical evidence is permissible.

The Supreme Court ruled unconstitutional an Indianapolis ordinance, authored by Catherine MacKinnon and Andrea Dworkin, that defined pornography in part as discrimination against women.

Congress enacted into law six of the 22 provisions of the Economic Equity Act, including pension rights for military spouses; private pension reforms; continued health insurance coverage for widows, divorced spouses, and their children; an increase in the deduction for single heads of households; and an increased tax credit for low-income families.

1987

Rotary International v. *Rotary Club of Durante*—The Supreme Court by a vote of 7–0 held that a California law against discrimination in public accommodation applied to Rotary Clubs. Rotary, Lion, and Kiwanis Clubs all decided to admit women.

California Federal Savings and Loan v. *Guerra*—The Supreme Court upheld a California law requiring employers to grant a new mother up to four months unpaid disability leave as well as job security. In another ruling, the Court upheld a Missouri law that disallowed pregnancy as a reason to award unemployment compensation and said that the law did not violate Federal Unemployment Compensation, which forbids discrimination on the basis of pregnancy.

Johnson v. *Transportation Agency, Santa Clara County*—The Supreme Court upheld in a 6–3 decision a voluntary affirmative action plan that permitted an employer to take into consideration the sex of a qualified applicant as one factor in making promotions.

New York State Club Association, Inc. v. *The City of New York*—The Supreme Court upheld as constitutional a New York City ordinance placing sharp limits on male-only clubs. The ordinance provided that private clubs with more than 400 members that regularly serve meals and regularly receive payment from or on behalf of non-members in furtherance of trade or business could not discriminate on the basis of race, sex, or other grounds in regard to membership.

The Hyde Amendment's prohibition on the use of Medicaid funds and other federal health program funds for abortion services is made permanent by Congress; the amendment also prohibited awarding Title X funds to organizations such as Planned Parenthood that provide abortion services, counseling, and referrals for abortion, or to advocates for abortion rights.

1988

Congress passed the Civil Rights Restoration Act, reversing the Supreme Court's 1984 Grove City decision and restoring full coverage of Title IX provisions prohibiting sex discrimination in education by recipients of federal funds. The act also restored full coverage of statutes prohibiting discrimination based on minority status, disability, or age.

Forrester v. *White*—In a unanimous decision, the Supreme Court ruled that although state judges were immune from lawsuits concerning their judicial rulings and acts, they could be sued for alleged discrimination in their administrative and employment decisions.

Congress passed the Women's Business Ownership Act, extending protection of the Federal Equal Credit Opportunity Act to applications by women for commercial credit. The act also created a National Women's Business Council to serve as an advocate for women who deal with government agencies.

1989

Webster v. *Reproductive Health Services*—The Supreme Court in a 5–4 decision upheld a Missouri statute that said that life begins at conception. The statute prohibited the use of public facilities or public personnel to perform abortions and required a physician to make determinations and perform tests concerning gestational age, weight, and lung maturity when he or she has reason to believe a woman to be 20 weeks or more pregnant.

Wards Cove Packing Co. v. Atonio, Patterson v. *McClean Credit Union*—The Supreme Court reinterpreted Title VII and Section 1981 of the Civil Rights Act of 1866 to place a heavier burden of proof on plaintiffs in suites that challenge sex and race discrimination in the workplace.

Price Waterhouse v. *Hopkins*—The Supreme Court ruled that once a plaintiff in a discrimination case demonstrates that the employer was motivated in part, in a particular action, by unlawful considerations, the burden of proof shifts to the employer to show that the same discisions would have been reached without the discriminatory motive.

Mansell v. *Mansell*—The Supreme Court held that military personnel could deny their ex-spouses a share of veterans' retirement pay by converting a portion of their pensions (divisible marital property) into non-divisible disability payments.

President George Bush vetoed a bill approved by Congress that would permit the use of Medicaid funds to pay for abortions for women who were victims of "promptly reported" rape or incest.

1990
President Bush signed legislation requiring the federal government to collect hate crime statistics based on race, ethnic background, religion, and sexual orientation. Excluded from this bill were crimes motivated by gender.

Hodgson v. *Minnesota*—The Supreme Court in a 5–4 decision invalidated as having no rational basis a Minnesota law requiring notification of both parents, without a procedure for judicial waiver, by minors seeking abortions. It also upheld a provision that required two-parent notification for minors but included a procedure for a judicial waiver, as well as a 48-hour waiting period.

Ohio v. *Akron Center for Reproductive Health*—The Court upheld an Ohio statute that required a minor woman seeking an abortion to notify one parent or obtain a judicial waiver.

1991
United Automobile Workers v. *Johnson Controls*—The Supreme Court declared that employers could not exclude women from jobs in which exposure to toxic substances could harm a developing fetus. All nine justices agreed that the policy violated the Civil Rights Act of 1964.

Rust v. *Sullivan*—The Supreme Court ruled that it was constitutional for the government to restrict Title X-funded clinics from counseling women on abortion, upholding a "gag rule" even if the continued pregnancy threatened a woman's life or health.

Planned Parenthood Federation v. *Agency for International Development*—The Supreme Court affirmed the federal government's right to deny foreign aid to overseas health-care organizations that promote abortion as a means of family planning.

Planned Parenthood of Southeastern Pennsylvania v. *Casey*—The Supreme Court upheld 7–2 the right of states to impose restrictions on abortions as long as those constraints do not impose an undue burden on women. Undue burden is defined as "a substantial obstacle in the path of a woman seeking an abortion." Some of the provisions of the Pennsylvania statute in question require: that physicians provide patients with anti-abortion information to discourage them from obtaining abortions; that a mandatory 24-hour delay follow these lectures; and that minors receive consent from at least one parent, with a judicial bypass.

Benten et al. v. *Kessler et al.*—By a 7–2 vote, the Supreme Court refused to order the return of abortifacient RU 486 pills to a pregnant American woman from whom they had been seized by U.S. Customs.

1993
St. Mary's Honor Center v. *Hicks*—In a 5–4 descision, the Supreme Court increased a worker's burden to prove employment discrimination. Previously it was sufficient for employees to show that their employers' asserted reasons for a decision were a pretext for a discriminatory motive. In this decision, the employee could now be required to present direct evidence of a discriminatory motive.

Bray v. *Alexandria Women's Health Clinic*—By a vote of 5–4, the Supreme Court held that blockades that obstruct access to reproductive health clinics do not constitute sex-based discrimination for the purpose of a federal civil rights law known as the Ku Klux Klan Act.

Wisconsin v. *Mitchell*—In a unanimous decision, the Court ruled that people who commit "hate crimes" motivated by bigotry may be given extra punishment. The court ruled that such punishment does not violate free-speech rights. Such crimes are "thought to inflict greater individual and societal harm" than crimes not motivated by bigotry.

Alexander v. *U.S.*—The Supreme Court decided, 5–4, that free speech rights are not violated when a federal anti-racketeering law (RICO) is used to confiscate all assets and inventory of pornographers convicted of selling some obscene materials.

President Bill Clinton reversed a U.S. policy that had denied foreign aid to countries providing abortion funding to women. He also rescinded the "gag rule" promulgated under President Reagan, which prohibited doctors in federally funded clinics from providing abortion counseling; lifted the ban on fetal tissue research; and encouraged research on RU 486 for eventual release in this country.

The Family and Medical Leave Act was passed by Congress. This provides workers in businesses with more than 50 employees up to 12 weeks of unpaid leave each year to care for a newborn, a newly adopted child, or a seriously ill family member, or in case of the worker's own illness.

1994

Harris v. *Forklift Systems, Inc.*—In a reaffirmation of its 1986 ruling in Meritor Savings Bank v. Vinson, the Supreme Court unanimously ruled that sexual harassment is a violation of a federal law barring employment discrimination. The new decision also clarified the 1986 ruling's ban on a "hostile" and "abusive" workplace by declaring that those conditions do not have to result in severe, or any, psychological harm.

Florence County School District Four v. *Carter*—The Supreme Court decided unanimously that a lower court may order reimbursement for parents who unilaterally withdraw their child from a public school that provides an inappropriate education under the Americans With Disabilities Act, even if the child is placed in a private school that doesn't meet all the ADA requirements.

National Organization for Women v. *Scheidler*—The Supreme Court unanimously ruled that the federal anti-racketeering law (RICO) may be invoked to sue protesters who block access to abortion clinics or in other ways conspire to stop women from having abortions. The ruling reinstates a lawsuit in which abortion rights advocates seek to prove that a coalition of anti-abortion groups and their leaders conspired to put abortion clinics out of business through arson and other crimes.

The Omnibus Budget Reconciliation Act was passed by Congress. A number of provisions of this act are significant for women, among them: state Medicaid programs are allowed to provide free vaccinations to children in need; states are required to increase child-support collection rates; the earned income tax credit is increased with the goal of helping to lift working poor families out of poverty; and funds are provided for state programs aimed at returning children to their families or keeping them out of foster care.

The following provisions from the Women's Health Equity Act of 1991 were passed by Congress as part of the 1993 National Institutes of Health (NIH) Revitalization Act: authority is given to the NIH Office of Research on Women's Health to monitor the inclusion of women and minorities in clinical studies sponsored by the NIH; research is expanded on reproductive tract cancers, contraceptives, fertility, osteoporosis, and the aging process in women, particularly menopause; and a loan repayment program is established to encourage health professionals to enter the field of contraceptive and fertility research.

A portion of the Department of Defense Authorization Act removed remaining limitations on women serving in the military, including the ban on women serving on combat ships. The act also authorized primary and preventive health-care services targeted at women to be provided at military hospitals and health clinics operated by the military, and created a Defense Women's Health Research Center to research and develop treatments related to women's health.

J.E.B. v. *Alabama*—By a 6–3 vote, the Supreme Court ruled that the Constitution's equal-protection clause forbids the use of peremptory challenges to exclude jurors on the basis of their sex.

FEDERAL GOVERNMENT AGENGIES OF INTEREST TO WOMEN

ADMINISTRATION FOR CHILDREN AND FAMILIES
Office of Child Support Enforcement
378 L'Enfant Promenade, S.W., 4th Floor
Washington, DC 20047
(202) 401-9373

CENTERS FOR DISEASE CONTROL
National Center for Chronic Disease Prevention and Health Promotion
Reproductive Health Division
Rhodes Building, Koger Center
4770 Buford Highway, N.E., m/s K20
Atlanta, GA 30341
(404) 488-5191

COMMISSION ON CIVIL RIGHTS
1121 Vermont Avenue, N.W.
Washington, DC 20425
(202) 523-5571

Regional Offices:

Central Region—Alabama, Arkansas, Iowa, Kansas, Louisiana, Mississippi, Missouri, and Nebraska
Old Federal Office Building
911 Walnut Street
Kansas City, MO 64106
(816) 426-5253

Eastern Region—Connecticut, Delaware, District of Columbia, Maine, Maryland, Massachusetts, New Hampshire, New Jersey, New York, Pennsylvania, Rhode Island, Vermont, Virginia, and West Virginia
624 9th Street, N.W.
Washington, DC 20425
(202) 376-7533

Midwestern Region—Illinois, Indiana, Michigan, Minnesota, Ohio, and Wisconsin
Xerox Center, Suite #410
55 W. Monroe Street
Chicago, IL 60603
(312) 353-8311

Rocky Mountain Region—Colorado, Montana, North Dakota, South Dakota, Utah, and Wyoming
1900 Broadway, Suite 701
Denver, CO 80290
(303) 844-6716

Southern Region—Florida, Georgia, Kentucky, North Carolina, South Carolina, and Tennessee
101 Marietta Street, Suite 2821
Atlanta, GA 30303
(404) 730-2476

Western Region—Alaska, Arizona, California, Hawaii, Idaho, Nevada, New Mexico, Oklahoma, Oregon, Texas, and Washington
3660 Wilshire Boulevard
Los Angeles, CA 90010
(213) 894-3437

COMMITTEE FOR THE UNITED NATIONS FUND FOR WOMEN (UNIFEM)
252 N. Washington Street
Falls Church, VA
(703) 241-8405

COMMODITY FUTURES TRADING COMMISSION
Office of Personnel
Federal Women's Program
2033 K Street, N.W.
Washington, DC 20581
(202) 254-9531

CONGRESSIONAL CAUCUS FOR WOMEN'S ISSUES
2471 Rayburn House Office Building
Washington, DC 20515
(202) 225-6740

CONSUMER PRODUCT SAFETY COMMISSION
Office of Equal Opportunity and Minority Enterprise
4330 EW Highway
Bethesda, MD 20814
(301) 504-0570

DEPARTMENT OF AGRICULTURE
Agriculture Research Service
Equal Employment Opportunity Office
Federal Women's Program
Administration Building
14th Street and Independence Avenue,S.W., Room 337
Washington, DC 20250
(202) 720-6161

Animal and Plant Health Inspection Service
Equal Opportunity and Civil Rights
South Agriculture Building
14th Street and Independence Avenue, S.W.,
Washington, DC 20250
(202) 720-6312

Cooperative State Research Service
Federal Women's Program
Aerospace Building
901 D Street, S.W.
Washington, DC 20024
(202) 401-6845

Extension Service
Federal Women's Program
South Agriculture Building
14th Street and Independence Avenue,S.W.,
Room 3913
Washington, DC 20250
(202) 720-8070

Food and Nutrition Service
Civil Rights Division
Federal Women's Program
Park Office Center
3101 Park Center Drive
Alexandria, VA 22302
(703) 305-2195

Supplemental Food Programs Division
National Advisory Council on Maternal, Infant and Fetal Nutrition
3101 Park Center Drive
Alexandria, VA 22301
(703) 756-3746

Supplemental Food Programs Division
Special Supplemental Food Program for Women, Infants, and Children
Park Office Center
3101 Park Center Drive
Alexandria, VA 22302
(703) 756-2746

Food Safety and Inspection Service
Federal Women's Program
Annex Building
300 12th Street, S.W.
Washington, DC 20250
(202) 205-0285

Foreign Agriculture Service
Federal Women's Program
South Agriculture Building
Washington, DC 20250
(202) 720-9335

Soil Conservation Service
Equal Opportunity Branch
Federal Women's Program
South Agriculture Building
14th Street and Independence Avenue, S.W.,
Washington, DC 20250
(202) 720-1710

DEPARTMENT OF THE AIR FORCE
Manpower, Reserve Affairs, Installations and Environment
Equal Opportunity Agency
SAF/MI
1660 Air Force Pentagon
Washington, DC 20330
(703) 607-3167

DEPARTMENT OF THE ARMY
Manpower and Reserve Affairs
Equal Employment Opportunity Agency

Federal Women's Program
Crystal Mall Building 4
1941 Jefferson Davis Highway
Arlington, VA 22202
(703) 607-1976

DEPARTMENT OF COMMERCE
Office of Small and Disadvantaged Business Utilization
Agency for International Development
Washington, DC 20523
(703) 875-1551

DEPARTMENT OF DEFENSE
Administration and Management Washington Headquarters Services
Federal Women's Program
400 Army Navy Drive
Arlington, VA 22202
(703) 693-1096

Defense Advisory Committee on Women in the Services and Military Women Matters
The Pentagon
Washington, DC 20301
(703) 697-2122

Defense Information Systems Agency
Federal Women's Program
701 Courthouse Road
Arlington, VA 22204
(703) 692-0042

Defense Investigative Service
Federal Women's Program
1340 Braddock Place
Alexandria, VA 22314
(703) 325-5344

DEPARTMENT OF EDUCATION
Office of the General Counsel
Educational Equity Division
400 Maryland Avenue, S.W.
Washington, DC 20202
(202) 401-2666

Women's Educational Equity Act Program
400 Maryland Avenue, S.W., Room 2049
Washington, DC 20202
(202) 260-2755

DEPARTMENT OF HEALTH AND HUMAN SERVICES
Substance Abuse and Mental Health Services Administration
Federal Women's Program EEO
Parklawn Building
5600 Fishers Lane
Rockville, MD 20857
(301) 443-4447

Alcohol, Drug Abuse, and Mental Health Administration
National Institute on Drug Abuse
Women and Drugs Section
5600 Fishers Lane
Rockville, MD 20857
(301) 443-6720

National Institute of Mental Health
Violence and Traumatic Stress Research Office
5600 Fishers Lane, Room 10-C-24
Rockville, MD 20857
(301) 443-3728

Office of the Administrator, Women's Council
Parklawn Building
5600 Fishers Lane
Rockville, MD 20857
(301) 443-4447

Office for Substance Abuse Prevention
Pregnant and Postpartum Women and Infants Review Committee
Rockwall 2 Building, 6th Floor
5600 Fishers Lane
Rockville, MD 20857
(301) 443-8923

Food and Drug Administration
Center for Devices and Radiological Health
Obstetrics-Gynecology Devices Panel
1390 Piccard Drive
Rockville, MD 20850
(301) 427-1186

Center for Drug Evaluation and Research
Fertility and Maternal Health Drugs Advisory Committee
5600 Fishers Lane HFD-510, Room 14B04
Rockville, MD 20857
(301) 443-3511

Federal Women's Program
Parklawn Building, Room 872 HF-16
5600 Fishers Lane
Rockville, MD 20857
(301) 443-3310

Office of Consumer Affairs
Advisory Group on Women's Health Issues
Parklawn Building
5600 Fishers Lane
Rockville, MD 20857

Health Resources and Services Administration
Maternal and Child Health Bureau
Parklawn Building
5600 Fishers Lane
Rockville, MD 20857
(301) 443-2170

Maternal and Child Health Bureau
Maternal and Child Health Research Grants Review Committee
Parklawn Building
5600 Fishers Lane
Rockville, MD 20857
(301) 443-2190

Maternal and Child Health Bureau
National Center for Education in Maternal and Child Health
2000 15th Street N., Suite 701
Arlington, VA 22201
(703) 524-7802

Maternal and Child Health Bureau
National Maternal and Child Health Clearinghouse
8201 Greensboro Drive, Suite 600
McLean, VA 22102
(703) 821-8955, x 254, 255

Office of Equal Opportunity and Civil Rights
Federal Women's Program
Parklawn Building
5600 Fishers Lane
Rockville, MD 20857
(301) 443-6824

Indian Health Service
Federal Women's Program
Parklawn Building
5600 Fishers Lane
Rockville, MD 20857
(301) 443-2700

National Institutes of Health
National Institute of Child Health and Human Development
Center for Research for Mothers and Children
Building 6100, Rm 4B05
Bethesda, MD 10892
(301) 496-5097

National Institute of Child Health and Human Development
Maternal and Child Health Research Committee
Scientific Review Program
Bethesda, MD 20892
(301) 496-1696

National Institute of Child Health and Human Development
Office of Research Reporting
Building 31, Room 2A-32
9000 Rockville Pike
Bethesda, MD 20892
(301) 496-5133

National Institute of General Medical Sciences
Coordinating Committee on Women's Health Issues
9000 Rockville Pike
Bethesda, MD 20892

Office of Disease Prevention
Scientific and Technical Committee on Women's Health Initiatives
9000 Rockville Pike
Bethesda, MD 20892
(301) 496-1058

Office of Equal Opportunity
Federal Women's Program
Building 31, Room 2B4C
9000 Rockville Pike
Bethesda, MD
(301) 402-3663

Office of Research on Women's Health
Building 1, Room 201
9000 Rockville Pike
Bethesda, MD 20892
(301) 402-1770

Task Force on Opportunities for Research on Women's Health
9000 Rockville Pike
Bethesda, MD 20892

Office of the Assistant Secretary for Health
Office on Women's Health
200 Independence Avenue, S.W.
Washington, DC 20201
(202) 690-7650

Office of Family Planning
Family Life Information Exchange
P.O. Box 37299
Washington, DC 20013
(301) 585-6636

Office of the Surgeon General
Panel on Women, Adolescents and Children with HIV Infection and AIDS
Working Group on Pediatric AIDS
Room 736E
200 Independence Avenue, S.W.
Washington, DC 20201
(202) 690-6467

Public Health Service
Agency for Health Care Policy and Research
Cesarean Section Patient Outcome Research Advisory Committee
Executive Office Center, Suite 601
2101 E. Jefferson Street
Rockville, MD 20852
(301) 594-1364 x175

Agency for Health Care Policy and Research
Panel on Development of Guidelines on Quality Determinants of Mammography
Office of Forum for Quality and Effectiveness in Health Care
600 Executive Boulevard,
Willco Building
Rockville, MD 20852
(301) 594-4015

Task Force on Women, Children, and AIDS
370 L'Enfant Promenade, S.W.
Washington, DC 20447
(202) 619-0257

Department of Justice

Special Counsel for Sex Discrimination Litigation
10th and Pennsylvania Avenue,
Room 574
Washington, DC 20530
(202) 633-4701

Department of Labor

Glass Ceiling Commission
Office of the Secretary
200 Constitution Avenue, N.W.
Washington, DC 20210
(202) 219-7368

Women's Bureau
Frances Perkins Building
200 Constitution Avenue, N.W.
Washington, DC 20210
(202) 219-6593

Network on Female Offenders
3535 Market Street
Philadelphia, PA 19104
(215) 596-1183

For regional offices of the Women's Bureau, see the Work chapter, p.57–8

Task Force on Women in Apprenticeships
200 Constitution Avenue, N.W.
Washington, DC 20210
(202) 523-8913

Work and Family Clearinghouse
200 Constitution Avenue, N.W.
Washington, DC 20210
(202) 219-4486

Department of the Navy

Bureau of Naval Personnel
Women in the Navy
Pers-OOW
II Navy Annex Quad D
Washington, DC 20370
(703) 695-9385

Department of State

Bureau of International Organizational Affairs
Human Rights and Women's Affairs
2201 C Street, N.W.
Washington, DC 20520
(202) 647-1534

International Women's Programs
21st and C Streets, N.W.
Washington, DC 20520
(202) 647-1155

Department of Transportation

Federal Aviation Administration
Office for Civil Rights
Federal Women's Program
800 Independence Avenue, S.W.
Washington, DC 20591
(202) 267-3259

Federal Highway Administration
Office of Civil Rights
Federal Women's Program
400 7th Street, S.W.
Washington, DC 20590
(202) 366-1596

Federal Railroad Administration
Office of Civil Rights
Federal Women's Program
400 7th Street, S.W.
Washington, DC 20590
(202) 366-0482

National Highway Traffic Safety Administration
Office of Civil Rights
Federal Women's Program
400 7th Street, S.W.
Washington, DC 20590
(202) 366-0972

Office of the Deputy Secretary
Office of Civil Rights
Departmental Federal Women's Program
400 7th Street, S.W.
Washington, DC 20590
(202) 366-9367

Department of the Treasury

Internal Revenue Service
Affirmative Action Section
Federal Women's Program
1111 Constitution Avenue, N.W.
Washington, DC 20224
(202) 724-3504

Customs Service
Office of the Commissioner
Federal Women's Program
1301 Constitution Avenue, N.W.
Washington, DC 20229
(202) 927-0210

Department of Veterans Affairs

Advisory Committee on Women Veterans
810 Vermont Avenue, N.W.
Washington, DC 20420
(202) 233-2621

Assistant Secretary for Human Resources and Administration
Affirmative Employment Service
Federal Women's Program
McPherson Square Building
1425 K Street, N.W.
Washington, DC 20005
(202) 233-3136

Veterans Health Administration
Women Veterans Program
810 Vermont Avenue, N.W.
Washington, DC 20420
(202) 535-7182

Environmental Protection Agency

Office of Civil Rights
National Federal Women's Program
401 M Street, S.W.
Washington, DC 20460
(202) 260-4585

Equal Employment Opportunity Commission

1801 L Street, N.W.
Washington, DC 20507
(202) 663-4001

For regional offices of the EEOC, see the Work chapter, p. 72

Federal Deposit Insurance Corporation

Office of Equal Opportunity
Minority and Women Outreach Program
550 17th Street, N.W.
Washington, DC 20429
(800) 753-9064

House of Representatives

Judiciary Committee
Subcommittee on Civil and Constitutional Rights
O'Neill House Office Building, Room 808
300 New Jersey Avenue, S.E.
Washington, DC 20515
(202) 226-7680

Information Agency

Office of Equal Employment Opportunity and Civil Rights
Federal Women's Program
301 4th Street, S.W.
Washington, DC 20547
(202) 619-5151

International Development Cooperation Agency

U.S. Agency for International Development
Women in Development Office
320 21st Street, N.W.
Washington, DC 20523
(703) 875-4411

Marine Corps Headquarters

Administration and Resource Management Division
Equal Employment Opportunity Office
2 Navy Annex, ARC-2 Room 1021
Washington, DC 20380
(703) 614-2046

NATIONAL AERONAUTICS AND SPACE ADMINISTRATION
Office of Equal Opportunity Programs
Federal Women's Program
NASA HQ
300 E Street, S.W.
Washington, DC 20546
(202) 358-2167

NATIONAL SCIENCE FOUNDATION
Experimental Projects for Women and Girls
Women's Programs Section
4201 Wilson Boulevard
Arlington, VA 22230
(703) 306-1637

NUCLEAR REGULATORY COMMISSION
Office of Small and Disadvantaged Business Utilization/Civil Rights
Civil Rights Program
Federal Women's Program
Manager, SBCR
M217 NMBB
Washington, DC 20555
(301) 492-7082

OFFICE OF PERSONNEL MANAGEMENT
Government-Wide Federal Women's Program
1900 E Street, N.W., Room 6332
Washington, DC 20415
(202) 606-0870

PEACE CORPS
Women in Development
1990 K Street, N.W., Room 8660
Washington, DC 20526
(202) 606-5279

POSTAL SERVICE
Employee Relations Department
Office of Equal Employment Opportunity
Affirmative Action, Room 3641
475 L'Enfant Plaza West, S.W.
Washington, DC 20260
(202) 268-6446

SMALL BUSINESS ADMINISTRATION
National Women's Business Council
409 3rd Street, S.W., Suite 7425
Washington, DC 20416
(202) 205-3850

Office of Women's Business Ownership
408 3rd Street, S.W., 6th Floor
Washington, DC 20416
(202) 205-6673

TASK FORCE ON LEGAL EQUITY FOR WOMEN
Social Security Administration
West High Rise, Room 4413
6401 Security Boulevard
Baltimore, MD 21235
(301) 965-4033

NEWSLETTERS AND PUBLICATIONS FOR WOMEN

ACTIVISM AND POLITICS

Action Agenda
Media Action Alliance
P. O. Box 391
Circle Pines, MN 55014
(612) 434-4343
Sexism in media

Advocacy Update
Public Voice for Food and Health Policy
1001 Connecticut Avenue, N.W., Suite 522
Washington, DC 20036
(202) 659-5930

Alternatives
National Center for Policy Alternatives
Women's Economic Justice Center
1875 Connecticut Avenue, N.W.
Washington, DC 20009
(202) 387-6030
For a variety of progressive issues

ASTRAEA Bulletin
ASTRAEA National Lesbian Action Foundation
666 Broadway, Suite 520
New York, NY 10012
(212) 529-8021

At the Crossroads
P.O. Box 112
St. Paul, AR 72760
(501) 677-2235

Bridges: A Journal for Jewish Feminists and Our Friends
P.O. Box 18437
Seattle, WA 98118

Challenging Media Issues of Women
P.O. Box 902
Framingham, MA 01701

Conscience and Instantes: Latina Initiative Quarterly Newsletter
Catholics for a Free Choice
1436 U Street, N.W., Suite 301
Washington, DC 20009
(202) 986-6093

CWI Newsletter
Clearinghouse on Women's Issues
P.O. Box 70603
Friendship Heights, MD 20813
(301) 871-6106

The Equal Rights Advocate
Equal Rights Advocates
1663 Mission Street, Suite 550
San Francisco, CA 94103
(415) 621-0672

Feminist Majority Report
Feminist Majority Foundation
1600 Wilson Boulevard
Arlington, VA 22209
(703) 522-2214

GLAD Briefs
Gay and Lesbian Advocates and Defenders
P.O. Box 218
Boston, MA 02112
(617) 426-1350

Heartnote
Nurturing Network
P.O. Box 2050
Boise, ID 83701
(208) 344-7200 or (800) 866-4666
Information on abortion alternatives

Letter from SHARE
Self-Help for Women with Breast or Ovarian Cancer
19 W. 44th Street
New York, NY 10036

LDEF In Brief
NOW Legal Defense and Education Fund
99 Hudson Street, 12th Floor
New York, NY 10013
(212) 925-6635

LFL Reports
Libertarians for Life
13424 Hathaway Drive
Wheaton, MD 20906
(301) 460-4141

Mom's Apple Pie
Lesbian Mothers' National Defense Fund
P.O. Box 21567
Seattle, WA 98111
(206) 325-2643

Mothers and Others Action
Mothers and Others for a Livable Planet
40 W. 20th Street
New York, NY 10011
(212) 727-4508

National Right to Life News
National Right to Life Committee
419 Seventh Street, N.W.
Washington, DC 20004
(202) 626-8833

off our backs: a women's newsjournal
2423 18th Street, N.W.
Washington, DC 20009
(202) 234-8072

On the Issues: The Progressive Woman's Quarterly
P.O. Box 3000, Department OTI
Denville, NJ 07834

Peace and Freedom and *Program and Legislative Action*
Women's International League for Peace and Freedom
1213 Race Street
Philadelphia, PA 19107
(215) 563-7110

Political Woman
Political Woman
276 Chatterton Parkway
White Plains, NY 10606
(914) 285-9761

Public Affairs Action Letter
Planned Parenthood Federation of America
Public Affairs Division
810 Seventh Avenue
New York, NY 10019
(212) 541-7800

Religious Coalition for Abortion Rights Newsletter and *Common Ground, Different Planes (Women of Color Partnership Newsletter)*
Religious Coalition for Abortion Rights
100 Maryland Ave., N.E., Suite 307
Washington, DC 20002
(202) 543-7032

The Republican Woman
National Federation of Republican Women
Republican National Committee
310 First Street, S.E.
Washington, DC 20003
(703) 548-9688

Resist
Resist
One Summer Street
Somerville, MA 02143
(617) 623-5110
Radical political newsletter

Sisterlife
Feminists for Life of America
811 E. 47th Street
Kansas City, MO 64110
(816) 753-2130

Standing Together
National Coalition Against Pornography
800 Compton Road, Suite 9224
Cincinnati, OH 45231
(513) 521-6227

WNDC News
Women's National Democratic Club
1526 New Hampshire Avenue, N.W.
Washington, DC 20036
(202) 232-7363

The Woman Activist
The Woman Activist
2310 Barbour Road
Falls Church, VA 22043
(703) 573-8716

Women's Rights Law Reporter
15 Washington Street
Newark, NJ 07102
(201) 648-5320

Education

About Women on Campus
National Association for Women in Education
1325 18th Street, N.W., Suite 210
Washington, DC 20036
(202) 659-9330

Action Alert
American Association of University Women
1111 16th Street, N.W.
Washington, DC 20036
(202) 785-7712

Centerpiece
The Women's Center
133 Park Street, N.E.
Vienna, VA 22180
(703) 281-2657

Correspondent
Big Brothers/ Big Sisters of America
230 N. 13th Street
Philadelphia, PA 19107
(215) 567-7000

NWS Action
National Women's Studies Association
University of Maryland
College Park, MD 20742
(301) 403-0525 or 403-0524

On Campus with Women
Association of American Colleges
1818 R Street, N.W.
Washington, DC 20009
(202) 387-3760

Research Report
Wellesley College Center for Research on Women
Wellesley College
Wellesley, MA 02181
(617) 283-2510

Talking at the Big Gate
Black Women Organized for Educational Development
518 17th Street, Suite 202
Oakland, CA 94612
(510) 763-9501

Women in Higher Education
1934 Monroe Street
Madison, WI 53711
(608) 251-3232

Family Life

ACES National News
Association for Children for Enforcement of Support (ACES)
723 Phillips Avenue, Suite J
Toledo, OH 43612
(419) 476-2511 or (800) 537-7072

The Child Advocate's Information Exchange
National Association of Child Advocates
1625 K Street, N.W., Suite 510
Washington, DC 20006
(202) 828-6950

Child Care ActioNews
Child Care Action Campaign
330 Seventh Avenue, 17th Floor
New York, NY 10001
(212) 239-0138

Childhelp
Childhelp USA
6463 Independence Avenue
Woodland Hills, CA 91367
(818) 347-7280

Children's Rights Council
220 I Street, N.E.
Washington, DC 20002
(202) 547-6227 or (800) 787-5437

The Children's Voice
National Coalition to End Racism in America's Child Care System
22075 Koths
Taylor, MI 48180
(313) 295-0257

Family Therapy News
American Association for Marriage and Family Therapy
1100 17th Street, N.W., Tenth Floor
Washington, DC 20036
(202) 452-0109

Fair Share: The Matrimonial Law Monthly
Prentice Hall Law and Business
270 Sylvan Avenue
Englewood Cliffs, NJ 07632
(201) 894-5222

The Matrimonial Strategist
New York Law Publishing Company
111 8th Avenue
New York, NY 10011
(212) 741-8300

The New Relationships
Equal Relationships Institute
Experimental Cities
P.O. Box 731
Pacific Palisades, CA 90272
(310) 276-0686

NRCCSA News
National Resource Center on Child Sexual Abuse
107 Lincoln Street
Huntsville, AL 35801
(800) 543-7006 or (205) 534-6868

Ours: The Magazine of Adoptive Families
Adoptive Families of America
3333 Highway 100 N.
Minneapolis, MN 55422
(612) 535-4829

Parent Post
Parent Action
2 N. Charles Street
Baltimore, MD 21201
(410) 727-3687

Shop Talk: Collection of Parenting Experiences
P.O. Box 64211
Lubbock, TX 79464

Speak Out for Children
Children's Rights Council
220 I Street, N.E.
Washington, DC 20002
(202) 547-6227 or (800) 787-5437

Welcome Home
Mothers at Home
8310-A Old Courthouse Rd.
Vienna, VA 22182
(703) 827-5903

Health

American Anorexia/Bulimia Association Newsletter
American Anorexia/Bulimia Association
418 E. 76th Street
New York, NY 10021
(212) 734-1114

Breast Cancer Action Newsletter
Breast Cancer Action
P.O. Box 460185
San Francisco, CA 94146
(415) 922-8279

Cancer Forum
Foundation for Alternative Cancer Therapies
P.O. Box 1242
Old Chelsea Station
New York, NY 10113
(212) 741-2790

CAnswers
Lesbian Community Cancer Project
Pat Parker Place
1902 W. Montrose
Chicago, IL 60613
(312) 561-4662

Caribbean Sun
Caribbean Women's Health Association
2725 Church Ave.
Brooklyn, NY 11226
(718) 826-2942

Center News
Women's Cancer Resource Center
3023 Shattuck Ave
Berkley, CA 94705
(510) 548-9272

Endometriosis Association Newsletter
The Endometriosis Association
8585 North 76th Place
Milwaukee, WI 53223
(800) 992-3636

Endometriosis Newsletter
The Endometriosis Program
St. Charles Medical Center
2500 N.E. Neff Rd.
Bend, OR 97701
(800) 446-2177

Focus: A Guide to AIDS Research and Counseling
UCSF AIDS Health Project
Box 0884
San Francisco, CA 84143
(415) 476-6430

HERS Newsletter
Hysterectomy Educational Resources and Services Foundation (HERS)
422 Bryn Mawr Avenue
Bala Cynwyd, PA 19004
(215) 667-7757

In Touch and *Women's Health Issues*
Jacobs Institute of Women's Health
409 12th Street, S.W.
Washington, DC 20024
(202) 863-4990

Journal of Pesticide Reform
Northwest Coalition for Alternatives to Pesticides
P.O. Box 1393
Eugene, OR 97440
(503) 344-5044
Includes information on women's health issues

LAP Notes
Lesbian AIDS Project, Gay Men's Health Crisis
129 W. 20th Street
New York, NY 10011
(212) 337-3532

Letter from SHARE
Self-Help for Women with Breast or Ovarian Cancer
19 W. 44th Street
New York, NY 10036

Menninger Perspective and *The Menninger Letter*
Menninger Clinic: The Women's Program
5800 S.W. Sixth Ave
P.O. Box 829
Topeka, KS 66601
(913) 273-7500

NABCO News
National Alliance of Breast Cancer Organizations
1180 Avenue of the Americas, 2nd floor
New York, NY 10036
(212) 719-0154

National Women's Health Report
National Women's Health Resource Center
2440 M Street, N.W., Suite 201
Washington DC 20037

NAWHO News
National Asian Women's Health Organization
440 Grand Avenue, Suite 208
Oakland, CA 94610
(510) 208-3171

Vital Signs
National Black Women's Health Project
1237 Ralph David Abernathy Blvd., S.W.
Atlanta, GA 30310

What's Happening in AMWA and *Journal of the American Medical Women's Association*
American Medical Women's Association
801 N. Fairfax Street, Suite 400
Alexandria, VA 22314
(703) 838-0500

Women's Community Cancer Project
Women's Community Cancer Project
c/o Women's Center
46 Pleasant Street
Cambridge, MA 02139
(617) 354-9888

WORLD
Women Organized to Respond to Life-Threatening Diseases
P.O. Box 11535
Oakland, CA 94611
(800) 933-3413 or (510) 658-6930

Y-Me Hotline
Y-ME, National Organization for Breast Cancer Information and Support
18220 Harwood Avenue
Homewood, IL 60430
(708) 799-8228

Lesbian Issues

Anything that Moves
Bay Area Bisexual Network
2404 California Street, Box 24
San Francisco, CA 94115
(415) 703-7977

ASTRAEA Bulletin
ASTRAEA National Lesbian Action Foundation
666 Broadway, Suite 520
New York, NY 10012
(212) 529-8021

CAnswers
Lesbian Community Cancer Project
Pat Parker Place
1902 W. Montrose
Chicago, IL 60613
(312) 561-4662

GLAD Briefs
Gay and Lesbian Advocates and Defenders
P.O. Box 218
Boston, MA 02112
(617) 426-1350

The Lambda Update
Lambda Legal Defense and Education Fund
666 Broadway
New York, NY 10012
(212) 995-8585

LAP Notes
Lesbian AIDS Project, Gay Men's Health Crisis
129 W. 20th Street
New York, NY 10011
(212) 337-3532

Momazons
Momazons
P. O. Box 02069
Columbus, OH 43202
(614) 267-0193
For lesbian mothers

Mom's Apple Pie
Lesbian Mothers' National Defense Fund
P.O. Box 21567
Seattle, WA 98111
(206) 325-2643

NCLR Newsletter
National Center for Lesbian Rights
1663 Mission Street
San Francisco, CA 94103
(415) 621-0674

North Bi Northwest
Seattle Bisexual Women's Network
P.O. Box 30645, Greenwood Station
Seattle, WA 98103
(206) 783-7987

PFLAGpole
Parents and Friends of Lesbians and Gays
1012 14th Street N.W., Suite 700
Washington, DC 20005
(202) 638-4200

Task Force Report
National Gay and Lesbian Task Force
1734 14th Street, N.W.
Washington, DC 20009
(202) 332-6483

Reproductive Health

BFHI News
The Baby Friendly Hospital Initiative
UNICEF
3 United Nations Plaza, H-9F
New York, NY 10017

Birth Gazette
42, The Farm
Summertown, TN 38483
(615) 964-2519

Bulletin
National Perinatal Association
3500 E. Fletcher Avenue, Suite 525
Tampa, FL 33613
(813) 971-1008

Heartnote
Nurturing Network
P.O. Box 2050
Boise, ID 83701
(208) 344-7200 or (800) 866-4666
Information on abortion alternatives

The Journal of Perinatal Education
ASPO/ Lamaze
1101 Connecticut Avenue, N.W., Suite 700
Washington, DC 20036
(800) 368-4404

Lamazebaby and *Lamaze Parents' Magazine*
Lamaze Publishing Company
372 Danbury Road
Wilton, CT 06897
(203) 834-2711

NACC News
National Association of Childbearing Centers
RD 1, Box 1
Perkiomenville, PA 18074
(215) 234-8068

NFPRHA News
National Family Planning and Reproductive Health Association
122 C Street, N.W., Suite 380
Wasington, DC 20001

Positive Pregnancy & Parenting Fitness
51 Saltrock Road
Baltic, CT 06330

Resolve
Resolve, Inc.
1310 Broadway
Somerville, MA 02114
(617) 623-0744 (helpline) or (617) 623-1156 (office)
Support for infertility

SHARE Newsletter
SHARE Pregnancy and Infant Loss Support
St. Joseph Health Center
300 First Capitol Drive
St. Joseph, MO 63301
(314) 947-6164

Retirement

AAHA News
American Association of Homes for the Aging
901 E Street, N.W., Suite 500
Washington, DC 20004
(202) 783-2242

Golden Page
National Caucus and Center on Black Aged
1424 K Street, N.W., Suite 500
Wasington, DC 20005

Senior Citizens News
National Council of Senior Citizens, Nursing Home Information Service
1331 F Street, N.W.
Washington, DC 20004

Self-Defense

AWSDA Newsletter
American Women's Self-Defense Association
713 N. Wellwood Avenue
Lindenhurst, NY 11757
(516) 226-8383

Chimera Newsletter
Chimera
59 E. Van Buren, Suite 714
Chicago, IL 60605
(312) 939-5341

Double-Time
National Clearinghouse for the Defense of Battered Women
125 South 9th Street, Suite 302
Philadelphia, PA 19107
(215) 351-0010

Dragon Times
Dragon Books
P.O. Box 6039
Thousand Oaks, CA 91359
(818) 889-3856
Martial arts

Fighting Woman News
6741 Tung Avenue West
Theodore, AL 36582

NCADV Update
National Coalition Against Domestic Violence
P.O. Box 34103
Washington, DC 20043
(202) 638-6388

Networks
National Victim Center
2111 Wilson Boulevard, Suite 300
Arlington, VA 22201
(703) 276-2880

NOVA Newsletter
National Organization for Victim Assistance
1757 Park Road, N.W.
Washington, DC 20010
(202) 232-6682

WAR Newsletter
Women Against Rape
Box 02084
Columbus, OH 43202
(614) 291-9751

Women's Recovery Network
c/o Tracie Anderson
423 Beharrall
New Albany, OH 47150
A forum for survivors of abuse

Spirituality

The Beltane Papers: A Journal of Women's Mysteries
1333 Lincoln Street, #240
Bellingham, WA 98226

Bridges: A Journal for Jewish Feminists and Our Friends
P.O. Box 18437
Seattle, WA 98118

Churchwoman
Church Women United
475 Riverside Drive, Room 812
New York, NY 10115
(212) 870-2347

The Flyer
The General Commission on the Status and Role of Women in the United Methodist Church
1200 Davis Street
Evanston, IL 60201
(708) 869-7330

Journal of Women and Religion
Center for Women and Religion
Graduate Theological Union
2400 Ridge Road
Berkeley, CA 94709
(510) 649-2490

New Women, New Church
Women's Ordination Conference
P.O. Box 2693
Fairfax, VA 22031
(703) 352-1006

On Wings
Women in Constant Creative Action
P. O. Box 5080
Eugene, OR 97405
(503) 345-6381

The Wise Woman
2441 Cordova Street
Oakland, CA 94602
(510) 536-3174
Spirituality, witchcraft

WORK

ABWA Newsletter
American Business Women's Association
P.O. Box 8728
Kansas City, MO 64114
(816) 361-4991

AWIS Magazine
Association for Women in Science
1522 K Street, N.W., Suite 820
Washington, DC 20005
(202) 408-0742

Breakthrough Strategies: The Management Newsletter for Women
70 Hilltop Road
Ramsey, NJ 07446
(800) 879-2441

CWAO News
Coalition of Women's Art Organizations
123 East Beutel Road
Port Washington, WI 53074
(414) 284-4458

Executive Female
National Association for Female Executives
30 Irving Place
New York, NY 10003
(212) 477-2200

FEMALE Forum (Formerly Employed Mothers at the Leading Edge)
P. O. Box 31
Elmhurst, IL 60126
(708) 941-3553

International Alliance Newsletter
The International Alliance
8600 LaSalle Road
Baltimore, MD 21286
(410) 472-4221

In Touch!
Mothers on the Move, an Alliance of Entrepreneurial Mothers
P.O. Box 40356
Tucson, AZ 85717
(602) 628-2598

NATIONAL WOMEN'S MAILING LIST

The National Women's Mailing List uses information technology to allow women to communicate with each other for networking and outreach purposes. Organizations as well as individuals can sign up, with members receiving mail on a variety of topics from politics and sports to spirituality. In addition, organizations sending out mailings of interest to women can use the mailing list for this purpose. The National Women's Mailing List also has speakers on women and technology, and offers two-day intensive classes on computer literacy. For further information, contact:

National Women's Mailing List
P.O. Box 68
Jenner, CA 95450
(707) 632-5763

Homeworking Mother
Mother's Home Business Network
Box 423
East Meadow, NY 11554
(516) 997-7394

Making Success Happen
National Association of Black Women Entrepreneurs
P.O. Box 1375
Detroit, MI 48321
(313) 559-9255

National Home Business Report
National Home Business Network
P.O. Box 2137
Naperville, IL 60567
(708) 717-0488

NAWBO News
National Association of Women Business Owners
600 S. Federal Street, Suite 400
Chicago, IL 60605
(301) 608-2590

NFWBO News
National Foundation for Women Business Owners
1377 K Street, N.W., Suite 637
Washington, DC 20005
(301) 495-4975

9 to 5 Newsline
9 to 5, National Association of Working Women
238 West Wisconsin Avenue, #700
Milwaukee, WI 53203

Pulse
Executive Women International
Spring Run Executive Plaza
965 E. 4800 South, Suite 1
Salt Lake City, UT 84117
(801) 355-2800

RWF News
Roundtable for Women in Foodservice
425 Central Park West, #2A
New York, NY 10025
(212) 865-8100

Tradeswomen: A Quarterly Magazine for Women in Blue-Collar Work
P.O. Box 40664
San Francisco, CA 94140
(510) 649-6160

Transition Times
Women Work! The National Network for Women's Employment
1625 K Street N.W., Suite 300
Washington, DC 20006
(202) 467-6346

Today's Insurance Woman
National Association of Insurance Women
P.O. Box 4410
Tulsa, OK 74159
(800) 766-6249

Women at Work
Wider Opportunities for Women
National Commission on Working Women
1325 G Street, N.W., Lower Level
Washington, DC
(202) 638-3143

Women Directors of the Top Corporate 1,000
National Women's Educational (Economic) Alliance Foundation
1440 New York Avenue, N.W., Suite 300
Washington, DC 20005
(202) 393-5257

Women Entrepreneur
American Woman's Economic Development Corporation
641 Lexington Avenue
New York, NY 10022
(212) 688-1900

Women in the Trades
Northern New England Tradeswomen
RR2 Box 66-17, Emerson Falls
St. Johnsbury, VT 05819
(802) 748-3308

Women Lawyers Journal
National Association of Women Lawyers
American Bar Center
750 North Lake Shore Drive
Chicago, IL 60611
(312) 988-6186

Working at Home
P.O. Box 200504 HM
Carterville, GA 30120

Miscellaneous

Feminist Bookstore News
P.O. Box 882554
San Francisco, CA 94188
(415) 626-1556

News and Views
Women's Environment and Development Organization
845 Third Avenue, 15th Floor
New York, NY 10022
(212) 759-7982

Newsletter
Organization of Pan Asian American Women
P.O. Box 39128
Washington, DC 20016
(202) 429-3824

PH Factor
National Panhellenic Conference
3901 W. 86th Street, Suite 380
Indianapolis, IN 46268
(317) 255-9384
National sorority newsletter

SIECUS Report
Sex Information and Education Council of the United States
130 W. 42nd Street, Suite 2500
New York, NY 10036
(212) 819-9770

Women's International Network News
187 Grant Street
Lexington, MA 02173
(617) 862-9431

THE NATIONAL WOMEN'S HALL OF FAME

Located in Seneca Falls, New York, where the first Women's Rights Convention was held in 1848, the National Women's Hall of Fame was founded in 1969 to honor the contributions of American women. The women honored by the Hall of Fame are:

Abigail Adams
Jane Addams
Marian Anderson
Ethel Percy Andrus
Susan B. Anthony
Clara Barton
Mary McLeod Bethune
Antoinette Blackwell
Elizabeth Blackwell
Emily Blackwell
Margaret Bourke-White
Gwendolyn Brooks
Ruth Colvin
Emily Dickinson
Dorothea Dix
Amelia Earhart
Marian Wright Edelman
Gertrude Belle Elion
Alice Evans
Betty Friedman
Ella Grasso
Martha Wright Griffiths
Fannie Lou Hamer
Alice Hamilton
Helen Hayes
Dorothy Height
Dolores Huerta
Mary Jacobi
Mae Jemison
Mary Harris "Mother" Jones
Lucretia Mott
Annie Oakley
Georgia O'Keeffe
Rosa Parks
Alice Paul
Frances Perkins
Margaret Sanger
Katherine Siva Saubel
Florence Seibert
Mother Elizabeth Seton
Bessie Smith
Margaret Chase Smith
Sojourner Truth
Harriet Tubman
Lillian Wald
Madam C. J. Walker
Faye Wattleton
Ida B. Wells-Barnett
Rosalyn Yalow
Gloria Yerkovich
Mildred "Babe" Didrikson Zaharias

LESBIAN/GAY ARCHIVES AND LIBRARIES

Northeast

Boston Lesbian and Gay History Project
285 Harvard Street, #202
Cambridge, MA 02139

Buffalo Woman's Oral History Project
255 Parkside Avenue
Buffalo, NY 14214

Center for Lesbian & Gay Studies
Center for the Study of Women in Society
Graduate Center
City University of New York
33 West 42nd Street
New York, NY 10036
(215) 787-8231

Connecticut Lesbian Archives
Hartford Women's Center
350 Farmington Avenue
Hartford, CT 06105
(203) 232-7393

Delaware Lesbian and Gay Archives
P.O. Box 974
Wilmington, DE 19899

Gay and Lesbian Archives of Philadelphia
201 South Camac
Philadelphia, PA 19103
(215) 923-7505

Gay Community News Library
62 Berkeley Street
Boston, MA 02116
(617) 426-4469

Herizon Archives
P.O. Box 1082
Binghamton, NY 13902

Latina Lesbian History Project
P.O. Box 627, Stuyvesant Station
New York, NY 10009

National Herstory Archives
P.O. Box 1258
New York, NY 10116
(212) 874-7232

National Museum of Lesbian and Gay History
208 W. 13th Street
New York, NY 10001
(212) 620-7310

New Jersey Gay and Lesbian Archives
P.O. Box 160
New Brunswick, NY 08903

New Alexandria Lesbian Library
P.O. Box 402, Florence Station
Northhampton, MA 01060
(413) 584-7616 or (202) 628-4166

SOUTHEAST

Contemporary Culture Collection
Howard Tilton Memorial Library
7001 Freret Street
Tulane University
New Orleans, LA 70188

The Feminist Library
c/o Y.W.C.A.
809 Rector Street
Durham, NC 27707
(919) 688-4396

Florida Collection of Lesbian Herstory
P.O. Box 5605
Jacksonville, FL

Gay and Lesbian Archives of Washington, D.C.
P.O. Box 4218
Falls Church, VA 22044
(703) 671-3930

Kentucky Collection of Lesbian Herstory
P.O. Box 1701
Louisville, KY 40201
(502) 895-3127

Kentucky Gay and Lesbian Archives
1464 South Second Street
Louisville, KY 40208
(502) 636-0935

Lambda, Inc., Barnes Library
516 South 27th Street
Birmingham, AL 35255
(205) 326-8600

Lesbian and Gay Archives of Naiad Press
P.O. Box 10543
Tallahassee, FL 32302
(904) 539-9322 or (904) 539-5965

Southeastern Lesbian Archives
Atlanta Lesbian Feminist Alliance Library
P.O. Box 5502
Atlanta, GA 30307
(404) 523-7786

Tennessee Lesbian Archives
c/o Hornsby
303 Kennon Road
Knoxville, TN 37909

Women's Library
362 West Dickson
Fayetteville, AR 72701
(501) 442-5598

Resource Library
World Congress of Gay and Lesbian Jewish Organizations
P.O. Box 18961
Washington, DC 20036

Midwest

American Radical History Collection
Special Collections Division
Michigan State University Libraries
East Lansing, MI 48824
(517) 355-2344

Chicago Gay/Lesbian History Project
P.O. Box 60046
Chicago, IL 60660

Cincinnati Gay/Lesbian Archives
408 Ludlow, #56
Cincinnati, OH 45220
(513) 861-6171

Kinsey Institute for Research in Sex, Gender and Reproduction
Room 313, Morrison Hall
Indiana University
Bloomington, IN 47405
(812) 335-7686

Lambda United Library
P.O. Box 6024
Bismark, ND 58502

Matrices
c/o Jacqueline Zita
Woman's Studies Department
492 Ford Hall
University of Minnesota
Minneapolis, MN 55455

Milwaukee Lesbian Archives
c/o MLA/Mary Frank
3363 North Richard Street
Milwaukee, WI 53212
(414) 372-3330

Ohio Lesbian Archives
c/o Crazy Ladies Bookstore
4039 Hamilton Avenue
Cincinnati, OH 45223
(513) 541-1917

Resource Room and Archives
Gay and Lesbian Resource Center
P.O. Box 11152
Fort Wayne, IN 46856

T.S. Library
2425 Indiana
P.O. Box 1144
Topeka, KS 66601
(312) 883-3003

Southwest

Baker Archives
350 S. Center Street, #350
Reno, NV 89501
(702) 747-5323

Dallas Gay/Lesbian Historic Archives
c/o Dallas Gay Alliance
4012 Cedar Springs
P.O. Box 190712
Dallas, TX 75219
(214) 528-4233

Gay and Lesbian Archives of Texas
P.O. Box 16401
Houston, TX 77222

Lesbian Resource Center Library
P.O. Box 180446
Dallas, TX 75218

Northwest

Douglas County Gay Archives
P.O. Box 942
Dillard, OR 97432
(503) 679-9913

Lesbian and Gay Heritage Alliance of the Pacific Northwest
1425 East Prospect Street
Seattle, WA 98112
(206) 323-3007

Out in Montana Resource Center
P.O. Box 7223
Missoula, MT 59807
(503) 697-9144

West

Blanche M. Baker Memorial Library
ONE, Inc.
3340 Country Club Drive
Los Angeles, CA 90019
(213) 735-5252

Constance Barber Collection on Lesbian History
Women's Resource Center Library
250 Golden Bear Center
University of California, Berkeley
Berkeley, CA 94720
(510) 643-8367

Gay and Lesbian Collection
Harvey Milk Branch Library
San Francisco Public Library
3555 16th Street
San Francisco, CA 94114
(415) 626-1132

Gay/Lesbian Historical Archives of Utah
341 North Center Street, #2
Salt Lake City, UT 84103

Gay and Lesbian Historical Society of Northern California Archives
P.O. Box 424280
San Francisco, CA 94142
(415) 626-0980

Harvey Milk Archives
3930 17th Street
San Francisco, CA 94114
(415) 621-4378

International Gay & Lesbian Archives
626 North Robertson Boulevard (side entrance)
West Hollywood, CA 90069
P.O. Box 38100
West Hollywood, CA 90038
(213) 854-0271 or (213) 962-6531

June Mazer Lesbian Collection
626 North Robertson Boulevard (side entrance)
West Hollywood, CA 90069
(213) 659-2478

Lavender Archives
P.O. Box 28977
Santa Ana, CA 92799

Lesbian Heritage Group
c/o Pacific Women's Resource
4523 Roosevelt Street, N.E.
Seattle, WA 98105

Nevada Women's Herstorical Society
1298 South Christy Lane
Las Vegas, NV 89122
(702) 431-1208

Research Library
Institute for Advanced Study of Human Sexuality
1523 Franklin Street
San Francisco, CA 94109
(415) 928-1133

Terry Mangan Memorial Library
Gay & Lesbian Community Center of Colorado
1245 East Colfax Avenue, #319
P.O. Drawer E
Denver, CO 80218
(303) 831-6268 or (303) 837-1598

Utah Gay and Lesbian Historical Archives
Utah Stonewall Center
450 South 900 East, Suite 140
Salt Lake City, UT 84102

West Coast Lesbian Collection
P.O. Box 25753
Oakland, CA 94623
(415) 465-8080

Lesbian/Gay Archives of San Diego
P.O. Box 40389
San Diego, CA 92164
(619) 260-1522

CANADA

Archives Gaies du Quebec
CP 395 succ Place du Parc
Montreal, Quebec H2W 2N9

Archives for the Protection of Gay History and Literature
P.O. Box 6368, Station A
St. John, New Brunswick E2L 4R8

Canadian Women's Movement Archives
P.O. Box 128, Station P
Toronto, Ontario M5S 2S7
(416) 597-9965

Gay Archives Collective
P.O. Box 3130 MPO
Vancouver, British Columbia U6B 3X6
(604) 669-5978

Gay History Project
P.O. Box 7508
Saskatoon, Saskatchewan

Hamilton-Wentworth Gay Archives
P.O. Box 44, Station B
Hamilton, Ontario L8L 7T5

James Fraser Library
Canadian Gay Archives
P.O. Box 639, Station A
Toronto, Ontario M5W 1G2
(416) 921-6310

Lesbian and Gay History Group of Toronto
c/o P.O. Box 639, Station A
Toronto, Ontario M5W 1G2

Librarie Lesbienne, Feministe, Gaie
3636 Boulevard St. Laurent
Montreal, Quebec H2G 3C9

Traces/Archives Lesbiennes
CP 244 succ Beaubien
Montreal, Quebec H2G 3C9

Winnipeg Gay/Lesbian Resource Center
1-222 Osborne Street South
Winnipeg, Manitoba R3C 2Z6

Source: Gay and Lesbian Task Force Clearinghouse

RESOURCES: BOOKS AND MAGAZINES

The following publications were of invaluable help in preparing this book.

Books

Alternative Health Care For Women, Patsy Wescott and Leyardia Black
The Alyson Almanac, Alyson Publications
The American Woman, 1992-93, Paula Reis and Anne J. Stone
American Women's History, Doris Weatherford
Back Off! How to Confront and Stop Sexual Harassment and Harassers, Martha Lagelan
Be an Outrageous Older Woman—A R.A.S.P. (Remarkable Aging Smart Person), Ruth Harriet Jacobs
The Beacon Book of Quotations by Women, Rosalie Maggio, ed.
Black Woman's Health Book, Evelyn White
The Book of Women's Firsts, Phyllis J. Read and Bernard Witlieb
Changing Bodies, Changing Lives, Ruth Bell
Closer to Home: Bisexuality and Feminism, Elizabeth Reba Weise
The Courage to Heal: A Guide for Women Survivors of Sexual Abuse, Ellen Bass and Laura Davis
Directory of Financial Aids for Women
Directory of Nontraditional Training and Employment Programs Serving Women, Women's Bureau
Directory of Personal Image Consultants
Eldercare: Choosing and Financing Long-term Care, Joseph Matthews
Employment and Retirement Issues for Women, National Center for Women and Retirement Research
Ending Men's Violence National Referral Directory, Pennsylvania Coalition Against Domestic Violence
Entrepreneurial Woman's Guide to Owning a Business, *Entrepreneur* magazine
Every Woman's Guide to The Body at 40, Marjorie Shafto and Gerald Hunt
Feminist Chronicles, 1953–1993, Toni Carabillo
Feminist Resources for Schools and College, Anne Chapman
For Each Other: Sharing Sexual Intimacy, Lonnie G. Barbach
For Yourself: The Fulfillment of Female Sexuality, Lonnie G. Barbach
The Fountain of Age, Betty Friedan
Gayellow Pages
Get Smart! A Woman's Guide to Equality on Campus, Montana Katz and Veronic Veiland
Grants for Women and Girls
Hardball for Women, Pat Heim
The Healthy Heart Handbook, National Institute of Health
Healthy People 2000, Department of Health and Human Services
How to Make the World a Better Place for Women in Five Minutes a Day, Donna Jackson

The Janus Report on Sexual Behavior, Samuel S. Janus and Cynthia L. Janus
Key Women in Executive Search
The Kinsey Institute New Report on Sex: What You Must Know to Be Sexually Literate, June Reinisch
Lesbian Lists, Dell Richards
Library and Information Sources on Women
Looking Ahead to Your Financial Future, National Center for Women and Retirement Research
The Maternity Sourcebook, Wendy and Matthew Lesko
Meeting at the Crossroads, Lyn Mikel Brown and Carol Gilligan
Money Smart, Esther M. Berger
National Directory of College Athletics
National Directory of Women Owned Business Firms, Business Research Services)
The New Hite Report, Shere Hite
The New Our Bodies Ourselves, Boston Women's Health Collective
Nobel Prize Women in Science, Sharon Bertsch McGrayne
Notable American Women, Edward T. James, ed.
An Older Woman's Health Guide, Joan Mintz
On Your Own: A Widow's Passage to Emotional and Financial Well-Being, Alexander Armstrong and Mary Donahue
Ourselves Growing Older, Boston Women's Health Collective
The Perfect Fit: How to Achieve Mutual Fulfillment and Monogamous Passion Through the New Intercourse, Edward Eichel and Philip Nobile
Places of Interest to Women: The Women's Guide: USA & Canada
Questions and Answers About Breast Lumps, General Services Administration
Report of the National Institutes of Health: Opportunities for Research on Women's Health, National Institutes of Health
Sexual Harassment —Women Speak Out, Amber Coverdale Sumrall and Dena Taylor, eds.
Sexual Violence: Our War Against Rape, Linda Fairstein
The Silent Passage, Gail Sheehy
Statistical Handbook on Women in America, Cynthia Taeuber, ed.
Statistical Record of Women Worldwide, Linda Schmittroth, ed.
Taking Control of Your Life: The Secrets of Successful EnterprisingWomen, Gail Blanke and Kathleen Walas
Untamed Tongues, Autumn Stephens
Vicki Lansky's Divorce Book for Parents, Vicki Lansky
WAC Stats—The Facts About Women, Women's Action Coalition
What Mona Lisa Knew, Dr. Barbara Mackoff
When in Doubt, Check Him Out, Joseph J. Culligan
A Woman's Place, Anne Stibbs
The Womanly Art of Breastfeeding, La Leche League
Women and Money, Frances Leonard
Women Business Owners: Selling to the Federal Government, Small Business Administration
Women in Love, Shere Hite
Women in the Business Game, Charlotte Taylor
Women Smokers Can Quit: A Different Approach, Sue F. Delaney
Women's Health Alert, Sidney M. Wolfe
Women's Information Directory, Shawn Brennan
The World Almanac of First Ladies, Lu Ann Paletta
Yale University School of Medicine Heart Book, Barry Zaret, Marvin Moser, and Lawrence Cohen
Your Home, Your Choice: A Workbook for Older People and Their Families, American Association of Retired Persons
9 to 5 Guide to Combatting Sexual Harassment, 9 to 5, National Association of Working Women

Magazines

Advertising Age
Allure
American Demographics
American Health
American Psychologist
Business Week
The Chronicle of Higher Education
Cosmetic Insiders Report
Cosmopolitan
Details
Entrepreneurial Woman
Essence
Family Law Quarterly
Financial World
Forbes
Glamour
Good Housekeeping
Harper's
Home Office Computing
Lambda Book Report
Ladies' Home Journal
Lear's
Media Women
Mirabella
Mother Jones
Ms.
The New England Journal of Medicine
New Moon
New York Magazine
off our backs
On the Issues: The Progressive Woman's Quarterly
Radcliffe Quarterly
Redbook
Scientific American
Self
Sports Illustrated
'Teen
Tokyo Journal
Vogue
Woman Engineer
Women and Guns
Working Mother
Working Woman

ORGANIZATION INDEX

SUBJECT INDEX

INDEX

Page numbers followed by M indicate information found in the margins.